Social Media Marketing

A STRATEGIC APPROACH

Social Media Marketing

A STRATEGIC APPROACH

Melissa S. Barker

Donald I. Barker

Nicholas F. Bormann

Krista E. Neher

SOUTH-WESTERN
CENGAGE Learning

Australia • Brazil • Japan • Korea • Mexico • Singapore • Spain • United Kingdom • United States

Social Media Marketing: A Strategic Approach, First Edition
Melissa Barker, Donald Barker,
Nicholas Bormann, Krista Neher

Senior Vice President of Editorial, Business:
Jack W. Calhoun

Vice President, Editor-in-Chief: Karen Schmohe

Publisher: Erin Joyner

Executive Acquisition Editor: Michael Roche

Developmental Editor: Daniel Noguera

Editorial Assistant: Megan Fischer

Marketing Manager: Gretchen Swann

Media Editor: John Rich

Manufacturing Planner: Ron Montgomery

Senior Marketing Communications Manager:
Jim Overly

Internal/Cover Designer, Production
Management, Composition and
Art Direction: PreMediaGlobal

Rights Acquisition Specialist, Text:
Amber Hosea

Rights Acquisition Specialist, Image:
Deanna Ettinger

Photo Researcher: Terri Wright

Cover Images:

Man with basketball:
© Juanmonino / iStockphoto

Man with mustache:
© Juanmonino / iStockphoto

Woman with long dark hair:
© iodrakon/ iStockphoto

Older Woman with glasses:
© Yuri Arcurs / Shutterstock

Woman with glasses:
© William Perugini/ iStockphoto

Smiling girl teen: © igor terekhov/ iStockphoto

Girl in white: © Juanmonino / iStockphoto

Woman in lavender shirt:
© Juanmonino / iStockphoto

Teen Boy with strap over shoulder:
© EDHAR / Shutterstock

i-phone/globe art:
© Kamruzzaman Ratan/iStockphoto

Man in glasses: © leungchopan/ iStockphoto

Young man in light blue button-down shirt:
© Juanmonino / iStockphoto

ExamView® is a registered trademark of eInstruction Corp. Windows is a registered trademark of the Microsoft Corporation used herein under license. Macintosh and Power Macintosh are registered trademarks of Apple Computer, Inc. used herein under license.

Library of Congress Control Number: 2012930782

Student Edition
ISBN-13: 978-0-538-48087-1
ISBN-10: 0-538-48087-4

South-Western
5191 Natorp Boulevard
Mason, OH 45040
USA

Cengage Learning products are represented in Canada by Nelson Education, Ltd.

For your course and learning solutions, visit **www.cengage.com**

Purchase any of our products at your local college store or at our preferred online store **www.cengagebrain.com**

Printed in the United States of America
3 4 5 6 16 15 14 13

Brief Contents

Contents

Chapter 4 | Rules of Engagement for Social Media   64

Chapter 5 | Publishing Blogs   84

Chapter 6 | Publishing Podcasts and Webinars   104

Chapter 11 | Microblogging   207

Chapter 12 | Discussion Boards, Social News, and Q&A Sites   228

Chapter 13 | Mobile Computing and Location Marketing   261

Chapter 14 | Social Media Monitoring   280

Chapter 15 | Social Media Marketing Plan   317

Preface

Social Media Marketing: A Strategic Approach is built upon an eight-step planning cycle that helps ensure the development of a winning social media marketing plan. This model incorporates the conceptual foundation and practical techniques necessary for creating a comprehensive and effective social media marketing plan.

This planning cycle begins with observing an organization's current presence and competition on the social web, followed by the establishment of realistic social media goals and effective strategies to achieve them. The next step is to define an organization's target markets on the social web. This process makes it possible for a company to identify the social media platforms with the highest concentrations of its target audiences and determine how they are participating on those platforms, which enables the organization to select the optimal social media platforms for reaching its target audiences.

Interaction on the social web is guided by informal rules of engagement and general principles of appropriate behavior (social media ethics). Marketers must be aware of these precepts before attempting to participate in social media or risk alienating the very market segments they hope to connect with and influence.

With these guidelines in mind, as well as the company's social media goals, strategies, target audiences, and prime social media channels, marketers can craft actionable platform-specific marketing tactics. The execution of these platform-specific tactics allows an organization to implement its general social media strategies across multiple social media platforms and realize the company's marketing goals. The bulk of this textbook is dedicated to learning how to create and deploy these platform-specific marketing tactics.

In addition, extensive consideration is given to monitoring and measuring the progress made in reaching social media goals. The most useful quantitative and qualitative social media measurements are introduced and explained in detail, along with various ways to estimate an organization's return on investment from social media marketing activities. This feedback provides the means to constantly and continuously adjust and improve the elements of a social media marketing plan to maximize the chances of success.

The final chapter draws upon all the proceeding material in the textbook to demonstrate and explain how to develop a thorough social media marketing plan, with multiple references and illustrations from a real world sample plan (presented in its entirety in the Appendix). Hence, this textbook provides a rich and robust cumulative learning experience, with deep contextual relevance that endows the reader with an enduring understanding of the process of effective social media marketing planning.

About the Authors

Melissa S. Barker

Melissa S. Barker (B.A. in public relations/advertising, Gonzaga University) is the social media manager at Jive Software, where she develops and oversees the implementation of social media campaigns and trains the sales team on social selling. She has coauthored three leading-edge textbooks, including *Internet Research Illustrated*, fifth and sixth editions, both bestsellers, as well as *Social Media Marketing: A Strategic Approach*. Melissa was instrumental in creating the first accredited social media marketing certificate in Washington State. She developed and teaches the certificate's core courses for Spokane Falls Community College, which include social media marketing, search engine marketing, and social media strategic planning courses. Melissa began her career as a social media marketing specialist for the international software company Siber Systems, where she more than doubled the company's presence on Facebook, Twitter, and LinkedIn within a few months. In recognition of her accomplishments, Siber Systems promoted her to the position of chief social media strategist. Melissa then became director of communications for Own Point of Sale, where she created and executed social media campaigns, as well as public relations, advertising, and other marketing efforts. As a social media strategist at Integra Telecom, Melissa developed and implemented comprehensive social media campaigns and taught executives and sales team how to build their personal brand with social media. She has established herself as an authority on LinkedIn, along with achieving expert author status on EzineArticles. In addition, Melissa is a sought after speaker at conferences such as InnoTech and ITEXPO. For more information about Melissa, visit: www.linkedin.com/in/melissasbarker.

Donald I. Barker

Donald I. Barker (M.B.A., Eastern Washington University) has authored, coauthored, and contributed to thirty-five cutting-edge textbooks, many bestsellers, on subjects ranging from computer operating systems and expert systems to Internet research and social media marketing. He pioneered the "hybrid" college textbook, combining the power of the Internet with the convenience of paper to deliver the most up-to-date learning experience possible, along with devising the process for putting textbook ancillary materials online. In addition, Don was instrumental in establishing the lucrative practice of packaging student versions of software with textbooks. As an assistant professor of information systems at Gonzaga University, he was honored as the winner of the Best Theoretical Paper Award by the International Business Schools Computer Users Group Annual North American Conference and received several Jepson Scholarship Awards for notable publications in the field of artificial intelligence. As senior editor of *PC AI Magazine*, he wrote popular columns for the magazine and BotSpot.com. Before commencing his academic career, Don was a business development specialist for the Small Business Development Center in Spokane, Washington, receiving the award for Outstanding Leadership and Service to Small Business. In addition, he was the sales manager for the largest consumer electronics retailer in Spokane. Today, Don continues to push the technology envelope by authoring trailblazing textbooks, as well as developing and teaching innovative online courses. For more information about Don, visit: www.linkedin.com/in/donaldibarker.

Nicholas F. Bormann

Nicholas F. Bormann is currently pursuing a Ph.D. in economics at George Mason University (expected 2014). He received his undergraduate education at Gonzaga University, graduating with a B.S. in economics and a B.A. in political science, with a concentration in women's/gender studies. He is a two-time recipient of the Albert Mann Award for intercollegiate policy debate and qualified for the National Debate Tournament four times, advancing to elimination rounds twice. A member of Omicron Delta Epsilon, the economics honor society, his 2010 paper on the effect of state minimum wage laws on unemployment was presented at the Spokane Intercollegiate Research Conference. For more information about Nick, visit: www.linkedin.com/in/nfbormann.

Krista E. Neher

Krista E. Neher (B.B.A., Wilfrid Laurier University) is the CEO of Boot Camp Digital, author of the *Social Media Field Guide*, international speaker and managing director of the Institute for Social Media at Cincinnati State Technical and Community College. Krista is a social media marketing pioneer, having created one of the first corporate Twitter accounts in 2007 when she was VP marketing at an Internet start-up company. By leveraging social media, Krista built the company to 40,000 registered users in four months, beating out competitors who spent millions of dollars on marketing. Prior to this work, Krista spent over five years at Procter & Gamble in a career spanning marketing and finance in which she worked on the largest global businesses. As the founder of Boot Camp Digital, a company that specializes in social media marketing training and consulting, Krista has worked with countless small and medium businesses as well as market leaders including Procter & Gamble, GE, 5/3 Bank, and the United States Senate Office of Education and Training. Krista speaks regularly at industry-leading trade shows, conferences, and corporate engagements around the world. As the managing director of the Institute for Social Media at Cincinnati State Technical and Community College, she created and manages the accredited social media marketing certification program. Krista is passionate about social media and has been an avid blogger and social network user since 2007. For more information about Krista, visit: www.linkedin.com/in/kristaneher.

Acknowledgement

A number of people have contributed to making this textbook possible. They include Michael Roche, the executive editor at South-Western Publishing/Cengage Learning, who saw the potential in this project long before anyone else and fought to make it happen; Daniel Noguera, our developmental editor and guide through the intricacies of authoring a textbook; Kailash Rawat, senior project manager at PreMediaGlobal, who oversaw with great forbearance the production of this book; James A. Corrick, a skilled copyeditor, and Sheila Joyce, a highly detailed proofreader, who both diligently sought out and corrected our errors; as well as Terri Wright and Melissa Tomaselli, who secured the rights to the key material necessary to codify the best practices in the field of social media marketing.

Why Social Media?

When an organizer for a national trade show was asked, "What is the biggest question your group has about building their business through social media?" his response was, "They hear about social media and are interested, but they don't know where to start. They know that the Yellow Pages don't work anymore, but social media can be overwhelming."[1]

If one is new to social media, there is a lot to grasp. This is a common problem for both small business owners and large multinational companies when looking at social media. This book is intended to help both students and businesses understand the social media landscape and how to approach it strategically.

Many businesses struggle with social media because they lack a definite plan. They start with an end in mind instead of creating a strategy and objectives. A company might start a Twitter account or a Facebook page, but it is not likely to see results unless there is a clear understanding of its marketing objectives. Like any form of marketing, a strong strategic plan for social media is required for success.

The advent of social media has also posed a challenge to traditional marketing methodologies. During the recession of 2009-2010, budgets for marketing and advertising were slashed, and big marketing firms have been forced to adjust. The job market for marketing professionals is changing (see the end--chapter case study and exercise set for details). Advertising revenue has increasingly moved to the Internet, with even long-time print magazines such as *The Atlantic* shifting to a largely digital-based revenue strategy.[2] For many firms, the focus is now online, which makes knowledge of social media marketing especially valuable for students and/or soon-to-be job-seekers.

LEARNING OBJECTIVES

After completing this chapter, students will be able to:

- Explain why social media is important
- Define social media marketing
- Explain the 7 myths of social marketing
- Describe a brief history of social media marketing
- Explain how social media marketing is different
- Identify the characteristics of a successful social media marketer
- Describe the careers in social media marketing

This book is organized into two core sections: the first four chapters will lay the foundation for engaging in social media, including marketing strategy and objectives, targeting specific audiences, and the background rules of social media. The remainder of the book will encompass more detailed elements of social media marketing and how to adapt the strategy to specific platforms and international audiences. By creating a solid content plan and choosing the right tools, a business can expediently and successfully navigate to its marketing goals and objectives.

Finding a Way Through Social Media

With the rising number and popularity of social media sites, as portrayed in Table 1.1, lots of people are "doing" social media marketing. Some trailblazers in the field have achieved notoriety for their mastery of certain platforms and for their written instructional manuals to assist others in doing the same. This textbook codifies the knowledge in the field of social media marketing, and examines the successful routes that others have already discovered. By learning about the successes and failures of others' media strategies, a student of social media marketing can use tools that help find an efficient and effective path. With a decisive strategy, combined with knowledge of where others have gone before, it will be possible to take aim across the field of social media, and make any necessary corrections along the way.

In social media marketing, businesses often start their efforts by heading in a random direction, and results take a long time or are never achieved at all. Alternately, the firm spends time trying many different approaches, and after substantial cost and effort, figures out how to accomplish its goals. Some businesses become exhausted by the journey and write off social media marketing as ineffective because it is too difficult to figure out. However, with the right tools and knowledge, any business can potentially gain from social media marketing, without getting lost along the way.

Social Media Site	Category	Monthly Visitors (millions)*	Google Page Rank**	Alexa Global Traffic Rank***
Facebook	Social Network	700	9	2
YouTube	Video Sharing Site	450	9	3
Wikipedia	Wiki-based Encyclopedia	350	8	6
Twitter	Microblogging Site	200	9	9
WordPress	Blog Hosting Site	150	9	93
LinkedIn	Social Network	100	9	13
Flickr	Photo Sharing Site	90	9	36
MySpace	Social Network	80.5	8	124
Photobucket	Photo Sharing Site	75.5	7	143
Blogger	Blog Hosting Site	75	9	7
eHow	Article Directory	55	7	149
Digg	Social News Site	25.1	8	190

Table 1.1 Popular Social Media Sites, as of December 2011

Estimated unique monthly visitors according to eBiz|MBA Inc.
**Google Page Rank uses the number and quality of links to a web page to determine its relative importance, using a scale of 0-10, with 10 indicating the highest rank and 0 the lowest.
***Alexa Global Traffic Rank estimates a site's popularity, with traffic data from Alexa Toolbar users and other diverse traffic sources, using an ascending scale where 1 represents the highest traffic rank.

What Is Social Media Marketing?

As a relatively new field, many have attempted to define "social media marketing." For example, the most popular online collaborative encyclopedia, *Wikipedia*, defines it thus:

Social media marketing is a term that describes use of social networks, online communities, blogs, wikis or any other online collaborative media for marketing, sales, public relations and customer service. Common social media marketing tools include Twitter, blogs, LinkedIn, Facebook, Flickr and YouTube.

In the context of Internet marketing, social media refers to a collective group of web properties whose content is primarily published by users, not direct employees of the property (e.g., the vast majority of video on YouTube is published by non-YouTube employees)…

Social media marketing has three important aspects:

1. *Creating buzz or newsworthy events, videos, tweets, or blog entries that attract attention, and become viral in nature. Buzz is what makes social media marketing work. It replicates a message through user to user contact, rather than the traditional method of purchasing an ad or promoting a press release. The message does not necessarily have to be about the product. Many successful viral campaigns have gathered steam through an amusing or compelling message, with the company logo or tagline included incidentally.*

2. *Building ways that enable fans of a brand or company to promote a message themselves in multiple online social media venues. Fan pages in Twitter, MySpace or Facebook follow this model.*

3. *It is based around online conversations. Social media marketing is not controlled by the organization. Instead it encourages user participation and dialogue. A badly designed social media marketing campaign can potentially backfire on the organization that created it. To be a successful [social media marketing] campaigns must fully engage and respect the users.*[3]

This *Wikipedia* definition captures the essence of social media marketing, although it lacks precision and conciseness, whereas the following definition provides both clarity and succinctness: **Social media marketing (SMM)** uses social media portals to positively influence consumers toward a website, company, brand, product, service, or a person. Typically, the end goal of social media marketing is a "conversion," such as the purchase of a product, subscription to a newsletter, registration in an online community, or some other desirable consumer action. As *Wikipedia* points out, this conversion is accomplished by creating a buzz online so that complementary content about an individual or company's offerings goes viral, with consumer-generated media endorsements spreading like wildfire across the Internet.

Fiskars Creates a Social Media Community around Scrapbooking

Introduction

Fiskars is a global consumer products corporation, which has a variety of international brands and has been in existence for over 360 years; established in 1649, it is the oldest company in Finland. It launched the world's first plastic-handled scissors in 1967, with a distinctive orange handle that is still easily recognizable today.[4] That classic model has now sold over a billion copies.

History

In the late 90s and early 2000s, Fiskars was faced with competition from a variety of other brands. While Fiskars had a groundbreaking product, they needed to make a bold move to cement its status.

Crafts and hobbies are a $30 billion industry, and high-quality scissors are integral to most crafting projects.[5] Fiskars decided to focus its efforts around scrapbooking hobbyists and to develop a better connection with its customers. In 2006, Fiskars hired consultants Brains on Fire to help implement a plan.[6] After interviewing people in crafting groups on Yahoo, the consultants' research paid off.

From the interviews, the company selected four women to become "The Fiskateers," who were to spread awareness of the Fiskars brand to their friends and acquaintances. The Fiskateers were hired part-time and encouraged to travel around the country and build relationships with store owners, tradeshow hosts, and hobbyists.

The Fiskateers also set up blogs to address customer questions and to gain feedback on the products.* The result was broader consumer engagement and a valuable source of information for the company. Later, other hobbyists could send in applications to join the Fiskateers. Few applications were rejected, but the process of joining the Fiskars network built a stronger sense of community. People from the online network could gather in person to trade crafting tips or product suggestions.

Fiskars' Well-known Scissors

© Cameramannz/ Shutterstock

Results

With a budget of less than $500,000, Fiskars was able to implement a revolutionary social media marketing campaign.[7] The Fiskars online community has grown

---

*See Fiskateers: Crafting Ambassadors, http://www.fiskateers.com/blog/

rapidly, with noticeable effects on Fiskars's bottom line. The fan community has increased sales by 300% and generated a large number of new product ideas.[8]

By connecting with the scrapbooking community using both online and word-of-mouth efforts, Fiskars has become a classic social media marketing success story. The company's dramatic results can be attributed to a strong strategy as well as to detailed demographic research. By targeting a group that already used the product, then connecting those individuals to others with a shared interest, Fiskars's online community has been a valuable resource to customers as well as to the company.

The Seven Myths of Social Media Marketing

Social media marketing is one of the best ways that businesses can drive sales, build relationships, and satisfy their customers. Although social media has increased in popularity over the years as a marketing tool,** there remain some common misconceptions about social media marketing. The following are seven of the most common myths that business professionals have regarding social media marketing.

SOCIAL MEDIA MYTH #1: SOCIAL MEDIA IS JUST A FAD

Businesses want to invest their time and energy in marketing tools that will be useful in the long-term, versus wasting limited resources on a flash-in-the-pan technology or a fad. Some business professionals question whether social media will remain a powerful marketing and communications tool or if it will eventually fall by the wayside. To resolve this issue, it is helpful to look at the foundations of social media, which are built on age-old concepts of community, socialization, and word of mouth marketing.

The "social" component of social media has been part of human interactions since the dawn of time. People are inherently social creatures to some extent. What has changed is the media by which people are able to express social impulses. As technology has advanced, so have the media available for social behavior. Initially, social interactions were limited to in-person meetings, then mail and letters, then telephones, then email, and now "social media," or web-based social interactions.

The underlying premise of social media—that people are social and want to connect with other people—has been stable over time. The difference is that people are now able to connect with each other in a more efficient and scalable way. Facebook allows users to see what friends from high school are up to without ever speaking to them. Photos of friends and family from across the world can be viewed on photo sharing sites. In these and many other ways, social media allows people to keep up to speed with many connections in quick and efficient ways.

Like the Internet, social media is a not a flash in the pan because of the human desire to socialize and because the media of the Internet continue to evolve at a rapid rate, providing new and attractive means for people to interact. Although social media will only expand in the foreseeable future, specific social media platforms (technologies

---

**It is estimated that nearly four out of five businesses with 100 employees or more will be using some form of social media in 2011, compared to 42% in 2008. The same study found that "social media ranked third among areas marketers [who] planned to focus their online marketing budget in 2011 after search and their own website." From eMarketer (2010, December 9), "How Many Marketers Are Using Social Media?" Retrieved January 5, 2011, from http://www.emarketer.com/Article.aspx?R=1008092

or applications such as Facebook and Twitter) change considerably over time. Rather than focusing on the latest and greatest sites or applications, economize on effort by looking at core trends and behaviors in social media interaction—these remain relatively stable over time.

In addition, social media marketing is a form of word-of-mouth marketing. It is common for people to share experiences with businesses or products with friends: for example, telling them about tasty food at a new restaurant or about the horrible customer service at a furniture store. The difference is that these conversations are now happening online, and they are happening on a larger scale than ever before.

Social media has reached a critical mass that is so interwoven in cultures around the world that it is clear there is no going back. Consider these statistics:

- Facebook now has over 700 million users. That is bigger than the populations of the United States, Canada, and Mexico combined.[9]

- According to the "Social Media Matters Study" of 2010, three-quarters of the online population is comprised of frequent social media users.[10]

- According to comScore, there are nearly 25 billion searches done online every month.[11]

- Forrester Research estimates that online U.S. retail spending accounted for $191.7 billion or roughly 7% of all retail consumer spending in 2010. It expects that online retail sales will reach $248.7 by 2014 or 8% of the entire retail market[12]

- Social media continues to grow steadily. The fourth annual "BlogHer 2011 Social Media Matters Study" found increases in the usage of Facebook, YouTube, blogs, and variety of other social media, as shown in Figure 1.1.[13]

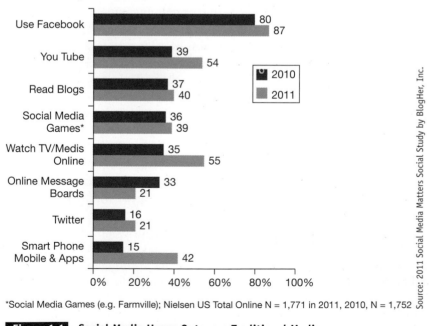

The general population:
Online media continues to grow steadily

Source: 2011 Social Media Matters Social Study by BlogHer, Inc.

*Social Media Games (e.g. Farmville); Nielsen US Total Online N = 1,771 in 2011, 2010, N = 1,752

Figure 1.1 Social Media Usage Outpaces Traditional Media

*Forrester Research Web-Influenced Retail Sales Forecast, Forrester Research, Inc., December 2009.

SOCIAL MEDIA MYTH #2: SOCIAL MEDIA IS JUST FOR THE YOUNG

Many social media skeptics think that social media is a tool primarily for the young: kids, teenagers, and college students. The reality is that older users are among the fastest growing demographics on most social media sites:

- YouTube reports that their user base is broad in age range, 18 to 55, evenly divided between males and females, and spanning all geographies.[14]

- People over 65 are adopting Facebook quicker than any other group.[15]

- 48% of people over 55 have Facebook accounts.[16]

- Facebook is more popular with younger people but has significant penetration in all age groups. According to Morpace research, 84% of those 18 to 34 have Facebook pages compared to 61% of those 35 to 54 and 48% of people over 55.[17]

Social networks are increasingly being adopted by older populations and are becoming incredibly diverse, with users spanning all age and income brackets. This diversity means that most businesses, if they are willing to look, can find their target consumers on social media sites.

SOCIAL MEDIA MYTH #3: THERE IS NO RETURN IN SOCIAL MEDIA MARKETING

Many social media skeptics are concerned about quantifying the return from social media marketing. The results from social media can be difficult to measure, and many businesses do not currently measure their social media efforts. The paucity of commonly accepted measuring tools does not demonstrate the lack of return from social media marketing but rather that the field and the metrics to access are still developing. Indeed, this textbook has an entire chapter dedicated to social media measurement.

One of the fastest growing and highest demand careers in social media marketing is in measuring the economic impact of social media marketing campaigns. The subject is a frequent topic for conferences of online marketing experts, and as a result, newer and more accurate tools for quantifying social media outcomes are constantly emerging.[18]

Although ROI (return on investment) is a specific monetary value determined by an established method, social media return is measured in a variety of different ways and is not always as clear-cut. That being said, the monetary return on a social media marketing campaign can be measured, and many businesses are doing so.

The following are just a few examples of businesses successfully measuring returns from their respective social media marketing efforts:

Dell generated $6.5 million dollars from its Twitter account.[19]

Marriott got over $500 million in bookings directly from its blog.[20]

Golden Tee saved tens of thousands of dollars running a contest on Facebook.[21]

VistaPrints sold $30,000 from social media marketing.[22]

Lenovo saved costs with a 20% reduction in customer service calls by using social media.[23]

Naked Pizza, a small regional pizza chain, had its highest-ever sales day from deals posted on Twitter.[24]

A number of case studies highlight the tangible dollar return from companies of all sizes using social media. Both small independent retailers and large multinational companies have seen success from social media marketing.

In addition to direct attributable sales, a number of other benefits arise from social media marketing: savings in customer service, online word-of-mouth promotion (buzz), improved brand awareness and reputation, increased brand loyalty, and sale lead generation, just to name just a few.

SOCIAL MEDIA MYTH #4: SOCIAL MEDIA MARKETING ISN'T RIGHT FOR THIS BUSINESS

Many companies have trouble determining if social media marketing is right for their specific industry or business. Although business-to-consumer (B2C) online sales continue to grow rapidly, business-to-business (B2B) transactions are increasingly moving online; some CEOs and sales experts think that the majority of B2B transactions may eventually be done over the Internet.[25] It is a common misconception that B2B firms can benefit little from social media marketing. However, B2B firms, like B2C companies, are made up of people who use social media. Hence, social media marketing is just as relevant to them as to B2C firms.

The reality is that for almost any business, there are opportunities in social media marketing. With the massive growth in social media over the past few years, a large part of the population is on at least one social media site. A third of U.S. adults already use social media to make either negative or positive comments about products and services.[26] This means that the people in any particular target audience are probably using some social media sites; the challenge is choosing the right place to look. Traditional marketing has shown that where consumer attention goes, so go marketing dollars. Marketers connect with people where they spend their time, and, increasingly, that time is being spent on social media. According to Nielsen's *State of the Media*: *Social Media Report* for the third quarter of 2011, "social networks and blogs reach nearly 80 percent of active Internet users and represent the majority of Americans' time online."[27]

In addition to more time shifting towards social media, an increasing number of people seek to interact with brands on social media platforms. According to Facebook, an average Facebooker is connected to over 80 brand pages, community pages and events.[28] A Morpace study found that the primary reasons people join fan pages is to let their friends know the products they like (word-of-mouth) and to receive coupons and discounts (direct sales opportunity).[29]

Social media has a powerful ability to drive word-of-mouth or recommendations from friends. Facebook is one substantial source for word-of-mouth advertising: 57% state that they use Facebook to discuss products and services with friends and nearly 68% of consumers say that a positive referral from a friend on Facebook makes them more likely to buy a specific product or visit a certain retailer.

According to ComScore, there are almost 25 billion online searches each month.[30] Regardless what industry a business is part of, people are searching for information about products and brand reputation to help guide their purchase. Search is the number one resource used when looking for information about a product online, with 92% of people using it. Social media influences search as a resource because search results frequently include social media sites. Facebook, LinkedIn, *Wikipedia*, Yelp, Yahoo!Answers, review sites, blogs, and other social media sites consistently show up on the first page of search results. Even if businesses don't believe in the value of engaging in social conversations as a part of marketing, there is no denying the value of a strong business or product presence in search results.

Businesses that don't monitor social media or search engine results may be unpleasantly surprised by what shows up. A search for "Comcast" returns a video of a Comcast technician falling asleep on a customer's sofa while on hold with Comcast customer service. This video, posted in 2006, is still a first-page Google search result for Comcast as of this writing.

Even companies that listen to the social web have been heavily penalized for being insensitive or slow to react to customer concerns, as painfully demonstrated by the case study: *United Breaks Guitars*. Despite United Airlines's active social media monitoring program, it failed to use social media to provide basic customer service.

Given the power that social media endows consumers with, it is little wonder that users are increasingly screening out traditional advertising media and focusing their attention toward social media where they control the content. Many businesses are familiar with marketing through television, radio, newspapers, yellow pages, or direct mail. However, these methods are losing their power in the marketplace. People are watching less traditional TV and are instead viewing videos online through YouTube and television through sites like Hulu.com. Radio is being replaced by online streaming music on sites such as Pandora.com or Slacker.com. Newspapers are in dramatic decline, while blogs such as the Huffington Post are growing in popularity. The Yellow Pages are more likely to be used to hold up a computer monitor than to locate a business, with the abundance of online white page and yellow page directories. Direct mail coupons end up in the garbage because the same coupons can be found online far more easily at sites like Groupon.com. To keep people's interest, marketing efforts have to adapt and evolve to ride the social media tsunami.

CASE STUDY

United Breaks Guitars

Introduction

In 2008, Dave Carroll, a musician flying United Airlines, witnessed baggage handlers throwing his $3,500 Taylor guitar.[31] Carroll immediately alerted airline's personnel to the problem, but was met with indifference and inaction. So Carroll began a nine-month effort to get United Airlines to pay for damages to the guitar, which ultimately proved fruitless. When it became clear United was not going to pay for repairs to the instrument, Carroll warned the airline that he was going to make three music videos portraying his negative experiences and post them on YouTube.

Unfortunately for United Airlines, the first video, titled "United Breaks Guitars" went viral on YouTube. Carroll's story, set to music and visuals, resonated across the social web, tarnishing United Airlines' reputation.[32] Mainstream media, like the *Today Show* and *CNN's Situation Room*, picked up the story.[33,34] In response, United Airlines called the video a "learning experience" and began using it for internal training purposes to improve customer service.[35]

Far more than a mere cautionary tale in the age of social media, this "Dave versus Goliath" saga signaled a not-subtle shift in the power of communicating a message.[36] Gone are the days when millions in advertising and PR could control the message—now when customer service is lacking, an individual can use the social web to communicate with the world, sometimes with nothing more than a song and clever video.[37]

History

Dave Carroll made a modest living as a musician for over two decades by performing pop-folk music with his band (Sons of Maxwell), traveling across Canada, with occasional visits to U.S. cities and overseas' music festivals.[38]

On March 31, 2008, the members of Carroll's band were flying from Halifax, Canada to Omaha, Nebraska to perform a week of shows.[39] While transferring planes in Chicago, a woman behind them yelled, "Oh my God, they are throwing guitars outside."[40] The band watched in horror as they recognized their instruments being thrown by the airline's baggage handlers. Carroll saw his $3,500 Taylor guitar being mishandled.

Carroll called a flight attendant and made her aware of what was going on. She responded, "Don't talk to me. Talk to the lead agent outside."[41] But the ground staff at O'Hare said, "Talk to the ground staff at Omaha."[42] After a flight delay, Carroll reached his destination in Omaha around midnight and the ground staff was gone. Upon opening the guitar case, he discovered that the base of his Taylor guitar was indeed smashed.

Challenge

Dave Carroll spent the next nine months phoning and emailing customer support at United Airlines trying to recover the $1,200 he spent to have the guitar repaired.[43] At each stage, United Airlines staff refused to take responsibility and passed him along to telephone representatives in India, the central baggage office in New York, and the Chicago baggage office.[44] He finally began exchanging emails with a customer service representative at United who appeared to have decision-making authority, but after 10 email exchanges with her, she

Dave Carroll with His Guitar

ended with, "This is it, there's going to be nothing you're going to get out of United Airlines."[45] Ms. Irlweg informed Carroll that the airline had concluded the damage was his responsibility and United considered the matter closd.[46]

Strategy ....

This was the final straw for Carroll. "At that moment, it occurred to me I've been fighting a losing battle all this time. I got sucked into their cycle of insanity. I called, emailed, and jumped through hoops, just as they told me to do…However, I realized, that as a musician, I wasn't without options…So, I said, 'I urge you to reconsider because I am a singer-songwriter and I am going to write three songs about United Airlines and post them on YouTube.'"[47] The customer service rep replied, "Good luck with that, pal."[48]

Carroll's first video cost $150, with friends pitching in for free to produce it—the local firehouse, where he volunteered as a firefighter, provided the "tarmac" backdrop for the video.[49] On July 6, 2009, the video was posted to YouTube.[50]

Result ....

Within 24 hours after uploading the video, it had over 50,000 views, which drew the attention of United Airlines.[51] They contacted Dave Carroll and offered to pay for the cost of repairing his guitar, plus $1,200 worth of flight vouchers, which he declined, but suggested that the airline donate the sum to charity.[52] Carroll felt that accepting the offer would be a form of "betrayal" to everyone who helped him make the video.[53]

Twenty-four days after uploading "United Breaks Guitars" on YouTube, the video had received over 4 million views, and more than 19,000 comments, "…fueling negative publicity for United Airlines."[54]

Carroll observed, "It's been said that in the 'old days' (maybe only a decade ago) that people who had a positive customer service experience would share that with 3 people. If they had a bad experience, they would tell 144…[A]s of today I have reached more than 6 million people on YouTube with my story and, according to some estimates, some 100 million people if you total all media references."[55] By August 2011, the YouTube video had received over 10 million views, with 51,485 likes.[56]

The "United Breaks Guitars" PR disaster has deep implications for marketing and branding in the era of social media. *Advertising Age* columnist David Stein opined that, "In these postmodern times, where every interaction with the customer is a marketing event, the real crunch point comes when the customer meets your customer-service department."[57] The value of good customer service and the power of social media are lessons that United Airlines learned the hard way.

SOCIAL MEDIA MYTH #5: SOCIAL MEDIA MARKETING IS NEW

Social media marketing is not really new. Most of the marketing principles, based on social, behavioral, and economic concepts, have been around for many years, but new technology and media are changing the role those concepts play in modern marketing efforts. For example, brands are very excited about the potential to harness online conversations on blogs, Twitter, and social networks. The behavior—talking about brands and businesses—isn't new and is more generally called word-of-mouth marketing. The difference is that these conversations are now public, online, and viewable for the indefinite future.

The newest aspect of social media is the technology which enables open and transparent online conversations. Some companies don't want to "get on" social media because they are afraid of what consumers might say about them. The reality is that consumers are already on social sites, talking about businesses on their Facebook pages, blogs, and Twitter accounts, whether a business acknowledges this or not.

SOCIAL MEDIA MYTH #6: SOCIAL MEDIA IS TOO TIME-CONSUMING

One of the biggest business concerns about using social media marketing is the amount of time and resources it will take. The time and resources required to manage social media marketing depends on the size of the business. Large companies that have thousands of online mentions a day will have to dedicate more resources to social media than a small business. The time commitment required to manage social media will also depend on the specific social media strategy and approach used.

Most of the concern about time and resources comes from small- and medium-sized businesses. After the initial setup and strategy, these businesses should be able to manage their social media programs effectively with only a few hours per week. Social media doesn't have to be time consuming when done right. The problem is that many people log on to Facebook, Twitter, or LinkedIn and become addicted to checking out what friends are up to, exchanging messages, or generally spending far more time than necessary for business promotion.

There are three key ways to limit the time investment in social media marketing. The first is to look for underutilized employees who can spend some of their time on social media marketing. For example, a receptionist may not be busy the entire day, and many retail stores and restaurants have downtimes during which human resources are not fully utilized.

The second opportunity is to leverage efficiency tools. There are a number of sites, such as HootSuite, TweetDeck, and CoTweet, which make managing social media easier. By using these tools, social media efforts can be streamlined.

Finally, using mobile devices is a key way to boost efficiency in social media marketing. This is especially helpful for publishing multimedia content. Smartphones (a Blackberry, iPhone, or Android phone) can take a picture or video and instantly post it onto Facebook, Twitter, or a blog in only a minute. This speed makes managing social media marketing even easier and less time consuming.

SOCIAL MEDIA MYTH #7: SOCIAL MEDIA IS FREE

Many businesses are excited about social media because it is free. Nevertheless, while most sites do not have a fee for usage, social media isn't really free. First, there is the cost in terms of time and resources, as well as the fee of using consultants or agencies involved in building and executing the social media strategy. Social media takes time, and that alone means it is not free.

Second, similar to other media and advertising, in addition to costs from posting content, there are also costs to producing and creating content. Imagine if it were free to run TV commercials. Companies would run lots of commercials, including more bad ones that drive fewer sales. Free access means no barrier to entry and greater competition for consumer attention. Good commercials would still have costs for creativity and production in order to produce a sequence memorable enough to be recognized and remembered. In a similar way, strong social media strategies may entail costs for top-quality creative or development efforts, depending on their scale.

Finally, many businesses engaging in social media invest in a guide or consultant to help them through the process. Consultants can help businesses get off to a quicker start and avoid common pitfalls, as well as save time and money.

Regardless of whether or not there are actual out-of-pocket expenses associated with social media, the resource and time costs should not be forgotten. As time spent on social media is not free, it must be allocated wisely in order to generate maximum results. Hopefully, this text will provide the tools necessary to get the most impact out of time spent on social media marketing.

The History of Social Media Marketing

Currently, social media is said to have reached critical mass, with over half of the adult U.S. population now using some form of social media.[58] Still, this trend emerged from humble beginnings, as illustrated by the social media timeline in Figure 1.2. Using a loose interpretation, one could say that the first social media existed as soon as the first postal service was created, which allowed people to communicate across great distances instead of just face-to-face. However, social media marketing in the most relevant sense for this book became viable with the development of the Internet in the late 1960s. The early Internet was created for the use of professors and researchers working for the Department of Defense. Those researchers began using the ARPANET (the Advanced Research Projects Agency Network, a core of what would become the Internet) resources for nonwork purposes, and usage quickly began to grow. Early online marketing efforts would soon follow; the first "spam" email message was sent in 1978![†]

The earliest ancestor of today's diverse social media platforms is most likely USENET, developed by Duke University graduate students Jim Ellis and Tom Truscott in 1979. Users can post articles, which are organized into "newsgroups" depending on the topic. Other users can subscribe to newsgroups they find interesting; often some post responses to an article they read, forming a "thread." Unlike bulletin boards or online forums that have an administrator or central hub, USENET is a conglomeration

---

[†]The first mass email message was sent to 393 people out of the 2,600 ARPANET users at the time in order to advertise a new computer model created by Digital Equipment Corporation. It was sent by Gary Turk. For more information, see: NPR News (2008, May 3), "At 30, Spam Going Nowhere Soon," hosted by Andrea Seabrook (transcript online, retrieved September 8, 2011 from http://www.npr.org/templates/story/story.php?storyId=90160617); Tom Abate (2008, May 3), "A Very Unhappy Birthday to Spam, Age 30," *San Francisco Chronicle*. Retrieved September 8, 2011 from http://articles.sfgate.com/2008-05-03/business/17155925_1_spam-e-mail-world-wide-web

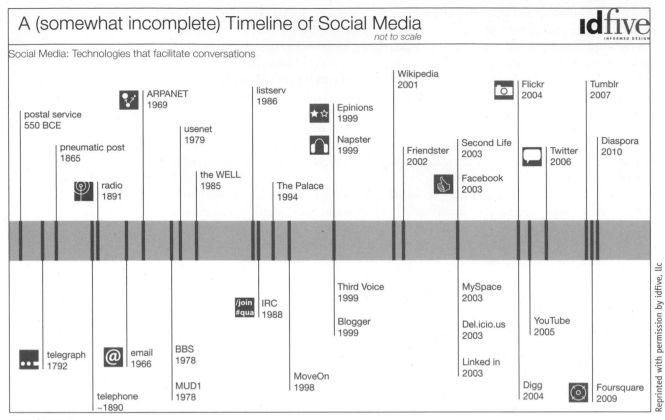

A (somewhat incomplete) Timeline of Social Media
not to scale

idfive
INFORMED DESIGN

Social Media: Technologies that facilitate conversations

- postal service 550 BCE
- pneumatic post 1865
- radio 1891
- ARPANET 1969
- usenet 1979
- the WELL 1985
- listserv 1986
- The Palace 1994
- Epinions 1999
- Napster 1999
- Wikipedia 2001
- Friendster 2002
- Second Life 2003
- Facebook 2003
- Flickr 2004
- Twitter 2006
- Tumblr 2007
- Diaspora 2010

- telegraph 1792
- telephone ~1890
- email 1966
- BBS 1978
- MUD1 1978
- IRC 1988
- /join #qua
- MoveOn 1998
- Third Voice 1999
- Blogger 1999
- MySpace 2003
- Del.icio.us 2003
- Linked in 2003
- YouTube 2005
- Digg 2004
- Foursquare 2009

Reprinted with permission by idfive, llc

Figure 1.2 Social Media Timeline

of separate servers run by different organizations or Internet service providers (ISPs), which exchange articles and threads with each other. In this way, articles posted by one user can reach many others eventually, and people can comment and have their voices heard. These are the core principles of social media.

Following USENET, there was an explosion of different web-based services designed for people with common interests to share information. The WELL (Whole Earth 'Lectronic Link) was created in 1985, starting out as a dial-up bulletin board system (BBS). This quickly developed into a dial-up ISP in the early 1990s, dramatically expanding its user base. Its online forums are still hosting discussions today. Other dial-up BBS systems like CompuServe and Prodigy were fulfilling a similar function by hosting user-driven discussions about various topics.

The growth of social media paralleled the increasing development of computing and Internet transfer technology. While in the 1990s most Internet users were on dial-up connections with speeds under 56 kilobytes per second, within ten years broadband technology such as DSL and cable Internet would become available, increasing transfer speeds by thousands of times. As more data was transferred quickly, social media networks became more advanced and included elements other than just plain text. In 1999 Napster was developed, allowing users to quickly share media files such as music and video with each other. *Wikipedia* was established in 2001 and continues to be a leading source of relevant user-contributed information. The year 2003 was highly significant for social media with the creation of MySpace, Delicious, SecondLife, and Facebook. The photo-sharing site Flickr was created in 2004 and YouTube for sharing videos in 2005. Twitter came along in 2006. Since then, numerous competitors have arisen for all of the above, each seeking to draw in more online participants and develop its own market share. As a result, the history of social media platforms is still being written.

The groundbreaking texts for social media as a serious academic and marketing field were also being written during that same time period. The possibilities for online social interaction and community were beginning to be explored. A seminal text for social media marketing came in 1993 when Howard Rheingold wrote *The Virtual Community: Homesteading on the Electronic Frontier.*[59] In 1999 Seth Godin authored another influential book, *Permission Marketing: Turning Strangers into Friends and Friends into Customers*, which still remains relevant today (some of its lessons will be discussed in Chapter 4).[60] Another important text was *The Cluetrain Manifesto*, which outlined ninety-five theses exploring business media of the future.[61] Since the mid-2000s, a slew of instructional books have been published, focused on specific areas of social media marketing, search engine optimization, and other web-based marketing tactics. Some experts have made their careers out of this developing field; Guy Kawasaki, Chris Brogan, and David Meerman Scott, to name just a few, have become household names in social media marketing. Obviously, this is a rapidly evolving field with opportunities in both business and academia.[††]

Why Social Media Marketing is Different

A common misconception is that social media marketing just means using new online social media sites to do traditional marketing. This view may be common because "[m]any look at social media as another outlet to pump their marketing messages into, especially companies which have found that success in other channels of marketing."[62] The traditional marketing approach, emphasizing the four Ps (product, price, place, and promotion) has become second nature to many professionals. While the traditional marketing perspective still has important lessons for future marketers, in the new terrain of social media, it has to be adapted or in some areas changed completely.

Several aspects distinguish social media marketing from so-called traditional marketing. The first is **control vs. contributions**. Traditional marketing seeks to control the content seen by the audience. Old school marketers attempt to dominate the territory and try to exclude their competitors' messages. Exclusivity agreements between retailers and suppliers are a classic example: a fast food restaurant will serve drinks under the Pepsi brand or under the Coca-Cola brand but almost never will it sell both brands due to agreement between the parent companies.

Traditional marketers try to export similar agreements into the digital terrain, but social media marketers "are more likely to host an online 'discussion' in which they welcome comparison to their competitors' products and group information sharing."[63] Social media marketing emphasizes audience contribution, and relinquishes

---

[††]Recently, social media and social media marketing have been topics of several post-graduate dissertations in a variety of fields. For some examples, see *Boyd, Danah Michele* (2008, Fall), "Taken out of Context: American Teen Sociality in Networked Publics," PhD diss., Information Management and Systems, Designated Emphasis in New Media, University of California, Berkeley; *Ivanauskas, Giedrius* (2009), "The Evaluation of Social Media Effects on Marketing Communications, London Metropolitan University: The UK Consumers' Perspective," M.A. thesis, International Business and Marketing; *Java, Akshay* (2008), "Mining Social Media Communities and Content," PhD diss., Department of Computer Science and Electrical Engineering, University of Maryland (all available online).

control over large parts of the content. Effective social media marketers can sometimes influence what participants say and think about their brand, but rarely can they control the conversation entirely. Indeed, the very nature of social media can make controlling the conversation seem rude and domineering. Avoiding this pitfall makes knowledge of social media important even for persons engaged in traditional marketing.

The second important distinction between traditional and social media marketing is **trust building**. Firms cannot fully control the content that users will create, so to build their image, companies must develop trusting relationships with their audience. Unlike traditional advertisements in which consumers expect some exaggeration or spin to be applied to the product's image, on social media it is important to be earnest and down-to-earth.

The importance of trust emerges from how social media messages are consumed. In traditional marketing, the signal is one-way: from the firm to potential customers. However, social media involves "two-way communication to an audience that is interested in the brand."[64] The audience's attention cannot be taken for granted; deliver boring, inaccurate, or irrelevant information and they will look elsewhere. Unlike an advertising campaign with a set stop and end, "social media doesn't have an end date. It is an ongoing conversation between the advertiser and the customer."[65] Companies that bend the truth will be eventually held accountable and have to explain their actions. This pattern appears in numerous case studies throughout the book. On social media, trust is slow to earn but very easy to lose. Successful social media marketers consider building trust with the audience to be of paramount importance.

What are the Characteristics of a Successful Social Media Marketer?

Social media marketing is a developing field, and the standards for success are still being fine tuned. Some social media marketers started with an education in marketing and then adapted those skills to social media, while others have been self-taught or have even been former programmers. In any case, the traits of a successful social media marketer can be divided into two categories: technical and personal.

The **technical** skills required for social media marketing involve basic computer skills, proficiency with search engines and navigating the web. Knowledge of coding or graphic design is helpful but far from necessary. Similarly, strong typing skills will increase a social media marketer's efficiency, but technological aids such as speech recognition, writing tablets, or others devices do exist. Generally, the technical skills for social media marketing are not beyond the grasp of most people.

The **personal** attributes required for success in social media are arguably more important than technical abilities. A good social media marketer is personable and able to make conversation and establish a connection with anyone, regardless of their location or background. Being a good listener is often the basis of this ability. Having a diverse vocabulary, strong reading and comprehension skills, and/or proficiency in multiple languages will all increase the effectiveness and job prospects of a social media marketer. Above all, having creativity and a passion for the field of social media marketing are necessary to achieve success. In any social media campaign, there will be unexpected challenges or setbacks, so be prepared to think quickly. Along the way, a sense of humor and a flexible ego will be of great assistance. Being able to respond to negative comments without losing composure or professionalism is an essential skill for social media marketing specialists.

The above characteristics may not sound very rare or difficult to develop. Arguably, large parts of the population have the skills to do social media; indeed, as shown by the enormous growth of sites like Twitter, Facebook, and LinkedIn, much of the population already is "doing" social media! An effective social media marketer must be able to translate business or marketing goals and objectives into the execution of social media strategy. While many people may be good at social media marketing, it often takes a great social media marketer in order to make a profit. It is common for social media specialists to work seventy-hour weeks and rarely to have weekends off. Developing the skills and knowledge emphasized in this book will help one compete against others in the growing field of social media marketing and to rise to the top in this dynamic area.

Careers in Social Media Marketing

While traditional marketing and public relations careers have been hit hard by the recent economic downturn, social media marketing has been a growth area for business spending. Spending on social media is forecast to expand substantially between 2009 and 2014 (see Figure 1.3). According to the 2009 CMO Survey, currently "marketers spend 3.5 percent of their budget on social media, but that number is expected to grow to 6.1 percent over the next 12 months and 13.7 percent in the next five years. The biggest growth is expected to come from the business-to-consumer service sector."[66]

Further, based on a Marketing Executives Networking Group (MENG) survey of over 1,800 high-ranking corporate marketers, "[o]ver 70% of respondents said their company is planning NEW social media initiatives in 2010."[67] Asked how they will do those social media initiatives, 71% said "internally," suggesting that many companies will need to hire additional social media marketers soon. As one example, the JetBlue Airways (which has around ten people working on Twitter) indicated that "[r]ather than hiring external social media savvy people . . . we looked internally for people who happened to be active on

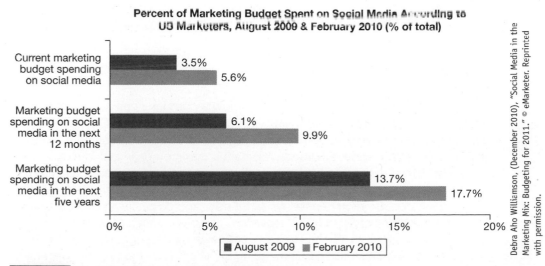

Figure 1.3 Firm Spending on Social Media Marketing

Debra Aho Williamson, (December 2010), "Social Media in the Marketing Mix: Budgeting for 2011." © eMarketer. Reprinted with permission.

social media in their personal lives."[68] Jobs in the field will continue to grow, as more companies decide to follow a similar strategy and realize that internal talent will not be enough to meet their needs. As a result, demand for social media marketers is likely to increase in the near future.

Currently "the majority of the jobs in social media are freelance rather than full-time. On the up side, hourly rates can be high—$200 an hour and more."[69] Even salaried social media marketers receive competitive pay. The median yearly pay for a social media marketer located in Washington, DC is $64,000, with those in the 75% percentile earning an average $103,500 per year.[70] Professional bloggers can be paid between $10 to $200 per post, depending on length and content, but the biggest money is to be found in consulting.[71] These types of jobs are typically offered only to seasoned professionals who have demonstrated results in the past.

Companies are increasingly looking for **power-users** or people who already have influence in the world of social media. Writers with popular blogs are sometimes hired to become corporate bloggers. For the rest of us who have no particular presence online, the first step toward landing a social media job is getting involved. Start a blog, develop a Twitter following, and so on, and companies are more likely to be convinced that results can be generated for them as well. As one commentator notes, "If you can't market your own brand, your own services, and something that you're passionate about—how can you expect any company to take you serious?"[72] Getting a social media position is increasingly possible but also highly competitive. A strong work ethic, determination, and background knowledge will help an individual stand out from the crowd. This textbook can only contribute to the last factor; the hard work and determination lie with the individual.

EXERCISE CASE STUDY

Exercise: JetBlue Uses Social Media to Connect with Customers

Introduction

JetBlue Airways provides a good example of how a company can successfully use social media to better connect with its customers.[73] Marty St. George, senior vice president of Marketing & Commercial Strategy at JetBlue, speaking at conference in June 2010, admitted that the airline industry comes in last in terms of American customer satisfaction ratings.[74] However, Mr. George, sees social media as a powerful way to 'bring humanity' back to travel.[75] In September 2006, JetBlue began with a corporate blog penned by its founder and CEO, David Neeleman, but the blog fell quiet by October 2007.[76] However, participation in other social media platforms, such as Twitter, YouTube, and Facebook, were started after an incident in February of 2007. This effort has proven highly effective in helping the airline get closer to its customers.[77]

Challenge

JetBlue's goal of 'bring the humanity' back to air travel was dealt a serious blow on February 14, 2007, when weather and "...a shoestring communications system that left pilots and flight attendants in the dark, and an undersized reservation system," caused about 1,000 flight cancelations within five days, stranding thousands of passengers on Valentine's Day.[78] This type of public relations disaster is what every airline fears. JetBlue reacted by using traditional and social media to make amends to its customers.

Strategy

In an effort to reach out to customers, CEO Neeleman, appeared in an unscripted YouTube video, apologizing for the airline's mistakes and announcing a "Customer Bill of Rights," which outlined steps the airline would take in response to service interruptions.[79] The admission of complete responsibility for the incident and an acknowledgement of the pain it caused passengers, coupled with a credible promise to fix it, amounted "to the perfect business apology—in fact, it is likely to become a generally accepted standard for how business errors should be handled."[80] As a consequence, the video apology received a significant number of comments, most of which were positive because it felt authentic and genuine.[81] The YouTube experience gave the company a glimpse of the power of using social media to establish a two-way dialogue with its customers. The recognition of just how effective social media can be in repairing a damaged image and improving customer relations set the airline down the path of crafting an overall social media marketing strategy.[82]

The centerpiece of that social media strategy has become JetBlue's Twitter account, which grew from a mere 700 followers, as of March 7, 2008, to approximately 1.1 million followers by August of 2009.[83] This kind of growth in just over 17 months is nothing short of phenomenal and can be directly attributed to the company's social media strategy of first using Twitter to see what people were saying about them, then responding to questions and finally engaging in full blown conversations with their customer base.[84]

JetBlue Airways

Results

Today, JetBlue has rebuilt its reputation and made enormous strides in improving its relationships with customer through the use of social media. Indeed, Todd Wasserman writes on Mashable, "JetBlue is one of the top airlines associated with the web . . . When it comes to social media, it's less about direct sales and more about brand building, and JetBlue has embraced it with gusto."[85]

As of the end of October 2011, the airline's YouTube Channel, jetBlue, had accumulated over a million views.[86] Its JetBlue Airways Twitter page had attracted over 1.6 million followers, with more than 12,000 tweets.[87] The company's Facebook page racked over 500,000 fans.[88] The effective use of video, microblogging and social networking has played a key role in helping the company strengthen its brand. In addition, JetBlue uses its social media properties to attract people to its web site jetblue.com, where they can purchase tickets, converting them from fans to customers.[89]

Review Questions for JetBlue Case Study

1. Why do you think JetBlue became active on more social media platforms following the February 2007 incident?

2. The apology of the CEO of JetBlue took place several years ago. Do you think that strategy would still be an effective one for a company today? Why or why not?

3. How does JetBlue's response to the stranding of passengers compare to United's response to the broken guitar (from the earlier case study)? Based on the information here, which do you think was more effective and why?

4. Why has Twitter become the most popular social media platform for JetBlue in helping them improve customer satisfaction?

Notes

1. Neher, Krista (2010, October 26), *Social Media Field Guide: Discover the strategies, tactics and tools for successful social media marketing* (Boot Camp Digital Publishing), p. 2.
2. Peters, Jeremy W. (2010, December 12), "Web Focus Helps Revitalize the *Atlantic*," *New York Times*. Retrieved July 3, 2011, from http://www.nytimes.com/2010/12/13/business/media/13atlantic.html?_r=1
3. "Social Media Marketing" (n.d.), *Wikipedia*. Retrieved July 3, 2011, from http://en.wikipedia.org/wiki/Social_media_marketing.
4. Fiskars (n.d.), About Us: Heritage. Retrieved July 3, 2011, from http://www2.fiskars.com/About-Us/Company
5. Ochman, B. L. (2007, March 27), "Case Study: Fiskateers: How a Social Community Became a Veritable Sales Force. What's Next?" blog. Retrieved July 3, 2011, from http://www.whatsnextblog.com/2008/10/fiskateers_how_a_social_community_became_a_veritable_sales_force /
6. Nally, Nancy (2008, October 2), "The Genius of Fiskateers: Leveraging Social Media to Promote Fiskars," Scrapbook Update. Retrieved July 3, 2011, from http://www.scrapbookupdate.com/2008/10/02/the-genius-of-fiskateers-leveraging-social-media-to-promote-fiskars/
7. Stairhime, Shannon, and Andy Sernovitz (2007, February 8), "Chrysler, Coke: New Brand Buzz Leaders," iMedia Connection. Retrieved July 3, 2011, from http://www.imediaconnection.com/content/13538.imc

8. Sernovitz, Andy (2010, June 3), "How Fiskars Created Their Amazing Fan Community," *Andy's Answers for SmartBlog*. Retrieved July 3, 2011, from http://smartblogs.com/socialmedia/2010/06/03/andys-answers-how-fiskars-created-their-amazing-fan-community/

9. Facebook (n.d.), Press Room, Statistics. Retrieved July 3, 2011, from http://www.facebook.com/press.php#!/press/info.php?statistics

10. Page, Elisa Camahort (2010), "2010 Social Media Matters Study," *The BlogHer—iVillage*. Retrieved July 3, 2011, from http://www.blogher.com/files/Social_Media_Matters_2010.pdf

11. "ComScore Releases June 2010 U.S. Search Engine Rankings" (2010, July 13), ComScore. Retrieved July 3, 2011, from http://www.comscore.com/Press_Events/Press_Releases/2010/7/comScore_Releases_June_2010_U.S._Search_Engine_Rankings

12. Schonfeld, Eric (2010, Mar. 8), "Forrester Forecast: Online Retail Sales Will Grow to $250 Billion by 2014," TechCrunch. Retrieved July 3, 2011, from http://techcrunch.com/2010/03/08/forrester-forecast-online-retail-sales-will-grow-to-250-billion-by-2014/

13. Collins, Jane (2011, April 11), "The 2011 Social Media Matters Study," BlogHer. Retrieved November 15, 2011, from http://www.blogher.com/2011-social-media-matters-study

14. YouTube Demographic Data (n.d.), Statistics. Retrieved July 3, 2011, from http://www.youtube.com/t/press_statistics

15. Wortham, Jenna (2010, July 17), "As Facebook Users Die, Ghosts Reach Out." *New York Times*. Retrieved July 3, 2011, from http://www.nytimes.com/2010/07/18/technology/18death.html?_r=1&scp=6&sq=facebook&st=cse

16. "Is Facebook an Effective Marketing Tool for Retailers to Influence Consumer Purchase Decisions?" (2010, April), Morpace Omnibus Report. Retrieved July 3, 2011, from http://www.morpace.com/Omnibus-Reports/Omnibus%20Report-Facebooks%20Impact%20on%20Retailers.pdf

17. Nussel, Stefanie (April 28, 2010), "How Facebook Pages Can Impact Customer Experience," Retail Customer Experience. Retrieved July 3, 2011, from http://www.retailcustomerexperience.com/article/21650/How-Facebook-pages-can-impact-customer-experience

18. Rangaswamy, Adarsh (2010, October 11), "Social Media Measurement: Defining the Metrics to Quantify ROI," eConsultancy. Retrieved July 3, 2011, from http://econsultancy.com/us/blog/6702-social-media-measurement-defining-the-metrics-to-quantify-roi

19. Ostrow, Adam (2010), "Dell Rides Twitter to $6.5 Million in Sales," Mashable. Retrieved July 3, 2011, from http://mashable.com/2009/12/08/dell-twitter-sales/

20. Halzack, Sarah (2008, August 25), "Marketing Moves to the Blogosphere." *Washington Post* Retrieved July 3, 2011, from http://www.washingtonpost.com/wp-dyn/content/article/2008/08/24/AR2008082401517_2.html?hpid=topnews

21. Personal interview with Dan Schrementi of Golden Tee (2010, June 4), conducted by Krista Neher.

22. Personal interview with Jeff Esposito of Vista Prints (2010, June 4), conducted by Krista Neher.

23. Petouhoff, Natalie (2010, January 12), "Case Study #2: How Lenovo Implemented Customer Service Social Media Best Practices," blog. Retrieved July 3, 2011, from http://blogs.forrester.com/business_process/2010/01/how-lenovo-implemented-customer-service-social-media-best-practices.html

24. Twitter 101 (n.d.), @NakedPizza, "Twitter becoming mission critical to the business." Retrieved July 3, 2011, from https://twitter.com/twitter101/case_nakedpizza

25. James, Geoffrey (2009, July 2), "Will B2B Sales Move Mostly Online?" BNET. Retrieved July 3, 2011, from http://www.bnet.com/blog/salesmachine/will-b2b-sales-move-mostly-online/3913

26. Sass, Erik (2010, June 4), "One-Third of Americans Criticize or Compliment Brands Online," *MediaPost Blogs*. Retrieved July 3, 2011, from http://www.mediapost.com/publications/?fa=Articles.showArticle&art_aid=129546

27. "State of the Media: Social Media Report" (2011, Q3), Nielsen Company. Retrieved November 28, 2011, from http://blog.nielsen.com/nielsenwire/social/

28. Facebook (n.d.), Press Room, Statistics. Retrieved July 3, 2011, from http://www.facebook.com/press.php#!/press/info.php?statistics

29. "Is Facebook an Effective Marketing Tool for Retailers to Influence Consumer Purchase Decisions?" (2010, April), Morpace Omnibus Report. Retrieved December 30, 2010, from

http://www.morpace.com/Omnibus-Reports/Omnibus%20Report-Facebooks%20Impact%20
on%20Retailers.pdf

30. "ComScore Releases June 2010 U.S. Search Engine Rankings" (2010, July 13), ComScore.
Retrieved July 3, 2011, from http://www.comscore.com/Press_Events/Press_Releases/2010/7/
comScore_Releases_June_2010_U.S._Search_Engine_Rankings

31. Taulbee Jackson. (2010, March 17) Case Study: United Airlines Loses Millions on Social
Media. Social Media Risk. Retrieved August 27, 2011 from http://socialmediarisk.
com/2010/03/case-study-united-airlines-loses-millions-on-social-media/

32. Harvey MacKay. (2011, February 17) A lesson in business from the not-so-friendly skies.
Buffalo Law Journal. Retrieved August 27, 2011 from http://www.lawjournalbuffalo.com/
news/article/current/2011/02/17/102893/a-lesson-in-business-from-the-not-so-friendly-
skies

33. Harriet Baskas. (2009, July 23) Get in tune with your airline's instrument policy. MSNBC.com.
Retrieved August 27, 2011 from http://www.msnbc.msn.com/id/32031049/ns/travel-travel_
tips/t/get-tune-your-airlines-instrument-policy/#.TlkcIagg3vY

34. Wolfe Blitzer. (2009, July 8) CNN, The Situation Room. Retrieved August 27, 2011 from
http://transcripts.cnn.com/TRANSCRIPTS/0907/08/sitroom.03.html

35. Ibid.

36. Social Media Experience. (no date) Beyond Philosophy: Building Great Customer
Experiences. Retrieved August 27, 2011 from http://www.beyondphilosophy.com/services/
social-media-experience

37. Ibid.

38. John Deighton and Leora Kornfield. (2010, August 25) United Breaks Guitars. Harvard
Business School. Harvard Business Review Case Studies. p 2

39. David Meerman Scott. (2010, November 2) Real-Time Marketing and PR: How to Instantly
Engage Your Market, Connect with Customers, and Create Products that Grow Your Business
Now. John Wiley & Sons. Hoboken, NJ. p 3

40. Singers Sweet Revenge. (2009, July 10) CBS. YouTube. Retrieved August 27, 2011 from http://
www.youtube.com/watch?v=PGNtQF3n6VY

41. Peter Greenberg. (2009, August 11) United Breaks Guitars, Dave Carroll Keeps Playing.
PeterGreenberg.com. Retrieved August 27, 2011 from http://www.petergreenberg.
com/2009/08/11/united-breaks-guitars-dave-carroll-keeps-playing/

42. David Meerman Scott. (2010, November 2) Real-Time Marketing and PR: How to Instantly
Engage Your Market, Connect with Customers, and Create Products that Grow Your Business
Now. John Wiley & Sons. Hoboken, NJ. p 4

43. Broken guitar song gets airline's attention: United ready to talk after Halifax band's song hits
YouTube. (2009, July 8) CBS News. Retrieved August 27, 2011 from http://www.cbc.ca/news/
arts/music/story/2009/07/08/united-breaks-guitars.html

44. David Meerman Scott. (2010, November 2) Real-Time Marketing and PR: How to Instantly
Engage Your Market, Connect with Customers, and Create Products that Grow Your Business
Now. John Wiley & Sons. Hoboken, NJ. p 4

45. Peter Greenberg. (2009, August 11) United Breaks Guitars, Dave Carroll Keeps Playing.
PeterGreenberg.com. Retrieved August 27, 2011 from http://www.petergreenberg.
com/2009/08/11/united-breaks-guitars-dave-carroll-keeps-playing/

46. John Deighton and Leora Kornfield. (2010, August 25) United Breaks Guitars. Harvard
Business School. Harvard Business Review Case Studies. p 1

47. David Meerman Scott. (2010, November 2) Real-Time Marketing and PR: How to Instantly
Engage Your Market, Connect with Customers, and Create Products that Grow Your Business
Now. John Wiley & Sons. Hoboken, NJ. p 4

48. admin. (2010, January 11) Social Media Taylor Guitar Success. Vestal Media: The Blog.
Retrieved August 28, 2011 from http://vestalmedia.com/2010/01/11/social-media-
taylorguitar-success/

49. Linda Laban. (2009, July 14) Dave Carroll Smashes YouTube Records with 'United Breaks
Guitars.' Retrieved July 3, 2011 from http://www.spinner.com/2009/07/14/dave-carroll-breaks-
youtube-records-with-united-breaks-guitars/#

50. Dave Carroll. (2009, July 6) United Breaks Guitars. YouTube. Retrieved August 27, 2011 from
http://www.youtube.com/watch?v=5YGc4zOqozo

51. Lee Otsubo. (2010, March 10) United Breaks Guitars – Song 3. Digital Photo Guy. Retrieved August 27, 2011 from http://www.thedigitalphotoguy.com/2010/03/10/united-breaks-guitars-song-3/

52. Singer gets his revenge on United Airlines and soars to fame. (2009, July 23) News Blog. guardian.co.uk. Retrieved August 27, 2011 from http://www.guardian.co.uk/news/blog/2009/jul/23/youtube-united-breaks-guitars-video

53. John Dodge. (2009, August 7) Dave Carroll v. United Airlines, social media lessons round two. Smart Planet Blog. Retrieved August 28, 2011 http://www.smartplanet.com/blog/thinking-tech/dave-carroll-v-united-airlines-social-media-lessons-round-two/999

54. United Breaks Guitars - Negative Publicity (2009, July 30) MktgCliks Blog. Retrieved August 27, 2011 from http://mktgcliks.blogspot.com/2009/07/united-breaks-guitars-united-airlines.html

55. Dave Carroll. (2009, November 25) Statistical Insignificance. AdWeek. Retrieved July 3, 2011 from http://www.adweek.com/aw/ content_display/community/columns/other-columns/e3ia7f0e1dcab3176840f88bf567f95ce7d

56. Dave Carroll. (2009, July 6) United Breaks Guitars. YouTube. Retrieved August 27, 2011 from http://www.youtube.com/watch?v=5YGc4zOqozo

57. David Klein. (2009, July 27) Your Most Crucial Moment Comes When the Customer Calls. Advertising Age. Retrieved August 27, 2011 from http://adage.com/article/guest-columnists/customer-service-crucial-moment-customer-calls/138116/

58. Mandese, Joe (2008, June 19), "OMG! UM Finds Web 2.0 Breeding Consumers 2.0, Social Media Attains Critical Mass," MediaPost News. Retrieved December 30, 2010, from http://www.mediapost.com/publications/?fa=Articles.showArticle&art_aid=85025

59. Rheingold, Howard (1993), The Virtual Community: Homesteading on the Electronic Frontier (Reading, MA: Addison Wesley).

60. Godin, Seth (1999), Permission Marketing: Turning Strangers into Friends and Friends into Customers (New York: Simon & Schuster).

61. Levine, Rick, Christopher Locke, Doc Searls, and David Weinberger, (2001), The Cluetrain Manifesto: The End of Business as Usual (New York: Basic Books).

62. Evans, Liana (2009, November 23), "Marketing Tactics vs. Social Media Strategy," Search engine Watch. Retrieved July 3, 2011, from http://searchenginewatch.com/3635721

63. Blumenfeld, Ciaran (2009, June 24), "No Room for Competitors on the Social Media Brandwagon?" Retrieved July 3, 2011, from http://www.ciaranblumenfeld.com/tag/traditional-marketing-vs-social-media/

64. Meckler, Brian (2010, March 18), "Social Media vs Traditional Media FAQs," Absolute. Retrieved July 3, 2011, from http://www.absolutemg.com/2010/03/social-media-vs-traditional-media-faqs/

65. Ibid.

66. "Spending on Social Media Marketing to Continue Rising, Survey Finds" (2009, August 27), Resources for Entrepreneurs. Retrieved July 3, 2011, from http://www.gaebler.com/News/Small-Business-Marketing/Spending-on-social-media-marketing-to-continue-rising-survey-finds-19333385.htm

67. Collier, Mack (2010, March 3), "Senior Marketing Execs See Their Companies Moving to Social Media in 2010," blog. Retrieved July 3, 2011, from http://moblogsmoproblems.blogspot.com/2010/03/senior-marketing-execs-see-their.html

68. Weisz, Elan (2009, July 15), "Explosion in Social Media Fails to Create Many Jobs—So Far," CNBC, Retrieved July 3, 2011, from http://www.cnbc.com/id/31893821/Explosion_in_Social_Media_Fails_To_Create_Many_Jobs_So_Far

69. "Emerging Jobs in Social Media" (2010, May 2), AOL Jobs, PayScale. Retrieved July 3, 2011, from http://jobs.aol.com/articles/2010/05/02/social-media-jobs/

70. Aquent and the American Marketing Association's Marketing Salary Survey (n.d.). Retrieved July 3, 2011, from http://www.marketingsalaries.com/home/search_results.htm

71. Kirkpatrick, Marshall (2008, October 9), "How Much Do Top Tier Bloggers and Social Media Consultants Get Paid? We Asked Them!" ReadWriteWeb. Retrieved July 3, 2011, from http://www.readwriteweb.com/archives/how_much_do_top_tier_bloggers_make.php

72. Curl, Patrick (2010, March 25), "How to Secure Your First Social Media Consulting Gig," QuickOnlineTips. Retrieved July 3, 2011, from http://www.quickonlinetips.com/archives/2010/03/first-social-media-consulting-gig/

73. Morrell, Dan (2008), "Case Study in Social Media Jet Blue," TechWag. Retrieved October 31, 2001, from archive at http://web.archive.org/web/20100903062110/http://techwag.com/index.php/2008/12/02/case-study-in-social-media-jet-blue/

74. McNaughtonmMarissa (2010, August 12), "JetBlue Case Study: Social Media, With Emphasis on the Social (Part 1 of 4)," The Realtime Report. Retrieved October 31, 2011, from http://therealtimereport.com/2010/08/12/social-media-with-emphasis-on-the-social-1/

75. Ibid.

76. jetBlue Blog (2011, October 31) Jetblue.com. Retrieved October 31, 2011, from http://www.jetblue.com/about/ourcompany/flightlog/index.html

77. Morrell, Dan (2008), "Case Study in Social Media Jet Blue," TechWag. Retrieved October 31, 2001, from archive at http://web.archive.org/web/20100903062110/http://techwag.com/index.php/2008/12/02/case-study-in-social-media-jet-blue/

78. Bailey, Jeff (2007, February 19), "JetBlue's C.E.O. Is 'Mortified' After Fliers Are Stranded," The New Your Times. Retrieved October 31, 2011, from http://www.nytimes.com/2007/02/19/business/19jetblue.html?pagewanted=all

79. Goolpacy, Peter F. (n.d.), "The Perfect JetBlue Apology," PerfectApology.com. Retrieved October 31, 2011, from http://www.perfectapology.com/jetblue-apology.html

80. Ibid.

81. 6 CEO apologies on YouTube (2009, September 14), Attention Digital. Retrieved October 31, 2011, from http://attentiondigital.com/6-ceo-apologies-on-youtube-Dirqy

82. McNaughtonmMarissa (2010, August 12), "JetBlue Case Study: Social Media, With Emphasis on the Social (Part 1 of 4)," The Realtime Report. Retrieved October 31, 2011, from http://therealtimereport.com/2010/08/12/social-media-with-emphasis-on-the-social-1/

83. Jetblue – this week's Twitter case study (2009, August 26), Lots of Small Fries. Retrieved October 31, 2011, from http://lotsofsmallfires.wordpress.com/2009/08/26/jetblue-this-weeks-twitter-case-study/

84. Ibid.

85. Wasserman, Todd (2011, June 1), "How JetBlue's Social Media Strategy Took Flight," Mashable. Retrieved October 31, 2011, from http://mashable.com/2011/06/01/jetblue-social-media-success/

86. jetBlue YouTube Channel (2011, October 31), YouTube.com. Retrieved October 31, 2011, from http://www.youtube.com/user/jetblue

87. JetBlue Airways Twitter Page (2011, October 31), Twitter.com.Retrieved October 31, 2011, from http://twitter.com/#!/jetblue

88. JetBlue Airways Facebook Page (20111, October 31), Facebook.com. Retrieved October 31, 2011, from http://www.facebook.com/JetBlue

89. Wasserman, Todd (2011, June 1), "How JetBlue's Social Media Strategy Took Flight," Mashable. Retrieved October 31, 2011, from http://mashable.com/2011/06/01/jetblue-social-media-success/

Goals and Strategies

The single most important action a marketer can take to improve an organization's chances of success in implementing a social media effort is creating a well-researched and carefully thought-out social media marketing plan. One of the major reasons social media marketing efforts fail is poor planning.

Beginning with this chapter, the remainder of the book will focus on the steps necessary to create a winning social media plan. Two of the most important steps in this planning process are goal setting and strategy determination. Before moving forward with social media marketing activities, an organization should first determine what it wants to accomplish and then how best to do it. Without goals, it will be unclear in which direction to go or how to ultimately measure success. With a well-defined destination in mind, appropriate strategies can be designed to achieve these goals. As such, the process of setting goals and determining strategies is crucial for success in the field of social media marketing.

LEARNING OBJECTIVES

After completing this chapter, students will be able to:

- Define a social media plan
- Explain the social media marketing planning cycle
- Describe each step in the social media marketing planning cycle
- Identify five ways to listen and observe the social web
- Explain how to set social media marketing goals
- Describe how to create social media strategies

(Continued)

What is a Social Media Marketing Plan?

A **social media marketing plan** details an organization's social media goals and the actions necessary to achieve them. Key among these actions is the creation of solid marketing strategies without which there is little chance of successfully executing the plan.

Social Media Marketing Planning Cycle

Creating a social media plan is a continuous process, as illustrated by the **Social Media Marketing Planning Cycle** in Figure 2.1. Skilled social media marketers constantly monitor the progress of the plan's foundational elements, test alternative approaches, and adjust the plan based on the results. It is important to think about all of the steps in Figure 2.1 when constructing a social media plan (Chapter 15 will demonstrate how to use these steps to build a social media marketing plan).

Figure 2.1 Social Media Planning Cycle

© Cengage Learning 2013

THE SOCIAL MEDIA MARKETING PLANNING CYCLE

- **Listening** to what people are saying about a company enables the organization to determine its current social media presence, which in turn guides the setting of social media goals and strategies to achieve them. Another important reason to listen to the social web is for competitive intelligence (i.e., information about what people are saying about competitors and what the competitors are saying about themselves). Finally, it is critical for a company find out what people are already talking about before becoming part of the conversation.

- **Setting goals** is done by pinpointing the location, behavior, tastes, and needs of the target audience and conducting a competitive analysis to determine an organization's strengths and weaknesses and the opportunities and threats in the environment. By performing these appraisals, marketers can then choose the social media goals that satisfy the unmet needs of consumers, capitalize on the strengths of the company, seize opportunities, while minimizing organizational weaknesses and external threats, such as those from competitors, advances in technology, industry trends, and general economic conditions.

- **Defining strategies** must be done on a case-by-case basis, using all available pertinent information. The "8 C's of Strategy Development" (covered below) provide guidelines to help an organization reach its marketing goals. These suggestions are intended as broad guidance for marketers and must be adjusted to each organization's unique strengths, weaknesses, opportunities, and threats.

- **Identifying the target audience (market)** enables a company to organize its marketing strategies to efficiently reach those most receptive and likely to become customers and even brand advocates.

- **Selecting tools** is accomplished by finding the social media sites where the target audience resides and then focusing the company's social media efforts on those platforms. (Other tools, such as mobile apps (applications) can play an important role in reaching a target audience, using location marketing techniques, as explained in Chapter 13.)

- **Implementing** is the process whereby the goals, strategies, target market, and tools are taken into consideration in creating actionable social media platform-specific marketing tactics. Executing well-defined tactics makes it possible for an organization to implement its general social media strategies across multiple social media platforms and realize the company's marketing goals.

- **Monitoring** is the process of tracking, measuring, and evaluating an organization's social media marketing initiatives.

- **Tuning** is the constant and continuous process of adjusting and improving the elements of the plan to maximize the chances of success.

The book is structured around this social media planning model. Listening, setting goals, and defining strategies are explained in detail below. Chapter 3 covers identifying the target audience. Chapters 5 through 12 discuss tools and implementation, providing guidance regarding the execution of strategies and social media platform-specific marketing tactics. However, it is first necessary to lay a foundation for learning how to successfully execute these platform-specific marketing tactics, which is why Chapter 4 presents the **Rules of Engagement** for participating on the social web.[1] Monitoring the progress of social media marketing is explored in Chapter 14. Finally, Chapter 15 puts it all together, by presenting how an example social media marketing plan is prepared, with special emphasis on the constant and continuous need to tune, adjust, and improve the plan and its implementation.

Listen and Observe: Five Stages

Before jumping into social media marketing, it is important to observe the surroundings, and consider the target audience as well as the social landscape in general. During the listening and observing stage, marketers should follow conversations about a particular brand and company, its competitors, and the relevant industry on as many social media platforms as possible. This procedure will not only gauge the overall tone of the communities, but more important, it will identify where the organization's target audience hangs out and what they are doing there.

STAGE #1: LISTEN TO CONVERSATIONS ABOUT A BRAND OR COMPANY

The first stage is listening to and observing conversations about a particular company. As advised by Brian Solis in his blog for the Harvard Business Review, "[l]isten to the conversations that are already taking place" and "[p]ay attention to the nuances of these conversations."[2] What are people saying about this brand? What good and bad comments have been made? How do people feel about the company? Listen to the conversations taking place on blogs, Twitter, discussion forums, websites, LinkedIn, Facebook, etc., to understand how the company is perceived. Both positive and negative remarks can show where opportunities may lie. In addition, knowing what consumers are already saying will help in preparing responses for common questions or problems. Anticipating areas to address will provide an advantage when entering into social media marketing.

STAGE #2: LISTEN TO WHAT PEOPLE SAY ABOUT THE COMPETITORS

Next, listen to what people say about a company's competitors, and what those competitors are saying about themselves. How do people perceive the pros and cons of the competitors in the social space? How do these comments influence business opportunities? In addition to listening to how people feel about competitors, it is helpful to identify the most *competitive areas* of the social media landscape. What are the competitors doing on social media? Who are they targeting? What seems to work? Assessing the competitive landscape on social media sites will show how buyers are meeting sellers on social media and may provide insights that can be leveraged when later building a strategy. Learning from others' social media approaches will help build a powerful strategy quickly while refining it to suit different needs.

STAGE #3: LISTENING TO WHAT PEOPLE SAY ABOUT THE INDUSTRY OR CATEGORY

After observing the competition, begin listening on a broader scale: the overall industry. What are consumers (or potential consumers or members of the target audience) saying about the industry? Is the sentiment strongly positive or negative surrounding certain issues? What conversations occur between firms in the industry? Does this create opportunities? Understanding the conversations taking place around a certain industry will help gauge what people are interested in and frequently talk about. We will discuss content in Chapter 5, but it is important to remember that social media content must connect with consumers on an issue they are passionate about (which typically is not a particular brand). Listening at the category or industry level will help one understand what the consumers in that industry are really interested in talking about.

STAGE #4: LISTENING FOR THE TONE OF THE COMMUNITY

The next stage is to observe the **Tone of the Community**. Essentially, this means observing how your consumers naturally interact with each other on social sites. What technical jargon, acronyms, or slang do they use? How do they interact with each other? What words are most often used to describe specific brands, competitors or industries? How are brands participating, and who is getting the most attention? What are the unwritten rules of participation? How do they talk, and what are they interested in? When engaging in social media, it is good to fit in and sound like other consumers. To accomplish this, it is essential to first know how relevant social media users communicate with each other and the etiquette of communicating on different social sites. This knowledge will facilitate integration and participation in the community.

STAGE #5: LISTENING TO DIFFERENT SOCIAL MEDIA CHANNELS

Finally, when listening to social media, be sure to access multiple social media channels to identify where target audiences hang out and what they do there. The participants on Facebook may be dramatically different from those on Twitter, LinkedIn, or blogs. Each social media channel has a distinctive audience (target market) with unique interests, behaviors, and characteristics (Chapter 3 explores this topic in depth). For example, according to Quantcast, Facebook users are mostly younger, between the ages of 13 and 34; LinkedIn users are more affluent, older, and educated; and Twitter users are less wealthy than either LinkedIn or Facebook users.[3] Since the users on each site and the social networking structure are different, it is important to listen to conversations across a variety of social media channels.

Listening and observing is the key first step in the social media planning stage. Time spent observing will pay off when planning the rest of the social media strategy and will help avoid an embarrassing faux pas along the way.

Setting Goals

By carefully listening to a wide range of social media sites and observing the location, behavior, tastes, and needs of the target audience, marketers can set optimal goals and determine the most suitable strategies to achieve them. The key in defining goals is to understand what will be accomplished through social media. What is the desired outcome? Social media marketing goals include brand building, increasing customer satisfaction, driving word-of-mouth recommendations, producing new product ideas, generating leads, handling crisis-reputation management, as well as integrating social media marketing with public relations and advertising. In addition, achieving one or more of these social media marketing goals is likely to increase site traffic, search engine rankings, and conversions (i.e., sales).

© szefei/ Shutterstock

It is important to keep in mind that goals must be flexible in the light of new developments while engaging in social media. Sometimes, unintended benefits from social media engagement are discovered. For example, after Vista Prints, an online printing company, got started on social media, they noticed that many people were seeking customer support through Twitter. In reaction the company engaged its customer service department, connecting that department to questions from Twitter so that service professionals could respond directly to the tweets. This clever adaptation allowed faster service for customers needing assistance and also resulted in cost savings to the firm through reduced phone time spent on customer support.

According to a CMO Survey, the most popular uses for social media include brand awareness and brand building, acquisition of new customers, introduction of new products and service, retention of current customers, and market research, respectively.[4] Although some of these uses of social media appear intuitive, such as brand strengthening, others are less obvious, such as customer retention and market research.

Many of these uses are unexpected benefits from social media and must have been discovered while other goals were being pursued. Many brands likely set out with a narrower objective for their social media campaigns and then broadened their usages as more benefits became apparent. The survey results demonstrate the importance of flexibility and an open mind in social media planning.

CASE STUDY

Dell Reinvents Itself Through Social Media

Introduction

Dell exemplifies a strong execution of the Social Media Marketing Plan shown in Figure 2.1: listen to the social web, establish social media strategies, define the company's target audience, create innovative content, pick the right social media tools, implement the plan with precision, track and measure results, and adjust the campaign to get the biggest bang for the buck.

History

Dell Computer Corporation (originally called PCs Limited) was founded in 1984 by Michael Dell in Austin, Texas, and was based on selling computers with customizable options directly to consumers.[5] This unique approach offered lower prices than other brand names and greater convenience than purchasing parts and putting them together at home. The company was first traded on the U.S. stock market in June 1988 and grossed over $73 million that year.[6] In 1996 Dell began selling computers though its website. By 2009 the company was grossing over $61 billion a year. Dell employs 96,000 workers and sells over 110,000 computers every day, which amounts to more than one per second.[7]

Challenge

In 2005 Jeff Jarvis, a noted print journalist and blogger, posted a rant on his blog, *BuzzMachine*, decrying a horrific customer experience with Dell after buying a laptop. He entitled the post, "Dell Lies, Dell Sucks."[8] Little did Jarvis suspect that his invective would create a firestorm in the blogosphere with a torrent of angry Dell customers piling on to complain about the computer maker. Thousands of unsatisfied consumers commented and linked to Jarvis's blog, supporting and adding to his statement that "Dell Sucks." A little under a month later, Jarvis followed up the post with another blog post, intended as an open letter to Michael Dell, "suggesting his company read blogs, write blogs, ask customers for guidance, and join the conversation your customers are having without you."[9] This social media tale came to be known as "Dell Hell."

Strategy

Michael Dell's company started listening and, more importantly, acting. Because of "Dell Hell," the company became one of the first large corporations to integrate social media throughout its organization. Starting in 2006, Dell launched a companywide social media marketing campaign to engage consumers, improve customer service, and turn round its badly damaged reputation.

Dell began by training its employees in how to listen and engage consumers on the social web. To accomplish this considerable task, Dell employed almost every conceivable social media tool. As an example, Dell launched an internal blog entitled *EmployeeStorm* and a Twitter-like microblog called *Chatter*. In addition, it held employee "unconferences" in each of its global sales regions. All of these efforts were dedicated to helping the organization adapt to the social web. These substantial training initiatives focused on getting employees recognized as social media professionals in the community. Within two months, over 2,000 Dell workers had been trained in social media marketing. Along with a certification, the Texas computer giant educated employees across the enterprise on how to listen and converse on the social web, using the latest in social media metrics and monitoring tools.

In 2007 Dell launched IdeaStorm, a corporate social network or community, where consumers are encouraged to contribute suggestions for new products, features, and services. The company not only actively participates in the discussions, but it often incorporates the best recommendations into its products and services.

In 2007 Ricardo Guerrero, a Dell employee, championed the use of Twitter as a means to push out information about his company's products. But to the surprise of Guerrero and his fellow company Twitterers, this one-way form of communication quickly evolved into two-way conversations as customers began asking questions. The Dell Twitterers soon realized that people were interested in having conversations with them, not just hearing about the latest deals. By engaging customers on Twitter, Dell not only raised its brand awareness, but it improved its reputation. The more enthusiastic Twitter participants became brand advocates for the company and vastly multiplied the effect, which is the real secret of any successful social media marketing campaign.

There are now more than 80 Dell-branded Twitter accounts, offering the latest products and providing customer service. They encourage employees to be active on Twitter, with more than 100 employee accounts. The company also uses Twitter to monitor any mentions of its brand.[10] In mid-2006 Dell launched the successful *Direct2Dell* blog (originally called *One2One*), with content that ranges widely from product deals and reviews to industry news and trends to corporate social responsibility and the impact of technology on the environment.[11]

Results

Before "Dell Hell" in 2005, the company had a strict policy prohibiting employees from responding to bloggers. Given the magnitude of changes within Dell since this time, what have been the net results? In short, the company now has a strong relationship with the social media world, and has fostered a great deal of goodwill among its customer base.

By mid-2009 Dell had sold more than $3 million in PCs and accessories through Twitter.[12] In 2005 Dell had a 49% negative blog post ratio, whereas since then, it has reduced that ratio to a mere 22%. The company's blog, *Direct2Dell*, ranks around 700 on Technorati. The blog receives more than 5 million unique views per month, making it one of the most popular corporate blogs. Well over 7,000 product suggestions and other ideas have been posted on the IdeaStorm social networking community.[13]

What is the secret ingredient to Dell's brand turnaround success? They discovered—perhaps the hard way—that to remain successful, a corporation must reach out to its current customer base. Dell hasn't become complacent, and it continually monitors, tracks, and measures the influence of its social media marketing efforts to maximize their impact. To keep current, Dell constantly evolves its social marketing plan, both to remain relevant to its intended audience and also to fully integrate social communication throughout every part of its corporate culture. The end goal is not just to become a better social communicator but to conduct business more productively, evolving from a twentieth-century enterprise into a twenty-first-century "socialprise."[14]

Social media marketing goals include but are not limited to:

- **Building a Brand**: Perhaps the most important task of social media marketing is to establish a company's brand.[15] Social brand building, unlike traditional branding, is more about what people say about a company than what it says about itself.[16] For example, consumer reviews on major retailers' discussion boards help define a brand (for better or worse). Bloggers, discussing a company's product or service (positively or negatively), impact brand perception. Employees can also have a large influence on a brand's image. As an example, Home Depot's How-to videos, featuring actual Home Depot associates demonstrating the best ways to accomplish home improvements, have established the company as a trusted expert as well as humanizing a faceless corporation.[17] On the flipside, Domino's Pizza, which spends millions a year on advertising, had its brand instantly tarnished by two employees posting a prank video on YouTube that showed a sandwich for delivery being prepared in an unsavory manner—the video received more than a million views within days after being uploaded.[18]

The following is a list of major brand building goals:

- **Increasing Brand Awareness**: For a new product or service, the first priority is often to build general awareness that the product or service exists and is being offered. This is true for large brands as well as for individuals. For instance, insurance and real estate agents use extensive networking to build awareness of their services. An agent's hope is that even individuals not needing his or her services will immediately think of the agent in their network as soon as the need arises. In this case, the natural goal may be to build connections with as many people as possible in order to increase consumer awareness. Alternately, a company producing consumable goods such as laundry detergent or potato chips may also initially aim to increase general awareness of its brand or of a newly released product. Even after a product has been launched, a firm might also want to educate an audience about the benefits of the company's particular product in comparison to that of others. For example, many new products boast that they "contain antioxidants" as a key health ingredient. Creating content that explains the importance of antioxidants could raise awareness for related products as well.

- **Improving Brand Perception**: Using social media to improve a company's brand perception is one of the most effective ways to increase sales over the long run. Every action a business takes on the social web can add or detract from brand perception. A company can positively influence brand perception by establishing online relationships with leaders in the industry (cool by association); gathering together and displaying testimonials, positive posts, tweets, reviews, comments, and discussions that lend credence to the company's desired brand perception; ensuring that all materials published by the company on social media sites consistently promote the preferred brand perception; consistently monitoring the social web for positive or negative content—rewarding brand advocates with attention, while handling less than favorable reviews and outright attacks against the company in an adroit, transparent, and honest manner so as to prevent ruining the company's brand perception.[19]

- **Positioning a Brand**: An already-known brand still has the opportunity to create a more positive impression with the target audience. Consider Tide laundry detergent: most people know of the brand, but still there may be equity-building opportunities in associating "the most clean" or "the best smell" with Tide. Car companies are among those who spend a lot of energy on equity and positioning—what does a BMW make consumers think of? This concept applies to more than just big brands. In any competitive industry, firms can gain by positioning themselves differently from the competition. A coffee shop might want to be known for serving the best coffee, for providing the best place to work, or for offering the freshest baked goods.

- **Expanding Brand Loyalty**: Social media thrives because people enjoy talking to each other. The loyalty of current customers may convince them to market a brand indirectly by telling friends and family about a product or service. Businesses that engage in the conversation are more likely to gain recommendations on social sites because they are at the front of people's minds. In addition, following the 80-20 rule, it can be assumed that 80% of a company's business will come from 20% of its customers.* What if a firm could have more of its customers be that loyal? Seeking repeat business may be easier—and more profitable—than expending energy on acquiring new customers, and building relationships through social media can increase customer loyalty. In everyday situations, many people will give repeat business to firms because they are friendly and familiar with the staff, and get more enjoyment from the transaction as a result. Social media can be used in the same way. Building loyalty from existing customers can be a powerful and profitable marketing strategy.

- **Increasing Customer Satisfaction**: Following up through social media channels and using a pleasant and professional tone can significantly influence customer satisfaction. Social media provides an opportunity for companies to build relationships and resolve issues that might otherwise taint a customer's view of the brand. Just knowing that a business cares enough to listen is often enough to increase customer satisfaction.

- **Driving Word-of-Mouth Recommendations**: Social media thrives because people enjoy talking to each other. Loyalty from current customers may convince them to market a brand indirectly by telling friends and family about a product or service. Businesses that engage in the conversation are more likely to gain recommendations on social sites because they are at the front of people's minds.

- **Producing New Product Ideas**: By engaging with current and potential customers, companies can discover new product ideas or requests for new features and services. Instead of running occasional focus groups, listening to the social space allows firms to learn continually from customers and to use this information to improve on or create new products. In addition to actively soliciting input, companies can listen to social networks to learn what consumers are saying about their products, their competitors, or their industry. Social media conversations

---

*Otherwise known as the Pareto principle, so named for economist Vilfredo Pareto's 1906 observation that 20% of the population owned 80% of the land in Italy. More generally, as the principle of factor sparsity, it states that 80% of the effects come from 20% of the causes for many events. For more information on the 80-20 rule, see: *Koch, Richard* (2005), *Living The 80/20 Way: Work Less, Worry Less, Succeed More, Enjoy More* (Boston: Nicholas Brealey), and Starak, Yaro (2006, March 29), "What Is the 80/20 Rule and Why It Will Change Your Life," Entrepreneurs Journey. Retrieved January 7, 2011, from http://www.entrepreneurs-journey.com/397/80-20-rule-pareto-principle/

occur in an unfiltered setting so that firms can gain valuable insights for improving products and even creating new ones.

- **Generating Leads**: Publishing web content can be a great strategy for generating leads, especially if that content requires an email address to register. E-books, white papers, and webinars are all publishing tools that typically require someone to enter their email address to receive the free content. In addition to collecting an email address, a brief survey prior to downloading the content can be used to qualify leads for sales teams. Acquiring an email address creates an opportunity to send marketing messages (newsletters, special offers, etc.) over a lifetime, provided the customer doesn't unsubscribe.

- **Handling Crisis Reputation Management**: "Corporate leaders in nearly every industry, regardless of size or geography, acknowledge that the dark clouds of impending social media crises are gathering. They also believe they know with some certainty how soon a crisis will occur—within the next year. An overwhelming majority of them—79%—said they believe their company is less than 12 months away from a potential crisis moment. Most of them believe that that crisis will arise from within social media networks." [20] To minimize the damage to a company's reputation, it is important to monitor what is being said about a company on the social web, have a predefined social media crisis plan in place for rapid response, regularly update and practice responding to a social media crisis, develop an employee social media policy, and train employees on how to use the social web within the guidelines. [21]

- **Integrating Social Media Marketing with Public Relations and Advertising**: Press and industry analysts increasingly look to social media sites when building their stories. Many large traditional publications like the *New York Times* or the *Wall Street Journal* pick up stories that start in blogs by using syndication services like *BlogBurst*, *Blogrunner*, and *Sphere*. [22] In addition, many journalists use search engines to research their stories. A larger social media presence increases the opportunity for unsolicited media coverage and quick publicity.

- **Search Engine Optimization**: With the exception of online contests that feature product giveaways on social media sites like Facebook and Twitter, using social media marketing to drive traffic to a company website occurs over time. As the effects of brand building slowly cumulate, people increasingly link to a company's website and social media properties. Search engines tend to favor the sites with the greatest number of inbound links from well-respected sites by ranking them higher in search results. Studies show that approximately 90% of traffic to a website comes via search engines and that search engines handle "more than half of all the E-commerce transactions." [23] In addition, "Studies show that 68% of search engine users only look at the first page of results . . . [so] if you're ranked number one on the first SERPs (Search Engine Results Page), you're ten times more likely to get a click than someone who is ranked number ten." [24] Hence, a high search engine ranking translates into increased traffic to a company's site (or social media property), which in turn results in a greater conversion rate (i.e., number of sales, newsletter registrations, etc.).

This list of eight goals is a start, but it is far from exhaustive. These are some common examples of social media marketing goals, which should be adapted to fit a particular social media plan. An integrated marketing strategy may combine a number of these goals, or different aspects of the social media plan may focus on different goals. Regardless of how many are chosen, having a clear idea of the goal is important when initiating a social media campaign.

Determining Strategies

There are some key considerations when setting social media marketing strategies.

WHAT ARE THE OVERALL GOALS?

Look at the mission and general marketing goals of the organization when creating social media marketing strategies. Social media marketing should not be an isolated part of the marketing strategy; rather, it should link into a broader marketing plan. The building of social media marketing strategies that support the overall strategic goals of a company will also make it easier for the strategies to win support within the company.

© Robert Churchill/ iStockphot

WHAT WAS LEARNED FROM LISTENING?

The listening stage should have unearthed information about the company, its target audience, competitors, and the industry as a whole. Marketers should be able to answer the following questions:

- How do people feel about a company, product, service, person, or issue?

- How are competitors using social media platforms?

- Which media platforms appear to be the most viable in order to achieve social media marketing goals?

- Where does a company's target audience hang out, and what do they do there?

- How can this information be used to identify strategic opportunities?

WHAT BEST PRACTICES CAN BE APPLIED?

This book offers a variety of best practices and case studies showing how to apply social media marketing for the building and expanding of an organization's presence. Best in-class examples of social media marketing can inspire future social media marketing plans. Look to best-in-class examples, even from firms outside the specific industry you are interested in, to help shape marketing goals and strategies.

GOALS MAY CHANGE . . . BE FLEXIBLE

The social media planning model is a fluid circle; it is flexible and adaptive. After gaining experience in social media, measuring the results may lead to a change in goals or strategies. For example, customers may primarily want to use Twitter for customer service, or perhaps most existing customers are only active on Facebook. Be open to adaptation, as social media may work in unanticipated ways.

THE EIGHT C'S OF STRATEGY DEVELOPMENT

From the above discussion, it is apparent that determining social media marketing strategies must be done on a case-by-case basis, using all available pertinent information. Nonetheless, it is worthwhile to consider some of the major social media marketing strategies that have helped other organizations achieve their marketing goals. The following eight C's of strategy development are intended as broad guidelines for marketers and should be adapted to each organization's unique strengths, weaknesses, opportunities, and threats.[25]

1. Categorize social media platforms by target market relevancy. In other words, a company should focus its efforts on the social media sites where its target audience resides in the greatest numbers. By listening and observing, it is possible to rank the social media platforms that offer the most target rich environments. Concentrating a company's social media marketing resources and efforts on the platforms with the largest number of potential or existing customers is more likely to result in a higher return on investment (ROI).

2. Comprehend the rules of the road on the platform by listening and learning how to behave, successfully spark conversation, and engage and energize the participants. Social media is a powerful way to connect with people if marketers first learn how to behave appropriately on the social web. Following the policies and guidelines on a social media site shows respect for and interest in the other participants. People prefer to do business with companies they know, like, and respect.

3. Converse by acknowledging and responding to other users of the platform, always remembering to be a contributor, not a promoter. Companies can establish trust with consumers by displaying both their knowledge of a product area and genuine concern toward topics that their customers are interested in. Creating and publishing relevant content is a key way to assure customers that a brand is worthy of their trust. Published web content can show a more personal side to a company's management and organization. Taking time to explain policies and practices, and sharing news in a human and conversational voice makes the company more appealing to consumers. By honestly and openly engaging in conversations, firms can further build the trust that ultimately earns sales. Many companies are using social media for customer service. Twitter, blogs, and discussion forums provide opportunities for customers to help each other solve issues, thus saving the company time and money.

4. Collaborate with platform members as a means of establishing a mutually beneficial relationship with the platform participants. Social media is a key way to build relationships. While most social media users look to build connections for nonmonetary reasons, relationships can matter to a firm as well. Social media sites are generally designed to make conversations between many people simple and easy. By using these tools, firms have the opportunity to not only build real relationships with their target audiences and encourage repeat business and word-of-mouth recommendations, they also show the human side of a business. People who feel a personal connection with a company are apt to like and trust the associated brand or product. A faceless corporation is unlikely to inspire confidence, but seeing the people behind the brand can build customer loyalty and support.

5. Contribute content to build reputation and become a valued member, helping to improve the community. A brand or company can be positioned as **thought leaders** or experts in an industry by showcasing their unique knowledge. This positioning can develop positive equity for that brand or company; if a firm knows more about the subject area than anyone else, it signals that its product will most likely be of higher quality. This thought leadership strategy involves creating content that highlights a firm's unique expertise in a particular subject area. For example, by providing product information for complex purchases, especially in the business-to-business (B2B) space, a company can establish itself as a valuable contributor to a sizeable community. In fact "81 percent of the B2B companies using social media maintain a presence on social media sites, versus 67 percent of the B2C companies surveyed [by eMarketer]."[26] Blogs and webinars are other examples of valuable content contribution and provide powerful and easy ways to share information about a product or category. Spreading knowledge about the general industry can build trust in potential customers, and trust is especially important for large-scale or repeat business.

6. Connect with the influencers so that you can enlist them to help shape opinions about your product or service. One of the best ways to impress and to connect with the influencers on the social web is to provide everyone with outstanding customer service, both on- and offline. The combination of these efforts will likely attract the attention of the movers and shakers on the social media platform, giving them ample reason to praise and promote a company.

7. Community participation (and creation) can elicit valuable consumer suggestions for improving products and innovative suggestions for new products or service. Carefully cultivated two-way dialogue on discussion boards can lead to insightful feedback and the solicitation of product ideas from customers. Blogs, podcasts, and even Facebook fan pages all allow for community building and company-consumer conversation. Many brands will poll their social media communities about new products (do you prefer red or green?) or other aspects of their business. For example, Google has a Product Ideas blog where community members can advocate for new services or propose changes to existing ones.[27] Their Product Ideas team interacts with consumers, gathering feedback and suggestions. Google is just one example of a large company using social media in this powerful way.

8. Convert strategy execution into desired outcomes such as brand building, increasing customer satisfaction, driving word-of-mouth recommendations, producing new product ideas, generating leads, handling crisis reputation management, integrating social media marketing with PR and advertising, and **increasing search engine ranking and site traffic**. Although the last two outcomes have traditionally been the province of search engine optimization, social media marketing can contribute toward these goals. Search engines, like Google, have a number of factors that impact where a website shows up when people search for a specific topic. Search engine marketing alone has generated an industry unto itself; in 2008 $13.5 billion was spent on search engine marketing in North America, and that is projected to increase to $26.1 billion in 2013.[28] The amount of money businesses are willing to spend on optimizing search engine results demonstrates the value that can be gained by this strategy. A blog that is content rich and uses many relevant key words can improve a business's search engine ranking considerably. Producing informative blogs, videos, e-books, and white papers can help make a website visible when people search for terms associated with that company, product, or industry. Additionally, social media profiles on sites like Twitter, LinkedIn, and Facebook often show up toward the top of search engine results. The consequence of higher search engine ranking is increased traffic, which frequently leads to more sales.

Again, these eight social media marketing strategies are just a beginning. It is most important to develop a goal-oriented approach that links the goals and strategies together. The specifics will depend on information from listening to and observing the target market. Depending on the circumstances, social media strategies may help accomplish multiple or overlapping goals. Looking at the eight goals and eight strategies listed above, how might a marketer link each strategy to one or more of these goals?

CASE STUDY

HubSpot Gets Results from Strategic Social Media Marketing

Introduction

HubSpot demonstrates how strategically approaching social media marketing can achieve tremendous results. In developing and executing its social media marketing plan, HubSpot followed a model very similar to the one described in this chapter. The company began by listening, and prior to launching a social media campaign, it clearly identified its marketing goals and objectives. Once it had selected the appropriate social media tools to reach its target audience, the firm was able to grow rapidly.

History

The founders of HubSpot met in 2004 at MIT. Both were interested in how the Internet could transform small businesses and entrepreneurship.[29] The discussions and preliminary work went on for two years, and in June 2006 the company was officially in business.

HubSpot Inbound Marketing Software now aids 4,000+ customers generate traffic through their websites, helping to convert more of those hits into sales. HubSpot software includes tools for blogging, landing pages, lead nurturing, marketing analytics, content management, social media, SEO, CRM integration, email marketing, and more.

HubSpot provides a software platform that helps small and medium businesses grow online, so it was intuitive that it should build its business through social media and Internet marketing. HubSpot avoided costly traditional marketing by utilizing the social web.

Strategy

HubSpot developed a social media marketing strategy based on its strategic objectives, its customer base, and the importance of content. The primary objective of HubSpot's social media marketing campaign is to generate leads. With that goal in mind, it was possible to craft content on each social media channel that would produce those leads.

To identify the target audience, HubSpot starts with buyer personas (covered in Chapter 3) that allow the firm to know its customer base at a detailed level. HubSpot makes an effort to know its customers as people, down to what they eat and what kind of cars they drive. This knowledge is essential for creating appealing content.

Mike Volpp, CMO of HubSpot, indicated that, "without content at the core you really aren't that interesting. We think a lot about the customer, what they are thinking about and how we use content to attract them. When you peel back the layers of any successful social media campaign, at the core is great content."[30]

When HubSpot got started in social media marketing, one of its early hires was a former editor of the *New York Times*. The editor was chosen because HubSpot knew that engaging content was essential to its social media marketing success. The company's content is mostly educational and not directly promotional. Its educational material begins an informal conversation, later leading to the question of "how can we help?" which eventually may conclude in a sale.

HubSpot uses a large number of social media tools including a blog, webinars, video, Twitter, eBooks, LinkedIn, Slideshare, and Facebook. According to Volpp, "different people like different kinds of content," so HubSpot aims to share meaningful content when and where the target audience is.[31] The type of content is based on the target audience and which of the audience's interests are related to the product. To stay current, HubSpot is constantly adapting its strategy by analyzing the quality of each social media site's traffic. Testing how effective each tool is allows the firm to fit different strategies to specific needs.

HubSpot completes its social media marketing campaign by creating calls to action for each social media channel. Its social media efforts aim to draw potential customers into further interaction with the company. For example, someone may follow HubSpot on Twitter, which leads that person to read a blog post on a social media topic, then download an eBook or attend a webinar. To access the eBook or webinar, the prospect provides her or his email address and answers lead qualification questions. This process converts random prospects into a solid leads.

Results

HubSpot has seen positive results from its multichanneled efforts in social media. However, the company still views its blog as the centerpiece for social media marketing because many of the other platforms drive traffic back to the blog. The blog is one of the company's top three sources of leads. Each article provides links to a webinar or an eBook, encouraging more interaction on the topic at hand. These clear calls to action help HubSpot achieve its marketing goals.

The traffic HubSpot generates from social media has a conversion rate of 5%, meaning that 5% of the people who visit the site become a lead or give an email address so that a sales representative can follow up. Compared to many other mass-marketing strategies, this conversion rate is astonishingly high.

Social media profiles have also increased traffic to HubSpot's website from search engines; social media now accounts for 70% to 75% of the firm's search engine traffic. According to Vlopp, of the traffic to the blog, 20% comes from other social media sources (such as Twitter, Facebook, and LinkedIn).[32]

HubSpot's success shows how taking a strategic approach to social media can produce solid business results. HubSpot entered social media marketing with a strong understanding of its goals, the customer, and the content. In addition, HubSpot has a clear call to action integrated into all of its online materials, which helps turn traffic into customers. Its strategic approach ensures that its marketing objectives can be achieved.

In order to stay competitive, HubSpot constantly tests and experiments with different social media marketing tools. It tracks the results to determine effectiveness, and it adapts its tactics as necessary. With a powerful strategy and openness to learning, HubSpot has created excellent results with social media marketing.

Linking Goals with a Call to Action

Once clear marketing goals are established, it is important to link those goals to a call to action. This process will help design and measure social media campaigns more effectively. In order to measure success, you need to clearly define what someone's desired action would be—your "call to action." With a clear and measurable call to action, it's possible to measure actual conversions due to a social media marketing campaign.

A **call to action** is simply the action that you want someone to take at each stage of your marketing campaign. There may be different calls to action for each aspect of an Internet marketing or social media strategy. For example, the goal may be to get blog readers subscribed to an email newsletter or webinar, so the call to action for webinar listeners may be for them to sign up. Following this, there may be a series of calls to action that increase the engagement level with the consumer, earning the right to ask for more information and eventually to close a sale.

Your call to action should flow naturally from your marketing goals. Table 2.1 shows some examples of calls to action based on different marketing strategies.

Marketing goal	Call to action
Lead generation	Sign up for webinar
	Call for consultation
	Complete form for consultation
Brand building	Watch video
	Click on links
	Read content
	Fan/friend/follow brand
	Sign up for newsletter

Table 2.1 Marketing Goals and Lead Generation

Getting to the sale is the final step in a chain of actions. For example, one chain of actions leading to a sale may be:

- Click on blog post from Twitter or Facebook

- Sign up for email newsletter

- Sign up for webinar (collect lead scoring and contact information)

- Have salesperson call

- Purchase

In each instance, the goal is to increase the level of interaction and engagement through small, incremental steps. Although the ultimate desired action is probably to generate a sale, the best way to get there involves intermediate steps that *end* in selling the product. It is also important that the call to action be integrated firmly with the actual content being provided. A call to action that seems artificial, forced, or overly aggressive is less likely to be successful. As author and CEO Sunita Biddu notes, "[b]eginning and nonprofessional writers often think that throwing in a few standard selling phrases will accomplish the call to action. The truth is that the call to action must be an extension and continuation of the entire marketing piece. If you have not convinced the potential buyer of the value of your product or service before they get to the call to action, it will not work."[33]

At every stage, the call to action must implicitly answer the consumer's question, "what's in it for me?"[34] Why should someone click on a link, give an email address, or sign up for a consultation? Having an effective call to action at every stage means answering these questions in advance. As one online entrepreneur claims, "[t]he whole point of using this very specific marketing design is to make sure that wherever on your site your visitor is, you are getting them closer to do what you want them to do."[35] Effective social media marketers should already have some idea what their audience's goals, motivations, and communication preferences are (through the listening process). A strong call to action will put that knowledge to work, by designing a compelling message that keeps consumers engaged and coming back for more.

Self-Promotion vs. Building an Army of Advocates

A final strategy point to consider when building a social media plan is the value of building an "army" of passionate brand defenders, advocates, and enthusiasts. Many businesses focus their social media efforts around themselves and publishing content about the brand. They measure social media "success" based on the number of followers or mentions.

While social media can be a platform for businesses to share their content, it can be even more valuable by building the number of people who are passionate about a business. These **brand advocates** will talk to their friends—not because of a contest or prize—but because they are truly passionate about a business and want to tell the world.

Building and cultivating these relationships can deliver direct value for a firm. First, this is basic word-of-mouth marketing that we previously discussed. Building relationships and rewarding or giving attention to your fans are key drivers of word of mouth. In addition, these are the people who will come to your defense if the company lands in hot water.

Some very passionate brand advocates can start off as disgruntled customers or skeptical purchasers. Many customers are flattered when businesses take time to respond personally to problems. If a company responds quickly to negative comments and resolves the situation professionally, it can change an initial bad impression into a lasting positive one. An angry customer may initially be hostile, but after the situation is resolved, this person feels relief and gratitude. People whose input has been taken seriously or who have been assisted in resolving a difficult problem know that the company respects them and values their time. In return, these people will be more likely to speak positively about the brand.

Building these positive relationships can result in natural positive recommendations from people who never need to be compensated; these relationships also pay dividends of goodwill and increased sales well into the future. An additional value of brand advocates comes when you get into trouble. As a result of circumstance or human error, eventually a business will offend or upset someone. Having honest, regular people who are not employed by the company defend the brand can turn an entire conversation around. These unpaid advocates can be one of the greatest assets to a social media campaign. In the next chapter, we discuss targeting and market segmentation to aid in finding these valuable brand advocates.

EXERCISE CASE STUDY

The Kryptonite Bike Lock Fiasco

In 2004, the well-known Kryptonite Bike Lock Company leaped into unwanted social media prominence when an online video demonstrated how to defeat a $50 Kryptonite lock using a Bic pen.[36] Kryptonite bike locks were a substantial improvement over locking technology at the time of the company's founding in 1972.

© Masterfile RF

Challenge ....

After biking enthusiast Chris Brennan posted onto a forum a demonstration of how to use a Bic pen to open a Kryptonite lock, the story quickly moved to other media as well. With potential consumers seeing an expensive bike lock being unlocked by extremely simple means, the company faced an unexpected public relations firestorm.

Strategy

Kryptonite did make a response but apparently not fast enough. The firm's actions were featured in a prominent book, *Naked Conversations: How Blogs Are Changing the Way Businesses Talk with Customers*, as a prominent example of what *not* to do in the face of a crisis.[37] After that negative exposure, Kryptonite became the benchmark of failure to respond to social media criticisms.

Interestingly, Kryptonite responded very quickly to the security problem with its locks. Five business days after the first forum post, Kryptonite announced a lock exchange program with existing customers in order to fix the lock's vulnerability, and the first exchanges were made a few weeks later.[38] Rather than being out of touch with social media, as some critics claim, Kryptonite took action quite fast, and its social media team was anything but unresponsive. Kryptonite's head of public relations, Donna M. Tocci, went on to contact Robert Scoble and Shel Israel, the authors of *Naked Conversations*, and asked to set the record straight (their book relied on secondary sources for the Kryptonite case study and had not asked for the company's input before publication).[39] In the conversation that resulted, when asked whether Kryptonite's PR department believes it could have handled the situation better, Tocci replied, "we could have posted to the website earlier, but other than that, there wasn't much different we could do."

Result

In spite of its proactive response, Kryptonite is still followed by negative publicity from the "Bic-picking" scandal. Although the security issue with its locks has been completely resolved, search engine results still show videos and demonstrations on how to defeat a Kryptonite lock using a pen. Some consumers, rather than digging deeper to find that the exploit has been resolved, leave with the impression that Kryptonite has done little to address the problem.[40] Some reports claim that Kryptonite was unaware of the problem until it reached the national media, an accusation the company denies. In any case it is undeniable that this experience has changed the way Kryptonite will approach social media in the future.

Review Questions for Kryptonite Case Study

1. What factors led to the social media explosion of the Kryptonite story?

2. Do you agree with Donna Tocci's claim that the company couldn't have done much differently? If so, why? If not, what about its response could have been improved?

3. What can Kryptonite do now to prevent customers from getting inaccurate information about its products?

4. What can other companies learn from this experience in terms of listening to the community and designing their social media strategy and objectives?

Notes

1. Uhrmacher, Aaron (2008, July 10) "How to Develop a Social Media Plan for Your Business in 5 Steps," Mashable. Retrieved August 5, 2011 from http://mashable.com/2008/07/10/how-to-develop-a-social-media-plan/

2. Solis, Brian (2010, July 19), The Conversation, *Harvard Business Review Blogs*. Retrieved January 13, 2011, from http://blogs.hbr.org/cs/2010/07/social_medias_critical_path_re.html

3. Aronsson, Laura, and Bianca Male (2010, Feb. 19), "Is Your Target Audience on Twitter, Facebook, or LinkedIn?" *Business Insider*. Retrieved January 1, 2011, from http://www.businessinsider.com/is-your-target-audience-on-twitter-facebook-or-linkedin-2010-2

4. "Org data" (n.d.), CMO Survey. Retrieved December 25, 2011, from http://www.cmosurvey.org/

5. Dell, Michael and Catherine Fredman (1999), *Direct from Dell* (New York: HarperCollins).

6. "Dell Overview" (n.d.), BetterTrades.com. Retrieved July 8, 2011, from http://www.bettertrades.org/companies/dell-ticker-dell.asp

7. Facts about Dell (n.d.), Dell. Retrieved January 1, 2011, from http://content.dell.com/us/en/corp/d/corp-comm/our-story-facts-about-dell.aspx

8. Jarvis, Jeff (2005, June 21), "Dell Lies, Dell Sucks," *BuzzMachine*. Retrieved December 25, 2010, from http://www.buzzmachine.com/archives/2005_06_21.html

9. Jarvis, Jeff (2005, August 17), "Dear Mr. Dell," *BuzzMachine,* Retrieved December 25, 2010, from http://www.buzzmachine.com/2005/08/17/dear-mr-dell/

10. Twitter 101 (n.d.), "Dell Case." Retrieved December 25, 2010, from http://business.twitter.com/twitter101/case_dell

11. Collier, Mack (2007, June 13), "Company Blog Checkup: Dell," blog. Retrieved December 25, 2010, from http://moblogsmoproblems.blogspot.com/2007/06/company-blog-checkup-dell.html

12. Taylor, Marisa (2009, June 12), "Dell Sells $3 Million through Twitter," *Wall Street Journal Blogs.* Retrieved December 25, 2010, from http://blogs.wsj.com/digits/2009/06/12/dell-sells-3-million-through-twitter/

13. Livingston, Geoff, as geoliv (alias) (2007, November 18), "Dell's Incredible Turnaround. Now Is Gone." Retrieved December 25, 2010, from http://nowisgone.com/2007/10/18/dells-incredible-turnaround/

14. Livingston, Geoff (2010, October 24), "Case Study: Dell Becomes a Socialprise." Retrieved January 1, 2011, from http://geofflivingston.com/2010/10/24/case-study-dell-becomes-a-socialprise/

15. Doreen (2011, May 6), "Social Media Marketing for Brand Building," *Social Media Marketing Blog,* ffreeLanceandmore.biz. Retrieved July 23, 2011, from http://freelancingandmore.biz/socialmedia/2011/05/06/social-media-marketing-for-brand-building/

16. Burnes, Rick (2009, October 6), "The Secret to Social Media Brand Building?" Cultivation. HubSpot. Retrieved July 23, 2011, from http://blog.hubspot.com/blog/tabid/6307/bid/5178/The-Secret-to-Social-Media-Brand-Building-Cultivation.aspx

17. Reinhard, Catherine-Gail (2009, June 1), "YouTube Brands: 5 Outstanding Leaders in YouTube Marketing." Mashable. Retrieved September 13, 2011 http://mashable.com/2009/06/01/youtube-brands/

18. Clifford, Stephanie (2009, April 15), "Video Prank at Domino's Taints Brand," *New York Times*. Retrieved July 23, 2011, from http://www.nytimes.com/2009/04/16/business/media/16dominos.html

19. "How to Improve Brand Perception with Social Media" (n.d.), Social Media Magic. Retrieved July 23, 2011, from http://socialmediamagic.com/blog/improve-brand-perception-social-media/

20. Rosendahl, Stephanie (2011, July 1), "Top 5 Tips for Reputation Management through Social Media," Articlebase. Retrieved July 23, 2011, from http://www.articlesbase.com/internet-marketing-articles/top-5-tips-for-reputation-management-through-social-media-4997832.html

21. Ibid.
22. Rowse, Darren (2008, November 5), "How to Get Featured on the *New York Times*, CNN, CNET and *Newsweek*," *ProBlogger*. Retrieved July 1, 2011, from http://www.problogger.net/archives/2008/10/05/how-to-get-featured-in-the-new-york-times-cnn-cnet-and-newsweek/
23. Kaushal, Navneet (2011, February 24), "Avoid Penalties—Optimize Your Site with White-Hat SEO Techniques!" *SEO Articles*. Retrieved July 23, 2011, from http://www.seoarticles.com/2011/02/24/avoid-penalties-%e2%80%93-optimize-your-site-with-white-hat-seo-techniques/
24. Shakour, Sarah (2011, January 7), "Search Marketing Strategies for 2011," webmarketing123. Retrieved July 23, 2011, from http://blog.webmarketing123.com/search-engine-optimization/search-marketing-strategies-for-2011/
25. Barker, Melissa (2011, April 14), "5 Steps to a Winning Social Media Marketing Plan," *New Social Media Marketing Blog*. Retrieved July 24, 2011, from http://www.new-social-media-marketing.com/blog/5-steps-to-a-winning-social-media-marketing-plan/
26. Evans, Dave (2010, May 12), "Social Media for Business (to Business)," *ClickZ*. Retrieved July 1, 2011, from http://www.clickz.com/clickz/column/1705525/social-media-business-business
27. "Updates from the Product Ideas team" (n.d.), Google Product Ideas. Retrieved July 1, 2011, from http://googleproductideas.blogspot.com/
28. "Survey of SEM Agencies and Advertisers, Nov 08–Jan 09" (2009, February), Search Engine Marketing Professional Organization, p. 6. Retrieved July 1, 2011, from http://www.sempo.org/learning_center/research/2008_exec_summary.pdf
29. Halligan, Brian (n.d.), "Brian Halligan, CEO & Founder, on the HubSpot Internet Marketing Company Vision," HubSpot. Retrieved May 27, 2011, from http://www.HubSpot.com/internet-marketing-company/
30. Personal interview, March 31, 2010.
31. Ibid.
32. Ibid.
33. Biddu, Sunita (2009, March 27), "Writing the Call to Action in Marketing Copy," *Ezine Articles*. Retrieved July 1, 2011, from http://ezinearticles.com/?Writing-the-Call-to-Action-in-Marketing-Copy&id=2150600
34. Pollard, Stefan (2007, May 8), "8 Tips for a Stronger Call to Action," LyrisHQ, Email Marketing. Retrieved January 7, 2011, from http://lyrishq.lyris.com/index.php/Email-Marketing/8-Tips-for-a-Stronger-Call-to-Action.html
35. Gislason, Jeremy A. (2010, March 5), "Marketing Call to Action—Strategies to Convert More Visitors into Sales and Leads," *Ezine Articles*. Retrieved January 7, 2011, from http://ezinearticles.com/?Marketing-Call-to-Action---Strategies-to-Convert-More-Visitors-Into-Sales-and-Leads&id=3879072
36. Torrone, Phillip (2004, September 14), "Kryptonite Evolution 2000 U- Lock Hacked by a Bic Pen." Engadget.com. Retrieved July 8, 2011, from http://www.engadget.com/2004/09/14/kryptonite-evolution-2000-u-lock-hacked-by-a-bic-pen/
37. Scoble, Robert, and Shel Israel (2006), *Naked Conversations: How Blogs Are Changing the Way Businesses Talk with Customers* (Hoboken, NJ: John Wiley).
38. Taylor, Dave (2005, December 13), "Debunking the Myth of Kryptonite Locks and the Blogosphere," Intuitive Systems. Retrieved January 12, 2011, from http://www.intuitive.com/blog/debunking_the_myth_of_kryptonite_locks_and_the_blogosphere.html
39. Israel, Shel (2005, July 26), "Kryptonite Argues Its Case," Global Neighbourhoods. Retrieved January 12, 2011, from http://redcouch.typepad.com/weblog/2005/07/kryptonite_argu.html
40. Keser, Alhan (2009, June 18), "Kryptonite Locks: You Need Reputation Management." Retrieved January 12, 2011, from http://www.alhankeser.com/kyrptonite-locks-reputation-management/

Identifying Target Audiences

Once marketing strategies have been defined, the next step is to understand the **target audience**. Who is the message designed to reach? This group should include consumers likely to purchase the company's product, and people who show interest in similar ideas or values. Defining an organization's target audience will reveal better strategies, which can be tailored to where and how the audience interacts online.

A **target audience (market)** is a group of consumers a company has decided to organize its marketing strategies to reach with their message.[1] One effective way to accomplish this task is through **personas**. Personas simplify the audience into groups so that it is easier to approach and understand them through social media marketing. According to Ian Lurie, in his book *Conversation Marketing: Internet Marketing Strategies*, a typical persona definition includes:

- **Demographics of the Persona**: Average age, level of Internet expertise, and spending habits.

- **Constraints**: A persona's technological limitations (type of Internet connection), a language barrier, or even vision impairment.

- **Needs and Wants**: What are the challenges facing this persona? What solutions do you offer that will turn this persona into a real-life customer?[2]

Since demographics are a core area of marketing that has been covered in great depth by other texts, we will only do a brief treatment here. Demographic information includes age, gender, income, education, ethnic

> **LEARNING OBJECTIVES**
>
> After completing this chapter, students will be able to:
> - Define a target (market) audience
> - Explain how personas can be used to define a group target audience
> - Describe the Persona Development Cycle
> - Explain how to determine the optimal target market
> - Describe an example persona and optimal target marketing
> - Explain the Social Technographics Profile
>
> *(Continued)*

- Identify where the target audience is participating online
- Describe what the target audience is talking about

background, and occupation.* All of these factors can be linked to both purchasing and social media participation rates. Another important factor is the family life cycle, "a series of stages determined by a combination of age, marital status, and the presence or absence of children."[3] While previously a married household was considered the traditional American family, now married couples make up around half of all households (versus about 80% of households in the 1950s).[4] Understanding the many family arrangements that now exist and understanding the different locations of single persons is essential for a sophisticated marketing campaign.

Next, consider the constraints that a persona may potentially face. These are too diverse to list fully here, but possible constraints can range from the technological to the extremely personal. It is important to note, however, that even personas with seemingly serious constraints—lack of computer skills, access to new technology, visual or bodily impairment—are still accessible audiences to a skilled social media marketer. Constraints should not be read as a sign to avoid that persona but rather as a sign to adapt the message and the medium of delivery to help overcome these barriers. People with constraints may even become a highly important market segment in themselves if a product and/or marketing campaign is able to add value by making that constraint less significant.

The final and perhaps most important aspect of a persona consist of needs and wants. What problems or desires will motivate that persona to action? These can be better understood through psychographic information, which consists of a person's activities, attitudes, beliefs, concept of self, interests, opinions, traits, and values. The sum of these attributes in context of a consumer setting results in certain purchasing and participatory decisions. While human behavior is never fully predictable, taking these motivating factors into account and considering a persona's needs and wants makes it possible to generalize about what sorts of messages are likely to be persuasive.

Essentially, a persona is a detailed profile of a particular subset of people within the broad target audience. It is obvious that people have many diverse interests and goals. Designing messages to reach a targeted audience may seem overwhelming and complex, "[b]ut if we break the buyers into distinct groups and then catalog everything we know about each one, we make it easier to create content targeted to each important demographic."[5] This ability is why personas are such a useful tool for social media marketing. By thinking about the needs of a fictitious, idealized persona, marketers and designers are able to "model" the interests of real people who share some common traits with that persona. This allows marketers to better understand the needs, preferences, and decision processes of their ideal customers.

Personas are often used by politicians in campaigns. Bill Clinton and George W. Bush both campaigned to soccer moms during their respective election cycles. Campaign staffs use dozens of personas like these to help focus their message and earn more votes. Some past references include "NASCAR Dads" and "Security Moms."[6] In the 2008 election, Republican vice presidential nominee Sarah Palin famously referred to "Joe Sixpack" and "Hockey Moms" during debates, and presidential candidate John McCain referenced "Joe the Plumber" when discussing how tax plans could hurt average Americans.[7] Even when these personas referred to specific people, they were intended to capture a broad (and in the candidate's mind, important) block of the electorate. These are just a few examples of how politicians from every ideological background use personas to build support from the public. Effective social media marketers can use the same tactic to gain a rapport with their audience.

For social media marketing, an in-depth understanding of the personas that make up the audience is essential in developing compelling and relevant content. Each persona will have a different set of interests, needs, and communication styles, so the content

---

*For a more detailed coverage of demographic segmentation according to these factors, see Lamb, Charles, Joseph F. Hair Jr., and Carl McDaniel (2011), *MKTG4 2010–2011 Edition*. (Mason, OH: South-Western/Cengage Learning), p. 119–25.

strategy must be targeted to specific personas that will help achieve the marketing objectives. Taking the time to create personas that include the demographics, constraints, and needs or wants of each group will assist in developing persuasive social media content.

The Persona Development Cycle

Many experienced marketers use personas, but the dilemma for a person new in the field is how to develop personas from scratch. There are many possible ways to create user personas, including intuition, trial and error, and costly market research, but only a few that have been modeled and studied academically. One such approach is the Three-Step Persona Development Cycle, which was created by Michelle Golden and which contains the following steps:

1. Identify Persona Roles, listing all relevant personas by role.

2. List Needs and Situational Triggers from personas' perspectives, defining concerns, symptoms, and problems.

3. Create Messaging Objectives suited to each persona's needs that you have the expertise to address (and note those that you don't).[8]

These steps can be broken down in more detail. First, think of a few well-known companies or consumer groups that are relevant to a specific industry or business. Then, consider the roles those people within these organizations take in their interactions with others. In particular, focus on **buyer roles** or **buyer personas**: those who make decisions about which products or services to spend money on. For a firm this could be the chief financial officer or general counsel, while in a household it would be the person who spends the majority of that household's income. Also, consider external stakeholders who are indirectly influenced by the buyer's decision; these may be taxpayers, donors, employees, or regulatory agencies. During this stage it is important to be specific and think of as many potential buyer roles as possible.

Second, consider the needs and situational triggers for the personas identified earlier. This step requires taking on the perspective of each persona and thinking about what needs, problems, or concerns that individual might frequently face. For example, if one were examining a student persona, typical problems or needs might include time management, convenient healthy food, access to recent social news and events, and the finding of low-cost textbooks. After listing these needs, consider the ones that would most likely induce a person to buy a product or service. These are the **situational triggers** that may cause that persona to seek the products or services of a firm. Thinking of personas in concrete terms—humanizing them—will make this step easier. The process should result in a detailed profile for all personas complete with a list of wants and situational triggers for each.

The third and final step is to create **messaging objectives**, which are "purpose-oriented goals for your communications" with each of the personas defined earlier.[9] In order to be effective, a social media marketer must tailor her or his message toward each group being addressed. Once the goals are clear, it is possible to become much more specific in addressing the needs of each persona. In other words, once a social media marketer knows what information a buyer will need before making a purchase, it is possible to design the social media strategy so that it provides a buyer with the relevant information, making the individual more likely to buy the product. Later, as feedback arrives, it will be possible to adjust these messaging objectives based on new information about the personas. Thus, like the social media planning cycle, persona development is also a fluid process that should be constantly evolving.

Determining the Optimal Target Audience

In traditional marketing, it was possible to take a broad approach and disseminate product information to everybody, thinking that they all were potential members of the target audience. In online communities, this practice has a bad reputation and is generally known as "spam." Mass messages are quickly dismissed by online consumers, and so social media marketing communications have to be finely targeted or they risk being ignored completely.

Once personas for potential buyers have been constructed, it is possible to narrow in and find the optimal target audience. At this point, it is helpful to "think about your buyer personas based on what factors differentiate them," within the broader category of potential customers.[10] What demographic traits do various personas have, and how do those combine to influence their buying decisions?

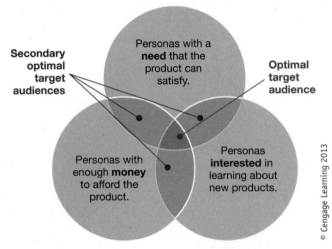

Figure 3.1 Relationships Between Types of Personas

© Cengage Learning 2013

A simple way to conceptualize how different personas might respond to a social media marketing campaign is using a relational diagram. Figure 3.1 uses a Venn diagram to illustrate the relationships between three sets of personas: personas with a need that the product being marketed satisfies, personas with enough money to purchase the product, and personas generally interested in receiving information about new products. All of the personas that fall into any of the three circles can be considered part of the target audience as they all have at least one attribute which might make them potential buyers. A spam marketing campaign could send the same message to all of this target audience, and would probably receive a very low rate of response. A sophisticated social media marketer, however, would target efforts toward the set of personas where all three attributes overlap, as shown in Figure 3.1: personas with a need for the product, enough money to buy it, and interest in receiving marketing messages. This group of personas makes up the **optimal target audience**. Intuitively, social media marketing efforts directed toward this segment have the highest probability of success.

It is important to note, both in real life and this diagram, that the optimal target audience makes up a fairly small proportion of the overall target audience and an even smaller fraction of the population as a whole. Also, because there are many firms providing any particular good or service, competition for the optimal target audience's attention is likely to be fierce. There is a much larger group of personas who have nearly all the traits of the optimal target audience but who are missing one attribute (money, need, or interest). We will refer to these personas as the **secondary optimal target audience**; personas with two of the three traits given above. Some marketers may prematurely write this group off, thus providing valuable openings for a skilled social media marketer to access otherwise untapped customers.

An advantage of social media marketing is that it allows unprecedented adaptation of the message depending on the group being targeted. After developing personas for potential customers, "use this buyer persona information to create specific marketing and PR programs to reach each buyer persona."[11] Using this approach, enterprising firms can reach out to groups outside the (small) optimal target audience by using specially tailored marketing strategies that meet the differing needs of secondary optimal groups. For example, if a persona has a need that the product can satisfy and is interested in learning about it but does not have enough money, a social media marketer could target the individual with deals, coupons, or promotions to make the product more affordable. Similarly, if a persona generally has money and is interested in learning but does not perceive a need for the product, the social media marketer could focus on demonstrating the product's worth or showcasing a need that it can satisfy. By adapting the message according to the target audience of which a specific persona is part, an intelligent social media marketer can generate a higher response rate than either a one-size-fits-all or an excessively selective marketing approach and consequently earn the firm more profits.

When deciding which part of the target audience to market toward, it is essential to keep the overall marketing goals and objectives in mind. Depending on the size of the industry and the number of relevant personas, taking a selective approach toward secondary groups may be overly time consuming and costly, so in some cases it may be most effective to focus just on the optimal target audience. However, there is almost always some room for improvement by adapting the message to meet some personas' specific needs. Further, by comparing the demographic information on personas with that from particular social media platforms, it is possible to focus efforts where they will be the most profitable. For example, as Twitter users tend to be in a lower socioeconomic class than social media users in general, Twitter might be a natural place to reach people looking for promotional coupons or a bargain. The specifics will depend on the industry, but using some basic logic and inference from demographic data can go a long way in improving the success rate for social media marketing efforts.

Example of Persona Development: Finding the Optimal Target Audience

The process of defining personas and finding the optimal target audience may seem abstract and complicated, so we will now work through a hypothetical example of this process at work. Suppose a company is selling online security tools designed to protect user privacy. How would the persona development process be implemented by such a company? The firm's social media marketing team could start with the broadest possible target market—people who use the Internet—and then develop personas for important sets within that larger group, as shown in Figure 3.2. Consider five buyer personas relevant to this imaginary company.** Here are the five buyer profiles for an online security company (with nicknames for convenience):

- Top executives or managers of companies (CEO)

- Beginning Internet users just starting out (new)

- High school/college-aged Internet users who spend large amounts of time on the web (student)

- Young professionals in tech-driven industries (yuppie)

- Middle-aged to senior citizens who are less familiar with the Internet (older)

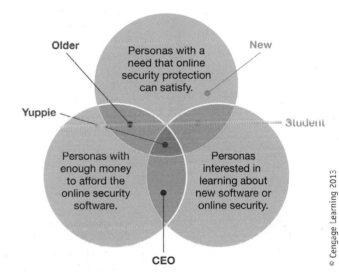

© Cengage Learning 2013

Figure 3.2 Relationships among Five Sets of Personas

The next step would be to gather relevant demographic information, assess the differing needs of each group, and consider which situational triggers may cause them to buy the product. After these considerations, the five personas might be categorized in a Venn diagram like that in Figure 3.1 to determine the best marketing strategy. Suppose that after their research, the social media marketers discovered that the personas fell into the

---

**In real life far more personas would be developed than just five. Depending on the product and the geographic or demographic distribution of potential customers, it would be possible to develop dozens or even hundreds of different personas.

categories shown in Figure 3.2.[†] According to this chart, students have a need for online protection (they spend large amounts of time on the Internet) and are generally interested in learning about new products, but they do not have much money. CEOs, on the other hand, have the money to buy the product and may be interested, but they probably already have some form of data protection in place; their need for the product is unclear. Older users might have money and a need for the product, but they are less interested in participating in social media marketing.[††] Young professionals (yuppies) might be identified as the optimal target audience; the combination of factors makes them theoretically the most likely to buy the product as a result of social media marketing messages.

Based on these categorizations, a strategy could be developed. Yuppies may be the best persona to market toward, but if that group is already saturated with competitors' messages, it would also be wise to direct some efforts toward the secondary optimal target audience: the older, student, and CEO personas. By creating persona-specific messages, social media marketing can direct coupons toward the students, demonstrate the product's usefulness to the CEO, and pass along information to the older users. This flexibility is the immense power of personas when doing social media marketing; learning about potential customers and identifying relevant traits before creating the message can improve both response rates and profits.

Developing Specificity within Personas

The most successful social media marketing plans are generally the most targeted. One common pitfall for those new to the field is that it often seems easiest to define the target audience very broadly. A food vendor might say the target is anyone who eats. While this categorization is technically correct, it is not very helpful when developing a social media marketing strategy. Remember, the broader the message, the more likely that receivers will interpret it as spam and ignore it. Exercising some thought and effort to clearly define personas will make a marketing campaign more successful, and avoid wasting money by targeting an overly vague segment of the population.

After conceptualizing a general persona, envision it as a target, filled with concentric rings and a bull's-eye in the center, as seen in Figure 3.3. The outer ring of the target represents the persona currently envisioned; consider the "student" from the example above. Now, move in a ring; increase the specificity of the persona by adding traits that would influence the response to the product. Again, taking the perspective of an online security software company, the next degree of specificity within the student persona might be "students who take online classes." One could go a degree further, specifying "students who take online classes and work part-time" or "students who take online classes and have recently lost data to a crash." This process is shown graphically in Figure 3.3. Considering the different needs of these subsets within the original student persona allows a social media marketer to develop a much more specific and persuasive message for those groups. As the persona gets more specific, it is like moving in closer and closer to the bull's-eye, which represents part of the optimal target audience.

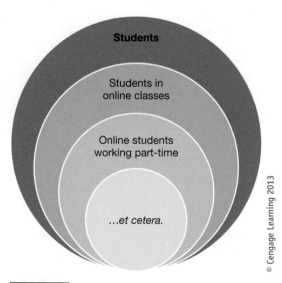

© Cengage Learning 2013

Figure 3.3 Specifying within Personas

[†]Categorization of these personas is intended to be instructional rather than informative; they were chosen for the purposes of the example and should not be read in any other context. In professional practice, persona development and categorization are based on demographic data rather than the ad hoc method employed (for simplicity) in this example.

[††]This is a generalization made for convenience; as discussed in the Seven Myths of Social Media Marketing section of Chapter 1, older Internet users are a growing and important demographic for social media marketers to consider.

The process of specifying down within a persona could be continued forever. There is obviously no inherent limit to how many different personas could be generated by applying this bull's-eye approach over and over again. So when does one stop specifying personas? The answer will differ according to the situation, but as a general principle, *stop specifying when the cost of finding information about a new subset within a persona is greater than the benefit to be gained by marketing uniquely to that subset.* At the simplest level, greater specification has two costs (the price of gathering information and down-sizing the audience that the message is designed for) and one benefit (making the message more persuasive). At some point any further specification will be of more cost than benefit. Where exactly this point will be found is hard to pin down precisely, but as firms experiment with different personas, interpretations of the results will become clearer.

As a social media campaign continues, new information about personas may expose areas for greater specificity that were previously unknown. One valuable aspect of customer input is that it provides information about needs, values, opinions, and desires that a social media marketer can use to refine a persona or divide it further into more useful groups. Much as a map may be improved as new geographic or landscaping tools become available, more accurate and specific personas to model the social media terrain can be developed as more information about the customer base is acquired.

CASE STUDY

How Wahoo's Fish Taco Created a Social Media Persona that Attracts a Unique Target Market

Introduction

Wahoo's Fish Tacos is a restaurant chain that appeals to 18- to 25-year-olds (Generation Y), especially those who attend concerts, surf, skateboard, and snowboard, and in general love extreme sports. Wahoo's has taken target marketing on the social web to a whole new level by crafting a social media persona that exemplifies the lifestyle and passions of their consumer base, enticing a typically hard-to-reach demographic to become not only fans but partners in helping the company expand its business and brand. This elusive audience comes to Wahoo's looking to promote extreme sports, music events, charities, and of course, the restaurant's unique cuisine.

History

Three brothers, Wing, Ed, and Mingo, opened their first restaurant in 1988, combining their love of surf and food to produce an eclectic Mexican/Brazilian/Asian menu with a Hawaiian north-shore vibe. The brothers, along with an entire generation of surfers, grew up taking surfing trips to Mexico, where they devoured a local specialty of charbroiled fish, salsa, and tortillas. This dish became the centerpiece of their Orange County, California, restaurant, **Wahoo's Fish Taco**. However, the Chinese brothers (who spent their early years in San Paolo, Brazil) gave it a twist, putting together the fish taco with their favorite Brazilian and Asian-inspired foods. The original restaurant was adorned with the donations of nearby surf shops.[12]

Challenge

Wahoo's strived to serve healthy fast food, and the fish taco filled the bill. The company did little to no conventional advertising. Instead, they relied on word of mouth to promote the restaurant. Unfortunately, beyond a loyal following in Orange County, the fish taco was little known outside the restaurant patrons and those who surfed or traveled south of the border to Baja, Mexico. So, in the beginning, getting the word out was very slow.

As social media began to emerge in the last decade, Wing Lam, often called the "coolest CEO in America" and an astute observer of trends, recognized the potential to quickly take the restaurant's word-of-mouth campaign to a much larger audience. The challenge was how to efficiently reach the target market using new media.

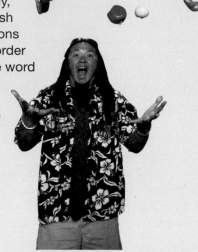

Wing Wahoo, Co-Founder/Partner of Wahoo's Fish Tacos

Strategy

The objective was simple; make Wahoo's food part of the lifestyle of Generation Y. To accomplish this goal the firm needed a way to broadcast itself while remaining true to its passion for surfing and eating healthily. Wahoo's began by sponsoring or taking part in sporting events (such as the X Games) and music concerts, as well as fostering partnerships, in the hopes of generating awareness of its restaurants. Part of the approach was to "provide food for benefits and charitable events, and do free tastings at places where their target market gathers."[13] With the advent of social networks, the company was able to efficiently target 18- to 25-year-olds, who consume the largest amount of fast foods, and made them aware of the events Wahoo's sponsored and the charities they contributed to.

Key to success of this strategy was the social media persona of Eddie Santos, Wahoo's art director and social media manager. His persona began with a few pictures of Wahoo's employees posted on a social network. The target audience immediately identified with Eddie Santos and his mullet haircut. His picture and conversations about him went viral, and he was dubbed RockdaMullet. Not missing a beat, RockdaMullet engaged with fans on Facebook and blogs and through YouTube videos and tweets (@RockDaMullet) about everything the Wahoo's lifestyle embraces, including rock tours, concerts, parties, and sporting events.

"Wahoo's team created a steady flow of content that was interesting to kids, teens, and young adults. Their fans collaborated and provided user-generated content filled with backstage concert experiences, compliments of Wahoo's, for bands, including Blink 182 and Green Day. A wide variety of events, music, action sports, charities, and celebrities provided plenty to talk about in the Wahoo's community."[14]

Results

Social media had provided Wing with a way to efficiently get the word out about Wahoo's. Millions of people follow Wahoo's social media presence, with Rockda-Mullet as their spokesperson. In addition, hundreds of famous athletes (such as Shaun White, gold medalist snowboarder), rock bands (such as Blink 182), and celebrities (such as Patrick Dempsey, TV and film star) endorsed Wahoo's Fish Tacos.

Today, the company has 1,500 employees in over fifty locations throughout California, Colorado, Texas, and Hawaii. Although privately held, the company provides franchising opportunities, with each store averaging $3,500 a day in sales, which puts the company's total annual gross sales for the brick-and-mortar operation in the neighborhood of $63 million. Moreover, the company sells its products online, which (notwithstanding a wide food menu) now include socks, watches, clothing, footwear, headwear, and gift cards and certificates. Online sale revenue for Wahoo's is unknown but likely to be substantial. Finally, Wahoo's vast social media exposure has also enabled it to raise noteworthy sums for charity.[15]

What does the future hold for Wahoo's? The firm hopes to expand into the U.S. Southwest and eventually go nationwide. None of these goals is unreasonable, given that the company continues to refine its target market for social media, as well as following new trends closely to determine what their audience wants and then giving that audience plenty to talk about.[16]

The Social Technographics Profile

Some social media researchers have already done pioneering work in developing personas, which can be of enormous use to new social media marketing professionals. The most influential methodology for creating social media personas is called the Social Technographics Profile, pioneered at Forrester Research by Charlene Li and Josh Bernoff.[17] The **Social Technographics Profile** uses demographics such as age, location, and gender to group social media users into personas based on their social media activities. **Technographics** is the methodology by which Forrester surveys consumers, similar to demographics and psychographics but restricted to technology behaviors. These personas are represented by rungs on the Social Technographics ladder shown in Figure 3.4.

The Social Technographics Profile consists of the following personas:

- **Creators** develop blogs, articles, videos, music, images, and art, and then upload them to social media platforms and are at the top of ladder

- **Conversationalists** participate in group discussions, engage in conversations on Twitter, and update their statuses on Facebook and LinkedIn

- **Critics** evaluate and comment on content produced by creators and conversationalists, post product ratings or reviews, comment on blogs, and participate in community's discussion forums, as well as correct wiki articles

- **Collectors** upload and save favorites on bookmarking sites such as Delicious; vote on content on sites such as Digg, tag photos on sites such as Flickr, and subscribe to RSS feeds to automatically receive new blog posts; and perform the valuable function of helping to organize and categorize content on the social web

- **Joiners** interact on social networks such as Facebook, LinkedIn, and Eon

- **Spectators** consume the content that others produce, such as blogs, videos, podcasts, forums, reviews, and so on

- **Inactives** Internet consumers not involved in social media

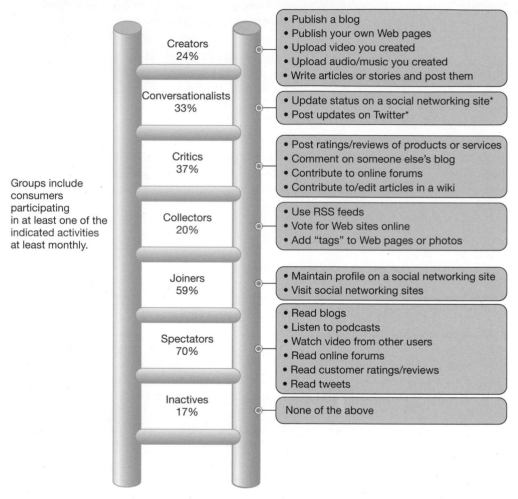

Base: US online adults

Figure 3.4 Social Technographics Ladder

*Bernoff, J., "Social Technographics: Conversationalists get onto the ladder," © Forrester Research Inc., January 19, 2010.

Forrester Research surveys have determined that Generation Y online users constitute the largest group of creators, making up 37% of consumers ranging between the ages 18 and 29.[18] In other words, young urban social media users are the most active of the personas in producing videos, blog posts, articles, discussion and forum text, among others.

The Social Technographics ladder not only reveals *what* people are doing on the social web but, perhaps just as important, *where* they are doing it (i.e., which social media platforms they are using). To reach their optimal target market, social media marketers must know where to aim and the Social Technographics ladder provides a helpful set of persona profiles to make that aim possible.

Using Video and Social Networks, Colgate-Palmolive Reached the Mobile Generation Y Target Market

Introduction

Colgate-Palmolive epitomizes how to create a target market persona that enables a company to successfully determine what its potential consumers are doing on the social web and, moreover, where they are doing it. By understanding how Colgate-Palmolive's intended audience participates on selected social media platforms, the company's social media marketing agency, Big Fuel, was able to craft content that not only attracted but engaged the particularly hard-to-reach Generation Y and make that group aware of a new product specifically designed for this generation.

History

Founded in 1806 by William Colgate, the Colgate-Palmolive Company began by producing soaps, perfumes, and candles.[19] In 1837 the company introduced oral health care products, including the first toothpaste—a fragrant dental cream packaged in jars. By 1991 Colgate-Palmolive dominated global sales of oral care products, with a 19% share of the toothbrush market.[20] Company growth had been steady, with total sales of $1.03 billion dollars and profits of $9.8 billion in 1991. Using conventional mass media channels, Colgate was successfully marketing several different types of toothbrushes, including the Colgate Classic and the Colgate Plus.

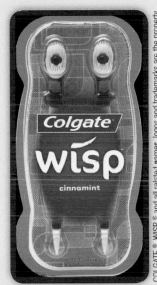

Colgate Wisp™ Toothbrush

Challenge

In April 2009, Colgate-Palmolive began rolling out a mini-disposable toothbrush called Wisp. The new product was intended for the on-the-go college student or urban professional, ages 18 to 25, both male and female. Colgate realized it had to tap into conversations relevant to these personas in the places where they hung out. This meant using the social web, which represented a unique marketing challenge for the company.

Since the social web was in its infancy, the firm enlisted Big Fuel, a social media marketing agency, to help tackle the challenge. However, conversing about a disposable toothbrush is not as buzz worthy as the latest reality TV episode. It was hard to imagine this audience following content about a disposable toothbrush on Twitter or Facebook. Consequently, Colgate and Big Fuel thoroughly explored the market and developed a variety of strategies to connect and interact with the target audience.

According to Avi Savar, founding partner and CEO of Big Fuel, "[w]e wanted to know, what does this product represent or mean to the audience? Wisp was almost a brand new product category. The biggest challenge for us was making the product and brand relevant to the young consumer market."[21] The research revealed that these young urban consumers are active daters, who rely heavily on mobile devices to establish times to meet with each other via instant text messaging.

Strategy

To fit with the behavior and satisfy the needs of this market, Big Fuel developed a Be More Kissable website for the Colgate Wisp product. It was designed to tap into the social media platforms where the market segment hung out and to encourage interaction by positioning the new product as a technology advancement that improved self-confidence. "Feeling kissable is about feeling confident. From a social media standpoint, we thought it was a good platform," said Savar.[22]

The key to the campaign was a series of irreverent videos uploaded to YouTube and other video-sharing hubs. Web celebrities, such as Kip Kay, known for his how-to and prank videos, help make the videos edgy and wacky, perfect for the niche tastes of the young target audience. The spots integrated Colgate Wisp into how-to, comedy, and talk show videos. This approach achieved a seamless integration of the product, without heavy-handed marketing.

In addition, Big Fuel launched a Be the Face of Wisp photo contest. The photo contest was designed to give anyone the chance to become "the most kissable person in America." Social media users participated by simply uploading their photos to colgatewisp.com and received a widget that enabled friends and peers to vote for them. The widget was delivered through Facebook, MySpace, and the colgatewisp.com site.

To further drive brand engagement, Big Fuel produced a Facebook app called Spin the Wisp, which collected the names of the user's Facebook friends. The app randomly picked Facebook friends for the game or the user could elect to handpick up to sixteen friends to fill in. Spin the Wisp was basically a digital

Be the Face of the Wisp

version of spin the bottle. In other words, in using the app, a woman might end up sending a virtual kiss to one of her male friends. Spin the Wisp evolved into a different way to flirt online.

Results

By mid-2010 the series of Be More Kissable videos had gone viral, racking up more than 4 million views on YouTube, with considerable exposure on other video-sharing sites as well. The Spin the Wisp app saw a solid 10% click-through rate—as measured by the notifications people received of virtual kisses appearing on their Facebook walls.[23]

The Be the Face of Wisp photo contest garnered over 40,000 installations of the widget and more than 1 million unique impressions of the widget, averaging 11 votes per person. The average number of spins per install on Spin the Wisp was 7.6. Combined, the video views, game (app) plays, widget installs, and pass-alongs totaled more than 6 million engagements for the Wisp campaign. This multipronged social media marketing effort produced a respectable $44 million in sales of the mini-toothbrush within the first seven months of the campaign's launch.[24]

In a consumer survey of product innovations, the Wisp was voted Product of the Year in 2010. Linda Tischler, a Fast Company editor, wrote that "I particularly loved Colgate's tiny 'Wisp' toothbrush, with its bead of embedded toothpaste. Perfect for going from the office to an evening event! Ideal for red-eye flights where you have to brush your teeth on a plane! Super cute!"[25] Even with the official conclusion of the campaign, people continue to watch the viral videos and play the Spin the Wisp game on Facebook, luring a steady stream of new customers to the Colgate Wisp.

The impressive results of this social media marketing campaign clearly demonstrate that Colgate and Big Fuel adeptly targeted the personas on the social media platforms where they hung out and offered them content that fostered the types of engagements that perfectly matched their behaviors.

The success of this process can be better understood by using Forrester Research's Social Technographics Profile Tool. It reveals that Colgate's Wisp target market of 18- to 24-year-olds make up 46% of the creators, 50% of critics, 38% of collectors, 85% of joiners, and 89% of spectators. These young personas gravitate toward creating, discussing, reviewing, voting, and watching **videos** and participating in **social networks**.[26] Hence, it is little wonder that a social media marketing campaign geared specifically to engage these personas on their preferred platforms with their favored activities should perform exceedingly well.

Colgate is now fully connected to social media marketing and uses it to help promote the company's more mature brands. Colgate is hoping to turn personas (target markets) into customers by meeting them where they live and by giving them what they want. The end game is to turn Colgate brands into social identities.

Where Is the Audience Participating Online?

As the Social Technographics Profiles section and the Colgate-Palmolive case study amply demonstrate, once an organization knows *who* the audience is through creating buyer personas, it is possible to determine where that audience's time is spent online. Social media marketing depends on building relationships and connections with the target group online, and so understanding where its members are online is vital to success.

In addition to using the Social Technographics Ladder to locate where a company's personas hang out on the social web, the following questions can help a firm zero in on the social platforms where its target audience participates:

- What news sites do members of the target audience go to?
- What discussion forums do they participate in?
- What social networks are they active on?
- What sharing sites are they active on?
- Are there significant social groups on these sites?
- Are there niche online groups that the target audience is part of?
- What blogs do they read?
- Who are the influential bloggers?
- Who is influential on Twitter?
- Who are the community leaders?
- Are they members of organizations?
- What social news sites are they a part of?

What Does the Target Audience Talk About?

The personas discussed above, especially in regard to the Social Technographics Ladder, enable an organization to locate its target market on the social web and gain an understanding of how the target audience participates in the social web. It is critical to understand what personas, such as creators, conversationalists, and critics, frequently talk about online. What are the subject areas they are passionate about and interested in? What areas do they have questions about? Look at blogs, microblogs, video and image-sharing sites, and news sites in the industry. What videos, posts, articles, and comments get the most comments or are the most popular? Identifying what the target audience wants to talk about is crucial in order to devise content that its members will respond to.

Once you understand who the target audience is, where it spends its time online, and what it is interested in talking about, the next important need is to understand *how* they talk to each other. In order to develop relationships with the customer community, it is necessary to fit in with the conversations and to sound "natural." To accomplish these goals means being able to relate to the target audience, using language that is familiar and comfortable to its members. Marketing messages that seem alien and unfamiliar are less likely to be successful. Building common ground with the audience members by sounding like one of them is a solid strategy when crafting marketing messages. Chapter 4 will explore guidelines to successfully engage social media consumers.

When reading the chapters to follow, always keep in mind that social media marketing efforts must center on the target market. This centering requires two complementary efforts: knowing where to find the target audience and understanding how to adapt the message to make it more appealing to each specific group. Always be thinking about the most relevant personas within the audience, and seek to adapt and refine your image of those personas as new information is encountered. This general advice will be helpful in creating content on each specific platform.

Lego's Market Segmentation Strategy

Introduction ....

The Lego Group provides a prime example of how insightful market segmentation and a fundamental understanding of different consumer personas can lead to successful social media marketing. By carefully targeting its intended audiences and using the social media platforms where these consumers actively participate, The Lego Group is able to effectively reach its customers and offer them the kind of online experience that helped win their Lego Brick the "Toy of the Century" award, one of most coveted honors in the toy industry."[27]

History ....

The Lego Group began in a carpentry workshop in Billund, Denmark, purchased in 1916 by the founder of the company, Ole Kirk Christiansen.[28] However, it wasn't until furniture sales slumped during the Great Depression that the company moved away from making chairs and tables to manufacturing toy versions of the furniture.[29] When plastics become available in Demark after World War II, the company began producing plastic toys.[30]

In 1949, the Lego Group developed blocks that could be stacked upon each other, much like wooden blocks, except the plastic ones, initially dubbed "The Automatic Binding Brick," had round studs on top and hollow holes on bottom, which allowed them to lock together, but not so securely that they couldn't be pulled apart and reassembled in another configuration.[31] In 1953, these plastic bricks were renamed "Lego Mursten" or "Lego Bricks."[32]

The company's line of Lego Bricks continued to expand in both type and popularity in the coming decades, employing innovative marketing techniques, such as featuring building block contests and tie-ins with

© tavi/ Shutterstock

Lego blocks

Hollywood themes like Star Wars® and Harry Potter®.[33] As a consequence, the Danish toy maker produced double-digit sales gains and swelling earnings during the mid-2000s, as well as a loyal following of enthusiasts.[34]

Challenge ....

With the advent of social media, the Lego Group faced the challenge of how to market their Lego Bricks on the social web. Jake McKee, a former social media practitioner at Lego, recalls that initially, "We as a company were walled off like crazy [from the social web] . . . I always joked that my task was really to jackhammer holes in that wall."[35]

McKee eventually was able to help change the culture within the organization, so they could use the social web to build relationships with customers, generate new product ideas by sharing proprietary information, and better understand their customers.[36]

Strategy ....

Understanding consumer behavior in regards to its products gives the Lego Group an edge in developing social media strategies. In fact, it enables the toy maker to effectively use personas to segment its markets. According to Conny Kalcher, a Lego Group representative, the company uses six distinct personas to categorize their customers based on purchase and usage rates:

"1. **Lead Users**—people LEGO actively engages with on product design

2. **1:1 Community**—people whose names and addresses they know

3. **Connected Community**—people who have bought LEGO and [have] also been to either a LEGO shop or a LEGO park

4. **Active Households**—people who have bought LEGO in the last 12 months

5. **Covered Households**—people who have bought LEGO once

6. **All Households**—those who have never bought LEGO"[37]

These six personas range from consumers who are highly involved with the Lego Group's products, such as those who help shape product design to those having no experience with the brand. The persona category of Lead Users has the fewest members, while All Households has the most. However, the first three personas represent the most fertile ground for social media interaction because of their deeper involvement with the brand.

Indeed, the Lego Group focuses its social media marketing initiatives on the upper three segments by co-creating products online with the Lead Users, and interacting with the Connected Community and 1:1 Community, using online communities and social networks.[38] By actively engaging these people and giving them special attention, the Lego Group stands the best chance of encouraging them to be the company's most ardent advocates.[39]

Moreover, proper customer segmentation and persona profiling enable the Lego Group to concentrate its efforts on the social media platforms with the highest number of brand active residents. In the words of Lars Silberbauer, the first global social media strategist for the Lego Group, "What platform you use depends on your target audience and the product you are marketing."[40]

Result ....

In 2010, the Lego Group became the world's fourth largest toy manufacturer, capturing approximately 6.9% of the global market share of toy sales and continues to sustain a high growth rate, as well as showing a net profit of about 688 million dollars for the year.[41]

According to Jake McKee (now the chief innovation officer of the social media consultancy, Ant's Eye View), "the Lego Group has never seen such tremendous success as they have in the past few years, since they began taking advantage of their most valuable resource – their fans. Not only have they received more coverage on the Internet, through the proliferation of cool LEGO pictures and fan-made viral videos, but have also turned feedback into new products."[42]

Review Questions for Lego Case Study

1. Which of the three personas does the Lego Group spend the most social media marketing time and effort? It is likely that different personas will emerge for the Lego Group over time? Explain.

2. What factors may have influenced the Lego Group's target marketing decisions?

3. This case study indicates that the Lego Group believes its optimal target audience are young boys. Based on principles from the chapter, who do you think the company's secondary optimal target audiences might be? What social media marketing efforts might help the company reach those other audiences?

4. How does identifying a target audience with personas help a company select the best social media platforms to focus its social media marketing efforts on?

Notes

1. Kurtz, Dave. (2010). *Contemporary Marketing*. (Mason, OH: South-Western Cengage Learning).
2. Lurie, Ian (2006). *Conversation Marketing: Internet Marketing Strategies* (Victoria, BC: Trafford), p. 20.
3. Lamb, Charles W., Hair, Joseph F., McDaniel, Carl (2011) *Essentials of Marketing. MKTG4 2010-2011 Edition* (Mason, OH: South-Western/Cengage Learning), p. 121.
4. Lamb, Charles, Joseph F. Hair Jr., Carl McDaniel (2011), *MKTG4 2010-2011 Edition* (Mason, OH: South-Western/Cengage Learning), p. 122.
5. Scott, David Meerman (2009), *The New Rules of Marketing & PR* (Hoboken: NJ: John Wiley), p. 32.
6. Ibid., p. 117.
7. "Gov. Sarah Palin at The RNC" (transcript) (2008, September 3), NPR, retrieved January 10, 2011, from http://www.npr.org/templates/story/story.php?storyId=94258995 and "McCain, Obama Go Head to Head in Last Debate" (2008, October 15), CNNPolitics, retrieved January 10, 2011, from http://www.cnn.com/2008/POLITICS/10/15/debate.transcript/index.html

8. Golden, Michelle (2011), *Social Media Strategies for Professionals and Their Firms* (Hoboken, NJ: John Wiley), p. 84–89.

9. Ibid., p. 87.

10. Scott, David Meerman (2009), *The New Rules of Marketing & PR* (Hoboken: NJ: John Wiley), p. 121.

11. Ibid., p. 121.

12. "Wahoo's Story" (n.d.), Wahoo's. Retrieved May 24, 2011, from http://wahoos.com/story.php

13. Jones, Susan (2010, August 17), "Do College Students Use Facebook to Find Restaurants?" Business.com, Answers. Retrieved May 24, 2011, from http://answers.business.com/Do-college-students-Facebook-find-restaurants-q21005.aspx

14. Macy, Beverly, and Teri Thompson (2011), *The Power of Real-Time Social Media Marketing* (New York: McGraw-Hill), p. 162.

15. "Wahoo's Fish Taco Partners with Blue C Advertising to Develop Cure Card Campaign" (n.d.), Blue C Advertising Agency. Retrieved May 24, 2011, from http://www.bluecusa.com/press/article.php?id=000046

16. Roberts, Kristen (2011, April 7), "The Problem with Being Cheap," *Brandtailers Blog*. Retrieved May 24, 2011, from http://www.brandtailers.com/tag/advertising

17. Li, Charlene, and Josh Bernoff, (2008), *Groundswell: Winning in a World Transformed by Social Technologies* (Boston: Harvard Business Press), p. 41–62.

18. Bernoff, Josh (2010, Jan. 19), "Social Technographics: Conversationalists Get onto the Ladder, *Forrester Research Blog*. Retrieved December 23, 2010, from http://forrester.typepad.com/groundswell/2010/01/conversationalists-get-onto-the-ladder.html

19. "A History of Suceess" (n.d.), Our Company History. Colgate. Retrieved December 24, 2010, from http://www.colgate.com/app/Colgate/US/Corp/History/1806.cvsp

20. Deveny, Kathleen (1991, Oct. 22), "Toothbrush Makers," *Wall Street Journal*.

21. Elkin, Tobi (2010, July 6), "Case Study: How Colgate Used Online Video, Social Media and Mobile to Drive Engagement and Purchase Intent," eMarketer. Retrieved September 13, 2011 from http://www.emarketer.com/blog/index.php/case-study-colgate-online-video-social-media-mobile-drive-engagement-purchase-intent/

22. Ibid.

23. Troung, H. (2010, July), "Colegate Wisp's 'Kissovation' Campaign," *DigiWave*. Retrieved December 24, 2010, from http://www.thedigiwave.com/2010/07/colgate-wisps-kissovation-viral.html

24. Elkin, Tobi (2010, July 6), "Case Study: How Colgate Used Online Video, Social Media and Mobile to Drive Engagement and Purchase Intent," *The eMarketer Blog*. Retrieved December 24, 2010, from http://www.emarketer.com/blog/index.php/case-study-colgate-online-video-social-media-mobile-drive-engagement-purchase-intent/

25. Tischler, Linda (2010, Feb. 2), "The 'Product of the Year' Awards: The Grammy's of the Walgreens Scene," Fast Company. Retrieved December 25, 2010, from http://www.fastcompany.com/blog/linda-tischler/design-times/teeny-toothbrush-salty-nasal-rinse-must-be-products-year-awards

26. Empowered. Social Technographics Profile Tool, Forrester, Tools. Retrieved December 24, 2010, from http://www.forrester.com/empowered/tool_consumer.html

27. 50th Birthday of the LEGO Brick (n.d.), LEGO.com. Retrieved November 5, 2011, from http://parents.lego.com/en-gb/LEGOAndSociety/50th%20Birthday.aspx

28. Ibid.

29. Wiencek, Henry (1987), *The World of LEGO Toys*. Harry N. Abrams, New York, p. 39.

30. Horn Hansen, Willy (1982) *50 Years of Play*, The LEGO Group, p. 25.

31. The Automatic Binding Block (n.d.), Technica. Retrieved November 5, 2011, from http://isodomos.com/technica/history/1940/1949.php

32. History of Lego (n.d.), Wikipedia. Retrieved November 5, 2011, from http://en.wikipedia.org/wiki/History_of_Lego#cite_ref-8

33. Schwartz, Nelson D. (2009, September 5), "Turning to Tie-Ins, Lego Thinks Beyond the Brick," The New York Times. Retrieved November 5, 2011, from http://www.nytimes.com/2009/09/06/business/global/06lego.html

34. Ibid.

35. Owyang, Jeremiah (2008, February 27), "The Tenacity of Jake McKee: A Social Media Case Study at Lego," Web Strategy, LLC. Retrieved November 5, 2011, from http://www.web-strategist.com/blog/2008/02/27/the-tenacity-of-jake-mckee-a-social-media-case-study-at-lego/

36. Ibid.

37. Paternoster, Leon (2011, September 2), "LEGO Brand Positioning" Legoman's Blog. Retrieved November 4, 2011, from http://eive.net/backtolego/?p=101

38. Rhodes, Matt (2009, March 31), "Engage Different Consumers in Different Ways—Why Segmentation Is Key," Fresh Networks. Retrieved November 5, 2011, from http://www.freshnetworks.com/blog/2009/03/engage-different-consumers-in-different-ways-%E2%80%93-why-segmentation-is-key/

39. Ibid.

40. Fernades, Ivan (2010, August 17), "The Building Block for Social Media." MediaCom. Retrieved November 4, 2011, from http://www.mediacom.com/en/news—insights/blink/issues/edition—3-2011/the-building-blocks-for-social-media.aspx

41. The LEGO Group increases its market share (2011, March 3), The LEGO Group Press Release. Retrieved November 6, 2011, from http://aboutus.lego.com/en-US/pressroom/Default.aspx?y=276303&l=200071&n=6

42. O'Neill, Megan (2010, June 9), "Then & Now: How Fans Changed The Face Of LEGO's Marketing Strategy," Social Times. Retrieved November 6, 2011, from http://socialtimes.com/how-fans-changed-the-face-of-legos-marketing-strategy_b14640

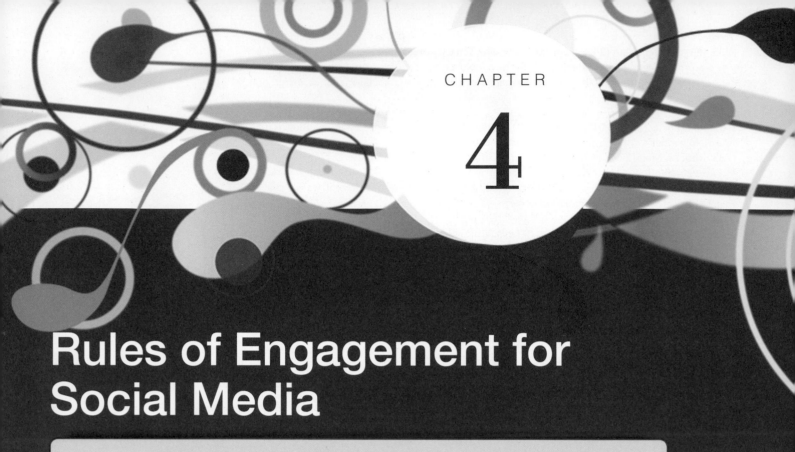

Rules of Engagement for Social Media

Marketers can find social media difficult to navigate because there are many unwritten practices and bits of etiquette that social media participants are expected to abide by. Slip up, and the unwary social media marketer could incur bloggers' wrath or be labeled a spammer. Hence, the rules of engagement in social media are as important as those in everyday life, but not always as familiar. A social media marketer must have a firm grasp of these rules and the norms that govern interactions on the social web.

This chapter will provide the general rules of engagement for success in social media marketing, as well as guidance on how to avoid costly mistakes by behaving properly on the social web. Something to keep in mind is that social media involves discussions between real people about issues or products that they care about. Typically, these conversations are not about the particular brand a social media marketer is hoping to promote. Therefore, one must *earn* people's attention, and that means playing by generally accepted standards.

Treat a person's social media properties, whether a blog, Twitter stream, or Facebook page, as though they were the individual's online homes. Depending on the circumstances, the social media marketer may be an invited guest (the person requested to follow or receive updates) or may be dropping in unannounced (by following someone and hoping to gain that person's attention or interest). It is polite, both in real life and online, to build some rapport before making requests of someone's time and attention. A first interaction should never be requesting a favor, especially when dropping by without an invitation!

LEARNING OBJECTIVES

After completing this chapter, students will be able to:

- Define the rules of engagement for social media
- Explain the difference between permission vs. interruption marketing
- Describe the initial entry strategy of Passive vs. Active
- Detail the principles for success in social media engagement

(Continued)

Permission vs. Interruption Marketing

- Describe the rules of effective social media interaction
- Define social media marketing ethics
- Explain how to make ethical social media decisions
- Describe the global perspective of social media marketing

Seth Godin coined the distinction between permission marketing and interruption marketing.[1] Old media or traditional marketing relies heavily on **interruption marketing**. When using interruption marketing, companies purchase the right to interrupt people and demand their attention. TV advertising, magazine ads, billboards, pop-ups, radio ads, and so on are all created to interrupt a viewer at what he or she is doing (trying to watch a show or listen to the radio, for instance) and make that person view or listen to a marketing message. Marketers in the interruption field don't have to worry about whether or not a consumer *wants* to see their ads, as firms paid for the right to display them regardless. Viewers or listeners realize that seeing ads is part of the cost they pay in order to consume some media content (TV shows, radio, magazines, etc.).

The content of interruption ads is focused around selling a product. It does not matter if the viewer has any interest in the ad or finds it useful. The goal of the ad is to showcase the product, highlight its benefits, and create a persuasive case for someone to make a purchase. Many boring ads can be highly effective at selling products due to their positioning or message. This marketing works because access to the audience's attention has already been bought.

From an optimistic standpoint, advertising is an effort to reduce information costs associated with acquiring a good or service. In addition to the dollar price paid, acquiring anything carries a number of intangible costs as well. For example, the price for a two-liter soda may be $1.99 at the grocery store, but the real cost of purchasing is actually higher. Consider the time spent driving or walking to the store, the chance of getting in an accident along the way, finding a parking spot and shopping cart, locating the drinks aisle, going through the checkout line, and then traveling home. Of course, this process assumes the consumer already know which grocery store to go to; he or she might also have to look up the address and get directions. After adding up all the time it takes to acquire the soda, the actual cost is much higher than the $1.99 price tag. The time spent driving, shopping, and so on could have been used to make money, enjoy leisure activities, or any number of other valuable pursuits. Thus, the real cost of acquiring goods may be very different from the price in dollars.

Thinking in this way helps explain why advertisements may have some value to consumers. By reducing the time spent gathering information about a product, ads make the real cost of purchasing lower, increasing both company revenue and customer satisfaction. Ads also serve a signaling function, because it is most profitable to advertise a high-quality product. In *Exchange and Production: Competition, Coordination and Control*, noted economists Armen Alchian and William Allen explain that "A seller's long-term survival rests on continued consumer acceptance—at least for products that continue under the same brand name. We therefore expect a positive correlation between a seller's *continued* advertising and quality of product and profitability: Good products make advertising more profitable."[2]

The logic behind this analysis is fairly intuitive. If a consumer buys a product based on an advertisement and is impressed by the quality, he or she is likely to recommend the product to friends, and the additional sales will make the ad profitable. If, however, the consumer finds the product subpar, that person will not buy again or recommend it to anyone, so the advertising may be a net loss. Therefore, consumers can expect that products with highly expensive advertisements are also of high quality. This is discussed as the *reputation effect* by some economists.*

---

*For more detailed economic models of advertising, see Hirshleifer, Jack, Amihai Glazer, and David Hirshleifer (2007), *Price Theory and Applications: Decisions, Markets and Information*, 7th ed. (Cambridge, U.K.: Cambridge University Press), and Philip Nelson (1974), "Advertising as Information," *Journal of Political Economy*," v. 82, p. 729–54.

Reducing information cost to consumers and the reputation effect are two justifications for traditional advertising. In spite of its downsides, interruption marketing in the form of mass TV and radio broadcasts and print publications does have its uses today, but it often helps consumers more than firms! More informed customers will drive a harder bargain, increasing competition between sellers and pushing down prices.** As more and more firms try to broadcast their products, the downsides of interruption marketing become more apparent. Companies end up shouting louder and louder with their ad campaigns, trying to be heard by the small segment that might need their products. At some point this advertising strategy becomes unprofitable, and companies search for more effective means of promoting their brands.

Permission-based marketing, on the other hand, relies on attention being earned from the audience. **Permission marketing** is when consumers consent to being marketed. This form of marketing may add value to consumers' lives, causing them to welcome and request certain marketing messages. Opting into an email newsletter, following an account on Twitter, or signing up for text message alerts are examples of permission marketing. Clearly, social media marketing is a form of permission marketing. Consumers choose to follow/friend/read/listen/watch a marketer's content because they see some value to be gained by doing so.

The problem for modern advertisers is that people are already bombarded by ads. According to the Media Dynamics publication *Media Matters*, a typical adult is exposed to between 600 and 625 ads per day.[3] Ads can be seen on urinal cakes, the backs of restroom stalls, napkins, airline peanuts, and even on sheep![4] Consumers are becoming increasingly talented at tuning out much of this advertising. People will record shows in order to fast-forward the commercials or change the station when an ad comes on the radio. There is also a growing trend toward "banner blindness": consumers know where to expect ads on a web page, and their eyes do not focus on those areas.[5] Internet viewers mentally block out the ads because their peripheral vision allows ads to be briefly seen and then ignored.

How is it possible to gain attention and build a brand in this sea of marketing? Unless a company has millions of dollars to spend, traditional advertising is unlikely to make an impact. The more economical answer is social media and permission-based marketing. In a permission-based marketing model, the budget is less important than a solid strategy combined with passion and compelling personalities. Permission marketing evens the playing field and allows new talent to compete more effectively against large, entrenched brands.

The basic rule of permission marketing is both a blessing and a curse: money is not enough to buy the way in. Effective permission marketers *earn* the attention of their audience. This need is part of what makes social media marketing difficult to navigate; it requires earning attention from people who *have a choice* about whether or not to engage with the marketing campaign. There are many strategies available, but people tend to choose engagement with brands that are authentic, are transparent, show care and empathy, respect consumers' time and opinions, and have a human presence online. This reality is illustrated in the case study: *Pepsi's Transition from Interruptive to Permission Marketing*.

The good news is that if social media marketing is done well, the ROI can be huge. Brands and businesses are witnessing tremendous growth by observing the rules of permission-based marketing and by being innovative in order to provide attention-worthy content for consumers.

Social media requires a permission-based or earned approach to marketing. Individuals generally feel that marketers don't have the *right* to be on their Twitter stream,

---

**For one example, an economic study examined Rhode Island liquor store prices before and after a 1996 Supreme Court ruling that permitted liquor prices to be advertised. After liquor stores were allowed to advertise, they cut prices of advertised beverages roughly 20%. Prices of other (non-liquor) products did not change. See Milyo, Jeffrey, and Joel Waldfogel (1999, December), "The Effect of Price Advertising on Prices: Evidence in the Wake of 44 Liquormart," *American Economic Review*, v. 89.

Facebook page, or blog. Outsiders have to earn an invitation and have permission (implicit or explicit) to market in someone's social media home. If a brand uses an annoying or intrusive sales pitch, potential customers are likely, at best, to cut off contact or may smear the brand's name on various social media platforms, at worst. The potential for a backlash against overeager social media marketing is one reason that it is important to start small. Listen first, and begin participating slowly after gaining an understanding of the community's language, etiquette, and conversational approach (as discussed in Chapter 2).

CASE STUDY

Pepsi's Transition from Interruption to Permission Marketing

History

Pepsi was first introduced as Brad's Drink in 1883 by Caleb Bradham, who created and sold it at his pharmacy in New Bern, North Carolina. It was later renamed Pepsi-Cola, possibly because of the digestive enzyme pepsin and kola nuts used in the recipe. Bradham sought to create a fountain drink that was delicious and would aid in digestion and boost energy.

In 1903, Bradham moved the bottling of Pepsi-Cola from his drugstore to a rented warehouse. Pepsi, which was at the time packaged in six-ounce bottles, sold 7,968 gallons that year. Sales continued to grow decade after decade, with the exception of the 1930s when financial and legal problems plagued the company. By the 1940s the company was back on track, making history with the first advertising jingle ever broadcast nationwide.

In 1961, recognizing the increasing importance of the younger, postwar baby boomer generation, Pepsi redefined its target audience with an innovative advertising campaign built around the slogan, "Now It's Pepsi, for Those Who Think Young."

The 1970s saw the cola wars heat up as Pepsi and its rival Coca-Cola fought over market share. Pepsi launched a clever and highly successful series of commercials called The Pepsi Challenge, which featured Coke drinkers claiming in a blind taste test that they preferred Pepsi. These commercials, along with the fact that Pepsi actually did taste sweeter than Coke, caused Coca-Cola sales to decline. Today, the cola wars continue to be fought locally and globally, inspiring the evolution of new marketing strategies by both companies.[6]

Challenge

As the shift from interruption to permission marketing began to emerge, Pepsi took the audacious leap of opting out of advertising during the 2009 Super Bowl in favor of spending its money on social media marketing. Pepsi ads had been seen during the Super Bowl every year from 1997 to 2008. As described by Larry Woodard, president and CEO of a New York-based advertising agency, "Pepsi's decision to pull its advertising from the Super Bowl telecast and concentrate on its Social Media strategy to try and create a movement will be the largest and most visible showdown between broadcast media and the Internet to date."[7] Frank Cooper, a senior vice president at Pepsico Americas Beverages, said, "The Super Bowl broadcast can be an amazing stage for advertisers if it aligns with their brand strategy . . . , [but] brands should not blindly anchor themselves to history."[8] Instead, Pepsi put the money toward a social media campaign called the Pepsi Refresh Project, which provides charitable grants to communities based on user suggestions. Through this program, "Pepsi estimates they will fund thousands of projects spending in excess of $20 million dollars."[9]

Engagement

Pepsi's choice to abandon the 2009 Super Bowl was a bold marketing move. Pepsi's market share was in danger at the time; "the brand's sales have been in decline for some years and in 2009 alone, volume declined 6 percent in each of the first three quarters of 2009."[10] However, the money saved from advertising in the Super Bowl—estimated to run between $2.5 and $3 million per commercial spot—opened up significantly more funds for social media marketing efforts. The shift in strategy was evident from Pepsi's public relations. According to the *Wall Street Journal*, "Pepsi says it will spend 60% more on online ads in 2010 than it did [in 2009]. It will be relying largely on Web ads and public relations to market its Pepsi brand because, it says, that's the best way to reach younger audiences—Pepsi's primary target—and to keep consumers involved with its brand."[11]

Vintage Pepsi ad

While Pepsi's strategy had many advantages, it also carried substantial risks for the company. From a traditional marketing perspective, allowing a chief competitor, Coke, to potentially control the content for a large viewing audience was a dangerous move. The Super Bowl audience is enormous from a marketing standpoint, but then so is social media. The numbers are difficult to compare; the "2009 Super Bowl attracted an impressive 95.4 million viewers (approximately 42.1 percent of U.S. TV homes) and many of those watch the commercials as attentively as the football game. By contrast, in the important 18–34 demographic, a whopping 85 percent use social media."[12]

Results

Analyzing Pepsi's decision in context of information costs and the reputation effect can shed some light on the company's reasoning. First, by increasing market saturation on social media, Pepsi could make more potential customers aware of its products and image. Second, by entering social media areas that users were already participating in by choice, Pepsi could influence an extremely broad audience. Finally, by creating the Pepsi Refresh Project the firm was able to direct more attention to itself as a creator of social media and as a valuable member of the community. By spending money on charitable causes, Pepsi was also relying on a reputation effect signaling that the company was of such high quality that it could afford to give away some of its profits. Simply being active on social media may be a sign of high quality; only a seller willing to stand behind its product would openly discuss the product and invite potential criticism.[†]

In short, Pepsi's decision to abstain from advertising during the 2009 Super Bowl shows that in its calculation, the gain to be had from social media marketing that year outweighed the benefit of interruption marketing through Super Bowl ads. Indeed, Pepsi continued its use of social media marketing in place of high budget advertising during the 2010 Super Bowl.[13]

© Austin MacRae

Social media has blurred the line between business and pleasure in the information arena so that now everyday people do valuable promotional work for businesses without thinking much about it. If Pepsi's Refresh Project is able to build the brand's social media presence, Pepsi may receive dividends of goodwill well into the future. Providing information, advice, and testimonials about worthy firms is now its own form of leisure for many people online. Companies able to tap into this activity will profit enormously from social media marketing.

© Cengage Learning 2013

[†]It is worth attaching a qualification to this point. A low-quality, thus low-cost, producer might also find it profitable to invest heavily in marketing, hoping to sell to a consumer once and then vanish with the money. For example, one New York-based online eyeglass retailer would loudly rebuke and threaten customers trying to return products. The retailer's negative online feeding boosted his Google page ranking, generating more sales. As a long-term strategy, this approach is less sustainable. Both the authorities and Google have been cracking down on this rogue eyeglass retailer. (For the full story, see Segal, David [2010, November 26], "A Bully Finds a Pulpit on the Web," *New York Time*). Generally, one would not expect a long-established or tightly managed company to attempt this strategy.

or thought leadership is especially useful in B2B markets or for those trying to build a personal brand.

There are two sides to credibility. The first is building a reputation for knowledge and expertise in the field, and the second is building a brand's trustworthiness.

The first type of credibility is discussed above. To build the second type of credibility, businesses have to be ready to share information and explain the rationale behind decisions to customers or potential customers. When problems emerge, businesses can gain credibility by admitting their mistakes, by asking the community for understanding or support, and by taking action to remedy the situation. Communicating openly can build credibility and make relationships with the audience stronger.

CASE STUDY

Trials and Tribulations: Walmart's Struggle with Social Media Marketing

Introduction

In spite of its commercial success, Walmart has walked a rocky path in its social media marketing efforts. If nothing else, the company should be commended for its persistence in social media. While there are many social media success stories, Walmart is an instructive example because of its many well-publicized gaffes and failed campaigns.

History

Walmart Stores, Inc. was created by Sam Walton in 1962. From humble beginnings, the company now has over 8,000 stores in 15 different countries. After making a name for itself with its highly efficient supply chain and its low retail prices, Walmart has also come under fire because of labor, environmental, and safety issues raised by activist groups. In addition to standard advertising, in the last decade Walmart has tapped into social media in order to defend and promote its brand name. These efforts have not met with complete success.

One of Walmart's ugliest social media problems arose from the *Wal-Marting across America* blog, started in September 2006. The subject was a couple traveling in their RV, using Walmart parking lots as rest areas. They would blog about how much all of the employees they encountered liked their jobs and other PR-friendly messages for Walmart.[18] However, when the significant financial relationship between Walmart and the bloggers was revealed, many people were displeased and felt the company had been dishonest. Even though the bloggers involved were real fans, Walmart's secretive approach drew negative media coverage and hurt the company's credibility.

Also in 2006 Walmart set up The Hub as part of its School Your Way promotion for back-to-school shopping. The Hub was a competitor with MySpace and was where teens could upload video and share pictures with friends. At the time Walmart already had a corporate MySpace account, but rather than developing a presence on existing platforms, the company decided to create its own service instead. Ten weeks after opening, the site went down.[19] Consumers were evidently not persuaded to participate on Walmart's social media bootstrapping.

To break into more platforms, Walmart set up a promoted Facebook account in 2007. Its page gained fans at a very slow rate; even after several months, membership in various anti-Walmart groups was still larger than Walmart's promoted account![20] The page had a feature tailored to college students, where roommates could input information and get fashion advice for their dorm room. Other forms of participation on the page were severely restricted. Users felt their comments were ignored and discussion was being quashed, and these feelings spawned even more negative remarks.[21] Walmart's Facebook campaign was largely regarded as a failure for the company.

Strategy

After some initial problems, Walmart's social media efforts became more sophisticated. In 2008 checkoutblog.com was introduced. It featured Walmart employees who would write about products in various categories, from gaming to sustainability, and provide helpful recommendations.[22] With a free comment policy and openness to discussion from users, the *Checkout* reoriented Walmart's image by putting focus on the employees rather than on a faceless corporation.

Building upon this strategy, Walmart sponsored the *Eleven Moms* blog.[23] Starting with eleven members, this blog quickly grew into a larger community of women discussing topics such as motherhood, health, and budgeting. This blog humanizes Walmart shoppers, with an option to "Meet All the Moms" on the front page, along with pictures and common discussion topics.

In addition to blogging and community building, Walmart has stayed involved with fresh technological trends in social media marketing. Smartphones are rapidly growing in popularity, and Walmart has been keeping pace by investing in mobile and location-based marketing services. There is a Walmart application for iPhone that provides guidance when shopping for electronics, reviewing products, and placing orders.[24] More of these services, which are both convenient and fun, signal a step in the right direction for Walmart's social media efforts.

In 2011 Walmart purchased social technology company Kosmix for $300 million. Analysts speculate that this purchase is primarily intended to acquire Kosmix's social media monitoring software and better expand Walmart's online business.[25] If this analysis is true, it is clear that social media marketing will continue to be an important aspect of Walmart's business strategy.

Results

Walmart has learned about managing social media the hard way. Already faced with a challenging audience due to the company's controversial business practices, effectively promoting the brand with social media has been uniquely difficult. In spite of many setbacks, Walmart continues to learn and adapt its message, and it appears to be meeting with greater success on the social net.

Regardless of the company's future plans, Walmart's journey of discovery in social media marketing is a helpful example to all others in the field. By analyzing the mistakes in Walmart's early social media efforts, it is possible for firms to avoid making the same blunders in the future. Walmart is also an excellent example of recovering from bad publicity. By moving between platforms and experimenting to find what works, Walmart's tenacity has helped preserve the corporation's image, even though the path to results has not the easiest.

Rules of Engagement

Social media involves *earning permission* to join in *personal conversations* with *real people* who don't usually want to be the target of advertising. Most people use social media to build personal relationships, and they are generally not looking for new products. Being aware of the following nine rules of engagement will help a new marketer avoid common mistakes entering the field of social media.

RULE #1: USE SOCIAL MEDIA CHANNELS AS INTENDED

Use all social media channels and their different communication methods as intended. Be aware of how the community is using channels and stay within the existing norms of communication. Look to how the general community is using each social media channel, then use some common sense about the channel's intended use, and keep usage within these standards.

For example, on Twitter, users can either send a *tweet*, which is a general public message to all followers, or a *direct message*, which is private and sent to a specific individual. Some people unfamiliar with this channel send direct messages promoting their blog/business/product to all of their Twitter followers. An untargeted message for all followers should be sent as a tweet, not as a direct message. Failing to follow site-specific conventions is one of the quickest ways to get unfollowed or called out on social media sites. Misusing social media channels in this way is a mistake made by people new to Twitter and self-styled social media experts alike.

RULE #2: DON'T BE A DIRTY SPAMMER

Don't send people in a network unwanted messages without their permission. Just because someone follows a page or group does not mean that they want promotional or sales messages.

For example, one LinkedIn member downloaded his entire list of LinkedIn contacts and sent an email promoting new products. There are two problems with his marketing approach. First, some people will feel that it is a form of unwanted spam. Connecting on LinkedIn does not constitute permission to be included on mass emails. Second, he violated rule #1 by using a channel (email) in a way not intended. Only a person requesting to be included or one who has opted in would expect emails. Taking email addresses from LinkedIn to do direct marketing is a violation of trust.

Many new marketers assume that average people *want* to receive their marketing pitches, but that is rarely the case. Give the audience the chance to opt out and don't mass-message people without their permission. People's general aversion to spam means sending unsolicited mass messages is a quick way to lose trust and annoy the audience. Don't send mass communications unless it is an urgently important issue or a person has opted in to receive group messages.

RULE #3: ASSUME PEOPLE DON'T CARE ABOUT THE PRODUCT

Related to the previous rule on spamming, it is helpful to assume that most people on social media sites do not care at all about the product being marketed. Sure, a few might, but most people are not interested. They care about saving money or solving a specific problem.

Just because someone follows or friends a company page does not mean they want to endlessly hear about that business. Consider: what is in it for them? Why would they care?

Some business owners think that they are doing a service by directing marketing at people. One small business owner thought he was doing people a favor by messaging them about his product. He would search on Twitter for people in his city with a keyword related to his product, follow them, and if they followed him back, he would send them a direct message with a sales offer. The reality is that this approach is still seen as marketing aggressively in a social space. Be aware of this attitude. If the approach is too forward, others will perceive it as a sales pitch, and it may taint their perception of the information provided. Be cautious of directly marketing to people, especially when it might not be expected or invited.

RULE #4: HAVE A PERSONALITY

Some people are hesitant to be personal on public social media sites. They want to keep their content strictly professional and business related. The reality is that people connect with other people on a deeper level than they can connect with a brand.

Sharing some personality helps build common ground and trust. A bureaucratic or forced tone is not a very appealing call to interact. Instead, building a feeling of trust and common interest makes it more likely that people will find the social media campaign to be engaging and worth participating in.

There is a professional line to be drawn, of course; it is a bad idea to get excessively personal or share intimate details. However, talking about music tastes, coffee brands, or other harmless character traits builds common ground and human connections. Always try to inject some personality into social media marketing and keep a sense of humor about the process.

RULE #5: PROVIDE CONTEXT WHEN SEEKING CONNECTIONS

Many social networks are intended for connecting with people already known. Facebook and LinkedIn are both sites where the network should ideally be centered on people one has met face to face. However, for social media marketing, it is necessary to expand that circle to people who may help provide business now or down the road. Therefore, having a tactful way to add new connections that may rarely or never be seen in person is extremely important.

When sending a request to connect with someone—whether it is on Twitter, Facebook, LinkedIn, or even via email—it is helpful to provide context for the connection. What is the reason for connecting with that person? Providing context is simple and just requires a quick note: "Hi, John, I saw that we are both members of group X, and you have posted some really smart discussion topics. I would like to add you to my network," or "Hi, Sally, we met last week at a networking event, and I wanted to follow up and say hi. You mentioned you were interested in social media marketing, so I went ahead and added you to my newsletter distribution. If you are not interested, you can opt out at any time." Adding a brief note for context will lead to higher acceptance rates on connection requests.

RULE #6: BE TRANSPARENT

Social media has changed the way information flows. Information is now available quickly, and it travels across the world in an instant. This means that businesses have to be more transparent in their interactions. Consumers can talk to each other and read about each other's experiences. They can research a company and its employees fairly easily.

This access to information means that companies have to be upfront with their information. Consumer reviews will inevitably highlight issues or problems. Be prepared to address them in an open and honest manner. Keeping secrets from customers is no longer a viable business strategy.

RULE #7: TALK ABOUT THE TOPIC

Businesses will often find discussion threads, Twitter conversations, groups, or blog posts that are related to their business line. Often their first instinct is to jump into the conversation with a marketing message. This is a mistake.

It is a good idea for the company to join the discussion, but it needs to make sure to focus on what the conversation is about, not just do self-promotion. A business that interrupts conversation threads to talk about its product is perceived like a loud braggart at a cocktail party. Pretty soon, no one wants to converse with the firm. Being overly self-centered is a quick way to be ignored at social gatherings, both in real life and online.

To avoid being shunned, talk about the conversation topic that is being addressed, not about the product or service being marketed. Don't hijack conversations and try to shift them to other purposes. People see through this easily, causing a loss of trust and in extreme cases getting the marketer kicked out of the group or off that social media site.

RULE #8: SOCIAL MEDIA PROFILES ARE NOT BILLBOARDS

Keep in mind that people do NOT create social media profiles for marketers to use. Marketers may think they are doing favors by leaving product messages on relevant blogs or discussions. However, most people are not excited to see posts from random businesses on their personal sites. What is intended as a useful product suggestion may be perceived as unwanted graffiti on someone's beloved blog and may generate a strong negative response.

Don't use other people's social media profiles or websites as a way to promote a message. It is best to engage in discussions without doing overt marketing unless it is directly on-topic. Generate original content and use that to get the message out instead of posting unwanted messages on others' sites.

RULE #9: BE NICE

Being pleasant and nice is very simple, but some businesses have a hard time grasping this principle. Politeness costs nothing, but it can make a huge difference in the responses that a social media marketing campaign receives.

An easy "please" and "thank you" can go a long way. Look for opportunities to publicly or privately thank people who help out or make positive comments about the product. On the other hand, when asking someone for a favor, be sure to ask nicely and not demand too much.

Look for opportunities to give back to other people in the same social community. Promote their events, blog posts, or products. Providing a link, positive recommendation, or other traffic-building measure for someone else can help a lot in earning his or her gratitude. In the long run, the return from these small favors add up.

Defining Social Media Marketing Ethics

What does it mean to be ethical while using social media marketing professionally? Generally speaking, the same code of ethics that applies to traditional marketing can be applied. However, due to its highly interactive as well as long-distance nature, social media brings its own set of challenges and complications to marketing ethics. Here are some principles to keep in mind when making those difficult decisions.

HONESTY

Social media marketing is based largely on personal interactions. Unlike traditional advertising, where it is often expected that some spin will be applied to the message, people use social media channels to

© Steven Wynn/ iStockphoto

communicate with friends so that honesty is highly valued. Social media messages are exposed to public view, so expect a high degree of scrutiny: facts will be checked, and promises will be expected to be kept. Building a reputation for honesty is a valuable asset in social media marketing. Honest and transparent communications should be a priority for both ethical and practical reasons.

PRIVACY

Do not collect or distribute personal information without consent. When implementing a social media campaign, it is helpful to have as much information about your target audience as possible, but obtaining that data should be balanced against protecting user privacy. More aggressive information-gathering software can be interpreted as malware, a computer virus, or just an annoyance to users. Violations of user privacy can quickly destroy a site's reputation and severely damage a company.[‡] When collecting user data, it is best to employ passive approaches that allow people to input information voluntarily. Do not collect any more information than is necessary about users, and be very careful that it does not leak to outside parties.

RESPECT

Showing respect for people means treating them as equals, as reasonable individuals with goals and lives of their own. While online interactions can be highly impersonal, there is always another person somewhere in front of a screen. Do not present manipulative messages, create false identities for testimonials, or hijack user profiles for promotional purposes. Using these questionable tactics hurts the quality of information online and inconveniences everyone. Show respect for online participants rather than attempting to herd them with deceptive claims.

RESPONSIBILITY

Mistakes or errors will inevitably occur during a social media marketing campaign. When a customer has a valid complaint, a technical problem arises, or some other crisis looms, there are three steps to take:

- **Acknowledge**: Find out what the problem is, and take responsibility for the situation.

- **Apologize**: If someone is angry, first attempt to calm her or him down. Apologize, and determine what would give the individual resolution.

- **Act**: Implement promised changes or make other restitution. Inform the complainant(s) that the problem is being addressed.

To responsibly handle a situation, all three of these steps must be undertaken. Still, it is important to avoid promising *too much* while apologizing because then it may be impossible to act! If the problem is beyond the realm of social media (that is, a technical problem or corporate policy), then a social media marketing specialist can only do so much. Taking responsibility must be done in realistic ways; an empty gesture is worse than a modest promise.

[‡]In April 2011 the PlayStation Network run by Sony Online Entertainment was breached by hackers, and around 77 million accounts were compromised. In early May it was revealed that another 25 million accounts could have had their credit card information stolen. Eventual damages to Sony are estimated in the billions. See Arthur, Charles (2011, May 3), "Sony Suffers Second Data Breach with Theft of 25M More User Details," *Guardian Technolog*. Retrieved May 24, 2011, from http://www.guardian.co.uk/technology/blog/2011/may/03/sony-data-breach-online-entertainment

Making Ethical Decisions

This set of ethical principles for social media marketing should be read as a starting-point rather than the final word. As technology and involvement in social media continue to evolve, new ethical situations will arise. Software tools to mine for user data are becoming ever more sophisticated but so are antiviral, ad-blocking, and anticookie programs to combat them. Deciding which practices to employ will be complex and will be based on both the tools available and the ethical limits and norms of the online community.

In a situation in which ethical standards could possibly be breached, it is best to err on the side of caution and avoid a potentially unethical action. The Internet has a long memory, and past actions can linger indefinitely. Gaining a reputation for unscrupulous tactics can seriously tarnish a social media marketing career and make finding employment more difficult. Even if questionable decisions seem like the only option, it is better to spend time doing more research and use creativity to solve the problem instead. It is better to learn through trial and experience rather than cut a career short by using unethical practices.

Global Perspective

Social media is an international phenomenon. As shown in Figure 4.1, a large number of countries have citizens who are active on social networks. As Internet access becomes more widely available, the number of people in online networks is certain to grow. As a result, communicating across national boundaries is an essential skill for any social media marketer.

CULTURAL DIFFERENCES

Adapting the message to fit the expected audience was discussed in Chapters 2 and 3, but this lesson is especially important when part of the community has an international background. Do some research beforehand to determine which regions or nationalities are active on each social media network. Then tailor communications on each platform to reference likely areas of interest or commonality.

Depending on their culture as well as personal preferences, different people have varying standards of contact and familiarity with others met through social media. Some will be more eager to participate in social media efforts than others. To avoid misunderstandings, be friendly but not invasive when seeking contacts.

HOW TO AVOID CONFUSING YOUR GLOBAL AUDIENCE

Expressions, proverbs, or folksy sayings that are clichés to a domestic audience may be unfamiliar to an international one. Some may be translated strangely or sound very odd to a foreign audience. Similarly, remarks intended as sarcasm or metaphor may not be interpreted as such if there is a language barrier. Avoid making jokes or references overly dependent on popular culture, puns, domestic sporting events, etc. A nonnative speaker is less likely to find these remarks interesting and may even find the reference irrelevant or confusing. This does **not** mean to dumb down material for international audiences but rather adapt to different cultural contexts. Making jokes that are only funny to native speakers or are easily lost in translation may leave international users feeling excluded.

To avoid confusion, it is best to make messages polite, concise, and direct. Before posting, mentally ask whether there is any part of a message that could easily be misinterpreted or cause your overall idea to be misunderstood. This is good practice when crafting messages to any audience, but especially when different languages and cultural backgrounds are involved.

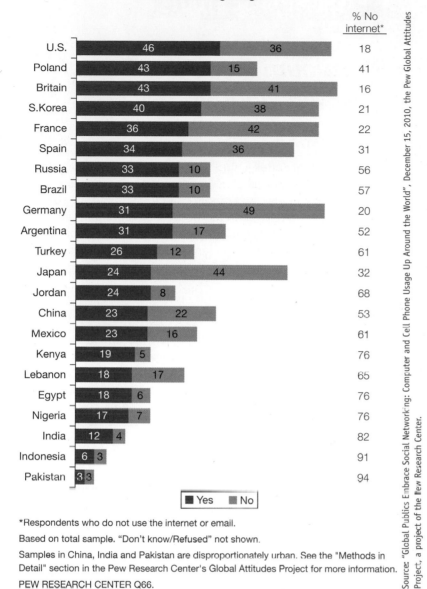

Social Networking Usage

Country	Yes	No	% No internet*
U.S.	46	36	18
Poland	43	15	41
Britain	43	41	16
S.Korea	40	38	21
France	36	42	22
Spain	34	36	31
Russia	33	10	56
Brazil	33	10	57
Germany	31	49	20
Argentina	31	17	52
Turkey	26	12	61
Japan	24	44	32
Jordan	24	8	68
China	23	22	53
Mexico	23	16	61
Kenya	19	5	76
Lebanon	18	17	65
Egypt	18	6	76
Nigeria	17	7	76
India	12	4	82
Indonesia	6	3	91
Pakistan	3	3	94

■ Yes ■ No

*Respondents who do not use the internet or email.

Based on total sample. "Don't know/Refused" not shown.

Samples in China, India and Pakistan are disproportionately urban. See the "Methods in Detail" section in the Pew Research Center's Global Attitudes Project for more information.

PEW RESEARCH CENTER Q66.

Source: "Global Publics Embrace Social Networking: Computer and Cell Phone Usage Up Around the World", December 15, 2010, the Pew Global Attitudes Project, a project of the Pew Research Center.

Figure 4.1 Global Social Media Usage Rates

GOOGLE TRANSLATE

Often, people who communicate globally through social media turn toward online translation services in order to bridge languages. Google offers one of several popular translation engines. Becoming familiar with Google Translate (or an equivalent website) is a valuable skill for social media marketing. Translation services can help gather what international audiences are saying about different brands.

Be careful when using online translations to create new content because sometimes the results can be rough or can lack important context. One good way to determine whether a message is likely to be misinterpreted is to translate that message into several other languages and then back into English. Is the content still recognizable? If not, revisions might be necessary.

Achieving familiarity with online translation will broaden the audience with whom a social media marketer can interact. These expanded contacts can be essential to the success of a marketing campaign. Learning to communicate and interact persuasively with an international audience requires skill and finesse, but the growing availability of online translations makes that task somewhat easier.

British Petroleum Runs the Social Media Gauntlet

Introduction

British Petroleum rose to media infamy after an unfortunate accident led to a three-month-long oil leak that despoiled the Gulf of Mexico and the southern coast of the United States. The disastrous offshore leak that occurred in the summer of 2010 continues to have serious repercussions for both the coastal environment and British Petroleum's public image. BP's efforts to combat this crisis through social media were largely regarded as unsuccessful, but this large company's failed attempt makes a valuable case study for future practitioners in the field.

History

With roots in the early twentieth century, the British Petroleum Company was formally established in 1954. At the time most of its operations were in the Middle East, but it quickly expanded to Alaska and struck oil in the North Sea. Today, it operates in more than eighty countries and is the third-largest energy company in the world. Its largest division is BP America, which produces more oil in the United States than any other American company.

Challenge

On April 20, 2010, an explosion on the BP-operated *Deepwater Horizon* oil-drilling platform released a rapid flow of oil on the bottom of the ocean. The explosion killed 11 workers aboard the rig and injured 17 others. The leak was finally stopped on July 15, 2010, after it had released nearly 5 million barrels of crude oil.

British Petroleum's early response to the crisis was generally seen as less about public engagement and more about spin control. BP's social media campaign did not start up in earnest until a month after the spill was announced. The company purchased promotional placement on Google and Yahoo to control search results for terms such as "oil spill" and sent viewers to positive articles about the clean-up. Later, the company spent $50 million on a TV campaign to promote BP's positive role. These expensive efforts did not help, instead "feeding a meme that BP is tone-deaf — more concerned with polishing its reputation than cleaning up its mess."[26]

Reaching for more social media platforms, BP's CEO, Tony Hayward, gave a public apology on YouTube. The video drew several parodies and was generally not received well.[27] More parody accounts were hounding BP on other social networks. On Twitter the account @BPGlobalPR quickly gathered 175,000 followers by mocking BP's failure to resolve the oil spill.[28] BP's official Twitter account, @BP_America, had been used by the company as a broadcasting channel and very little for community interaction.[29] The parody account had more than ten times as many followers as the company's official Twitter page, allowing the parody to dominate the online conversation. Meanwhile, dozens of anti-BP Facebook groups sprang up, dwarfing the company's presence on that platform as well.

Results ....

For many years BP's core business did not seem to call for, or even suggest, pursuing a social media strategy. The unfortunate result was that when a crisis occurred and BP desperately needed to communicate its message to the public, the company's attempt to bootstrap a social media presence by purchasing public attention was seen as inauthentic. This negative reaction illustrates the importance of starting a social media campaign immediately before problems arise and have to be cleaned up.

After engaging the media, BP's initial strategy was to refuse direct responsibility for the leak. When Tony Hayward was interviewed on the *Today Show* he said, "It wasn't our accident, but we are absolutely responsible for the oil, for cleaning it up, and that's what we intend to do."[30] This statement may have been partly motivated by legal concerns, as a full apology would open BP up to greater liability in court. However, this half-hearted approach did little to win over the general public. As a consequence of the accident and the weakly perceived PR response, BP fell from being the most highly ranked in customer loyalty in the oil industry to being the lowest ranked.[31] It will clearly be some time before its reputation fully recovers.

Rather than engaging in a top-down image management campaign, British Petroleum could have been better served by a more subtle social media campaign. One of its biggest mistakes was "failing to take advantage of social networking to open a clear line of communication with people living on the Gulf Coast and around the world."[32] There was an opportunity for BP to take revolutionary steps by engaging with those affected by the spill in more personal ways than grants of aid or clean-up assistance. That chance was missed in BP's case, but other companies can learn from its mistake by creating social media accounts for damage control, hopefully well before they are needed.

Review Questions for British Petroleum Case Study

1. What benefits would BP have gained from starting a serious social media campaign a year before instead of a month after the oil spill? Be as specific as possible.

2. While the parody account was posting on Twitter, BP asked for the account to be shut down. The social media site refused, saying that parodies were allowed under its terms of service. Is there a better way BP could have handled the accounts making fun of them?

3. BP was criticized for underestimating the extent of the oil spill at first: the company is said to have underestimated the leak's size by as much as a fifth the real amount. Would BP have been better off to report a higher number and perhaps risk overestimating the extent of the leak? Why or why not?

4. Go on YouTube and view Tony Hayward's apology. Was this a well-constructed social media message? Should YouTube have been used differently, the same, or not at all in presenting BP's case? Explain your argument.

5. Do some external research and look up the Exxon Valdez oil spill. Compare and contrast Exxon's and BP's responses to their respective crises. How successful were they in comparison? How much of the difference can be attributed to a change in the times, different corporate cultures, or media strategies? Cite your sources.

Notes

1. Godin, Seth (1999), *Permission Marketing: Turning Strangers into Friends, and Friends into Customers* (New York: Simon & Schuster).

2. Alchian, Armen, and William R. Allen(1983), *Exchange and Production: Competition, Coordination and Control,* 3rd ed. (Belmont, CA: Wadsworth), p. 278.

3. "How Many Advertisements Is a Person Exposed to in a Day?" (2007, March), American Association of Advertising Agencies. Retrieved December 30, 2010, from http://ams.aaaa.org/eweb/upload/FAQs/adexposures.pdf

4. Carvajal, Doreen (2006, April 24), "Advertiser Counts on Sheep to Pull Eyes over the Wool," *International Herald Tribune.* Retrieved January 11, 2011, from http://www.nytimes.com/2006/04/24/world/europe/24sheep.html

5. Benway, J. P., and D. M. Lane (1998, December), "Banner Blindness: Web Searchers Often Miss 'Obvious' Links," *Internetworking,* vol. 1.3. Retrieved January 11, 2011, from http://www.internettg.org/newsletter/dec98/banner_blindness.html

6. *The Pepsi-Cola Story* (n.d.). Retrieved December 11, 2010, from http://pepsiusa.com/downloads/PepsiLegacy_Book.pdf

7. Woodard, Larry D. (2009, December 23), "Pepsi's Big Gamble: Ditching Super Bowl for Social Media." ABC News. Retrieved December 30, 2010, from http://abcnews.go.com/Business/pepsis-big-gamble-ditching-super-bowl-social-media/story?id=9402514&page=1

8. Rooney, Ben (2009, December 18), "Pepsi Takes a Pass on Super Bowl Ads," CNN Money. Retrieved December, 30 2010, from http://money.cnn.com/2009/12/17/news/companies/pepsi_super_bowl/

9. Woodard, Larry D. (2009, December 23), "Pepsi's Big Gamble: Ditching Super Bowl for Social Media," ABC News. Retrieved December 30, 2010, from http://abcnews.go.com/Business/pepsis-big-gamble-ditching-super-bowl-social-media/story?id=9402514&page=1

10. Ibid.

11. Vranica, Suzanne (2009, December 17), "Pepsi Benches Its Drinks: Beverages Will Snap Long Streak by Sitting out Super Bowl," *Wall Street Journal.* Retrieved December 30, 2010, from http://online.wsj.com/article/SB10001424052748703581204574600322164130250.html?mod=googlenews_wsj

12. Woodard, Larry D. (2009, December 23), "Pepsi's Big Gamble: Ditching Super Bowl for Social Media," ABC News. Retrieved December 30, 2010, from http://abcnews.go.com/Business/pepsis-big-gamble-ditching-super-bowl-social-media/story?id=9402514&page=1

13. Warren, Christina (2009, December 23) "Pepsi to Skip Super Bowl Ads in Favor of $20M Social Media Campaign," Mashable Business. Retrieved September 13, 2011 from http://mashable.com/2009/12/23/pepsi-super-bowl/

14. Gilbreath, Bob (2009), *The Next Evolution of Marketing: Connect with Your Customers by Marketing with Meaning* (New York: McGraw-Hill).

15. Twitter 101(n.d.), @jetblue. Retrieved December 30, 2010, from http://twitter.com/JetBlue

16. Customer Community Software—Love Your Customers, Get Satisfaction (n.d.). Retrieved 12-30-2010, from http://getsatisfaction.com/

17. Scott, David Meerman (2009), *The New Rules of Marketing & PR* (Hoboken, NJ: John Wiley), p. 133.

18. Gogoi, Pallavi (2006, October 9), "Walmart's Jim and Laura: The Real Story". *Bloomberg Businessweek.* Retrieved May 23, 2011, from http://www.businessweek.com/bwdaily/dnflash/content/oct2006/db20061009_579137.htm

19. Rosmarin, Rachel (2006, October 3), "Walmart's MySpace Experiment Ends," *Forbes.com.* Retrieved May 23, 2011, from http://www.forbes.com/2006/10/02/myspace-walmart-youtube-tech-media-cx_rr_1003walmart.html

20. Kwan, Ming (2007, November 7), "Poor Walmart: A Social Networking Nightmare Scenario," *Wikinomics.* Retrieved May 23, 2011, from http://www.wikinomics.com/blog/index.php/2007/11/07/poor-Walmart/

21. Wilson, David (2007, October 11), "A Failed Facebook Marketing Campaign," *Social Media Optimization.* Retrieved May 23, 2011 from http://social-media-optimization.com/2007/10/a-failed-facebook-marketing-campaign/

22. Braziel, Lisa (2008, March 4), "Walmart's Latest Social Media Effort," *Ignite Social Media*. Retrieved May 23, 2011, from http://www.ignitesocialmedia.com/social-media-examples/walmarts-latest-social-media-effort-the-checkout-blog/

23. Walmart Moms (n.d.), *Eleven Moms*. Retrieved May 23, 2011, from http://site.elevenmoms.com/

24. Emery, Kevin (2011, April 25), "Not Sure if Mobile Marketing Is Worthwhile? Walmart Certainly Does." Retrieved May 23, 2011, Mojo. from http://www.mojosocialmediamarketing.com/not-sure-if-mobile-marketing-worthwhile-walmart-certainly-does/

25. Robles, Patricio (2011, April 19), "Walmart Makes Social Media Acquisition," *Econsultancy*. Retrieved May 23, 2011, from http://econsultancy.com/us/blog/7434-walmart-makes-social-media-acquisition

26. Van Buskirk, Eliot (2010, June 9), "BP's Social Media Campaign Going about as Well as Capping That Well," *Wired*. Retrieved May 23, 2011, from http://www.wired.com/epicenter/2010/06/bps-social-media-campaign-going-about-as-well-as-capping-that-well/

27. Schaal, Dennis (2010, June 11), "Will BP Social Media and Public Relations Efforts Appease Worried Hoteliers?" *Tnooz*. Retrieved May 26, 2011, from http://www.tnooz.com/2010/06/11/news/will-bp-social-media-and-public-relations-efforts-appease-worried-hoteliers/

28. Wauters, Robin (2010, June 26), "When Social Media Becomes the Message: The Gulf Oil Spill and @BPGlobalPR," *TechCrunch*. Retrieved May 26, 2011, from http://techcrunch.com/2010/06/26/bp-pr-bpglobalpr/

29. Kullin, Hans (2010, May 2), "BP Oil Spill and Social Media," *Media Culpa*. Retrieved May 26, 2011, from http://www.kullin.net/2010/05/bp-oil-spill-and-social-media/

30. "Fire booms neglected in oil cleanup?" (2010, May 3) NBC, msnbc.com and news services. Retrieved September 13, 2011 from http://www.msnbc.msn.com/id/36912754/ns/us_news-environment/t/fire-booms-neglected-oil-cleanup/#.Tm-KBtQg3vY

31. Sorg, Rosemary (2010, May 24), "BP's Social Media Disaster—4 Examples of What Not to Do," *InBoundMarketingPR*. Retrieved May 26, 2011, from http://inboundmarketingpr.com/Blog/bid/40716/BP-s-Social-Media-Disaster-4-Examples-of-What-Not-to-Do

32. Gaudin, Sharon (2010, June 15), "BP, in Crisis Mode, Misses Social Networking Target," *Computerworld*. Retrieved May 26, 2011, from http://www.computerworld.com/s/article/9178044/BP_in_crisis_mode_misses_social_networking_target

Publishing Blogs

Twenty years ago, the term "blog" did not exist. Today, blogs are an important source of news for millions, and professional blogging has been a path to wealth and fame for many people. For some companies the corporate blog is the centerpiece of a social media marketing strategy. Understanding how to utilize blogging to position a brand and to generate business is an essential skill for successful social media marketing.

The history of blogs has been a relatively short one. Justin Hall, student at Swarthmore College, was one of the first bloggers when he started writing about video games and consoles around 1994. The term "blog" had not yet been coined; in December 1997 the word "weblog" (combination of "web" and "log") was created and was then eventually shortened to blog.[1]

Blogging really took off after 1999 when LiveJournal and Blogger were launched. These sites allowed users with little or no technical ability to start their own blogs. At the end of 2008, 346 million people were reading blogs, and 184 million had begun writing their own blogs. These numbers continue to grow; "[a]ccording to Technorati, the number of blogs has doubled about every six months. Every day, more than 100,000 new blogs are created and 1.3 million new posts are added to existing blogs."[2] This large number represents a potentially huge audience that can be reached through blogging.

LEARNING OBJECTIVES

After completing this chapter, students will be able to:

- Define a blog
- Explain how to set up a blog
- Describe why everyone is a publisher on the social web
- Identify why content clutter is a problem
- Explain the marketing benefits of a blog
- Describe how to link a blog to marketing objectives

(Continued)

What Is a Blog?

Most people who are active online have heard of blogs, but a concise definition is helpful. According to *Wikipedia*, "[a] blog (a blend of the term web log) is a type of website or part of a website. Blogs are usually maintained by an individual with regular entries of commentary, descriptions of events, or other material such as graphics or video. Entries are commonly displayed in reverse-chronological order. Blog can also be used as a verb, meaning to maintain or add content to a blog."[3]

Most importantly, a blog is a website that has regular updates (or blog posts) where the most recent updates are displayed first. Blogs often allow readers to leave comments and respond to the blog posts. A blogger is then a person who administrates, writes, and updates a blog.

What distinguishes a blog from other types of social media? In their oft-cited book, *Naked Conversations*, authors Robert Scoble and Shel Israel present Blogging's Six Pillars, which make blogs different from other communication methods.[4] To paraphrase, these pillars are:

1. **Publishable**: It is cheap and easy for anyone to set up a blog. Posting is free and can be seen worldwide.

2. **Findable**: People can find blogs with search engines. Typically, the more posts a blog has, the easier it will be to find.

3. **Social**: Conversations about mutual interests can occur on blogs, either through direct comments or by linking to others with related content. These practices allow people to form connections with others regardless of their location.

4. **Viral**: Blogs can often spread information faster than a news service. The more interesting people find a topic, the more rapidly they will spread it to others.

5. **Syndicatable**: Viewers can easily subscribe to a blog using RSS and be notified about its updates in real-time. This ability saves time in searching and makes content easily findable.

6. **Linkable**: As blogs can link to each other, each blogger has access to a potentially huge audience.

Successful blogs take advantage of these six pillars to distinguish themselves and build influence on the social web. Blogs can be created for both personal and professional reasons, and they vary widely in topics and reader base. An individual may blog in order to develop his or her own position in relation to others in the field or a company blog might help position a firm as an expert in its industry. In any case sticking close to the core pillars of blogging is necessary for success.

SETTING UP A BLOG

Creating a blog is almost always the easiest part of blogging. A starter blog can be created on WordPress, Blogger, or other free sites.* These are examples of **hosted blogs**, which are run on some other company's website and server. Such blogs will typically have a suffix at the end of the URL address, indicating which service is hosting the blog. Businesses that want to invest more in blogging can **self-host** a blog on their

---

*See http://wordpress.com and http://blogger.com/

website, usually for relatively little cost. Self-hosted blogs have the advantage of being taken more seriously because they require a larger time investment to create and maintain.

Deciding how to set up the blog will depend on the circumstances; more information about hosted vs. self-hosting can easily be researched online. The difficult parts of blogging are creating a compelling and relevant subject area for the blog, writing effectively, and improving the content over time based on reader feedback.

CASE STUDY

Robert Scoble: The First Prominent Corporate Blogger within a Large Corporation (Microsoft)

Introduction

Robert Scoble became a trailblazer in corporation communications by establishing a position as the first high-profile and influential corporate blogger. He accomplished this feat by telling the truth (as he saw it) in his blog posts, which often meant criticizing his employer, Microsoft Corporation, and its products while heaping praise on the company's fiercest competitors (Apple Computer and Google) and their wares. Scoble's brutal honesty and invitation to open communication with consumers endowed his employer with a renewed credibility, which Microsoft's much-maligned business practices had previously eroded.[5]

Scoble's corporate blog, called the *Scobleizer*, employed podcasts, RSS, and Web video to give Microsoft a human face. He published his cell phone number and invited fans and critics alike to contact him directly or comment on his blog posts. This form of transparent and earnest corporate communication was more appealing to people than the bland press releases issued by the public relations department. Hence, Scoble's success quickly inspired other large companies to follow with their own corporate blogs (such as Sun, Adobe, and General Motors). Using his blog, Scoble "ushered in a new era of interaction among companies, customers, critics and the general public."[6]

Robert Scoble

History

Microsoft Corporation was officially launched on April 4, 1975, by Paul Allen and Bill Gates. They began by creating software (Altair BASIC) for the hardware manufacturer Micro Instrumentation and Telemetry Systems (MITS). In November 1980, after negotiations with Digital Research failed, IBM contracted with Microsoft to provide a DOS (Disk Operating System) for their forthcoming IBM PC. Gates was clever enough to negotiate a contract with IBM that allowed Microsoft to market a version of the operating system, MS-DOS. This operating system became the foundation of an empire built around the (in)ability of other hardware manufactures to compete with IBM in the PC arena. Relations with IBM eventually became strained, despite an ill-fated effort to mutually develop OS/2, a graphic user interface OS similar to Apple Computer's Mac OS. Microsoft eventually broke with IBM to market Windows, its own graphic user interface built on MS-DOS. The company also moved into application development, creating the Office Suite; first for the Apple Mac and later for the PC market.

Although *Microsoft* dominated the software industry, the mid-1990s brought the emergence of the World Wide Web, which posed a new threat to the company. Microsoft met it by buying, modifying, and giving away a web browser dubbed Internet Explorer. This effort was intended to dominate the browser market and run rival Netscape out of business. Gates was often quoted as saying that he thought Microsoft deserved a 100% share of the software market. All of these apparent predatory business practices eventually resulted in a lawsuit by the Department of Justice (DOJ) that almost resulted in the software titan being split apart.

Challenge

Despite escaping the worst consequences of the DOJ lawsuit, the perception of Microsoft as a ruthless competitor grew, with other lawsuits to follow in Europe and elsewhere. In addition, the company's rapidly growing size added layers of bureaucracy, pushing developmental programmers and their managers further and further away from end consumers. Over time, stories of Microsoft's aggressive business practices and the company's seeming indifference to consumers earned the Redmond software giant an unenviable nickname, the Evil Empire. The challenge then was to give this monolith a means to change its public image by directly interacting with everyday consumers, software developers, and even its critics.

Strategy

In 2000 Robert Scoble discovered blogging while organizing a tech conference for the publisher Fawcette. A couple of programmers at the conference, Dave Winer and Dori Smith, both avid bloggers, suggested he start blogging. As a consequence, he launched *Scobleizer* and gained an immediate readership. His big break came when a Microsoft executive, who read *Scobleizer*, suggested that he work for the company.[7]

Scoble used his blog to not only listen to the company's many constituencies but to build a network of resources so that he could help Microsoft respond appropriately to user needs.[8] At times, this practice meant criticizing poorly built Microsoft products and recommending competitors' offerings instead. Despite talking about some very touchy subjects (with legal implications), Scoble was never blocked from posting a blog by Microsoft.

Although many found it surprising that Microsoft would let Scoble criticize his employer in this manner, the software giant actually had a history of tolerating a certain amount of employees bashing Microsoft, especially when it ultimately helped the bottom line. For example, three Microsoft programmers, Alex St. John, Eric Engstrom, and Craig Eisler, were able to develop a close relationship with software game developers by ridiculing Microsoft (they were so unconventional and wild that they became known within the company as the Beastie Boys). However, the Beastie Boys' message resonated with the game developers, and they gained the developers' trust. By listening to the game developers, this oddball team was able to build the critical programming code (Active-X) that enabled game developers to create computer games that run on Microsoft Windows, a hugely profitable achievement for Microsoft.[9]

Scoble knew more had to be done than listening. He garnered support from the highest levels, arguing that if Microsoft didn't improve its products based on feedback from the blogosphere, consumers would catch on that the company didn't value their input, and his efforts would be viewed as just a PR stunt. Senior management bought this argument, and Scoble began searching the web for any mention of Microsoft on blogs. He interacted with these bloggers, even if they had no readers and were just ranting. The strategy was simple—let these bloggers know someone at Microsoft was listening and engaged. Over time, Scoble built an invaluable blog-based focus group.

Scoble confronted the appropriate product team leaders within Microsoft with these suggestions and criticisms, demanding to know what they were going to do about them. The responses he got from team leaders gave Scoble more to blog about, letting consumers know what Microsoft was going to fix, improve, make more secure, and so on. Scoble was also able get some Microsoft executives to blog within the company instead of sending out endless streams of email few had the time to read. These blogs later became a great repository of knowledge within the company for employees to search when necessary.

Results

According to an article published in 2005 in *The Economist*, "[Scoble has] become a minor celebrity among geeks worldwide, who read his blog religiously. Impressively, he has also succeeded where small armies of more conventional public-relations types have been failing abjectly for years: he has made Microsoft, with its history of monopolistic bullying, appear marginally but noticeably less evil to the outside world, and especially to the independent software developers that are his core audience."[10]

A 2006 Northwestern University *Blogging Success Study* went further, quoting blogger Jeremy Pepper: "I can say without any issue that Robert Scoble has given Microsoft a friendly persona out there on the Internet. He's given a face to the organization that's different than Steve Balmer or Bill Gates. He's made it warm and fuzzy. It's no longer the evil empire. It's just, 'Oh this is the company Scoble works for!' It helps take off the taint that the company has had. . . . He doesn't talk about Microsoft all that much, but he is known as a Microsoft blogger."[11]

Although Robert Scoble left Microsoft in late 2006, he had accomplished the impossible: he made Microsoft not only approachable but likable—along with becoming a brand unto himself, with more than 20,000 subscribers to his *Scobleizer* blog. In addition, Scoble had shepherded in a new era in corporation communications, which he documented in a book, *Naked Conversations: How Blogs Are Changing the Way Businesses Talk with Customers*.[12]

Everyone Is a Publisher

"Publisher" used to be a term restricted to those who produced magazines, newspapers, and books. However, with the tools available on the web, anyone can become a publisher at minimal cost. This radical change poses both challenges and opportunities for the marketing professional.

Early in the Internet's development, creating a website required either strong HTML[†] coding knowledge or the hiring of a programmer and designer to do the work. Website development was time consuming and costly. Only the experts or the well funded could create and publish content.

Today, a website can be created in under an hour with no expert coding knowledge using Google Sites, EditSpot, or other web-development tools.[††] Editing websites has also become much easier. Even many large corporate websites are built on some Content Management System (CMS) that allows users with no programming knowledge to easily edit the site's content.

The online space has changed from a *read web,* where people would go to the Internet primarily to consume content and information, to *a read-write web,* where it is possible to create in addition to consuming content. Rather than passively taking in information, users can create and interact with the content they see.

CONTENT CLUTTER

With publishing tools so accessible, anyone can be a publisher, and as a result there are millions of blogs, websites, and podcasts published. There is such a proliferation of content online that even the highest-quality material has difficulty standing out and building an audience.

According to a 2008 survey by Universal McCann, there are 26 million blogs and about 60 million blog readers in the United States, each of whom read about three blogs.[10] That would mean about six blog readers per blog if divided evenly, but that is not the case. Realistically, a few blogs have lots of readers while many blogs have almost no readers. That trend is likely to continue, as shown in Figure 5.1.

This reality sets a higher bar for publishers and content creators. In addition to creating interesting and relevant content to publish, part of the strategy must include how to build an audience and where to syndicate content online. Many of the social media tools covered elsewhere in this book (Facebook, Twitter, social news sites, etc.) can be excellent syndication platforms to build a following for a blog.

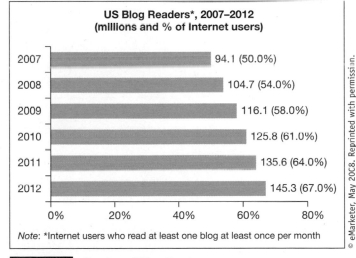

**US Blog Readers*, 2007–2012
(millions and % of Internet users)**

2007	94.1 (50.0%)
2008	104.7 (54.0%)
2009	116.1 (58.0%)
2010	125.8 (61.0%)
2011	135.6 (64.0%)
2012	145.3 (67.0%)

Note: *Internet users who read at least one blog at least once per month

© eMarketer, May 2008. Reprinted with permission.

Figure 5.1   **Number of Blog Readers**

In addition to leveraging social media to find an audience, consider ways to connect with current customers, direct mail subscribers, email newsletter readers, and so on with whom to blog content. An existing client base will generally be more interested in viewing the related blog, so finding ways to draw them into reading blog content is a valuable way to build readership.

[†]HTML stands for HyperText Markup Language; it is the most frequently used markup language for websites.

[††]See http://sites.google.com/ and http://ditspot.com/

The Marriott CEO Blog

The blog run by Marriott International's CEO, J. W. Marriott, has been praised for its accessibility and down-to-earth tone. Unlike many other corporate blogs, *Marriott On the Move*‡ does not focus on disseminating press releases. Instead, it provides the CEO an avenue to share stories, and information on the business and to develop a likable public personality. The success of Marriott's blog is an instructive lesson for other social media marketers.

In 1927, J. Willard Marriott and his wife started a root beer stand in Washington, D.C. At the time they likely never imagined that from this humble beginnings would grow a global hotel chain with over 3,000 lodging properties in the United States. At one time the company ran a series of theme parks, but those were shut down in order to focus on the core lodging business. As of 2008 the company had revenue of $13.3 billion and employed more than 150,000 people.

In January 2007 J. W. Marriott was convinced to start a blog. The idea was to give a personal angle on the CEO and to worry less about the corporate image.

As Kathleen Matthews, Marriott's spokeswoman, said, "This is going to be Bill Marriott's blog. It's not going to be the corporate blog. He's going to decide what he wants to say."[14]

Marriott hotel building

© AP Images/Paul Sakuma

As someone who typically preferred paper and pen to a keyboard, J. W. Marriott was not immediately sold on the idea. Indeed, relatively few begin their blogging career at the age of 75! Eventually, his method of blogging was to audio-record his thoughts and then provide them to his staff for transcription. On the website both audio and text versions of the blog are then available.

In spite of its creator avoiding computers, Marriott's blog has been a resounding success. Marriott employees make up about a fifth of the blog's readership, and they comment often. The blog gives a sense of camaraderie with the CEO that workers enjoy. The blog has also generated some tangible monetary gains, generating more than $5 million worth of revenue from bookings that originate from the blog.[15]

In the time since its creation, the Marriott blog has become a classic example of corporate blogging done well. J. W. Marriott himself has been highly praised for his blogging efforts. In 2008 he won the Excel Award given by the International Association for Business Communicators. When discussing his return on investment for the blog, Marriott said, "I would recommend it to any CEO. It's worth it."[16]

© Cengage Learning 2013

---

‡See http://www.blogs.marriott.com/

Marketing Benefits of Blogging

As one of the oldest and best-known social media outlets, blogging has several unique advantages. The potentially large audience and strong focus on content produces several benefits for blogging being part of an active social media marketing campaign.

COMMUNICATING WITH (POTENTIAL) CUSTOMERS

More so than the audience of most other social media platforms, that of blogs rewards thoughtful posts and fully developed ideas. As Brian Solis explains, "blog posts inherently boast the ability to share expanded content, text, video, audio, images, tags, links, to more effectively and deeply express, explain, and support the ideas and context related to any given topic."[17] This attribute makes blogs valuable in a broad variety of industries (as the case studies in this chapter demonstrate). Every business entails some form of expertise that can potentially be shared with and interest online viewers. In this context blogging can help to both position a company's brand as well as bring in new leads.

WORD-OF-MOUTH MARKETING

Some recent studies have found that word of mouth may be more than twice as effective as traditional marketing; it results in more new customer acquisitions and has longer-lasting results.[18] While many social media platforms can be valuable in creating buzz about a product or service, blogs are especially important. Blogging facilitates word-of-mouth marketing in several ways. First, they make messages portable and easy for others to link to or share. Second, they create new topics, much like mini-press releases, that spur public discussion, Third, a blog provides a center for conversation via comments or replies. And finally, blogging builds credibility with other bloggers, making it more likely that others will pass the word along.[19] As an inexpensive way to tap into the powerful marketing method of word of mouth, blogs are an invaluable tool for a social media marketer.

RECEIVING FEEDBACK Due to its comments feature, a blog makes it easy for viewers to respond to the topic at hand. On a company blog, posting recent news or questions to the community can bring valuable insights about the public mood on relevant issues. Both positive and negative responses are useful; supportive comments may influence other viewers to feel similarly, while criticisms may offer suggestions about potential changes. Some companies are able to develop new product ideas based on blog comments or to make improvements to existing goods. As an accessible and informal way for customers to provide feedback, a blog can save time and money a company would otherwise have to spend seeking out that same information.

Communicating with customers, word-of-mouth marketing, and getting feedback are just a few potential benefits from a blog. As a social media campaign develops, more creative uses can certainly be found.

Linking a Blog to Marketing Objectives

While there are many blogs on the Internet, a much smaller fraction of them generate tangible returns for the blog's creator(s). Many blogs are personal and function like an online journal; their authors do not generally expect an outside return. However, there are also many professional or corporate blogs that do not accomplish their objectives or are unclear even on what objectives should be accomplished! The difficulty of blogging successfully is why over 50% of blogs are abandoned within the first ninety days.[20]

When deciding on whether to start a blog and what the goals of blogging should be, it is important to consider the overall marketing goals and objectives. Such consideration will help to determine the right type of content to create based on the audience being reached. It will also make following up on and maintaining a blog more achievable. Indeed, "the single biggest risk in business blogging is setting the wrong strategy, resulting in discouragement and abandonment" of the blog.[21] A half-hearted blogging attempt may be worse than nothing at all, so it is crucial to set a long-term strategy before creating a blog for social media marketing.

One of the advantages of publishing content as a part of a social media marketing strategy is that it can achieve a wide variety of marketing goals and objectives. Defining those goals clearly (as discussed in Chapter 2) will help to develop a content plan that will reach the target audience and deliver the most relevant results.

Creating a Content Strategy

> *"If you want us to talk to you, tell us something. Make it something interesting for a change."*
>
> —*Cluetrain Manifesto,* "Thesis #75"

The key to successfully publishing content online is to have a clear and meaningful content strategy. As discussed in Chapter 3, a strong social media strategy starts with a clear understanding of how the marketing objectives relate to the target audience or buyer personas. To create content that will engage with the audience, the driving question is "what subject areas will members of the audience be interested in?"

Chances are that your audience is not really that interested in your brand or your product. They are interested in a problem and a solution to that problem. Ask yourself, "What subjects related to my brand is my audience passionate about?"

One additional key consideration in developing a publishing strategy is to overcome the fear of being too specific. Many companies don't want to pigeonhole themselves into a small and specific niche of content that they will cover. With the proliferation of content, the best strategy to building an audience is to be as niche and specific as possible.

In his book *The Long Tail*, Chris Anderson discusses how the web has created large opportunities for Long Tail content.[22] The Long Tail is small niche content that motivates smaller, highly specific audiences as contrasted with a generic "best seller." For example, the *New York Times*, which produces generic news content with broad mass appeal, would not be in the Long Tail, whereas a small, locally focused newspaper or a newspaper focused on industry-specific news and updates might be. The evolution of the web has shown that there are consumers looking for that very specific Long Tail content. Combined with the low cost of online publishing, this highly specialized content can be developed.

The future of publishing and content creation lies in serving niche markets effectively on a large scale. The lesson for bloggers is to keep in mind what specialized interests they might be able to market toward and to develop content that will appeal to such interests. Generalized content is commonly found elsewhere, and consequently, in order to build a blog's viewership and influence, the blogger must focus on specialized content that is not easily replicated.

Engadget Engages

Introduction

Engadget is an extremely popular multilingual blog network dedicated to gadgets and consumer electronics. These blogs are typically updated multiple times a day with the latest news stories, opinion articles, and rumors about gadgets and the world of technology. In addition, the network produces the weekly "Engadget Podcast," which recaps tech news for the week.

History

Engadget was cofounded by Peter Rojas as part of Weblogs, Inc., a blog network. Before Engadget, Peter Rojas had also cofounded the Gizmodo blog in 2002.[23] In 2005 AOL executive vice president Jim Bankoff (best known for helping build the wildly successful TMZ blog) convinced AOL to acquire a network of bleeding-edge technology blogs to help in AOL's transition from a dial-up to high-bandwidth service provider. He facilitated the purchase of Weblogs, Inc., for a reported $25 million. This included 85 blogs, one of which was Engadget.[24]

Challenge

Engadget's innovative coverage of tech gadgets and the latest developments in the tech industry propelled the blog into the consciousness of those interested in consumer electronics. The challenge for AOL and Peter Rojas was to continue and hopefully improve upon the progress Engadget had made with Weblogs in competing with Gizmodo (owned by Gawker Media).

Strategy

When AOL acquired Engadget as part of Weblogs, it inherited Peter Rojas, along with his professional editorial and technology staff, as well as dozens of prominent contributing writers. Building on these strengths, AOL-backed Engadget retained and expanded its impressive bullpen of writers to include Jason Calacanis, Paul Boutin, Phillip Torrone, Joshua Fruhlinger, Nilay Patel, Marc Perton, and Susan Mernit.[25] The most prolific Engadget blogger is Darren Murph. As an associate editor for Engadget, he was named the World's Most Prolific Professional Blogger by Guinness World Records, with over 17,212 posts and counting.[26]

Engadget's collection of top-notch writers and experienced editorial and technology staff worked together to produce clear, concise, and frequently updated posts full of information about the happenings in the tech world, giving it a real competitive advantage over rival Gizmodo. In addition, Engadget received rapid dissemination of news from industry giants, such as Microsoft and Apple, enabling them to scoop rival Gizmodo for breaking news. Moreover, Engadget staff avidly participates in the major technology conferences and shows, capturing exclusive pictures and video. Finally, Engadget blog posts are optimized for search engines, helping push them to the top of search results, attracting an even wider readership.[27]

Engadget Site

Results

Today, Engadget ranks in the top fifteen most popular blogs not only in the United States but around the world, eclipsing its rival Gizmodo.[28] Although Pete Rojas left in 2007, Ryan Block stepped in as editor-in-chief, taking over from the founder. Block continued the strategies that made the site so successful. "Thanks to tips from its millions of loyal readers seeded through the tech industry, the site has posted hundreds of juicy, top-secret product specification lists, photos and road maps, including the first photos of the then-unannounced Microsoft . . . Zune."[29]

Block was eventually replaced by other equally astute editors, enabling Engadget to remain hugely popular. However, in March 2011, it was reported that the current editor-in-chief, Joshua Topolsky, "and as many as eight of the more prominent editorial and technology staff members at Engadget have left or are leaving AOL and are about to build a new gadget site by joining forces with, yes, you guessed right, their old friend Mr. Bankoff, who now runs a federation of sports sites called SB Nation."[30]

"Topolsky . . . felt that the Engadget team was being held back by AOL's less-than-ideal management. . . .The blog will likely continue to exist in some form at AOL, but for now, its most vital talent has sided with Topolsky."[31] Only time will tell whether AOL's Engadget will remain a top-rated blog or whether it will be usurped by the new gadget blog at SB Nation or some other new contender. The fate of both blogs will likely depend on who the most prominent and prolific writers side with.

Tips for Successful Blogging

While no "secret formula" exists for becoming a popular blogger, the following tips provide advice for maximizing the chances of success. Keep in mind that these are only guidelines and success in blogging can be attained in many ways.

USE CATCHY TITLES

A great title attracts attention and gives people a reason to read the post, while a mediocre title either goes unnoticed or actually discourages people from reading the post. Although there are no hard and fast rules for writing great titles, there are useful guidelines. First, use the title to communicate a benefit.[32] In other words, people search for blogs that provide information about topics of interest (e.g., "10 Ways to Write Great Blog Titles"). Second, ask a question in the title. Readers love to be challenged. This is one of the most effective ways of drawing readers into the post and also helps elicit comments, especially if the question is personalized (e.g., "How Should You Ask for a Raise?").[33] Finally, be sure to include keywords in the title so that search engines will pick them up, hence, improving the search engine ranking of the post so people can find it.[34]

UPDATE FREQUENTLY

The most common advice for successful blogging is that a corporate blog should be updated at least twice a week; some blogs even update daily. Online audiences can quickly lose interest if content is spaced too far apart. Before creating a blog, you should be sure that you will have enough interesting posts for the blog, perhaps even writing some up in advance to be posted later. If updates occur less than once a week, expect to be perceived as disengaged and expect the possibility of losing blog viewers.

KEEP POSTS FOCUSED

People will often find a blog while browsing or researching other topics. Generally, net surfers do not want to sift through a rambling post to find the bits of information they are interested in. Blog updates should be long enough to cover one topic with sufficient depth but should avoid using filler or trying to combine several topics into one post. If one blog post covers two topics, a person who is looking for information on just one of the topics will find half of the material superfluous. Concise, focused posts are easy to read and will keep readers coming back for more.

INVITE COMMENTS

Perhaps the best way to encourage interaction on a blog is to end each post with a question that asks for help or is provocative. For example, "What other tips have I missed?" or "Is the social media about to bust?" Be sure to reply to comments in order to make readers feel they are part of the blog and help shape its direction. Interaction is often essential in creating an avid and involved readership.[35]

PROMOTE THE BLOG

With so many blogs out there, it takes effort to be seen in the crowd. Begin by signing up with popular blog listing services, such as Technorati.‡ Look around at other blogs, check to see what blog communities they are involved in, and join ones that look reputable. These initial actions will make it easier for search engine users to find the blog. However, this step is only the beginning: developing a blog presence takes time, so never overlook an opportunity to subtly self-promote (in a tactful fashion, of course).

ENGAGE WITH OTHERS

Make thoughtful comments on other relevant blogs, and respond to comments that others make. Developing an online personality is important for a blog to be successful, and that requires a high degree of interaction with others. Take advantage of the two-way nature of online communication by engaging those with related interests or with companies having products complementary to yours. Offering to provide a link or a review to someone else in exchange for their doing the same is a tried-and-true method for building blog connections, and it remains a useful strategy. However, the most valuable engagement will often come from unplanned interactions, so be open to those possibilities.

---

‡See http://technorati.com/

AVOID NEGATIVITY

Do not make insulting or aggressive statements toward other people, brands, or companies. It may be true that conflict draws a crowd, but that group is unlikely to become a productive part of the target market. Negative comments also invite others to respond in turn, potentially harming both sides' reputations. Even worse, it could result in a lawsuit if taken too seriously. Criticism can be given without being offensive, but you should be sure that any controversial comments are heavily researched, well-founded in fact, and presented in an even tone that is not accusatory or aggressive. In general, sticking to positive and constructive comments is both safer and more effective for building a blog's standing.

STAND BY THE CONTENT

Not every blog post will be well received. Sometimes, one may generate controversy or negative attention. If that happens, deleting the affected blog post is *not* a solution. Once content is published online, it will be viewable through syndication services even if the original post is taken down. Trying to hide the evidence, so to speak, may draw attention to the controversy and make dissatisfied viewers even more determined to spread the word. Instead, stand by what was written (which should not be too difficult if the original post was well conceived). If it is necessary to make a correction, consider leaving the original text with a strike-through mark and an explanation of why the revision was made. Internet controversies can either blow over quickly, or they can linger indefinitely in the public consciousness. Whenever possible, avoid compounding the situation by going back on what was said because it will make the mistake memorable and generate more negativity.

CROSS PROMOTE

Use other social media channels to get word out about the blog. When a new post is made, provide links to it on other platforms. Keep in mind that not every member of the target audience will be on every platform, so provide as many opportunities as possible for them to stumble over the content. Blogs offer the best opportunity for sharing thoughts and information, so use other, less content-heavy platforms to promote the deeper ideas found in blog posts.

Monitoring the Blogosphere

One of the primary benefits from blogging is to learn about the "tone" of the online community with regard to certain subjects, but the problem is that relevant comments are likely to be dispersed through a huge number of different blogs. While staying current on important blogs in the industry and looking at reader comments is a good start, you must mount a monitoring effort that goes considerably farther in order to see a broad segment of opinions, especially if a blog is still in its infancy and has few active commentators.

One crude metric for public sentiment is a look at how many views that posts on different topics generate (number of blog views or visits is typically easily available on hosted blogs). In theory the more that people enjoyed a certain post, the more likely they are to pass along or recommend it to others, boosting the number of views. However, view counts alone give no insight on whether overall sentiment is positive or negative or if any of these people will ever become potential leads.

The difficulty of determining what people think about a brand has driven an enormous growth in social media monitoring software, much of which is directed toward blogs. While many paid software suites exist for this purpose, they can cost hundreds of dollars a month in order to license and run. The World Bank has developed a program,

BuzzMonitor, that is based on open source software and is freely available to the public. It allows an organization to segment blog chatter into different categories that are based on topic matter as well as, perhaps more importantly, the authority of the person or group commenting.[36] While the interface is less user friendly and the software requires a dedicated server in order to operate, BuzzMonitor is one example of free software with powerful monitoring applications. As time goes on, it is likely that more such tools will begin to appear.

How many resources you should dedicate toward monitoring blog chatter will depend on your industry, your marketing budget, and the size of your existing blog following as well as how widely dispersed online opinion is on the relevant topics, to name just a few factors. However, time and money spent in monitoring general opinion is almost always well spent; it is impossible to finely tune a blogging strategy without some feedback on what needs to be changed or which content people find most attractive. Developing knowledge about public sentiment and response on other blogs makes social media marketing efforts through blogging much more fruitful.

EXERCISE CASE STUDY

The Huffington Post: *How a Single Voice Became Many*

Introduction

The *Huffington Post* began life as just another liberal blog in an already crowded field; it aggregates news from other sources, but eventually it grew into a full-fledged news organization. The *Huffington Post* is an unlikely success story, built in large part on the notoriety of Arianna Huffington and her allies. According to a *Washington Post* article, "skeptics dismissed it as a vanity outlet for [Arianna Huffington] and her Hollywood friends. But the Huffington Post has become an undeniable success, its evolution offering a road map of what works on the Web."[37]

History

Arianna Huffington was born Arianna Stasinopoulos in Greece, educated in England, and gained wide fame as an author, conservative columnist, and popular commentator in the 1980s and early 1990s. She is the ex-wife of former Republican congressman Michael Huffington. In the late 1990s her views shifted radically to the left. She explains her change in political leaning during a 2008 *Time* interview: "I left the Republican Party [because] my views of the role of government changed."[38]

Arianna Huffington

On May 9, 2005, Arianna Huffington, Kenneth Lerer, and Jonah Peretti launched the *Huffington Post* with about $2 million in seed capital. The website consisted of little more than a few blogs and some basic political news. It drew on news stories published by reputable news organizations, as well as the general public, "but what set the Huffington Post apart was the humor with which it was delivered. This is not to say the publication did not have a serious point to get across."[39] Indeed, the *Huffington Post* positioned itself to be the liberal counter to right-wing media.[40]

In August 2006 the *Huffington Post* announced its first round of venture capital funding, with a $5 million investment from SoftBank Capital, which enabled the publication to increase its staff with in-house reporters who could update the site around the clock as well as a multimedia team to produce video reports.[41] Among the new hires was a political editor, Melinda Henneberger, a former *Newsweek* magazine print journalist, who brought conventional journalistic credibility to the publication. Just a year after its launch, the site drew approximately 2.3 million unique visitors a month, thus making it one of the more popular blog sites.

In early 2008 the site garnered 3.7 million unique visitors and enabled it to beat out its conservative competitor, the *Drudge Report*, for the first time.[42] Its success drew further funding in 2008, with an additional $15 million investment, which allowed the publication to "finance the expansion of HuffPo, as it is known, into the provision of local news across the United States and into more investigative journalism."[43]

Challenge ....

Ms. Huffington faced several significant challenges in cofounding the *Huffington Post*. At the time, the landscape was dominated by powerful conservative voices, such as the *Drudge Report*. Moreover, the failure of other liberal blogs to draw huge audiences or active participation had produced a conventional wisdom that progressives were simply not interested in this type of content or interaction. Hence, convincing advertisers to support a liberal blog site would be a herculean undertaking. In addition, "[w]hen she launched her group blog in 2005, skeptics dismissed it as a vanity outlet for her and her Hollywood friends."[44] Lastly, the meager seed capital of $1 million had to be supplemented before long.[45]

In short, Arianna Huffington had to quickly prove that a liberal blog site could not only capture but sustain a sizable readership before investors or advertisers would make any commitments.

Strategy ....

Ms. Huffington's two objectives were obvious: drive traffic to the blog site and keep them coming back. "In 2006, she was named to the Time 100, Time magazine's list of the world's 100 most influential people."[46] As a popular cable talk show pundit, author, and notable proponent of the political left, she took every opportunity to promote the *Huffington Post*. With appearances on shows ranging from *Real Time with Bill Maher* and *Charlie Rose* to *The McLaughlin Group* and *Larry King Live*, she continually drove traffic to her namesake fledging blog site.[47]

In addition, the staff of the *Huffington Post* became adept as news aggregators in identifying the most compelling content on the web that matched its left-leaning editorial slant, as well as some juicy celebrity gossip, and reposting portions of these articles on the blog site. Ms. Huffington's editors are especially skillful at optimizing these story snippets "for search engine results, so that in a Google search, a Huffington Post summary of a Washington Post or a CNN.com report may appear ahead of the original article."[48] This practice is not without its critics. Indeed, Jack Shafer, who covers media for Reuters.com opinion section, characterized it this way: "Huffington glories in carving the meat out of a competitor's story, throwing a search-engine optimized (SEO) headline on it, and posting it."[49] The company site defends the practice as falling under the fair use doctrine. As the funding and ad revenues for the *Huffington Post* grew, the site eventually hired in-house reporters, columnists, and investigative journalists to create original news items to complement the content it aggregates.

To achieve *Huffington Post*'s second goal of retaining readership, it was clear from the start that it had to provide quality content from well-known political posters. Ms. Huffington led the way as a prolific blogger. In addition, she initially relied heavily on her impressive "rolodex of A-list celebrities and high-powered friends, soliciting early contributions from the likes of Larry David, Diane Keaton and Alec Baldwin."[50] Soon other notable voices followed, and, perhaps most importantly, the site threw open its doors to a legion of bloggers. Although bloggers received no remuneration, tens of thousands of posts poured in. This approach was not without its critics, as CNET writer Josh Wolf indicates, "[i]n most industries refusing to pay your labor force is not only unethical, it would likely border on slavery and be illegal as well. Apparently in the world of blogging it's considered good business practice."[51] The company justified the practice by saying they offer bloggers "visibility, promotion, and distribution with a great company" in exchange for their contributions.[52] Finally, Ms. Huffington's role in fundraising played a key role in the blog site's success because it gave the site the capital necessary to rapidly expand its staff and infrastructure.

Results

Today, the *Huffington Post* is the number one blog in the blogosphere.[53] It has over 9,000 bloggers,[54] with approximately 25 million visitors every month. The viewership, content, and success of the *Huffington Post* have not gone unnoticed. The site won the Webby Award for the best political blog in 2006 and 2008 and was the People's Voice Winner in the political blog category in 2009, 2010, and 2011.[55] *Time* named it the second best blog in 2009.[56]

As with other successful blog sites, AOL snapped up the *Huffington Post* in February 2011 for $315 million.[57] Arianne Huffington was appointed president and editor-in-chief of the Huffington Post Media Group at AOL in order to help ensure continuity in the quality of content and contributions.[58] Some fear that *HuffPo*'s distinctive viewpoint may be compromised by a loss of independence. However, *Huffington Post* executives claim that "[t]he AOL deal has the potential to create an enterprise that could reach more than 100 million visitors in the United States each month . . . [and we] estimate that the Web site will generate $60 million in revenue this year, compared with $31 million in 2010."[59] Whether such optimism is justified remains to be seen. It is worth noting that publication expanded into Canada in May 2011, a promising sign that the site is aggressively attempting to expand its readership.[60]

AOL Social Media Properties

However, there has been a dark cloud on the horizon for the blog site. In April 2011 Jonathan Tasini, a well-known labor advocate, filed suit against the *Huffington Post* in the United States District Court of New York on behalf of 9,000 uncompensated bloggers. He is alleging damages of over $105 million.[61] Ms. Huffington was quick to counter, asserting the blog site is two things, "[a] journalistic enterprise, hiring hundreds of journalists with benefits, great salaries and we are a platform that is available to anyone who does quality work to disseminate their ideas, promote their books, movies, political candidacies or whatever it is they are engaged in."[62] The courts will determine if this is, indeed, the case.

Review Questions for the *Huffington Post* Case Study

1. Arianna Huffington drew on some of her celebrity contacts early on to popularize the website. Do you think a person without her connections could have been equally successful? What strategy changes would a non-celebrity have to make to succeed?

2. Do you expect that AOL's purchase of the *Huffington Post* will have a largely positive or negative effect on its viewership? Name some pros and cons, and compare them.

3. Beyond Arianna Huffington using her celebrity contacts, what other strategies did the staff implement to make this the number one blog in the blogoshere? Can these same strategies be applied to other blogs? Explain why or why not?

4. What are the possible strategic marketing benefits and drawbacks of the acquisition of the Huffington Post by AOL? Explain.

Notes

1. Zarrella, Dan (2010), *The Social Media Marketing Book* (Sebastopol, CA: O'Reilly Media), p. 11.

2. Weber, Larry (2009), *Marketing to the Social Web: How Digital Communities Build Your Business* (Hoboken: NJ: John Wiley), p. 168.

3. Blog (n.d.), *Wikipedia*. Retrieved September 14, 2011 from http://en.wikipedia.org/wiki/Blog

4. Scoble, Robert, and Shel Israel (2006), *Naked Conversations: How Blogs Are Changing the Way Businesses Talk with Customers* (Hoboken, NJ: John Wiley), p. 28.

5. "Embrace, Extend, and Extinguish" (n.d.), *Wikipedia*. Retrieved June 1, 2011, from http://en.wikipedia.org/wiki/Embrace,_extend_and_extinguish

6. Cone, Edward (2006, September 29), "Robert Scoble: Life after Microsoft," CIO Insight. Retrieved June 1, 2011, from http://www.cioinsight.com/c/a/Expert-Voices/Robert-Scoble-Life-After-Microsoft/

7. Ibid.

8. Kim (2009) "Case Study: Robert Scoble," Social Media Coaching Center. Retrieved June 1, 2011, from http://socialmediacoachingcenter.com/2009/case-study-robert-scoble/

9. Drummund, Michael (1999), *Renegades of the Empire: How Three Software Warriors Started a Revolution behind the Walls of Fortress Microsoft* (New York: Crown).

10. "Chief Humanising Officer" (2005, February, 10), *The Economist*. Retrieved June 1, 2011, from http://www.economist.com/node/3644293?story_id=3644293

11. *Blogging Success Study* (2006, November 6), Northwestern University. Retrieved June 2, 2011, from http://www.scoutblogging.com/success_study/

12. Scoble, Robert, and Shel Israel (2006), *Naked Conversations: How Blogs Are Changing the Way Businesses Talk with Customers* (Hoboken: NJ: John Wiley).

13. Universal McCann (2008, March), Power to the People: Wave 3 Social Media Tracker, Scribd. Retrieved 6-9-2011, from http://www.scribd.com/doc/3836535/Universal-Mccann-on-Social-Media

14. Rosenwald, Michael S. (2007, January 16), "An Old Dog Learns to Write a New Blog," *Washington Post*. Retrieved June 10, 2011, from http://www.washingtonpost.com/wp-dyn/content/article/2007/01/15/AR2007011501348_pf.html

15. Halzack, Sarah (2008, August 25), "Marketing Moves to the Blogosphere: Business Model Shifts to Engage Customers Online," *Washington Post*. Retrieved June 10, 2011, from http://www.washingtonpost.com/wp-dyn/content/article/2008/08/24/AR2008082401517.html

16. Fernando, Angelo (2008, June 23), "Marriott CEO Blog: 'A Cool Way to Tell Stories," *Social Media Today*. Retrieved June 10, 2011, from http://socialmediatoday.com/index.php?q=SMC/38200

17. Solis, Brian (2010), *Engage! The Complete Guide for Brands and Businesses to Build, Cultivate, and Measure Success in the New Web* (Hoboken: NJ: John Wiley), p. 168.

18. Trusov, Michael, Randolph E. Bucklin, and Koen Pauwels (2009, September), "Effects of Word-of-Mouth Versus Traditional Marketing: Findings from an Internet Social Networking Site," *Journal of Marketing*, vol. 73, no. 5.

19. Sernovitz, Andy (2009), *Word of Mouth Marketing: How Smart Companies Get People Talking* (New York: Kaplan Publishing), p. 140-41.

20. Meyerson, Mitch (2010), *Success Secrets of the Social Media Marketing Superstars* (Irvine, CA: Entrepreneur Media), p. 166.

21. Borges, Bernie (2009), *Marketing 2.0: Bridging the Gap between Seller and Buyer through Social Media Marketing* (Tucson, AZ: Wheatmark), p. 174.

22. Anderson, Chris (2006, July 11), *The Long Tail: Why the Future of Business Is Selling Less of More* (New York: Hyperion).

23. "Gizmodo vs. Engadget: What Is the Difference?" (n.d.), noComparison. Retrieved June 6, 2011, from http://recomparison.com/comparisons/100619/gizmodo-vs-engadget-what-is-the-difference/

24. Noon, Chris (2005, October 6), "Parson's AOL in Weblogs Acquisition," *Forbes.com*. Retrieved June 6, 2011, from http://www.forbes.com/2005/10/06/twx-aol-weblogs-cx_cn_1006autofacescan06.html

25. "Engadget Blogs" (n.d.), *Wikipedia*. Retrieved June 6, 2011, from http://en.wikipedia.org/wiki/Engadget#Engadget_Blogs

26. Topolsky, Joshua (2010, October 5), "Engadget's Darren Murph Nabs Guinness World Record for Most Blog Posts Ever Written!" Engadget. Retrieved June 6, 2011, from http://www.engadget.com/2010/10/05/engadgets-darren-murph-nabs-guinness-world-record-for-most-blog/

27. "5 Reasons Why Engadget.com Is Successful" (2011, June 3), GeekSyrup. Retrieved September 14, 2011, from http://www.geeksyrup.com/news/why-engadget-is-successful/

28. "Top 10 Most Popular Blogs in the World" (2011, February 11), TopYaps, retrieved June 6, 2011, from http://www.topyaps.com/top-10-most-popular-blogs-of-the-world/ and "Top 15 Most Popular Blogs" (2011, June), eBizMBA Rank, retrieved June 6, 2011, from http://www.ebizmba.com/articles/blogs

29. Rosmarin, Rachel (2007, December 18), "The Gadget Guru," *Forbes.com*. Retrieved June 6, 2011, from http://www.forbes.com/2007/12/18/ryan-block-engadget-tech-cx_rr_07webceleb_1218block.html

30. Carr, David (2011, April 3), "No Longer Shackled by AOL," *New York Times*. Retrieved June 6, 2011, from http://www.nytimes.com/2011/04/04/business/media/04carr.html?_r=1&partner=rss&emc=rss

31. Bazilian, Emma (2011, April 4), "Staff of AOL's Engadget Leaving En Masse," *AdWeek*. Retrieved June 6, 2011, from http://www.adweek.com/news/technology/staff-aol-s-engadget-leaving-en-masse-126144

32. Rowse, Darren (2008, August 20), "How to Craft Post Titles that Draw Readers Into Your Blog," ProBlogger. Retrieved August 20, 2011 from, http://www.problogger.net/archives/2008/08/20/how-to-craft-post-titles-that-draw-readers-into-your-blog/

33. Gwen (2011, February 18), "You Had Me at 'Hello World' or How to Write a Killer Blog Title," Endurance Marketing. Retrieved August 20, 2011 from, http://endurancemktg.com/you-had-me-at-hello-world-or-how-to-write-a-killer-blog-title

34. Noguchi, Yo (2011, June 1), "6 Tips for Writing Oustanding Blog Titles," Techshare. Retrieved July 23, 2011 from, http://www.technshare.com/writing-outstanding-blog-titles/

35. Grey, Jim. (2011, July 25), "Six ways to build blog readership," Down the Road Blog. Retrieved August 20, 2011, from http://jimgrey.wordpress.com/2011/07/25/six-ways-to-build-blog-readership/

36. Tobin, Jim, and Lisa Braziel (2008) *Social Media Is a Cocktail Party: Why You Already Know the Rules of Social Media Marketing* (Cary, NC: Ignite Social Media), p. 97.

37. Kurtz, Howard (2007, July 9), "A Blog That Made It Big," *Washington Post*. Retrieved June 7, 2011, from http://www.washingtonpost.com/wp-dyn/content/article/2007/07/08/AR2007070801213.html

38. Stanford, Chris (2008, July 3), "10 Questions for Arianna Huffington," *Time* Magazine. Retrieved June 7, 2011, from http://www.time.com/time/magazine/article/0,9171,1820145,00.html#ixzz1Of7TCPF5

39. Rowe, Colin (2011, February 7), "History of the Huffington Post—Internet Success Story," Suite101.com. Retrieved June 8, 2011, from http://www.suite101.com/content/history-of-the-huffington-post--internet-success-story-a344735#ixzz1Oe7eNmin

40. Sarno, David (2011, February 7), "A Brief History of the Huffington Post: *Los Angeles Times*. Retrieved June 8, 2011, from http://articles.latimes.com/2011/feb/07/business/la-fi-huffington-post-timeline-20110207

41. "SoftBank Capital Invests in The Huffington Post" (2006, August 8), TechWhack. Retrieved June 8, 2011, from http://business.techwhack.com/1028-softbank-capital-huffington-post/

42. "The Huffington Post" (2011, February 7), *New York Times*. Retrieved June 8, 2011. from http://topics.nytimes.com/top/reference/timestopics/organizations/h/the_huffington_post/index.html

43. King, Ian (2008, November 21), "Business Big Shot: Arianna Huffington, Online Entrepreneur," *The Times*. Retrieved June 8, 2011, from http://business.timesonline.co.uk/tol/business/movers_and_shakers/article5201252.ece

44. Kurtz, Howard (2007, July 9), "A Blog That Made It Big," *Washington Post*. Retrieved June 7, 2011, from http://www.washingtonpost.com/wp-dyn/content/article/2007/07/08/AR2007070801213.html

45. "The Huffington Post" (2011, February 7), *New Your Times*. Retrieved June 7, 2011, from http://topics.nytimes.com/top/reference/timestopics/organizations/h/the_huffington_post/index.html

46. "Arianna Huffington" (2010, May 4), Planned Parenthood of the Heartland. Retrieved June 9, 2011, from http://www.plannedparenthood.org/heartland/arianna-huffington-31384.htm

47. Filmography by Year for Arianna Huffington (n.d.), Internet Movie Database. Retrieved June 9, 2011, from http://www.imdb.com/name/nm0400251/filmoyear

48. "The Huffington Post" (2011, February 7), *New York Times*. Retrieved June 7, 2011, from http://topics.nytimes.com/top/reference/timestopics/organizations/h/the_huffington_post/index.html

49. Maneker, Marion (2011, February 8), "AOL-Huffington Post: Why the Heavy Breathing?" *Big Picture*. Retrieved June 9, 2011, from http://www.ritholtz.com/blog/2011/02/aol-huffington-post-why-the-heavy-breathing/

50. Sarno, David (2011, February 7), "A Brief History of the Huffington Post," *Los Angeles Times*. Retrieved June 8, 2011, from http://articles.latimes.com/2011/feb/07/business/la-fi-huffington-post-timeline-20110207

51. Wolf, Josh (2007, September 26), "Huffington Post Doesn't Plan to Pay Its Bloggers," CNET News. Retrieved June 9, 2011, from http://news.cnet.com/8301-13508_3-9785908-19.html#ixzz1Oe4oLZ3y

52. Ibid.

53. "Top 10 Most Popular Blogs in the World" (2011, February 11), TopYaps, retrieved June 6, 2011, from http://www.topyaps.com/top-10-most-popular-blogs-of-the-world/ and "Top 15 Most Popular Blogs" (2011, June), eBizMBA Rank, retrieved June 6, 2011, from http://www.ebizmba.com/articles/blogs

54. "The Huffington Post: Contributors" (n.d.), *Wikipedia*. Retrieved June 9, 2011, from http://en.wikipedia.org/wiki/The_Huffington_Post#Contributors

55. The Webby Awards (2006-2011). Retrieved June 8, 2011, from http://www.webbyawards.com/webbys/current.php

56. McNichol, Tom (n.d.), "25 Best Blogs 2009," *Time*. Retrieved June 8, 2011, from http://www.time.com/time/specials/packages/article/0,28804,1879276_1879279_1879302,00.html

57. Ho, Erica (2011, February 7), "AOL Acquires Huffington Post for $315 Million," *Time*. Retrieved June 9, 2011, from http://newsfeed.time.com/2011/02/07/aol-acquires-huffington-post-for-315-million/

58. "The Huffington Post" (n.d.), *Encyclopedia Britannica*. Retrieved June 9, 2011, from http://www.britannica.com/EBchecked/topic/1192975/The-Huffington-Post

59. "The Huffington Post" (2011, February 7), *New York Times*. Retrieved June 7, 2011, from http://topics.nytimes.com/top/reference/timestopics/organizations/h/the_huffington_post/index.html

60. Noronha, Charmaine (2011, May 27), "The Huffington Post Crosses the Border to Launch Its First International Edition in Canada," *Star Tribune*. Retrieved June 9, 2011, from http://www.startribune.com/world/122753984.html

61. Peters, Jeremy W. (2011, April 12), "Huffington Post Is Target of Suit on Behalf of Bloggers," *New Your Times*. Retrieved June 7, 2011, from http://mediadecoder.blogs.nytimes.com/2011/04/12/huffington-post-is-target-of-suit-on-behalf-of-bloggers/

62. Noronha, Charmaine (2011, May 11), "Huffington Post Launches Canadian Site," *Chicago Sun Times*. Retrieved June 9, 2011, from http://www.suntimes.com/business/5654972-420/huffington-post-launches-canadian-site.html?print=true

Publishing Podcasts and Webinars

There are many ways to publish content on the social web. As the bandwidth of the Internet has increased, it has made it possible to publish audio and even large video files. The challenge has been to create the means to encode, deliver, and receive these files in a user-friendly manner. When these component technologies came together in the early 2000s, a new publishing platform was born—podcasting.

LEARNING OBJECTIVES

After completing this chapter, students will be able to:

- Define a podcast
- Describe briefly the history of podcasting
- Explain how to create and share podcasts
- Describe how to choose a podcast format
- Explain how to create podcast content
- Identify some of the key ways to produce and deliver a podcast

(Continued)

The word "podcast" was "*Oxford American Dictionary's* Word of the Year in 2004" but not everyone knows its precise definition.[1] Speaking generally, **podcasts** are media files distributed via subscription on the Internet. According to *Wikipedia,*

> *[a] podcast (or non-streamed webcast***) is a series of digital media files (either audio or video) that are released episodically and often downloaded through web syndication. . . . The mode of delivery differentiates podcasting from other means of accessing media files over the Internet, such as direct download, or streamed webcasting. A list of all the audio or video files currently*

---

*Note that the word "webcast" is functionally a synonym of "podcast" in most circumstances, except that webcasts may use streaming audio or video, while podcasts are almost always downloaded in their entirety before viewing. We will use the term "podcast" in this text exclusively in order to reflect common usage and avoid excessive jargon, but note that webcasts may also be a useful social media marketing tool and should not be discarded out of hand due to their omission here.

associated with a given series is maintained centrally on the distributor's server as a web feed.[2]

- Detail how to market with podcasts
- Describe the benefits of hosting webinars

To distill the core aspects of podcasting, this definition from the *Journal of Information Technology & Politics* is also helpful: "A podcast is a digital audio or video file that is episodic, downloadable, and program-driven, mainly with a host and/or theme; and convenient, usually via an automated feed with computer software."[3] The client software used to check web feeds and download new podcasts is occasionally referred to as a **podcatcher**.

A podcast may contain only audio or audio and video recording together. Podcasts that have both audio and video recording are sometimes called a **vodcast**.[4] Podcasts can be consumed one of three ways: (1) played directly off the website on a computer (clicking the play button), (2) downloaded to a computer and listened to offline, and (3) downloaded to portable MP3 players for listening offline.[5] Note that podcasts are not usually streaming content; they are recorded and then published on the Internet for later access by listeners.

A Brief History of Podcasting

From the mid-1990s to the early 2000s, key pieces of technology were being developed to improve the encoding, delivery, and reception of audio and video files via the Internet. One of the key breakthroughs came in the form of a technology called an RSS (Really Simple Syndication), which enabled users to subscribe to content for automatic delivery.

Although RSS was initially developed by the Netscape Communication Corporation in 1999, it wasn't until around 2000 that innovator Dave Winer extended the protocol to handle audio files, creating

> *the forerunner to podcasting, the audioblog. These audioblogs were recorded on MP3 files. By the mid-2000s entrepreneur Adam Curry became heavily involved in developing podcasting technology. [He is] credited with coming up with the idea to automate the updating and delivery of audioblogs. Curry's idea is the manifestation of the podcast. Working together, Curry suggested to Winer that he rethink the RSS feed so that when a new MP3 file was posted it would automatically be updated via the RSS feed. Winer added a 'file enclosure,' which told a computer where to download a new audio file that had been posted. With that innovation, the modern podcast was born.[6]*

In February 2004 Ben Hammersley, writing an article for *The Guardian*, coined the term "podcasting" in reference to audioblogging.[7] The word "podcasting" was a combination of "iPod" and "broadcasting." Numerous companies struggled to establish a variety of different names for audio and video downloads, such as AudioBlogs, Blogcasts, NanoCasts, vlogs, and NetCasts. It wasn't until Apple put audio and video together in their iTunes's podcast directory that the term "podcast" became the standard for both formats.[8]

Challenge

In order for Adam Curry to realize his vision of a profitable podcasting medium for broadcasters, he had to overcome a number of obstacles. First, he had to find a way of convincing both content producers (broadcasters) and listeners that podcasting was worth their time. Second, there was a serious lack of software tools for producing, encoding, and delivering podcasts. Facing these complex tasks, and without easy-to-use software programs to facilitate the process, few content providers would be willing to create material for this new medium. Third, listeners needed a simple way to find and then listen to podcasts. This required both robust hosting for podcast shows and user-friendly podcatching software so that people could automatically subscribe, download, and listen to podcasts. Fourth, Curry needed funding to develop these technologies, establish a hosting site, and create podcasts. This funding had to be sufficient to carry his fledgling business until it became a profitable enterprise. Finally, Curry had to come up with a way to make money for himself and the other content producers without turning off listeners who were expecting to receive the podcasts for free.

Strategy

The *Daily Source Code* was a proof-of-concept podcast show, showing the power and reach of the new medium. Curry's witty conversational style set the standard for high-quality podcasts, spreading the popularity of podcasting. To produce the show, Curry helped create Castblaster, a computer program that automated the time-consuming and technically complex tasks of recording, encoding, and uploading a podcast for dissemination to end users.[23] These software tools made it possible for other content providers to inexpensively edit and produce their own podcasts.

To lay the groundwork that would make it feasible for users to easily subscribe to and download podcasts, Curry codeveloped ipodder, which automated the process of downloading and listening to audio files.[24] He also cofounded the *PodShow* network, a hosting site for podcast shows, which inspired others to set up similar sites offering podcast production, dissemination, and subscription services. These full-featured podcast sites made it easy for listeners to find and subscribe to the content they wanted using a client program like ipodder.

In May 2006 Curry said, "It's not hard for us to bring in more shows . . . but we're selective about what podshows we promote as part of the PodShow brand."[25] That selectivity in programming was rewarded with a series of investments from high-profile venture capitalists, totaling over $38 million by July 2008.[26] Curry's early success in fundraising provided the resources to grow the *PodShow* network (now *MEVIO*) and contributed to the creation of the software necessary to make podcasting readily available to the masses. Furthermore, the funds enabled *MEVIO* "to launch new vertical entertainment networks that offer advertisers a 'brand-safe' platform to reach audiences on the scale and frequency offered by traditional broadcast networks"[27] but with the scalability, interaction, and data capacity only available on the web.

Initially, some industry luminaries had qualms about the advertising model, with some podcasts promoted over others because they had commercial endorsements. Curry was not concerned, saying that "[w]e're not going to see another Howard Stern of podcasting, we'll see a thousand Howard Sterns, all with one-thousandth of his audience. We're not restricted to listening to one particular show because there's no other channel. We have infinite channels."[28] In the end listeners tolerated Curry's promotion of podcasts with commercial sponsors, leading to the commercialization of the medium.

Results

The company Adam Curry cofounded, *PodShow* (now *MEVIO*), has enabled millions to download their favorite music and videos using devices ranging from computers and iPods to smart phones and televisions.[29] Although *MEVIO* is a privately held company and doesn't release download metrics, Curry did reveal that "in December 2006 the network produced 52 million download requests."[30] In May 2007 the *Daily Source Code* claimed it "was averaging more than 1 million downloads a month since the last quarter of 2005."[31] In May 2008 *MEVIO* reported it had attained "a top 20 comScore ranking in both music (May, #10) and Multimedia (May, #16)…[and] dramatic increases in unique monthly visitors, page views, video streams and registration."[32]

Curry's *Daily Source Code* is the oldest and longest running podcast show, popularizing the medium by showing others how podcasting can deliver interesting content.[33] The *Daily Source Code* distinguished itself early on by winning the 2005 People's Choice Award for the Best Produced podcast show.[34] In addition, Curry's efforts in developing the software tools and services to edit, produce, disseminate, receive, and host podcasts, as well as his relentless advocacy of the medium, were instrumental in bringing podcasting to the masses. Perhaps most impressive, he found a way to commercialize podcasting without alienating its listeners. As of 2010 Adam Curry now ends his podcast shows with, "Live your life with passion—and, as long as it lasts, enjoy your freedom," a fitting signoff for the Podfather.[35]

PODCAST CONTENT

In deciding the content focus for a podcast, there are three different possibilities: *instructional*, *informative*, or *entertainment*. While these three can be combined to some extent, it is best to stay with a common theme that connects the entire series of podcasts. While some podcasters choose to rotate between the different themes, such rotation may lose listeners if done incorrectly. A particular target audience is more likely to be drawn by a unique and distinctive theme, so regularity in content can help to draw more subscribers.

Recall the advice on content from Chapter 5 about blogging: specificity is valuable. This advice holds true for podcast content as well. Do not attempt to create a one-size-fits-all content; focus instead on the interests of a specific target audience. The benefit of podcasts from a listener's point of view is the enormous variety and minimal cost of subscribing. In a medium with so few entry barriers, the content being offered must have tangible appeal to some subset of the online audience, or it will be ignored in favor of more exciting presentations.

PRODUCING PODCASTS

While a podcast can theoretically be recorded in minutes, producing polished content that will draw an audience takes more time and effort. Many factors can contribute to a podcast's success or failure. Especially for a business using podcasts to demonstrate thought leadership or expertise, an amateurish-sounding podcast can be embarrassing. When creating podcasts, it is important to keep in mind the following:

- **Choose an articulate moderator**: Recorded audio often amplifies people's speaking quirks. When creating audio podcasts, it is especially important to find a moderator who has minimal verbal static (such as "um," "ah," or "like") and who has a strong vocal presence.

- **Create talking points, not scripts**: It is a difficult balance to strike but an important one. Having a full script can make the audio recording sound wooden or overly rehearsed, while having no outline can cause the speaker to lose focus. Ideally, the podcast should be presented in a relaxed and conversational manner.

- **Brevity**: When creating a podcast, determine the content first and the length second. Avoid the temptation to stretch out content to make keep people listening. Listeners value their time, so do not take up any more than necessary to cover the topic.

- **Avoid overediting**: Verbal static like "um" can be removed. However, if significant editing would be required to remove bad phrasing, consider rerecording instead. Too much editing can make the podcast sound choppy and forced, and consequently, the less audio editing, the better.

- **Include Music**: Introducing the podcast with a brief clip of music lends a professional air to the production and keeps the audience engaged. It also makes the podcast more memorable. To avoid infringing on copyrights, look for music that has a Creative Commons-type license or is podsafe licensed.

Of course, following all of these tips is still no guarantee of attracting a large audience. Gaining subscribers will depend on a combination of engaging content, a charismatic presentation, and consistent updates. For a podcast to be successful, new content must be posted with some regularity (i.e., daily, weekly, or biweekly), similar to a radio show. Mainstream news channels (such as CBS, CNN, and MSNBC) have jumped on board with this format and are regularly releasing podcasts to disseminate information.[36] Competition from professional news outlets has raised the bar for small-time podcasters and has increased podcast audiences' expectation of frequent updates with interesting content.

DELIVERING PODCASTS TO CONSUMERS

The advantage of podcasts is that they exploit the ways in which public media-viewing habits have changed in recent years. People desire information and entertainment to be available on demand, commercial free, and anywhere. Podcasts are a perfect fit in that they allow the listener to download the audio file and listen at her or his convenience. With the ease of finding and downloading podcasts, they cost almost nothing for consumers to access. Podcasts can be shared at no cost on iTunes, Zune, Sony, and Phillips, to name just a few.[37]

Delivering podcasts to listeners is the easiest part. The more difficult aspect of distributing podcast content is ensuring that it is found by the target audience. There are a host of directories available for listing podcasts; "[a]mong the best are Podcast Alley (owned by PodShow Network), Podcasting News, Podcast.net, and iPodder.

org."[38] In addition to directories, there are separate search engines for finding podcasts. Since podcasts are more difficult to index than text-based websites and media, specialized search engines became a necessity. Two podcast search engines are Podscope and GetAPodcast.[†]

To assist a search engine in finding podcasts, it is important to fill in the ID3 tag. ID3 is a file data tagging format that is recognized by most media-playing software.[39] It includes the title, author's name, description, and running time of the media file. Music devices, which are often used to listen to podcasts, can show this information to the listener. Since editing software does not require that these fields be filled in, it is important to remember to enter this information manually. Search engines read and index the information provided in ID3 tags, making it more likely that an online viewer will see the podcast in search results.[40]

Marketing with Podcasting

While many possible goals can be accomplished by podcasting, choosing which to focus on will depend on the larger marketing objectives being pursued. Podcasts have the advantage of both sharing information and putting a human voice or face on a brand. As such, podcasts can complement a broad variety of other social media efforts as part of a social media marketing campaign.

A podcast can be a strategic component of the marketing plan, but it requires a strong commitment to creating content that is tailored to the marketing objectives. This commitment will not only provide focus when developing content, but it helps ensure some payoff from the effort. As an example, suppose one is promoting a catering business, and the objective is to gain new clients from the podcast. The focus could be to demonstrate expertise, by creating a vodcast of the owner assembling delicious hors d'oeuvres. Additionally, it could teach the audience about the ingredients being used without giving away the exact recipe, building up demand for the service and product.

In addition to indirect marketing, podcasts can bring in independent revenue. There are two very different methods to monetize podcasts. The first option is to recruit paid sponsors to advertise on the podcast, much like with any radio or television station. This model of advertising is well established but has potential negative side effects on subscribership. Advertisements that interrupt content will annoy people and may cause them to stop listening. The second method to monetize podcasts is to offer fee-based content. Taking this approach requires the creator to produce top-notch content that viewers will find worth paying for. With so many free podcasts floating around, it may be difficult to convince consumers to pay for one unless it is truly unique and superior. While monetizing is a fine ultimate goal in a podcast-based strategy, it should not be pursued from the start, or there may never be enough subscribers to accomplish anything at all!

Perhaps more important than direct revenue are the advantages a brand can gain from regular podcasting. Speaking persuasively about a field demonstrates confidence and expertise, helping to distinguish a company as a thought leader in the industry. While setting up a website and blog is relatively easy, podcasting well requires both more determination and talent. Still, while it requires a significant commitment of time and energy, podcasting can be a valuable tool in a social media marketing campaign.

[†]See http://www.podscope.com/ and http://www.getapodcast.com/

MuggleCast *Makes Podcast Magic*

Introduction

In the late 1990s the Harry Potter series of fantasy novels, written by British author J. K. Rowling, made reading fashionable again for children and spawned a series of blockbuster films based on the books. Over the years Harry Potter has become a fixture of the pop-culture landscape. Not surprisingly, "a flurry of podcasts sprung up to report Harry Potter news, debate Harry Potter theories and celebrate beloved (or despised) Harry Potter characters."[41] *MuggleCast* emerged from the pack to not only become one of the most popular podcasts with Potter fans but one of the most popular podcasts, period. Indeed, *MuggleCast*'s journey from inception to domination of the podcasting world is a magical story in itself.

History

As young wizard with a dark past, Harry Potter is the central character in the bestselling fantasy novels by J. K. Rowling. By 2008 the Harry Potter books had sold more than 400 million copies, with the final four titles becoming the fastest selling on record.[42] The highly popular books inspired an equally successful series of major motion pictures, all of which rank among the top thirty grossing films worldwide.[43] In addition, Harry Potter merchandising has created a brand worth more than $15 billion.[44] It is little wonder that the millennial generation remains fascinated with Harry Potter.

The term "Muggles" refers (in Harry Potter's universe) to ordinary people without magical powers. So it would seem that the *MuggleCast* show has its intended audience built right into the name. Andrew Sims founded *MuggleCast* at the age of 17, while still in high school.[45] The first edition of the podcast was published on August 7, 2005, by his employer *MuggleNet*, a Harry Potter fan site launched by Emerson Spartz.

MuggleCast, hosted by Andrew Sims

The *MuggleCast* show covers a wide variety of subjects about Harry Potter. According to Andrew Sims' LinkedIn profile, "[he] produces, hosts, and edits this semi-monthly podcast for MuggleNet."[46] The *MuggleNet* fan site originally hired him to manage its content, but in 2007 it made him president. Andrew Sims is the main host for *MuggleCast*

© Gerald S. Williams/MCT/Newscom

and has taken part in every episode except one, which was aptly named, "Andrew-less."[47] The show also regularly features a variety of other cast members, guest hosts, and *MuggleNet* staffers.[48]

Challenge

The biggest challenge for *MuggleCast* was to convert the massive Harry Potter fandom into loyal listeners. The show had to come up with a format and content that would draw in the fans and keep them coming back for more. In addition, the podcast faced competition from other fan-based podcasts, especially the popular *PotterCast*. The show was looking for a way to gain a competitive advantage but still remain fan friendly because many of the same listeners might become subscribers to both podcasts.

Strategy

In an interview with Andrew Sims, he recalls the initial strategy for the show: "At the time, podcasts were still just blooming in popularity so we weren't sure how much of a success ours would be. Our original idea was to just do a short podcast with a roundup of the latest Potter news. As we started brainstorming, though, we kept thinking up bigger and better ideas. Eventually by release time we worked up a great show that everyone who visits MuggleNet loved from the start."[49]

MuggleCast sought to create superior programming and content that featured a unique mixture of interviews, breaking news, and give-and-take with fans by reading fan email and responding to it. *MuggleCast* strives to personalize the listening experience by this reading of fan email (MuggleMail), which typically consists of listeners arguing with statements made by the hosts. Fans are encouraged to submit audio questions for a panel of Potter experts to answer.[50] Character analyses and a discussion on a theory of the week are intended to provoke audience participation, keeping the interaction between hosts and fans lively. [51]

The hosts of the podcast try to make their commentaries entertaining by frequently interjecting wit and humor. The show segment, "Spy on Spartz," features a phone call to *MuggleNet*'s founder Emerson Spartz, asking him where he is and what he is doing. A British joke of the week is read by U.K. native Jamie Lawrence, and Sims reads the weird email sent to the show, often with strange or incoherent requests.[52] As one fan wrote, "I simply can't put into words how funny these people are."[53]

Another tactic is to get interviews with the major players in the Harry Potter movie series. For episode 200 of *MuggleCast*, Sims and company snagged the producer of the motion pictures, even getting him to record a new opening for the show: "Hello, this is David Heyman, and I'm the producer of the Harry Potter films. And this is MuggleCast!"[54]

MuggleCast insightfully pursued a friendly rivalry with its chief competitor *PotterCast*, occasionally having the host of *PotterCast* appear on *MuggleCast*. The two shows even jointly produce podcasts, which are titled "The Leaky Mug".[55]

Finally, one of the most important strategic decisions was to list *MuggleCast* on Apple's iTunes, which provided a sizeable potential audience for the podcast.[56] In the words of Andrew Sims, "[t]he day I saw MuggleCast finally up on iTunes I couldn't believe my eyes that we were actually published—that's when I realized we could really make something out of this."[57]

Results

Today, *MuggleCast* consistently appears in the top ten of Podcast Alley's most popular podcasts, based on listener votes. [58] The show has also claimed the top spot of Apple's iTunes podcast rankings.[59] *MuggleCast* has clearly succeeded in getting the fans of Harry Potter to become avid followers of the podcast.

Underscoring the success of the show's podcasting strategies is the significant public and media industry recognition that it has received: it has won the Podcast of the Year from the Weblog Awards in 2005[60]; the People's Choice Award in 2006 at the Second Annual Podcast Awards in Ontario, California; the Best Entertainment Podcast in 2008; and the Best Entertainment Podcast at the 2009 Podcast Awards.[61] As the Harry Potter book and movies series draws to an end, new generations of readers appear to be developing an appetite for Pottermania, which is likely a good omen for this podcast.

Hosting Webinars

While podcasts can be analogized to an online radio show, webinars more resemble a conference or seminar. A **webinar**, or teleseminar, is a seminar that is conducted live over the web and (unlike a podcast) is designed to be interactive.[62] The term "webinar" was coined from the phrase "web-based seminar."[63] To attend a webinar, the listener can call a phone number (much like a conference call) or listen live on a computer's speakers by accessing the webinar through the Internet. The specifics depend on how the webinar is set up by the host.

Webinars sometimes contain a visual aspect such as a slide show presentation or live-stream video. They require scheduling in advance so that people can make time to participate. Since it is a live experience, it is important to post and promote the date and time that the webinar will be held. On average the duration of a webinar is one to two hours. Many webinars are free, but some companies charge a fee to attend their webinars.

Webinars are still relatively new as a social media marketing tool. Up until fairly recently, webinar software was expensive and not very reliable with large numbers of participants. Now, many companies offer webinar services: Adobe Connect Pro, WebEx, GoToWebinar, and iLinc, to name just a few. [††] Webinar technology has evolved over the past few years, making the medium an effective, low-cost marketing solution.

HOW TO SET UP A WEBINAR

Webinar services vary in their abilities, but their webinars are relatively easy to set up and run. There are a number of free to low-cost webinar sites available, and so the first step is selecting the right webinar service. When selecting where to host the webinar, one should consider the following factors: the number of attendees, the visual content, and the frequency with which the webinar is held. Because some webinar hosting sites have a cap on the number of attendees, it is important to get an estimate beforehand. If there will be visual content, it will be necessary to

---

[††]See http://www.adobe.com/products/adobeconnect.html; http://www.webex.com/; http://www.gotomeeting.com/fec/webinar; and http://www.ilinc.com/

have a website host the webinar rather than using a conference call system. Lastly, establishing the frequency with which the webinar will be held will determine if it is better to pay a monthly subscription fee or if a one-time webinar fee will be most economical.

There may be some other technical details to decide on after a webinar service has been chosen. Webinar hosting sites often allow the creation of multiple choice questions (polls) for attendees to answer during the webinar; the results will be displayed. The poll can provide information about the attendees' general sentiments, as well giving the webinar participants a feeling of interaction. Through the survey, the webinar can also mimic a focus group and provide valuable information to the webinar's creator and participants.

The next step is creating the webinar outline, which contains a list of the main points to be covered during the webinar. These points should be kept brief to avoid any temptation of reading directly off the outline. Having a clear schedule for the talk will help avoid going off on unnecessary tangents and will ensure that the relevant material gets covered.

After an outline has been created for the webinar, the event must be scheduled. Most services have a simple user interface that allows a webinar to be scheduled in under ten minutes. Webinar sites like the ones listed above require the host name, email, company, webinar title and description, date and time, reoccurrence information, and category.[64]

Once the webinar is scheduled and listed online, it is time to start promoting it on other social media channels. As webinars are not usually available after they are presented, promoting the webinar to ensure a sufficient number of attendees is essential.

PREPARING FOR AND EXECUTING THE WEBINAR

While webinars can be a valuable component in a social media marketing campaign, they also carry some risks and dangers. One downside is that when hosting a webinar, there is no way to gauge the audience's reaction. Without faces or expressions to read, feedback may be hard to immediately assess. Another potential problem is that webinars are live with no chance to rerecord if the speaker is stumped or misspeaks. Because of these risks, time spent preparing for the webinar will be very well spent indeed.

Some webinar hosting sites have a moderator monitoring the webinar. If that is the case or if there are several speakers planned, coordination will be needed regarding introductions, which person will begin the call, and so forth. A few minutes of planning can avoid an awkward start to a webinar.

Webinars need to remain focused on the core content while still providing openings for listener participation and questions. Decide in advance if questions will be answered as they arise or held until the very end. Either approach can work, but it should be determined beforehand in order to avoid wasted time. Also, take steps to prevent interruptions. Be sure the speaker's surroundings will be quiet with little background noise. Simple measures like closing the door, turning off phones and alarms, and a "Do Not Disturb" sign are important matters to consider in advance. Finally, keep any relevant materials to be used during the webinar within easy reach so that there will be no unnecessary distractions.

Once preparations have ended and the webinar's scheduled beginning has arrived, be sure to start on time! As it is a live event, starting late leaves the audience waiting. Being inconvenienced makes it less likely that attendees will sign up for another webinar by the host.

When taking questions, answer them concisely and avoid rambling. It is difficult to anticipate the number of questions that will be asked, so leave enough time to cover them by giving brief but informative responses whenever possible. If there is extra time at the end, it is possible to readdress an earlier question, but if time runs out, people whose questions were not addressed will be frustrated.

Even if the ultimate goal of the webinar is to get business leads, avoid selling a service or product overtly during the webinar. People attend webinars to learn, and it is critical to meet that expectation or the audience may go elsewhere. If the content provided is valuable enough, then the presenter's expertise will signal a high quality of work, inspiring the audience to seek that person's services (see the exercise case study below for an example).

At the conclusion of the webinar, always invite the attendees to make contact with further questions or to connect on networking platforms after the webinar is completed. This is the time when business leads can be generated. Take advantage of the expertise that conducting a webinar conveys to accomplish other marketing goals.

Marketing with Webinars and/or Podcasts

One of the biggest advantages to using webinars is the ability to gather an enormous audience (in some cases over 500 people) in a seminar-type format without anyone needing to travel.[65] This characteristic of the webinar makes it an ideal format for training sessions or information sharing. Yet another benefit to webinars is that the audience can ask questions and get immediate answers. Unlike prerecorded podcasts, the audience can engage directly with the speaker, making webinars an ideal way to establish expertise and impress customers.

Clever social media marketers have also used webinars to gather information about potential clients. Webinars typically require participants to provide an email address in order to participate. This email list can later be used to send targeted messages based on the person's interest in the webinar. To gather further insight on the audience, a number of lead qualification questions can be asked prior to webinar registration. Especially if the webinar is popular, it can accumulate a large amount of data to better reach the target audience.

How does one decide between podcasts and webinars as components in a social media marketing strategy? While clearly not mutually exclusive, many campaigns choose to focus their efforts on either one or the other or to emphasize one medium more than the other. This choice may reflect available technology and resources (podcasts are typically less expensive to produce than webinars) or, more likely, a difference in the content or product being marketed.

With their interactive focus, webinars are highly valuable as a tool for learning or collaboration. The primary disadvantage of webinars is that they require planning and coordination beforehand because the event is live and must be attended at the time of its presentation. Podcasts, on the other hand, are less interactive because the viewer downloads and then listens to the file at leisure. While this may restrict the use of podcasts as a teaching tool, the advantage is broader access by viewers and less effort on coordinating because a podcast can still be accessed many months after it has been recorded. This continuing accessibility makes podcasts a natural fit for opinion, information, or entertainment products and services.

Depending on the industry, some organizations use both webinars and podcasts in their social media marketing campaign; others use just one or the other. Both offer valuable opportunities to engage consumers on a more personal level than text-based communication. Marketing strategies that leverage that deeper connection can be highly successful in using webinars and/or podcasts.

To create succes
a good title. As mos
whether to read the
an article's distribut
descriptive, as well
est, the title should
This need creates a
bring to mind any i
to view the article.

Above all, the art
that the content add
ing to trick readers
disappoint, frustrate
guidelines that titles
ter of every word or
unnecessary compli
will be willing and a

Using

Introductio

Launched in Nover
by other article dir
world and the favo
site allows authors
improve search en
tion by employing
tent, thus attracting
each month.[6] In tu
around the world.

Although most
themselves as an
Slick, a dedicated,

---

* The title itself does not h
method). Even a plain stat
simple title, "Successful M
"what are those methods?
content will support that t

Inspired Marketing LLC Generates Sales from Webinars

After selling education products in person at conferences and through other Internet marketing channels, Inspired Marketing LLC found that webinars were an extremely efficient and powerful way to generate leads and drive sales of its products. Inspired Marketing launched a free webinar program, which has now become their primary source of sales. Through webinars, they have been able to connect with prospects and convert them into customers for their business.

History

Inspired Marketing LLC, located in Columbus, Ohio, was cofounded by Sean Malarkey and Lewis Howes in 2009. After an injury interrupted his football career, Howes focused his attention on the web.[66] Malarkey and Howes had a strong background in social media and Internet marketing prior to founding Inspired Marketing, and they discovered the power of webinar marketing early on. Initially, based on his own experience and success on LinkedIn, Howes wrote a book on LinkedIn marketing.[67] Then, according to Howes, "I started creating digital products to sell, but I didn't have a good way to reach potential buyers. I was traveling all over the country to sell books, speak at conferences and host events. I was hustling, sleeping on couches and pulling in only a couple of thousand dollars a month."[68]

Inspired Marketing's challenge was to find a scalable way to market its educational products. The targets for the products are entrepreneurs, small business owners, and professionals across many industrial sectors. The company needed a marketing tool that would allow it to reach many people in different geographies, without high travel costs.

Strategy

Inspired Marketing discovered webinar marketing when Howes participated in a webinar and offered a $150 product for sale at the end of the session. Surprised by the high initial sales, he began to explore ways to take advantage of webinar marketing.[69]

Inspired Marketing began by offering free webinars on a variety of educational topics. The webinars allow the firm to reach large numbers of people around the globe and to serve two main objectives. First, webinars are powerful lead generation tools. To generate leads, or potential new customers, Inspired Marketing offers webinars on relevant topics. When a participant signs up for the webinar, he or she provides an email address that allows Inspired Marketing to send offers on future webinars or products.

Second, Inspired Marketing generates direct sales from the webinars. For example, at the end of a webinar on Twitter tips, attendees are able to take advantage of

listen to math information than read it. I haven't yet finished a series so that plan is still on hold. Right now, I am analyzing what kinds of articles garner publishers and what is getting the most reads. I'm also using Google Analytics to see if there is a pattern to where my website is being accessed, what on my website is of interest and what needs to be changed."[18]

Slick has one final thought to pass on: "A special THANKS to my mother for pushing and helping this math geek master grammar, punctuation and spelling. I wouldn't be a Diamond without you, Mom!"[19]

Creating White Papers and E-Books

The term "white paper" is derived from "white book," an official publication by a national government.[20] In public policy, white papers are delivered to policy makers to inform them on important issues. Businesses eventually began to adopt the term, referring to informative documents for important clients as white papers. In this context a "good white paper is written for a business audience, defines a problem, and offers a solution, but it does not pitch a particular product or company."[21] Marketing messages in a white paper should be as subtle as possible, if they appear at all. According to Michael Knowles, a **white paper** "is a technical document that describes how a technology or product solves a particular problem. It's a marketing document and a technical document, yet it doesn't go too far in either direction"[22] (see Figure 7.1 for an example).

What will be an effective white paper is defined mostly by its audience's expectations. A white paper is expected to have at least six pages of text and to provide useful information about a business or technical issue. A white paper should contain sources, facts, and figures.[23] Further, white papers are typically intended for the reader to review before making a purchase.† Online distribution, which avoids warehousing and printing costs, has made white papers both easier to access and more popular for businesses.[24]

Most of all, writing content-heavy but appealing marketing content, such as white papers, takes strong writing skills and practice. Having a solid process to guide the writing effort will make these potentially daunting publications more manageable. Business owner and white paper author Al Kemp lays out his nine-step process for writing white papers.[25] In order, these steps are Assess Needs; Plan; Acquire Information; Organize Content; Design the Look and Feel; Write; Illustrate; Review, Revise, and Approve; and finally Publish. A brief description of the process, along with insights from other white paper authorities, appears below.

STEP #1. ASSESS NEEDS

In order to make decisions about the white paper's structure and content, it is necessary to have a clear vision of the goals one is attempting to achieve. These may be *overt* goals that are clear to the reader (such as educating the public about a product or providing information about a problem) or *covert*

White Paper on Electronic Journal Usage Statistics

by Judy Luther
October 2000

COUNCIL ON LIBRARY AND INFORMATION RESOURCES

Figure 7.1　**Example of a White Paper**

---

†So-called white papers that are intended for postpurchase reading are more accurately termed technical support documents.

Inspired Marketing LLC Generates Sales from Webinars

After selling education products in person at conferences and through other Internet marketing channels, Inspired Marketing LLC found that webinars were an extremely efficient and powerful way to generate leads and drive sales of its products. Inspired Marketing launched a free webinar program, which has now become their primary source of sales. Through webinars, they have been able to connect with prospects and convert them into customers for their business.

History

Inspired Marketing LLC, located in Columbus, Ohio, was cofounded by Sean Malarkey and Lewis Howes in 2009. After an injury interrupted his football career, Howes focused his attention on the web.[66] Malarkey and Howes had a strong background in social media and Internet marketing prior to founding Inspired Marketing, and they discovered the power of webinar marketing early on. Initially, based on his own experience and success on LinkedIn, Howes wrote a book on LinkedIn marketing.[67] Then, according to Howes, "I started creating digital products to sell, but I didn't have a good way to reach potential buyers. I was traveling all over the country to sell books, speak at conferences and host events. I was hustling, sleeping on couches and pulling in only a couple of thousand dollars a month."[68]

Inspired Marketing's challenge was to find a scalable way to market its educational products. The targets for the products are entrepreneurs, small business owners, and professionals across many industrial sectors. The company needed a marketing tool that would allow it to reach many people in different geographies, without high travel costs.

Strategy

Inspired Marketing discovered webinar marketing when Howes participated in a webinar and offered a $150 product for sale at the end of the session. Surprised by the high initial sales, he began to explore ways to take advantage of webinar marketing.[69]

Inspired Marketing began by offering free webinars on a variety of educational topics. The webinars allow the firm to reach large numbers of people around the globe and to serve two main objectives. First, webinars are powerful lead generation tools. To generate leads, or potential new customers, Inspired Marketing offers webinars on relevant topics. When a participant signs up for the webinar, he or she provides an email address that allows Inspired Marketing to send offers on future webinars or products.

Second, Inspired Marketing generates direct sales from the webinars. For example, at the end of a webinar on Twitter tips, attendees are able to take advantage of a special offer on an educational product about Twitter. This approach allows Inspired Marketing to directly reach thousands of prospects with a targeted sales message that can lead to immediate sales.

In addition to recording free webinars for lead generation, Inspired Marketing produces a number of fee-based webinars in which participants pay to participate. The fee-based webinars are also recorded and made available for sale, creating an additional revenue stream.[70]

Results

The results from the webinars have been tremendous. During its first webinar in 2009, Inspired Marketing generated over $12,500 in sales through a single sixty-minute call. Over the next year, Howes devoted substantial time to webinars, leading him to later estimate that he had "done about 300 of them live over 2010."[71] Currently, he continues to do between three to five webinars per week.[72]

Inspired Marketing has come a long way since its initial webinar, and in January 2011 the company had sales of $250,000 from seven webinars. The firm currently reaches over 50,000 people worldwide.[73] It also anticipates $2.5 million in sales during 2011.[74]

According to top leadership in the company, free webinars have been the most effective tool for Inspired Marketing in finding prospects and in driving sales. By providing valuable content for free, Inspired Marketing is able to build relationships and showcase its expertise, which makes people want more information and services from the firm.

Inspired Marketing shows how a company of any size can leverage webinars to find and connect with potential customers, generate leads, and drive sales.[75] Even companies that don't directly sell products through their webinars have the opportunity to build closer relationships with their customers and prospects and to derive positive brand equity.

By providing free content that is highly valuable to prospective customers, webinars provide a starting point for building a relationship. Since webinars tend to be longer (about an hour for most) and fairly in-depth, they provide an opportunity to build trust and position a company as thought leaders.

Review Questions for Inspired Marketing Case Study

1. What was it about Inspired Marketing's product that made webinar promotion so successful?

2. Part of the company's strategy, as described in the case study, was to provide some information and then hope that listeners would pay to get more. Is there a danger that people will listen in for free, then never buy anything? Why or why not?

3. Compare and contrast the benefits of selling a product in person at a conference versus via webinar. While Inspired Marketing obviously chose to focus on webinars, other firms still go to conferences. Which types of products do you think are more likely to be sold in person and which online? Are there any changes in technology that might cause these practices to change?

4. Compare the revenue-generating strategy of the Podfather (first case study in the chapter) with that of Inspired Marketing. How do podcasts and webinars differ in these cases, as well as generally in their revenue strategies? Make an argument why one medium would be more effective than the other, and then provide the most compelling counterargument against this position.

Notes

1. Brogan, Chris, and Julien Smith (2009), *Trust Agents* (Hoboken, NJ: John Wiley), p. 20.
2. "Podcasts" (n.d.), *Wikipedia*. Retrieved June 14, 2011, from http://en.wikipedia.org/wiki/Podcast
3. Gil de Zúñiga, Homero, Aaron Veenstra, Emily Vraga, and Dhavan Shah (2010), "Digital Democracy: Reimagining Pathways to Political Participation," *Journal of Information Technology & Politics*, vol. 7, no. 1, p. 47.
4. Weber, Larry (2009), *Marketing to the Social Web: How Digital Communities Build Your Business* (Hoboken, NJ: John Wiley), p. 181.
5. Borges, Bernie (2009), *Marketing 2.0: Bridging the Gap between Seller and Buyer through Social Media Marketing* (Tucson, AZ: Wheatmark), p. 221.
6. Martell, James (2011, April 5), "The History of Podcasting—How'd We Get Here?" TheHistoryOf.net. Retrieved July 8, 2011, from http://www.thehistoryof.net/the-history-of-podcasting.html
7. "History of Podcasting (n.d.), Voices.com. Retrieved July 8, 2011, from http://www.voices.com/podcasting/history-of-podcasting.html
8. "A Podcast by Any Other Name Is Still a . . ." (2010, September 28), PostCast411's Podcast (originally posted in *Blogger and Podcast Magazine* in June 2007). Retrieved June 12, 2011, from http://podcast411.libsyn.com/a-podcast-by-any-other-name-is-still-a-
9. Meyerson, Mitch (2010), *Success Secrets of the Social Media Marketing Superstars* (Irvine, CA: Entrepreneur Media), p. 251.
10. Ibid., p. 254.
11. Gillin, Paul (2009), *Secrets of Social Media Marketing* (Fresno, CA: Quill Driver Books), p. 212-13.
12. Campbell, Garner (2005, November/December), "There's Something in the Air: Podcasting in Education," *EDUCAUSE Review*, vol. 40, no. 6, p. 32-47. Retrieved June 11, 2011, from http://www.educause.edu/EDUCAUSE+Review/EDUCAUSEReviewMagazineVolume40/TheresSomethingintheAirPodcast/158014
13. "Daily Code Source" (n.d.), *Wikipedia*. Retrieved June 12, 2011, from http://en.wikipedia.org/wiki/Daily_Source_Code#History
14. Miller, Martin (2007, May 25), "'Podfather' Plots a Radio Hit of His Own: LA Times," *PodShow*. Retrieved June 12, 2011, from http://pressroom.mevio.com/2006/05/23/podfather-plots-a-radio-hit-of-his-own-la-times/
15. Ibid.
16. Bazeley, Michael (2005, September 6), "PodShow's First Acquisition: Podcast Alley," *SiliconBeat*. Retrieved June 12, 2011, from http://www.siliconbeat.com/entries/2005/09/06/podshows_first_acquisition_podcast_alley.html
17. Curry, Adam (n.d.), No Agenda Wiki. Retrieved June 12, 2011, from http://noagenda.wikia.com/wiki/Adam_Curry
18. "Audio: NA-001-2007-10-26" (2007, Oct 26), @SpokenWord.org. Retrieved June 12, 2011, from http://www.spokenword.org/program/152092
19. West, Jackson (2008, October 2), "Mevio, Née Podshow, Replaces Cofounder with New CEO," Gawker. Retrieved June 12, 2011, http://gawker.com/5057864/mevio-ne-podshow-replaces-cofounder-with-new-ceo?tag=valleywag

20. Lewin, James (2007, December 28), "Podfather Adam Curry Backing Ron Paul," *Podcasting News*. Retrieved June 12, 2011, from http://www.podcastingnews.com/content/2007/12/podfather-adam-curry-backing-ron-paul/

21. Curry, Adam (2008, August 8) "Confessions of a Multimedia Hitman," Daily Source Cod*e*, episode 781, CastRoller. Retrieved September 14, 2011 from http://castroller.com/Podcasts/DailySourceCode/272268

22. *MEVIO* (n.d.). Retrieved June 12, 2011, from http://www.mevio.com/video/

23. Campbell, Garner (2005, November/December), "There's Something in the Air: Podcasting in Education," *EDUCAUSE Review*, vol. 40, no. 6, p. 32-47. Retrieved June 11, 2011, from http://www.educause.edu/EDUCAUSE+Review/EDUCAUSEReviewMagazineVolume40/TheresSomethingintheAirPodcast/158014

24. Jardin, Xeni (2005, May 4), "Audience with the Podfather," *Wired*. Retrieved June 11, 2011, from http://www.wired.com/culture/lifestyle/news/2005/05/67525

25. Harmanci, Reyhan (2006, May 17), "How an Ex-VJ Transformed Conventional Media into the Vox Populi. Ever Hear of Podcasting?" *San Francisco Chronicle*. Retrieved June 13, 2011, from http://www.sfgate.com/cgi-bin/article.cgi?f=/c/a/2006/05/17/DDGE0I3DP5146.DTL&ao=all#ixzz1P6mBA8iB

26. *MEVIO* Company Summary (n.d.), LinkSV: Link Silicon Valley. Retrieved June 13, 2011, from http://www.linksv.com/companySummary.aspx?co_;idURL=30875&partnerID=

27. MEVIO (2008, July 9) Fiercewireless. Retrieved September 14, 2011, from http://www.fiercewireless.com/press-releases/mevio

28. Harmanci, Reyhan (2006, May 17), "How an Ex-VJ Transformed Conventional Media into the Vox Populi. Ever Hear of Podcasting?" *San Francisco Chronicle*. Retrieved June 13, 2011, from http://www.sfgate.com/cgi-bin/article.cgi?f=/c/a/2006/05/17/DDGE0I3DP5146.DTL&ao=all#ixzz1P6mBA8iB

29. "Joy Daniels" (no date), *MEVIO*. Retrieved June 11, 2011, from http://pressroom.mevio.com/

30. "Adam Curry" (2007, March 3), curry.com Retrieved June 11, 2011, from http://curry.podshow.com/?p=548

31. Miller, Martin (2007, May 25), " 'Podfather' Plots a Radio Hit of His Own: LA Times," *PodShow*. Retrieved June 12, 2011, from http://pressroom.mevio.com/2006/05/23/podfather-plots-a-radio-hit-of-his-own-la-times/

32. "MEVIO Secures $15 Million in Funding to Support Rapid Growth and Move into Vertical Entertainment Networks" (2008, July 9), *MEVIO*. Retrieved June 13, 2011, from http://pressroom.mevio.com/2008/07/09/mevio-secures-15-million-in-funding-to-support-rapid-growth-and-move-into-vertical-entertainment-networks/

33. Adam Curry Source Code—Sourcecode—BS Source (n.d.), *Sourcecode Directory*. Retrieved June 12, 2011, from http://www.bssource.net/Sourcecode/Adam-curry-source-code-2101.html

34. Cochrane, Todd (2005, August 4), "2005 People's Choice Award Winners," *PodCast Connect*. Retrieved June 13, 2011, from http://www.podcastconnect.com/archive/2005/08/2005_peoples_choice_podcast_aw.html

35. 840 Podcast (2010, July 30), *Daily Source Code*. Retrieved June 12, 2011, from http://www.dailysourcecode.com/"http://www.dailysourcecode.com/

36. "Podcasts" (n.d.), CBS News, retrieved June 14, 2011, from http://www.cbsnews.podcast.com/" http://cbsnews.podcast.com/; "Audio & Video Podcasts" (n.d.), CNN, retrieved June 14, 2011, from http://www.cnn.com/services/podcasting/; and "Get Podcasts from NBC News, MSNBC and msnbc.com" (n.d.), MSNBC, retrieved June 14, 2011, from http://www.msnbc.msn.com/id/8132577/t/get-podcasts-nbc-news-msnbc-msnbccom/

37. Meyerson, Mitch (2010), *Success Secrets of the Social Media Marketing Superstars* (Irvine, CA: Entrepreneur Media), p. 259.

38. Gillin, Paul (2009), *The New Influencers*. (Fresno, CA: Quill Driver Books), p. 166.

39. Welcome (n.d.), ID3.org. Retrieved June 14, 2011, http://www.id3.org/

40. Gillin, Paul (2009), *Secrets of Social Media Marketing* (Fresno, CA: Quill Driver Books), p. 215-16.

41. Maltese, Racheline (2006, August 25), "The Weird, Wacky World of Harry Potter Podcasts," Associated Content from Yahoo! Retrieved June 11, 2011, from http://www.associatedcontent.com/article/53830/the_weird_wacky_world_of_harry_potter.html?cat=9

42. "Rowling Makes £5 Every Second" (2008, October 3), BBC News. Retrieved June 15, 2011, from http://news.bbc.co.uk/2/hi/entertainment/7649962.stm

43. "All Time Worldwide Box Office Grosses" (n.d.),5 Box Office Mojo. Retrieved June 15, 2011, from http://www.boxofficemojo.com/alltime/world/

44. "Business Big Shot: Harry Potter Author JK Rowling" (2008, April 2), *The Times*. Archived from the original on November 14, 2011, http://web.archive.org/web/20110611194604/http://business.timesonline.co.uk/tol/business/movers_and_shakers/article3663197.ece

45. "Andrew Sims in the News" (2006, October 22), YouTube. Retrieved June 15, 2011, from http://www.youtube.com/watch?v=7jXIoWKheOk

46. Andrew Sims Profile (n.d.), LinkedIn.com. Retrieved June 15, 2011, from http://www.linkedin.com/in/sims89

47. "MuggleCast" (n.d.), *Urban Dictionary*. Retrieved June 15, 2011, from http://www.urbandictionary.com/define.php?term=MuggleCast

48. "Muggle Cast" (n.d.), tvtropes.org. Retrieved June 15, 2011, from http://tvtropes.org/pmwiki/pmwiki.php/Main/MuggleCast

49. Holmes, Julian Bennett (2007, March 19), "Interview with Andrew Sims of Mugglecast," *GigaCom*. Retrieved June 11, 2011, from http://gigaom.com/apple/interview-with-andrew-sims-of-mugglecast/

50. "MuggleNet, Podcast" (n.d.), *Wikipedia*. Retrieved June 16, 2011, from http://en.wikipedia.org/wiki/MuggleNet#Podcast

51. "Harry Potter Fandom" (n.d.), *Wikipedia*. Retrieved June 16, 2011, from http://en.wikipedia.org/wiki/Harry_Potter_Fandom

52. Ibid.

53. "MuggleNet's Harry Potter Podcast!" (2006, December 8), *Electrify My Life*. Retrieved September 14, 2011, from http://stellarnostalgia.multiply.com/reviews/item/8

54. "MuggleCast #200: Admit Defeat—Now Available! Featuring Harry Potter Film Producer David Heyman" (2010, June, 9), *MuggleNet* News. Retrieved June 16, 2011, from http://www.mugglenet.com/app/news/show/3569

55. "PotterCast Is the Harry Potter Podcast Brought to You by The Leaky Cauldron" (2007, January 2), *PotterCast*. Archived from the original on June 16, 2011, from http://web.archive.org/web/20070102134107/http://www.the-leaky-cauldron.org/pottercast/page/what

56. "Secret Podcasting" (2005, September 8), Book Corner, Apple. Retrieved June 11, 2011, from https://www.apple.com/enews/2005/09/08enews1.html#top

57. Holmes, Julian Bennett (2007, March 19), "Interview with Andrew Sims of Mugglecast," *GigaCom*. Retrieved June 11, 2011, from http://gigaom.com/apple/interview-with-andrew-sims-of-mugglecast/

58. "Top 50 Rated Podcasts" (2011, June), Podcast Alley. June 11, 2011, from http://www.podcastalley.com/top_podcasts.php?num=50

59. "Mugglenet.com Taps Limelight's Magic for Podcast Delivery of Harry Potter Content" (2005, November 8), *PR Newswire*. Retrieved June 16, 2011, from http://www.prnewswire.com/news-releases/mugglenetcom-taps-limelights-magic-for-podcast-delivery-of-harry-potter-content-55453037.html

60. McWilliams, Ryan (2009, June 24), "Mugglecast: The #1 Harry Potter Podcast," Associated Content from Yahoo! Retrieved June 16, 2011, from http://www.associatedcontent.com/article/1830661/mugglecast_the_1_harry_potter_podcast.html

61. "What Is MuggleCast: Awards Won" (n.d.), *The LeakyPedia*. Retrieved June 16, 2011, from http://www.the-leaky-cauldron.org/wiki/index.php?title=MuggleCast

62. Weber, Larry (2009), *Marketing to the Social Web: How Digital Communities Build Your Business* (Hoboken, NJ: John Wiley), p. 31.

63. Brown, Georg (2008), *Social Media 100 Success Secrets* (Newstead, Australia: Emereo Publishing), p. 110.

64. Webinarlistings.com (n.d.). Retrieved July 8, 2011, from http://www.webinarlistings.com/calendar/events/index.php?com=submit

65. Karten, Naomi (2010) *Presentation Skills for Technical Professionals* (United Kingdom: IT Governance Publishing Company) p. 208.

66. Garland, David Siteman. (2010), "How Lewis Howes Went from Sleeping on His Sister's Couch to Becoming THE Authority on LinkedIn," Rise to the Top. Retrieved June 20, 2011, from http://www.therisetothetop.com/interviews-guests/how-lewis-howes-became-the-authority-on-linkedin/

67. Agin, Frank, and Lewis Howes (2009), *LinkedWorking: Generating Success on the World's Largest Professional Networking Website* (Columbus, OH: Four Eighteen Enterprises).

68. (2011)"Inspired Marketing Turns Social Media Savvy into Mega-sales with GoToWebinar (2011), Citrix. Retrieved June 16, 2011, from http://www.citrix.com/English/aboutCitrix/caseStudies/caseStudy.asp?storyID=2311441

69. Howes, Lewis (2010), "8 Ways to Boost Your Business with Webinars." Retrieved June 20, 2011, from http://www.lewishowes.com/webinars/webinar-marketing-tips-and-resources/

70. Howes, Lewis (2010), *How to Create Magnetic Webinars: 10 Ways to Generate More Leads, Increase Sales, and Captivate Your Target Audience with Webinars.* Retrieved June 16, 2011, from http://magneticwebinars.com/free/Webinar_Report_Finished.pdf

71. Howes, Lewis (2011, June), "The Only Inbound Marketing Plan You'll Ever Need." Retrieved June 16, 2011, from http://www.lewishowes.com/marketing/inbound-marketing-plan/

72. Howes, Lewis (2011), "Top 10 Ways to Create Magnetic Webinars." Retrieved June 16, 2011, from http://www.lewishowes.com/webinars/webinar-marketing/

73. Dellatorre, Erika (2011, March 28), "PowerSuit, with Lewis Howes," *614 Magazine.* Retrieved June 16, 2011, from http://614columbus.com/article/powersuit-632/

74. "Inspired Marketing Turns Social Media Savvy into Mega-sales with GoToWebinar," Citrix. Retrieved June 16, 2011, from http://www.citrix.com/English/aboutCitrix/caseStudies/caseStudy.asp?storyID=2311441

75. Barr, Corbett (2011, April), "How to Get Massive Traffic from LinkedIn and Webinars (with Lewis Howes)," Think Traffic. Retrieved June 20, 2011, from http://thinktraffic.net/massive-traffic-from-linkedin-and-webinars-with-lewis-howes

Publishing Articles, White Papers, and E-Books

This chapter will discuss several "conventional" publishing methods, which have been adapted and expanded for online distribution and social media marketing. Articles, books, and white papers all existed long before the Internet, but as technology has advanced, the reach and application of these media has broadened substantially.

An **article directory** is a website where users submit original articles for approval and syndication (free distribution to other websites with proper attribution).[1] The articles are organized into categories, such as technology, business, and health, so that they can be more easily found by readers and website owners for dissemination.

An **article** submission generally runs 400 to 500 words in length with a 2–3% keyword density (the percentage of times a word appears in an article).[2] A directory article also tends to have a highly descriptive title. Article brevity, appropriate keyword density, and careful titling are done to optimize the chances the piece will be ranked at the top of search engine results. However, directory articles lack the copyediting and editorial oversight of professional publications, such as magazines or newspapers, and they are typically meant to not only inform but also to promote an author, business, brand, website, or issue.

LEARNING OBJECTIVES

After completing this chapter, students will be able to:

- Define an article directory
- Define an article submission
- Explain how to publish and distribute articles
- Detail the steps in creating e-books and white papers, including how to assess needs, plan, acquire information, organize content, design the look and feel, write, illustrate, review, revise and approve, and publish
- Explain how to market with article directories, e-books, and white papers

Publishing and Distributing Articles

The first step in article-based marketing is to produce article content that the target audience will be interested in reading, as demonstrated by the first case study: *Using EzineArticles to Raise Awareness about Math Education.* In many ways the requirements for strong article content are very similar to those for blogs, as discussed in Chapter 5. Most of the advice found there will apply just as much when writing an article as a blog. Indeed, some blog posts can be adapted and transformed into articles with very little modification.

What really distinguishes an article from a blog is the length of the piece and the depth of content. A good article can range in length from several hundred to several thousand words, depending on the topic and the target audience. While readers may be forgiving of a typo, offhand reference, or colloquialism in a blog, the expectations for an article are higher. As an article takes time and forethought, readers will typically expect more research, fact checking, and polish than they do from blogs.

The power of article marketing comes from the many easy syndication services that exist to share online articles. A few of the more popular article directories are listed in Table 7.1. A well-written and topical article appearing on one (or more) of these sites can garner a significant viewership.

Note the "No Follow" (NF) column, which identifies the article directories that prevent search engines from following article links. Marketers are among the heaviest contributors to article directories, and a site that automatically inserts the no-follow attribute in article links defeats its objective of gaining a higher placement in search engine ranking because it blocks search engines from associating articles with that site. Hence, most marketers favor article directories without the no-follow requirement; however, some are willing to submit articles to NF directories to improve awareness and establish their authority on highly trafficked sites.

There are other rewards to be had from writing online articles. Some article directories offer "Expert" or "Frequent Contributor" status to their best authors and feature

Article Directory	Alexa Global Traffic Rank (TR)	Google Page Rank (PR)	No Follow
1. eHow.com	149	7	NF
2. Squidoo.com	206	7	
3. EzineArticles.com	280	6	
4. Hubpages.com	288	6	
5. examiner.com	762	8	NF
6. Articlesbase.com	976	6	NF
7. Technorati.com	1,120	8	
8. associatedcontent.com	1,470	7	NF
9. Buzzle.com	1,618	5	
10. suite101.com	1,980	6	

Table 7.1 Ten popular Article Directories, as of November 2011

these writers' works more prominently. Much like print authors can develop a following for their work, online article directories make further writings available to readers interested in a particular author.

To create successful article content, one of the most important steps is to choose a good title. As most viewers will see the title first, and have to decide from that whether to read the rest of the article, creating an appealing title can make or break an article's distribution success. To draw in readers, the title should be concise and descriptive, as well as give a solid idea of what the article is about. To generate interest, the title should bring to mind a question that the reader wants to have answered.[*] This need creates an incentive to view the content. If the title is boring or does not bring to mind any interesting questions, it is unlikely that readers will take the time to view the article.

Above all, the article itself should deliver on the promise made by the title; be sure that the content adequately addresses the question or issue being discussed. Attempting to trick readers with a title that does not match the article body is a sure way to disappoint, frustrate, or annoy the viewer. Finally, some article directories have specific guidelines that titles must meet for publication; for example, capitalizing the first letter of every word or avoiding certain forms of punctuation.[3] Follow these rules to avoid unnecessary complications on the path to publication, and produce articles that people will be willing and able to read.

CASE STUDY

Using EzineArticles to Raise Awareness about Math Education

Introduction

Launched in November 1999, EzineArticles.com has attained a standing unequaled by other article directories.[4] It is one of the most popular article directories in the world and the favorite among Internet marketers because this highly trafficked site allows authors to link articles back to their websites, which can substantially improve search engine rankings.[5] EzineArticles has earned an authoritative reputation by employing human reviewers, who impose strict criteria for style and content, thus attracting real-world experts to publish tens of thousands of new articles each month.[6] In turn, these articles have been syndicated on millions of sites around the world.

Although most contributors are Internet marketers, others seek to establish themselves as an authority in a field or gain recognition for a brand or issue. Shirley Slick, a dedicated, experienced math educator, falls into this latter category. Slick

---

[*] The title itself does not have to be in the form of a question (although some article authors do successfully use that method). Even a plain statement can bring to mind a question the reader wants to have answered. For example, the simple title, "Successful Methods for Running a Social Media Marketing Campaign," might lead the reader to ask "what are those methods?" As long as the title is interesting and descriptive, it can lead the reader to wonder what content will support that title, causing the individual to read further.

uses EzineArticles to raise awareness about the problems with the way math is being taught in the United States along with suggesting possible solutions to the problem.

History**

Slick completed college degrees in Mathematics, Education, and Psychology. In addition, she sought out training in a variety of teaching techniques, with an emphasis on the latest in brain research.[7] Along with a unique combination of degrees, Slick has more than thirty years' experience in mathematics education. During these years Slick has held a number of roles in mathematics education.[8] She has been a "high school mathematics teacher for 20+ years, a private mathematics tutor, an adjunct mathematics professor for IUPUI in Indiana, and a teacher for the Automaker's Jobs' Banks Program."[9]

Slick saw that an evolution was occurring. Leading experts were changing the way they were thinking about educating people (of all ages) in mathematics. New theories were being developed, and conventional wisdom was being challenged. Optimistic about these changes, Slick was well positioned to further this movement thanks to her background in mathematics, education, and psychology.[10]

Challenge

Getting a Passing Grade

In Slick's eyes there is still a lot more progress left to be made. According to some estimates, the failure rate of general algebra classes in the United States is about an astonishing 50%. Since retiring from full-time teaching in 2005, Slick has sought new and innovative ways to combat this high failure rate.

Article writing is one of the ways Slick has found that she can make a difference. By publishing articles online, Slick is now able to reach and educate an audience well outside of her city, county, and even state.

Admittedly a math geek, Slick initially felt outside of her comfort zone when she took up article writing. Over time, though, Slick has become more comfortable with writing and realized the power of publishing articles online. Between her new-found confidence in writing and her expansive range of knowledge, Slick has become even more determined to accomplish her goal. That goal is twofold: to vastly reduce the algebra failure rate and to teach parents how to help their children learn how to do math.[11]

Strategy

Advice for New Authors

When asked about her choice of article writing as her communication method, Slick said, "When I retired from teaching, I knew I wanted to have a positive impact on parents with respect to mathematics without having to give speeches. (I'm great in

**Marc (2011, June 16), "Expert Author Showcase: Shirley Slick: The 11th edition in a series of posts showcasing quality-driven Diamond level Expert Authors and their article writing insights," EzineArticles Blog. © EzineArticles.com and Shirley Slick. Reprinted with permission.

front of high school students. Adults are a totally different issue!) I just had no idea how to start. This past fall, a friend recommended EzineArticles; and here I am."[12]

With Slick's new-found understanding of article publishing, she now has a number of helpful tips for people who want to become authors. Slick states that "[t]here were two things I did in the beginning before I ever wrote an article that I strongly suggest to every new author: (1) I read and re-read the Editorial Guidelines (http://ezinearticles.com/editorial-guidelines.html) until I practically had them memorized (I have never had an article rejected), and (2) I decided on my initial important niches—I chose four – and then wrote either title ideas or at least potential topics for each."[13] Slick continues:

I have a notebook of topics divided by category. I initially wrote 40 to 50 topic ideas for each niche. Now, when I write an article, I tend to think of several related articles that need to be written, which I try to write next or add to the notebook. If I read an article I disagree with, I write about that before touching my initial list. If I decide on a series to write, I put those topics on a separate page. Any new ideas I get, I generally try to write immediately because the article is taking shape in my mind right then. If I wait, I sometimes "lose the fire."

Writing Titles

Another good piece of advice from Slick for those starting out is to "do [your] homework" on writing titles. Slick's biggest regret so far is not paying enough attention to the power of title writing. She said, "I spent too much time trying to think up 'cutesy' titles which didn't do a good enough job of explaining what the article was about. I think I was trying to write titles for EzineArticles editors rather than the people who would be reading the articles."[14]

For those just beginning their writing career, Slick recommends they look up top authors in their area of interest and spend time analyzing the titles in use. Ask questions like "What titles grab your attention and make you want to read the article? Is there anything that for sure turns you away from an article?"[15] There will be distinct differences. It is important to note which titles are "bad" and why. Another great resource, according to Slick, is EzineArticles: "EzineArticles offers as suggestions (http://blog.ezinearticles.com/2011/06/article-titles-for-you.html)."[16] It is also worth checking out their tips for writing article titles (http://media.ezinearticles.com/pdf/ezinearticles/training/full/article-title.pdf). Slick further suggests doing a similar analysis for articles read on the EzineArticles.com homepage, as the articles that appear are by writers with a wide range of skill levels.

Results

The quality and quantity of articles contributed by Shirley Slick to EzineArticles have netted her Diamond-level status, EzineArticles's most prestigious ranking for expert authors. It signifies genuine expertise on a topic, consistent contributions, and top-notch writing skill.[17] This status clearly demonstrates her success in using EzineArticles to make people aware of the serious problems and possible solutions for the problems with math education in this country.

Although Slick's primary focus right now is writing articles, she is also looking at a variety of other avenues. She says, "The plan that is taking shape in my brain is to turn these [articles] into ebooks and CDs. I think most parents would rather listen to math information than read it. I haven't yet finished a series so that plan is still on hold. Right now, I am analyzing what kinds of articles garner publishers and what is getting the most reads. I'm also using Google Analytics to see if there is a pattern to where my website is being accessed, what on my website is of interest and what needs to be changed."[18]

Slick has one final thought to pass on: "A special THANKS to my mother for pushing and helping this math geek master grammar, punctuation and spelling. I wouldn't be a Diamond without you, Mom!"[19]

Creating White Papers and E-Books

The term "white paper" is derived from "white book," an official publication by a national government.[20] In public policy, white papers are delivered to policy makers to inform them on important issues. Businesses eventually began to adopt the term, referring to informative documents for important clients as white papers. In this context a "good white paper is written for a business audience, defines a problem, and offers a solution, but it does not pitch a particular product or company."[21] Marketing messages in a white paper should be as subtle as possible, if they appear at all. According to Michael Knowles, a **white paper** "is a technical document that describes how a technology or product solves a particular problem. It's a marketing document and a technical document, yet it doesn't go too far in either direction"[22] (see Figure 7.1 for an example).

What will be an effective white paper is defined mostly by its audience's expectations. A white paper is expected to have at least six pages of text and to provide useful information about a business or technical issue. A white paper should contain sources, facts, and figures.[23] Further, white papers are typically intended for the reader to review before making a purchase.[†] Online distribution, which avoids warehousing and printing costs, has made white papers both easier to access and more popular for businesses.[24]

Most of all, writing content-heavy but appealing marketing content, such as white papers, takes strong writing skills and practice. Having a solid process to guide the writing effort will make these potentially daunting publications more manageable. Business owner and white paper author Al Kemp lays out his nine-step process for writing white papers.[25] In order, these steps are Assess Needs; Plan; Acquire Information; Organize Content; Design the Look and Feel; Write; Illustrate; Review, Revise, and Approve; and finally Publish. A brief description of the process, along with insights from other white paper authorities, appears below.

STEP #1. ASSESS NEEDS

In order to make decisions about the white paper's structure and content, it is necessary to have a clear vision of the goals one is attempting to achieve. These may be *overt* goals that are clear to the reader (such as educating the public about a product or providing information about a problem) or *covert*

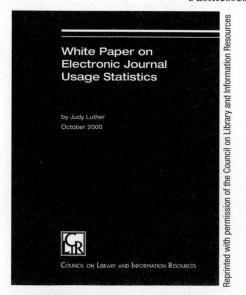

White Paper on
Electronic Journal
Usage Statistics

by Judy Luther
October 2000

COUNCIL ON LIBRARY AND INFORMATION RESOURCES

Reprinted with permission of the Council on Library and Information Resources

Figure 7.1 **Example of a White Paper**

[†]So-called white papers that are intended for postpurchase reading are more accurately termed technical support documents.

goals that might not be directly mentioned (such as increasing sales or creating doubts about the capabilities of competing products).

After considering the goals, define the audience that the white paper is being written for. It is generally agreed that to write a successful white paper, it is necessary to understand the audience.[26] What are the personal characteristics, jobs, and work responsibilities of the audience members? How large a company is each associated with and in what sector of the economy? Ideally, identify different segments of the audience based on job descriptions because such knowledge will provide more specific insight about audience members' behavior. Further, having a clear idea of the ideal audience for a white paper will help later when deciding which material to include and what to leave out. It is possible that several white papers on similar subjects must be produced, each tailored to a different set of readers.

STEP #2. PLAN

After or during the first step, start planning how the white paper will be constructed. Consult with the sales department to see how the white paper will be integrated into the sales process, and determine how the white paper will be distributed. This process will help to further define the audience and to inform the structure and tone of the final white paper. Next, decide responsibilities and estimate costs. A polished white paper will require research, writing, illustration, editing, and review. Calculate out-of-pocket expenses as well as labor costs in order to provide a rough figure for the time and resources needed. Then prepare a schedule and project plan to lay out when the white paper will be completed.

STEP #3. ACQUIRE INFORMATION

In order to write a good white paper, expertise is necessary. The relevant knowledge can be gained from reading and research or through interviews with authorities in the field. Interviews are especially valuable for unearthing information that may not yet be broadly available. After gathering the facts, analyze how they can support the goals set for the white paper. Obviously information about functionality of the product will be important, but that should be supplemented with other, less product-specific facts as well.

STEP #4. ORGANIZE CONTENT

It is likely that step number three may have uncovered an unmanageable amount of information, or at least more than will be needed for the white paper being written. To determine what is most important, one option is to create a simple outline with groups and subgroups to represent different themes or strands of information. Too many subgroups can make later organization complicated, so do not create too many specific groups. After this process is complete, hopefully the outline that has been created will become a roadmap for the final case study. Choose the starting point for the case study (perhaps a story or anecdote that will draw in the reader), and then put the major topics in order to follow.

STEP #5. DESIGN THE LOOK AND FEEL

Different audiences may have varying expectations for document presentation and formatting. Think about what the model reader would prefer. If a graphic illustration professional is available, he or she should be able to create the "look" after being given some general guidelines. If no professional is available, consider using one of the preconstructed page templates that come with many word processing programs.

Almost always, the page layout should center on ease of browsing. Keep in mind, most readers will not go word by word through a white paper. Instead, online viewers tend to scan over text quickly.[27] This reading practice makes informative headings, visual aids, and short paragraphs serious advantages. Big blocks of text are less pleasant to read and may turn off a reader altogether. While white papers should convey a lot of information, they should also be easy on the eyes and appealing to online consumers. Most white papers will not be printed, so be sure that the final product will look good on a computer screen.

Remember to create a catchy title page. In the planning stage, some sort of rough title should have been considered. Choose a layout that is aesthetically pleasing and draws the reader in further into the paper. Also, consider including an abstract on the first page to give a general idea of the topic and conclusions. Further, in this stage, select the font, line length, spacing, page size, and color scheme that will be applied to the document. Avoid cramped layouts; keep some white space to make the text more readable.

STEP #6. WRITE

Fill in the content that was outlined earlier using details gathered through research. White paper audiences expect to be educated, but they want technical elements to be combined with narrative and other interesting content. If the product is technology based, some space to explain how the item works is necessary, but do not become bogged down in technical details. To inspire action, white papers have to move beyond purely technical topics.[28] Ultimately, most readers want to see what the benefits of a product are, not just its functionality. Make sure the white paper fulfills both objectives. Whenever possible, quantify costs and benefits in specific ways, and estimate amounts of money that can be gained or lost by certain problems or solutions. Tangible information that assists in decision making will draw the most significant viewers toward a white paper.

Prevent miscommunication with readers by explaining all acronyms and by using consistent wording when defining each concept. White papers may be accessed by people with a broad range of familiarity with the topic at hand. Readers expect to learn and be challenged but are not generally excited to read a condensed user's manual. Use examples whenever possible to illustrate ideas as well as any other means to avoid losing the audience in obscure technical discussions.

When writing, keep the style direct and uncomplicated. For the first draft, focus on explaining the material well, and worry about eloquence during the revisions. At all stages, avoid excessive jargon or puffed-up marketing rhetoric. When studying news releases for word usage that David Meerman Scott refers to as "gobbledygook," he finds that that the phrases "next generation," "flexible," "world class," "scalable," and "easy to use" are employed thousands of times.[29] Other overused marketing phrases include "industry standard," "groundbreaking," and "user friendly." When employed in a white paper, these words call to mind a marketing press release, not an educational document. Such usage sacrifices the main advantage of white papers, which is that they can "penetrate most organizations' anti-marketing defenses because they are sought after and brought into the organization by decision-makers."[30] Be sure to eliminate unhelpful buzzwords to convey the correct impression about the white paper.

While some will say that it deviates from classic white paper format, forming the paper around a list can occasionally be a helpful design.[31] While more detailed than a list of tips, a list-based white paper can provide valuable information in an easily digested fashion for the hurried reader. The danger is that a list may seem too shallow or overly simplified and thus alienate the audience. The term "white paper" implies a level of information and analysis that must be upheld or risk disappointing readers. However, keeping the white paper light and readable by using bullet points or lists is an intelligent tactic.

STEP #7. ILLUSTRATE

Good white papers contain a visual as well as textual element to keep readers engaged. Especially with more complicated material, visual aids are essential in order to focus the audience's attention and to explain complicated concepts. Creating visual elements should occur at the same time as the writing process so that both elements complement each other.

Keep in mind that some viewers will skim through the white paper before deciding to read it in full. To draw in these readers, ensure that the illustrations convey the primary content and selling points of the white paper. Using charts to display data, well-chosen pictures to illustrate examples, and documenting the sources will help convince an unsure reader that the paper contains valuable material that is worth the reading time.

STEP #8. REVIEW, REVISE, AND APPROVE

In a first round of reviewing, the white paper should be evaluated by experts in the field or ideally by some of the people interviewed during step three. These reviewers can catch factual errors or correct imprecise explanations. The final draft should also be reviewed by the senior management of the company who is sponsoring the white paper. As a result of these reviews, there may be changes to both organization and content. Improvements for the final draft might include writing style revision, improved flow of the text with images, a grammar check as well as a check of the spelling of names, and so on. Before sending the white paper to publication, also check with the legal and accounting departments to avoid later conflicts.

STEP #9. PUBLISH

If the white paper will be published electronically, this step can be rather simple. Before publishing, always check the final output to ensure that it correctly transferred from final draft to final product version. If a print version is to be produced, check for errors in the proofs before printing, and avoid the potential high cost of reprinting to correct errors.

This nine-step formula for crafting a white paper may seem overly exhaustive. However, it reflects an industry standard and the very high expectations of white papers. Making a half-hearted attempt at writing a white paper may be worse than doing nothing at all: while an excellent white paper signals expertise, a poor one demonstrates just the opposite. White papers have existed for many years, and the process for creating them is well established. Failing to meet the standards or using the term "white paper" loosely for publications that do not meet the formula is an easy way to lose credibility with social media professionals.

While the process described above is tailored toward white papers, it can also be applied, with minor modification, to writing e-books (discussed below) or lengthier articles. In many ways the steps to writing either will be similar. As e-books have existed for less time than white papers, there is much more flexibility of opinion as to the "correct" way to write an e-book. On the one hand, this flexibility is a disadvantage because e-books convey less prestige and authority than the official-sounding white paper. On the other hand, the flexibility of e-book formatting makes it a useful platform for creative authors to showcase their thoughts.[††] In any case, applying a level of organization and detail that would be found in an industry white paper toward writing an e-book is sure to generate better results than a haphazard approach to authoring.

[††]Due to their success, some e-books have traveled from the online world into print. For example, David Meerman Scott's *The New Rules of Marketing & PR*, which we have quoted extensively in this chapter and other chapters, was first published as an e-book before reaching a paper edition.

The Mises Institute Advances Knowledge of Economics through Online Articles and E-Books

Since 1995 the Ludwig von Mises Institute has been publishing online content to further the cause of classical liberalism (libertarianism) in favor of free markets and against state intervention in the economy. Its contributors are strongly influenced by Austrian School, which emphasizes the role of individuals and the danger of aggregative thinking. While this stance may be controversial, the Mises Institute has grown to fame as one of the largest and best-known think tanks in the classical liberal (libertarian) tradition. Publishing articles, journals, and e-books has been a primary feature of the institute's social media strategy.

History

The institute's namesake, Ludwig von Mises, was born September 29, 1881, in the city of Lemberg. While initially an economic leftist, at an early age Mises discovered Carl Menger's *Principles of Economics*, which impressed on him the importance of individual action rather than mechanistic equations as a methodology for studying economics.[32] This conviction would influence Mises and generations of future Austrian School economists to come.

Mises's first well-known publication, *The Theory of Money and Credit* (1912), established a connection between micro- and macroeconomics that had been little appreciated before that time. This perceived connection became the core of Mises's (and later, many Austrian economists') theory of boom and bust driven by monetary expansion. According to his theory, expanding the money supply fuels malinvestment due to artificially low interest rates.[33] When the plans of savers and investors become disjointed by monetary injections, it makes a correction (economic recession) inevitable, as the amount of real savings proves inadequate to meet the demands of investors. This model contradicted the widely held belief that a government could adjust the money supply to manage and avoid economic hardship.

As time went on, the sophistication of Mises's critique of government intervention continued to develop. In 1920 Mises published his famous article "Economic Calculation in the Socialist Commonwealth," which convincingly argued that socialist planners could not successfully manage an economy (an unpopular conclusion at

> The social function of economic science consists precisely in developing sound economic theories and in exploding the fallacies of vicious reasoning. In the pursuit of this task the economist incurs the deadly enmity of all mountebanks and charlatans whose shortcuts to an earthly paradise he debunks.
>
> —Ludwig von Mises, *Economic Freedom and Interventionism*, pp. 51–52

the time, but one later vindicated by the collapse of the USSR and other socialist states). He would continue to write other noteworthy books and articles throughout his career, some of which are still frequently read, referenced, and cited for their relevance and insight in modern times.

> **The sharper the competition, the better it serves its social function to improve economic production.**
>
> —Ludwig von Mises, *A Critique of Interventionism*, p. 84.

In 1940 Mises immigrated to the United States to avoid persecution under Hitler's Germany. There, he taught at New York University until his retirement in 1969. While he had difficulties in finding paid teaching work at either Austrian or American universities, Mises's intellectual legacy would go on to influence several other important economists. In 1974 Mises's disciple Friedrich August von Hayek would win the Nobel Prize in Economics for development and exposition of his mentor's theories on monetary policy and economic calculation.

Following Mises's death in 1973, several intellectual admirers sought permission from his widow Margit von Mises to create an institution that would honor and uphold the Misesian contribution to economics. The Ludwig von Mises Institute was founded in October 1982. The institute's motto, *Tu ne cede malis, sed contra audentior ito* (Latin for "Do not give in to evil but proceed ever more boldly against it," from Virgil's *Aeneid*, Book VI), is a fitting tribute to Mises's unrelenting determination to expose what were, in his view, dangerous economic fallacies of the time.[34] Institute founder Llewellyn H. Rockwell, Jr. was the organization's president until 2009 when Douglas French assumed responsibility for guiding the Ludwig von Mises Institute into the twenty-first century.

Challenge

The Austrian School approach to economics has never been a popular one because it rejects the mathematical focus and emphasis on government control that has driven most "mainstream" economic thought in the last century. Further, many conclusions of the Austrian School are radically libertarian, and even by the most optimistic estimates, only around 15% of the U.S. population identifies with libertarianism.[35] Even fewer would likely agree with the conclusions of the Austrians, who are especially radical in their antigovernment beliefs. As a result, the potential audience that the Mises Institute seeks to reach is a limited one. Providing valuable content, which could both develop and expand the reach of Austrian School economic thought, became a primary challenge.

Strategy

While the Mises Institute now publishes daily articles and hosts several economic journals, the core of its content revolves around electronic books, both modern and historical.[36] The institute hosts community forums, blogs, and chat rooms but, perhaps most importantly, possesses a huge collection of literature featuring thousands of free e-books.[37]

In addition to hosting content on its primary website, the Mises Institute uses other platforms, such as Scribd, to bring its material to readers.[38] The institute's website now serves as a meeting place where libertarians and followers of Austrian

School economics share news and opinion pieces that they find relevant. The institute has also made available writings from well-known libertarian politician Ron Paul, who has impacted American political thinking in recent years.[39] With in-depth content and a presence on nearly every major social media platform, the Mises Institute has employed e-books, articles, and other social media marketing tools to great success.

Results

Thanks in part to its thought leadership on a unique branch of economics, the Ludwig von Mises Institute now draws students from over twenty countries to study and learn at its campus in Auburn, Alabama. Some have wondered "How does a world-class think tank end up in east Alabama?" The answer is found in the quiet setting, the low cost of living, and the proximity to Auburn University, one of the few Austrian School-tolerant colleges at the time of the institute's founding.[40] Beyond this standard reply, however, the role of social media must also be mentioned. With its focus on free high-quality content, the institute's physical location has become much less important than its prominent position online. While it is common for think tanks to place themselves close to the seat of power, the Austrian School's distaste from central control makes both its location and emphasis on social networking seem a natural choice.

> **It is a widespread fallacy that skillful advertising can talk the consumers into buying everything that the advertiser wants them to buy. The consumer is, according to this legend, simply defenseless against high-pressure advertising. If this were true, success or failure in business would depend on the mode of advertising only.**
>
> —Ludwig von Mises, *Human Action*, pp. 317, 321.

Although it is a nonprofit organization, the Mises Institute has generated a brisk business in both direct sales and viewer contributions, with thousands of donors from the United States as well as eighty other countries.[41] While it continues to struggle for recognition from university economics departments as well as seek approval in the court of public opinion, the Ludwig von Mises Institute's publishing strategy has ensured that the founding texts and knowledge of Austrian School economics will not disappear. As time goes on and the institute's online library grows, the Mises Institute will most likely continue to become more influential in the world of ideas.

© Cengage Learning 2013

Marketing with Articles, E-Books, and White Papers

An **e-book** (which stands for electronic book and is also sometimes called a digital book, ebook, or eBook) is defined by the Oxford English Dictionary as "an electronic version of a printed book that can be read on a computer or handheld device designed specifically for this purpose."[42] While precise, this definition does not add much for a social media practitioner. For the purposes of social media marketing, David Meerman Scott "define[s] an e-book as a PDF-formatted document that identifies a market problem and supplies an answer to the problem…. Well executed e-books have lots of white space, interesting graphics and images, and copy that is typically written in a lighter style than the denser white paper."[43] However, both e-books and white papers require strong written communication skills, content, and great presentation to be implemented successfully.[‡]

In most cases the ultimate goal for article, white paper, or e-book marketing will be the same: draw attention and develop a company's reputation for thought leadership and then use that expertise to generate sales. In order for this strategy to be successful, however, the audience must not perceive the content to be overt marketing material. As mentioned above in step one of writing a white paper, keeping a distinction between overt and covert goals is crucial.

If the end goal is to sell a product, doing so effectively with an article, white paper, or e-book will require more subtle framing than with a standard advertising pitch. Do not include the product name in the description or title.[44] Instead, describe a problem, some common solutions, and then finally discuss what special benefits the product being marketed has in solving that problem. In every instance, "solutions are only introduced after a significant case has been established, demonstrating a clear need."[45] Put valuable, general information first and then specific details about the product's advantages toward the end (if they need be mentioned at all). The real benefit of publications may be much greater than a few sales leads; indeed, a "single well-written white paper can propel a business to the thought leadership position and lead to enormous business opportunities."[46] Keep an open mind, and be prepared for unexpected benefits from authoring content-heavy material.

The style of white papers, articles, and e-books has evolved over time. Tighter budgets due to recent economic conditions have caused a shift to shorter white papers, with more sales-oriented content and less information.[47] In order to compete in this environment, new white paper publishers would do well to include pictures and easily read information in order to keep up with the flood of brief documents that now exist online. However, it is still a wise move to avoid overt sales pitches in order to help distinguish from less sophisticated white papers that confuse information delivery with direct marketing. Do not miss the larger opportunity to advance a brand's image and reputation by making the mistake of treating these publications as purely a marketing platform.

Another question now arises. How many white papers or e-books should be published as part of a social media marketing campaign? According to Gordon Graham, who has built a reputation around his expertise on white papers, there are five factors to consider: experience, market segments, problems solved, competition, and budget.[48] A company with little experience should write one or two white papers and then evaluate what the firm has learned before writing more. If there are many market segments, more white papers may be required in order to cover all of them. Depending on how many different problems the company can solve and depending on the degree of differences between these problems, more white papers may be needed for each problem area. If there are many competitors in the field publishing white papers, it

---

[‡]What distinguishes a white paper from an e-book? Arguably, very little, and what difference exists is likely more of style than substance. Users typically expect white papers to be on technical subjects and contain large amounts of information, while they expect an e-book to be both educational and entertaining. To generalize, white papers are written for business decision makers, while e-books are aimed at a general audience.

can also influence the optimal amount of publishing to do. Finally, the budget available will determine how much research and publishing an organization can afford to fund.

An advantage of e-books and white papers is that they have high-perceived value to the recipients, and they typically require the reader to provide an email address or other information to download or access. Sometimes e-books or white papers are only available for purchase and are directly monetized in this fashion. However, for most marketing purposes, the goodwill and customer information that can be gained from giving these publications away for free is much more valuable. Collecting email addresses through the distribution of a white paper gives valuable leads to the sales team and can also generate information on customer demographics, common areas of interest, and more.

White papers are primarily used by business-to-business marketers because the tone and content is designed for business executives. E-books are more commonly used in the consumer market. However, there can be substantial overlap between the two forms. For example, a bicycle shop might publish a white paper on how to find the right-sized bike, a beginner's guide to cyclist lingo, bicycling etiquette, or tips for new riders. These white paper topics might be valuable to general readers and help generate new customers. To connect with seasoned riders, the white papers could contain more advanced topics. The most important part is to find relevant content for the marketing goals and to target audiences and then put that content into a clear and useful format as either a white paper or e-book.

EXERCISE CASE STUDY

Soroptimist International of the Americas: Using White Papers to Raise Awareness about Issues Affecting Women and Girls Worldwide

Introduction

In nineteen countries and territories, Soroptimist International of the Americas (SIA) works to improve the lives of women and girls. SIA club members strive to accomplish this goal by participating in a wide variety of programs and local projects that involve education, employment, healthcare, disaster recovery, and the prevention of domestic violence, sexual assault, and sex trafficking.[49] The term "Soroptimist" is a combination of the Latin words *soror* meaning "sister" and *optimus* meaning "best," which loosely translates to "best for sisters."

History

The parent organization, Soroptimist International, was founded in 1921 as "a world-wide volunteer service organization for business and professional women who work to improve the lives of women and girls, in local communities and throughout the world."[50] The vision statement for the organization is to "[b]e the leading international organization of business and professional women united through volunteer efforts to enable women and girls to live their dreams, take control of their lives, and live according to their own values."[51]

The worldwide organization consists of four divisions (or federations): Soroptimist International of the Americas (SIA), SI of Great Britain and Ireland, SI of Europe, and SI of South West Pacific. The organization's world headquarters is located in Cambridge, United Kingdom.[52] Today, with over 95,000 members in more than 125 countries, the organization donates time and money to local projects and international efforts to make the lives of girls and women better. The SIA "was formed at the Washington, DC, conference in 1928."[53]

Challenge[‡‡] ....

Soroptimist has been researching and publishing white papers on issues important to women and girls for several years. Each year, new white papers are added and existing papers are updated to ensure that information is current. Soroptimist white papers focus on topics important to Soroptimists and women and girls worldwide. Currently, Soroptimist white papers are offered free of charge on the Soroptimist website (http://www.soroptimist.org/members/program/SoroptimistLocalClub-Projects.html).

The specific goal of Soroptimist white papers is to raise awareness of issues important to Soroptimist and to influence others to work to improve the lives of women and girls in local communities and throughout the world. Also, the white papers help to promote Soroptimist as an expert on international women's issues and as an organization addressing those issues.

Strategy ....

Soroptimist white papers can be used by Soroptimist members and clubs in a number of different ways. This resource contains a number of suggestions for club use. In addition, it includes abstracts for each of the current papers, the URL address, significant dates with which to use the white papers, and suggestions for other federation resources to use in conjunction with the papers.

Soroptimist Club Use for White Papers

1. **Educate Club Members**
   Using white papers as the center of a club program meeting is a simple and easy way to educate members about an issue of interest to them. Some specific ideas are:

   - A club can design a quiz on the white paper and give awards to those members scoring the highest. It can appoint a member to lead the discussion.

   - A club can email the white paper to all members prior to the club meeting. It can have a member-led discussion—like a book club.

[‡‡]Raising Awareness about Issues Affecting Women and Girls Worldwide, Soroptimist White Papers. © Soroptimist International of the Americas. Reprinted with permission.

- A club can hand out or email a white paper to all members. It can ask members to read the paper, highlighting information they did not previously know. Go around the room asking each member to discuss what she learned.

- A club can use the white papers to launch a discussion about ideas for new club projects. After presenting the information in the paper, members can brainstorm about ways the club could address the issue in the community or worldwide.

2. **Promote Soroptimist Programs**

   Because white papers focus on topics important to Soroptimists, frequently a tie exists between federation projects and the white papers. When promoting Soroptimist programs in the community, a club can use the white papers to give depth to an argument about why the programs are important. For instance, white papers are available on women and education (Women's Opportunity Awards), women and disaster relief (the Soroptimist Disaster Grants for Women and Girls), domestic violence in the workplace (Soroptimist Workplace Campaign to End Domestic Violence), and women and trafficking (Soroptimists STOP Trafficking). The white papers can help the club to promote the importance of Soroptimist programs in the community. If applicable, the club can use the white papers to promote local club projects as well.

3. **Educate the Community**

   Soroptimist Home Page

   White papers can serve as the centerpiece of awareness activities in the community. For example, if a club wants to present a program to a local school about women and education, it can use the white paper as a starting point to build a compelling case about the importance of women's education. Oftentimes, club members are asked to speak on topics important to women in their local communities. To find out important background information about a topic—and what Soroptimist is doing about it—these members check to see if Soroptimist offers a white paper on the topic.

4. **Interest the Media**

   The best time to announce these white papers is when related topics come up in the media... White papers can be used to create impressive opinion editorials or letters to the editor around these dates or when the topics are in the news. In addition, if the club is holding an event and inviting media, it can include a white paper addressing the theme of the event in the press kit.

5. **Strengthen Advocacy Efforts**

   When the club chooses a position to advocate for or against, the Soroptimist white papers can provide the information needed to prepare an advocacy statement and plan a campaign. It can provide the background information needed to build a coherent argument and an effective campaign.

6. **Raise Funds**

Donors want to know why their contributions are needed and where they are being used. If the club is holding a community event or giving out federation awards, it can appeal to the audience to support the Soroptimist programs. It can distribute white papers that correspond to the topic of the event or the award. For example, if the club is disbursing Women's Opportunity Awards, it can distribute the Women and Education white paper in order to educate donors about the importance of the award and to provide information about what Soroptimist is doing to ensure women's access to education. Or, if the club is holding a breast cancer event, it can hand out the "Breast Cancer and Low Income Women" to possible donors. White papers can also be given out to donors as a thank-you. If a donation is received from a community member who was responding to a specific club project, the club can send that person the white paper on that topic, along with a thank-you for the donation.

Results ....

The Soroptimist's cumulative impact has been significant. According the organization's 2009-2010 *Program Impact Report*, "more than $2 million was distributed through federation programs, helping more than 10,000 women and girls live their dreams of a better life."[54] Soroptimist participates and funds programs to ensure their strength and effectiveness. For example, recipients of their Women's Opportunity Awards, who have typically suffered hardships such as poverty and abuse, receive skills training and education so that they can find employment and reclaim their lives. Soroptimist also provides Disaster Grants for Women and Girls around the world, offering funding to rebuild homes and lives after natural disasters strike. These programs, along with numerous other awards, grants, and programs, have made SIA club members an important part of the international effort to improve the lives of girls and women.

Review Questions for Soroptimist International of the Americas Case Study

1. What are some of the ways SIA uses white papers to raise awareness about issues affecting girls and women?

2. How might this organization's white paper strategy and tactics be applied to other organizations or companies?

3. What are some of the possible drawbacks to using white papers in an attempt to influence people?

4. How could SIA use article directories and e-books to further raise awareness about issues affecting girls and women?

Notes

1. Barker, Donald I., Melissa S. Barker, and Katherine Pinard (2012), *Internet Research Illustrated*, 6th ed. (Boston, MA: Course Technology/Cengage Learning). Retrieved September 7, 2011, from http://www.cengage.com/search/productOverview. do?N=+16+4294922451&Ntk=P_Isbn13&Ntt=9781133190387
2. "Article Directory" (n.d.), *Wikipedia*. Retrieved July 3, 2011, from http://en.wikipedia.org/wiki/Article_directory
3. "The EzineArticles.com Article Writing: Article Title Training" (2008), EzineArticles. Retrieved June 26, 2011, from http://media.ezinearticles.com/pdf/ezinearticles/training/full/article-title.pdf
4. "Ezine Articles Review" (2009, July 23), IM Report Card. Retrieved June 24, 2011, from http://www.imreportcard.com/services/ezine-articles
5. "Top 50 Article Directories by Traffic, PageRank" (2011, June 24), Virtual Real Estate Toolbar. Retrieved June 24, 2011, from http://www.vretoolbar.com/articles/directories.php
6. "What Can EzineArticles.com Do for You?" (n.d.), About EzineArticles. Retrieved June 24, 2011 from http://ezinearticles.com/about.html
7. About Me (n.d.), "My Slick Tips," myslicktips.com. Retrieved June 26, 2011, from http://myslicktips.com/
8. Marc (2011, June 16), "Expert Author Showcase: Shirley Slick: The 11th edition in a series of posts showcasing quality-driven Diamond level Expert Authors and their article writing insights," *EzineArticles Blog*. Retrieved September 16, 2011, from http://blog.ezinearticles.com/2011/06/showcase-shirley-slick.html
9. Ibid.
10. Ibid.
11. Shirley Slick (2010, January), LinkedIn Profile. Retrieved June 26, 2011, from http://www.linkedin.com/pub/shirley-slick/28/502/574
12. Marc (2011, June 8), "Expert Author Showcase: Shirley Slick: The 11th edition in a series of posts showcasing quality-driven Diamond level Expert Authors and their article writing insights," *EzineArticles Blog*. Retrieved September 16, 2011 from http://blog.ezinearticles.com/2011/06/showcase-shirley-slick.html
13. Ibid.
14. Ibid.
15. Ibid.
16. Ibid.
17. "New 'Diamond' Account Level Unveiled" (2011, March 7), *EzineArticles Blog*. Retrieved June 24, 2011, from http://blog.ezinearticles.com/2011/03/diamond-account-level.html
18. Ibid.
19. Ibid.
20. Stelzner, Michael A. (2009), "How to Write a White Paper—A White Paper on White Papers." Retrieved June 22, 2011, from http://www.stelzner.com/copy-HowTo-whitepapers.php
21. Scott, David Meerman (2009), *The New Rules of Marketing & PR* (Hoboken, NJ: John Wiley), p. 135.
22. Knowles, Michael (2002), "How to Write a White Paper," Michael Knowles Consulting. Retrieved June 22, 2011, from http://www.mwknowles.com/free_articles/white_paper/white_paper.html
23. Graham, Gordon (2009, July 7), "When Is a White Paper NOT a White Paper?" WhitePaperSource. Retrieved June 21, 2011, from http://www.whitepapersource.com/writing/when-is-a-white-paper-not-a-white-paper/
24. Kantor, Jonathan (2009, September 9), "Understanding White Paper Longevity: Why White Papers Survive in the Midst of a Printing Industry Downturn," WhitePaperSource. Retrieved June 21, 2011, from http://www.whitepapersource.com/writing/understanding-white-paper-longevity-why-white-papers-survive-in-the-midst-of-a-printing-industry-downturn/
25. Kemp, Al (2005), *White Paper Writing Guide: How to Achieve Marketing Goals by Explaining Technical Ideas* (Arvada, CO: Impact Technical Publications). Retrieved June 22, 2011, from http://www.impactonthenet.com/wp-guide.pdf

26. Graham, Gordon (2010, January 5), "The First Key to White Paper Success," WhitePaperSource. Retrieved June 21, 2011, from http://www.whitepapersource.com/writing/the-first-key-to-white-paper-success/

27. Golden, Michelle (2011), *Social Media Strategies for Professionals and Their Firms* (Hoboken, NJ: John Wiley), p. 265.

28. Belfiore, Michael (2009, August 11), "Avoiding Information Overload: Strategies for Researching and Writing Clearly," WhitePaperSource. Retrieved June 21, 2011, from http://www.whitepapersource.com/writing/avoiding-information-overload-strategies-for-researching-and-writing-clearly/

29. Scott, David Meerman (2009), *The New Rules of Marketing & PR* (Hoboken, NJ: John Wiley), p. 145.

30. Stelzner, Michael A. (2006), *Writing White Papers: How to Capture Readers and Keep Them Engaged* (Poway, CA: WhitePaperSource), p. 5.

31. Graham, Gordon (2010, April 3), "How to Write a White Paper, by the Numbers," WhitePaperSource. Retrieved June 21, 2011, from http://www.whitepapersource.com/writing/how-to-write-a-white-paper-by-the-numbers/

32. Rothbard, Murray N. (2005, July 27), "Ludwig von Mises (1881-1973)," Ludwig von Mises Institute. Retrieved June 26, 2011, from http://mises.org/daily/1876

33. Mises, Ludwig von (1912 [1953]), *The Theory of Money and Credit* (New Haven, CT: Yale University Press). Available online at http://mises.org/books/Theory_Money_Credit/Contents.aspx

34. "Ludwig von Mises Institute" (n.d.), *Wikipedia*. Retrieved June 26, 2011, from http://en.wikipedia.org/wiki/Ludwig_von_Mises_Institute

35. Boaz, David, and David Kirby (2006, October 23), "The Libertarian Vote," Cato Institute. Retrieved June 26, 2011, from http://www.cato.org/pub_display.php?pub_Id=6735

36. Literature (n.d.), Ludwig von Mises Institute. Retrieved June 26, 2011, from http://mises.org/literature.aspx?action=subject&Id=117

37. "About the Mises Institute" (n.d.), Ludwig von Mises Institute. Retrieved June 15, 2011, from http://mises.org/about.aspx

38. "Ludwig von Mises Institute" (n.d.), Scribd. Retrieved June 26, 2011, from http://www.scribd.com/Ludwig%20von%20Mises%20Institute

39. "Ron Paul Literature Archive" (n.d.), Ludwig von Mises Institute. Retrieved June 26, 2011, from http://mises.org/literature.aspx?action=author&Id=392

40. Wingfield, Kyle (2006, August 4), "Sweet Home Alabama," *Wall Street Journal*. Retrieved June 15, 2011, from http://online.wsj.com/article/SB115466297072926763.html?

41. "About the Mises Institute" (n.d.), Ludwig von Mises Institute. Retrieved June 15, 2011, from http://mises.org/about.aspx

42. e-book(e-book) (2011), Oxford Dictionaries. Retrieved June 22, 2011, from http://oxforddictionaries.com/definition/e-book?region=us

43. Scott, David Meerman (2009), *The New Rules of Marketing & PR* (Hoboken, NJ: John Wiley), p. 136.

44. Kranz, Jonathan (2010, March 9), "Do the Flip: How to Turn Product/Service Features into White Paper Topics," WhitePaperSource. Retrieved June 21, 2011, from http://www.whitepapersource.com/writing/do-the-flip-how-to-turn-productservice-features-into-white-paper-topics/

45. Stelzner, Michael A. (2006), *Writing White Papers: How to Capture Readers and Keep Them Engaged* (Poway, CA: WhitePaperSource), p. 4.

46. Ibid., p. 1.

47. Kantor, Jonathan (2010, January 5) "The Recession's Impact on White Papers," WhitePaperSource. Retrieved June 21, 2011, from http://www.whitepapersource.com/writing/the-recessions-impact-on-white-papers/

48. Graham, Gordon (2009, August 11), "How Many White Papers Are 'Enough'? Some Thoughts for Marketers," WhitePaperSource. Retrieved June 24, 2011, from http://www.whitepapersource.com/marketing/how-many-white-papers-are-enough-some-thoughts-for-marketers/

49. *Soroptimist International of the Americas Program Impact Report* (2009-2010), Soroptimist. Retrieved July 2, 2011, from http://www.soroptimist.org/members/program/ProgramDocs/GeneralInformation/English/ProgramImpactReport.pdf

50. "Soroptimist International" (n.d.), *Wikipedia*. Retrieved July 2, 2011, from http://en.wikipedia.org/wiki/Soroptimist_International

51. "Soroptimist Vision & Mission" (2010, September), Soroptimist. Retrieved July 2, 2011, from http://www.soroptimist.org/whoweare/vision_mission.html

52. Ibid.

53. "Soroptimist—A Brief History" (2010, January), Soroptimist. Retrieved July 2, 2011, from http://www.soroptimist.org/members/membership/MembershipDocs/NewMembers/History.pdf

54. *Soroptimist International of the Americas Program Impact Report* (2009-2010), Soroptimist. Retrieved July 2, 2011, from http://www.soroptimist.org/members/program/ProgramDocs/GeneralInformation/English/ProgramImpactReport.pdf

Sharing Videos

Video sharing has increased in popularity as the cost of video recording and editing equipment has declined. Many computers now come with video editing software built in.

Such tasks as editing clips or adding graphics and music to videos that previously took serious expertise can now be accomplished with a computer program. While it is still a time-consuming process, the lower cost of recording and processing video content has led to an explosion of popularity in video sharing. This trend can be utilized to help in a social media marketing campaign.

A **video sharing site** allows users to upload video clips to a website that can later be viewed publicly or privately. These sites generally let registered users comment on the videos and tag them with keywords in order to group common topics together, thus making it easier to locate similar videos. Many sites let users rank videos, with the most popular ones featured on the front page. Getting a video on the front page of a high-traffic video sharing site such as YouTube can turn a video creator into an overnight sensation. In addition, organizations and individuals sometimes use video sharing sites to promote products and provide training in specific skills.

A Brief History of Video Sharing

Since the first video was uploaded in April 2005, YouTube has been a leader in online video sharing. After its founding and subsequent purchase by Google in October 2006, YouTube has grown rapidly. In 2010, 13 million

LEARNING OBJECTIVES

After completing this chapter, students will be able to:

- Define video sharing
- Describe a brief history of video sharing
- Explain benefits of marketing with online videos
- Detail how to create appealing video content
- Describe how to share online videos
- Explain how to generate video content
- Identify how to monetize online videos

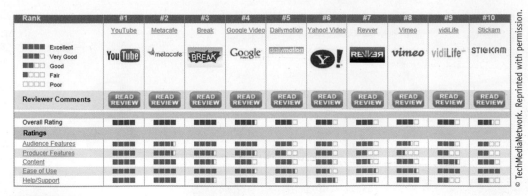

Rank	#1	#2	#3	#4	#5	#6	#7	#8	#9	#10
	YouTube	Metacafe	Break	Google Video	Dailymotion	Yahoo! Video	Revver	Vimeo	vidiLife	Stickam
Reviewer Comments	READ REVIEW	READ REVIEW	READ REVIEW	READ REVIEW	READ REVIEW	READ REVIEW	READ REVIEW	READ REVIEW	READ REVIEW	READ REVIEW
Overall Rating										
Ratings										
Audience Features										
Producer Features										
Content										
Ease of Use										
Help/Support										

Legend: Excellent, Very Good, Good, Fair, Poor

Table 8.1 2011 Comparison of Video Share Sites

hours of video were uploaded onto YouTube; thirty-five hours of video are now uploaded every minute. The site gets over 100 million views per day and draws from a wide age demographic: 18 to 54.[1] At the time of this writing, YouTube is the most popular video sharing site on the Internet, with a dominating 78.5% share of the market,[2] but it faces competitors, such as those described in Table 8.1. Clearly, the attraction of online video sharing is a phenomenon that is here to stay.

Part of YouTube's wide popularity lies in its easy integration with other social media platforms. Early in its history YouTube was primarily used as a resource by other social media sites. That has changed: "In October 2005, 52% of the traffic to YouTube came from social networking sites like MySpace and Facebook. 'Within just one month, the method by which users arrived at the YouTube site began to shift dramatically,'" and YouTube began to develop its very own online community.[3] Around half of all videos have user-created comments, and over 5 million people have subscribed to at least one friend on YouTube.[4]

Social media interactions are vital to the success of video sharing websites because they are typically supported through ad revenue. Depending on the site, guidelines for posting ads may vary. YouTube is among the most vigilant over which sorts of products are advertised on its site: "All advertisements must follow YouTube's Community Guidelines and advertising content policies."[5] Advertisers are willing to accept these limitations because of the extremely high viewership and targeted nature of YouTube advertisements.

Advertising revenue depends on appealing content, so video sites provide incentives to upload quality material. YouTube has a Content Partners program that rewards the makers of popular videos by splitting some of the ad revenue that is generated. According to the manager of that program, this relies on "a *performance-based* model. In other words . . .[.]if you upload a video and it gets one million views, for instance, we put an ad on every single view. And so that ad revenue starts to accrue, and, in many cases, can become significant for a lot of the Content Partners we have."[6] This feature makes high viewership on YouTube a valuable commodity, creating hot competition for top-ranked, front-page video placement.

Benefits of Marketing with Online Videos

Three of the main advantages of marketing with online videos include the ability to engage viewers, reach large audiences, and showcase products. Each of these benefits is explained in detail below.

ENGAGING VIEWERS

Video is a very popular medium because it can create a stronger connection with consumers. For many people video stimuli are more appealing than dry text or listening to a podcast. Also, "[t]he more senses that are involved in gathering information, the more engaging the process becomes."[7] Viewers become more vested in the content when a human face is attached to it. Further, communication studies estimate that between 50% to 80% of meaning is conveyed through body language. Thus, video deepens the communication experience, making the message (hopefully) more persuasive.

LARGE AUDIENCES

Most online or print ads have a serious disadvantage: they require the viewer to read them, and reading in general has become less popular over time. For example, "a 2007 study by the National Endowment for the Arts reports that 'on average, Americans aged 15 to 24 spend almost two hours a day watching TV, and only seven minutes of their daily leisure time on reading.' And… web video is only further fueling this difference in time spent watching versus reading across all age groups."[8] More people choose to consume their information visually, and online video marketing taps into this growing trend.

SHOWCASING THE PRODUCT

Demonstrating how to use a product has several benefits as a video marketing strategy. Viewers with no experience with the product may watch the video, be impressed with its quality or other appealing features, and consider making a purchase. In this respect an online video can function much like an old-fashioned infomercial. However, instructional videos also have the advantage of assisting those who have already bought the product. By providing value to the existing customer base, it may cause them to write positive reviews or otherwise participate in the social media campaign. Even if the viewership is limited, this factor makes videos demonstrating a product's utility potentially highly profitable.

CASE STUDY

Blendtec: Will It Blend?

Introduction

In tough economic times, marketers face improving performance with dwindling resources. One way to reach millions on a shoestring budget is shifting from traditional venues to social media. That is exactly what George Wright did. As Blendtec's new director of marketing, in November 2006 he launched a viral video campaign that featured the company's CEO, Tom Dickson, blending seemingly nonblendable items in a blender. The company's Will It Blend? brand videos quickly went viral on YouTube, bringing the company incredible brand recognition, website traffic, and most importantly, a five-fold increase in sales, all for a pittance of what a traditional media campaign would have cost.

History

Tom Dickson founded K-TEC, Inc., in 1987, based on his patent for "micronizing" grain mill, "which revolutionized the home grain mill market."[9] The company, which does business under the name Blendtec, manufactured the Champ blender for bread mixing, general blending, and food processing. In November 2006 Blendtec produced and posted the first in what would become a series of Blendtec YouTube brands videos.

Challenge

Blendtec's challenge was how to convince consumers to buy a pricey $400 kitchen blender without a significant marketing budget. George Wright and his team knew that the key was to grow the company's brand awareness. YouTube seemed like a great place to freely disseminate brand videos to an enormous audience, but the denizens of the social web are not prone to look favorably on overtly advertising a product. The company wanted to figure out a way to demonstrate the strength and durability of its entry-level 13-amp home blender without appearing to be blatantly advertising the product.

Strategy

Innovation often results from the ability to recognize the potential for an accidental discovery rather than an actual intent to create an innovation. The invention of the transistor at Bell Labs is a prime example. It happened by accident, but its creators saw the potential for innovation. On a smaller scale, the story of how Blendtec came with up its strategy to create viral brand

iPhone about to "blended" by Blendtec

Courtesy of Blendtec, Inc.

videos appears also to have been part accident and part recognition and capitalization on the opportunity. Apparently, "on the days that employees at the Blendtec plant smelled sawdust, they knew Tom (Blendtec's founder and CEO) was experimenting again and would flock to see the show. Tom was stuffing things like 2x2s into his blender. Noticing how entertained the staff was, Tom's marketing manager, George Wright, caught it on video, and with an advertising budget of only $50 it all began."[10] Of course, that doesn't count the cost of Tom Dickson's personal iPhone, which was still playing a video when it was halfway destroyed.[11]

So, in November 2006, George Wright and his team of Blendtec marketers bought "a white lab coat, marbles, a garden rake, a McDonalds Extra Value Meal, a Rotisserie Chicken and some Coke."[12] The idea was to blend things people might find amusing to watch being demolished and hence demonstrate that the powerful blender could handle any household foods. An in-house videographer recorded a series of brief videos, featuring Tom Dickson blending the various items into smithereens in the company's break room. The break room had been converted to resemble a cheesy game show set. The company posted the video clips on YouTube and its website.

Results

The Will It Blend? videos were an instant hit on YouTube. Blendtec had found a way to generate word-of-mouth advertising by creating rather jarring and at times shocking brand videos. By simply filming the company's CEO blending up outrageously funny nonfood items, viewers flocked to see if the items would really blend. The videos are not only hilarious, but they engender a true sense of wonder and anticipation while the audience eagerly waits to see if the blender can actually grind up objects as hard as diamonds.

Within five days of publishing the videos, "...[they] had garnered six million YouTube views. Blendtec's stated initial objective for the Will It Blend videos was increased brand awareness for their line of blenders. As a result of the campaign, however, they retail sales have increased by over 700%."[13]

By 2007 Blendtec's YouTube Channel already had over 60,000 subscribers,[14] so it is of little wonder that in delivering a keynote at PubCon in November 2008, George Wright, then the vice president of marketing and sales at Blendtec, attributed the entire success of Blendtec's brand recognition to the company's viral video campaign.[15] Indeed. By April 2009 the Blendtec iPhone video had attracted over 6,000 links, resulting in the top ten ranking on Google for the keyword, "blender."[16]

The 64-year-old engineer sees no end sight for the Will It Blend? videos. With new blenders scheduled for release to the marketplace and an endless supply of unusual items to grind up, Dickson sees nothing mixed about Blendtec's future.

How to Create Appealing Video Content

Creating a video to share online is fairly easy, but making the *right* video that will be widely viewed and will accomplish marketing objectives is much more difficult. The challenge may vary depending on the industry or sector being promoted. Some organizations lend themselves especially well to video marketing: "For example, many churches routinely shoot video of weekly services and offer it online for anybody to watch .... Many amateur and professional sports teams, musicians, and theater groups also use video as a marketing and PR tool."[17] For other products that are more technical and perhaps less immediately engaging, more creative approaches may be necessary.

A variety of authors have offered recommendations for developing online video content to be posted on YouTube and other video sharing sites. Perhaps the most authoritative advice comes from conversations with accomplished online video creators, which author Paul Gillin used to develop the AEIOU rule: video content should be *authentic*, *entertaining*, *intimate*, *offbeat*, and *unusual*.[18]

AUTHENTIC

Use real people in actual locations, as illustrated in the exercise case study: *Home Depot Shows You How*. Online viewers often see high production values as a sign of slick professional marketing and may be more skeptical of the content. Plenty of viral videos are recorded using just a webcam. Viewers will not only forgive, but they will also frequently reward a "homemade" feel in online video because the content appears more believable.

ENTERTAINING

Put simply, people enjoy fun content. At times it can be valuable to focus less on company branding and more on entertainment value. If a video is viewed millions of times because it is funny, the brand will be carried along for the ride even if it is mentioned very briefly. Entertaining videos can also spawn imitations and spinoffs, which further expand the brand's influence.

INTIMATE

It is part of human nature to follow stories or personal drama experienced by peers. A video that tells a story, perhaps focusing around one person and showing how others react, is more appealing because it creates a connection with the viewer. A prime example is Burger King's Whopper Freakout campaign in which customers' reactions were secretly filmed when they were told that BK had discontinued the Whopper. Run as both a TV ad and a longer web video, this highly personal (some would say voyeuristic) campaign created a huge response for the company.

OFFBEAT AND UNUSUAL

Offbeat and unusual tend to work together, as underscored by the case study: *The 'Old Spice Guy' Viral Videos*. A video needs to be distinct and memorable to stand out among the millions uploaded regularly. Videos that challenge a taboo or that seem otherwise strange and unlikely can be highly popular. Most viral videos feature these qualities. Bland content is easily skipped or ignored, so video marketing teams have to constantly innovate and find new ideas. An unusual image or clip may be further edited by other content creators, an action that amounts to free advertising for the company.

Beyond the AEIOU rule, keep in mind that brevity is important. Online video audiences typically have very short attention spans. Often, people will skim past content that does not immediately capture their interest. This reaction is supported by research. "[A]s reported by the video distribution service TubeMogul:

- Within the first ten seconds of a video, 10.39% of viewers are gone.

- Within the first thirty seconds of a video, 33.84% of viewers are gone.

- By the one-minute mark of a video, 53.56% of viewers are gone.

- By the two-minute mark of a video, 76.29% of viewers are gone."[19]

A successful video will get to the point quickly, or otherwise convince the viewer to keep watching. Keeping important material for the end may be stylistically appealing, but a large number of people will end up skipping the climactic finish if the video takes too long to watch. Good marketing videos should be as short as possible while still conveying the message.

After developing a concept, try to keep continuity of theme between videos. An individual or organization can maintain a channel on YouTube that others can view or subscribe to. Having a common theme or element that runs through several videos is more likely to convince a viewer to watch previous entries or to subscribe to the channel to receive future updates. The most successful video marketing campaigns (for example, the Blendtec mad scientist featured in the first case study of this chapter) have recurrent appearances centered on a common, easily understood theme. This strategy for video creation has generally been more effective at holding viewer interest.

Finally, do not focus solely on creating a viral video. Many videos go viral purely by accident, so attempting to imitate that feat can be a path to frustration. Predicting the viewing patterns of online audiences is difficult, so the risk of attempting to create viral videos is having a series of flops and no meaningful content. Sometimes it is more important to deliver valuable content to a core audience, and posting video can be helpful even if it does not go viral; other benefits include higher conversion rates and greater interest in the product.[20]

CASE STUDY

The "Old Spice Guy" Viral Videos

Introduction

Old Spice, a brand of Procter & Gamble, successfully created videos that went instantly viral and ultimately drove sales. Multiple videos featuring Isaiah Mustafa, who became known as the "Old Spice Guy," showed a man in masculine settings promoting body wash. The over-the-top campaign also included a variety of 30-second response videos of the Old Spice Guy responding to celebrities who mentioned him online. The campaign was an instant YouTube success.

History

Old Spice is a prominent American brand of male grooming products, manufactured by Procter & Gamble, which acquired the brand in 1990 from the Shulton Company. The Old Spice brand was originally created in 1938, which included men's shaving products, with a nautical theme in the branding.[21]

In recent years, the Old Spice brand began losing sales. According to Marc Pritchard, the Global Brand-Building Officer at Procter & Gamble, "this is a 70 year old brand that was getting its 70 year old butt kicked."[22] Indeed, the brand was losing its relevancy with younger audiences, and needed a makeover to revive sales in a highly competitive market.[23]

Challenge

As the men's body wash category has grown, the amount of competition in the market increased dramatically. With business slowing, Procter & Gamble sought a strategy to increase the sales of Old Spice and find a compelling purpose for the brand. In the past, the company had tried ads comparing the effectiveness of the product with competitors' offerings, but these efforts failed to show any significant returns. The brand had an outdated image and lacked a relevant purpose.

Since women make over half of all body wash purchases for their households (70%), Procter & Gamble decided to target women, as well as men in their Old Spice videos.[24] The objective was to encourage couples to discuss body wash, so that women would purchase an additional male scented body wash (Old Spice) for the men in their lives.[25] The main challenge for Proctor & Gamble was to market the body wash to female purchasers, but still position the product as masculine to lure men away from using bar soap or other body wash.[26]

Strategy ···

When Wieden + Kennedy, the advertising agency working on Old Spice, began designing the Old Spice campaign for Procter & Gamble, they drew on the heritage of the brand. The "Old Spice Guy" campaign centered on the actor Isaiah Mustafa (the "Old Spice Guy") in a video that was over-the-top in masculinity. The commercial opened with, "Hello, Ladies. Look at your man. Now back at me. Now back at your man. Now back to me. Sadly, he isn't me, but if he stopped using ladies scented body wash and switched to Old Spice, he could smell like he's me."[27]

Isaiah Mustafa appears in Old Spice video

Courtesy of The Advertising Archives

According to Jason Bagley, the creative director at Wieden + Kennedy, "We kept turning up the dial, the satire and the ridiculousness of the category advertising."[28] The campaign helped Old Spice to define its purpose. Pritchard says that Old Spice's goal is to "help guys navigate the seas of manhood" and the creativity of the videos delivered on this message.[29]

During the week of July 12, 2010, Old Spice launched their social media promotion of the video, focusing on YouTube and Twitter. The main idea was to get more traction than the initial video views. To achieve this, the team created over 180 response videos, where the "Old Spice Guy" recorded video replies to comments left by online influencers and celebrities.[30]

In addition, the agency ran a Twitter ad promotion, which featured the product as a trending topic.[31] The campaign was also supported by traditional media buys in targeted environments, as well as discount coupons to further help encourage sales of the product.[32] Hence, Old Spice did not rely solely on word-of-mouth to spread the video. They produced a powerful video, but seeded it with traditional marketing as well.

Result ···

In the first day of the Old Spice Campaign, the video received 6 million views, 20 million views by the third day, and 40 million views by the end of the week.

As a consequence, the Old Spice Twitter account shot up to over 43,000 followers and the company's YouTube Channel was viewed over 58 million times.[34] This traction drove a 300% increase in traffic to the web site: OldSpice.com, and increased the number of interactions on the company's Facebook page by 800%.[35] Clearly, the video's success had a significant impact on engagement in other social media channels for Old Spice.[36]

Furthermore, the Old Spice campaign spurred hundreds of parody videos, including one by Grover on Sesame Street, as well as invitations for the actor, Isaiah Mustafa, to appear on popular TV talk shows, such as "The Oprah Winfrey Show" and "Ellen," to discuss the ad.[37]

Most important, the videos were successful in driving sales of the Old Spice Body Wash. Nielson estimated that sales of the product jumped 55% in the three months during the campaign, with a 107% lift in July 2010 alone, when the social media campaign was launched.[38] And the Old Spice videos were effective in reaching the target demographic - women. Old Spice accounted for 75% of the conversations in the category during 2010 and half of those conversations came from women.[39]

It is worth noting that the immense success of the Old Spice video campaign is difficult to replicate. The basic concept of the "Old Spice Guy" had been tested a number of times by Procter & Gamble without success. The right creative aspects, which took many years to hone, were what made the campaign so effective. As David Hallerman of Advertising Age so clearly puts it, "the most clever marketers saw a major sticking point in making the Old Spice [Guy] into a model for their own campaigns: its success depended on excellent, compelling creative. And while every brand would like to think all its video assets are compelling, that's clearly not the case. Making advertising videos that consumers want to watch is, in truth, very, very difficult."[40]

Sharing Online Videos

Creating strong video content is challenging, but that is only the beginning. In order to have influence, videos must be found online and watched. While some content is so creative, funny, or engaging that it spreads organically, not all online video producers are so fortunate. Especially when the topic is a more serious company, brand, or organization, finding the best way to share an online video so that it reaches the target audience can be a significant obstacle to marketing success.

In order to overcome this barrier and successful distribute an online video, there are several different levels of sharing that must occur. First, the **primary** sharing occurs when the video creator posts it online; then, the **secondary** sharing happens as insiders or friends of the creator share the video; and finally, **tertiary** sharing occurs when online viewers begin sharing the video of their own accord. To be widely disseminated, an online video must pass through all three stages, so each will be discussed in turn.

PRIMARY SHARING

Primary sharing is perhaps the simplest step, as it can be done by just one person. A video must be posted online, often on several different video sharing sites, so that more people will have the opportunity to find and watch it (see Table 8.1). The poster can also use other social networking, link sharing, or microblogging websites to distribute links to the video. Even if the video is posted at multiple locations, consider funneling all link traffic through the most popular portal (YouTube) or wherever the target audience is concentrated so that the video will be ranked higher by search engines. Posting a blog entry to refer to the video is also helpful because the post may be picked up and further distributed by syndication services.

SECONDARY SHARING

Secondary sharing occurs when fans, friends, customers, or early viewers begin spreading the video within their own social circles. Ideally, the video creator will already have some following on one or more platforms. If those people enjoy the video, they will pass it along to their other contacts. This stage is perhaps the most crucial in establishing a video's audience, because the majority of online videos that fail to spread within the first forty-eight hours never become popular.[41] Encouraging immediate contacts to spread video content is crucial in reaching the broader Internet audience.

The groundwork for secondary sharing can be laid much earlier by participating in the online video community. It is important to interact with other content creators. Like other online networks, there are YouTube opinion leaders, whose content has more influence than that of the average user. It is possible to "identify opinion leaders by their behavior" because they are more likely to have rated an online video or posted comments regarding an online video.[42] These are the people who are likely to lead general opinion, influence others toward specific content, and perhaps determine the success of a video marketing campaign.

In order to encourage fans to spread their video content, some companies are using contests or featuring user-submitted videos on the corporate website or blog. For example, Doritos ran a contest in which people submitted commercials to be run during Superbowl 2009.** Even less dramatic incentives can allow a company to leverage user-generated videos. Offering to share content created by outsiders makes those people more likely to reciprocate by sharing the company's content, or telling others about the contest. Even small, informal fan competitions have proved a successful way to facilitate secondary sharing.

TERTIARY SHARING

Lastly, **tertiary sharing** is when content is spread on the Internet by people who likely do not know or have connections with the original video's creator. It is in this stage that most viral videos are found. Of course, viral videos are just the examples when primary and secondary sharing was highly successful, making the final stage of distribution huge and often global. To reach anything close to that scale, however, a video's creator likely spent considerable effort on the earlier stages.

Keep in mind that sharing of online information, particularly videos, happens on more than just social networks. ShareThis has compiled data about how people share content (see Figure 8.1). Email is still the most popular way to share information, with 46% of all content sharing. The next most popular is Facebook, with 33%, followed by other social networks at 14% and then Twitter at only 6%. The lesson is that video content should be sharable on as many platforms as possible but especially optimized for email. It is hard to anticipate how any single individual may decide to share content, but knowing the overall trends can help focus video sharing efforts where they will be most fruitful.

In order to make tertiary sharing easier, be sure that each video has a descriptive and memorable title. Those words may be all that someone has for reference when she or he sees a link or recommendation from a friend, especially if it comes through email. Also consider having different titles, tags, or keywords associated with the video on each online video sharing website. The more ways there are to find and share a particular video, the more likely it will be that it will be widely viewed and influence the target audience.

**The winning video was created by two unemployed brothers from Batesville, Indiana. This winning ad earned them $1 million as a reward from Doritos's parent company, Frito-Lay. For more information,, see Horovitz, Bruce (2009, December 31), "Two Nobodies from Nowhere Craft Winning Super Bowl Ad," *USA Today*.

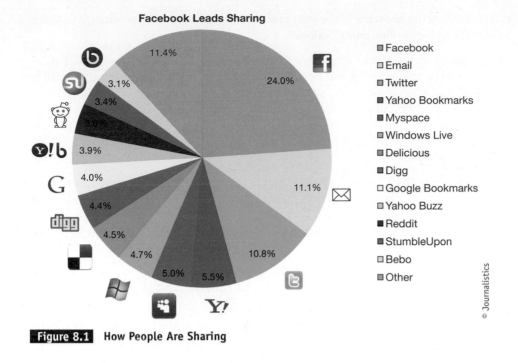

Facebook Leads Sharing

- Facebook — 24.0%
- Email — 11.1%
- Twitter — 10.8%
- Yahoo Bookmarks — 5.5%
- Myspace — 5.0%
- Windows Live — 4.7%
- Delicious — 4.5%
- Digg — 4.4%
- Google Bookmarks — 4.0%
- Yahoo Buzz — 3.9%
- Reddit — 3.8%
- StumbleUpon — 3.4%
- Bebo — 3.1%
- Other — 11.4%

© Journalistics

Figure 8.1 How People Are Sharing

Encourage User Generated Content

Some of the best online product marketing videos are not even created by the company in question but by admirers or fans. Encouraging others to share content related to the brand is a powerful social media marketing strategy that can be especially effective with video. This is often referred to as user generated content (UGC), and it is highly useful in a social media campaign.

Contributions from nonaffiliated individuals are often taken more seriously by online audiences because they assume the content is independent of the company being promoted. Video UGC is particularly valuable to a company because, unlike other online media platforms, a user video is considerably harder to fake than written text. This quality of video adds to the authenticity and appeal of the message.

Encouraging UGC can be as simple as highlighting customers who share their content or by running a contest (as discussed above). Just providing links and recognition to user contributions may be enough to spur more content submissions. When some fans start sharing, others may also. The result can be a series of testimonials, how-to tutorials, or other indirect promotions that cost nothing for a social media campaign but that achieve substantial results.

How to Monetize Online Video Sharing

While many people post online videos for fun and amusement, a much smaller number are able to make money or even a comfortable living by creating online videos. The YouTube partners program (mentioned earlier in the chapter) is one way for talented video creators to see their efforts rewarded. Other similar video sharing sites also have methods to make money from high-quality online videos (although this is not universal; Vimeo, for example, does not have a monetized option at the time of this writing).[43] In any case, the following are some of the best practices for aspiring video producers to make money from their online contributions:

- **Focus on Content First:** It hardly needs saying, but without solid content, there is no chance to make money from videos. YouTube, for example, will not consider people for their partner program unless they have a substantial number of views and frequently posted content. Build up the video content first, and then (with luck), the website the videos are posted to will seek to monetize them without being prompted. If the content is lacking, the chance of success is close to zero.

- **Promote the Channel:** There are a variety of ways to build awareness for a YouTube (or other video sharing site) channel, including blog posts, merchandise, other social networks, and more.[44] Use every tool available to get more eyes on the video content because successful monetization requires high traffic.

- **Update Frequently:** Some video sharing sites (such as YouTube) make this an explicit requirement in order to join their partners program, but even if not required, it is still good advice.[45] Obviously, more videos available means more clicks and potential advertising revenue, which can be directed back toward the video's creator(s). Also, having a steady stream of content demonstrates commitment to the project and keeps viewers coming back for more, and is therefore highly valuable to advertisers.

- **Keep Up with Analytics:** Video sharing sites will often give their partners information about how many people are viewing particular video content as well as their demographics.[46] With this knowledge it is possible to better craft content for advertisers to spread their message or to craft material that viewers will watch on rental. Good content depends on reaching the correct audience, so use every tool available to refine the material being produced.

EXERCISE CASE STUDY

Home Depot Shows You How

Introduction ....

Home Depot® is the world's largest home improvement retailer, the fourth-largest retailer in the United States, and the fifth-largest retailer in the world, with stores in every state in the United States, as well as in the District of Columbia, the U.S. Virgin Islands, ten provinces of Canada, Mexico, and China.[47] With a strong emphasis on customer service and well-trained, helpful employees to deliver on that promise, the retail giant has built one of the most-valued and desirable brand names in retail. According to surveys by Interbrand, a global brand consultancy, Home Depot has consistently scored among the top ten most-valued retail brands, hitting the number three spot for 2010, with an estimated brand value of over $23 billion.[48]

It is little wonder that Home Depot entered the world of social media marketing with a great deal of anxiety about potential damage to its sterling reputation. However, the company quickly discovered a huge fan base awaiting them. The retailer soon found new ways to satisfy its customers using social media, such as how-to videos published on YouTube and other video sharing sites. Unlike viral videos, it took time for Home Depot to attract a sizable viewership for its how-to videos, but eventually the retailer discovered that "[i]f you build it, they will come."[49]

History ....

Home Depot was founded in 1978 by Bernie Marcus and Arthur Blank. To change the way people thought about home care and improvement, the company created "the 'do-it-yourself' concept, spawning an entire industry that now spans the globe."[50] The first store was opened on June 22, 1979 in Atlanta, Georgia. Although Home Depot's corporate headquarters remains in Atlanta, it has become the fastest-growing retailer in history, with more than 2,200 retail stores around the world and with revenues exceeding $16 billion in the first quarter of 2011,[51] as well being listed on the Dow Jones Industrial Average and Standard & Poor's 500 index.

A typical Home Depot warehouse stocks an enormous variety of building materials, wall and floor coverings, paint, plumbing supplies, hardware, tools, electrical supplies, and items for landscaping and gardening. The initial concept for Home Depot was to be a discounter, marking down merchandise to increase sales while lowering overhead. However, the founders recognized that the major problem plaguing most cut-rate retailers was poor service, because they hired low-paid employees with few skills and no training in order to minimize costs.

According to the company, "[a]t the time, do-it-yourselfers made up more than 60 percent of the building supply industry's sales volume, but the majority of them did not have the technical knowledge or expertise to accomplish most home repair or improvement projects."[52] So, from the start, Marcus and company hired knowledgeable do-it-yourselfers and professional tradespeople, who then underwent thorough product knowledge training. With this level of expertise, these store associates were able to skillfully guide customers through projects, eliminating the mystery surrounding home improvement. Taking it one step further, Home Depot began offering clinics to educate customers on how to do home renovations themselves. Having gained the knowledge and confidence to take on complex home projects, customers returned to Home Depot warehouses to buy additional materials and gain further guidance for undertaking other home improvement jobs.

By providing customers with low prices, project know-how, and the right tools for the job, Home Depot revolutionized the home improvement industry and has become widely known for delivering the best customer service in the business. As the company says, our "philosophy of customer service—'whatever it takes'—means cultivating a relationship with customers rather than merely completing a transaction. As [cofounder Marcus] says…[,] 'At the end of the day, we're in the people business.'"[53]

Challenge ....

Given the careful planning and many years of hard work that have gone into crafting Home Depot's highly valued brand image, it is little wonder that the company at first perceived the social web as a potential threat to its brand. They feared that by participating on social media platforms, the company would lose control of its marketing message. Overcoming this corporate anxiety was the biggest obstacle faced by Nick Ayres, Home Depot's interactive marketing manager.[54] Ayres sought a way to not only calm the top executives' concerns but to convince them there were tangible benefits for Home Depot's active participation in the social media space. Ayres also had to come up with a way to translate the close relationships established between the company's store associates and customers to the social web.

Strategy ....

In order to garner the necessary buy-in of the top brass at Home Depot, Nick Ayres needed allies in and champions of using social media. By moving slowly into social media marketing and by racking up successes, Ayres could gain allies and find people within the company to champion his cause, without making management nervous about the possibly of damaging the Home Depot brand.

Ayres's first tentative foray into social media involved inviting people to review products sold by the home improvement giant. This low-risk approach was designed to demonstrate the power of social media, without exposing the Home Depot brand to criticism. As Ayres put it, "[i]t's a lot less of a concern when you start with product reviews as that's a logical extension of what we've been doing . . . . This is one of the few areas where we can tactically say that there's a good financial upswing for us that you can really see in the general marketplace. Generally speaking, products that have higher ratings and reviews do better from a sales perspective."[55]

Online videos show how to perform home repairs and renovations

During the June 2010 BlogWell Atlanta conference, Nick Ayres described Home Depot's next move into social media. The fact that the fastest-growing category on YouTube is how-to videos wasn't lost on Ayres.[56] His team came to the realization in December 2008 that "people just don't come to [our site], they might also go to Google or YouTube, where there happens to be a whole lot of videos. So, perhaps it would be of value to have [our] how-to content on…places like YouTube and others as well."[57]

So Ayres's team published a sizable collection of how-to videos on YouTube and other specialized video sharing sites, such as Howcast and 5 Minutes. The videos, featuring everything from home renovations to energy efficiency, were well received, garnering over 2 million views by June 2010. Ayres stresses that the most effective way for Home Depot to use social media is to provide what customers are requesting. He says, "If they want to know how to install a toilet or pick paint color, then that is the content you should provide them."[58] In addition, the company constantly seeks feedback about its ventures into social media as a means to shape future endeavors.

According to Kristina Proctor of SocialMediaMarketing.com, Home Depot's YouTube videos succeed because they have great educational content as opposed to blatant commercials, remain consistent in producing new and relevant content in a timely manner, diversify the offerings by featuring such things as seasonal content, offer transparency through showing raw footage of what it is like to go through a job interview or how hard the work can be as a store associate, and use real workers, not actors or spokespeople.[59]

Results ....

As of June 18, 2011, Home Depot's YouTube videos have been viewed over 8 million times, with more than eight thousand subscribers to the company's official YouTube Channel.[60]

Influential bloggers have lavished praise on Home Depot for its adept YouTube brand videos. In 2009 Catherine-Gail Reinhard, a blogger on Mashable (the most popular and respected social media marketing site), named the retailer as one of the five outstanding leaders in YouTube marketing. She wrote, "[t]he Home Depot stands out in their category because they publish content about subject matter that is relevant to their brand without being over-the-top in promoting the specific products that they sell."[61]

Home Depot's YouTube brand videos have established the company as a reliable and knowledgeable source of information and materials for home repairs and improvements. The videos are easy to follow and feature products Home Depot sells, effectively promoting its tools and materials without appearing like pushy advertisements. Finally, the videos have managed to put a human face on one of the world's largest retailers by using actual store associates to dispense advice in a straightforward and informative manner.

Due to the success with YouTube, Home Depot plans to expand its "digital orange apron" (the in-store uniform) to other social media. At the 2010 Social Media Success Summit, it was noted that Home Depot's "YouTube has been helping create awareness around the videos they have to offer. Home Depot believes their level of current involvement in social media is just the tip of the iceberg for them. They are actively engaging in blogs and forums and are piloting an informal network for their store associates."[62]

In fact, on December 10, 2010, the company launched its "online 'How-To' Community . . . where do-it-yourselfers can discuss home improvement projects and share their expertise with other members."[63] Do-it-yourself questions may be answered by peers or a featured number of Home Depot store associates from around the country, and because its customer service department will be monitoring for response opportunities, in-store associates will be available to respond to users.[64]

So, when a question about painting a room is posted, it may be answered by the resident Home Depot expert, "PatInPaint," with a short YouTube video showing exactly how to accomplish the task. Thus, social media is taking Home Depot to a whole new level of customer service, further expanding the company's brand recognition and perception.[65]

© Bloomberg via Getty Images

Producing a do-it-yourself short video

Review Questions for Home Depot Case Study

1. What in particular about Home Depot's business made this how-to series of videos so successful? What other industries might be able to use a similar strategy?

2. Are these instructional videos actually more effective than overt commercials? Why or why not?

3. Why did Home Depot choose to focus on producing YouTube videos? Would videos exclusively hosted on its company web site or on other video sharing platforms have been equally effective?

4. What advantages did Home Depot gain from having in-store representatives featured in the videos? Name at least two advantages, and explain why they are important.

Notes

1. "Statistics" (n.d.), YouTube. Retrieved June 12, 2011, from http://www.youtube.com/t/press_statistics

2. "The Top 10 Video and Multimedia Websites" (2011, April), MediaBlitzz. Retrieved July 3, 2011, from http://mediablitzz.com/2011/06/the-top-10-video-sharing-sites-by-market-share/

3. Bill Tancer, quoted in Jarboe, Greg (2009), *YouTube and Video Marketing: An Hour a Day* (Hoboken, NJ: John Wiley), p. 413.

4. "Statistics" (n.d.), YouTube. Retrieved June 12, 2011, from http://www.youtube.com/t/press_statistics

5. Jarboe, Greg (2009), *YouTube and Video Marketing: An Hour a Day* (Hoboken, NJ: John Wiley). p. 317.

6. George Strompolos, quoted in Safko, Lon, and David K. Brake (2009), *The Social Media Bible: Tactics, Tools & Strategies for Business Success* (Hoboken, NJ: John Wiley), p. 258.

7. Safko, Lon, and David K. Brake (2009), *The Social Media Bible: Tactics, Tools & Strategies for Business Success* (Hoboken, NJ: John Wiley), p. 237.

8. Kabani, Shama Hyder (2010), *The Zen of Social Media Marketing: An Easier Way to Build Credibility, Generate Buzz, and Increase Revenue* (Dallas, TX: BenBella Books), p. 112.

9. "About Blendtec" (n.d.), Blendtec. Retrieved June 16, 2011, from http://commercial.blendtec.com/Company/About

10. "How the Videos Got Started: Sawdust Day at Blendtec" (n.d.), SquidWho. Retrieved June 16, 2011, from http://www.squidoo.com/tomdickson

11. Money, Rachelle (2008, June 11), "Viral Marketing Insights from WillItBlend.com," Wordtracker. Retrieved June 16, 2011, from http://www.wordtracker.com/academy/case-study-willitblend

12. "Corporate Social Media Case Study: Blendtec" (n.d.), DemingHill. Retrieved June 16, 2011, from http://www.deminghill.com/blog/corporate-social-media/corporate-social-media-case-study-blendtec/

13. Ibid.

14. Money, Rachelle (2008, June 11), "Viral Marketing Insights from WillItBlend.com," Wordtracker. Retrieved June 16, 2011, from http://www.wordtracker.com/academy/case-study-willitblend

15. "PubCon: "'Blending' Viral Marketing into Your Marketing Strategy" (2008, November 21), WPN Videos. Retrieved September 16, 2011 from http://videos.webpronews.com/2008/11/21/pubcon-blending-viral-marketing-into-your-marketing-strategy/

16. Oden, Lee (2009, April 15), "Social Media and SEO: 5 Essential Steps to Success," Mashable. Retrieved June 16, 2011, from http://mashable.com/2009/04/15/social-media-seo/

17. Scott, David Meerman (2009), *The New Rules of Marketing & PR* (Hoboken, NJ: John Wiley), p. 223.

18. Gillin, Paul (2009), *Secrets of Social Media Marketing* (Irvine, CA: Quill Driver Books), p. 216–19.

19. Kabani, Shama Hyder (2010), *The Zen of Social Media Marketing: An Easier Way to Build Credibility, Generate Buzz, and Increase Revenue* (Dallas, TX: BenBella Books), p. 116.

20. Evans, Liana (2010), *Social Media Marketing: Strategies for Engaging in Facebook, Twitter, & Other Social Media* (Indianapolis, IN: Que Publishing), p. 299.

21. Old Spice (n.d.), *Wikipedia*. Retrieved November 6, 2011, from http://en.wikipedia.org/wiki/Old_Spice

22. Ibid.

23. Pritchard, Marc (2010, October 15), "Pritchard Deconstructs Old Spice Campaign Success," Advertising Age. Retrieved November 6, 2011, from http://adage.com/article/special-report-ana-2010/pritchard-deconstructs-spice-campaign-success/146486/

24. Newman, Andrew Adam (2010, July 15), "Old Spice Argues That Real Men Smell Good," The New York Times. Retrieved November 6, 2011, from http://www.nytimes.com/2010/07/16/business/media/16adco.html?scp=1&sq=old%20spice%20video&st=cse

25. Mauro (2011, July), "Old Spice Responses Campaign," Vimeo. Retrieved November 6, 2011, from http://vimeo.com/25187993

26. Newman, Andrew Adam (2010, July 15), "Old Spice Argues That Real Men Smell Good," The New York Times. Retrieved November 6, 2011, from http://www.nytimes.com/2010/07/16/business/media/16adco.html?scp=1&sq=old%20spice%20video&st=cse

27. Old Spice | The Man Your Man Could Smell Like (2010, February 4), YouTube. Retrieved November 6, 2011, from http://www.youtube.com/watch?v=owGykVbfgUE

28. Parpis, Eleftheria (n.d.), "Spice It Up," Adweek. http://www.adweek.com/news/advertising-branding/spice-it-102895

29. Pritchard, Marc (2010, October 15), "Pritchard Deconstructs Old Spice Campaign Success," Advertising Age. Retrieved November 6, 2011, from http://adage.com/article/special-report-ana-2010/pritchard-deconstructs-spice-campaign-success/146486/

30. Newman, Andrew Adam (2010, July 15), "Old Spice Argues That Real Men Smell Good," The New York Times. Retrieved November 6, 2011, from http://www.nytimes.com/2010/07/16/business/media/16adco.html?scp=1&sq=old%20spice%20video&st=cse

31. Brian Morrissey (2010, July 14), "How Old Spice Ruled the Real-Time Web," Adweek. Retrieved November 6, 2011, from http://www.adweek.com/news/technology/how-old-spice-ruled-real-time-web-102823?page=2

32. Mauro (2011, July), "Old Spice Responses Campaign," Vimeo. Retrieved November 6, 2011, from http://vimeo.com/25187993

33. Wieden + Kennedy (2010, August 11), "Old Spice Social Campaign Case Study Video," Digital Buzz Blog. Retrieved July 26, 2011, from http://www.digitalbuzzblog.com/old-spice-social-campaign-case-study-video/

34. Brian Morrissey (2010, July 14), "How Old Spice Ruled the Real-Time Web," Adweek. Retrieved November 6, 2011, from http://www.adweek.com/news/technology/how-old-spice-ruled-real-time-web-102823?page=2

35. Wieden + Kennedy (2010, August 11), "Old Spice Social Campaign Case Study Video," Digital Buzz Blog. Retrieved July 26, 2011, from http://www.digitalbuzzblog.com/old-spice-social-campaign-case-study-video/

36. Neff, Jeff (2010, July 26), "How Much Old Spice Body Wash Has the Old Spice Guy Sold?" AdvertisingAge. Retrieved November 6, 2011, from http://adage.com/article/news/spice-body-wash-spice-guy-sold/145096/

37. Gibson, Ellen (2011, June 24), "Cannes ad prize asks novel question: Did it work?" Huffington Post. Retrieved November 6, 2011, from http://www.huffingtonpost.com/huff-wires/20110624/us-ads-that-work/

38. Old Spice Viral Campaign Translates into Sales - Lots of Them (2010, July 28), MarketingVox.com. Retrieved November 6, 2011, from http://www.marketingvox.com/old-spice-viral-campaign-translates-into-sales-lots-of-them-047427/?utm_campaign=newsletter&utm_source=mv&utm_medium=textlink

39. Morrissey, Brian (2010, August 4), "Old Spice's agency flexes its bulging stats," Adweek. Retrieved November 6, 2011, from http://www.adweek.com/adfreak/old-spices-agency-flexes-its-bulging-stats-12396

40. Hallerman, David (2010, August 26), "What Marketers Can Learn From the Old Spice 'Your Man' Campaign," AdAge Digital. Retrieved November 6, 2011, from http://adage.com/article/digitalnext/marketers-learn-spice-man-campaign/145603/

41. Weinberg, Tamar (2009), *The New Community Rules: Marketing on the Social Web* (Sebastopol, CA: O'Reilly Media), p. 290.

42. Jarboe, Greg (2009), *YouTube and Video Marketing: An Hour a Day* (Hoboken, NJ: John Wiley), p. 47.

43. "Which Video Sharing Service is Best for You?" (2011, April 10), No Film School. Retrieved June 30, 2011, from http://nofilmschool.com/2011/04/best-video-sharing-service-you/

44. Van Marciano, Fabrizio (2011, March 27), "45 Ways to Promote Your YouTube Channel!" Magnet4Marketing.Net. Retrieved June 30, 2011, from http://www.magnet4marketing.net/2011/03/27/45-ways-to-promote-your-youtube-channel/

45. Beamond, Sam (2011, April 28), "Benefits of the YouTube Partner Program," Internet Marketing Source. Retrieved June 30, 2011, from http://www.internetmarketingsource.net/2011/04/benefits-of-the-youtube-partner-program/

46. "Benefits & Qualifications" (n.d.), YouTube. Retrieved June 30, 2011, from http://www.youtube.com/t/partnerships_benefits

47. "The Home Depot, Inc—News Releases" (n.d.), Home Depot, retrieved June 18, 2011 from http://corporate.homedepot.com/wps/portal/corpHome and "Did You Know?" (n.d.), Home Depot, retrieved June 18, 2011 from http://corporate.homedepot.com/wps/portal/!ut/p/c1/04_SB8K8xLLM9MSSzPy8xBz9CP0os3gDdwNHH0tDU1M3g1APR0N3lxBjAwgAykfC5H1MzN0MzDycDANMYdIGBHT7eeTnpuoX5EaUAwCu61v4/dl2/d1/L2dJQSEvUUt3QS9ZQnB3LzZfMEcwQUw5MTU1RjBVSEExR0xUMzAwMDAwMDA!/

48. Ibsen, David Allen (2010, March 12), "Who Ranks Top in Brand Value? Walmart, Target, Best Buy, Home Depot, Walgreens, CVS, Sam's Club, Dell, Coach and Amazon.com—That's Who," *Five blogs before lunch*, Typepad.com, retrieved June 18, 2011 from http://daveibsen.typepad.com/5_blogs_before_lunch/2010/03/who-ranks-top-in-brand-value-walmart-target-best-buy-home-depot-walgreens-cvs-sams-club-dell-coach-a.html and *Best Retail Brands 2011* (n. d.), Interbrand, retrieved June 18, 2011 from http://www.interbrand.com/Libraries/Branding_Studies/Best_Retail_Brands_2011.sflb.ashx

49. "List of misquotations" (n.d.), *Wikiquote*. Retrieved June 18, 2011, from http://en.wikiquote.org/wiki/List_of_misquotations

50. "Our Company" (n.d.), Home Depot. Retrieved June 18, 2011, from http://corporate.homedepot.com/wps/portal/!ut/p/c0/04_SB8K8xLLM9MSSzPy8xBz9CP0os3gDdwNHH0sfE3M3AzMPJ8MAV0sDKNAvyHZUBABGeSMx/

51. "Corporate Fact Sheet" (n.d.), Home Depot. Retrieved June 18, 2011, from http://corporate.homedepot.com/en_US/Corporate/Public_Relations/Online_Press_Kit/Docs/Corp_Financial_Overview.pdf

52. "The Home Depot, Inc." (n.d.), Funding Universe. Retrieved June 18, 2011, from http://www.fundinguniverse.com/company-histories/The-Home-Depot-Inc-Company-History.html

53. "Our History" (n.d.), Home Depot. Retrieved June 17, 2011, from http://corporate.homedepot.com/wps/portal/!ut/p/c0/04_SB8K8xLLM9MSSzPy8xBz9CP0os3gDdwNHH0sfE3M3AzMPJ8MAN0sDKNAvyHZUBAA_E14g/

54. Weinberg, Tamar (2009), *The New Community Rules: Marketing on the Social Web* (Sebastopol, CA: O'Reilly Media), p. 70.

55. Ibid., p 71.

56. Bullas, Jeff (2011, May 9), "50 Awesome YouTube Facts and Figures." Retrieved June 18, 2011, from http://www.jeffbullas.com/2011/05/09/50-awesome-youtube-facts-and-figures/

57. "The Home Depot: Our Social Media Road Trip, by Nick Ayres and Sarah Molinari; presented by GasPedal and the SMBC." (2010, June), Vimeo. Retrieved June 17, 2011, from http://vimeo.com/8422890

58. Ibid.

59. Proctor, Kristina (2010, February 14), "5 Reasons Why the Home Depot Is a YouTube Success," Social Media Marketing. Retrieved June 17, 2011, from http://www.socialmediamarketing.com/blog/5-reasons-why-the-home-depot-is-a-youtube-success

60. "Home Depot's YouTube Profile" (2011, June 18), YouTube. Retrieved June 18, 2011, from http://www.youtube.com/user/HomeDepot

61. Reinhard, Catherine-Gail (2009, June 1), "YouTube Brands: 5 Outstanding Leaders in YouTube Marketing," Mashable. Retrieved September 16, 2011 from http://mashable.com/2009/06/01/youtube-brands/

62. Duermyer, Randy (2010, May 12), "Day 3 Wrapup: Social Media Success Summit 2010," Market it Right. Retrieved June, 17, 2011, from http://marketitwrite.com/blog/2010/05/day-3-wrapup-social-media-success-summit-2010-smss10/

63. "The Home Depot Launches 'How-To' Community for Do-it-Yourself Enthusiasts" (2010, December 10), Home Depot. Retrieved June 18, 2011, from http://multivu.prnewswire.com/mnr/homedepot/47702/

64. Defren, Todd (2010, October 25), "Home Depot's Big Bet: Participation is Marketing," pr-squared. Retrieved June 18, 2011, from http://www.pr-squared.com/index.php/2010/10/home-depots-big-bet-participation-is-marketing

65. "HomeDepot 'How to' Community Video from Home Depot" (2010, December 14), YouTube. Retrieved June 18, 2011, from http://www.youtube.com/watch?v=aOBCNx9R6H4

Sharing Photos and Images

Photo sharing is a relatively nascent and sometimes overlooked area of social media marketing.[1] Some companies find it hard to believe that sharing pictures on the web can be an effective marketing strategy. However, photo sharing is experiencing an unprecedented growth surge, in large part due to the ubiquity of smart-phones equipped with constantly improving cameras.[2]

According to eMarketer, one in four people in the United States have smart phones; by 2015 one in three will have them.[3] With tens of millions snapping pictures with smart-phones and mobile applications that make it easy to instantly upload and share these pictures, people are flocking to photo sharing sites for personal and business use. Photo sharing is, by its very nature, a social activity. Hence, for companies, nonprofits, and government agencies, photo sharing sites now represent a wealth of social media marketing opportunities.

A **photo sharing site** lets users upload photos and other images for public or private consumption, allowing them to comment, rate, and tag the pictures.[4] These sites provide permanent and centralized access to a user's images (and in some cases video clips, too). Most photo sharing sites create albums or galleries, where visitors can view all the works of individual authors on the site. Many provide desktop-like photo management applications for organizing and presenting images. Photo sharing sites typically permit registered users to comment on the images and tag them with descriptive keywords, which the site uses to group the images by topic, making it easier to locate similar graphics.

According to *Wikipedia*, photo sharing sites fall into two primary categories:

[1] Sites that offer photo sharing for free and [2] sites that charge consumers directly to host and share photos." *Of the sites that offer free photo sharing, most can be broken up into advertising-supported media plays and online photo finishing sites, where photo sharing is a vehicle to sell prints or other merchandise. Paid sites typically offer subscription-based services directly to consumers and dispense with advertisements and sometimes the sale of other goods.*[5]

The copyright protection afforded to users varies among photo sharing sites. In general, copyright holders of photos, artwork, and other images can grant users the right to use their creations without fees or royalties and still retain their copyrights.[6] It is critical to check the copyright policy of a photo sharing site before posting images to it or using images from it for commercial or personal purposes.

- Detail how to market on photo sharing sites
- Describe the future of photo sharing

A Brief History of Photo Sharing

Launched in September 1995, Webshots was one of the first photo sharing sites.[7] Webshots began life as a sports-oriented screen saver sold at retail for PCs, but in 1999 it morphed into a social network, which by April 2000 became the most popular photo sharing destination online.[8] A number of similar sites were founded in the late 1990s, although the two photo sharing sites that would come to dominate the field, Photobucket and Flickr, didn't come into existence until the early 2000s, as shown in Table 9.1.

Photo Sharing Sites	Alexa Global Traffic Rank*	Google Page Rank**	Dated Started	Description
Flickr	37	9	February 2004	Free upload 300MB of photos per month (pro account available at $24.95 per year).
Photobucket	143	7	June 2003	Free, Unlimited Photo Storage (pro account available for $2.99/month or $24.95/year).
SmugMug	1,834	7	November 2002	Free trial, then packages from $5/month to $150/year.
Shutterfly	1,106	6	December 1999	Picture storage is free and unlimited.
SnapFish	2,792	7	April 2000	Free photo storage is unlimited, but to Maintain your account, you must make one purchase per year.
Webshots	3,065	6	September 1995	Free (pro account available for $19.95/year).
Kodak Gallery	5,822	6	December 2001	You must spend $4.99 per year for 2GB. For accounts over 2GB, the fee is $19.99 per year to maintain your account.
PBase	3,889	6	August 1999	$23 yearly for 1,000MB of photo storage, $43 for 2,000MB, $60 for 3,000MB.

© Cengage Learning 2013

Table 9.1 Popular Photo Sharing Sites, as of December 2011

*Alexa Global Traffic Rank estimates a site's popularity, with traffic data from Alexa Toolbar users and other diverse traffic sources, using an ascending scale where 1 represents the highest traffic rank.
**Google Page Rank uses the number and quality of links to a web page to determine its relative importance, using a scale of 0-10, with 10 indicating the highest rank and 0 the lowest.

Photobucket was founded on June 1, 2003, by Alex Welch and Darren Crystal.[9] This photo sharing site is well known for personal photo albums and (more recently) as a way to store and share videos, as depicted in Figure 9.1. Since the acquisition of Photobucket by News Corp. in 2007, the site has gained a more social networking feel similar to MySpace (formerly a News Corp. property).[10] Although News Corp. divested its majority stake in both Photobucket (December 2009) and MySpace (June 2011), Photobucket's image storage facilities continue to serve as a place for MySpace members to store photos.[11] Users may keep their photo albums private, permit password-protected guest access, or open them to the public.[12]

By June 2006 Photobucket had become the most popular photo sharing site, capturing 44% of the market.[13] However, starting in 2007, complaints began surfacing about not enough free storage, photo editing tools, and options in pro accounts, as compared with Flickr.[14] In August 2009 Photobucket reduced free storage space from 1GB to 500GB, further angering users, who were unable to upload more images to their accounts unless they were willing pay the upgrade fee.[15] Eventually these missteps were corrected, including the removal of storage limits for free accounts.[16]

Flickr was founded in February 2004 by Stewart Butterfield and Caterina Fake, pictured in Figure 9.2.[17] The Vancouver-based parent company, Ludicorp, was originally launched to develop a social network-based massively multiplayer online game. As the funding began to run low, the only portion of the game fully developed was the user-interface. So Ludicorp

Figure 9.1 **Photobucket Categorizes Images to Make Browsing and Searching Easier**

Figure 9.2 Flickr cofounders Stewart Butterfield and Caterina Fake take a photo of themselves during a photo shoot in San Francisco

opted to use the game's user interface as the basis for a photo sharing service dubbed Flickr.[18]

The game's user-interface provided a chat room on Flickr. Fake recalls that "George Oates [a Flickr employee] and I would spend 24 hours, seven days a week, [in the chat room] greeting every single person who came to the site. We introduced them to people, we chatted with them. This is a social product. People are putting things they love—photographs of their whole lives—into it. All of these people are your potential evangelists. You need to show those people love."[19]

Over time the chat room was dropped, as new versions of the site did away with the original gaming codebase and as the focus shifted to file uploading and sharing. The site's growing popularity attracted the elite of Silicon Valley, including Google and Yahoo!, as potential buyers of the fledgling company. In March 2005 Yahoo! acquired Ludicorp and Flickr for a reported $35 million.[20] In a move to take advantage of Photobucket's storage restrictions, Flickr lifted the previous size upload limits for free accounts on April 9, 2008.[21]

In spite of their success, the founders of Flickr, husband-and-wife team Butterfield and Fake, were experiencing a growing frustration in working for a large enterprise like Yahoo![22] According to Butterfield, "Yahoo failed to provide some resources needed during the first couple of years [after the acquisition]. Decision-making slowed because of bureaucracy."[23] In June 2008 both founders resigned from the company.[24] In fact, "Stewart Butterfield and Caterina Fake had already distanced themselves from Flickr, with Fake working in another Yahoo! division and Butterfield on an extended paternity leave."[25]

Despite the departure of the founders, the photo sharing site continued to gain popularity, fostering an environment where professional photographers felt comfortable posting and discussing their work.[26] In May 2009 White House official photographer Pete Souza began using Flickr as a conduit for releasing White House photos.[27]

In September 2010 Flickr announced its 5 billionth photo upload.[28] By July 2011 Flickr had an estimated 90 million unique monthly visitors,[29] and just a month later, the site announced its 6 billionth photo upload.[30]

Benefits of Marketing with Online Photos and Other Images

Photo sharing sites function much like other social networks. Users must be active in the community in order to produce results. Indeed, the social communities surrounding image sharing sites are the most important factor because they will circulate and share the content.[31] On Flickr, for example, the most influential users not only share photos but interact with others, making thoughtful comments on many pictures. Staying connected will draw people back to connect or to look at other targeted content.

From a marketing standpoint, there are several advantages to photo sharing. Photos can be used to showcase a product, document offers, and influence buyer mood.[32] Most directly, images of the product can generate interest and online buzz, leading to sales. Showcasing a product is most effective when the presentation is highly detailed. Some companies shy away from distributing product images and specifications, fearing that their trade secrets will be uncovered. While this is a legitimate worry, the potential risk is often outweighed by the sales benefits of sharing product information. Giving detailed

- To gain a better understanding of how social tagging and community input could benefit both the Library and users of the collections
- To gain experience participating in the emergent web communities that would be interested in the kinds of materials in the Library's collections

The Commons on Flickr

Once the popular photo sharing website Flickr was selected as a venue that would meet the Library's requirements, the pilot team contacted Flickr to discuss its available rights statement options, none of which was appropriate for the Library's content. These discussions began the collaboration that resulted in the launch of the Commons (see http://www.flickr.com/commons), a designated area on Flickr where cultural heritage institutions can share photographs that have no known copyright restrictions in order to increase awareness of these collections. Flickr members are invited to engage with Commons collections by describing the items through tags or comments.

"A growing number of libraries, museums, and archives, intrigued by the possibilities of this model, have followed the Library's lead and launched accounts within the Commons framework." (See *For the Common Good: The Library of Congress Flickr Pilot Project*, http://www.loc.gov/rr/print/flickr_report_final.pdf).

Results...

Two collections of historical photographs were made public on a Library account on the Flickr photo sharing site in January 2008. The response from Flickr members and observers of the pilot was overwhelmingly positive and beneficial. The following statistics from *For the Common Good: The Library of Congress Flickr Pilot Project* (http://www.loc.gov/rr/print/flickr_report_final.pdf) attest to the popularity and impact of the pilot:

- As of October 23, 2008, there have been 10.4 million views of the photos on Flickr.
- 79% of the 4,615 photos have been made a "favorite" (i.e., are incorporated into personal Flickr collections).

- Over 15,000 Flickr members have chosen to make the Library of Congress a "contact," creating a photostream of Library images on their own accounts.
- For Bain News Service photographs placed on Flickr, views/downloads rose approximately 60% for the period January to May 2008, compared to the same time period in 2007. Views/downloads of Farm Security Administration and Office of War Information Collection image files placed on Flickr rose approximately 13%.
- 7,166 comments were left on 2,873 photos by 2,562 unique Flickr accounts.
- 67,176 tags were added by 2,518 unique Flickr accounts.
- 4,548 of the 4,615 photos have at least one community-provided tag.
- Less than twenty-five instances of user-generated content were removed as inappropriate.
- More than 500 Prints and Photographs Online Catalog (PPOC) records have been enhanced with new information provided by the Flickr Community.
- Average monthly visits to all PPOC web pages rose 20% over the five-month period of January to May 2008, compared to the same period in 2007.

This project significantly increased the reach of Library content and demonstrated the many kinds of creative interactions that are possible when people can access collections within their own web communities. The contribution of additional information to thousands of photographs was invaluable. Performance measures documented in [*For the Common Good* report] illustrate how the project has been successful in achieving the objectives and desired outcomes of the Library's strategic goals. The Flickr project increases awareness of the Library and its collections; sparks creative interaction with collections; provides LOC staff with experience with social tagging and social web community input; and provides leadership to cultural heritage and government communities . . .

Concerns about loss of control over content will continue to be discussed, but such loss can also be mitigated. Community practices and forums like the new Flickr Commons, where cultural organizations can now offer collections, help reduce the risks. Pilots like the Flickr project provide practical experience and concrete data on the risks and rewards of the social web, and they help staff learn to operate in less formal environments that enhance recognition for a library's valuable cultural roles.

As the Library of Congress considers new strategies to make its resources available, discoverable, and useful, pilots of the Flickr Commons type are essential for learning how best to engage audiences with library collections in ways that benefit the public at large. The Flickr team recommends that this experiment in use of the social web become an ongoing program with expanded involvement in Flickr Commons and other appropriate social networking opportunities for nonphotographic collections. The benefits appear to far outweigh the costs and risks.

Marketing with Photo Sharing Sites

The first step in marketing on photo sharing sites is to determine the target market for the images because different photo sharing sites cater to different clientele. Identifying the demographics and behavioral characteristics of the target market enables the marketer to select an optimal series of photo sharing sites on which to upload images. Check out the sites to determine whether they are primarily trafficked by, for example, college-age viewers, women, or professional photographers and artists.

Who Are You with Nikon?

Introduction[†] ....

Nikon has been incredibly successful in the digital SLR category. However, it was steadily losing ground when it came to compact cameras. Hence, Nikon launched a competition encouraging people to share and promote their photos on social media platforms.

History ....

In 1917, three leading optical manufacturers merged to form an optical company called Nippon Kogaku K.K.[56] The company manufactured a variety of products using optical lenses. Nippon Kogaku K.K. experienced turbulent times after World War II, but eventually regained its footing and went on to produce the highly popular and well-respected line of Nikon cameras. In fact, the company was renamed after the cameras in 1988, becoming the Nikon Corporation.

In 1991, as a research project for NASA, Nikon helped build some of the first digital single-lens reflex (D-SLR) cameras.[57] By 1999, Nikon was building its own D-SLR camera for consumers. A D-SLR camera enables the user to see an accurate representation of what the lens picks up, takes high-resolution pictures, and can handle a variety of lenses, including wide-angle and telephoto. Up though the mid-2000s, Canon D-SLRs used larger light sensors and hence produced better quality pictures than equivalent Nikon models. However, in late 2007, Nikon introduced a powerful new series of D-SLRs, regaining "much of its reputation among professional and amateur enthusiast photographers as a leading innovator in the field, especially because of the speed, ergonomics, and low-light performance of its latest models."[58]

Challenge ....

Despite having 35% of the D-SLR market, the Nikon brand had just 8% of the EU compact sector, and in some markets the situation was even worse. The challenge was to drive sales of compact cameras while also not alienating the core D-SLR consumer base.

The insight was that Nikon was perceived as a conservative brand.

Nikon widely used by professional and amateur photographers

© Lee Webb/Alamy

[†] "Who Are You with Nikon?" (2011, June 8), Marketing Case Study. © Bizcommunity.com. Reprinted with permission.

Consumers knew the company made high-quality products for the professional market, and as a result they thought Nikon's compacts would be too expensive.

The brand's success in the professional market was actually isolating them from the more casual consumer. The brand was regarded as old-fashioned and unapproachable.

Rival technology brands such as Panasonic and Sony, as well as Nikon's key competitor Canon, all performed much stronger than Nikon both in terms of brand awareness and brand perception metrics.

Strategy ....

If Nikon wanted to perform as well in the compact sector as it did in the D-SLR segment, it would have to build an emotional connection with the brand that could run alongside the respect it generated among more serious photographers.

© AP Images/Vincent Thian

Nikon wanted to make an emotional connection with social consumers

The first insight was that technology has democratized photography. A cheap camera phone suffices to make someone a photographer.

The second insight was that photography now plays a much more important role in people's lives thanks to the ease of sharing. Digital platforms have made photography more social than ever before. A major reason for taking pictures is now to share them with friends and family.

This insight was applicable to both the serious amateur who posts creative work on Flickr to receive peer recognition and the social recorder who posts on Facebook to generate 'likes.' The bottom line was that a key motivation for taking pictures was the ability to share online.

Establishing a presence in social media

The campaign strategy used this understanding to create a more emotional connection with both target groups. Nikon would incentivize sharing, encourage it, and inspire it.

For the first time, the brand would have a presence in social media with dedicated spaces populated by the two target groups: Flickr for the serious hobbyist D-SLR market and Facebook to reach out to social photographers.

Nikon would provide the platforms to let both groups of consumers show who they were.

Nikon would be the first photography brand to really come to grips with the social media space—a democratic platform for an art form that had become democratic through the encouragement of all consumers to be truly creative.

Nikon would not set any barriers to participation in the *"Who are you with Nikon?"* contest. All the participant needed was a camera or a camera phone, and the winners would be selected for their ability to meet the brief, not for light metering or composition.

'I AM NIKON'

'I AM NIKON' pages were set up on Flickr and Facebook, using ads to drive traffic to the pages and to swell the numbers in the respective groups.

Simple questions such as, "What camera do you own?" were used to build interaction with the sites. Regular updates included tips on how to take better pictures and new product launches. The pages ran in six European markets and were moderated with an agreeable tone of voice (more serious on Flickr and more playful, without losing an authoritative edge, on Facebook).

Once the groups were large enough, Nikon launched *"WHO ARE YOU WITH NIKON"* competitions on both platforms. Every Friday, Nikon created massively popular showcases highlighting the best work on both sites.

On Flickr, since the more serious target audience liked a challenge, the brand set specific tasks. A dedicated microsite was created by Yahoo to house the competition, and advertising was used to drive more traffic to the "I AM NIKON" Flickr page.

Results ....

The campaign successfully brought the more emotional, creative attributes of Nikon to the fore.

On the Facebook page, users have uploaded nearly 40,000 photos. On Flickr the Nikon community, despite only being open since March 2010, is already in the top 2% in terms of group size, with more than 8,500 members. Members have now contributed nearly 80,000 photos, with 200 more added each day.

Nikon's share of the compact camera market has doubled in its six key markets.

Astronaut Taking Picture with a Nikon Camera

NASA Johnson Space Center (NASA-JSC)

Today, Nikon is one of the biggest brand groups on Flickr, with almost 30,000 members and 120,000 photos uploaded.[59] Its Nikon Digital Learning Center provides Flickr members with help on taking better pictures through its useful tutorials and a discussion board, where professional photographers and enthusiasts answer questions and offer advice on such topics as the best lens to use and lighting tips. In addition, members upload their Nikon photos and tag them. The catchphrase, "Nikon is doing more to make picture taking easier (and fun) for everyone,"[60] succinctly sums up why this brand is doing so well on Flickr.

Review Questions for Nikon Case Study

1. What incentives did Nikon provide to spur its fans to share more pictures? Should the company have done more?

2. Nikon was identified more with the professional market than consumer photography. Has that changed following this social media marketing campaign? Why or why not?

3. How did Nikon leverage its technical superiority in photo taking with its social media strategy? Could it have been done differently? If so, how? If not, explain why not.

4. Nikon had an initial edge in photo sharing as a company specializing in camera gear. What specific tactical advantages did this give Nikon?

Notes

1. Bard, Mirna (2011, May 11), "Are Photo-sharing Sites Overlooked?" *SmartBlog* Social Media. Retrieved July 16, 2011, from http://smartblogs.com/socialmedia/2011/05/11/are-photo-sharing-sites-overlooked/

2. Golden, Michelle (2011), *Social Media Strategies for Professionals and Their Firms* (Hoboken, NJ: John Wiley), p. 57.

3. Pladson, Craig (2011, April 26), "Social + Mobile: Shaping The Future Of Photo Sharing," Posterous. Retrieved July 16, 2011, from http://craigpladson.posterous.com/social-mobile-shaping-the-future-of-photo-sha

4. Barker, Donald I., Melissa S. Barker, and Catherine T. Pinard (2012), Unit D, *Internet Research—Illustrated*, 6th ed. (Boston, MA: Cengage Learning), p. 15.

5. "Photo Sharing Revenue Models" (n.d.), *Wikipedia*. Retrieved July 16, 2011, from http://en.wikipedia.org/wiki/Photo_sharing#Revenue_models

6. "Explore/Creative License" (n.d.), Flickr from Yahoo! Retrieved July 16, 2011, from http://www.flickr.com/creativecommons/

7. "Webshots Celebrates 15 Years!" (2010, September 22), *Webshots Blog*. Retrieved July 16, 2011, from http://blog.webshots.com/?p=1376

8. Excite@Home's Webshots Ranked #1 Online Photo Destination (2000, April 20), Excite@Home, Press Release. Retrieved September 16, 2011 from http://www.webshots.com/corporate/index.cgi?h=PRESS&t=press_release03.html

9. Arrington, Michael (2009, August 3), "Photobucket Founders to Leave News Corp.," TechCrunch. Retrieved July 17, 2011, from http://techcrunch.com/2009/08/03/photobucket-founders-to-leave-news-corp/

10. Huang, Gregory T. (2010, February 5), "It's Official: Ontela Bought Photobucket from News Corp," xconomy. Retrieved July 17, 2011, from http://www.xconomy.com/seattle/2010/02/05/it%E2%80%99s-official-ontela-bought-photobucket-from-news-corp/

11. Huang, Gregory T. (2010, February 5), "It's Official: Ontela Bought Photobucket from News Corp," xconomy, retrieved July 17, 2011, from http://www.xconomy.com/seattle/2010/02/05/it%E2%80%99s-official-ontela-bought-photobucket-from-news-corp/ and "Specific Media Acquires MySpace from News Corporation" (2011, June 29), MySpace Press Room, retrieved July 17, 2011, from http://www.myspace.com/pressroom/2011/06/specific-media-acquires-myspace-from-news-corporation/

12. Sheehy, Ryan (n.d.), "Photobucket," You are 1 in 7 billion. Retrieved July 17, 2011, from http://youare1in7billion.com/2011/04/05/photobucket/

13. Prescott, LeeAnn (2006, June 21), "Hitwise US: PhotoBucket Leads Photo Sharing Sites; Flickr at #6," Hitwise. Retrieved July 17, 2011, from http://pic.photobucket.com/press/2006-06-HitwiseBlog.pdf

14. Schroeder, Stan (2007, May 7), "Photobucket Gets MySpaced—Time to Switch to Flickr?" Mashable. Retrieved July 17, 2011, from http://mashable.com/2007/05/07/photobucket-myspaced/

15. Photobucket (n.d.), *Wikipedia*. Retrieved December 10, 2011, from http://en.wikipedia.org/wiki/Photobucket#cite_note-6

16. "Photobucket Now Has Unlimited Storage!" (2011, June 1), *Photobucket Blog*. Retrieved July 17, 2011, from http://blog.photobucket.com/blog/2011/06/photobucket-now-has-unlimited-storage.html

17. Butterfield, Stewart, and Caterina Fake (2006, December 1), "How We Did It: Stewart Butterfield and Caterina Fake, Co-founders, Flickr," *Inc*. Retrieved July 17, 2011, from http://www.inc.com/magazine/20061201/hidi-butterfield-fake.html

18. Graham, Jefferson (2007, February 27), "Flickr of Idea on a Gaming Project Led to Photo Website," *USA Today*. Retrieved July 17, 2011, from http://www.usatoday.com/tech/products/2006-02-27-flickr_x.htm

19. Ibid.

20. "Butterfield, Stewart and Fake, Caterina—Creators of Flickr, Career, Sidelights" (n.d.), *encyclopedia.jrank*. Retrieved July 17, 2011, from http://encyclopedia.jrank.org/articles/pages/3928/Butterfield-Stewart-and-Fake-Caterina.html

21. "Video for all + HD!" (2009, March 2), *Flickr Blog*. Retrieved July 17, 2011, from http://blog.flickr.net/en/2009/03/02/video-for-all-hd/

22. Butterfield, Stewart, and Caterina Fake (2006, December 1), "How We Did It: Stewart Butterfield and Caterina Fake, Co-founders, Flickr," *Inc*. Retrieved July 17, 2011, from http://www.inc.com/magazine/20061201/hidi-butterfield-fake.html

23. Kopytoff, Verne B. (2011, January 30), "At Flickr, Fending off Rumors and Facebook," *New York Times*. Retrieved July 17, 2011, from http://www.nytimes.com/2011/01/31/technology/31flickr.html?_r=1

24. Robinson, Gavin (2008, June 19), "Flickr Founders Resign from Yahoo!" Geek. Retrieved July 17, 2011, from http://www.geek.com/articles/blurb/flickr-founders-resign-from-yahoo-20080619/

25. Ibid.

26. Pormit, Jack (2011, May 20), "War of the Networking Sites Pt. 2: Flickr vs Photobucket," *Wordpress Blog*. Retrieved July 17, 2011, from http://jacopormit.wordpress.com/2011/05/20/war-of-the-networking-sites-pt-2-flickr-vs-photobucket/

27. "Flickr History" (n.d.), *Wikipedia*. Retrieved September 16, 2011, from http://en.wikipedia.org/wiki/Flickr#History

28. Sutter, John D. (2010, September 20), "5 Billionth Photo Uploaded to Flickr," CNN. Retrieved July 16, 2011, from http://articles.cnn.com/2010-09-20/tech/flickr.5.billion_1_photo-sharing-site-flickr-facebook?_s=PM:TECH

29. "Top 15 Most Popular Web 2.0 Websites" (2011, July), eBizMBA, retrieved July 16, 2011, from http://www.ebizmba.com/articles/web-2.0-websites and Kessler, Sarah (2011, February 14), "Facebook Photos by the Numbers [INFOGRAPHIC]" Mashable, retrieved July 16, 2011, from http://mashable.com/2011/02/14/facebook-photo-infographic/?asid=c228f21b

30. 6,000,000,000 (2011, August 4), Flickr Blog. Retrieved December 10, 2011, from http://blog.flickr.net/en/2011/08/04/6000000000/

31. Solis, Brian (2010) *Engage! The Complete Guide for Brands and Businesses to Build, Cultivate, and Measure Success in the New Web* (Hoboken, NJ: John Wiley), p. 63.

32. "Use Photos as Part of Your Marketing Arsenal" (n.d.), Fun Careers. Retrieved July 17, 2011, from http://www.funcareers.com/work_at_home_articles/49/Use-Photos-as-Part-of-your-Marketing-Arsenal.html

33. Scott, David Meerman (2009), *The New Rules of Marketing & PR* (Hoboken, NJ: John Wiley), p. 185.

34. Borges, Bernie (2009), *Marketing 2.0* (Tucson, AZ: Wheatmark), p. 85.

35. Bard, Mirna (2011, May 11), "Are Photo-sharing Sites Overlooked?" *SmartBlog*, Social Media. Retrieved July 18, 2011, from http://smartblogs.com/socialmedia/2011/05/11/are-photo-sharing-sites-overlooked/

36. Golden, Michelle (2011), *Social Media Strategies for Professionals and Their Firms* (Hoboken, NJ: John Wiley), p. 307.

37. Safko, Lon, and David K. Brake (2009), *The Social Media Bible: Tactics, Tools & Strategies for Business Success* (Hoboken, NJ: John Wiley), p. 194.

38. Doctorow, Cory (2008, December 16), "New York Public Library Joins Flickr Commons," BoingBoing. Retrieved June 29, 2011, from http://boingboing.net/2008/12/16/new-york-public-libr.html

39. Bray, Paula, Sebastian Chan, Joseph Dalton, Dianne Dietrich, Effie Kapsalis, Michelle Springer, and Helena Zinkham (2011, April), "Rethinking Evaluation Metrics in Light of Flickr Commons," Archives & Museum Informatics. Retrieved June 29, 2011, from https://conference.archimuse.com/mw2011/papers/rethinking_evaluation_metrics_in_light_of_flic

40. "History" (2010, November 12), Library of Congress. Retrieved June 29, 2011, from http://www.loc.gov/about/history.html

41. "More about the Commons" (n.d.), Flickr. Retrieved June 29, 2011, from http://www.flickr.com/commons?GXHC_gx_session_id_=6afecb2055a3c52c

42. Bayo, Cary (2010, April 26), "The Use of Flickr in Public Libraries: What Were the Goals of the Library of Congress Flickr Project?" LIS 5313 Course Wiki. Retrieved June 29, 2011, from http://lis5313.ci.fsu.edu/wiki/index.php/The_use_of_Flickr_in_Public_Libraries#What_were_the_goals_of_the_Library_of_Congress_flickr_project.3F

43. Ibid.

44. Gillin, Paul (2009) *Secrets of Social Media Marketing* (Irvine: CA: Quill Driver Books), p. 210.

45. "How to Market on Photo Sharing Sites" (n.d.), Stepforth.com. Retrieved July 17, 2011, from http://www.stepforth.com/resources/web-marketing-knowledgebase/diysmm/smm9-photo-sharing-sites/

46. Weinberg, Tamar (2009), *The New Community Rules: Marketing on the Social Web* (Sebastopol, CA: O'Reilly Media), p. 280.

47. Pladson, Craig (2011, April 26), "Social + Mobile: Shaping the Future of Photo Sharing," Posterous. Retrieved July 16, 2011, from http://craigpladson.posterous.com/social-mobile-shaping-the-future-of-photo-sha

48. Safko, Lon, and David K. Brake (2009), *The Social Media Bible: Tactics, Tools & Strategies for Business Success* (Hoboken, NJ: John Wiley), p. 198.

49. Weinberg, Tamar (2009), *The New Community Rules: Marketing on the Social Web* (Sebastopol, CA: O'Reilly Media), p. 271.

50. Golden, Michelle (2011), *Social Media Strategies for Professionals and Their Firms* (Hoboken, NJ: John Wiley), p. 292.

51. Odio, Sam (2010, July 1), "Making Facebook Photos Better," *Facebook Blog*. Retrieved July 16, 2011, from http://blog.facebook.com/blog.php?post=403838582130

52. "Flickr Sell off Rumors by Yahoo" (2011, February 1), Online Marketing Trends. Retrieved July 17, 2011, from http://www.onlinemarketing-trends.com/2011/02/flickr-sell-off-rumors-by-yahoo.html

53. Kopytoff, Verne B. (2011, January 30), "At Flickr, Fending Off Rumors and Facebook," *New York Times*. Retrieved July 17, 2011, from http://www.nytimes.com/2011/01/31/technology/31flickr.html?_r=1

54. Ibid.

55. Gannes, Liz (2011, June 10), "Photobucket Gets New Life With Twitter Deal," Yahoo Finance. Retrieved July 17, 2011, from http://finance.yahoo.com/news/Photobucket-Gets-New-Life-allthingsd-161293006.html

56. "Corporate History" (n.d.), Nikon. Retrieved July 4, 2011, from http://www.nikon.com/about/info/history/corporate/index.htm

57. "NASA F4 Electronic Still Camera" (n.d.) NikonWeb. Retrieved July 4, 2011, from http://www.nikonweb.com/nasaf4/

58. Nikon (n.d.), *Wikipedia*. Retrieved September 16, 2011, from http://en.wikipedia.org/wiki/Nikon_Corporation

59. Miss Onetrouser (2009, February 25), "Brands on Flickr: Success Case Studies," OneTrouser.com. Retrieved April 24, 2011, from http://www.onetrouser.com/gaumina_blog/brands_on_flickr_success_case_studies_/472

60. Northcott, Geoff (2008, July 12), "Brands on Flickr." Retrieved July 5, 2011, from http://geoffnorthcott.com/blog/2008/07/brands-on-flickr/

CHAPTER

10

Social Networks

While social networking is as old as humanity, the practice moved online much more recently. The 2000s saw the explosive growth of social networks, with names like Facebook, LinkedIn, and MySpace becoming part of the common vernacular.[1] More interactions could take place online, lessening the need for face-to-face or phone conversation.

The Millennial Generation (especially those born in the 1990s) grew up using social network sites to interact in ways that closely paralleled the culture of cliques and exclusivity commonly found on both high school and university campuses. For example, Facebook's invitation and approval process for entrance into an individual's sphere of friends and acquaintances ensures exclusivity, which is largely credited with making the social network an immediate hit among millennials.[2] Eventually, social networks were introduced that appealed to other demographic groups, such as business professionals. Today, social networks are among the most popular sites on the social web.[3]

A **social network site** is an online service on which members can establish relationships based on friendship, kinship, shared interests, business advantage, or other reasons. A social network site facilitates these interactions by letting members build a public or private profile, specify who can connect with them, and share their connections with others. Social network services simplify the process of sharing information, such as interests, events, status, and pictures, within individual networks.

Social network sites are the latest development of a prior Internet phenomenon, discussion boards (discussed in Chapter 12). Instead of just sharing thoughts and information, users began to develop communal relationships. A **virtual community**, a term first coined by Howard Rheingold in his 1993 book by the same name, focuses on building relationships using discussion boards to converse about topics of shared interest.[4] Technology's ability to aggregate personal characteristics makes it easier than ever to connect to others with similar background or interests.[5]

Online communities are the forerunners of social networks. While other virtual communities are driven by thoughts and ideas, social networks are primarily organized around people, not interests.[6] People join to connect with existing contacts and to keep in touch with old friends, not primarily to engage in discussion. Understanding the background and general expectations that members have of social networks is essential when developing a marketing presence on these platforms.

- Explain the global perspective of social networking
- Identify the benefits of marketing with social networks
- Define a white label social networking
- Explain the pros and cons of creating a white label social network
- Describe how nonprofit organizations can benefit from a private social network
- Summarize some predictions about the future of social networks

A Brief History of Social Networks

One of the first social network sites was SixDegrees.com, launched in 1997 by Andrew Weinreich, a well-known entrepreneur and Internet executive.[7] Weinreich drew his inspiration for the site from the "six degrees of separation" theory, which claims that "anyone on the planet can be connected to any other person on the planet through a chain of acquaintances that has no more than five intermediaries."[8] SixDegrees.com let users build profiles, display a list of their Friends, and transverse these lists. Although each of these functions had already been implemented by dating services and virtual communities, SixDegrees.com was the first to combine them. Despite attracting millions of users, the site could not attract sufficient funding or advertising to sustain its business model and closed in 2000. Nonetheless, "it paved the way for the likes of Facebook, LinkedIn and many more [social networks]."[9]

In 2001 Ryze.com was launched by Adrian Scott to help people make connections and grow their personal networks.[10] Scott introduced Ryze.com to his close friends in San Francisco, many of whom went on to become the entrepreneurs and investors behind such social network sites as Friendster, Tribe.net, and LinkedIn. This tight-knit group believed that its respective social networks could coexist without competition.[11]

However, Ryze.com never achieved critical mass, while Friendster enjoyed a meteoric rise and suffered an equally precipitous fall, with *Inc.* magazine calling it "one of the biggest disappointments in Internet history".[12] At the heart of Friendster's catastrophic failure was the alienation of its early adopters, which (in large part) came about because of continued intermittent service problems and the routine practice of deleting user accounts that appeared suspicious. On the upside, Tribe.net eventually carved out a loyal niche audience, while LinkedIn grew to become the second-most popular social network.

In August 2003 MySpace was launched by a group of eUniverse employees with Friendster accounts who were inspired by its potential, and decided to mimic the social network's more popular features.[13] The founders of MySpace "wanted to attract [the] estranged Friendster users," according to cofounder Tom Anderson.[14] However, it was the 2004 mass influx of teenagers into MySpace that accounted for its swift rise in popularity. By May 2005 MySpace had become the fifth-ranked web domain in terms of page views, according to ComScore's Media Metrix.[15] The notoriety of MySpace attracted the attention of News Corporation, which purchased the social network site for $580 million in July 2005.[16] On August 9, 2006, MySpace reached its 100 millionth account.[17] By 2007 MySpace was considered the leading social networking site in the U.S., valued at $12 billion.[18]

On February 4, 2004, Mark Zuckerberg, an undergraduate at Harvard University, launched "Thefacebook," originally located at thefacebook.com.[19] Unlike previous social network sites, membership was initially limited to only people with a harvard.edu email address, a restriction that created the perception of an intimate, exclusive community.

Within twenty-four hours of launch, 1,200 Harvard students became members. A month later, over half of the undergraduate population of Harvard had created a profile.[20] The social network quickly spread to other Boston-area universities, then to other Ivy League universities, and gradually to most of the colleges and universities in the U.S.[21]

The name of Zuckerberg's social network was officially changed to Facebook.com in August 2005, after the domain name was purchased for $200,000.[22] On September 2, 2005, U.S. high school students were allowed to join Facebook, substantially increasing its target market.[23] Then, the social network spread to universities in other countries, beginning with schools in the U.K.

In September 2006 Facebook expanded its registration policy to anyone older than thirteen with a valid email address.[24] This expanded access foreshadowed a boom in Facebook's popularity. On April 19, 2008, Facebook overtook MySpace in traffic.[25] MySpace continued to experience a steady decline in membership, attributed to such factors as "the failure to execute product development," a failure to innovate, sticking with a "portal strategy," and too many ads.[26] However, membership in Facebook skyrocketed, reaching 100 million by August 2008, 350 million by December 2009, 500 million by July 2010, and 750 million active monthly users in June of 2011.[27]

As of this writing, Facebook is the most popular social network, as shown in Table 10.1. Facebook has raised more than $1.3 billion in funding, with the *New York Times* estimating the value of the privately held company at a whopping $200 billion.[28] Of course, this success has spawned many competitors, as can also be seen in the table.

Social Network	Monthly Visitors (millions)*	Google Page Rank**	Alexa Global Traffic Rank***
Facebook	700	9	2
LinkedIn	100	9	13
MySpace	80.5	8	124
Ning	60	7	324
Google+	32	8	N/A
Tagged	25	6	280
Orkut	15.5	8	145
hi5	11.5	6	746
myYearbook	7.4	7	1,726
Meetup	7.2	7	454
Badoo	7.1	6	113
bebo	7	6	3,227
mylife	5.4	6	1,503
Friendster	4.9	6	7,116

Table 10.1 Popular Social Network Sites, as of December 2011

*Estimated unique monthly visitors according to eBiz|MBA Inc.
**Google Page Rank uses the number and quality of links to a web page to determine its relative importance, using a scale of 0–10, with 10 indicating the highest rank and 0 the lowest.
***Alexa Global Traffic Rank estimates a site's popularity, with traffic data from Alexa Toolbar users and other diverse traffic sources, using an ascending scale where 1 represents the highest traffic rank.

How Two Coke Fans Brought the Brand to Facebook Fame*

Introduction ....

Pop quiz: [As of March 2009, who had] the most popular page on Facebook? Barack Obama. Who's second? Coca-Cola. Yes, sugared water runs second only to the [president]. Who was it again that said people don't want to be friends with brands?

The Coke page, which totals 3.3 million "fans," wasn't even created by Coca-Cola, but by a pair of Los Angelinos who just love Coke.

In late August 2008, aspiring actor Dusty Sorg was hunting for a Coca-Cola fan page he could join on Facebook. He didn't find one that seemed legitimate so he hunted down a high-resolution digital image of a Coke can, uploaded it to Facebook and made a page.

History ....

And the page grew. And grew. There are 253 pages on Facebook devoted to Coca-Cola, but for some reason, Mr. Sorg's page—which he runs with his friend Michael Jedrzejewski, a writer—took off.

The guys weren't sure why theirs ended up with millions of fans—Facebook fan pages, at least last year, were relatively static, and the guys said they had been pretty inactive on it as they got busy during the winter holidays. And most people can't actually do that much with branded page—unless a brand is putting dollars behind it. Which Coke didn't.

Coca-Cola still remains perplexed over why Messrs. Sorg and Jedrzejewski's page took off.

Facebook gave Coca-Cola fans a place to voice their enthusiasm for the brand

© Greg Balfour Evans/Alamy

"We've discussed a dozen hypotheses about why it took off," said Michael Donnelly, director of worldwide interactive marketing at Coca-Cola Co. One theory the company keeps coming back to, he said, was the quality of the photo—a crisp,

*Klaassen, Abbey (2009, March 16), "How Two Coke Fans Brought the Brand to Facebook Fame: Soda Has Most Popular Page after President, in Collaboration between Creators and Marketer," AdAge Digital. © Crain Communications. Reprinted with permission.

high-resolution image of a Coke can covered with a thin layer of condensation. "For us as marketers, luckily it was exactly right—the can we had in the marketplace. . . . It grabs you." He said another theory is that Messrs. Sorg and Jedrzejewski had very active, expressive "social graphs," i.e., their network of Facebook friends. But "we can't measure that," he said.

Challenge

As the page picked up fans, it also racked up spam and obscene comments—issues that can plague many large pages on the social network. In November, Facebook decided to start enforcing a policy that says anyone creating a branded Facebook "page" must be authorized by or associated with the brand. Independent Facebook users could still create homages to brands, but they must live as a "group" or fan club.

"The problem was they had created a page, not a group," said Mr. Donnelly. Facebook made the decision to either close the page or let Coca-Cola take it over. Coca-Cola instead proposed an alternative: Let the creators keep the page but share it with a few of Coca-Cola's senior interactive folks. "We threw a variable to Facebook and said we're interested, but we'd rather walk away from it than have it be perceived that we caused this action," Mr. Donnelly said. Over the December holidays, he got in touch with Messrs. Sorg and Jedrzejewski to explain to them that this was a Facebook-driven change, and asked if they'd want to join him in administering it.

Strategy

Now normally when a giant multinational company calls a consumer about something the consumer has created in that company's brand name or image, it's not a good sign. And initially Mr. Jedrzejewski said he was worried about it.

"Everyone has this vision that if something like this happens, the big company will send you off to Guantanamo," he said. "This was exactly the opposite."

Coke instead flew the guys down to Atlanta for a few days of meetings, a tour of the World of Coke museum and a visit to the company's legendary archives. It was a friendly, not heavy-handed approach, Mr. Jedrzejewski said. "We talked openly about ideas, the future of the fan page," he said.

Coke's actions in sharing the page are indicative of not only the lessons the beverage giant has learned in the social-media space but also proof that big brands can tread gracefully in social media.

Results

The company has come a long way. Its initial reaction to a Diet Coke-Mentos viral video sensation in 2006 was that the stunt didn't fit the brand's personality—after all, people are meant to drink Diet Coke, not use it to make geysers. Now the company appears to be more at ease with its consumers creating content on its behalf—and it's largely eschewed a destination-centric philosophy as it has recognized that its expressive fans are everywhere.

Mr. Donnelly recounts how in the early days of the web, big marketers would define success by how much traffic came to their websites—and they've only recently become comfortable with the fact they can deliver a message through gaming, rich video and other places across the web. The same thing happened in

FACEBOOK PAGE LEADERBOARD

Sorted by Fans

Name	# of Fans	Daily Growth	Weekly Growth
1. Facebook	49,697,716	45,028	418,460
2. Texas Hold'em Poker	47,763,199	57,981	396,816
3. Eminem	44,465,700	55,742	471,744
4. YouTube	42,709,639	47,289	383,838
5. Rihanna	41,888,446	57,106	479,703
6. Lady Gaga	41,671,499	42,379	381,136
7. Michael Jackson	38,801,235	42,770	303,674
8. Shakira	38,119,665	50,429	443,548
9. Family Guy	35,707,765	34,917	325,941
10. Justin Bieber	33,806,925	45,691	306,117
11. Linkin Park	33,112,555	39,491	321,209
12. KatyPerry	33,052,582	40,534	439,310
13. Coca-Cola	32,999,207	39,030	306,663
14. The Simpsons	32,834,907	36,135	370,405

© Facebook

Facebook Page Statistics, as of August 1, 2011

Second Life, when marketers busily built islands, or destinations, within the virtual world. And it's a natural tendency in social networking.

"This page is a fan page and happens to be the biggest one, but we recognize that when you do a search you see 253," he said. And when it comes to communities, they recognize they need to ask advice, counsel and permission before engaging. "We don't want to be a big brand there doing big-brand advertising."

[As of August 1, 2011, the Coca-Cola Facebook page still ranked a respectable thirteenth place in fan popularity, with almost 33 million fans.[29]]

A GLOBAL PERSPECTIVE

With a plethora of social networks launching, as illustrated in Figure 10.1, most of the attention has gone to the U.S. superstars, such as Facebook and LinkedIn. However, in other countries, different social network sites have risen to prominence, even ones built by major corporations. As an example, Google launched Orkut on January 22, 2004, and although the social network never gained significant U.S. market share, it became popular in both India and Brazil.[30] Despite recent trends showing Facebook making strong inroads in India and Brazil, Orkut remains a well-known brand in these countries.[31] Renren is the leading social network in China, with more than 117 million users,[32] Vkontakte dominates in Russia, with over 100 million members.[33] And Bebo, according

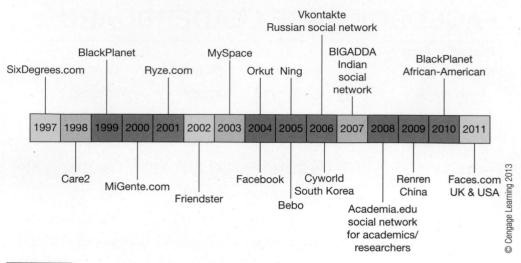

Figure 10.1 Timeline of the Launch Dates for Major Social Network Sites

to the BBC, has 22 million users in the United Kingdom.[34] As a consequence, marketers who want to reach a global audience should take into consideration these other social networks.

Benefits of Marketing with Social Networks

One consequence of online social networks has been to blur the line between business and personal life. With contacts overlapping between business, family, school, and so on, keeping private life out of the public eye is increasingly difficult. While previously only celebrities and politicians could expect public scrutiny of their actions, much personal information (especially contributed by young people) can now be found on the Internet.[35] While some are concerned about the implications of widespread information sharing, it can also be argued that this "transparency is in sum a good thing for individuals and society."[36] In any case, online sharing of popular interests is highly valuable to a social media marketer.

Marketing with social networks has several advantages for firms, allowing them to "find talent, build brand awareness, find new customers, and help conduct brand intelligence and market research."[37] Job search portals and professional networking platforms (such as LinkedIn) have become a popular way to match job seekers with employers. Further, with the large population segment participating on social networks, such networks have become an excellent way to seek out clients or customers. The term **brand intelligence** refers to information that businesses can collect about their customers, from basic demographics to topics of discussion to detailed feedback. Instead of costly market research, monitoring social networks can gather general sentiments, opinions, and customer needs with great efficiency.

Due to their information-sharing capacity, social networks can also be used as a new distribution channel for marketing messages. Marketers must be aware that people participate on social networks primarily to connect with friends, not to search out new products. However, an advantage of networks such as Facebook is that they encourage users to have many conversations with different people or brands, all occurring at once.[38] If marketing messages are engaging and valuable to social network users, they may be welcomed by users. Social networks allow a brand to engage its target audience in ongoing conversation, which can both draw in new business and increase customer loyalty (as demonstrated by the case study: *How Two Coke Fans Brought the Brand to Facebook Fame*).

Some business executives worry that participating on social networks might make their company appear unprofessional or invite negative commentary. To some extent these fears are justified; if there is negative sentiment about a company, some of it will show up in comments on the firm's social networking profiles. Negative comments, however, are not the disaster that many predict them to be. Instead of searching the Internet for negative reviews, false information, or bad press to refute, a social network profile can become the lightning rod for criticism, concentrating it in one location for easy response. Instead of controlling what people say, build their trust with earnest communications.[39] As a space to respond to criticism and receive feedback, participating on a social network has many benefits to a firm.

Marketing with Social Networks

Many businesses are motivated to interact on social networks, but large numbers of these companies do not have much payoff from their efforts. On a social network, it is especially important to enter with a strong understanding of the strategies and objectives (discussed in Chapter 2). The first step is to decide on goals and objectives that should be achieved.[40] Otherwise, due to its informal nature, for firms social networking can easily become a distraction rather than an aid. To avoid this problem, develop a solid plan before marketing on a social network.

The next decision involves the target market. Different social networks attract extremely different clientele, so knowing who the audience is and where to find them is essential. For online marketing, most campaigns will fall into one of two categories: business-to-consumer (B2C) and business-to-business (B2B) marketing. Facebook and LinkedIn are two networks frequently used for these respective purposes. These two will be used as instructional examples for B2C and B2B marketing, but similar tactics may likely apply on other social networks with equal results.

BUSINESS-TO-CONSUMER MARKETING

For businesses specializing in consumer products or services, social networks can be a great way to locate and market to potential customers. Most social networks make it easy for members to like, share, or become fans of a brand. Therefore, the emphasis needs to be on content, more specifically, creating content that is "share-worthy" in the eyes of the consumer. The end goal is to share content that makes the audience want to discuss it further with friends. This can function as word-of-mouth advertising as consumers share their likes with each other.[41] Social networks can also advance a brand's position in relation to competitors by making a company seem more memorable or personable. However, accomplishing these lofty goals demands "persistence, consistency, and genuine intentions."[42]

To have maximal reach to consumers, focus on the places where most consumers are spending time. At the present time, Facebook is the giant of casual social networking, so establishing a presence there is crucial for B2C marketing.[43] While Facebook is the "most marketer-friendly" of the major social networks, it still requires finesse in order to market on its social network effectively.[44] There are a huge number of professionals and brands operating on Facebook, so the competition can be fierce.

To begin marketing a brand on Facebook, start an account. Do **not** create a profile; those are intended for private users and are not as helpful for marketing. Instead, create a page that will represent the business.[45] Pages allow users to follow or become fans of a company without giving access to their personal information as would occur from friending a profile. This feature makes pages more functional and engaging for marketing to consumers.[46] A page is Facebook's recommended approach for creating an officially branded business presence.[47] Customize the page to reflect the company's style and values, but provide some content distinct from the firm's primary website.[48]

Once a page has been created, it must be updated frequently with new content. How often? Too-frequent updating can overwhelm a fan's newsfeed and become an annoyance. Do not update more than three times per day. Quality is much more important than quantity because boring or repetitive content can be easily hidden on Facebook.[49] Focus on content that is relevant and engaging for Facebook users.[50] Generally, Facebook content should be light, funny, and informative, or it should give a special deal or value. Give useful tips, or ask open-ended questions that will interest the audience.[51] Not every content item must be original: sharing links to interesting items can also be valuable.[52]

One avenue for Facebook content to go viral is through "likes." When a Facebook user likes a page, comment, or other material, it is displayed to her or his friends, who have an opportunity to like the item as well. In this way an appealing post or idea can spread rapidly through Facebook friend networks. However, users are often picky about which items they will like. To get an idea of what sort of content to post, look at others' Facebook pages—particularly those of businesses offering a product or service similar to the one being marketed—and see which statuses or comments are being liked the most. This survey will give some insight into what potential fans want to see. Often, less serious posts will be liked more, so keep content funny, personable, and entertaining.

To gain viewers for a page, put links on other websites and email signatures, business cards, and outgoing communications. To make the URL for the Facebook page easy to write and remember, it is important to "secure shorter 'vanity' URLs."[53] A customized URL makes the page more memorable, increasing the chance Facebook users will visit and become fans. Running contests or offering discounts to Facebook members are also good ways to convince people to follow a Facebook profile. Contests should be tailored to the product being offered. The risk is that if a contest goes poorly, it can be an embarrassment for the brand.[54] To avoid this, do not ask too much from members: pictures or stories are faster to submit than fully edited videos. More entries will be made if there are few or no barriers to joining the contest.

Groups are a classic and useful way to spread information about a product. However, on Facebook the groups' functionality presents some problems for marketing purposes.[55] Groups are very loosely organized and have many redundancies, overlaps, and competing groups on the same topics. Further, in groups beyond a certain size, mass messaging is blocked by Facebook, making communication with all the members difficult or impossible. While groups are a potential avenue for viral marketing, they are much more challenging to employ than a Facebook page.

While few brands have successfully marketed with groups, a great number have used Facebook Places to expand their social presence. Aimed toward small- to medium-sized local businesses, Places is a location-based service that allows users to check in online before or after they visit. A relatively recent feature (launched in late 2010), many Facebook users are already engaged by checking in with their favorite businesses.[56] Companies have found that integrating their physical and online locations has increased traffic to both. Offering special deals when visitors check in online is a reliable way to draw more attention.[57] It is also possible to create local market events, or host a charity drive to bring visitors to a Places page.[58] With some creativity, integrating a business into Facebook Places is a strong social media marketing tool.

Facebook derives much of its revenue from advertising. It offers an advertising program that is designed to be approachable by small businesses as well as global corporations. Ad costs can be set very low (well under $100 per month) depending on the budget. There are multiple purposes for ads. They can direct more viewers to like a page or send them to an external website. Ads can display a picture as well as text; choose these carefully to attract more clicks. While Facebook ads can be useful to market a product, they also provide valuable information about users. The Facebook ad tool can be specified for demographics, including race, gender, interests, and location, and the "Estimated Reach" section can give an idea of how many users fit the target market.[59] This insight can be gained at minimal cost by employing the Facebook ads interface, and it can help to fine-tune other aspects of a marketing campaign even beyond Facebook and social networking.

While Facebook offers many technical tools to assist a social media marketer (and will doubtless continue to offer more in the future), do not lose sight of the service's social nature. Keep in mind that while people may have hundreds of page likes or friends, the trend on "Facebook is that most of its millions and millions of members communicate with relatively few people."[60] Having a large number of likes or fans is a good step but no guarantee of actual results if nobody pays attention or responds to page updates. To avoid this problem, focus on relationships. Facebook is about personal connections, so let some personality through in updates.[61] Giving a human voice to a brand is one of the most powerful advantages of this social networking platform. Engage with users to create an emotional connection; this tactic will build brand loyalty.[62] Used correctly, Facebook is an excellent tool for B2C marketing.

BUSINESS-TO-BUSINESS MARKETING

While most people might associate social media marketing exclusively with the consumer side, business-to-business firms have also made a huge impression with social networking. The most dominant platform for B2B marketing is the professional networking site LinkedIn: "according to a study by BtoB Magazine and the Association of National Advertisers, 81% of business-to-business marketers use LinkedIn."[63] While there are obviously other platforms available for B2B, the current dominance of LinkedIn earns it the focus of this section.

LinkedIn is designed to facilitate interactions between business professionals. Users fill out profiles including their past education, job experience, skills, and so on. Like any social network site, people can connect with friends or colleagues, but the professional focus of LinkedIn causes many to take connections more seriously. As people are less prone to connecting with strangers or casual acquaintances, someone's connections can provide much more information about them. It is this "information about millions of people, including their connections, [that] makes LinkedIn such a powerful tool."[64] Before attempting to market on LinkedIn, complete the member profile in as much detail as possible. Unlike Facebook, putting more professional information on a profile can increase its chance of building connections.[65] Completing the profile signals seriousness and determination to use LinkedIn correctly.

Although some will screen their contacts, LinkedIn is still an enormously valuable networking or broadcasting tool to reach a huge audience. LinkedIn displays a broader network than just immediate contacts, including other people in the extended network. This "degrees-of-separation principle amplifies the value of contacts. A person who has only 100 direct contacts, for example, may have indirect access to over a million others."[66] LinkedIn recently implemented a status and newsfeed feature, which allows sharing of news topics or possibly marketing messages. Be aware, however, that LinkedIn is not

Do you really belong in Marketing & Advertising, or does Online Media describe you more succinctly? Help yourself get found by choosing your category wisely.

4. **The "Who Cares?" Summary.** Is your summary a third-person regurgitation of useless "accomplishments"? Sales guru Jeffrey Gitomer says: "They don't care how much you know until they know how much you care." In other words, people do not read your summary to learn more about you. They read to learn more about what *you* can do for *them.* Write your summary in first person for better engagement and personalization. Ask a few trusted friends to give you feedback. If the collective reaction is "No, it's good. *Really*!" you've got some work to do.

5. **Ignoring Critical Profile Areas.** Have you put effort into your headline or summary only to ignore the Contact Me section? You *do* want prospects to contact you, right? Don't simply check off the standard boxes provided by LinkedIn. Think! Tell people why there is value in contacting you, and add your business phone and/or email address so that they can. Realtors selling million dollar homes would never allow toys, debris, and overgrown grass to clutter the property and detract from the view. Your profile is the exterior of *your* million dollar home—the skills, accomplishments, and personality that make you who you are. Do everything in your power to make your LinkedIn profile attractive to buyers, and watch your business grow.

Victoria Ipri is a LinkedIn marketing expert and high caliber copywriter specializing in the VSB (very small business) B2B market. She is the author of the popular ebook, LinkedIn for the Clueless and regularly blogs at www.Linked-In-Sanity.com, as well as contributing frequently as a guest blogger. Victoria enjoys a healthy following across social media channels, manages several LinkedIn groups, and is regularly cited as a Top Influencer. She maintains a consistently superb ranking on LinkedIn for key search terms. Victoria holds a Masters certificate in Advanced Internet Marketing Strategies from the University of San Francisco, and resides in suburban Philadelphia, PA.

as marketer friendly as some other social networks, and overt broadcasting is not generally rewarded by the user base.

To facilitate connections, LinkedIn has several useful features for an aspiring networker. InMail, the internal messaging service for the site, can be used to contact others. LinkedIn offers several premium, paid account options that include more usage of InMail and better messaging functionality. These options can be useful if LinkedIn is a substantial part of the social media strategy. However, the same function of the premium accounts—contacting others outside one's immediate network—can be accomplished in more subtle and less expensive ways as well. The introductions feature on LinkedIn allows users to mention others and to suggest potential contacts. Some people require potential contacts to know their email address before inviting them to connect; getting an introduction can avoid this problem if there is a valuable contact whose email is unknown. Use introductions to expand a network and broaden the base of connections available from which to draw.

To reach a broader B2B audience, some of the most useful LinkedIn features are groups and Answers. Groups can be set up as private or open allowing anyone to join. Nearly every profession or industry specialization has some form of associated group. Joining these can be a quick way to build contacts, as membership in a common group can be an excuse to connect with future business partners. Groups also have associated discussion boards for conveying information on relevant topics. These boards can be the best way to meet people in the group. Before posting a new topic or question, spend some time reading and responding to others' posts. While general rules of online etiquette apply (see Chapter 12 for more details), the expectations on LinkedIn are especially high. Show courtesy and respect for other users' time by posting only relevant, well-considered, and valuable thoughts to group discussion boards.

To find an even more targeted audience, participate on LinkedIn Answers. Members can pose questions for others to answer. Contributing valuable, well-considered answers can draw in business leads by highlighting personal expertise. Reading and responding to others' answers can also build a larger network; compliment someone on his or her good response, explain why it was useful, then ask that person to join as a contact. After asking a question, be sure to choose a best answer, and then follow up with that individual to give her or him a personal thanks (through a private message). This is an effective way to build professional contacts with other experts in a field. Done well, networking through answers can generate revenue for a business.[67]

LinkedIn is targeted toward individuals, so interact under a personal account rather than a company or brand name. Instead of profiles, companies can set up pages, which LinkedIn members can follow in order to receive updates. These updates may include job openings, new positions, or similar information. At the time of this writing, there is no way to directly contact a company's followers on LinkedIn, limiting its applications for marketing. However, developing a large company following will raise awareness of a brand because more people will see that company as a suggestion based on their contacts' interests.

To channel more people toward following a company or being aware of a product, some firms are creating their own groups from the group up. This is a highly involved process and should not be taken lightly. If this path is chosen, first create a descriptive group name, which should address a common issue or problem or otherwise make clear why someone would be influenced to join. Next, start formulating content, which should follow the group's theme but not be overly promotional. Ask contacts, past customers, industry analysts, and employees to join the group and/or follow the brand. The result can be a beneficial co-branding opportunity for all parties.[68] This co-branding is especially useful if coworkers or clients write recommendations for each other.

Having many contacts or followers for a company can build an image of being LinkedIn savvy, but on its own it will not generate new business leads. Even a high response rate can be misleading: many contacts may come from other marketers, consultants, or job seekers hoping for work.[69] While these contacts are not directly useful, they help to expand the extended network and open up more business options in the future. Be aware that the "most successful business users of LinkedIn focus on providing professional services."[70] While other industries or products can also successfully use this networking service, for some it may be an uphill battle. While LinkedIn is an excellent professional networking tool, as a way to market products, it requires more sophistication.

Much more can, and has been, said about marketing on LinkedIn. Out of necessity this textbook covers only the most essential elements. Other features of the platform, such as recommendations, LinkedIn advertising, and applications, are important, but their usage is so specific that no general treatment could do them full justice. A social media marketer who intends to specialize in LinkedIn as a career path should examine some of the many more-detailed trade books on the subject. However, for most purposes that matter, the lessons of other social networks will hold true here, albeit with minor modifications. Keep in mind that the primary purpose for LinkedIn is to find, and be found by, other professionals.[71] The standards for conduct and conversation are high due to the background of most LinkedIn members. By building goodwill, responding thoughtfully, and keeping the audience in mind, a social media marketer can employ LinkedIn or other B2B networks to achieve great results.

CASE STUDY

Quantivo Uses LinkedIn for Lead Generation[†]

Introduction

Marketers frequently cite LinkedIn as one of the most valuable social networks to incorporate in a marketing strategy. But even marketers who have LinkedIn on their radar screens still wonder how to participate. What works, what doesn't, and what should you expect? We asked a marketer who is using LinkedIn for lead generation, to share his lessons on joining groups, sharing marketing collateral, and qualifying the leads that come through the channel.

[†]Using LinkedIn for Lead Generation: 6 Lessons" (2009, July 29), © MarketingSherpa, LLC. Reprinted with permission.

History ....

When the recession deepened [in the fall of 2009] Jason Rushin, Director, Marketing, Quantivo, needed to broaden the focus of his team's marketing efforts. The company's behavioral analytics tools had been originally positioned for retailers, but as the economy took its toll on that sector, the team wanted to expand its focus on the Web analytics and business intelligence markets.

Challenge ....

Rushin's team saw social media as a means to raise awareness about the products and generate leads from these new audiences. So, in addition to using Twitter, blogs, and YouTube videos, the team experimented with joining LinkedIn groups and sharing marketing collateral there to generate leads.

On one level, the tactic was a success: Rushin has connected with a community of prospects in the analytics world, received valuable feedback from those potential users, and was routinely seeing upwards of 70-90 registrations for marketing collateral shared with his network. "This is all gravy for us," says Rushin. "It's essentially free, other than requiring a little bit of time, and every lead that comes through is an incremental increase."

But the team also learned that LinkedIn requires a special approach to lead generation, and presents some unique challenges for marketers. We asked Rushin to share his top six lessons for using LinkedIn to generate leads.

Strategy and Results ....

Lesson #1. Target groups by activity level, not just size

Rushin began his LinkedIn experiment by searching for groups related to his company's key target industries:

- Retail
- Business intelligence
- Web analytics

The search turned up dozens of groups to explore. To winnow the list, he first eliminated any groups that were more geared toward job opportunities, rather than discussing business concerns.

Then, he examined the size of the groups, but had to actually join groups to assess each one's typical activity level. His goal was to find a highly engaged audience, rather than simply the largest audience.

"Some groups had 15,000 members, but every discussion had received only one or two comments."

For each group, Rushin spent 15 or 20 minutes reading through recent posts to assess group members' interest areas, and how much activity each post generated. In the end, he identified 17 groups that matched his needs.

Lesson #2. Join groups under an individual name, not a company identity

Social media is a two-way channel, which makes it especially important to assign a point-person to oversee your social media initiatives, establish themselves as a community member, and respond to feedback.

Rushin joined LinkedIn groups under his own name and title, to establish a presence within the industry audiences the company targets. Joining under a personal name also helps avoid the temptation to simply push company marketing

© AP Images/Minnesota Public Radio, Tim Post

into a community discussion group. "These are people who are potentially important in our industry, and I don't want to horn my way into a networking group and just start selling."

Lesson #3. Place collateral in the context of a conversation

Every time the team had a new piece of collateral to promote—such as a webinar or a white paper—Rushin looked for opportunities to share that information with the team's LinkedIn groups. Rather than just posting a message that promoted the team's marketing content, Rushin created messages that invited a conversation with group members. For example, when promoting a white paper, he would write a message to the group announcing the new title, sharing a link, and asking group members to provide feedback on the white paper itself. "Just from a pure marketing improvement point of view, it's almost like a blog where people can comment," says Rushin. "Now I have a place where people can comment on my white papers, and that's good feedback for me."

Rushin also monitored ongoing conversations to find opportunities to comment on other people's topics. He would include a link to marketing collateral when appropriate, but often would just share an opinion or give feedback on other group members' comments. "That's totally a conversation, not necessarily a marketing thing," he says. "People see my name as an actual contributor to the conversation."

Lesson #4. Response rate is highly variable

By participating in several groups, Rushin quickly saw that response to his lead-generation offers (in the form of landing page registrations) was highly variable. Each group has its own characteristics and dynamics, which make some white paper or webinar offers highly successful and others relative duds.

Testing content offerings among different groups is essential. Beyond that, Rushin also saw two factors that affected response rate:

Placement in the weekly or daily update newsletters

LinkedIn group members receive either daily or weekly email dispatches that high-light recent discussion activity within that group. Rushin discovered that placement on those email lists is akin to your placement on a search engine results page: The higher you are in the dispatch, the more views your topic will receive and the more registrations you're likely to capture.

Because there's no way to control the amount of activity within a group, there's no way to guarantee a topic you post will be among the top discussions listed in the email dispatch.

White paper or webinar topic

Not surprisingly, discussion group members are more interested in white papers or webinars that address industry trends, operational issues, and other educational topics. Product-focused white papers tend to receive a lackluster response. "Even with webinars, you want to use as little salesmanship as possible," says Rushin. "Our white papers now contain almost no Quantivo messaging in there, except for some boilerplate at the end."

Lesson #5. Create social media-specific landing pages

Rather than taking LinkedIn members to a standard landing page, Rushin created landing pages that specifically addressed the LinkedIn audience. The tactic did not require a complete landing page redesign. Instead, the team modified the landing page text to create continuity for visitors arriving from LinkedIn, using phrases such as: "Thank you for your interest in this discussion."

Lesson #6. Quality can be an issue with leads from LinkedIn

Rushin's team noticed a trend when they began qualifying leads generated through LinkedIn: Many responses came from job seekers and independent consultants looking for work.

Career networking is a major component of LinkedIn, so response from job-seekers is to be expected. However, minimizing response from these non-qualified leads can be tricky.

To discourage job-seekers, the team changed its registration form to require prospects to use an email address from a company domain—forbidding the use of free email accounts such as Yahoo! or Gmail. The technique backfired, though, when LinkedIn members began complaining to Rushin (and sometimes to their Twitter followers) that the company was preventing unemployed people or inde-pendent consultants from viewing their thought-leadership content.

Rather than risk alienating LinkedIn members, you may have to rely on inside sales follow-up or further nurturing to eliminate non-qualified leads from your mar-keting funnel.

What Is a White Label Social Network?

A **white label social network** is an online service that shares many, if not most, of the characteristics of a public social network like Facebook, with the key difference being the white label is privately run by a corporation or nonprofit organization. Hence, a white label social network is sometimes referred to as a corporate, private, or internal social network. A number of software vendors make platforms for organizations to use in constructing a white label social network. Some large corporations choose to build their own private social networks from scratch. However it is built, the chief purpose of a white label social network is to promote the goals of the organization that owns it.

White label social networks took off in popularity in the late-2000s. By 2007 there were dozens of services offering white label networking services to companies.[72] In 2008 ABI Research forecast that white label social networks would be a $1.3 billion industry within five years.[73] This forecast presaged a boom in white label social network companies until there were over 100 offering community management solutions.[74] This profusion of services contracted somewhat, as companies were sold and acquired, leaving fewer white label social network providers.[75] After the industry settled, the outcome left some services, such as Ning, RealityDigital, and Salesforce's Chatter, established as market leaders with large corporate clients. However, there remain many competitive, low-cost white label social network solutions available.

Pros and Cons of Creating a White Label Social Network

There are several readily apparent advantages for business purposes to using a white label social network as opposed to a mass audience social network. The first and most obvious is the ability to customize features to suit the user base. White label social networks are typically integrated directly into the company's home website and can be tweaked easily. Some aspects of other social networking sites, such as real-time chat, status updates, or birthday reminders, may be more or less useful to a particular company's social media campaign. Being able to pick and choose which will be implemented can be very helpful. Turning off nonessential social features can encourage employees who are less enthusiastic about networking by making the service appear more professional.[76] It can also bring more focus to the desired aspects of the platform, improving the quality of results. Customized features can aid in member retention by taking in feedback and implementing suggestions that can continue to improve the service.

Another advantage to white label social networks is that they provide much more detailed information to the administrators. The companies that provide white label social networks keep detailed statistics on each of them and their usage to provide more value to their corporate clients. This extremely useful data is collected and organized by the hosting company, reducing the amount of time and effort needed to gather it by hand.

Keeping members engaged after they follow the brand is a serious issue faced by other social network campaigns.[77] The reduced clutter imposed on members, as well as the specialized social atmosphere, tends to increase user loyalty on white label social networks. Employees or customers who already have a relationship with the company and people within it are less likely to leave the platform or become inactive. While white label social networks can be useful for generating sales leads or metrics on the target audience, their core value is still in building relationships.[78] Providing a custom platform for members to interact can be a boon to many social media marketing campaigns.

The many advantages to creating a white label social network are balanced by some substantial costs. The most obvious are measured in time and money; establishing and maintaining a whole social network is very time consuming, and requires a significant capital investment (by comparison to the other free social networking options). Pricing for white label social networking services can vary, but these direct costs are only the beginning. Integrating the network into an existing corporate site may incur web development costs. Most white label social networks also require a full-time administrator or community manager to maintain the service. Until a community becomes self-sustaining, company staff may have to do much of the work stimulating conversation and providing content.[79]

There is also the substantial risk that a social network never does become self-sustaining. Drawing in new members can be difficult unless a brand already has large public recognition. Even if it is sponsored by a popular brand, a network must demonstrate some purpose for participating, or it may resemble a ghost town. There are already so many platforms available for people to stay in touch with friends that any new service must provide some unique value to draw in users. Before starting a white label social network, be sure that there is sufficient draw for it to gain an audience or it may become simply an echo chamber of internal company discussions with little outside input.

While some organizations can obviously benefit from white label social networks, it is a tool not suited to every occasion. White label networks can be useful for reaching groups that might otherwise not participate, guiding which content members will view, and tracking the results easily. Whether these benefits are worth the costs will depend on the organization and the other aspects of its social media marketing strategy. Creating an in-house social network demands a huge commitment from the organization, but only if that is met with engagement by consumers is the project likely to be a wise investment.

CASE STUDY

Starbucks's Social Network Gathers Feedback from Its Customers

Introction ....

Starbucks, the largest chain of coffee shops in the world, unexpectedly fell on hard times in early 2008, with sales and foot traffic declining for the first time in its history. Howard Schultz, founder of Starbucks, returned to his company with a turnaround plan, which relied heavily on social media to improve the customer experience.

As part of this strategy, the coffee store chain launched MyStarbucksIdea.com, a highly successful discussion board, where consumers can suggest ideas, pose questions, and voice complaints.[80] This corporate social network, along with the company's other social media properties, have helped put Starbucks back on the path to growth.

History ....

In 1971 Starbucks was launched in Seattle, Washington. Three friends, Jerry Baldwin, Zev Siegl, and Gordon Bowker, opened a small shop and began selling fresh-roasted gourmet coffee beans as well as brewing and roasting accessories. The company thrived, making Starbucks the largest roaster in Washington, with six retail outlets by 1980.[81] In 1982 Jerry Baldwin hired a plastics salesman, Howard Shultz, as head of marketing.[82] Schultz would become the key to company's future.

Startbucks Coffee Shop

Shortly after being hired, Schultz was sent to Milan, where he immediately became thrilled with the coffee culture in Italy. Moreover, he noticed the unique atmosphere, where cafe drinkers sat around chatting and enjoying themselves while sipping coffee in the elegant surroundings. This Italian experience was his inspiration. Schultz had the idea to duplicate that great coffee experience in the United States.[83]

In 1987 the owners of Starbucks Coffee Company decided to sell their coffee business. Schultz raised the money to buy it and found investors to fund 125 more elegant, comfortable coffee houses. In 2004 Starbucks had 1,344 stores worldwide. Within a few more years, the company became a truly international corporation, with more than 9,000 locations in thirty-four countries, serving more than 20 million customers a week.[84]

By the time Schultz stepped down as chief executive officer in 2000, Starbucks had become one of the world's most recognizable brands.[85] However, in 2006 the company started running into overexpansion troubles. A management strategy of rapidly opening coffee shops in subprime locations, coupled with a weakening economy, led to a traffic decline for the first time ever in its domestic coffee shops.[86] A November 2007 announcement of the traffic loss shocked investors. Within days the coffee shop titan's market value tumbled by half what it was a year before.[87] Howard Schultz returned to his former position as CEO in January 2008 in hopes of turning the company around.[88]

Challenge

Schultz envisioned turning around the company he founded by "providing customers with the distinctive 'Starbucks Experience' and building on Starbucks's legacy of innovation." [89] He had another epiphany. This time, however, it did not come from another country's culture but rather the culture of the social web.

He soon began an incredibly aggressive and highly comprehensive, integrated social media marketing campaign. And "[a]s part of Mr. Schultz's multifaceted turnaround plan, the chain launched MyStarbucksIdea.com in July 2008 as a forum for consumers to make suggestions, ask questions and, in some cases, vent their frustrations."[90]

Creating a viable corporate (white label) social network is no easy task. According to a 2008 Deloitte report, *Tribalization of Business Survey*, the majority of corporate social networks at the time had "fewer than 500 active members and their biggest challenge [was] to keep members engaged."[91] If MyStarbucksIdea.com was going to succeed and help bring traffic back into the physical coffee shops, it first had to attract traffic to the website and then keep the customers engaged, excited, and involved.

Strategy

MyStarbucksIdea.com set out to provide a forum where customers could receive responses directly from the company and submit ideas that would be reviewed and promoted within the company. The idea was that "[c]ustomers join the online community to submit suggestions/comments and vote on others' ideas. There are also forums where customers can talk directly to Starbucks representatives (roughly 200 moderators) from departments like beverages, cards, food and Human Resources."[92]

This social network has an easy-to-use interface that encourages customers to share their ideas for improving the customer experience in the coffee shops. Users submit and vote on suggestions and see what changes have been implemented as a consequence of their feedback, as well as see what ideas are under review or approved for implementation. Not every idea is acted upon. But "Starbucks knows that engaged customers stick around, buy more (often) and refer friends."[93]

Starbucks adopted a six-pillar strategy for maintaining an active sustainable online community:

1. **Visible Action:** Show the number of changes made based on customer suggestions.
2. **Great Discussions:** Encourage conversations with the company and with other customers.
3. **Promotion:** Place ads in the stores to let customers know that specific changes were made as a result of online community involvement.
4. **New Features:** Introduce new fun and useful features to keep customers interested, such as polls that ask questions like "If the baristas were able to have tattoos, would you still come?"
5. **New Geographies:** Plan to include more countries in the mix.
6. **New Ways to Use Site to Have People Engage in Brand:** Encourage customers to become involved in decisions about the stores (e.g., picking the music, art, and books that will appear in a new or renovated store).[94]

Results

Right out of the gate, MyStarbucksIdea.com garnered customer participation. In November 2008, just eight months after its March 2008 launch, the white label social network site had 3 million unique visitors, 60,000 ideas submitted, 100,000 comments, 460,000 votes, and 2,500 moderator posts.[95] By August 2009, 75,000 ideas had been submitted to the website, with 25 of the suggestions implemented in the first year.[96] As of February 2010, the site had 180,000 registered users, with 80,000 submitted ideas, 50 of which have been implemented in-store.[97]

The company's shift of resources from traditional advertising campaigns, like TV media blitzes, to innovative social media marketing efforts, such as MyStarbucksIdea.com, has proved to be a good one. In November 2010 the site reached the milestone of the 100,000th idea submitted by a customer. As one commentator noted, "[t]he site is dynamic with customers posting one new idea on average every hour, ranging from new product suggestions about technology to techniques to improve the coffee beans."[98]

As evidenced by the numbers above, Starbucks has been successful in creating a vibrant white label social network, which not only energizes its customer base but also gathers valuable feedback from a highly engaged community of customers.

How Nonprofit Organizations Can Benefit from a Private Social Network

While corporations have used white label social networks to some effect, many nonprofits have started to employ them as well. Change.org, which provides private social networks to nonprofits, already has clients including CARE, Greenpeace, and Amnesty International using its services. Other networks include Wiser Earth, Care2, PickensPlan and the Sierra Club Activists Network. The appeal of a social network, without the commercial trappings of most mainstream platforms, has drawn nonprofits toward white label social networks instead. These private networks offer some substantial advantages for organizing and implementing an activist strategy, conducting a charity or service campaign, or otherwise influencing the world for the better.

Nonprofits have several advantages when opening a private social network. Most are organized around a recognizable cause or in response to a well-known problem. This characteristic creates an immediate user base, of people who are informed and interested in those particular issues. Nonprofits already operate in a circle of concerned individuals, and this operational sphere can be naturally transitioned into a social network.[99]

Once it is established, a white label social network can provide many benefits to a nonprofit. Deeper engagement between members can bring out new ideas and encourage people to work together for the common cause. Also, private social networks can serve a revenue-gathering function without requiring member dues by soliciting donations or selling advertisement space.[100] Some nonprofits have in-person meetings in addition to online collaboration; for such a private network can boost turnout, while at the same time live events can direct more people into the social network. Once people become involved, networking increases loyalty and member retention as well. This virtuous cycle helps explain why so many nonprofits have made use of white label social networks.

While they enter with some inherent advantages, nonprofit organizations still face the same challenge of building a membership for a private social network. Sometimes, a cause alone is not enough to get people involved. To draw in members, tailor features to the audience being targeted. The audience for networks on antipoverty or veterans support, for example, might be very different. Further, use general-purpose social networks (such as Twitter or Facebook) as beachheads to gather up a more specific following, and bring them back to the private network.[101] In this way, a general social network presence can be used to serve the particular goals of the organization.

The Future of Social Networks

Interest in social networks has grown at a constantly increasing pace since 2005, with no indication of tapering off.[102] Although Facebook dominates the landscape today, Google entered the fray in early June 2011 with its network, Google+, which has grown at a rapid pace, reaching an estimated 50 million members by October 2011.[103] Eric Schmidt, CEO of Google, believes that there is room for multiple social networks and for more cooperation among them.[104] This belief is evidenced by the many niche social networks that have survived and even thrived by catering to specific interests. One such example is Ravelry, which targets people with a passion for knitting, or My Own Car Show, which caters to hot-rod and antique car enthusiasts. These and other targeted social networks illustrate the power of specificity in audience selection.

However, Google+ and Facebook want to capture the masses, not small target markets. Schmidt is on record saying that Facebook with its 750 million users may well have too many entrenched users to face serious competition, but Google+ seems well positioned to give Facebook a run for its money.[105] Even though large networking sites are not always the best place to invest a marketing budget, they set social media trends and thus are worth developing a presence on.[106] Whatever the outcome, marketers who follow the precepts set forth in this chapter are likely to be the biggest beneficiaries of the competition and growth in social networking.

EXERCISE CASE STUDY

Anvil Media Uses LinkedIn for Brand Building[††]

Introduction ....

Compelling content, strategic connection building and search engine optimization (SEO) are just a few tools that Anvil Media president Kent Lewis uses to gain prestige via LinkedIn.

[††]Smith, Kimberly (2010), "LinkedIn Success Stories: How 11 Companies Are Using the Global Networking Site to achieve Their Business and Marketing Goals," © MarketingProfs LLC. Reprinted with permission.

History ....

Founded in 2000 by [Kent] Lewis, Anvil Media, Inc., is a search engine marketing agency specializing in SEO, pay-per-click management, search engine marketing public relations, online reputation management, and social media marketing services.

Courtesy Kent Lewis, www.anvilmediainc.com

Kent Lewis of Anvil Media

Challenge ....

Lewis [wanted] to continuously cultivate both his firm's reputation and his personal brand.

Strategy ....

To proactively connect with prospective clients and partners, Lewis requests introductions from existing contacts and uses the "People you may know" feature on his LinkedIn homepage. His goal is not to make as many connections as possible, but to make quality connections. The main reason Lewis makes an effort to grow his contact base is to "flatten out the six degrees of separation" to the people he wants to meet.

A high number of recommendations was a priority for Lewis, however. "Recommendations show quality and depth," he says. To strengthen his profile, Lewis reached out to associates from every line item of his experience with a request for recommendations. Today, his profile boasts 84 recommendations and covers every position but the oldest listed.

Lewis also optimizes his profile by incorporating keywords so that his information shows up in both LinkedIn and Google search results. For example, he lists every bit of experience he's ever had—every board membership, group affiliation, award received, you name it—and includes pertinent keywords in each description. He also lists key industry terms under his "Interests." "Social sites are highly trusted by Google," Lewis says, "and you can gain control of your brand through profile optimization."

LinkedIn lets users list three links on their profiles, so Lewis uses this space to describe each link with industry keywords instead of the default titles of "my website" or "my portfolio."

He also leverages applications, such as SlideShare, WordPress, and Events, to showcase his expertise and keep his name prominently featured on connections' homepages. "SlideShare on its own is a great SEO/brand management tool, but it's also good for marketing when others see your slides," he says.

His Twitter profile is synced, too. He uses it to broadcast interesting industry news. Lewis says he gets as much (and sometimes even more) interaction with these posts on LinkedIn as he does through Twitter.

LinkedIn Polls is another application he leverages. His network is notified each time a new poll is launched. Plus, Lewis takes the opportunity to share both the initial

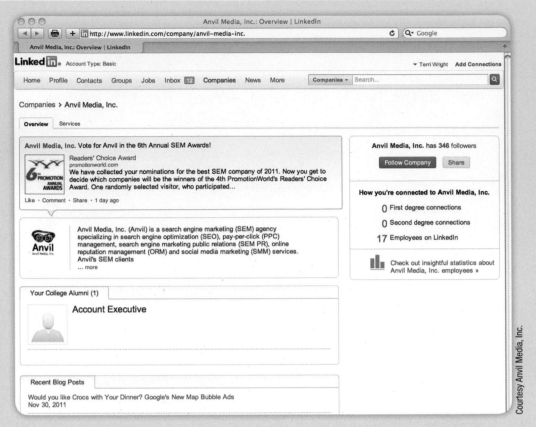

Anvil Media's LinkedIn Profile

feedback and final results he collects from respondents—which exhibits credibility and his understanding of the marketplace.

Perhaps the most advantageous resource Lewis uses for establishing authority is LinkedIn Answers. He searches for questions relevant to his line of work, then answers anywhere from three to 10 per week. So far, 28 of his responses have been nominated as "best answers," which means he usually appears as one of the top five experts in his contacts' networks. "Create messaging so compelling that people are likely to share it, vote it a 'best answer' and contact you directly," Lewis says. "When someone reads your answers and then takes the time to learn about who answered it, they're already sold by that point."

Results ....

Lewis's responses on LinkedIn Answers, supported by various elements of his profile, have been instrumental in positioning both himself and Anvil Media as highly competent. Lewis reports that LinkedIn is one of the top three sources of qualified leads for the agency. It has helped him identify and connect with key clients, such as the firm's largest one, a global book retailer. It also helped him secure a keynote speaking engagement at SEM4SMB in Austin, Texas, and aided in the development of an important partnership with an out-of-state company, for whom he may become a strategic advisor.

Review Questions for Anvil Media Case Study

1. How did connecting with quality industry contacts bridge the gap between Anvil Media and the people they would like to meet?

2. Why should one seek recommendations from people on LinkedIn?

3. Why is it important to optimize a LinkedIn profile with keywords?

4. What is the value of adding applications such as SlideShare and WordPress to a LinkedIn profile?

5. How can LinkedIn Answers be used to showcase a person's expertise to a broader audience?

Notes

1. "Searches on Google for Social Networks" (2011, July 13), Google Trends. Retrieved July 13, 2011, from http://www.google.com/trends?q=social+networks&ctab=0&geo=all&date=all&sort=0

2. Vik (2010, October 14), "What We Can Learn From Facebook's Success," There's Money Everywhere, retrieved July 13, 2011, from http://theresmoneyeverywhere.com/what-we-can-learn-from-facebook%E2%80%99s-success/ and Morales, Mitchell (2011, July 11), "Why Facebook Succeeded." *Social Network Revolution Blog*, retrieved July 13, 2011, from http://mitchellmessi.posterous.com/why-facebook-succeeded

3. "Top 15 Most Popular Social Networking Sites" (2011, July), eBizMBA. Retrieved July 13, 2011, from http://www.ebizmba.com/articles/social-networking-websites

4. Rheingold, Howard (2000 [1993]), *The Virtual Community: Homesteading on the Electronic Frontier* (Cambridge, MA: MIT Press).

5. Weber, Larry (2009), *Marketing to the Social Web* (Hoboken, NJ: John Wiley), p. 198.

6. "Social Networking Service" (n.d.), *Wikipedia*. Retrieved July 13, 2011, from http://en.wikipedia.org/wiki/Social_networking_service

7. Boyd, Danah M., and Nicole B. Ellison (2007), "Social Network Sites: Definition, History, and Scholarship," *Journal of Computer-Mediated Communication*, vol. 13, no. 1, article 11. Retrieved July 13, 2011, from http://jcmc.indiana.edu/vol13/issue1/boyd.ellison.html

8. "Six Degrees of Separation" (n.d.), WhatIs. Retrieved July 13, 2011, from http://whatis.techtarget.com/definition/0,,sid9_gci932596,00.html

9. Prall, Laura (2010, September 15), "Sixdegrees.com—Social Networking in Its Infancy," *Afri Design Ad Blog*. Retrieved July 13, 2011, from http://blog.afridesign.com/2010/09/sixdegrees-com-social-networking-in-its-infancy/

10. "About Ryze" (n.d.), Ryze. Retrieved July 13, 2011, from http://www.ryze.com/faq.php

11. Festa, Paul (2003, November 11), "Investors Snub Friendster in Patent Grab," CNET. Retrieved July 13, 2011, from http://news.cnet.com/2100-1032_3-5106136.html

12. Chafkin, Max (2007, June 1), "How to Kill a Great Idea!" *Inc.* Retrieved July 13, 2011, from http://www.inc.com/magazine/20070601/features-how-to-kill-a-great-idea.html

13. "The History of MySpace" (n.d.), WebHostingReport. Retrieved July 14, 2011, from http://www.webhostingreport.com/learn/myspace.html

14. Boyd, Danah M., and Nicole B. Ellison (2007), "Social Network Sites: Definition, History, and Scholarship," *Journal of Computer-Mediated Communication*, vol. 13, no. 1, article 11. Retrieved July 13, 2011, from http://jcmc.indiana.edu/vol13/issue1/boyd.ellison.html

15. "News Corporation to Acquire Intermix Media, Inc." (2005, July 8), press release, News Corporation. Retrieved July 14, 2011, from http://www.newscorp.com/news/news_251.html

16. Ibid.

17. "MySpace History" (n.d.), *Wikipedia*. Archived from the original on September 5, 2008, and retrieved July 14, 2011, from http://web.archive.org/web/20080905142107/http://profile.myspace.com/index.cfm?fuseaction=user.viewprofile&friendID=100000000

18. "MySpace Loses 10 Million Users in a Month" (2011, July 15), *The Telegraph*. Retrieved July 14, 2011, from http://www.telegraph.co.uk/technology/myspace/8404510/MySpace-loses-10-million-users-in-a-month.html#

19. Seward, Zachary M. (2007, July 25), "Judge Expresses Skepticism about Facebook Lawsuit," *Wall Street Journal*. Retrieved July 15, 2011, from http://online.wsj.com/article/SB118539991204578084.html?mod=googlenews_wsj

20. Phillips, Sarah (2005, July 25), "A Brief History of Facebook," *The Guardian*. Retrieved July 15, 2011, from http://www.guardian.co.uk/technology/2007/jul/25/media.newmedia

21. Rosmarin, Rachel (2006, September 11), "Open Facebook," *Forbes*. Retrieved July 15, 2011, from http://www.forbes.com/2006/09/11/facebook-opens-up-cx_rr_0911facebook.html

22. Yadav, Sid (2006, August 25), "Facebook—The Complete Biography," Mashable. Retrieved July 15, 2011, from http://mashable.com/2006/08/25/facebook-profile/

23. Arrington, Michael (2005, September 7), "85% of College Students Use Facebook," TechCrunch. Retrieved July 15, 2011, from http://techcrunch.com/2005/09/07/85-of-college-students-use-facebook/

24. Abram, Carolyn (2006, September 26), "Welcome to Facebook, Everyone," *Facebook Blog*. Retrieved July 15, 2011, from http://blog.facebook.com/blog.php?post=2210227130

25. "Facebook Overtakes MySpace" (2008, May 7), Alexa. Retrieved July 15, 2011, from http://blog.alexa.com/2008/05/facebook-overtakes-myspace_07.html

26. Tsotsis, Alexia (2011, June 28), "Sean Parker on Why MySpace Lost to Facebook," TechCrunch, retrieved July 15, 2011, from http://techcrunch.com/2011/06/28/sean-parker-on-why-myspace-lost-to-facebook/ and Chmielewski, Dawn C., and David Sarno (2009, June 17), "How MySpace Fell off the Pace," *Los Angeles Times*, retrieved July 15, 2011, from http://articles.latimes.com/2009/jun/17/business/fi-ct-myspace17

27. "Timeline" (n.d.), Facebook Press, retrieved July 15, 2011, from http://www.facebook.com/press/info.php?timeline and Scott, Hilary (2011, June 27), "Report: Facebook Hits 750 Million Users." *PCMag*, retrieved July 15, 2011, from http://www.pcmag.com/article2/0,2817,2387680,00.asp

28. Parr, Ben (2011, January 3), "Facebook Raises $500 Million in Funding, Now Worth $50 Billion." Mashable, retrieved July 15, 2011, from http://mashable.com/2011/01/03/facebook-raises-500-million-now-worth-50-billion-report/ and Goldfarb, Jeffery (2011, May 4), "Renren May Skew Facebook's Value," *New York Times*, retrieved July 15, 2011, from http://www.nytimes.com/2011/05/05/business/05views.html

29. "Top 100 Most Popular Facebook Pages In The World 2011" (2011, July 6), Facebook Page Leaderboard. Retrieved July 6, 2011, from http://www.facebook.com/pages/Top-100-Most-Popular-Fac%E1%BA%BBbook-Pages-In-The-World-2011/165408200173753

30. Spertus, Ellen, and Mehran Sahami (n.d.), "Evaluating Similarity Measures: A LargeScale Study in the Orkut Social Network," *Google Papers*, retrieved July 15, 2011, from http://static.googleusercontent.com/external_content/untrusted_dlcp/labs.google.com/en/us/papers/orkut-kdd2005.pdf and Jain, Sorav (2010, October 6), "40 Most Popular Social Networking Sites of the World," socialmediatoday, retrieved July 15, 2011, from http://socialmediatoday.com/soravjain/195917/40-most-popular-social-networking-sites-worlds

31. Bonfils, Michael (2011, April 13), "Why Facebook Is Wiping Out Orkut in India & Brazil," Search Engine Watch. Retrieved July 15, 2011, from http://searchenginewatch.com/article/2064470/Why-Facebook-is-Wiping-Out-Orkut-in-India-Brazil

32. Spears, Lee, and Danielle Kucera (2011, May 4), "Renren Surges on First Day of Trading with Price-to-Sales Beating Facebook," *Bloomberg*. Retrieved July 15, 2011, from http://www.bloomberg.com/news/2011-05-04/renren-raises-743-million-in-china-social-networking-site-ipo.html

33. "Russian Social Network Vkontakte Has More Than 100M Registered Users (2011, February 9), Digital Stats. Retrieved July 15, 2011, from http://blog.gigya.com/tag/vkontakte/

34. "Top 10 Social Networking Websites" (2011, March 28), *Geeks Desk Tech Blog*. Retrieved July 15, 2011, from http://www.geeksdesk.com/top-10-social-networking-websites/

35. Weinberg, Tamar (2009), *The New Community Rules* (Sebastopol, CA: O'Reilly Media), p. 150.

36. Qualman, Erik (2009), *Socialnomics* (Hoboken, NJ: John Wiley), p. 122.

37. Bolotaeva, Victoria, and Teuta Cata (2010), "Marketing Opportunities with Social Networks," *Journal of Internet Social Networking and Virtual Communities*, vol. 2010, article ID 109111. Retrieved July 13, 2011, from http://www.ibimapublishing.com/journals/JISNVC/2009/109111.pdf

38. Golden, Michelle (2011), *Social Media Strategies for Professionals and Their Firms* (Hoboken, NJ: John Wiley), p. 213.

39. Weber, Larry (2009), *Marketing to the Social Web* (Hoboken, NJ: John Wiley), p. 217.

40. Barker, Melissa (2010, July 27), "5 Steps to a Winning Social Media Marketing Plan," EnzineArticles. Retrieved July 31, 2011, from http://ezinearticles.com/?5-Steps-to-a-Winning-Social-Media-Marketing-Plan&id=4748691

41. Sernovitz, Andy (2009), *Word of Mouth Marketing: How Smart Companies Get People Talking* (New York: Kaplan Publishing), p. 143.

42. Borges, Bernie (2009), *Marketing 2.0* (Tucson: AZ: Wheatmark), p. 195.

43. Halligan, Brian, and Dharmesh Shah (2010), *Inbound Marketing* (Hoboken, NJ: John Wiley), p. 89.

44. Gillin, Paul (2009), *Secrets of Social Media Marketing* (Irvine, CA: Quill Driver Books), p. 122.

45. Gannet, Kim Komando (2011, March 11), "Market Your Business on Facebook in 4 Easy Steps," *USA Today*. Retrieved July 14, 2011, from http://www.usatoday.com/tech/columnist/kimkomando/2011-03-11-komando-facebook_N.htm

46. Weinberg, Tamar (2009), *The New Community Rules* (Sebastopol, CA: O'Reilly Media), p. 159.

47. Golden, Michelle (2011), *Social Media Strategies for Professionals and Their Firms* (Hoboken, NJ: John Wiley), p. 211.

48. Ibid., p. 208.

49. Parker, Donna (2011, April 12), "10 Ways to Market to Women on Facebook," All Facebook. Retrieved July 14, 2011, from http://www.allfacebook.com/10-ways-to-market-to-women-on-facebook-2011-04

50. Weinberg, Tamar (2009), *The New Community Rules* (Sebastopol, CA: O'Reilly Media), p. 154.

51. Shaw, Sarah (2011, January 31), "How to Market Your Business (or Yourself) on Facebook," *Maria Shriver Blog*. Retrieved July 14, 2011, from http://www.mariashriver.com/blog/2011/01/how-market-your-business-or-yourself-facebook

52. Treadaway, Chris, and Mari Smith (2010), *Facebook Marketing: An Hour a Day* (Hoboken, NJ: John Wiley), p. 58

53. Golden, Michelle (2011), *Social Media Strategies for Professionals and Their Firms* (Hoboken, NJ: John Wiley), p. 226.

54. Gillin, Paul (2009), *Secrets of Social Media Marketing* (Irvine, CA: Quill Driver Books), p. 223.

55. Smith, Justin (2007, December 9), "The Facebook Marketing Bible: 24 Ways to Market Your Brand, Company, Product, or Service inside Facebook," InsideFacebook. Retrieved July 14, 2011, from http://www.insidefacebook.com/2007/12/09/inside-facebook-marketing-bible-24-ways-to-market-your-brand-company-product-or-service-in-facebook/

56. Howard, Justyn (2010, August 21), "A Local Business Guide to Facebook Places," Sprout Social Insights. Retrieved July 28, 2011, from http://sproutsocial.com/insights/2010/08/a-local-business-guide-to-facebook-places/

57. Axon, Samuel (2011, January 19), "How to List Your Business on Facebook Places," Sprout Social Insights. Retrieved July 28, 2011, from http://sproutsocial.com/insights/2011/01/how-facebook-places-local-business/

58. Ibid.

59. Halligan, Brian, and Dharmesh Shah (2010), *Inbound Marketing* (Hoboken, NJ: John Wiley), p. 91.

60. Weber, Larry (2009), *Marketing to the Social Web* (Hoboken, New Jersey: John Wiley), p. 208.

61. Shaw, Sarah (2011, January 31), "How to Market Your Business (or Yourself) on Facebook," *Maria Shriver Blog*. Retrieved July 14, 2011, from http://www.mariashriver.com/blog/2011/01/how-market-your-business-or-yourself-facebook

62. Parker, Donna (2011, April 12), "10 Ways to Market to Women on Facebook," All Facebook. Retrieved July 14, 2011, from http://www.allfacebook.com/10-ways-to-market-to-women-on-facebook-2011-04

63. "LinkedIn Success Stories: How 11 Companies Are Using the Global Networking Site to Achieve Their Business and Marketing Goals" (n.d.), MarketingProfs. Retrieved July 29, 2011, from http://www.marketingprofs.com/store/product/37/linkedin-success-stories

64. Halligan, Brian, and Dharmesh Shah (2010), *Inbound Marketing* (Hoboken, NJ: John Wiley), p. 94.

65. Golden, Michelle (2011), *Social Media Strategies for Professionals and Their Firms* (Hoboken, NJ: John Wiley), p. 219.

66. Gillin, Paul (2009), *Secrets of Social Media Marketing* (Irvine, CA: Quill Driver Books), p. 123–24.

67. Schaffer, Neal (2009), *Understanding, Leveraging, & Maximizing LinkedIn* (Charleston, SC: Booksurge), p. 193.

68. Borges, Bernie (2009), *Marketing 2.0* (Tucson, AZ: Wheatmark), p. 193.

69. "Using LinkedIn for Lead Generation: 6 Lessons" (2009, July 29), Marketing Sherpa. Retrieved July 29, 2011, from http://www.marketingsherpa.com/article.php?ident=31315#

70. Weinberg, Tamar (2009), *The New Community Rules* (Sebastopol, CA: O'Reilly Media), p. 164.

71. Schaffer, Neal (2009), *Understanding, Leveraging, & Maximizing LinkedIn* (Charleston, SC: Booksurge), p. 284.

72. Owyang, Jeremiah (2007, February 15), "Social Networking White Label Market Overcrowded, Reminiscent of CMS and Portal Craze of Yesteryear," Web Strategy. Retrieved July 31, 2011, from http://www.web-strategist.com/blog/2007/02/15/social-networking-white-label-market-overcrowded-reminiscent-of-cms-and-portal-craze-of-yesteryear/

73. McKay, Lauren (2008, July 23), "'White-Label' Social Networking to Hit the Enterprise: ABI Research Predicts the Industry Will Reach $1.3 Billion within Five Years," Destination CRM. Retrieved July 31, 2011, from http://www.destinationcrm.com/Articles/CRM-News/Daily-News/White-Label-Social-Networking-to-Hit-the-Enterprise--50038.aspx

74. Owyang, Jeremiah (2007, February 12), "List of 'White Label' or 'Private Label' (Applications You Can Rebrand) Social Networking Platforms, Community Platforms," Web Strategy. Retrieved July 31, 2011, from http://www.web-strategist.com/blog/2007/02/12/list-of-white-label-social-networking-platforms/

75. Kanaracus, Chris (2008, February 11), "'White label' Social Networking Set for Shake-up," InfoWorld. Retrieved July 31, 2011, from http://www.infoworld.com/d/developer-world/white-label-social-networking-set-shake-277

76. "Internal Social Networks: Pros & Cons" (2010, June 23), *SNAP Blog*. Retrieved July 14, 2011, from http://snapblogger.wordpress.com/2010/06/23/internal-social-networks-pros-cons/

77. Meldrum, Scott (2010, October 28), "Fans Are Fickle: How to Inspire Loyalty after the 'Like.'" IMedia Connection. Retrieved July 31, 2011, from http://www.imediaconnection.com/content/27915.asp

78. Owyang, Jeremiah (2008, June 3), "When Social Media Marries CRM Systems," Web Strategy. Retrieved July 31, 2011, from http://www.web-strategist.com/blog/category/white-label-social-network/page/3/

79. "Internal Social Networks: Pros & Cons" (2010, June 23), *SNAP Blog*. Retrieved July 14, 2011, from http://snapblogger.wordpress.com/2010/06/23/internal-social-networks-pros-cons/

80. York, Emily Bryson (2010, February 22), "Starbucks Gets Its Business Brewing Again with Social Media," *Advertising Age*. Retrieved September 19, 2011, from http://adage.com/article/special-report-digital-alist-2010/digital-a-list-2010-starbucks-brewing-social-media/142202/

81. "Who Founded Starbucks?" (n.d.), *YourDictionary*. Retrieved July 7, 2011, from http://answers.yourdictionary.com/business/who-founded-starbucks.html

82. "The History of Starbucks" (2009, July 8), BizAims. Retrieved July 7, 2011, from http://www.bizaims.com/coffee%20break/curiosities%20events%20funny/the%20history%20starbucks

83. "Starbucks Coffee History" (n.d.), Ultimate Coffees Info. Retrieved July 7, 2011, from http://www.ultimate-coffees-info.com/starbucks-coffee-history.html

84. "Starbucks Coffee Company" (n.d.), Smell the Coffee. Retrieved July 7, 2011, from http://www.coffee.great-recipe.net/25142.php

85. Ignatius, Adi (2010, July-August), "The HBR Interview: 'We Had to Own the Mistakes,'" interview with Howard Schultz, *Harvard Business Review*. Retrieved July 7, 2011, from http://www.ceo.com/tag/starbucks-ceo-interview/

86. "Shakeup at Starbucks" (2009, February 11), CBS News. Retrieved July 7, 2011, from http://www.cbsnews.com/stories/2008/01/07/business/main3684458.shtml

87. Usborne, David (2008, March 21), "Change of Tune at Starbucks as Lattes Lose Their Allure," *The Independent*. Retrieved July 7, 2011, from http://www.independent.co.uk/news/world/americas/change-of-tune-at-starbucks-as-lattes-lose-their-allure-799038.html

88. "Starbucks Chairman Schultz Returning as CEO" (2008, January 8), MSNBC. Retrieved July 7, 2011, from http://www.msnbc.msn.com/id/22544023/ns/business-consumer_news/t/starbucks-chairman-schultz-returning-ceo/

89. "Will Restructuring Help Starbucks Turnaround?" (2008), casestudyinc.com. Retrieved July 6, 2011, from http://www.casestudyinc.com/Starbucks-Turnaround-Strategy-Case-Study

90. York, Emily Bryson (2010, February 22), "Starbucks Gets Its Business Brewing Again with Social Media," *Advertising Age*. Retrieved July 7, 2011, from http://adage.com/article/special-report-digital-alist-2010/digital-a-list-2010-starbucks-brewing-social-media/142202/

91. "Retailers Experimenting with Social Networks" (2008, August), Retailnet Group. Retrieved July 7, 2011, from http://archive.constantcontact.com/fs028/1102142477435/archive/1102205036940.html

92. Lynn, Christopher (2008, November 20), "Three Killer Social Media Case Studies from SMC San Francisco," socialTNT. Retrieved July 6, 2011, from http://socialtnt.com/2008/11/20/three-killer-social-media-case-studies-from-smc-san-francisco/

93. Bains, Linda (2010, July 8), "Starbucks Listens to Customer Feedback: A Case Study," Cvent, *Web Surveys*. Retrieved July 6, 2011, from http://survey.cvent.com/blog/market-research-and-survey-basics/starbucks-listens-to-customer-feedback-a-case-study

94. Cubicans (2010, April 19), "Make Your Business Boom: Social Media Style," *Cubic*, retrieved July 7, 2011, from http://www.cubiccreative.com/blog/index.php/2010/04/19/make-your-business-boom-social-media-style/ and Lynn, Christopher (2008, November 20), "Three Killer Social Media Case Studies from SMC San Francisco," socialTNT, retrieved July 6, 2011, from http://socialtnt.com/2008/11/20/three-killer-social-media-case-studies-from-smc-san-francisco/

95. Lynn, Christopher (2008, November 20), "Three Killer Social Media Case Studies from SMC San Francisco," socialTNT. Retrieved July 6, 2011, from http://socialtnt.com/2008/11f/20/three-killer-social-media-case-studies-from-smc-san-francisco/

96. Adamson, Walter (2009, August 12). Retrieved July 6, 2011, from http://www.walteradamson.com/2009/08/my-starbucks-ideas-action.html

97. Boese, John (2010, March 3), "Crowdsourcing: Getting Others to Do Your Work for You," Ogilvy Digital Labs. Retrieved July 7, 2011, from http://nydigitallab.ogilvy.com/2010/03/01/crowdsourcing-getting-others-to-do-your-work-for-you/

98. Anand, Raj (2011, February 2), "A Holistic Approach to Social Media Marketing: Part 1," *Que*. Retrieved July 6, 2011, from http://www.quepublishing.com/articles/article.aspx?p=1665789

99. Barry, Frank (n.d.), "What Nonprofit Organizations Should Know about Launching a Private Label Social Network," Blackbaud. Retrieved July 14, 2011, from http://www.blackbaud.com/files/resources/downloads/WhitePaper_LaunchingAPrivateSocialNetwork.pdf

100. Ibid.

101. Livingston, Geoff (2010, February 12), "5 Tips for Creating Non-Profit Online Communities," Mashable. Retrieved July 31, 2011, from http://mashable.com/2010/02/12/non-profit-communities/

102. "Social Networks" (n.d.), Google Trends. Retrieved December 15, 2011, from http://www.google.com/trends?q=social+networks

103. "Introducing the Google+ Project: Real-life Sharing, Rethought for the Web" (2011, June 28), *Official Google Blog*. Retrieved December 5, 2012, from http://googleblog.blogspot.com/2011/06/introducing-google-project-real-life.html and onelily (2011, October 11) "Current State of Social Media – The BIG Four," Visual.ly. Retrieved December 5, 2012, from http://visual.ly/current-state-social-media-big-four?ref=nf

104. Gayomali, Chris (2011, July 11), "Eric Schmidt: There's Room for Multiple Social Networks, More Cooperation," TechLand. Retrieved July 14, 2011, from http://techland.time.com/2011/07/11/eric-schmidt-theres-room-for-multiple-social-networks-more-cooperation/

105. Ibid.

106. Gillin, Paul (2009), *Secrets of Social Media Marketing* (Irvine, CA: Quill Driver Books), p. 118.

Microblogging

While many of the social media market-ing tools discussed up to this point have had similar, historical mediums to draw guidance from, microblogging is almost entirely without precedent. Some other media encourage brevity, but microb-logging positively enforces it. These changes present unique challenges for the modern marketing professional.

The popularity and growth of microblogging as a communication technology reflect broader social trends in how people view, consume, and digest infor-mation. The ability to focus on long messages or arguments has declined with access to digital technology: a 2002 BBC article reported that the average web browser's attention span was just seconds, comparable to that of a goldfish![1] In the decade since that column was written, consumers have become even more inundated with brief, catchy digital messages as advertisers try to cap-ture those crucial few seconds.

In this short and fast environment, microblogging tools like Twitter are an increasingly relevant component for a marketing strategy. Companies are discovering that microblogging can play an important role in brand build-ing, viral marketing, and increasing sales.[2] This chapter will explore a brief history of microblogging, some best practices for employing it in a social media marketing campaign, and how to leverage a microblogging presence to achieve the marketing objectives.

LEARNING OBJECTIVES

After completing this chapter, students will be able to:

- Define microblogging
- Describe a brief history of microblogging
- Identify different uses for microblogging
- Explain the benefits of marketing with social networks
- Describe ways to build brands with Twitter
- Summarize how to create an effective Twitter channel
- Identify microblogging and the market objectives

What Is Microblogging?

The term "microblogging" is not frequently used in conversation; instead, people typically refer to the name of their favorite microblogging platform, such as Twitter. However, for the purposes of this chapter, a definition to distinguish microblogging from other social media outlets is useful. **Microblogging** is a form of blogging, with the main difference being significant limits on the length of posts, typically consisting of short sentences and links.[3] *Wikipedia* defines microblogging as

> a broadcast medium in the form of blogging. A microblog differs from a traditional blog in that its content is typically smaller in both actual and aggregate file size. Microblogs "allow users to exchange small elements of content such as short sentences, individual images, or video links.* As with traditional blogging, microbloggers post about topics ranging from the simple, such as "what I'm doing right now," to the thematic, such as "sports cars." Commercial microblogs also exist, to promote websites, services and/or products, and to promote collaboration within an organization. Some microblogging services offer features such as privacy settings, which allow users to control who can read their microblogs, or alternative ways of publishing entries besides the web-based interface. These may include text messaging, instant messaging, E-mail, or digital audio.[4]

The most essential aspect of microblogging is that messages are required to be short. *Platforms enforce a limit (most often 140 characters) to restrict the length of users' posts, and force ideas to be communicated succinctly.* To visualize how long is allowed, see the italicized sentence preceding this one; it is exactly 140 characters, including the period.

A Brief History of Microblogging

Where did microblogging originate? The earliest ancestors of microblogs were referred to as "tumblelogs" and contained links or stream of consciousness posts, all in quick succession. Tumblelogs were first described by Jason Kottke in October 2005.[5] The concept of microblogging, as it exists today, leapt to prominence in 2006 with the launch of Twitter by its founder, Jack Dorsey. Originally an internal company service for Odeo, Twitter grew into a public sensation.[6] In February 2011 Twitter passed beyond 200 million accounts.[7] As of July 2011, Twitter has over 333 million accounts, with 8.9 more being added every second.[8] At this pace Twitter will pass 400 million accounts by early 2012.

Twitter has a solid lead in microblogging membership; a Pew Research report found that 13% of online adults now use Twitter.[9] However, other microblogging sites have also gained an audience as well, as shown in Table 11.1. Some noteworthy sites include Jaiku, AOL Lifestream, and Soup.io, to name just a few. In addition, social networking sites, such as Facebook, LinkedIn, Google Buzz, and Yahoo Pulse, have a microblogging aspect in the form of status updates.

These sites offer varying features and post guidelines, and they also draw very different demographics; for example, Plurk (http://www.plurk.com) draws 38% of its traffic from Taiwan.[10] Other international microblogging sites are also rising in importance, such as Identi.ca, which is a popular in the Philippines, Thailand, and Indonesia.[11]

---

*Kaplan, Andreas M., and Michael Haenlein (2011), "The Early Bird Catches the News: Nine Things You Should Know about Micro-blogging," *Business Horizons*, vol. 54, no. 2.

**See http://www.jaiku.com/; http://lifestream.aol.com/; and http://www.soup.io/

Microblogging Sites	Alexa Global Traffic Rank*	Google Page Rank**
Twitter	9	9
Tumblr	44	8
Posterous	525	7
FriendFeed	1,414	N/A
Plurk	1,708	7
Yammer	3,518	7
Indenti.ca	5,381	7
Soup.io	5,773	6
DailyBooth	5,812	6
Jaiku	11,700	6
Meemi	31,693	4
Qaiku	45,957	5
Plerb	47,053	4
Hictu	52,362	5
Koornk	690,856	5

© Cengage Learning 2013

Table 11.1 Popular Microblogging Sites, as of December 2011

*Alexa Global Traffic Rank estimates a site's popularity, with traffic data from Alexa Toolbar users and other diverse traffic sources, using an ascending scale where 1 represents the highest traffic rank.

**Google Page Rank uses the number and quality of links to a web page to determine its relative importance, using a scale of 0-10, with 10 indicating the highest rank and 0 the lowest.

From this plethora of sites, microblogging has evolved into an important source of news and citizen journalism. The ease of posting and sharing allows relevant news to reach interested groups quickly. The material covered can range from celebrity gossip to world events. During the Iranian elections, Twitter was frequently updated with news, making it possible to follow along with events in real-time.[12] When Osama bin Laden was killed by an American intervention in Pakistan, a Twitter user was the first to announce the operation. These and many other examples help to illustrate the power of microblogs for distributing information. The hashtag (#) feature of Twitter (discussed later in the chapter) makes news topics easily searchable so that important items can be found and shared.

Different Uses for Microblogging

While millions of people now participate in microblogging, the platform's usage is deceptively simple from a marketing perspective. Its purpose can be broken down into two main divisions: one is to convey information, and the second is to start a discussion or to participate in an ongoing conversation.[13] Both of these goals will be familiar from other social media platforms, but the special challenges of microblogging require a different format to accomplish them. The give-and-take nature of the format makes Twitter, and other microblogging platforms, a "very multidirectional communication medium."[14]

In his book *Twitter Power 2.0*, Joel Comm describes six different categories of microblog posts (written in context of Twitter, these are referred to as **tweets**). Different types of tweets include:

1. **Classic Tweets**: "This is What I'm Doing Now."
2. **Opinion Tweets**: "This is What I'm Thinking Now."
3. **Mission Accomplished Tweets**: "This is What I've Just Done."
4. **Entertainment Tweets**: "I'm Making You Laugh Now."
5. **Question Tweets**: "Can You Help Me Do Something Now?"
6. **Picture Tweets**: "Look at What I've Been Doing."[15]

Depending on the industry, audience, and objectives, a different mix of these six components might be appropriate. Selecting the proper ratio between them is where much of the artistry behind microblog marketing is involved. While Twitter asks users to post "What's happening?" (the classic tweet), this may be one of the less-used categories employed by a marketing professional. Saying "I'm at the store" or "getting lunch" is not uncommon on a personal Twitter account but less useful for conveying a product-oriented message (unless the classic tweet is given some extra relevance or pizzazz). Indeed, sharing excess personal details can become a "mistweet" that is contrary to or does not serve the marketing objectives at all.[16]

While some personal "What's happening" posts are good to establish a human voice, for the purposes of social media marketing, the other five categories will probably be used more frequently. The following sections will offer guidelines for good microblog content and posting strategies. While reading, consider which category each tweet might fall into and how to balance all of the categories in a strategic way.

Tips for Brand Building with Twitter

While other microblogging platforms offer unique benefits and target markets, Twitter remains the largest and best-known microblog site online, so in most cases it will be the starting point for establishing a brand's presence through microblogging. As such, the rest of the chapter will focus on Twitter, although similar strategies (with some intelligent modification) may likely be applicable to any other microblogging platform. This focus reflects not only Twitter's large market share for microblogging, but also the incredible utility of Twitter as a branding tool, especially for small businesses.[17] With the low start-up cost and speed of content creation, Twitter will be a common entry point for many social media marketing strategies.

Why is there so much focus on Twitter? The platform has a number of advantages for a clever social media marketing team. Unlike a blog or podcast, it takes less time to reach large numbers of readers on Twitter. The ability to directly contact other users with thoughts or questions invites a more interactive and engaging strategy. As a result, Twitter can draw attention from high-profile people and connect with opinion leaders in a variety of industries.[18] More and more celebrities, business leaders, and other public figures have become involved, deepening the pool of talented individuals with whom to communicate. An increasing number of CEOs are now active on Twitter in order to take advantage of these tangible benefits.[19]

The ease of connecting and the wide audience to reach caused one author to describe Twitter as "somewhat intoxicating."[20] Success from microblogging can indeed be a heady experience. However, failure is publicized and very sobering, so it is wise to enter with a plan and some basic guidelines to avoid mistakes.

SEARCH TO GATHER INFORMATION

One of the most powerful Twitter features is the ability to search users, posts, and subjects. For the former. Twitter can operate as a "global human search engine."[21] In almost any field of expertise, it is possible to find someone on Twitter with relevant information to share. In a live conversation, listening is the best way to learn; on Twitter that function is filled by searching.[22] Developing good search skills is necessary to get familiar with the audience being addressed and to see what they will respond to.

Further, search can turn up information about specific topics. As tweets are displayed in reverse–chronological order, a researcher can look to see how frequently a specific topic is updated to get a feel for what the audience is interested in. A topic that receives many tweets is obviously important to more people. When beginning a social media marketing campaign, start using Twitter by looking up the brand's name, the competition, and what is being said about each.[23] This approach will give a feel for the social landscape and suggest intelligent future tactics.

The ease of topic searching is aided by **hashtags**. Included in the form of "#topic" in tweets, clicking on the word with "#" in front (the hashtag topic) will draw up a list of other tweets that have been tagged with the same topic. For example, if someone were looking for news about the economy and Federal Reserve, that individual could try searching *#economy* or *#Fed*. To find information about social media marketing, one could search *#socialmedia* or *#smm*. Users place hashtags in their tweets to make them more visible, so take advantage of this feature both when gathering information and attempting to pass messages on to others.

KNOW THE AUDIENCE

Using the search function to navigate through Twitter is helpful for building a portrait of the target audience. Think back to Chapter 3 and the persona development cycle. Twitter, with its easily searched database of faces attached to personal interests and hobbies, provides an optimal arena to study and develop different user personas. To do this, find one person whose profile seems to exemplify a certain persona. Then, look at the list of similar people to follow, which Twitter provides. Make note of how their expressed interests are similar to or different from the first profile. Continue this process until a more fleshed-out persona emerges. Aggregating together different characteristics of Twitter users who all might be interested in a brand or product allows a picture of the target market to emerge.

A word of caution on using Twitter to estimate more general target audiences: the demographics on Twitter do not necessarily reflect those of the general public. Adoption of Twitter is more pronounced in some groups than others. For example, there tend to be more young (18- to 34-year-old) Twitter users and more African-American and Hispanic Twitter users than would be found in a random sample of the population.[24] While this skewing introduces complications into statistical research, it should not affect the persona development process described above. Twitter is such a large and diverse community that many people can be found possessing any particular value or need that a social media marketer might be interested in. Focus on the segment that will be drawn to the marketed product, and then aggregate demographics become less important.

CUSTOMIZE THE PROFILE PAGE

When deciding whether or not to follow someone, the profile page (see Figure 11.1) plays an enormous role in a viewer's decision. Generally, looking at the profile is the most research that a Twitter user will do before deciding to follow or not. A good profile page will help to develop a solid following and also provide external benefits such as views to the main site and more interest in the marketed product.

Twitter offers many options to customize a profile's home page. Background, text color, avatar picture, and description are the most noticeable features that can be modified. The first, and perhaps most important choice, is selecting a good avatar

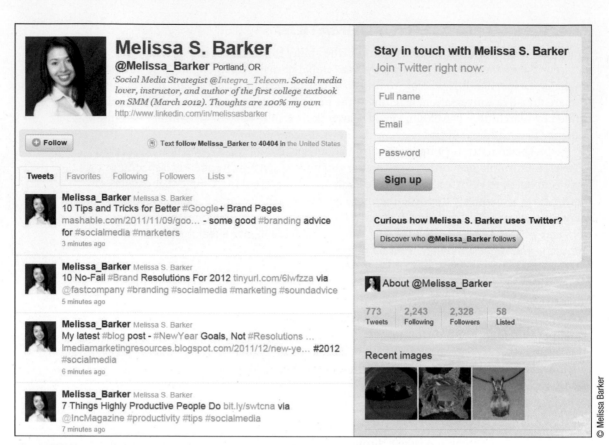

Figure 11.1 Twitter Profile Page

picture, which will appear next to every tweet, so the avatar should be recognizable and eye-catching for best results. It is very common, and perhaps the best practice, to use a face picture as the avatar. Generally, people follow faces more readily than logos.[25] Consequently, putting a brand or corporate image as the avatar is less personable than a facial picture. The avatar picture does not have to be overly polished; casual photos can outdo studio photography by transmitting a more relaxed image.

The profile's description should complement the avatar by providing context and important details. Writing space is limited, so the description will have to be concise. The background image can fill in the rest that cannot be conveyed in the description. A custom-made background image can display personality, longer explanation of the product or services, and past accomplishments. The background is also a place to put URLs for other social networking profiles, websites, or blogs.[26] The combined result in a profile page should both encourage viewers to follow and to give links to other social media platforms in order to allow deeper engagement.

TWEET CONTENT

On a Twitter feed, it is especially easy to miss tweets that do not immediately catch the eye. If an account does not provide appealing content, users will ignore it. As a golden rule, the best content is "interesting, fun, and valuable."[27] The first two are self-explanatory, but creating valuable content is more complex because it must be both timely and relevant. Think about the sorts of concerns, interests, or values that the target Twitter audience might have, and address those first. Also, refer back to the six types of Tweets (covered earlier in the chapter). Keeping a balance between different categories will make the content fresher and more engaging.

While it is important to have varying content, do not cover too many different topics in quick succession. Having multiple streams of thought going at once can make replies from followers confusing and can prevent outside viewers from understanding the overall message(s). Even if several tweets are sent out each day, keep each day's tweets to a common theme or idea.[28] This practice will help prevent miscommunication.

With a limited space to write on Twitter, some content will be too large for a tweet, so it only makes sense to provide a link to another site. Distributing links to interesting articles, images, or websites can be valuable to readers and draw a positive response. However, sharing a link is no guarantee anyone will visit it, especially if the content is poorly described, is uninteresting, or seems untrustworthy. In particular, links without a title attached are unlikely to get a response.[29] To save room for describing the linked content, use shortened URLs. A few link-shortening services include tinyurl.com, is.gd, ow.ly, and bit.ly.[30] Some of these services also provide free analytics to determine how many people clicked each link, a metric that can be valuable feedback for choosing later content.

Aside from clicking on links, another way to know if followers listen or care about what is being discussed is to look at how many retweets are given.[31] Users can **retweet** a post, displaying its author on their own timeline, or they can use "RT @*[author]*" and mention for a similar effect. Twitter will show which posts are retweeted and who did the retweet. Twitter users retweet content they enjoy or are willing to vouch for, so it is a signal of approval when a retweet occurs. This process gives insight into which sorts of content are most popular.

CASE STUDY

Zappos Tweets Its Way to Customer Service Nirvana[†]

Introduction

What's more stereotypically trivial than shoe shopping? Using Twitter, of course! Online shoe retailer Zappos does shoes and social media remarkably well. Scores of bloggers, lots of video blogging and 198 employees on Twitter help keep the company's profile high and humanize the folks behind the shoe sales.

Of all the different types of social media the company uses, none are as interesting as its use of Twitter. Twitter may sound cliché, but it's not just about Twitter as one single service. Twitter is symbolic of rapid, short, synchronous and public conversations. Zappos has bitten off a big chunk of that paradigm.

History

[Zappos was founded in 1999 by Nick Swinmum. His frustration in trying to find the right-sized shoes in a color and style that matched his tastes inspired Swinmum to launch an online shoe store.[32] It turned out that a lot of other people were looking for a wider shoe selection too: "[i]n 2001, Zappos more than quadrupled their yearly sales, bringing in $8.6 million."[33] By 2008 Zappos reached $1 billion in annual sales, stocking over 3 million shoes, clothing items, and accessories from

---

[†]Kirkpatrick, Marshall (2008, April 30), "Zappos Shows How Social Media Is Done," © ReadWriteWeb.

more than 1,100 brands. [34] Zappos attracted the attention of Amazon.com, which announced on July 22, 2009, that they had acquired the online shoe retailer for $928 million in stock and cash.[35]]

Challenge

It's a daring step for a brand to take; you never know when someone is going to post a message like "I <3 clubbing baby seals. =)" on your company website. Zappos employees also drink a lot, but always in moderation—a Tweetscan search finds that no one inside or outside the company has ever tweeted the words Zappos and "drunk" in the same message! I'd have thought excessive drinking would lead to shoe loss and thus replacement but apparently the company is taking a longer-term approach to its social media strategy.

Instead, the aggregation site highlights words throughout the page that link back to search results pages in the Zappos catalog. Could this really drive sales? Conceivably, I suppose.

Strategy

[Retailer Zappos has always had an excellent reputation for customer service. It prides itself on being customer focused, and Twitter provided it with another opportunity to show its commitment to its customers. Zappos' involvement with social media is driven by its CEO, Tony Hsieh. He's engaged, enthusiastic, and honest, and it's paid off—his Twitter account has over one million followers. His personal accessibility sets the standard for Zappos on Twitter. Over 500 of its employees use Twitter, and they have even created a special section of the company website to aggregate all of their tweets. [36]]

There's also an employee leaderboard that shows who's on Twitter and how many followers they have. [Hsieh] has five times as many followers as anyone else [in the company], perhaps because there's a link on every page encouraging people to follow him and perhaps because CEOs are always the most interesting people at any company (sarcasm). Notably, [Hsieh] has taken the time to follow even more people than are following him—he's got 2800+ followers and 3200+ friends.

[Hsieh has] also penned a prominently placed introduction to using Twitter. Check out the intro paragraph:

> Remember back when sending SMS text messages on your cell phone was a new thing, and it seemed kind of strange to use your cell phone to do that? And today, you probably wonder how you ever lived without text messaging. Well, Twitter is the same way. It's going to seem a little weird at first, but I promise you if you can talk your friends into joining it and you all use it for 2 weeks, it will change your life. You will wonder how you ever lived without it.

Talk about drinking the kool-aid! The introduction is actually one of the most accessible introductions to Twitter I've seen and something that anyone interested in getting started could learn from.

Transparent Brand Tracking

Additionally, there's a page that aggregates all the public mentions of Zappos from Twitter users at large. This is a great example of openness and transparency—something the company would probably be less inclined to do had they not already developed a wildly loyal customer base thanks to their famous customer service.

Who wouldn't like to have [positive messages] on their website, though, without exercising any control over what appears there?

Now if there were shoe factory employees in China or Indonesia tweeting in English about their working conditions making shoes that will be sold on Zappos ("carpal tunnel for dollars an hour pays rent on hovel-like family dorm in company compound. damn these shoes. pic: tinyurl.com/ . . . ")—that might not be so desirable. Luckily for the brand, like people say—Twitter isn't mainstream yet.

© Ethan Miller/Getty Images

Zappos.com

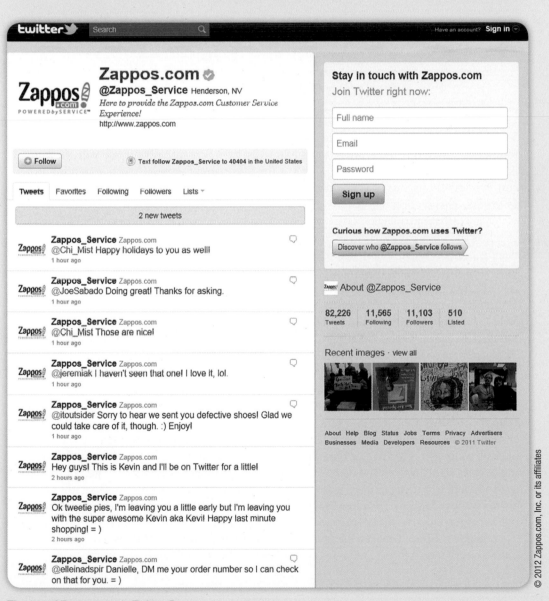

The top of Zappos.com's Twitter Page

© 2012 Zappos.com, Inc. or its affiliates

Celebrating Your Super Fans

Finally, Zappos has set up special Twitter tracking pages for some of its favorite outside fans. Check out this page [http://twitter.zappos.com/garyvee] for the super charming WineLibrary.TV founder Gary Vaynerchuk, and this page [http://www.horsepigcow.com/] for author and social media consultant Tara Hunt. That's a great little way to say thanks to Twitter savvy brand super fans.

Results

There are lots of companies using Twitter these days. Not because it's a reaching a mass audience but because it's reaching an early-adopter, tech-savvy, presumed-influencer audience...If the spammiest business Twitter users are on one end of the spectrum, that's the heavy side, unfortunately. The air is clearer and the examples are sparser on the high end of the Twitter engagement spectrum, [where Zappos "claims it is twittering with over 9 million customers, or 3% of the U.S. population."[37]] Clearly, Zappos is a great model for other companies seeking to get engaged.

Build a Twitter Following

Twitter is set up such that users only receive tweets in their feed from people they are following. Therefore, if a profile has no followers, then functionally no one will see what is being posted![††] Because of this, as well as the status some associate with a high follower count, many thousands of words have been written about the best ways to gather Twitter followers. This section will cover some basics.

Many different strategies have been employed to gain Twitter followers quickly. One classic is the **mass follow** strategy in which one follows lots of other profiles and hope they decide to follow back. Stefan Tanase, one researcher studying this issue, "found that simply following almost 50,000 people [gave] him nearly 8,000 followers in return, a follow-back rate of about 17 percent."[38] However, this approach has several pitfalls. The first is technical: Twitter implemented new rules that block users from following more than 2,000 profiles unless they are also being followed by a similar number.[39] A policy intended to deter automated accounts, mass marketing and spam, this reform makes mass following difficult. The second problem is practical: most of the users who follow back automatically will be mass marketers and spammers, who will never read the tweets from profiles they follow. This reality makes followers gained from the mass follow strategy largely worthless.

Another approach to gathering followers is the **equal ratio** strategy, which aims to keep the profile's following and follower counts as close to equal as possible. With this system the profile will only follow users who seem likely to follow back; it also follows back all followers. This strategy handily avoids Twitter's imposed ratio for those following over 2,000. However, the downside is that this approach is very slow to get off the ground. When starting a new Twitter profile, it may take weeks or months to gather even a hundred followers unless the brand is already well-known. For many social media marketing strategists, that period will be too long to wait.

A happy medium between the two methods above is the **targeted follow** strategy. The first step is to search for and follow a few (somewhere between 50 and 150) profiles with

---

[††]This statement is not entirely true. If a mention (e.g., @FoxNews) is made in a post, the user who is mentioned will see the tweet in his or her @Mention section on the Twitter home page. This is one way to be noticed without having many followers. Unfortunately, this fact has been taken advantage of by spammers and automated accounts that mention thousands of people daily. Sending too many mentions that lack relevance or content can get an account banned for spam; using mentions alone cannot guarantee a real audience.

similar interests and ideas or those that already have members of the target audience following them. For a business this may mean following the competition! Ideally, choose accounts that have roughly equal following/follower counts, as such counts indicate these accounts are more likely to follow back. However, focus more on the content and interests, and do not be overly concerned about following some that are unlikely to return the favor immediately.[40]

To increase the chance of being followed back, consider sending a mention (perhaps also with the hashtag #NowFollowing or similar) to inform the person about gaining a follower. On Twitter, the **mention** feature makes directed messages very simple; a tweet with "@[name]" will be viewable on the @Mention section of that person's home page. Notifying someone she or he has been followed and promoting that individual's name with a tweet signals the follower is active and worth following back.

Even with best efforts, do not expect perfect results when gaining followers, especially early on. Not everyone will respond. Following an unknown Twitter account is somewhat like leaving an old-fashioned calling card.[41] If the person finds the "card" (the profile, avatar, and description) interesting enough, he or she may decide to follow also. From this starting point, some of those early follows can become core connections to draw from later. Strike up dialogue when appropriate, and begin developing relationships.

The advantage of following relevant accounts with similar topics of interest is granted by Twitter's "Suggested People" feature. Users see lists of similar accounts as well as suggested people to follow based on which profiles they view and follow. This feature can lead interested viewers back to related profiles. For example, consider a small café starting up a Twitter presence; it could follow other coffee companies (such as Seattle's Best and Starbucks), coffee wholesalers/retailers (such as Maxwell House and Folgers), as well as other local businesses in town. Then, if someone was searching through Twitter profiles related to either coffee or the local town, that person might find that small café's profile as a suggestion. In this way the suggestion feature can help to access the target audience.

The second stage of the targeted follow strategy is more passive: choosing which profiles to follow back. Hopefully, many followers will be interested in the brand or business, but others may be following indiscriminately in hopes of boosting their own numbers. Early on, with less than 500 to 1,000 followers, it is worthwhile to follow back nearly everyone.‡ Twitter accounts with few followers tend to lack credibility and draw in followers more slowly, so do not risk losing the first few! After the account has grown, one can afford to be more selective in choosing who to follow back. Ultimately, the goal of this targeted follow strategy is to draw in followers who will read and respond to messages or who will become future recommenders or sources of expertise. In this respect quality of followers is far more important than quantity.

While a targeted follow strategy is often the best match for the marketing objectives, it is not the fastest way of gaining Twitter followers. For those with less patience, there is the **purchase** option. Many different services offer to provide Twitter followers for a fee. While this option may be tempting in order to get an account started, it is *not* advisable. Much like the mass follow approach, bought followers will likely be some combination of automated accounts, inactive accounts, and accounts not in the target audience. Joel Comm observes that "the price to be paid for having a large number of followers is often a less-targeted market and a lower conversation rate of followers to customers or users of your own site."[42] This observation is especially true when there is no guarantee that all of the followers are real people! Although it takes time, this pitfall is the reason that a Twitter following must be built, not bought.‡‡

---

‡Why "nearly" everyone? Some Twitter accounts are overtly racist, sexualized, or otherwise in poor taste. For almost any industry, following a problematic Twitter account is a potential scandal waiting to happen. If a profile's background, tweets, or avatar image is offensive, it may be better to avoid association and not follow back.

‡‡There are also more subtle ways of "buying" followers on Twitter. Some companies do giveaways, offering a chance to win some new technology product for users who follow and then mention the company's Twitter profile. While this is a way to gain followers quickly, and is more likely to draw in actual people (instead of automated accounts), it suffers the same flaw of drawing an untargeted following. While giveaways can be useful for building community good will or awareness of a brand, they are still not the best way to gain valuable targeted followers.

Finally, synergize with other communication media to draw existing contacts into the Twitter following. It is possible to easily integrate Twitter with Facebook, LinkedIn, Digg, and other social media platforms, but this tactic is just the beginning. Provide a link from the company website or blog requesting viewers to follow on Twitter. People browsing a page may be drawn to the attached Twitter account. When asking people to follow on Twitter, phrasing is important. According to one study,

> the way web sites tell users to follow them on Twitter has a dramatic effect on the click-through rate. Saying simply "I'm on Twitter" produces a clickthrough rate of 4.7 percent . . . Ordering users to "Follow me on Twitter" increased that clickthrough rate by 55 percent, pushing it up to 7.31 percent. Making the phrase more personal by saying "You should follow me on Twitter" increased the clickthrough rate to 10.09 percent, and providing a link for people to click in the phrase "You should follow me on Twitter here" was the most effective of all with a clickthrough rate of 12.81 percent.[43]

A higher click-through rate indicates more people going from the linking website to the Twitter profile. On a high-traffic page, a well-worded Twitter follow request can bring in a large number of followers.

Twitter can be integrated into even more communication media. After a variety of content has been posted, consider assembling a string of tweets into a blog post; it will draw attention to the Twitter page as well as providing an easy, interesting blog update.[44] A Twitter account can also be promoted through personal contacts. Attach the Twitter handle to business cards, email signatures, and other outbound communications.[45] People who are already known from other interactions make great Twitter contacts because they might have some interest in the brand or business already. Collecting followers is especially fruitful when there is a prior relationship to build from.

CASE STUDY

Dell Uses Sina to Reach Chinese Professionals[†]

Introduction

Dell recognizes that global markets are unique and require unique approaches and channels for engaging with customers. So, following successful social media programs like Direct2Dell, IdeaStorm, @DellOutlet and Direct2Dell Chinese, the company assessed how to leverage its existing social media best practices for China's unique social media marketplace and in a manner that would relevantly engage existing and potential customers there while staying authentic to the brand and culturally sensitive.

History

Dell, Inc., was founded in 1984 by Michael Dell.[46] In 2010 Dell retook the number-two spot in global computer sales in 2010.[47] As of 2011 the computer maker was ranked number 41 in the list of Fortune 500 corporations.[48] The company has long been the leader in using social media for marketing.[49]

[†]"Dell, Inc." (2010), © Society for New Communications Research. Reprinted with permission.

Challenge

Define the Target Audience

Dell's goal is to build awareness and affinity among key demographic audiences: students and young professionals in China. The Chinese social media scene is unique compared with those of most other technologically advanced international markets. . . . [In January 2011 China's total Internet users reached 457 million, a 19.1% increase year after year. The booming Chinese Internet market naturally attracts U.S. companies such as Dell. [50]] The estimated [457] million users participate in an online world of animation, pop-culture expression and humor.

Goals and Objectives

Dell's goal is to build awareness and affinity among key demographic audiences: students and young professionals in China through relevant social media channels. [The question, however, becomes "how can one reach and connect with Chinese professionals online?" [51]]

Strategy

The Plan

With the success of microblogging channels such as @DellOutlet and @DellCares, Dell assessed social media channels relevant to China to reach the company's target audience. Dell quickly discovered that China's online population is not using Twitter as a primary microblogging service but rather a platform unique to the Chinese marketplace: ["Sina Weibo (pronounced Way-Boh and meaning microblog in Chinese)...was the Internet phenomenon of China in 2010, reaching 50 million users by the end of October—and is likely fast approaching 100 million users." [52]]

The Deployment

Dell created a mini-blog on [Sina Weibo] and immediately set the bar high for corporate presence on the channel. Dell began to offer exclusive coupons on the platform, implemented customer surveys and formed a team of Employee Ambassadors to engage with customers—becoming the first international company to do any of these activities, much less all three, via Sina.com.

With customer outreach in China, it was important for conversations to be customized, topically and culturally. Messaging and tactics that work on Twitter.com in the United States would not necessarily work on [Sina Weibo] users. Dell conducted research and focus groups that provided insight on topics of interest to Chinese technology customers who were considering Dell hardware and services. An important next step was to define success metrics and identify how the program would be measured.

The Team

Dell's Employee Ambassadors interact with customers to share news and information regarding Dell products, services and technology trends and proactively reach out to customers to answer questions, solve service issues and thank them for choosing Dell. These activities combined with timely customer surveys, coupons and discounts, make up the components of Dell's Sina presence.

Results

Within six months of launching, Dell became the third most followed international brand on Sina.com, with 20,000 followers, and transformed the way an international brand talks to its customers on this platform. Dell succeeded in reaching the online population in China with relevant content and conversation about its products while effectively targeting support for customers in need. Dell continues to receive valuable direct feedback from consumers that is constantly integrated into marketing and production for the region. Dell's interactions on Sina.com have made the company even smarter on reaching and interacting with customers in China. It has helped Dell recognize the value of social media interactions not just in marketing, communications and customer support, but in other aspects of the brand's business as well.

Crafting an Effective Twitter Channel

The tips above provide a baseline of knowledge to start a Twitter account and begin using it successfully. Many businesses have developed a Twitter presence and have had positive results. One new derivative product is Twitter brand insurance, which will compensate companies for lost reputation on Twitter.[53] Intended to hedge against unauthorized tweets or image smears online, this insurance (in million-dollar quantities) demonstrates how much businesses invest in microblogging as well as how easily those efforts can be ruined.

Twitter can become an extremely effective marketing channel, but only when it is used with forethought. Making a profile pay off over time will require a commitment of time, energy, and attention to detail. Keep the following in mind over the long-run execution of a Twitter social media marketing campaign.

SELF-PROMOTE CAUTIOUSLY

The first lesson in marketing on Twitter is to not market too much. In principle this advice may sound contradictory, but in practice it is essential in order to reach an audience and to keep that audience's attention. Do not assume that Twitter users will care about product announcements, updates, or promotions; there are thousands, if not millions, of obvious (sometimes automated) Twitter marketing accounts vying for their attention.

To distinguish oneself from the crowd of advertisers, focus on relationships first. Do favors for others, providing links or mentions, and they may reciprocate. A good ratio to keep in mind is 10:1.[54] In other words, promote others or share information ten times for each self-promotional tweet. The best Twitter "advertising" will come as a result of mentions or recommendations by contacts and followers, so foster those connections early on by generously promoting others.

CHOOSE OPTIMAL TWEET TIMES

Without a direct mention, someone will probably never see a tweet unless that individual is online and looking at his or her home page in the minute that it is posted. Especially for users who follow many people, it can take just minutes or seconds for a tweet to escape that person's view. Therefore, putting out updates when people are online to see them is essential for making an impact.

Some simple logic can illuminate when the best time to post is: people must sign on in order to make their own updates, so that is the time they are certain to be online. Therefore, in order to be seen, post updates at times that followers are also updating the most.[55] Some have found "midday and midweek tend to produce the best results."[56] Also keep time zones in mind. Depending on where the audience is located, it might be asleep when a tweet is posted. Adapt the posting schedule to allow more viewers to see and react to each update.

RESPOND TO QUESTIONS

If the prior steps have been done well and if useful content and links have been shared, this air of expertise may lead other users to ask questions. This is one of the most frequent uses of Twitter for firms: quickly responding to consumer questions and comments.[57] As users can access Twitter from many different devices, engaging their questions in a forthright manner can create a sense of closeness unparalleled by other platforms.[58]

Microblogging encourages users to seek input from others, and in a business context, this practice means responding to comments, questions, or issues that potential customers might have. Providing useful information can build a brand's reputation and thought leadership (see the case studies in this chapter for some examples).

GATHER FEEDBACK

While it is possible to passively observe and respond on Twitter, a more proactive strategy is to request answers directly. Asking for opinions or product reviews is a cheap alternative to focus groups; Twitter users are generally happy to share their thoughts when asked politely. Take advantage of this impulse, and seek feedback whenever possible. If the following is interested and engaged, some are likely to respond.

In addition to gauging general sentiment, it is also possible to solicit expert advice through microblogging platforms.[59] For example, one real-estate agent asked his Twitter following whether a client could get a mortgage for a property where the well had not undergone a safety test.[60] After receiving a quick response of "Yes" from one of the agent's expert Twitter contacts, the client was able to get the loan. Instead of paying a lawyer or doing extensive research himself, the real estate agent was able to save time and money and ultimately serve the client better. This represents just one potential usage of microblogging to find useful advice, and undoubtedly far more applications also exist.

As feedback from Twitter can be very helpful, it is good to encourage and reward users who are willing to provide it. After asking a question, acknowledge the people who respond or provide an answer.[61] If followers are left feeling unappreciated, they will be less likely to help in the future. These give-and-take relationships, which may seem insignificant individually, can aggregate into a powerful machine for gathering input and information. Being kind, polite, and appreciative helps to grease that apparatus and keep it running smoothly.

PROVIDE UNIQUE VALUE

Implicitly, every successful Twitter marketing profile must answer the question "why follow and listen to the messages being offered?" If the answer to this question is unclear, it is unlikely that many users will pay attention to what is said. While stellar content can draw in viewers, even that alone may not be enough to guarantee results.

A simple way to keep viewers' attention that many companies have employed is to offer special deals on Twitter. These can include coupons, promotional discounts, special products, free shipping, and so on. The most important aspect is that the deal is only seen or available to Twitter users.[62] Followers get a sense of exclusivity and privilege from the special bargain, and everyone has more reason to follow closely for future deals.

Good deals are one sort of unique value that a Twitter page can offer, but there are nonmonetary incentives that also can be valuable. Access to training, unique informational resources, or ground-breaking news are all reasons to follow a Twitter feed. The specifics will depend on the audience being targeted, but one should always try to find some unique value that the Twitter channel can provide.

Team TurboTax uses Twitter to provide better customer service

TurboTax has found that on Twitter customers can help each other. Corporate communications became the hub that farms out questions to the appropriate spokes. The company also uses CoTweet to [ferret] out all the incoming customers.

Now if a customer has a complaint or a problem, it is assigned to the right person. As their Twitter feed bio reads, "TeamTurboTax is who you ask when you have tax, tech or TurboTax questions!"

Results

[As] the 2010 tax season progressed, the company realized people were using the feed differently than they expected. Mostly twitterers were coming to ask TurboTax personal tax issues.

"We set out thinking we'd have more technical questions," says Marti. "But we found out quickly we were getting tax questions."

The company had employed tax experts for their effort. They enabled them to find a buddy, train a buddy, or recruit a buddy. That effort added 10 to 12 people to the team. Says Marti: "For us, Twitter was a great way to help customers, but it wasn't the be all and end all. What really made it for us was the expertise that people brought to Twitter."

Marti acknowledged if the feed had been staffed by her and corporate communications alone, it would have been far less effective. With experts on deck, the response time was fast. It took an average of four minutes for TurboTax to get back to Twitter questions.

At least half of the people who came to the feed were about to finish a return. The company also found that most of the people seeking out tax help from TurboTax turned out to be existing customers. And they found those customers were 71% more likely to recommend TurboTax because of their interactions with the company on Twitter.

In the end, TurboTax' expanded efforts on Twitter became a great customer retention program. Says Marti: "Everyone knows it's less expensive to keep a customer than create a new one."

Review Questions for TurboTax Case Study

1. TurboTax has strong name recognition from Intuit's software Quicken. How did this affect the company's Twitter strategy?

2. Name the pros and cons of asking for tax advice on Twitter. What specific social media marketing tactics does the company use to better manage the rush around tax day?

3. How does the seasonal nature of TurboTax's work make social media marketing easier? More difficult? What specific steps do you think the company takes to make the rush around tax day easier to manage?

4. The article names word-of-mouth recommendations as one advantage of TurboTax's Twitter strategy. What other advantages exist that weren't mentioned?

Notes

1. "Turning into Digital Goldfish"(2002, February 22), BBC News. Retrieved July 11, 2011, from http://news.bbc.co.uk/2/hi/science/nature/1834682.stm
2. Comm, Joel (2010), *Twitter Power 2.0* (Hoboken, NJ: John Wiley), p. 179.
3. Barker, Donald I., Melissa S. Barker, and Catherine T. Pinard (2013), Unit D, *Internet Research—Illustrated,* 6th ed. (Boston, MA: Cengage Learning), p. 12.
4. "Microblogging" (n.d.), *Wikipedia.* Retrieved July 11, 2011, from http://en.wikipedia.org/wiki/Microblogging
5. Kottke, Jason (2005, October 19), "Tumblelogs." Retrieved July 11, 2011, from http://www.kottke.org/05/10/tumblelogs
6. Arrington, Michael (2006, July 15), "Odeo Releases Twttr," TechCrunch. Retrieved July 11, 2011, from http://techcrunch.com/2006/07/15/is-twttr-interesting/
7. Johansmeyer, Tom (2011, February 3), "200 Million Twitter Accounts . . . But How Many Are Active?" Social Times. Retrieved July 11, 2011, from http://socialtimes.com/200-million-twitter-accounts-but-how-many-are-active_b36952
8. "What Does 300 Million Registered Twitter Accounts Mean?" (n.d.), Twopcharts. Retrieved July 11, 2011, from http://twopcharts.com/twitter300million
9. Smith, Aaron (2011, June 1), "Twitter Update 2011," Pew Internet. Retrieved July 11, 2011, from http://pewinternet.org/Reports/2011/Twitter-Update-2011/Main-Report.aspx
10. "Plurk.com" (n.d.), Alexa. Retrieved July 11, 2011, from http://www.alexa.com/siteinfo/plurk.com
11. "Identi.ca" (n.d.), Alexa. Retrieved December 16, 2011, from http://www.alexa.com/siteinfo/indenti.ca
12. Kabani, Shama Hyder (2010), *The Zen of Social Media Marketing: An Easier Way to Build Credibility, Generate Buzz, and Increase Revenue* (Dallas: TX: BenBella Books), p. 76.
13. Comm, Joel (2010), *Twitter Power 2.0* (Hoboken, NJ: John Wiley), p. 117.
14. Borges, Bernie (2009), *Marketing 2.0* (Tucson, Arizona: Wheatmark), p. 204.
15. Comm, Joel (2010), *Twitter Power 2.0* (Hoboken, NJ: John Wiley), p. 123-29.
16. Glaser, Mark (2007, May 15), "Your Guide to Micro-Blogging and Twitter," PBS, "Media Shift." Retrieved July 12, 2011, from http://www.pbs.org/mediashift/2007/05/your-guide-to-micro-blogging-and-twitter135.html
17. Kukral, Jim (2008, October 29), "How and Why to Use Twitter for Small Businesses," Small Business Trends. Retrieved July 12, 2011, from http://smallbiztrends.com/2008/10/how-why-twitter-small-businesses.html

History

Lenovo Group Limited (Lenovo) is a Chinese multinational computer technology corporation, which develops, manufactures, and markets desktops and notebook personal computers and a variety of other technology products and services. It acquired the ThinkPad link of notebook computers from IBM in 2005, and as of 2009 Lenovo was the fourth-largest vendor of personal computers in the world.[33]

Challenge

Lenovo found that customers were talking about its products and services on independent forum and review sites such as notebookreview.com and thinkpads.com. Since the conversations were happening across the web, Lenovo didn't always have the opportunity to participate in the discussions. The firm wanted to have more ownership over the conversations and to provide leadership since the conversations were about its products.[34]

Lenovo, a multinational computer technology company

In addition, with tech-savvy computer purchasers increasingly looking online for ratings, reviews, and customer support, there was an opportunity for Lenovo to leverage discussion forums to better meet the needs of its customers. According to the 2010 Cone Customer New Media Study, U.S. new media users are looking for companies online to solve problems and provide product or service information (46%) and solicit feedback on products and services (39%).[35]

According to Mark Hopkins, the social media project manager at Lenovo, "[a]fter monitoring the blogosphere for substantive discussions about Lenovo and some of the major product brands like ThinkPad, we noted that the majority of the content originated in several forums. Passive viewing only took us so far and we wanted to learn more, be able to ask questions, and offer guidance."[36]

Additionally, because Lenovo wants to reach out to the 18- to 34-year-old demographic of young adults who spend the bulk of their time and activities on the Internet, social media and digital support are even more important. In 2011, Lenovo invested in a digital and social media hub in Singapore, "designed to increase Lenovo's digital investments for branding and marketing worldwide."[37]

Strategy

Lenovo determined that launching a peer-to-peer discussion forum would help them connect with its key demographic while reducing customer service costs and providing better customer service to their customers.

The discussion forums at forums.lenovo.com allowed customers to ask and answer each other's questions. In addition, moderators monitored the forums

Review Questions for TurboTax Case Study

1. TurboTax has strong name recognition from Intuit's software Quicken. How did this affect the company's Twitter strategy?

2. Name the pros and cons of asking for tax advice on Twitter. What specific social media marketing tactics does the company use to better manage the rush around tax day?

3. How does the seasonal nature of TurboTax's work make social media marketing easier? More difficult? What specific steps do you think the company takes to make the rush around tax day easier to manage?

4. The article names word-of-mouth recommendations as one advantage of TurboTax's Twitter strategy. What other advantages exist that weren't mentioned?

Notes

1. "Turning into Digital Goldfish"(2002, February 22), BBC News. Retrieved July 11, 2011, from http://news.bbc.co.uk/2/hi/science/nature/1834682.stm
2. Comm, Joel (2010), *Twitter Power 2.0* (Hoboken, NJ: John Wiley), p. 179.
3. Barker, Donald I., Melissa S. Barker, and Catherine T. Pinard (2013), Unit D, *Internet Research—Illustrated*, 6th ed. (Boston, MA: Cengage Learning), p. 12.
4. "Microblogging" (n.d.), *Wikipedia*. Retrieved July 11, 2011, from http://en.wikipedia.org/wiki/Microblogging
5. Kottke, Jason (2005, October 19), "Tumblelogs." Retrieved July 11, 2011, from http://www.kottke.org/05/10/tumblclogs
6. Arrington, Michael (2006, July 15), "Odeo Releases Twttr," TechCrunch. Retrieved July 11, 2011, from http://techcrunch.com/2006/07/15/is-twttr-interesting/
7. Johansmeyer, Tom (2011, February 3), "200 Million Twitter Accounts . . . But How Many Are Active?" Social Times. Retrieved July 11, 2011, from http://socialtimes.com/200-million-twitter-accounts-but-how-many-are-active_b36952
8. "What Does 300 Million Registered Twitter Accounts Mean?" (n.d.), Twopcharts. Retrieved July 11, 2011, from http://twopcharts.com/twitter300million
9. Smith, Aaron (2011, June 1), "Twitter Update 2011," Pew Internet. Retrieved July 11, 2011, from http://pewinternet.org/Reports/2011/Twitter-Update-2011/Main-Report.aspx
10. "Plurk.com" (n.d.), Alexa. Retrieved July 11, 2011, from http://www.alexa.com/siteinfo/plurk.com
11. "Identi.ca" (n.d.), Alexa. Retrieved December 16, 2011, from http://www.alexa.com/siteinfo/indenti.ca
12. Kabani, Shama Hyder (2010), *The Zen of Social Media Marketing: An Easier Way to Build Credibility, Generate Buzz, and Increase Revenue* (Dallas: TX: BenBella Books), p. 76.
13. Comm, Joel (2010), *Twitter Power 2.0* (Hoboken, NJ: John Wiley), p. 117.
14. Borges, Bernie (2009), *Marketing 2.0* (Tucson, Arizona: Wheatmark), p. 204.
15. Comm, Joel (2010), *Twitter Power 2.0* (Hoboken, NJ: John Wiley), p. 123-29.
16. Glaser, Mark (2007, May 15), "Your Guide to Micro-Blogging and Twitter," PBS, "Media Shift." Retrieved July 12, 2011, from http://www.pbs.org/mediashift/2007/05/your-guide-to-micro-blogging-and-twitter135.html
17. Kukral, Jim (2008, October 29), "How and Why to Use Twitter for Small Businesses," Small Business Trends. Retrieved July 12, 2011, from http://smallbiztrends.com/2008/10/how-why-twitter-small-businesses.html

18. Stelzner, Michael (2008, December 31), "How to Use Twitter to Grow Your Business," *CopyBlogger*. Retrieved July 12, 2011, from http://www.copyblogger.com/grow-business-twitter/

19. MacMillan, Douglas (2008, September), "CEOs' Take on Twitter," *Business Week*. Retrieved July 12, 2011, from http://images.businessweek.com/ss/08/09/0908_microblogceo/index.htm

20. Borges, Bernie (2009), *Marketing 2.0* (Tucson, Arizona: Wheatmark), p. 203.

21. Kabani, Shama Hyder (2010), *The Zen of Social Media Marketing: An Easier Way to Build Credibility, Generate Buzz, and Increase Revenue* (Dallas, TX: BenBella Books), p. 80.

22. Ibid., p. 87.

23. Brogan, Chris (2008, August 20), "50 Ideas on Using Twitter for Business." chrisbrogan.com. Retrieved July 12, 2011, from http://www.chrisbrogan.com/50-ideas-on-using-twitter-for-business/

24. Lee, Amy (2011, June 1), "Twitter Statistics: 13 Percent of Americans Tweet, Growth Led by African-Americans," *Huffington Post*. Retrieved July 13, 2011, from http://www.huffingtonpost.com/2011/06/01/twitter-pew-statistics_n_869790.html

25. Warnke, Marc (2009, February 10), "Top 10 Things New People to Twitter Should Know," blog. Retrieved July 12, 2011, from http://www.marcwarnke.com/blog/marcwarnke/top_10_things_new_people_twitter_should_know

26. Borges, Bernie (2009), *Marketing 2.0* (Tucson, Arizona: Wheatmark), p. 206.

27. Comm, Joel (2010), *Twitter Power 2.0* (Hoboken, NJ: John Wiley), p. 76.

28. Rowse, Darren (2008, May 8), "5 Tips to Grow Your Twitter Presence," *ProBlogger*. Retrieved July 12, 2011, from http://www.problogger.net/archives/2008/05/08/5-tips-to-grow-your-twitter-presence/

29. Brantner, Eric (2009, January 11), "7 Ways to Get Your Twitter Followers to Click Your Links," SEOHosting. Retrieved July 12, 2011, from http://www.seohosting.com/blog/social-networking/7-ways-to-get-your-twitter-followers-to-click-your-links/

30. Ludwig, Sean (2009, February 16), "Top 10 Twitter Tips for Beginners," *PCMag*. Retrieved July 12, 2011, from http://www.pcmag.com/article2/0,2817,2341095,00.asp

31. Gage, Randy (2009) "Tweet This! A Twitter Manifesto." Retrieved July 12, 2011, from http://www.randygage.com/blog/tweet-this-a-twitter-manifesto/

32. "In the Beginning—Let There Be Shoes" (n.d.), Zappos. Retrieved July 1, 2011, from http://about.zappos.com/zappos-story/in-the-beginning-let-there-be-shoes

33. FN Staff (2009, May 4), "Zappos Milestone: Timeline," *Footwear News*. Retrieved July 1, 2011, from http://www.wwd.com/footwear-news/zappos-milestone-timeline-2121760

34. Mitchell, Dan (2008, May 24), "Shoe Seller's Secret of Success," *New York Times*, retrieved July 1, 2011, from http://www.nytimes.com/2008/05/24/technology/24online.html and "Twitter: On Emerging Business Case Studies & Participatory Marketing" (2009, February 25), Off the Grid PR, retrieved July 1, 2011, from http://offthegrid-pr.com/socially-responsible-pr/2009/2/25/twitter-on-emerging-business-case-studies-participatory-mark.html

35. Lacy, Sarah (2009, July 22), "Amazon Buys Zappos; The Price is $928M, Not $847M," TechCrunch. Retrieved July 1, 2011, from http://techcrunch.com/2009/07/22/amazon-buys-zappos/

36. Griffin, Chris (2010, December 22), "Social Media Tips from the Major Players—Part One," WSI IMS. Retrieved July 1, 2011, from http://www.readwriteweb.com/archives/zappos_twitter.php

37. "Twitter: On Emerging Business Case Studies & Participatory Marketing" (2009, February 25), Off the Grid PR. Retrieved July 1, 2011, from http://offthegrid-pr.com/socially-responsible-pr/2009/2/25/twitter-on-emerging-business-case-studies-participatory-mark.html

38. Comm, Joel (2010), *Twitter Power 2.0* (Hoboken, NJ: John Wiley), p. 78.

39. "Following Rules and Best Practices" (2011), Twitter Help Center. Retrieved July 13, 2011, from https://support.twitter.com/entries/68916-following-rules-and-best-practices

40. Kabani, Shama Hyder (2010), *The Zen of Social Media Marketing: An Easier Way to Build Credibility, Generate Buzz, and Increase Revenue* (Dallas, TX: BenBella Books), p. 78.

41. Dykeman, Mark (2009, January 26), "Getting More Twitter Followers—or Losing Them." Pistachio Consulting. Retrieved July 12, 2011, from http://pistachioconsulting.com/twitter-followers/

42. Comm, Joel (2010), *Twitter Power 2.0* (Hoboken, NJ: John Wiley), p. 79.

43. Ibid., p. 93-94.

44. Golden, Michelle (2011), *Social Media Strategies for Professionals and Their Firms* (Hoboken, NJ: John Wiley), p. 205.

45. Norgard, Brian (2009, February 24), "5 Ways to Find & Acquire Customers on Twitter," Shoe Money. Retrieved July 12, 2011, from http://www.shoemoney.com/2009/02/24/5-ways-to-find-acquire-customers-on-twitter/

46. "Our Story" (n.d.), Dell. Retrieved July 1, 2011, from http://content.dell.com/us/en/corp/about-dell-our-story.aspx#

47. netbook fan (2011, March 23), "Dell Retakes Number-two Spot in Global PC Sales," Cheap Notebook Deals. Retrieved July 1, 2011, from http://www.cheapnetbookdeals.net/dell-netbook/dell-retakes-number-two-spot-in-global-pc-sales/

48. "Fortune 500" (2011), *Fortune*. Retrieved July 1, 2011, from http://money.cnn.com/magazines/fortune/fortune500/2011/full_list/

49. Tobin, Jim (2011, April 7), "Dell and Social Media: How the Four R's Help Manage 25,000 Conversations a Day," Cross Pollination Media. Retrieved July 1, 2011, from http://crosspollinationmedia.com/social-media-optimization/social-media-marketing/dell-and-social-media-how-the-four-r%E2%80%99s-help-manage-25000-conversations-a-day/

50. "How to Connect with Chinese Professionals Online" (2011, February 23), TELL Fleur. Retrieved July 1, 2011, from http://telfleur.wordpress.com/2011/02/23/how-to-connect-with-chinese-professionals-online/

51. Ibid.

52. Epstein, Gady (2011, February 16), "China's Social Network: Zuckerberg and Sina Chat over the Great Firewall," *Forbes*. Retrieved July 1, 2011, from http://blogs.forbes.com/gadyepstein/2011/02/16/chinas-social-network-zuckerberg-and-sina-chat-over-the-great-firewall/

53. Rowinski, Dan (2011, April 26), "Worried about Brand Damage from Social Media? Get Tweet Insurance," ReadWriteWeb. Retrieved July 15, 2011, from http://www.readwriteweb.com/archives/worried_about_brand_damage_from_social_media_get_tweet_insurance.php

54. Golden, Michelle (2011), *Social Media Strategies for Professionals and Their Firms* (Hoboken, NJ: John Wiley), p. 196.

55. Comm, Joel (2010), *Twitter Power 2.0* (Hoboken, NJ: John Wiley), p. 204.

56. Ibid., p. 204.

57. Weinberg, Tamar (2009), *The New Community Rules: Marketing on the Social Web* (Sebastopol, CA: O'Reilly Media), p. 127.

58. Ibid., p. 125.

59. Comm, Joel (2010), *Twitter Power 2.0* (Hoboken, NJ: John Wiley), p. 29.

60. Vascellaro, Jessica E. (2008, October 27), "Twitter Goes Mainstream," *Wall Street Journal*. Retrieved July 12, 2011, from http://online.wsj.com/article/SB122461906719455335.html

61. Rowse, Darren (2008, November 21), "How to Ask Effective Questions on Twitter," Twitip. Retrieved July 12, 2011, from http://www.twitip.com/how-to-ask-effective-questions-on-twitter/

62. Weinberg, Tamar (2009), *The New Community Rules: Marketing on the Social Web* (Sebastopol, CA: O'Reilly Media), p. 129.

63. Borges, Bernie (2009), *Marketing 2.0* (Tucson, Arizona: Wheatmark), p. 208.

64. "TurboTax Again Rated No. 1 Tax Software" (2011, March 8), Intuit, press release, Reuters. Retrieved June 30, 2011, from http://www.reuters.com/article/2011/03/08/idUS133247+08-Mar-2011+BW20110308

65. "Intuit Inc." (n.d.), Funding Universe. Retrieved June 30, 2011, from http://www.fundinguniverse.com/company-histories/Intuit-Inc-Company-History.html

66. "Intuit Twitter Display Campaign" (2009, June 24), Slideshare.net. Retrieved June 30, 2011, from http://www.slideshare.net/ralphpaglia/intuit-twitter-display-campaign

67. "Intuit's Turbo Tax: Turning Customers into Marketers" (n.d.), Gigya. Retrieved June 30, 2011, from http://www.gigya.com/solutions/casestudies/TurboTax.aspx

Discussion Boards, Social News, and Q&A Sites

This chapter will cover three different types of social media networks, which are note-worthy for their many similarities but also their subtle differences. Understanding the benefits of discussion boards, social news, and question-and-answer sites is essential to integrate these tools into a social media marketing campaign.

LEARNING OBJECTIVES

After completing this chapter, students will be able to:

- Describe the purpose of a discussion board
- Detail the typical structure of a discussion board
- Explain discussion board netiquette
- Describe how to how to use discussion forums for marketing
- Detail the guidelines for moderators of online discussion groups
- Explain the purpose of a social news site

(Continued)

Discussion boards are perhaps the oldest form of social media, even predating the Internet itself. Review sites continue this general theme. Social news sites are a new innovation in discussion boards that allow users to vote on which topics are most important. Finally, Q&A sites evolved to combat the increasing complexity of business and online interaction by providing forums for experts to respond to questions.

Many social trends led up to this online democratization of information and commentary. However, from a pragmatic marketer's perspective, the most important changes regarded which sources were given authority and trust. Instead of the touted experts or company representatives prominently featured in old broadcasting, new online forums give voice to anonymous strangers who can share their experiences with others.

A Nielsen Survey of 2007 found that "the most trusted form of advertising was recommendations from other consumers—cited by 78% of respondents."[1] Many consumers feel a greater sense of commonality with other ordinary people rather than with rich and famous media professionals. Thus, "[c]itizen endorsers benefit from perceptions of similarity that are typically absent from celebrity endorsers."[2] This fact undergirds the utility of discussion boards, social news, and Q&A sites because they are all user-driven wells of information. By understanding the usage for each of these three platform types, a social media marketer can advance a brand and boost sales results.

What Is a Discussion Board?

As the oldest kind of social media, discussion boards are a natural choice to discuss first. A **discussion board** is a service where participants can exchange messages with each other. Organization of these messages may vary or be customizable by the individual user. Often a sense of **virtual community** develops around discussion boards, which have regular members that share common interests. This sense of community can motivate either online friendships or feuds, depending on the tone and topics being discussed.

Discussion Forum Structure

A discussion board is typically organized into groups based on topics of interest. A **discussion group** is made up of **forums**, which frequently arrange **posts** and **replies** about a specific subject in an indented hierarchical fashion so that users can easily follow the flow of a conversation. The treelike structure of a forum is called a **thread** because it reveals the chronological order of posts and replies in a forum.

A **moderator** monitors and facilitates forum discussions, enforcing discussion board policies and rules. If users engage in abusive exchanges, known as **flaming**, or post inappropriate material, the forum moderator acts as an arbitrator to settle disputes and remove disallowed content. An **administrator** of a discussion board manages the technical details required to maintain the site, such as granting (or revoking) moderator privileges along with performing such routine maintenance as fixing technical glitches and backing up the discussion board to minimize the risk of data loss.

Many of the major portal sites, such as Google Groups, Yahoo! Groups, and Microsoft's Window Live Groups, have discussion boards. Social network sites, such as LinkedIn, have active discussion groups, but they usually require the user to join the site to search for groups and/or participate in them. In addition, there are branded discussion boards, which are hosted by companies and nonprofits and which attempt to build online communities of brand enthusiasts and evangelists,

Figure 12.1 CompuServe Helped Pioneer Dial-Up Discussion Boards

Virtual Worlds

A **virtual world** is an online community where users can interact with one another and create and use objects.[3] Typically, a virtual world involves a computer-based simulated environment that is interactive and often three-dimensional where users can move around and interact with each other. A user in a virtual world usually takes the form of an **avatar**, which is a two-dimensional or three-dimensional representation or character that is visible to others.[4]

A virtual world may be a part of a game, like that in the popular World of Warcraft game, or simply be a place where users communicate without any game objectives, as in Second Life. Communication between users in virtual worlds may range from text to voice communication and voice command.

In 2007, when virtual worlds like Second Life were gaining popularity with users and brands, some analysts expected up to 80% of the U.S. population would have avatars in virtual worlds by 2011.[5] Although those predictions have proven overly optimistic, participation in virtual worlds more than doubled from 2009 to 2011.[6] In the second quarter of 2011, usage of virtual worlds accelerated, with 214 million new users.[7] In fact, data from both KZero and Nielsen show that virtual worlds continue to grow in popularity.[8]

Virtual worlds are especially popular in social games, which are experiencing tremendous growth.[9] Virtual worlds present a number of opportunities for social media marketers, including virtual goods, brand placement, advertising and even selling.

Marketing companies can promote in virtual worlds by introducing branded virtual goods, such as better weapons, buildings or accessories. For example, a clothing company may create virtual versions of their outfits that can be purchased or used for free to dress avatars. This provides these companies with brand exposure and awareness in the virtual world.

Advertising in virtual worlds typically takes a different form than advertising online. On the web most ads are banner ads in standard format sizes. In virtual worlds advertising is usually integrated directly into the world and may appear as a billboard on a

facilitate customer support by answering user questions, and increase brand awareness. Government agencies also use discussion boards to answer questions and disseminate information. Specialized search services exist to help locate discussion groups, such as groups.google.com, groups.yahoo.com, boardreader.com, and boardtracker.com.[12]

A Brief History of Discussion Boards

Internet discussion forums grew out of local neighborhood bulletin boards, "basic places where communities would come together and find information about various topics."[13] These pen-and-paper-based information exchanges were eventually replaced by electronic methods. The first Internet discussion boards functioned much like an electronic mailing list with people posting messages about a single topic and others responding. As discussion boards evolved, multiple topics (forums) became commonplace.[14] Soon, there was a vast list of forums, with discussion centered on everything from technology, online games, and music to movies, celebrity gossip, and sports. More scholarly forums sprung up to converse about such subjects as the sciences and liberal arts, as well as forums dedicated to politics, religion, and news events.

One of the earliest dial-up discussion boards was CompuServe, founded in 1969; the company started offering dial-up online services in 1979, including an electronic bulletin board, which quickly became a popular feature on the service (see Figure 12.1).[15] Usenet, launched in 1980, is the oldest online discussion board still in use; however, it has been largely displaced by modern discussion boards.[16] Prodigy, founded in 1984, hosted a widely used dial-up discussion board in the late 1980s to early 1990s.[17] Modern web-based discussion forums began appearing in 1994 and have since quickly proliferated, with over 1.7 billion posts and 22 million members on the largest forums.[18]

As of April 2011, the most popular threads (topics) on discussion forums were as follows:

1. **Words that don't exist in the English language**, posted by Jessica Fletcher (viewed 18,116 times)

2. **I have $10,000 to blow, where can I live comfortably for a year?** posted by ArghMonkey (viewed 8,715 times)

3. **Spontaneous travel**, posted by traveller1990 (viewed 4,931 times)

4. **The world's friendliest countries**, posted by Kano_Jim (viewed 2,955)

5. **Using an iPad across France, Germany, and Italy**, posted by benelli (viewed 2,475 times)[19]

It is worth noting that traffic is not the only measure of the popularity of a discussion thread. The number of responses in a thread can provide a more accurate indication of how involved viewers are in the topic. When many people are engaged in a discussion, its appeal is likely to spread to more viewers.

Discussion Board Netiquette

While forums are generally open and welcoming to newcomers, there are some basic guidelines that all participants are expected to follow. Sometimes known as "netiquette" (a contraction of Inter*net* and et*iquette*), these largely unspoken rules define interactions in online discussion boards. In some cases the rules are enforced by a forum administrator and in others the community is self-policing.[20] For those not observing these guidelines, the response from discussion board veterans is likely to be both swift and harsh. While different forums have variations on these general rules, what follows are some commonly accepted pillars of discussion board etiquette.

virtual street, branding on virtual vehicles or even buildings.

Retailers like Brookstone have created storefronts in virtual worlds where users can enter a virtual store to shop for real goods that are purchased with actual money and shipped to the user's home. Traditional retailers like Sears have also created simulated stores in virtual worlds.[10]

In addition to the marketing activities taking place in virtual worlds, many companies and organizations are using virtual environments to host meetings. For example, Procter & Gamble has a presence on Second Life that includes a replica of their global headquarters. Procter & Gamble has used Second Life for virtual meetings in virtual conference rooms, for education and marketing purposes.[11]

© Cengage Learning 2013

STICK TO THE TOPIC

Discussions, or threads, always have a title and general topic that is obvious from reading just a few posts. This focus is essential for people to quickly gather specific information. Avoid tangents, chit-chat, or diversions from the main topic because they inconvenience other users. For general comments or discussion, seek out forums in the "off topic" section.

SEARCH BEFORE POSTING

Some forums see frequent repeats of common questions or have dealt with an issue in depth before. Prior to asking the community for an answer, search the forum to see if the topic has already been discussed. Most discussion boards have extensive archives that can be mined for information. Asking questions that have been answered before makes the poster seem lazy or inexperienced.

USE GOOD GRAMMAR AND CAPITALIZATION

Many forum users will employ Internet shorthand, loose grammar, or generally poor writing in their posts. For a social media marketer, however, this practice can damage a professional image or reduce credibility of the information presented. While minor grammar errors are easily forgiven, they should not impact readability. Having solid grammar, good spacing, and proper punctuation all makes a post easier and more enjoyable to read. For a similar reason, do not use ALL CAPITALS when posting; it is interpreted as shouting by forum users and will generate negative responses.

NO FEEDING THE TROLLS

In discussion forum parlance, a **troll** is someone who attacks or personally insults another user, driving a thread off topic with negative comments. Similarly, "trolling" may refer to posting unsupported, controversial claims intended to anger others and provoke a response. It should go without saying that a good social media marketer never resorts to trolling in order to get a point across. It is also best to avoid interacting with other users who are acting like trolls. The most effective response is to ignore them and refuse to give them the attention they are seeking. Without a response or someone taking the bait, users who troll eventually become bored and go away.

DO NOT POST REPETITIVELY (OR DOUBLE-POST)

If a question or comment does not receive a response on one thread, it is unwise to post it elsewhere. If both posts eventually generate comments, it splits the conversation and is inconvenient to view. Users find it annoying when someone litters a forum with comments that disrupt the flow of discussion. If a post has not generated immediate response, just wait. It is possible that no one is interested in responding at the time, and posting again will only aggravate those who were ambivalent to start with.

NO SOCK PUPPETS

According to *The New York Times*, a sock puppet is "the act of creating a fake on-line identity to praise, defend or create the illusion of support for one's self, allies or company."[21] Several large companies have attempted this tactic and have been caught. For savvy forum users, it is fairly easy to spot sock puppets or other fake accounts. It is better to endure some negative comments than destroy a brand's credibility online by creating fake accounts.

None of these guidelines is groundbreaking, and many will likely seem obvious to the reader. Most online etiquette issues can be resolved with some common sense and by reading the rules of the discussion board before posting messages. Online discussion forums function like other communities in which social norms and mores influence interaction. The danger when executing a social media campaign is letting the end goals dominate all decision making, as a result leading to questionable decisions that violate forum etiquette. When rules are broken, most often the offender will get one warning. After that, a forum administrator may institute a ban on the offender or delete the account altogether. For a marketer, this outcome can represent the loss of substantial time and effort.

These penalties can be easily avoided. Resist the temptation of shortcuts such as spamming users or creating sock puppets, and discussion forums can be a valuable tool for social media marketing. The list above is a starting point for interacting on discussion forums and should also be remembered later in the chapter when we discuss social news, Q&A, and review sites.

Marketing with Discussion Forums

As consumers increasingly look to each other for guidance on which products to buy or what companies to avoid, discussion boards can play a prominent role in a social media marketing campaign. However, keep in mind that forums are not designed or intended to be portals for marketing. Members join and follow a discussion board because it provides useful information or entertainment. Therefore, all posts should serve one or both of those goals. Marketers who aggressively promote their products, spam users with advertisements, or drive topics off track are negatively received on discussion forums. Focus on the core goals of forum participation (information and entertainment) before any marketing efforts occur at all.

Depending on the product being marketed, different discussion forums may be more fruitful. As there are so many forums available online, with a little searching, it should be possible to find several highly relevant discussion boards that may have viewers interested in the product. Before participating, spend some time observing each forum to see if it is a good fit. At the end of this process, there should be a list of forums that are potentially receptive to the marketing campaign.

In the first post on a new forum, include a brief self-introduction. New posters are judged more critically because they have yet to establish a reputation. Be especially sure that early posts are thought out and well composed so that they are taken more seriously. Earning trust and credibility in a discussion forum may take some time. Respond to others' threads for a while before posting new topics.

Most posts to discussion boards will be about other people's questions or interests and rarely if ever about the product being marketed. While to scatter around in forum posts overt marketing or links back to the product home page would be in poor judgment, the signature line (which is enabled by many discussion boards) allows marketing goals to be achieved more subtly. A signature can contain brief information about the account, and perhaps a link back to the product page. As it will appear following all of the constructive posts on others' topics in the forum, a link in the signature can draw interested people back to the product site and lead to sales.

Many of the payoffs from discussion board marketing are indirect and may take time to materialize. To some extent, following online discussions can be a preventative measure that takes in feedback or notices upset customers before a problem has time to grow. Being active even before there are issues to deal with is ideal because after seeing active participation in online forums, customers will be more sympathetic and patient if problems or bad press arise later.[22] By giving generously to a forum community in time and effort creating quality posts, a social media marketer can create good will to call upon when needed.

Guidelines for Moderators of Online Discussion Groups

Out of necessity almost all online forums have a moderator, and due to the person's importance in maintaining a discussion community, many have several moderators. The job of a moderator is to keep the forum organized (by moving off-topic posts and deleting old or irrelevant ones), to provide content and topics for discussion when needed, and to handle disputes between members. These tasks, while simple in theory, can become very complex in practice. What follows are some guidelines to assist future moderators in their performance and to help administrators choose and evaluate effective moderators.

The most important skill a moderator can have is the ability to communicate effectively. This requires strong writing skills but even more crucially the capability to listen and convey ideas to others. As moderators are expected to uphold a level of quality in content, their own contributions to the forum should be top quality. Good moderators lead discussions by example, providing informative and content-rich posts. These posts should be of a high standard that other users can strive for.

How to Build an Online Community

For some companies the existing selection of online discussion boards and forums will not be enough to accomplish their marketing goals. In some cases it can be better to start fresh and create a new social discussion space that can advance the aims of a specific organization. While many brands, both large and small, have attempted this tactic, only a select few have been successful. We will briefly discuss the best ways to build an online community, expand its membership, and accomplish the external social media marketing objectives.

When creating an online community, having an image of the target audience is crucial. Who might be attracted to join a new community? Chris Brogan observes that "[f]or the most part, the people who join and participate in online communities are those who want more out of their product or service experience."[23] However, people tend to join and participate for their own reasons that are not necessarily connected to a product. Do not anticipate areas of discussion or direct conversation toward particular topics.[24] Instead, try to appeal to the buyer personas that might be interested in items like the product, and then let conversation develop organically.

For many young online communities, finding more members and convincing them to join and participate is the most challenging part. Often new communities fail at this stage and never take root at all. When a community is first started, offer memberships to close contacts, friends, customers, employees, business partners, and so on. Due to their prior engagement with the brand or product, some of these people may become core members (and potentially moderators) as the community develops.

After the first invitations are sent, the next step is to encourage members to invite their friends to the community as well. There are two diametrically opposed strategies that can be used: open or limited invitations.[25] With **open invitations**, members are told to invite as many people as they can. While this strategy can grow a community quickly, it also depends on solid incentives for members to send convincing invitations. Keeping lists of top recruiters, having an invitation competition with prizes, or giving other forms of recognition are some ways to reward members for bringing in new people.[26] While effective, these mechanisms require time and effort to administer. The **limited invitations** strategy allows members to invite only one person per month. Making invitations scarce causes them to be more highly valued. A sense of exclusivity makes participating in a forum more exciting and draws more outside interest than an open community.

Having members is important for a successful community, but it is also essential that the members are active and contribute. A forum administrator can take a variety of steps to encourage member engagement. Asking open-ended questions, having polls in which users vote, and recognizing quality posts are some classic methods. Allowing some democratic input makes forums more interesting for users: for example, having members vote on who will be moderator, which posts should be featured up top, and so on.

There are many advantages to be gained by creating an online community from the ground up. Compared to using a third-party platform, where another company's goals and objectives may be given precedence, hosting conversations independently offers many benefits.[27] The ability to customize discussion topics, direct the tone of the forum, and build interest in a brand or product is enormously useful in a social media marketing campaign. While not all new online communities will succeed, the rewards for those that do are substantial.

© Cengage Learning 2013

Maintaining continuity of discussion is one of the most important jobs a moderator has.[28] Forum threads will naturally wander slightly as different users post their thoughts. Distinguishing between a shift in conversation and a derailment of the topic is a judgment call that moderators will frequently have to make. Moderation should never become overly controlling because it may stifle member participation. The goal of organizing threads is to make information easy to find and discussions simple to follow, so avoid micromanaging threads too closely. An overzealous moderator can quickly destroy member engagement with a forum.

Moderators are also expected to cull out old topics that have not been recently discussed. This practice saves space on the forum and makes users' search results more recent and relevant. When constructive exchange has ended, ending dialogues is appropriate, often done by "closing" a thread.[29] Choosing when to delete an old thread is also complicated because occasionally new members may revive a previous topic of discussion. Delete threads that are past a time-sensitive date, do not present useful information, or have gone over twelve months without new comments. It is better to leave a thread in place for too long rather than disappoint members who feel the topic had value and was deleted unnecessarily.

A forum moderator upholds the rules or code of conduct of the forum. This code will typically resemble the list of netiquette items provided earlier in the chapter. Moderators should reprimand users who troll, flame, or otherwise hurt the quality of discussion. However, this duty does not mean to quash all disagreements.[30] Heated debates are often the most exciting part of contributing to an online forum! Moderators can encourage healthy argument and intellectual competition, while still upholding clear guidelines on acceptable behavior (accordingly, political disagreements are okay, but racial or sexual slurs are not). Online debates can be entertaining and are typically harmless. Moderators can spotlight controversial threads and topics in order to draw more member engagement, without letting the fracas get out of hand.

A successful forum moderator should have a soft touch and resort to overt reprimands or punishment as little as possible. Members will only participate when they feel that their contributions are valued, so the primary job of a moderator is to give more people that sense of appreciation. The best moderators promote top-quality posts, reward insightful members, and keep the experience fun for everybody. As they are so important to maintain the tone and content of a discussion forum, the choice of moderators will be among the most important decisions that an administrator makes.

Get Product Creation Ideas from Discussion Forums

Companies spend many millions of dollars on product research, market analysis, and focus groups each year. By observing discussion forums and asking the right questions, much of the same information can be garnered at little or no cost. The practice of "crowd sourcing," mining a group such as customers or employees for product development ideas, has caught on in many industries.[31] Several companies have used this strategy and other applications of discussion forums successfully (see the case study: *Lenovo Turns to Discussion Forums to Cut Customer Service Costs, Attain Feedback, and Improve Productivity*). With basic knowledge of forum etiquette and some well-considered questions, a social media marketer can bring back valuable insight to assist a company's product development team.

Keep in mind that different forum members will have different reasons and goals for joining. To get high-quality feedback, it is best to give an incentive for users to provide information. The effectiveness of the offerings will depend on each member's motivation for participating in the forum. Some will be experts in the field already, while others will be new and searching for basic information. Ask broad, open-ended questions to draw in thoughts from as many sources as possible.[32] Even users with little time on the forum may have valuable product marketing insights that are based on their recent exposure to the brand.

If a product is already partway through development, asking discussion boards for feedback can be helpful to test the market before going to final production. Ask forum members about desired features and possible improvements or customizations. The prospect of influencing a product's development is exciting for many discussion board members, who will respond enthusiastically with ideas and suggestions. Especially on discussion boards that are already populated by people interested in the product (the target market), high-quality feedback can be received. Companies that use the product-screening resource that online forums provide can save substantially on research and development and gain detailed insight on ways to improve their product and bottom line.

CASE STUDY

Lenovo Turns to Discussion Forums to Cut Customer Service Costs, Attain Feedback, and Improve Productivity

Introduction

Lenovo, a global leader in computers, wanted to leverage social media technologies to better reach its customers and respond to customer service and product questions. The company noticed that many of the discussions were happening on blogs and third-party discussion forums online.

After spending some time understanding and participating in the existing conversations, Lenovo decided that it wanted more ownership and wanted to provide stronger leadership to the discussions about its products. Accordingly, Lenovo launched its own discussion forums. The results exceeded expectations with a 20% reduction in call-service volume as well as increases in productivity and cost savings.

History

Lenovo Group Limited (Lenovo) is a Chinese multinational computer technology corporation, which develops, manufactures, and markets desktops and notebook personal computers and a variety of other technology products and services. It acquired the ThinkPad link of notebook computers from IBM in 2005, and as of 2009 Lenovo was the fourth-largest vendor of personal computers in the world.[33]

Challenge

Lenovo found that customers were talking about its products and services on independent forum and review sites such as notebookreview.com and thinkpads.com. Since the conversations were happening across the web, Lenovo didn't always have the opportunity to participate in the discussions. The firm wanted to have more ownership over the conversations and to provide leadership since the conversations were about its products.[34]

Lenovo, a multinational computer technology company

In addition, with tech-savvy computer purchasers increasingly looking online for ratings, reviews, and customer support, there was an opportunity for Lenovo to leverage discussion forums to better meet the needs of its customers. According to the 2010 Cone Customer New Media Study, U.S. new media users are looking for companies online to solve problems and provide product or service information (46%) and solicit feedback on products and services (39%).[35]

According to Mark Hopkins, the social media project manager at Lenovo, "[a]fter monitoring the blogosphere for substantive discussions about Lenovo and some of the major product brands like ThinkPad, we noted that the majority of the content originated in several forums. Passive viewing only took us so far and we wanted to learn more, be able to ask questions, and offer guidance."[36]

Additionally, because Lenovo wants to reach out to the 18- to 34-year-old demographic of young adults who spend the bulk of their time and activities on the Internet, social media and digital support are even more important. In 2011, Lenovo invested in a digital and social media hub in Singapore, "designed to increase Lenovo's digital investments for branding and marketing worldwide."[37]

Strategy

Lenovo determined that launching a peer-to-peer discussion forum would help them connect with its key demographic while reducing customer service costs and providing better customer service to their customers.

The discussion forums at forums.lenovo.com allowed customers to ask and answer each other's questions. In addition, moderators monitored the forums

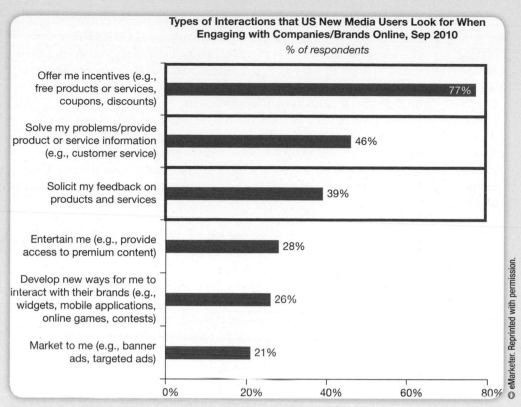

Types of Interactions that US New Media Users Look for When Engaging with Companies/Brands Online, Sep 2010

% of respondents

Offer me incentives (e.g., free products or services, coupons, discounts)	77%
Solve my problems/provide product or service information (e.g., customer service)	46%
Solicit my feedback on products and services	39%
Entertain me (e.g., provide access to premium content)	28%
Develop new ways for me to interact with their brands (e.g., widgets, mobile applications, online games, contests)	26%
Market to me (e.g., banner ads, targeted ads)	21%

© eMarketer. Reprinted with permission.

Types of Interactions among Social Media Users and Brands

to make sure that forum posts were appropriate and to help answer additional questions.

Lenovo had already been blogging for some time, and there were a variety of customer service inquiries left in the comments section of the blog. The forums provided Lenovo with a more appropriate place for customers to ask and answer these questions.

Prior to launching the discussion forums, Lenovo did a lot of listening online, including monitoring blogs and a variety of industry discussion forums. This listening helped the company understand what people were already saying about its products and brands and where the information gaps were.[38] Rather than simply launching a discussion forum, the firm had a clear purpose and objective for the forums based on an assessment of the landscape.

In creating the initial approach for the launch of the discussion forums, Lenovo used a collaborative internal approach and engaged multiple departments in the company in multiple locations. This approach included the legal department, public relations, sales and marketing, product development, engineering, and customer service. All of the departments were encouraged to provide input and help improve the process of launching the forums.[39]

Results

One year after the initial launch of the Lenovo discussion forums, Lenovo posted on its blog that "I believe the underlying value and persistence of relationships found in forums continues to be one of the highest value, and most enduring social investments a company can make."[40]

The bottom-line results from the Lenovo discussion forums are outstanding. According to a Forrester case study, the community "resulted in a 20% reduction in laptop support call rates, an increase in agent productivity, a shortened problem resolution cycle and an increase in Net Promoter Scores (a Net Promoter Score tracks how likely a consumer is to recommend [company X] to a friend). This has led to better products and a reduction in support costs."[41]

The discussion forums at Lenovo have been a lasting success. "The Lenovo Support Community has been growing steadily over the last two and a half years along with other social channels like Facebook and Twitter," said Mark Hopkins.[42] On June 15, 2010, the forum registered the 75,000th member. Since the launch in December of 2007, millions have viewed the site content and thousands of discussions occurred on the site.[43]

There are a number of lessons that can be learned from the successful launch of discussion forums at Lenovo. First, it is important to listen and understand the existing conversations and discussions to determine the purpose and objectives of the forums. For discussion forums to be successful, they must provide a mutual benefit for both the customer and the company. By listening to its customers on existing discussion forums, Lenovo was able to identify both the purpose of the forums and their mutual benefit for the company and customer.

Second, Lenovo engaged existing discussion forums and began participating in them first. Prior to creating its own discussion community, the company gained experience and built relationships with key influencers in its community by actively participating in existing discussion forums.

Third, many companies of varying sizes are successfully using social media and discussion forums to increase sales and reduce customer service costs. "Companies using social media for customer service include Wells Fargo (NYSE: WFC), Dell, Lenovo, General Motors (NYSE: GM), and Zappos," Pam Abbazia, manager of SEO and social media programs for Digital Brand Expressions, told *CRM Buyer*. She continued, "Many report that they've been able to reduce the size of their call center operations and have increased sales as a result of their online customer service efforts."[44]

Finally, social media and discussion forums can provide multiple benefits to an organization. As the results show, Lenovo experienced cost savings through customer service, increased agent productivity, better products from customer feedback, and an increase in overall satisfaction as measured by the Net Promoter Score.

What Is a Social News Site?

A **social news site** lets users submit links to news stories or other web pages to be ranked and displayed. Although every social news site permits users to submit content, sites differ in how they rank and display it. For example, Digg, Reddit, and Newsvine organize content based on votes by readers, with the most popular articles appearing on the front page, while Slashdot and Fark use human editors to determine which articles show up on the front page. StumbleUpon combines user voting and machine learning (in a process called collaborative filtering) to automatically rank and present web pages to users.[45]

Most social news sites also provide the means for readers to discuss and comment on articles. Several social news sites even let users vote on comments and then they rank

Social News Sites	Alexa Global Traffic Rank	Google Page Rank	Dated Started	Description
Reddit	114	8	January 2005	Site displays news based on personal preferences and what the community prefers.
StumbleUpon	120	8	November 2001	Ratings from people with similar interests are used to recommend web pages based on collaborative opinions.
Digg	192	8	December 2004	Users vote to determine the ranking of news items, a process referred to as "Digging."
Slashdot	1,628	8	September 1997	Site features user-submitted and critiqued technology-related and science-oriented news items.
Fark	2,576	8	Mid-1997, active February 1999	Users submit articles to the site administrators from which fifty articles are selected to appear on the front page.
Newsvine	2,733	7	July 2005	Users submit articles on which they vote, and comment; additionally, users can write their own articles and author news columns.

© Cengage Learning 2013

Table 12.1 Popular Social News Sites, as of December 2011

and display the most popular comments first.[46] Popular social news sites include Reddit, StumbleUpon, and Digg, as shown in Table 12.1.

As a consequence of user involvement in shaping the content of social news, these sites appear to be fundamentally altering the way news is consumed.[47] Today, instead of journalists or editors, readers are taking control of the news they view. News comes from many more sources than in the past, popularizing stories that traditional media outlets might not have deemed newsworthy. Since some social news sites let readers create custom views of the news or automatically personalize the news for them, users now have access to individualized news that features content relevant to that person.

A Brief History of Social News Sites

Slashdot, first online in September 1997, was one of the first social news sites.[51] The site's motto is "News for Nerds. Stuff that Matters." It features technology and

What Is the Difference between a Social News Site and a Bookmarking Site?

How to categorize sites as either social news or bookmarking is a fuzzy exercise at best. Both rely on user-submitted links, involve a social aspect, and can be utilized in a social media marketing campaign. However, there are some important distinguishing features that separate the two, as well as differentiating their utility in marketing. We now will briefly examine those differences, and discuss the best ways to use both.

Social news sites' biggest distinction from bookmarking is the community-voting aspect. On social news platforms, member submissions are voted up or down by other users. Posts also tend to be time specific because relevant news topics as a category often get the most up-votes. By contrast, bookmarking sites are more centered on individual interests. Rather than submitting sites for others' approval, bookmarking sites allow users to store whatever strikes their fancy.

The different emphasis on content makes usage of social news and bookmarking sites differ as well. Bookmarking sites can be the best place to find product reviews, useful background information, and other less time-sensitive material.[48] Even on sites that encourage sharing bookmarks with friends, it is an extended process and may occur over a long period of time. Further, as bookmarking sites rely on diversity of content rather than ranking content by votes, there is less immediate input on what others find interesting.[49] While social bookmarking sites can be valuable to get information about a product or idea, they are less useful at gaining insight on recent consumer behavior and opinions, of top importance to marketers.

Some social bookmarking sites, such as Delicious, have been used to market products or organizations, but these applications are less common than marketing via social news websites.* A social news site posts singular articles rather than full websites, thus allowing more detailed information to be quickly filtered and displayed to viewers.[50] This characteristic is also helpful to marketers, because each separate page of a product website can potentially go onto a social news site. For example, a seasonal sale, coupon, or discount could be quickly popularized through social news. This excellent feature has made social news sites a more popular destination for online marketers.

Generally speaking, the more gradual dissemination process of bookmarking sites makes them difficult to use effectively for social media marketing. While social bookmarking sites are, and will likely continue to be, an important part of the online terrain, they will not be discussed in great detail by this text. While bookmarking should not be forgotten, it is less likely to appear as part of a strategic social media marketing campaign.

© Cengage Learning 2013

*See http://www.delicious.com/

science-related news stories, submitted by users. As of 2011 Slashdot continued to be popular among technology enthusiasts, typically serving up approximately 40 million pages each month to a loyal audience of 5 million unique monthly visitors.[52]

Fark, which also started in mid-1997 but which didn't become active until February 1999, targeted a more general audience with what is often a humorous view of the news.[53] According to founder Drew Curtis, "[t]he idea was to have the word Fark come to symbolize news that is really Not News. Hence the slogan 'It's not news, it's Fark.'"[54] However, when major events occur, such as 9/11, the site's traffic spikes, and its discussion forums and news aggregation take the role of a more serious news outlet.[55] Fark typically receives approximately 1,800 to 2,000 link submissions per day, but it only posts about 50 hand-picked news items.[56]

StumbleUpon was launched in November 2001 and billed as a discovery engine, but it is typically classified as a social news site.[57] Although StumbleUpon was sold to eBay in May 2007, the original founders bought it back in April 2009 and the company has remained independent ever since.[58] StumbleUpon works by using collaborative filters,

meaning that the user picks categories, and the computer serves links from across the web that [match what] the user would [likely] be interested in. The user can give each page a thumbs up or down, and StumbleUpon takes each rating into consideration and works to optimize its suggestions to the user's preferences. When the [users are] ready for a new page, they simply click "Stumble" and the engine will serve a new page. Users never know which page is going to come next—called serendipitous discovery— and pages served are often not ones that would typically be found in search engines.[59]

Digg, which started in December 2004, was the first social news site to introduce voting on articles. The site lets users "digg" or "bury" articles, equivalent to voting up or down, respectively, causing the articles with the most Diggs to appear at the top. Burying an article does not decrease its popularity, but if an article accumulates enough buries, it will be automatically deleted.[60] Digg's pioneering interface helped it become the dominant social news site during the last half the 2000s (see the case study: *Digg: How News Became Social!*).

Longtime rival to Digg, Reddit was launched in January 2005.[61] Unlike Digg, the up- and down-votes of users directly affect an article's ranking.[62] An "upvote" increases an article's score, while a "downvote" decreases it. Top scoring articles appear on the front page of Reddit. According to the site's FAQ, "[article] links that receive community approval bubble up towards #1, so the front page is constantly in motion and (hopefully) filled with fresh, interesting links."[63] Reddit was acquired by Condè Nast, owner of *Wired* and other magazines and websites, in October of 2006.[64] Reddit's simple interface and minimal advertising, along with missteps by Digg's new interface that reduced user influence, enabled Reddit to pull ahead of Digg in 2011 to become the most trafficked social news site.[65]

Marketing with Social News Sites

Perhaps the most powerful draw of marketing on social news sites is the incredible payoff to stories that become popular or end up on the front page.[66] Top stories may receive tens of thousands of views by a targeted, relevant audience. However, for every influential social news story, there are thousands that languish in obscurity with very few up-votes at all. Stories that remain on the bottom will receive little if any traffic. The feast-or-famine nature of social news can be either exhilarating or frustrating, so learning from the experience of others is essential to boost the chance of marketing success.

One appeal of StumbleUpon, in contrast to other social news sites, is that it can generate moderate amounts of traffic even for smaller stories or websites. If a few people up-vote a site over time, it will slowly build more and more traffic.[67] This characteristic of the site allows less flashy, but high-quality content to gain an audience. StumbleUpon is easy to use and a great fallback to drive traffic toward a website. Encourage people to up-vote a page, and more people will stumble across it.

The rest of this section, however, will focus on other social news sites, such as Digg or Reddit, because they require much more effort and finesse to generate site traffic. On social news sites, perhaps the most important determinant of an article's success or failure will be the title. Many hurried users will vote a story up or down based solely on the title and never view the attached content. Make the title appeal to short attention spans because those tend to dominate the space on social news sites. To see what sorts of titles have generated a response, look at items from the Top News or front page of a social news site. What attributes do those titles have? Emulate the form of other successful headlines to hopefully draw traffic to new offerings.

In addition to a catchy title, some sorts of content are favored more by social news readerships. In particular, lists are a popular format because they are easy on the eyes and quick to read. In every case content should be well spaced so that it can be skimmed easily and highlight the main points. Much like a successful blog or microblog post, social news content should be relevant, entertaining, and informative. These are the factors that may lead other members to up-vote a story.

Good content alone is not enough to reach the top of social news sites. The sheer volume of articles submitted is a barrier because the vast majority will never be seen. To increase an article's visibility, having a good relationship with a power user, who can influence many others to view a story, is essential. This article volume makes networking with other members a top priority on social news sites.[68] Vote up submissions by other users with similar interests, and they may return the favor. Without genuine participation, it is unlikely a marketer will achieve her or his goals from social news; users who only submit their own content are quickly identified as spammers and ignored.[69] Avoid this pitfall by supporting others' content frequently and building relationships with users to create a springboard for marketing messages.

Even if an article becomes popular and generates tens of thousands of visits to the webpage, not every one of those viewers will stay to look at the rest of the site or consider purchasing a product. Luckily, web traffic is only one potential benefit of social news as a marketing strategy. By providing space for discussion and comment by a wide reader base, social news can draw comments and input (much like a discussion board). It can also build an organization's thought leadership by contributing valuable content to the community.[70] Many conversations occur on social news sites, regarding breaking news and hot products, which cannot be found anywhere else. Observing and engaging in these discussions can provide an edge to any business.

In addition to broadly popular general-purpose social news sites that have been discussed above, there are also platforms targeted toward narrower audiences. For example, Sphinn is geared toward online marketing and search engine optimization experts and represents a useful pool of knowledge for marketing professionals to share links and ideas. Kirtsy, another social news site, is similar to Digg but targeted toward women. For finding good deals, people can go to Dealigg or Kaboodle. New niche social news sites are being developed constantly. With some research a social media marketer can find social news platforms that will be receptive to almost any product. A combined approach, which uses both the large, mainstream platforms as well as specialty social news sites, will have the best chance of reaching target audiences.

CASE STUDY

Digg: How News Became Social!

Introduction

Digg was the first social news site to introduce the voting system, whereby subscribers and reviewers determine the ranking of news stories by voting them up or down.[71] Instead of having editors decide what news should appear on the front page, the wisdom of the crowd makes this decision on a social news site.[72]

"Digg is a place for people to discover and share content from anywhere on the web. From the biggest online destinations to the most obscure blog, Digg surfaces the best stuff as voted on by our users. You won't find editors at Digg—we're here to provide a place where people can collectively determine the value of content and we're changing the way people consume information online."[73]

The immense popularity of Digg spawned an entire industry, with a slew of imitators creating their own story submission and voting sites.[74] Social media marketers were quick to recognize the power of getting a story on the front page of Digg because it both increased brand awareness and attracted massive website traffic.

Kevin Rose, cofounder of Digg

© David Paul Morris/Bloomberg via Getty Images

History

With a mere $2,000 from Kevin Rose, Digg begin life in December 2004 as a non-commercial enterprise, founded by Rose, Owen Byrne, Ron Gorodetzky, and Jay Adelson.[75] To assist readers in navigating the site's rapidly growing content, Digg offered categories for topical news items, such as Technology, Science, World & Business, Videos, Entertainment and Gaming. With increasing fame, the owners of Digg decided to monetize the site by Google AdSense. Digg received its first round of venture capital, $2.8 million, in Octobe 2005.[76]

According to Kevin Rose, the point at which he knew Digg was going be big occurred "with the Paris Hilton cell phone incident. That was a major turning point for us. A user close to the hacker submitted the story to Digg, and due to its [interest] with the Digg audience it was quickly Dugg to the homepage. That same night Google and Yahoo! both indexed Digg and gave us the top position for the keywords 'Paris Hilton hack'. At the time we were only running one webserver. As you can imagine, for the next two days the site was hammered with traffic and Digg hardly functioned."[77]

Digg was a poster child "for [social media] success," and in 2008 it became a potential target for a Google acquisition; although the Google deal fell through, acquisition rumors persisted.[78] However, as of June 2011, Digg remained a privately held company. To bring in additional revenue, Digg entered into an advertising partnership with Microsoft.[79] Traffic to the site and user participation continued to increase from 2005 to 2010.

© AP Images/Kevork Djansezian

Paris Hilton on the phone

Challenge

The first obstacle Digg had to face was finding a way to convince power users to invest their time in an unproven platform and submit news stories.[80] The social media site had to build a critical mass of submitters in order to attract sufficient traffic to the site to warrant interest by venture capitalists and advertisers.

Over time Digg built up a large cache of power users, who submitted enough stories to draw readers in increasing numbers to Digg. The social media site's next big challenge appeared to be shifting "from fostering story submission to figuring out how to ensure that relevant stories are matched to each Digg reader and the entire community."[81]

Strategy

Kevin Rose was a big fan of Slashdot.com. He began wondering what would happen if you let readers vote on stories as a way to rank them.[82] This idea builds on a process known as "crowdsourcing," in which tasks are performed by an undefined large group of people or community.[83]

Rose decided to initially focus on technology news and to build a loyal following among a group he knew well as the former host of *Screensavers*, a technology cable TV show.[84] In fact, Rose announced the launch of Digg on *Screensavers*, reaching a prime target market of over a 95,000 viewers.[85]

Another factor that made this community so appealing to Digg was that techies tend to set up websites and blog, so they are always looking for ways to improve their ranking in search engine results. Digg provides techies with a powerful tool to build inbound links to their sites, hence improving their rankings on search engines such as Google.[86]

Digg's lack of editors, with story placement entirely dependent on votes, created a level of transparency that lured in these power users and helped create a critical mass of story submitters. Digg then built a community feature so that contributors could become better acquainted with each other, interact, and create a sense of rivalry among top submitters by showing them how they stacked up against others in terms of submissions and hit rates. Using these tactics, Digg was able to form a community of devoted submitters.[87]

Finally, Digg enabled readers to comment on and discuss stories, often improving the original content with their own views and suggestions. This site provided discussion forums for readers to exchange ideas and chat about new items and related topics of interest. These tactics helped generate enthusiasm for the site among the masses.

Results

Digg's strategies struck a chord with the public, especially among power users (techies, Internet marketers, and bloggers), who flocked to the site to submit and rate content. In just two years after its launch, Digg had achieved impressive site participation and traffic. By 2006 it had 600,000 registered users, 10 million daily page views, 1.5 million daily unique visitors, and 10 million unique monthly visitors.[88] An August 2006 *Business Week* cover story estimated

Kevin Rose (pictured right), retakes control of Digg in April 2010

Digg's value at $60 million.[89] By 2008 Digg had nearly 20 million unique monthly visitors.[90] In 2009 it won the Webby Award for Best Social Networking.[91] As a privately held company, 2008 valuations of Digg ran the gamut, from $167 to $300 million.[92]

In late 2009 the picture for Digg looked bright, with about 40 million users and more than $40 million in venture capital funding from investors such as Highland Capital Partners and Greylock Partners. According to Digg's CEO, Jay Adelson, the company was on the path to profitability by convincing advertisers "to create content as advertising. Instead of the standard [Internet] billboard . . . [we] create ads that are literally content, so if you click on it you read an interesting story or article, and you put branding next to it. And we get literally get 100 times the click-through-rate of what a typical ad would get, so that's good for advertisers."[93]

However, the landscape for Digg suddenly darkened after it released the much ballyhooed Digg v4 website system on August 25, 2010. Describing massive changes to Digg, Jay Adelson said, "Every single thing has changed. The entire website has been rewritten."[94] The entry point for Digg became a "My news" page instead of the traditional front page in order to give readers a personalized home page that matches relevant stories to a user's interests based on the individual's diggs (votes). To diminish the chances of power users dominating the site with their submissions by pushing those submissions to the front page, Digg v4 incorporated a revised ranking algorithm, which took into consideration where the votes come from and the source of new items.

However, the radical changes of Digg v4 were widely disliked.[95] Digg v4 was unstable, and moreover, many users suspected the changes were really made to help monetize the site and appease the venture capitalist, who had sunk so much funding into Digg. In addition, users claimed that the social news site now favored items from such major sites as the BBC, Techcrunch, CollegeHumor, and *Wired* over smaller content providers. The Internet marketers and bloggers, who helped make the site successful, no longer saw value in actively submitting and voting on Digg content. About 10% of the users on Digg (the power users) contributed roughly 90% of the popular stories.[96] Unsurprisingly, in 2010, just from beginning of September to the 18th, "traffic from UK Internet users to Digg . . . declined by 34%. In the US, which is Digg's primary market, visits . . . dropped by 26%."[97] On October 27, 2010, Digg had to let 37% of its staff go and began refocusing the service.[98]

Fortunately, there may be a light at the end of the tunnel. Kevin Rose, who was an ardent defender of Digg v4 and who resisted rethinking the decisions made in its design, resigned his role in the company on March 18, 2011.[99] The relatively new CEO, Matt Williams, has quickly moved to stabilize the performance of Digg and is actively talking with both power users and regular users to help make changes that revitalize the site. As a consequence, traffic to Digg has picked up a bit after the mass exodus with the introduction of Digg v4. As one blogger put it, "there's life left in the old lady yet."[100]

What Is a Q&A Site?

A **Q&A (question-and-answer) site** lets people pose questions and receive answers back from anyone willing and (hopefully) knowledgeable enough to reply. Most Q&A sites can also provide fast answers by looking up questions that have already been asked; the other option is waiting to see if someone answers the query. When the user

Social News Sites	Alexa Global Traffic Rank	Google Page Rank	Dated Started	Description
Ask.com	49	8	April 1996	Originally known as "Ask Jeeves," Ask.com allows users to pose questions in natural language or using keywords, and supports math, dictionary, and conversion questions.
Answers.com	183	9	May 1996	Combines community-driven questions and answers with hundreds of authoritative editorial reference books as well as drawing on community answers from WikiAnswers and Reference Answers database, along with licensed reference topics.
Yahoo! Answers	N/A	7	July 2005	Accepts questions and provides answers in twelve languages, with status points awarded to encourage participation.
Quora	1,042	6	January 2010	Experts have flocked to the site to answer questions in specific fields, such as programming, cooking and photography.
JustAnswer	1,596	6	August 2003	A fee-based service, which matches user questions with topic experts, such as lawyers, veterinarians, mechanics, physicians, and contractors.
ChaCha	2,330	6	December 2005	Provides answers to questions via the website, or through texting and mobile apps.
AllExperts	3,405	6	Early 1998	Volunteer experts in a wide variety of fields are available to answer user questions.
Answerbag	4,910	6	July 2003	A collaborative database of FAQs, where multiple answers to a question are displayed, with the best-rated responses at the top.
Blurtit	5,405	5	June 2006	Offers a community-based approach to answering users' questions.

© Cengage Learning 2013

Table 12.2 Popular Q&A Sites, as of December 2011

types a question, the Q&A site instantly begins to search for similar queries posted days or months earlier. With luck, the answer is already there. Some Q&A sites can classify questions by category, increasing the odds it will be seen and answered by a person who knows about the subject. Popular Q&A sites include Ask.com, Answer.Yahoo. com, Answers.com, and Quora.com (see Table 12.2 for a list of other Q&A sites). Of these, Answers.com is unique in that is combines responses from common users with authoritative sources such as *Wikipedia*, the *Encyclopedia Britannica*, and the *American Heritage Dictionary*.[101]

A Brief History of Q&A Sites

Launched April 1997, Ask Jeeves was one of the first question-and-answer sites. Jeeves was the name of the butler pictured on the original site that fetched answers to question, which could be posed in conversational language or by using keyword searches.[102] In later incarnations the Q&A site added support for math, dictionary, and conversion questions. In 2001 the name was shortened to Ask.com.[103] On September 23, 2005, the company announced Jeeves was going into retirement, and the character was removed from Ask.com on February 27, 2006.[104] On May 16, 2006, Ask.com introduced a "Binoculars Site Preview" into its search results so that users could use the "Binoculars" to get a sneak peek at search results pages.[105] In September 2010 Ask.com launched its mobile Q&A app for the iPhone, which brought the service to mobile users in an easy-use format.[106]

Yahoo! Answers, launched July 5, 2005, lets users both pose questions and respond to questions submitted by other users.[107] The Q&A site accepts and answers queries in twelve languages and awards status points to encourage participation.[108] As of December 2006, Yahoo! Answers had already amassed 60 million registered users and a database of 65 million answers.[109]

Answers.com was founded by Bill Gross and Henrik Jones at Idealab in May 1996, but it didn't launch its free Q&A site until January 2005.[110] By August 2009 the site had 56.4 million unique monthly visitors in the United States and 83.0 million globally.[111] Bob Rosenschein, CEO of Answers.com, announced that the site had reached 5.5 million registered users and its database of answers had topped 10 million as of November 2010.[112]

This social media category has long been controlled by high-traffic industry giants such as Yahoo! Answers and Answers.com, which each had nearly 50 million unique monthly visitors in December 2010, according to the analytics firm comScore.[113] However, more recent players, like Quora, have reinvigorated this lethargic field with new innovations, such as celebrity experts and video questions and answers.[114]

Marketing with Q&A Sites

While Q&A sites are primarily intended to deliver information, they can also be an avenue for social media marketing. However, Q&A sites are not an appropriate place to promote a product (unless, by some amazing coincidence, the marketed product happens to be the answer to someone's question). Members of Q&A sites gain a reputation for providing detailed and useful answers.[117] This process can be a natural way to demonstrate thought leadership and build trust in a brand through the knowledge of its spokespeople.

Sharing information through Q&A sites builds an aura of expertise, especially because many services provide points or rankings to members who provide the best

Review Sites

A **review site** is a service that lets people post opinions about brands, companies, products, and services. Starting in 1995 (one year after its launch), Amazon.com was one of the first sites to encourage reviews.[115] By 2006 more stores were clamoring for the user input and valuable information that online product reviews could provide.[116] Now most large retailers permit product and service reviews, including Walmart and Costco. In addition, there are dedicated review sites, such as Yelp or Epinions.com, and specialized review sites like RateMds.com for help finding a doctor or dentist. There are also membership services that compile and verify consumer ratings of local service companies and contractors, such as Angie's List. Finally, there are professional review sites, which either hire experts in specific fields to write reviews or use in-house staff to prepare reviews.

While product reviews are undeniably important in influencing consumer purchases, their role as a marketing tool is more tenuous. Most sites have explicit guidelines that bar overt marketing. Reviews are checked, either by human editors or computer algorithms, to detect manipulation of rating scores. The punishments can be harsh: On Yelp a business is permanently barred from being rated if it is found to have cheated the system. This banishment represents a serious loss of credibility for a firm. While a business can encourage past clients to go and write positive reviews, that is almost the full extent of possible marketing strategies on a review site. Valuable for their product feedback in addition to informing other customers, review sites are best when the results are completely organic. While review sites might be passively involved in a social media marketing strategy, companies should refrain from attempting to influence rating results because of the serious potential consequences.

© Cengage Learning 2013

answers (either decided by community vote, or chosen by the question's asker). It does not require a tricky agenda to be successful on Q&A sites; simply share answers in a thorough, detailed way.[118] In addition to building a reputation, there are some tangible benefits as well. Q&A sites can help build links back to a personal profile or a product page, drawing more attention from the target audience.[119]

Much has been said about succeeding on Yahoo! Answers, Ask.com, or Answer.com alone, but the most essential parts of general Q&A strategy have been addressed above. However, due to its distinct target market and format, the relatively young Q&A site Quora deserves some special attention. A combination of professional networking and an advice service, Quora presents unique opportunities for a social media marketer.

Upon joining Quora, users are encouraged to follow areas of interest. The site is integrated with other social networking platforms, such as Facebook, and will suggest trends and contacts to follow based on prior connections. After following topics of interest, start observing what other users have posted. Members are encouraged to establish areas of expertise by answering questions and posting news. This practice makes Quora an excellent platform to get breaking information about specific industries.[120] Do not rush into asking questions immediately; first tap into the resources that already exist.

The advantage of Quora is that each of the topics can function like a targeted social news site. Following some topics of expertise and building a reputation opens up discussion with other industry leaders. These members may later become potential leads for a business. When answering a difficult or detailed question, consider adapting the answer into a blog post and directing others back to it.[121] By encouraging interaction between people in similar industries, Quora is an excellent networking tool for business contacts, in addition to gathering information.

Providing valuable answers is the core of any successful Q&A site member's strategy, and Quora is no exception. By communicating about topics with unique insight, these platforms are a perfect avenue for building thought leadership online. By integrating professional networking and by placing a premium on specificity of knowledge, Quora is especially well positioned for developing a brand's reputation for expertise.[122] By creating and sharing answers, a social media marketer can advance his or her brand and organization.

Future of Discussion Boards, Social News, and Q&A Sites

Discussion boards have become a mainstay of many sites, even in online games. Some companies have found discussion boards a great source of product innovation. Most online retailers have review sites, which often include discussion boards for posting consumer opinions and receiving company feedback. Although discussion boards are one the oldest forms of social media, they continue to grow in importance, and marketers who fail to include them in their social media marketing plans do so at their own peril.

Social news sites continue to gain ground over traditional news media outlets as new generations move from traditional news media to the Internet. In 2011 online news readership overtook newspapers: "[f]or the first time, more of us are getting our news from the Web than from newspapers, according to a new report, which finds that the Internet now 'trails only' television among American adults as a destination for the news."[123] And the 2011 Project for Excellence in Journalism by Pew Research reported that the gap between Internet and TV news consumption was closing.[124] Moreover, "[s]eventy-seven percent of social-media users . . . get their news from social media. . . .

People tend to be 'news grazers' getting their information from a variety of sources, with just 33 percent of Internet users saying they have a favorite site for their news gathering," according the Future of Media website.[125]

For better or worse, today, news has become more personalized and social. The days of editors choosing what people read or see are fading as social news sites provide the means to customize what news appears and how it is ranked. These news aggregators may well be the next stage in the evolution of journalism. Some argue that losing the editorial function means people will have an increasingly myopic view of the world from less than trustworthy sources; however, others reply that diverse perspectives (i.e., the "wisdom of the crowd") and the inherent value in immediately breaking news outweigh these objections to social news.[126] Only time will tell how this evolution will impact society; but for marketers, having these self-defining market segments presents vast opportunities.

Arnold Brown, in an article published by *The Futurist* in 2008 anticipating the rise of social media marketing, wrote that "[u]nderstanding that public-opinion trends are driven not by a few influentials influencing everyone else but by many impressionable people influencing one another should change how companies incorporate social influence into their marketing campaigns."[127] This trend is a common theme in all of the social media platforms that have been discussed in this chapter. With online consumers now influencing each other more and more, modern marketing professionals have to engage in the conversation. Discussion forums and Q&A sites are some of the best ways to do just that.

Once considered a dead or dying service, new Q&A sites such as Quora and VYou have breathed life into this social media category. Long plagued with clutter, repetitive questions, and answers that vary widely in quality, Q&A sites are enjoying a resurgence. According to a *New York Times* article, "[a] flurry of start-ups in this field are gathering speed and attracting the eyes and wallets of venture capitalists. . . . The entrepreneurs behind the newer sites say there is a big opportunity to be captured in revamping the question-and-answer model."[128] Whether this renaissance succeeds is an open question. In the meantime, traditional and second-generation Q&A sites provide marketers with innovative ways to build brands. By answering questions about products and services, marketers create good will among consumers and improve brand perception. By establishing themselves as experts in a field, social media marketers can lend credibility to the companies they represent.

EXERCISE CASE STUDY

How Business Pioneers Take Advantage of Quora[**]

Introduction ....

Quora, the easy to navigate question-and-answer service built on a social-media backbone, has soared in popularity since launching in 2009. Founded by [Adam D'Angelo and Charlie Cheever], the site has already attracted high-level

---

[**]Republished with permission of Mansueto Ventures LLC, from "10 Tips on Using Quora for Business," Inc. Magazine, Tim Donnelly, February, 28, 2011; permission conveyed through Copyright Clearance Center, Inc.

executives, journalists, industry insiders, and entrepreneurs, all eager to answer a vast array of questions for free. The site is rife with crowd-sourced queries, with a comprehensive listing and incentive to stay in touch with a network of people.

[What makes Quora unique as compared to other Q&A sites, such as LinkedIn Answers or Yahoo Answers, is its utilitarian interface and active member community. Quora's design creates a positive user experience. Members can post and answer questions by category, making information retrieval a relatively painless process. Quora's streamlined interface entices "users to share their knowledge and expertise to create an ever-deepening (and searchable) database of answers."[129] The design also makes it easy for users to vote on answers, moving them up or down in ranking based on the perceived quality of the answers, a factor that tends to push the best answers to the top.

In addition to a superior design, Quora's growing and active community of area experts, provide in-depth, accurate, and relevant answers: "[t]he expertise of the people [who answer] questions on Quora is incredibly impressive and adds to the value of using the application."[130] In short, Quora has found a way to connect with people's insatiable search for answers, explaining its explosive growth.[131]]

History

[Quora was founded in June 2009 by Adam D'Angelo, former CTO and VP of engineering at Facebook, and Charlie Cheever, former product developer and manager at Facebook.[132] Quora won the TechCrunch award for "Best New Startup or Product of 2010" and received funding from Benchmark Capital in March 2010. [133]]

Challenge

[For marketers the question begging an answer is whether Quora is worth their time and effort.] [O]n a site whose range of topics stretches from "Do Silicon Valley VCs invest in European early-stage startups?" to "Given our current technology and with the proper training, would it be possible for someone to become Batman?" how can you maximize its potential for your business? We asked a few Quora [business] pioneers who've quickly found ways to take advantage of the site for their tips:

Strategy

1. **Find new ideas to talk about.**
   "It's pretty much the perfect way to beat writer's block for your blog. Go to your topic of expertise, find the un-answered question that has the most followers, and assuming that you have an opinion on it, write an answer. Use it as inspiration or the meat for your blog post."
   —Naval Ravikant, founder, CEO, and chairman at online marketplace Vast.com

2. Open the lines of communication.

"I'm not encouraging people to begin handling their business development and cold calling via Quora. It's a terrible idea, in fact. My advice on how to connect with a tech rockstar? Follow them on Quora. Start answering the questions that you are notified that they are following. If they ultimately choose to 'like' your answer or comment on your answer, only then would I suggest reaching out to them via direct message. If you do so in a respectful manner you'd be surprised at the great people you'll connect with offline. It happened for me with one of the co-founders of The Huffington Post."
—Tyler James, co-founder, Conversated Media

3. Sharpen your communication skills.

"Honestly I can't say Quora has helped me win new business or do a great deal of networking. The value I've gotten out of my interaction with Quora has more been one of sharpening some of my own communication skill sets. It's helped me evaluate concise, clear responses to questions instead of waffling. This happens both in my own evaluation of questions/answers as well as the feedback I get from the community. Just like blog writing or Tweeting, this constant evaluation of 'what works and why' makes me a better communicator, something that comes in handy given I work in communications."
—Vlad Ivanovic, head of Innovation at Blue Barracuda London

4. Don't self-promote.

"The secret of building your reputation on Quora is to answer questions in which you have a deep level of knowledge. Your own company is obviously a thing in which you have expertise and that's where you could start. You should then look at the area your company focuses on and provide answers to questions related to that area. Remember that Quora is not about self-promotion but about providing the best answer to a specific question. The way you build your business with Quora is by helping the Quora community. Its members will eventually notice you and, hopefully, start using your services."
—Tristan Louis, CEO of Keepskor and writer at TNL.net

5. Ask good questions.

"Questions are more important than answers. There is some spirit of competitiveness in how Quora works that encourages people not only to provide the best answer but also the best question. Picasso once said computers are useless because they only provide answers. In Quora the value is in the fact that you need to ask a good/interesting/intriguing question to get feedback from all those people out there. A lot of the work I do with entrepreneurs revolves around just that: focus on asking the right question and answers will arrive. For a business or a business leader, having the knowledge of which are the key questions driving his/her business provides a great advantage."
—Hod Fleishman, founder and chief of safety at GreenRoad, a maker of driver technology

6. **Build a presence.**

"Use your real name, mention your business, and have a full, succinct profile. Quora, like Twitter, is not a social network where you follow friends a la Facebook, but rather, you should follow thought-leaders in your industry, colleagues, competitors, and anyone else who is making contributions that seem interesting. Everyone is an expert on something: contribute to the community and answer questions. I've engaged in some interesting conversations and found some very smart people to follow this way. I thought I would overwhelm myself by following too many questions and topics, but Quora actually curates interests well and so feel free to mark down many."
—Alexander Niehenke, associate at San Francisco venture capital firm Crosslink Capital

7. **Monitor and engage.**

"Using Google alerts with the query 'Quora jess3' for instance, will in real time for free send me e-mails mentioning (my company) Jess3. Start threads for areas you sell an expertise in, and stay engaged. Be a part of the conversations in your industry. This is how you build [the reputation of your business] on Quora. You might also want to put a Google alert for your competition's mentions on Quora. In general, you want to know what your industry is talking about, and this will include your rivals, partners and everything in between. Quora is an active version of Wikipedia. A business has to respond to any mentions of their brand."
—Jesse Thomas, CEO and founder, Jess3, an interactive creative agency

8. **Do market research.**

"It's easy to look up topics and questions that are currently top-of-mind for my prospective customers. In this way, Quora excels as a market research tool. When I can contribute value to a question—whether through an authoritative answer, or a suggested refinement to the question itself—I can also help subtly market whatever I'm working on as well. From a marketing perspective, Quora is about being authoritative on a subject, and building relationships over the course of multiple questions with the people who share similar interests. In a sense, it's very similar to other forms of online marketing. The key for me is this: The extremely tight subject matter focus and smaller scope allows for greater intimacy, and lowers the barriers to being a consistent and useful contributor—even compared to something like Twitter!"
—Dean Blackburn, founder of NaviDate.com

9. **Prove your worthiness.**

"This includes providing quality answers and brushing up on Quora icons such as The Scobelizer. Learn how to recognize and avoid the 'dumb neighborhoods.' Posting there offers a very poor ROI. If you have an easily stimulated sarcasm gland, fight hard to resist the temptation to troll the dumb neighborhoods. This will only get you banned. Buddy up with other newbies by 'following' them so that you have someone to talk to because the coolest kids will most likely continue to ignore you. Finally, understand and appreciate that Quora is a good place to connect with interesting people."
—Peter Ireland, former CEO at Rubicon Capital Corp., who now runs www.tycoonplaybook.com

10. **Don't over-promote yourself.**

"Don't try and market your site or product—put information about what you are working on, what you own, etc., in your bio/profile, but don't market it unless there is a specific situation that it adds value. Figure out how to give back to the community. Answer questions that are related to your area of competency and that you have a unique vantage point (based on your experience) that can add value and benefit the community. Don't be afraid to talk about your product/service, but only do it when there is value added. The bottom line rule is: add value by giving the askers of questions a useful and insightful answer."

—Marc Gayle, founder of CompVersions.com

Results

[Clearly from the advice and comments above, businesses are successfully using Quora for a variety of marketing purposes. Quora itself is off to a fast start with 200,000 members regularly returning each month, and a March 2010 infusion of $11 million in funding from Benchmark Capital, which valued the start-up at $86 million.[134] Just how effective Quora will become as social media marketing channel remains to be seen.]

Review Questions for Quora Case Study

1. Why has Quora taken off so quickly?

2. Explain the major differences between Quora and other Q&A sites. How do these differences influence a marketing strategy?

3. What advice given in the Strategy section of this case study seems most applicable to Quora? Why?

4. Go on the Quora site and look at the topics. What are some of the topics that appear most engaging and how might marketers use these topics to establish a reputation for expertise?

Notes

1. Burmaster, Alex (2007, December 6), "Consumers Trust Others' Opinions More Than Ads," *New Media Age.* Retrieved July 22, 2011, from http://www.nma.co.uk/opinion/consumers-trust-others-opinions-more-than-ads/36100.article

2. Tuten, Tracy L. (2008), *Advertising 2.0: Social Media Marketing in a Web 2.0 World* (Westport, CT: Praeger), p. 119.

3. Bishop, Jonathan (2009, January 1). Retrieved September 12, 2011, from http://www.jonathanbishop.com/214/unplugged-and-uncut/structure-of-online-communities-as-genre/

4. Cook, Ann D. (2008, August). "A case study of the manifestations and significance of social presence in a multi-user virtual environment," University of Saskatchewan Library Electronic Theses & Dissertations. Retrieved September 12, 2011, from http://en.wikipedia.org/wiki/Virtual_world

5. "Gartner Says 80 Percent of Active Internet Users Will Have A 'Second Life' in the Virtual World by End of 2011" (2007, April 24) Gartner Group: Press Release. Retrieved September 12, 2011, from http://www.gartner.com/it/page.jsp?id=503861

6. "Q2 2011 VW cumulative registered accounts reaches 1.4 billion" (2011, July 27). KZero. Retrieved September 12, 2011, from http://www.kzero.co.uk/blog/?p=4625

7. Korolov, Maria (2011, July 28), "Virtual world usage accelerates," Hypergrid Business. Retrieved September 12, 2011, from http://www.hypergridbusiness.com/2011/07/virtual-world-usage-accelerates/

8. Ibid.

9. Jansen, Monika. (2011, February 3) "Social Game Developer Pure Bang Games Poised for Growth," Tech Cocktail. Retrieved September 12, 2011, from http://techcocktail.com/social-game-developer-pure-bang-games-poised-for-growth-2011-02#.Tm7aydQg3vY

10. "IBM to Build Virtual Stores in 'Second Life' for Sears, Circuit City" (2007, January 09) Associated Press. Retrieved September 12, 2011, from http://www.foxnews.com/story/0,2933,242564,00.html

11. "P&G Second Life Channel 9 News - Red Dog Willie" (2008, July 22) YouTube: WCPO Channel 9. Retrieved September 12, 2011, from http://www.youtube.com/watch?v=8q_IyfOfqYg

12. Barker, Donald I., Melissa S. Barker, and Catherine T. Pinard (2013), Unit D, *Internet Research—Illustrated*, 6th ed. (Boston, MA: Cengage Learning), p. 8.

13. "What Is an 'Internet forum'?" (n.d.), Videojug. Retrieved July 19, 2011, from http://www.videojug.com/expertanswer/internet-communities-and-forums-2/what-is-an-internet-forum

14. Ibid.

15. Red, James (2010, October 1), "When Did Compuserve, AOL and Prodigy Begin to Offer Internet Online Services?" eHow.com. Retrieved July 19, 2011, from http://www.ehow.com/facts_7266921_did-offer-internet-online-services_.html

16. Lueg, Christopher, and Danyel Fisher (2003), *From Usenet to CoWebs: Interacting with Social Information Spaces* (New York: Springer).

17. Red, James (2010, October 1) "When Did Compuserve, AOL and Prodigy Begin to Offer Internet Online Services?" eHow.com. Retrieved July 19, 2011, from http://www.ehow.com/facts_7266921_did-offer-internet-online-services_.html

18. "Forum Software Timeline 1994–2010" (2010, December 24), Forum Software Reviews. Retrieved July 19, 2011, from http://www.forum-software.org/forum-software-timeline-from-1994-to-today

19. Flowers, Frankie (2011, May 3), "5 Most Popular Threads," Lonely Planet Post. Retrieved July 19, 2011, from http://www.lonelyplanet.com/thorntree/thread.jspa?threadID=2052833

20. Beal, Vangie (2008, April 18), "All about Online Forums," *Webobedia*. Retrieved July 19, 2011, from http://www.webopedia.com/DidYouKnow/Internet/2008/forum_etiquette.asp

21. Stone, Brad (2007, July 16), "The Hand That Controls the Sock Puppet Could Get Slapped," *New York Times*. Retrieved July 19, 2011, from http://www.nytimes.com/2007/07/16/technology/16blog.html?ex=1342238400&en=9a3424961f9d2163&ei=5088&partner=rssnyt&emc=rss

22. Scott, David Meerman (2009), *The New Rules of Marketing & PR* (Hoboken, NJ: John Wiley), p. 85.

23. Brogan, Chris (2010), "Build Strong Online Communities Using Social Media," in Mitch Meyerson, ed., *Success Secrets of the Social Media Marketing Superstars* (Irvine, CA: Entrepreneur Media), p. 87.

24. Millington, Richard (2010, January), "The Right and Wrong Way to Grow a Forum," FeverBee Community Consultancy. Retrieved July 18, 2011, from http://www.feverbee.com/2010/01/the-right-and-wrong-way-to-grow-a-forum.html

25. Millington, Richard (2008, November 21), "Giving Members Invites," FeverBee Community Consultancy. Retrieved July 23, 2011, from http://www.feverbee.com/2008/11/giving-members-invites.html

26. Millington, Richard (2008, September 15), "Basic Tactics to Grow Your Online Community without Any Promotion," FeverBee Community Consultancy. Retrieved July 23, 2011, from http://www.feverbee.com/2008/11/giving-members-invites.html

27. Brogan, Chris (2010), "Build Strong Online Communities Using Social Media," in Mitch Meyerson, ed., *Success Secrets of the Social Media Marketing Superstars* (Irvine, CA: Entrepreneur Media), p. 93.

28. "Top Tips for Moderators of Online Discussion Groups" (n.d.), adapted from William Spitzer, Kelly Wedding, and Vanessa DiMauro, "Fostering Reflective Dialogues for Teacher Professional Development" (1994), TERC, Leader Networks. Retrieved July 18, 2011, from http://www.leadernetworks.com/download.php?file=Online_Discussion_Tips.pdf

29. Ibid.

30. Millington, Richard (2009, April 28), "Why Fights Are So Important," FeverBee Community Consultancy. Retrieved July 23, 2011, from http://www.feverbee.com/2009/04/importantfights.html

31. Brown, Arnold (2008, January-February), "The Consumer Is the Medium," *The Futurist*. Retrieved July 22, 2011, from http://www.agriworldsa.com/article-archive/technology/consumer.pdf

32. Spijkstra, Menno (n.d.), "Get Product Creation Ideas from Discussion Forums," EzineArticles. Retrieved July 18, 2011, from http://ezinearticles.com/?Get-Product-Creation-Ideas-From-Discussion-Forums&id=3614736

33. "Lenovo" (n.d.), *Wikipedia*. Retrieved July 5, 2011, from http://en.wikipedia.org/wiki/Lenovo

34. Petouhoff, Natalie (2010, January 12), "Case Study #2: How Lenovo Implemented Customer Service Social Media Best Practices," *Forrester Blog*. Retrieved July 5, 2011, from http://blogs.forrester.com/business_process/2010/01/how-lenovo-implemented-customer-service-social-media-best-practices.html

35. Cohen, Heidi (2011, February 22), "How to Integrate Customer Service into Social Media Marketing," ClickZ. Retrieved July 5, 2011, from http://www.clickz.com/clickz/column/2027223/integrate-customer-service-social-media-marketing

36. "The Lenovo Community: Spotlight on Success" (2009, September 1), *Lithium Blog*. Retrieved July 5, 2011, http://lithosphere.lithium.com/t5/Best-Practice-the-Community-Blog/The-Lenovo-Community-Spotlight-on-Success/ba-p/3780

37. Lau, Adaline (2011, May 16), "Lenovo Sets up Digital and Social Media Hub in Singapore," ClickZ.asia. Retrieved July 5, 2011, from http://www.clickz.asia/3353/lenovo_sets_up_digital_and_social_media_hub_in_singapore

38. Collier, Mack (n.d.), "5 Ways Companies Are Using Social Media to Lower Costs." Retrieved July 5, 2011, from http://mackcollier.com/5-ways-companies-are-using-social-media-to-lower-costs/

39. Joel (2011, April 8), "Mini Case Study: How Lenovo Reduced Customer Service Costs Using Social Media," Fluxe Digital Marketing. Retrieved July 5, 2011, from http://www.fluxedigitalmarketing.com/2011/04/08/mini-case-study-how-lenovo-reduced-customer-service-costs-using-social-media/

40. "Happy 1st Birthday Lenovo!" (2008, December 1), *Lenovo Blog*. Retrieved July 5, 2011, from http://www.lenovoblogs.com/connections/2008/12/happy-1st-birthday-lenovo-forum/

41. Petouhoff, Natalie L. (2009, August 14), "Case Study: Lenovo Takes Ownership of Social Media to Reduce Customer Service Costs," Forrester. Retrieved July 5, 2011, from http://www.forrester.com/rb/Research/case_study_lenovo_takes_ownership_of_social/q/id/54318/t/2

42. "Lenovo Delivers Full Social Support with Lithium" (2010, October 20)," Lithium. Retrieved July 5, 2011, from http://www.lithium.com/who-we-are/events/press-releases/2010/lenovo-delivers-full-social-support-with-lithium

43. "Community Milestones" (2010, June 16), *Lenovo Blog*. Retrieved July 5, 2011, from http://www.lenovoblogs.com/connections/2010/06/community-milestones/

44. Baker, Pam (2010, April 30), "CRM News: E-Marketing: Social Media Adventures in the New Customer World," *CRMBuyer*. Retrieved September 23, 2011, from http://www.crmbuyer.com/story/emarketing/69895.html

45. Barker, Donald I., Melissa S. Barker, and Catherine T. Pinard (2013), Unit D, *Internet Research—Illustrated*, 6th ed. (Boston, MA: Cengage Learning), p. 18.

46. Ibid.

47. Baekdal, Thomas (2009, June 1), "What the Heck Is Social News?" Baekdal. Retrieved July 20, 2011, from http://www.baekdal.com/media/social-news-explained

48. Gilson, David (2008, December 22), "The Difference between Social News and Social Bookmarking: A guide." Retrieved July 23, 2011, from http://www.davidgilson.co.uk/2008/12/the-difference-between-social-news-and-social-bookmarking-a-guide/

49. "Social Bookmarking and Social News Sites . . . Same Difference?" (2009, May 19), Social Maximizer. Retrieved July 18, 2011, from http://blog.socialmaximizer.com/difference-between-social-bookmarking-and-social-news-sites/

50. Nations, Daniel (n.d.), "How to Get Started with Social News," About.com. Retrieved July 19, 2011, from http://webtrends.about.com/od/socialbookmarking/a/socialnews_how.htm

51. "Rob Malda" (2007), *Encyclopedia of the World Biography*. Retrieved July 20, 2011, from http://www.notablebiographies.com/newsmakers2/2007-Li-Pr/Malda-Rob.html and "Slashdot FAQ" (n.d.), Slashdot. Retrieved July 19, 2011, from http://slashdot.org/faq

52. "Slashdot FAQ" (n.d.), Slashdot. Retrieved July 19, 2011, from http://slashdot.org/faq

53. "Fark Frequently Asked Questions (FAQ): Random Stuff" (n.d.), Fark. Retrieved July 20, 2011, from http://www.fark.com/farq/misc/

54. "About Fark" (n.d.), Fark. Retrieved July 20, 2011, from http://www.fark.com/farq/about/#What_is_Fark.3F

55. McBride, Kelly (2009, June 22), "Archived Chat: Frat House Meets Debate Club When It's News and It's Fark," Poynter Institute for Media Studies. Retrieved July 20, 2011, from http://www.poynter.org/latest-news/everyday-ethics/96384/archived-chat-frat-house-meets-debate-club-when-its-news-and-its-fark/

56. "About Fark: What is TotalFark" (n.d.), Fark. Retrieved July 20, 2011, from http://www.fark.com/farq/about/#What_is_Fark.3F

57. Stern, Allen (2006, December 12), "Interview with Garrett Camp, StumbleUpon Co-Founder," CenterNetworks. Retrieved July 20, 2011, from http://www.centernetworks.com/interview-with-garrett-camp-stumbleupon

58. "eBay Acquires StumbleUpon" (2007, May 30), press release, Yahoo! Finance. Originally archived August 25, 2007, retrieved July 20, 2011, from http://web.archive.org/web/20070707122554/http://biz.yahoo.com/bw/070530/20070530006201.html and "StumbleUpon's Founders Buy Service Back from eBay" (2009, April 13), *Salon.com*, originally achieved April 17, 2009, retrieved July 20, 2011, from http://web.archive.org/web/20090417043638/http://www.salon.com/wires/ap/scitech/2009/04/13/D97HSSH00_ebay_stumbleupon/index.html

59. Vosters, Mike (2011, May), "StumbleUpon: Everything You Need to Know." Retrieved July 20, 2011, from http://mikevosters.com/blog/social-media/research-everything-you-need-to-know-about-stumbleupon/2011/05/04/

60. Spiliotopoulos, Tasos (n.d.), "Votes and Comments in Recommender Systems: The Case of Digg," Madeira Interactive Technologies Institute, University of Madeira. Retrieved July 20, 2011, from http://hci.uma.pt/courses/socialweb/projects/2009.digg.paper.pdf

61. Wauters, Robin (2010, July 13), "Reddit Convinced Roughly 6,000 Users to Subscribe So Far," TechCrunch. Retrieved July 20, 2011, from http://techcrunch.com/2010/07/13/reddit-gold-update/

62. "Social News: Reddit" (n.d.), *Wikipedia*. Retrieved July 20, 2011, from http://en.wikipedia.org/wiki/Social_news#Reddit

63. "Reddit Frequently Asked Questions: What Is Reddit?" (n.d.), Reddit. Retrieved July 20, 2011, from http://www.reddit.com/help/faq#Whatisreddit

64. Reddit. (n.d.) CrunchBase. Retrieved July 20, 2011 from http://www.crunchbase.com/company/reddit

65. O'Dell, Jolie (2011, April 28), "Is Reddit Eclipsing Digg in Traffic?" Mashable. Retrieved July 18, 2011, from http://mashable.com/2011/04/28/reddit-digg-traffic/

66. Halligan, Brian, and Shah, Dharmesh (2010), *Inbound Marketing: Get Found Using Google, Social Media, and Blogs* (Hoboken, NJ: John Wiley), p. 110.

67. Ibid., p. 115.

68. Green monster (2011, July 4), "The Best Uses of Social News Sites," Article Directory, Submit Articles. Retrieved July 18, 2011, from http://whydir.com/articles/3513/1/The-Best-Uses-Of-Social-News-Sites/Page1.html

69. Garrett, Chris (2010), "Using Social Bookmarketing to Improve Your Traffic, Links, and Visibility," in Mitch Meyerson, ed., *Success Secrets of the Social Media Marketing Superstars* (Irvine, CA: Entrepreneur Media), p. 266.

70. Go, Gregory (n.d.), "Six Reasons Why You Should Care about Social News," About.com. Retrieved July 18, 2011, from http://onlinebusiness.about.com/od/onlinecommunities/a/whysocialnews.htm

71. Spiliotopoulos, Tasos (n.d.), "Votes and Comments in Recommender Systems: The Case of Digg," Madeira Interactive Technologies Institute University of Madeira. Retrieved June 20, 2011, from http://hci.uma.pt/courses/socialweb/projects/2009.digg.paper.pdf

72. "What Is Digg" (n.d.), Digg. Archived from the original, June 19, 2011, from http://web.archive.org/web/20080329121633/http://digg.com/about/

73. What is Digg? (n.d.), About Digg. Retrieved September 23, 2011, from http://about.digg.com/faq

74. Snoggle Media (2010, February 25), "Utilizing DesignMoo for Social Media Traffic to Your Design Blog," Inside the Web. Retrieved June 20, 2011, from http://www.insidethewebb.com/2010/02/utilizing-designmoo-for-social-media-traffic-to-your-design-blog/

75. Techknow, Juixe (2006, September 24), "Kevin Rose—The Digg Story," retrieved June 20, 2011, from http://juixe.com/techknow/index.php/2006/09/24/kevin-rose-the-digg-story/ and Jenin, John (n.d.), "HISTORY OF DIGG—the Kevin Rose Empire," Squidoo, retrieved June 20, 2011, from http://www.squidoo.com/the-digg

76. "Digg" (n.d.), *Wikipedia*. Retrieved June 20, 2011, from http://en.wikipedia.org/wiki/Digg

77. Berger, Doug (2006, January 25), "Gadgetell Exclusive: Interview with Digg's Kevin Rose," Gadgetell. Retrieved June 20, 2011, from http://www.gadgetell.com/technologytell/article/gadgetell-exclusive-interview-with-diggs-kevin-rose/

78. Gabbay, Nisan (2006, October 15), "Digg Case Study: Why Techies Are an Important Audience," Startup Review, retrieved June 20, 2011, from http://www.startup-review.com/blog/digg-case-study-why-techies-are-an-important-audience.php and Arrington, Michael (2008, July 22), "Google in Final Negotiations to Acquire Digg for 'around $200 Million,'" Tech Crunch, retrieved June 20, 2011, from http://techcrunch.com/2008/07/22/google-in-final-negotiations-to-acquire-digg-for-around-200-million/

79. Holahan, Catherine (2006, June 10), "The Future of Digg," Video View, *Bloomberg BusinessWeek*. Retrieved June 20, 2011, from http://www.businessweek.com/mediacenter/video/technology/dbde5e08b496e1bd7516512fb519244c0d0073de.html

80. Gabbay, Nisan (2006, October 15), "Digg Case Study: Why Techies Are an Important Audience," Startup Review. Retrieved June 20, 2011, from http://www.startup-review.com/blog/digg-case-study-why-techies-are-an-important-audience.php

81. Ibid.

82. "Digg: Five Years in 5 Minutes" (2010, Jan. 25), YouTube. Retrieved June 20, 2011, from http://www.youtube.com/watch?v=0fkIjOP0aug

83. "Definition of crowdsourcing" (n.d.), *encyclopedia, PC*. Retrieved June 20, 2011, from http://www.pcmag.com/encyclopedia_term/0,2542,t=crowdsourcing&i=57732,00.asp

84. "Alex Albrecht: Career" (n.d.), *Wikipedia*. Retrieved June 20, 2011, from http://en.wikipedia.org/wiki/Alex_Albrecht#Career

85. Byrne, Own (2006, September 20), "Kevin Rose Shows off Digg.com on The Screen Savers," YouTube. Retrieved June 20, 2011, from http://www.youtube.com/watch?v=W1_YoG7lqI4

86. Rooney, Mascar (n.d.), "How Digg Can Help Your Website in SEO," Tech Seeker. Retrieved June 20, 2011, from http://tech-seeker.com/blog/how-digg-can-help-your-website-in-seo/

87. Khabiri, Elham, Chiao-Fang Hsu, and James Caverlee (n.d.), "Analyzing and Predicting Community Preferences of Socially Generated Metadat: A Case Study on Comments in Diggs Community," white paper, Department of Computer Science and Engineering, Texas A&M University. Retrieved June 20, 2011, from http://faculty.cs.tamu.edu/caverlee/pubs/khabiri09icwsm.pdf

88. Gabbay, Nisan (2006, October 15), "Digg Case Study: Why Techies Are an Important Audience," Startup Review. Retrieved June 20, 2011, from http://www.startup-review.com/blog/digg-case-study-why-techies-are-an-important-audience.php

89. "Valley Boys: Digg.com's Kevin Rose Leads a New Brat Pack of Young Entrepreneurs" (2006, August 14), *Bloomberg BusinessWeek*. Retrieved June 20, 2011, from http://www.businessweek.com/magazine/content/06_33/b3997001.htm

90. "Digg Site Statistics" (n.d.), site analytics. Retrieved December 7, 2010, from http://siteanalytics.compete.com/digg.com/?metric=uv

91. Chakraborty, Angsuman (2009, May 6), "Trent Reznor, Twitter, Digg Win at Webby Awards," *Gea Times*. Retrieved June 20, 2011, from http://tech.gaeatimes.com/index.php/archive/trent-reznor-twitter-digg-win-at-webby-awards/

92. Ante, Spencer E. (2008, December 8), "A Wrench in Silicon Valley's Wealth Machine," *Bloomberg BusinessWeek*. Retrieved June 20, 2011, from http://www.businessweek.com/magazine/content/08_52/b4114082618241.htm

93. Austin, Scott (2009, November 17), "CEO: Profitability Is Not a Problem Anymore," *Wall Street Journal*. Retrieved June 19, 2011, from http://blogs.wsj.com/venturecapital/2009/11/17/digg-ceo-profitability-is-not-a-problem-anymore/

94. Calore, Michael (2010, March 15), "SXSW: Digg's Big Redesign Taps into Social Web," *Wired*. Retrieved June 20, 2011, from http://www.wired.com/epicenter/2010/03/digg-redesign-social-web/

95. Finn, Greg (2010, September 21), "Digg v4: How to Successfully Kill a Community," Search Engine Watch. Retrieved June 20, 2011, from http://searchengineland.com/digg-v4-how-to-successfully-kill-a-community-50450

96. Sanjay, Vishal (2011, May 12), "Reddit vs Digg: Reddit Now Leads the Way [Stats]," *Dumb Little Blogger*. Retrieved June 20, 2011, from http://www.dumblittleblogger.com/2011/05/12/reddit-vs-digg-reddit-now-leads-the-way-stats/

97. "Digg's Traffic Is Collapsing at Home and Abroad" (2010, September 23), Next Web. Retrieved June 20, 2011, from http://thenextweb.com/socialmedia/2010/09/23/diggs-traffic-is-collapsing-at-home-and-abroad/

98. Arrington, Michael (2010, Oct 25), "Digg to Layoff 37% of Staff, Product Refocus Imminent," TechCrunch. Retrieved June 20, 2011, from http://techcrunch.com/2010/10/25/digg-to-lay-off-37-percentof-staff/

99. Warren, Christina (2011, March 18), "Kevin Rose Resigns from Digg [CONFIRMED]," Mashable. Retrieved June 20, 2011, from http://mashable.com/2011/03/18/kevin-rose-resigns-from-digg-report/?utm_source=feedburner&utm_medium=feed&utm_campaign=Feed%3A+Mashable+%28Mashable%29

100. Vernon, Amy (2011, March 14), "The Future of Digg," Soshable. Retrieved June 20, 2011, from http://soshable.com/the-future-of-digg/

101. Barker, Donald I., Melissa S. Barker, and Catherine T. Pinard (2013), Unit D, *Internet Research—Illustrated*, 6th ed. (Boston, MA: Cengage Learning), p 20.

102. "Ask.com: History" (n.d.), *Wikipedia*. Retrieved July 20, 2011, from http://en.wikipedia.org/wiki/Ask.com#History

103. "Who Created Ask Jeeves?" (2010, September), answers.ask.com. Retrieved July 20, 2011, from http://answers.ask.com/Reference/Other/who_created_ask_jeeves

104. "Ask.com" (2007, October 7), World's Most Famous Websites. Retrieved July 20, 2011, from http://worldsfamouswebsite.blogspot.com/2007_10_01_archive.html

105. "Ask Us—Ask.com" (n.d.). infoBrainz. Retrieved July 20, 2011, from http://infobrainz.blogspot.com/2010/09/about-us-askcom.html

106. Zibreg, Christian (2010, September 24), "Ask.com Has an iPhone App That Lets You Ask and Get Local Answers," Geek.com. Retrieved July 20, 2011, from http://www.geek.com/articles/mobile/ask-com-has-an-iphone-app-that-lets-you-ask-and-get-local-answers-20100924/

107. "What Year Did Yahoo Answers Come Out?" (2011, March), Yahoo! Answers. Retrieved July 20, 2011, from http://answers.yahoo.com/question/index?qid=20110411213332AALGS2t

108. Ibid.

109. "What Kind of Site is Yahoo! Answers?" (2009, July), askville.com. Retrieved July 20, 2011, from http://askville.amazon.com/kind-site-yahoo-answers/AnswerViewer.do?requestId=56620676

110. "Answers.com" (n.d.), eNotes.com. Retrieved July 20, 2011, from http://www.enotes.com/topic/Answers.com

111. Ibid.

112. Wauters, Robin (2010, November 10), "Answers.com Hits 10 Millionth Answer, Launches Its First iPhone App (blufr)," TechCrunch. Retrieved July 20, 2011, from http://techcrunch.com/2010/11/02/answers-com-blufr/

113. Worthham, Jenna (2011, February 6), "The Answers Are out There, and New Q. and A. Sites Dig Them Up," *New York Times*. Retrieved July 19, 2011, from http://www.nytimes.com/2011/02/07/technology/07question.html?pagewanted=all

114. Ibid.

115. Zarrella, Dan (2010), *The Social Media Marketing Book* (Sebastopol, CA: O'Reilly Media), p. 133.

116. Benderoff, Eric (2006, October 25), "Stores Rave about Web Reviews: Online Analysis Provides Instant Feedback and Maybe New Customers," *Chicago Tribune*. Retrieved July 22, 2011, from http://articles.chicagotribune.com/2006-10-25/business/0610250155_1_customer-reviews-ratings-and-reviews-online-store

117. Weinberg, Tamar (2009), *The New Community Rules: Marketing on the Social Web* (Sebastopol, CA: O'Reilly Media), p. 189.

118. "Use Q&A Sites to Market Your Business" (2011, June 22), OperationROI.com. Retrieved July 18, 2011, from http://www.operationroi.com/2011/06/social-marketing/use-qa-sites-to-market-your-business?utm_source=TW&utm_medium=tweet&utm_content=40&utm_campaign=Social%2BMedia

119. Weinberg, Tamar (2009), *The New Community Rules: Marketing on the Social Web* (Sebastopol, CA: O'Reilly Media), p. 193.

120. Sundar, Mario (n.d.), "How Can You Use Quora Professionally?" Quora. Retrieved July 18, 2011, from http://www.quora.com/How-can-you-use-Quora-professionally

121. Whalley, Brian (2011, February 9), "A Marketer's Guide to Quora," HubSpot. Retrieved July 18, 2011, from http://blog.hubspot.com/blog/tabid/6307/bid/9167/A-Marketer-s-Guide-to-Quora.aspx

122. O'Toole, Brian (2011, July 1), "Establishing Yourself as the Go-Expert," What's Next Marketing. Retrieved July 18, 2011, from http://www.whatsnextmarketing.com/blog/quoratwitterexpert/

123. Choney, Suzanne (2011, March 14), "Online News Readership Overtakes Newspapers," Technolog, MSNBC. Retrieved July 20, 2011, from http://technolog.msnbc.msn.com/_news/2011/03/14/6267015-online-news-readership-overtakes-newspapers

124. Rosenstiel, Tom, and Amy Mitchell (2011), "The State of the News Media: An Annual Report on the State of Journalism," Pew Research Center's Project for Excellence in Journalism. Retrieved July 20, 2011, from http://stateofthemedia.org/2011/overview-2/

125. Admin (2011, Jan 20), "The Future of News? Media Trends Suggest Social Media, Partisan Reporting and Brevity," Future of Media. Retrieved July 20, 2011, from http://www.futureofmediaevents.com/2011/01/20/the-future-of-news-media-trends-suggest-social-media-partisan-reporting-and-brevity/

126. Cherubini, Federica (2011, March 13), "'10 Best Practices for Social Media' by the American Society of News Editors," editors.weblog.org. Retrieved July 20, 2011, from http://www.editorsweblog.org/multimedia/2011/05/10_best_practices_for_social_media_by_th.php

127. Brown, Arnold (2008, January-February), "The Consumer Is the Medium," *The Futurist*. Retrieved July 22, 2011, from http://www.agriworldsa.com/article-archive/technology/consumer.pdf

128. Worthham, Jenna (2011, February 6), "The Answers Are out There, and New Q. and A. Sites Dig Them Up.," The *New York Times*. Retrieved July 19, 2011, from http://www.nytimes.com/2011/02/07/technology/07question.html?pagewanted=all

129. Hempel, Jessi (2011, June 27), "As the Q&A Website's Top Designer, Rebekah Cox Has Found a Way to Make Sharing Information Addictive," *Fortune* and CNN. Retrieved July 5, 2011, from http://tech.fortune.cnn.com/2011/06/27/quoras-designing-woman/

130. Whalley, Brian (2011, February 9), "A Marketer's Guide to Quora," HubSpot. Retrieved July 5, 2011, from http://blog.hubspot.com/blog/tabid/6307/bid/9167/A-Marketer-s-Guide-to-Quora.aspx

131. Goodson, Scott (2011, January 11), "Why Is Quora Exploding?" *Forbes*. Retrieved July 5, 2011, from http://blogs.forbes.com/marketshare/2011/01/11/why-is-quora-exploding/

132. "Quora" (n.d.), CrunchBase. Retrieved July 5, 2011, from http://www.crunchbase.com/company/quora

133. Rao, Leena (2011, January 21), "Congratulations Crunchies Winners! Twitter Takes Best Startup of 2010," TechCrunch, retrieved July 5, 2011, from http://techcrunch.com/2011/01/21/congratulations-crunchies-winners-twitter-takes-best-startup-of-2010/ and "Press" (n.d.), Quora.com, retrieved July 5, 2011, from http://www.quora.com/press

134. Hempel, Jessi (2011, June 27), "As the Q&A Website's Top Designer, Rebekah Cox Has Found a Way to Make Sharing Information Addictive," *Fortune* and CNN, retrieved July 5, 2011, from http://tech.fortune.cnn.com/2011/06/27/quoras-designing-woman/ and Arrington, Michael (2010, March 28), "Quora Has the Magic: Benchmark Invests at $86 Million Valuation," TechCrunch, retrieved July 5, 2011, from http://techcrunch.com/2010/03/28/quora-has-the-magic-benchmark-invests-at-86-million-valuation/

Mobile Computing and Location Marketing

Mobile computing and location marketing are changing the way people interact on the social web and in the physical world. Today, users can access the social web from any urban and many rural areas using such mobile computing devices as smartphones, tablets, and netbooks. In fact, according to a white paper from Deloitte, consumers and companies are starting to shift online spending away from desktops and laptops to mobile computing devices.[1]

The growing abundance of mobile computing devices and the ever-expanding social web are merging to create a mobile social lifestyle in which people are on the move, interacting with social media and effortlessly connecting those interactions with physical locations. This mobile social lifestyle presents limitless opportunities for marketers.

What Is Mobile Computing?

Mobile computing is the use of portable wireless devices to connect to the Internet. It enables people to access data and to interact on the social web while on the move as long as they are in range of a cellular or WiFi (Wireless Fidelity) network.

Common mobile computing devices include cell phones, PDAs, smartphones, tablet PCs, and netbooks. **Cell phones** provide wireless voice communications and short message service (SMS) for sending and receiving texts messages. **PDAs** (portable digital assistants) are handheld computers that

LEARNING OBJECTIVES

After completing this chapter, students will be able to:

- Define mobile computing devices, such as cell phones, PDAs, smartphones, tablet PCs, and netbooks
- Describe a brief history of smartphone growth and adoption
- Explain how social networks go mobile
- Identify how social media marketers can take advantage of mobile computing
- Describe how branded mobile social networks work

(Continued)

- Define location-based social networks
- Explain the growth of location-based social networks
- Summarize the key predictions of the future of mobile computing and location marketing

frequently fuse pen-based input to function as personal organizers, thus allowing users to synchronize files with larger computers. **Smartphones** combine the power of cell phones and PDAs; using mini-keyboards for either mechanical or touchscreen input, they can receive and store text messages and email, act as web browsers, run mobile applications to perform a growing variety of tasks, and take pictures with increasingly high-quality miniaturized digital cameras.[2]

Tablet PCs are similar to laptop computers, but they use touchscreens to replace bulky keywords, offering a more compact form with maximum screen size. **Netbooks** are basically laptop computer, but on a smaller scale, more lightweight, and about the size of a hardback book; they tend to focus on web browsing and email with limited support for productivity applications, such as word processing and electronic spreadsheets. Netbooks provide another convenient way to stay connected to the social web while on the move.

A Brief History of Smartphone Growth and Adoption

While the term "mobile computing" applies to a wide variety of mobile devices, the impact of smart phones on social media has been by far the most significant. Although cellular phones have been in existence for many years, the mass adoption of smartphones has had significant implications for social media. Cell phones provided powerful marketing opportunities through text messaging and even voice. However, these communications were still one-to-one, and they were not taking place in social media. Smartphone technology has brought new social networks and new opportunities for marketers that could not have taken place without applications and Internet access.

A smartphone is defined by *Wikipedia* as "a high-end mobile phone built on a mobile computing platform, with more advanced computing ability and connectivity than a contemporary feature phone . . . Modern smartphones typically also include high-resolution touchscreens, web browsers that can access, and properly display, standard web pages rather than just mobile-optimized sites, and high-speed data access via Wi-Fi and mobile broadband."[3]

Each smartphone runs a mobile operating system such as Apple iOS, Google Android, Microsoft Windows Phone 7, or Research In Motion BlackBerry OS. Mobile phones typically run third-party applications that are created using an application programming interface, commonly referred to as an API. Applications for a smartphone are accessed through an application marketplace. Each operating system has a unique marketplace of applications that are compatible with its operating system.

According to research by Gartner, in the first quarter of 2011, smartphone sales globally grew 19%, underscoring the quick global growth of these devices. The most popular global operating system was Android, followed by Symbian and iOS (Apple).[4] The Android operating system has demonstrated rapid market share growth, while Apple's iOS made only a moderate gain and the respective market shares for Symbian, Research In Motion, and Microsoft have declined, as shown in Table 13.1.

In the United States, smartphone usage is also growing quickly and approaching mass adoption. According to a 2011 study conducted by Pew Internet, over one-third of American adults (35%) own a smartphone, as illustrated in Table 13.2. According to the study, 87% of smartphone owners access the Internet or email on the device. Twenty-five percent of those surveyed also said that they typically use their smartphone to go online rather than a computer.[5]

Company	1st Quarter 2011 Units	1st Quarter 2011 Market Share (%)	1st Quarter 2010 Units	1st Quarter 2010 Market Share (%)
Android	36,267.8	36.0	5,226.6	9.6
Symbian	27,598.5	27.4	24,067.7	44.2
iOS (Apple)	16,883.2	16.8	8,359.7	15.3
Research In Motion	13,004.0	12.9	10,752.5	19.7
Microsoft	3,658.7	3.6	3,696.2	6.8
Other	3,357.2	3.3	2,402.9	4.4
Total	100,769.3	100.0	54,505.5	100.0

Table 13.1   Smartphone Growth Globally, as of May 2011

Smartphone ownership and Internet use summary

% of smartphone owners, cell owners and all adults who...

	% of smartphone owners who...	% of all cell owners who...	% of all adults who...
Own a smartphone	100%	42%	35%
Use the internet or email on smartphone	87	36	30
Use smartphone to go online on a typical day	68	28	23
Go online mostly using smartphone	25	10	8

Table 13.2   Smartphone Owner Comparison

Source: The Pew Research Center's Internet & American Life Project, April 26 — May 22, 2011 Spring Tracking Survey. n=2,277 adult Internet users ages 18 and older, including 755 cell phone interviews. Interviews were conducted in English and Spanish.

As reported in the 60 Second Marketer, "Mobile is one of the fastest-growing platforms in the world. With 40% of U.S. mobile subscribers regularly browsing the Internet on their phone and a projected 12.5% of all e-commerce transactions going mobile by the end of the year, it's a channel that you need to be aware of. According to Google, mobile web traffic will surpass PC traffic by 2013."[6]

Social Networks Go Mobile

One of the key implications of the growth of smartphones is that social networks are increasingly being accessed through mobile devices. In March 2010 ComScore reported social network access through mobile browsers grew by triple digits.[7] Rather than accessing Facebook, LinkedIn, and Twitter from a computer, many consumers are accessing these sites directly from their smartphones and Internet-connected phones.

The majority of people have their mobile device within arm's reach and thus are connected with their social networks 24/7. This reality means that participants in the social networks are always on and always connected. As a result, people tend to post and share content on social networks more often. According to Facebook, over 250 million of its 750 million active users (roughly one-third) are currently accessing Facebook through their mobile devices. Additionally, people who use Facebook on their mobile devices are twice as active on Facebook than nonmobile users.[8] Twitter shows similar statistics, with reports that 95% of Twitter users own a mobile phone, and half of the users access Twitter through their mobile device.[9]

The other implication of social networks on mobile devices is the ease of sharing and posting content, especially multimedia content. In only a few seconds, one can take a picture on a smartphone and with the click of a button post it to Twitter or Facebook. One can tweet or update social network statuses directly from a mobile device without the need of connecting and uploading to a computer. Google's social network, Google+, launched with a highly integrated mobile application that allows multimedia to flow seamlessly from mobile devices to the social network.

From a marketer's perspective, the ability to access and interact with social networks quickly and easily from a mobile device can be used as a powerful strategy for staying in touch with consumers on social networks. For example, businesses can inform consumers about new product features or a special sales event, or they can instantly address customer complaints to prevent problems from going viral. The following section will discuss ways that social media marketers can take advantage of this new technology trend to market their business.

Marketing with Mobile Computing

Mobile computing provides a plethora of marketing opportunities, such as text messaging, mobile applications, and mobile advertising. The focus of this section will be on how mobile computing and smartphones are impacting social media for both consumers and marketers.

There are two key opportunities for marketers to leverage mobile as a part of a social media marketing strategy: branded social networks delivered through applications and location-based social networks and applications. Mobile devices are key enablers of social lives, so it makes sense that they play a big role in social media marketing as well.

BRANDED MOBILE SOCIAL NETWORKS

A number of branded social networks are emerging to leverage mobile devices. A **branded social network** is a social network created by and for a specific brand. Branded social networks are usually delivered through an application on a mobile device, and they typically allow users to connect with each other in some way that links back to the brand that created the application.

Branded social networks can be difficult to create and must have a strong value incentive for the user to create yet another social media account. Before creating a branded social network, a company should first investigate the pros and cons of using existing social networks such as Facebook or LinkedIn, versus creating a branded social network. Many companies have used the strategy of creating a popular Facebook page first and then directing Facebook followers to the company's branded social network.

A growing number of pharmaceutical companies are using branded social networks such as Children with Diabetes, an online community for kids, families, and adults with diabetes, which offers an online newsletter, FAQs, private chat rooms, and discussion forums for specific topics.[10] These branded social networks allow patients to connect with other people with the same type of disease in order to form support groups so that they can share experiences. Through the monitoring of conversations among patients, the company can provide better customer service by addressing the issues facing these patients as well as being able to track information related to the disease and collecting valuable statistics regarding their medication. With the addition of mobile application to the branded social network, patients will have easy and instant access to information, and companies can provide real-time support to customers.

Another example of a branded social network that is driven by a mobile application is the SitOrSquat application (www.sitorsquat.com) that is sponsored by Charmin®. The mobile application allows users to add, find, and rate nearby restrooms. For example, if you are in the middle of Times Square and in need of a restroom, you can launch the SitOrSquat application and view the location of nearby restrooms including ratings and photos. The application leverages user-generated content, ratings, and reviews (all social media tools) to deliver content. The application lets consumers find bathrooms that have different facilities including changing tables and handicap access. There are over 55,000 restrooms in over thirty-two countries included in the application, all of which have been added by users. The brand gains value through branding and awareness, and the application provides a valuable service to the users, creating a win-win proposition.[11]

Branded mobile social networks are typically delivered through applications. The key challenge for brands is that in addition to creating the application for their social network, there is a significant discovery problem, as shown in Figure 13.1. In order for consumers to join a branded social network, they have to discover the application for doing so. According to data from Nielsen, branded smartphone applications must rely on advertising and paid marketing to build an audience for the application.[12] Creating a new social network can be expensive and time consuming, but it can have great results when it is based on the right strategy and has a significant value proposition for the customer.

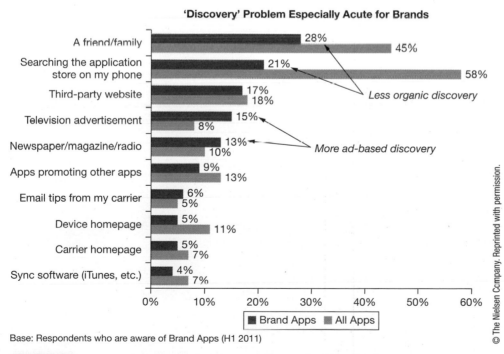

'Discovery' Problem Especially Acute for Brands

Discovery Method	Brand Apps	All Apps
A friend/family	28%	45%
Searching the application store on my phone	21%	58%
Third-party website	17%	18%
Television advertisement	15%	8%
Newspaper/magazine/radio	13%	10%
Apps promoting other apps	9%	13%
Email tips from my carrier	6%	5%
Device homepage	5%	11%
Carrier homepage	5%	7%
Sync software (iTunes, etc.)	4%	7%

Less organic discovery

More ad-based discovery

■ Brand Apps ■ All Apps

Base: Respondents who are aware of Brand Apps (H1 2011)

Figure 13.1 Discovery Method of All Apps vs. Brand Apps—Smartphones

Dunkin' Donuts Gets You Running with Mobile Marketing

Introduction

In 2009 Dunkin' Donuts, the world's leading coffee and baked goods chain, created a branded mobile social network called Dunkin' Run. The insight behind Dunkin' Run was that many groups had a single "runner" who would go to Dunkin' Donuts for the entire group. For example, at an office multiple people would write down their Dunkin' Donuts orders, and a single person would go to Dunkin' Donuts to place and pick up the order.

The Dunkin' Run application and social network simplifies the process of doing a Dunkin' Run. The Dunkin' Run application allows people to connect with each other, send notifications for a "run," and place their order with the runner online and from their mobile phones.

The Dunkin' Run iPhone application was extremely successful at both meeting a real customer need while serving a real business purpose. Six months after the launch, there were over 25,000 downloads from the iTunes store.

History

In 1950 the first Dunkin' Donuts store was opened in Quincy, Massachusetts, and by 1955 the first franchise was licensed. Today, Dunkin' Donuts is the world's leading baked goods and coffee chain with 6,772 franchised restaurants in the United States.[13] The chain serves over 3 million customers a day and sells 4 million donuts and 2.7 million cups of coffee each day.[14]

Challenge

An average Dunkin' Donuts customer visits the franchise a few times a week and spends twice as much as the casual customer. The lightest Dunkin' Donuts customers spend less than 25% of the average spending. The challenge for Dunkin' Donuts was to grow the relationship and grow the revenue contributions of the lighter customers[15].

According to Cynthia Ashworth, vice president of consumer engagement for Dunkin' Donuts, "[o]ur campaign theme is America Runs on Dunkin'. We provide food and drink for busy, on-the-go-people, so portability is

America Runs on Dunkin'®

built into all of our product propositions."[16] The portability aspect of the company's products and its physical stores make the chain a strong fit for mobile marketing.

Strategy

Dunkin' Donuts has two rules for engaging in interactive campaigns: (1) make them fun and (2) make them cheap. Dunkin' Donuts's aim in using digital marketing is to build advocates, not merely followers and likes. Its digital marketing focuses on the little interesting things that allow fans to engage and be entertained.[17]

Location marketing is about activating people while they are at a certain place or business. The next step is to turn those people into loyal, repeat customers for that business.[18]

To achieve these objectives, Dunkin' Donuts launched a mobile application and desktop social network called Dunkin' Run (www.dunkinrun.com). Dunkin' Run is a social network that allows for group ordering. Using the application, a Runner can initiate a group order for Dunkin' Donuts using a computer or a mobile application and can invite others to place an order.

Upon receiving an invitation, each user can input her or his order from each individual's own computer or mobile phone, making sure that each order is accurate. Using the mobile application the Runner goes to a Dunkin' Donuts and shows his or her phone or a printout to the Dunkin' Donuts crew member, who fills the order. The application also serves as a checklist to make sure that each person received her or his order correctly.[19] The application also tracks past orders and favorite menu items, receives run reminders, and syncs with Facebook to display the run status, making the process of going on a Dunkin' Run even easier.[20] The goal of the Dunkin' Run application is to increase sales by making it easier to place group orders.

The Dunkin' Donuts application serves a real customer need and also supports a real business objective. By making it easier to invite friends or coworkers to place orders for a Dunkin' Run and by making it easier for the Runner to receive the orders, there is the potential to increase sales. The application also increases the accuracy of orders, which can increase customer satisfaction.[21]

Results

The Dunkin' Run application received 25,000 downloads within six months after the launch, and *Forbes* ranked it number six in its Best Branded Mobile Applications list.[22] Dunkin' Run was a successful application because it is useful instead of focusing only on marketing. An application that builds on brand equity and promise while providing real value to customers is most effective.[23]

According to Dunkin' Donuts's brand marketing officer, Frances Allen, Dunkin' Run is a powerful example of the company's commitment to bring value to people in new and innovative ways. According to Allen, "Dunkin' Run extends that same spirit and commitment to the office, the dorm or any group, leveraging fun and exciting online and mobile tools to make it even faster and easier to keep yourself and others running with a great cup of coffee or a breakfast sandwich any time of day."[24]

One additional potential benefit of the application is the information about consumers and the insights that Dunkin' Donuts can gain from the application. The application provides valuable information on location, customer history and group consumption habits.[25]

Marketing in Online Social Games

A **social network game** is conducted online with multiplayers and asynchronous communications primarily through social networks.[26] Social network games are among the most popular games in the world, played at least once a month by 24% of U.S. Internet users.[27] By 2012, social gaming is projected to grow to 69 million social gamers in the U.S. alone.[28]

Popular social network games include Mafia Wars and FarmVille, which can be played on their own platforms or through applications on existing social networks like Facebook. Social network games are different than other online games because they typically leverage social networks to recruit game allies or integrate social networks into the game design by linking social media activity and influence into the game design.

One other relevant feature of social network games is the inclusion of **virtual currencies**. Virtual currencies are typically used to purchase virtual goods in social network games and may be earned during the game or purchased with real money.[29] For example, virtual currency may be used to purchase land, accessories for an avatar or character or weapons or tools to be used in the game. eMarketer projects that revenues from social gaming will grow from $856 million in 2010 to $1.32 billion in 2012.[30]

Online social games and virtual goods present a number of opportunities for social

(continued on next page)

What Is a Location-based Social Network?

A **location-based social network**, also known as a **mobile social network**, refers to a social network where people can share their location with friends. The main location-based social networks include Foursquare, Gowalla, and Facebook Places. While each of these services has slightly different functionality, they generally work in a similar way.

According to *Wikipedia*, Foursquare is "[a] location-based social networking website based on hardware for mobile devices. The service is available to users with GPS-enabled mobile devices such as smartphones. Users 'check-in' at venues using a mobile website, text messaging or a device-specific application by running the application and selecting from a list of venues that the application locates nearby."[36]

Location-based social networks answer the key question "Where are you?" and allow users to "check-in" to inform friends of their current location. For example, a user might be checked in on Foursquare to a cafe in the neighborhood, and the individual's friends on Foursquare can see the location and have the option of meeting them there if they so choose. Essentially, social networks like Foursquare allow you to share where you are and what you are doing with your friends. Users of location-based social networks share their activities and loyalty with their social network.

In addition to the location-based network Foursquare, other companies provide competing services and should be considered when determining the best mix of tactics to implement the overall strategies for reaching social media goals. The following list describes some of the other popular social location-based networks and mobile apps:[37]

- **Gowalla** – currently the main rival of Foursquare. Gowalla has partnered with the Travel Channel, *National Geographic*, and *The Washington Post* to offer users the ability to check

in at locations as part of a "Trip" game, where upon completion of a "Trip," users earn rewards. These partnerships also provide Gowalla users with rich sources of content. In addition, Gowalla's social location app has a unique interface, featuring stylish caricatures of people hanging out at a coffee shop and looking trendy—immediately revealing the target market this service is aiming for.

- **Facebook Places** – a location-based service that lets Facebook users view where their friends are and share their locations. It enables marketers to develop campaigns around the check-in service "… to build awareness, grow their fan base and engage and reward customers. Each time a Facebook user checks in to a particular location on Facebook Places, Facebook broadcasts the check-in to that user's friends' news feeds. This is not only viral marketing for the company—it also allows businesses to provide incentives for people to come to their physical locations or events."[38]

- **Google Hotpot** – Google's Hotpot social location app works in conjunction with Google Places to let users rank, review, and recommend local businesses.[39] Given Google's dominant search engine, its social location service Hotpot has the potential to create a synergy between location marketing and search engine optimization (SEO), which will be a compelling reason for marketers to use this service.[40]

- **Yelp** – a user review and search service that draws upon its thousands of regular reviewers (called Yelpers) to place reviews about venues using the site's mobile social location service. Hitting 20 million reviews in July 2011,[41] Yelp continues to grow at a brisk pace. One of the most powerful marketing features of the Yelp's mobile app is the Monocle option, which activates the camera in a mobile device to capture a photo of what the viewer sees, then overlays it "… with the names, star rating, and number of reviews of the various venues that are within a set radius of the user and are in the directions the mobile device is pointing."[42] As a consequence, the decision to purchase can be directly affected by this incredibly rich collection of information. Naturally, this can significantly increase foot traffic to a venue, making the use of Yelp's social location service and app an attractive marketing tactic.

- **Others** – many other social location sharing services and apps exist, such as MyTown, SCNVGR, (Whrrl no longer exists after being acquired by Groupon in April 2011), Loopt, and Brightkite, as shown in Table 13.3.[43] With any social location service, app, or tool, marketers should carefully consider what tactical advantages they bring to the execution of the social media marketing plan.

Location-based social networks are still relatively new, but they are demonstrating considerable growth. In 2010 there were 33 million users of U.S. location-based services, almost three times the number of users in 2009 (see Table 13.4).[44]

media marketers. Businesses are participating in online social games through branded virtual goods, incorporating offers and ads into games, running campaigns that include virtual and real items and through creating their own branded social games. The projected growth of social gaming and the amount of time already spent in social networks makes social games a popular choice for marketers.

Farmers Insurance, for example, created a branded blimp that appeared in the popular social network game FarmVille.[31] Farmers Insurance has an actual real-life zeppelin, and in October of 2010 it launched a campaign where the blimp hovered over crops to protect them from wilting.[32] The Farmers FarmVille blimp linked back to their marketing objectives of attaching the Farmers brand to the idea of protection in a relevant way. The FarmVille Blimp was also supported by a Facebook contest where the winner received a ride on the actual blimp.[33] The Farmers Blimp is an example of a company integrating directly into a social network game.

Brands are also creating their own online branded virtual goods in virtual games. As an example, Century 21, a real estate company' launched a social gaming campaign in April of 2011, where players could incorporate the company's branded buildings into the virtual cities they were constructing in the social game We City.[34] Following the campaign, Century 21 reported that 92% of We City players had integrated Century 21-branded buildings into their cities.[35]

As these examples show, there are a variety of opportunities for brands to participate in social games.

Location-based Social Networks and Gaming

In addition to allowing users to post their current location, some location-based social networks like Foursquare have additional features based on game mechanics in order to increase user engagement. First, each location may have a mayor, who checks into the location most frequently. In reality, being the mayor of a location doesn't mean much beyond bragging rights; however, Foursquare users compete for mayorship over locations.

The second part of the gaming mechanics built into Foursquare is the concept of badges. Users can earn badges by engaging in certain behaviors. For example, a user may earn the Don't Stop Believing badge for checking into three karaoke bars in a month. There are a variety of badges created by Foursquare, but brands can also create custom badges that users can earn. For instance, a shopping magazine has created a badge that can be earned by checking into stores featured in the magazine.

Profile of Select Mobile Geolocation Apps

Game-focused

foursquare	Check-ins unlock badges for various activities/achievements, many of which earn rewards or discounts; users become "Mayor" through repeat check-ins. Nearby specials are highlighted.
Gowalla	Check-ins earn stamps in a "passport." Users can label locations, post photos/comments and follow trips mapped out by friends or brands.
MyTown	Closer in spirit to social games like FarmVille. Players visit real-life locations and "buy" them for their virtual town.
SCVNGR	Checking in to location reveals challenges; users complete challenges to earn badges and real-world rewards.
Whrrl	Check-ins unlock "societies," matching users by interest based on check-in patterns. Users earn points/rewards from businesses.

Deal-focused

Checkpoints	Users receive points when entering participating businesses or scanning select products.
Facebook Places	Check in to update Facebook status, tag friends who are with you. "Deals" feature currently in limited testing.
Loopt	Check-ins earn points toward rewards from businesses; users become "Boss" through repeat check-ins. Users IM with friends and track their whereabouts.
shopkick	Users receive "kickbucks" when entering participating businesses or scanning select products. In-store rewards vary by business.

Other

Brightkite	Provides group testing service, with a greater focus on staying connected with friends than on badges/achievements. Offers traditional mobile ad options.
buzzd	Compiles check-ins from other services to formulate trend info for a given city.
CauseWorld	Check-ins earn "karmas," which users can turn into real-world donations to charitable causes from brand sponsors.
WHERE	Recommends new locations based on what the user marks as favorites. Offers guides curated by local experts. Businesses can pay for sponsored results.
Yelp	Users review local restaurants, stores, etc. Businesses can respond to reviews and pay for sponsored results.

Source: Company Reports, © eMarketer 2010. Reprinted with permission.

Table 13.3 Profile of Mobile Users

Note: Game-focused apps emphasize achievements such as badges, while deal-focused apps emphasize rewards/discounts from businesses; a given app may have elements of both.
Source: Company reports, 2010

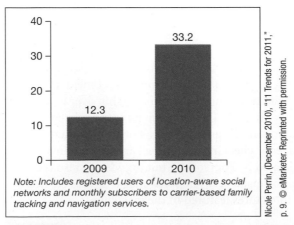

Note: Includes registered users of location-aware social networks and monthly subscribers to carrier-based family tracking and navigation services.

Nicole Perrin, (December 2010), "11 Trends for 2011," p. 9. © eMarketer. Reprinted with permission.

Table 13.4 US Location-based Service Users, 2009–2010

The third aspect of social gaming built into Foursquare is the leader board. Four-square awards points for different things—checking in, adding a new venue, multiple check-ins, and checking in at a new place—and compiles leader boards to track points within a user's network. Again, the points are not really worth anything; however, it is another fun way that Foursquare engages users and keeps them active. Thus, users of Foursquare check in at locations to gain points, with badges and mayorships being fun ways of showing their friends where they spend their time.

While gaming through Foursquare increases both consumer and marketing opportunities, studies show that gaming is not among the top reasons that consumers claim they use location-based applications. Studies show that most U.S. users of location-based services employ them to get informed (64.6%), followed by meeting up with friends (43.2%) and meeting new people (14.8%), with gaming being a reason for only 8.6%.[45]

The Growth of Location-based Social Networks

Location-based applications where users check in are becoming increasingly popular for smartphone users, and they represent a large opportunity for marketers, as illustrated in Table 13.4. According to a 2011 comScore study, nearly one in five smartphone owners access location-based social networks via their mobile device with almost 70% of mobile users checking in from an Android or Apple iPhone.[46]

While mobile location-based check-in services are still in their infancy, they have impressive adoption among smart phone users. As smart phone adoption continues to increase, it is expected that location-based social networks will grow significantly as well.

Marketing with Location-based Social Networks

There are many different ways for marketers to connect with consumers on location-based social networks. The opportunities are most obvious for businesses with a physical presence, but location-based marketing also works for events and brands.

One of the most popular opportunities for marketers to connect with consumers on location-based social networks is by offering deals and discounts. Most of the major location-based marketing platforms offer merchants the opportunity to create a deal or discount. In a study by JiWire, users of location-based applications were asked why they check in. Twenty-nine percent said they check in for deals and discounts, 17% to share their location, 14% to be associated with cool places, and only 7% checked in to receive points.[47] These percentages shows that consumers are interested in receiving deals and discounts through location-based social networks.

Coupons, deals, and discounts are the most popular form of marketing on location-based social networks. The opportunities differ between each particular site and are still emerging, However, there are some consistent trends in how deals can be offered. The most basic form of a location-based deal is to offer a discount coupon when an individual checks in to a location. For example, a restaurant may run a deal that says "Check in to get a half-price appetizer with the purchase of a meal." Upon checking in, the customer would show the coupon to the server to receive the discount.

In addition to basic coupons, many location-based social networks have created unique coupon offerings to reward customers. Foursquare offers a mayor deal in which

QR Codes Facilitate Mobile and Location Marketing

A **QR (quick response) code** is a two-dimensional matrix-style image readable by smartphones, QR scanners, and other hand-held devices (see Figure 13.2). Scanning a QR code eliminates the need to type in information on a mobile device, making it quick and easy to capture a significant amount of information.[48]

Figure 13.2 Scanning the above QR code will display pertinent information about this textbook

© Cengage Learning 2013

As mobile device use increases, the social media marketing possibilities for QR codes become almost boundless. For example, placing a QR code on coupons, business cards, and other printed promotional material can provide instant links to a corporate website, branded social network, company blog, discussion board, or online contest.[49]

In addition, marketers can place a QR code on a product, advertisement, or catalog so that when consumers scan the code, they are immediately connected to the department selling the item. A QR code can also be used to quickly link customers to service departments, product reviews, price comparisons, nutritional information, and so on.[50] Hence, QR codes provide a powerful way to link mobile computing with location-based marketing.

the mayor of an establishment receives a special offer. This offer is intended to reward loyalty and encourage customers to fight for mayorship with their check-ins. In 2010 Starbucks launched a deal on Foursquare in which the mayor received $1 off a Frappuccino. This offer was an innovative way for Starbucks to reward its loyal customers and to encourage check-ins at their stores.[51]

Both Foursquare and Facebook offer other loyalty coupons, which reward customers after a certain number of check-ins. The offer may be a free coffee on your fifth check-in, or, similar to a punch card, it may be a free drink after purchasing ten cups of coffee. Deals can also be offered only on the first check-in to reward a new customer or to encourage an individual to try a new product. Both of these deal offerings persuade customers to check in and share their location with their friends while being rewarded for loyalty.

Deals can also be created to encourage customers to bring their friends. Many location-based social networks offer customers rewards when they check in with a certain number of friends. This deal encourages people to ask their friends to check in, therefore increasing the social spread of a location.

The idea behind location-based coupons is to reward customers for checking in and sharing locations with their friends. These mass check-ins offer a number of benefits for merchants. First, they build awareness for a business as the sharing of the whereabouts via check-ins on the location-based social networks. Second, they have the opportunity to reward loyalty and keep the most valuable customers coming back.

Location-based deals can also drive new customers into a business. For example, when a user checks in to a downtown location on Foursquare, the individual will see an icon that says "special offers nearby." This icon shows a list of places in the area that are offering a reward for checking in. This knowledge can increase awareness of your business and also drive someone who is in the area into your establishment.

By encouraging customers to check in, businesses are increasing the social spread of their brand. If an individual constantly sees his or her friends checking in to a particular place, that person is more likely to be interested in visiting the place. In addition, upon checking in, the user can leave comments or reviews about the business, which will be broadcasted to the individual's social networks. If a positive comment is posted after checking in, it can be a very powerful way to promote a business. On the other hand, a negative experience shared by a customer on the location-based social network would have a devastating effect on the business.

The Future of Mobile Computing and Location Marketing

As the number and functionality of mobile computing devices continues to expand exponentially, it is hard to imagine what is coming next. It is likely that mobile computing may become so ubiquitous that the term itself becomes passé. Indeed, Jake Joraanstad, a software developer and Android team manager at Myriad Devices, writes

"It will not need to be called 'mobile' computing anymore because everything will be mobile."[52]

Another trend is "context-aware" mobile computing, which basically involves a smartphone tracking a person's daily routine. Context awareness enables marketers to target people based on their activities, online behavior, and location, making it possible to display advertisements tailored to a specific individual's lifestyle. "The more 'stitched-in' your mobile is to your everyday life patterns, the more it will know about you without you having to explicitly 'tell' it; just like your housemate, partner, family or friends might know your routine, so will your phone," according to Cath Wilcox of Overlay Media.[53]

The future of location marketing is just as difficult to predict. However, Chris Brogan, president of Human Business Works, believes that for location-based apps to reach their full potential, they must become smarter, informing users not only about the location of nearby restaurants, but making restaurant recommendations based on the person's food preferences.[54] Taking this a step further, marketers can offer "location-based advertising," using a combination of smartphone GPS tracking and opt-in services, to let users sign up for advertising alerts that match their culinary preferences, which are automatically triggered when users cross "geo-fences" (i.e., virtual fields that detect mobile devices when users enter or exit specific areas).[55]

Such avant-garde examples of mobile computing and location marketing merely touch upon the potential of these rapidly evolving social media technologies. How will marketers take advantage of highly portable and powerful mobile computing devices that provide easy access to the social web from almost any location? What new mobile apps will be developed to leverage these gadgets? What new social media platforms will emerge to cater to the users of these advanced devices? The answers to these questions will likely shape the future of social media marketing well into this decade and beyond.

EXERCISE CASE STUDY

Conan O'Brien Flies High with Foursquare Blimp and Badges

Introduction ....

On the afternoon of January 12, 2010, Conan O'Brien began winning the hearts and minds of the social web with his announcement to the "people of earth" that he would resign as host of *The Tonight Show* if it were moved to a later time slot.[56] In the ongoing saga revolving around NBC's late night lineup, O'Brien's heart-felt message said (in part) that, "My staff and I have worked unbelievably hard and we are very proud of our contribution to the legacy of The Tonight Show. But I cannot participate in what I honestly believe is its destruction."[57] The transparency and sincerity of his statement resonated with the Twitterverse. When his statement hit the top of

Conan O'Brien on Twitter

© Turner Broadcasting System / Photofest

Twitter's trending topics, it caused an enormous spike in tweets using #teamconan, and the responses were overwhelmingly positive.

This massive response by Twitterers alerted O'Brien and Team Conan to the potential opportunity of promoting his new talk show on TBS by reaching out to mobile mass influencers. On February 4, 2010, O'Brien, a.k.a. Coco, officially joined the Twitterverse with the Twitter account @conanobrien.[58] O'Brien's next move was to court the Mass Mavens of Twitter by dropping in on Twitter HQ and entertaining the movers and shakers, less than two months after joining Twitter.[59] In an obvious strategy to draw further attention of mass influencers, O'Brien visited and entertained other mega-Web players, such as Google (Conan visits GooglePlex).[60] By the end of 2010, he had amassed over 1.8 million Twitter followers.[61]

History

Conan O'Brien is a TV show host, comedian, writer, producer, and performer. He is currently the host of *Conan*, a late-night talk show that airs on TBS. From 1993 to 2009, Conan was the host of *Late Night with Conan O'Brien*.

In 2004 when O'Brien negotiated his contract with NBC, it was agreed that he would take over *The Tonight Show* from Jay Leno in 2009. In January 2010 NBC executive Jeff Zucker met with Jay Leno and Conan O'Brien and proposed moving O'Brien's *The Tonight Show* to a later time slot to accommodate an earlier time slot for Jay Leno. O'Brien was unhappy with the new arrangement and negotiated a deal to leave *The Tonight Show* and begin working for another network.[62]

The conflict over the timing of *The Tonight Show* and moving Conan's time slot back to give Leno a better time resulted in a public outcry and public demonstrations. People began sharing their support for Team Coco (Conan O'Brien) or Leno.[63] In April 2010 O'Brien announced that he would host a new show on TBS.

Challenge

While there was significant support on social media for Conan during the dispute with NBC, Conan had to build awareness and viewership for his new show on TBS. TBS was a smaller network than NBC, and despite initial support for O'Brien, mainstream networks still owned the late-night television show audience.

When the *Conan* show was set to launch on TBS, an innovative marketing solution was needed to break through the clutter of TV commercials. TBS is not a major network, so making the public aware of the show would normally take a lot of advertising dollars. By leveraging social media, however, TBS and Conan could rely on social spread to help the message go further.[64]

Strategy

To generate buzz and connect with influencers through mobile, Conan O'Brien launched the Conan Blimp, which even has its own website (www.blimp.teamcoco.com). The website for the blimp included a live map and a livecam with which users can track the exact location of the blimp at any time. The Conan Blimp was launched in partnership with AT&T to fly over select locations on the east coast.[65]

Conan and AT&T worked together to promote the launch of the blimp. The blimp launch included a series of commercials that were repurposed for YouTube and posted as high-resolution images on Flickr.[66] In addition, fans used the hashtags on Twitter (#TheConanBlimp) to talk about the blimp and share spottings.[67]

The most powerful part of the blimp strategy was the use of Foursquare to connect with audiences. During the tour of the blimp in October of 2010, users could check in to the blimp on Foursquare when they saw it flying overhead.[68] Upon checking in to the Conan Blimp, users earned their Conan Blimpspotter badge, which was displayed on their profile. When the badge was unlocked, the user received a message that read "You've spotted The Conan Blimp! A big orange bag of slow moving gas has never looked so pretty. Visit www.teamcoco.com for more Conan!"[69]

In addition to the use of the blimp and Foursquare, Conan also leveraged mobile applications by creating his own mobile app, which included the latest photos, videos, and more from the cast and crew of the show.[70] The idea was to leverage the large mobile fan base and to build a stronger relationship with those fans.

Results

The Conan Blimp received over 21,000 check-ins and over a hundred comments on Foursquare for the duration of the promotion (the blimp is no longer in the air, and the location is closed).[71] The Conan Blimp also received considerable attention in the media, and it was a finalist for Location of the Year in the Shorty Awards.[72] There is also a general Conan check-in on Foursquare for Team Coco that has over 1,500 check-ins, and "Team Coco" is followed by over 51,000 people on Foursquare.[73]

The blimp promotion on Foursquare shows how location, check-ins, and entertainment marketing can work together. The check-ins on the blimp were distributed across the social web to spread the message, in addition to the value of the physical impressions of the blimp.[74]

Review Questions for Conan O'Brien Case Study

1. How did the blimp drive additional support for the new show on TBS?

2. Why were Foursquare and social media an appropriate choice for Conan and TBS?

3. How did a badge and social gaming make the Conan Blimp more successful?

4. What other mobile marketing tools could have made the Conan Blimp more successful?

Notes

1. "Mobile Devices to Overtake PCs This Year" (2011, January 25), MC Marketing Charts. Retrieved July 22, 2011, from http://www.marketingcharts.com/direct/mobile-devices-to-overtake-pcs-this-year-15836/

2. Beal, Vangie (2008, May 2), "The Difference between a Cell Phone, Smartphone and PDA," *Webopedia*. Retrieved July 22, 2011, from http://www.webopedia.com/DidYouKnow/Hardware_Software/2008/smartphone_cellphone_pda.asp

3. "Smartphone" (2011, July 11), *Wikipedia*. Retrieved November 22, 2011, from http://en.wikipedia.org/wiki/Smartphone

4. "Gartner Says 428 Million Mobile Communication Devices Sold Worldwide in First Quarter 2011, a 19 Percent Increase Year-on-Year" (2011, May 19), Gartner, Inc. Retrieved November 4, 2011, from http://www.gartner.com/it/page.jsp?id=1689814

5. Smith, Aaron (2011, July, 11), "Smartphone Adoption and Usage," Pew Internet. Retrieved July 21, 2011, from http://pewinternet.org/Reports/2011/Smartphones/Summary.aspx

6. Wilson, Rebecca (2011, June 7), "Top 5 Features of Next Generation Mobile Websites," 60 second marketer. Retrieved July 21, 2011, from http://60secondmarketer.com/blog/2011/06/07/mobile-website-best-practices-2/

7. "Facebook and Twitter Access via Mobile Browser Grows by Triple-Digits in the Past Year" (2010, March 3), ComScore. Retrieved July 21, 2011, from http://www.comscore.com/Press_Events/Press_Releases/2010/3/Facebook_and_Twitter_Access_via_Mobile_Browser_Grows_by_Triple-Digits

8. "Statistics Page" (2011, July 24), Facebook. Retrieved July 21, 2011, from https://www.facebook.com/press#!/press/info.php?statistics

9. "Twitter Update 2011" (2011, June 1), Pew Internet. Retrieved July 21, 2011, from http://www.pewinternet.org/Reports/2011/Twitter-Update-2011.aspx

10. Children with Diabetes: The Online Community for Kids, Families, and Adults with Diabetes (2011, July 27), vol. 17, no. 30. Retrieved August 1, 2011, from http://www.childrenwithdiabetes.com/

11. Khan, Mickey Alam (2009, April 10), "Procter & Gamble's Charmin Brand Runs First Mobile Sponsorship," Mobile Marketer. Retrieved July 21, 2011, from http://www.mobilemarketer.com/cms/news/advertising/3017.html

12. "You Have an App for That . . . Now What?" (2011, June 22), Nielsen. Retrieved September 27, 2011, from http://blog.nielsen.com/nielsenwire/consumer/you-have-an-app-for-that-now-what/

13. "Company Snapshot" (2011, July 15), Dunkin' Donuts. Retrieved July 21, 2011, from http://www.dunkindonuts.com/content/dunkindonuts/en/company.html

14. "Video Case Study (Dunkin' Donuts)" (n.d.), Pearson. Retrieved July 21, 2011, from http://wps.pearsoned.co.uk/ema_uk_he_hollensen_globalmark_4/64/16425/4204963.cw/content/index.html

15. "Dunkin' Donuts Case Study: Going Online to Strengthen Customer Relationships" (2010, May), Yahoo! Retrieved July 21, 2011, from http://advertising.yahoo.com/industry-knowledge/dunkin-donuts-case-study.html

16. Butcher, Dan (2009, June 23), "Dunkin' Donuts Sweetens Dunkin' Run Campaign with Mobile," Mobile Marketer. Retrieved July 21, 2011, from http://www.mobilemarketer.com/cms/news/advertising/3528.html

17. Paynter, Ben (2010, May 1), "Five Steps for Consumer Brands to Earn Social Currency," Fast Company. Retrieved July 21, 2011, from http://www.fastcompany.com/magazine/145/next-tech-five-steps-to-social-currency.html

18. Kats, Rimma (2011, March 3), "Dunkin' Donuts Bolsters Iced Coffee Sales via Mobile Reward Challenges," Mobile Marketer. Retrieved September 27, 2011, from http://www.mobilemarketer.com/cms/news/content/9256.html

19. Rosenberg, Dave (2009, June 22), "Dunkin' Donuts iPhone App Makes Coffee More Social," CNET. Retrieved July 21, 2011, from http://news.cnet.com/8301-13846_3-10270431-62.html

20. Hepburn, Aden (2009, June 23), "Dunkin' Donuts Online Ordering and iPhone App," digitalbuzz. Retrieved from http://www.digitalbuzzblog.com/dunkin-donuts-launches-online-ordering-iphone-app/

21. "The Social Smarts of Dunkin Run" (2009, June 23), SociaLens. Retrieved July 21, 2011, from http://www.socialens.com/blog/2009/06/23/the-social-smarts-of-dunkin-run/

22. Burkitt, Laurie (2009, November 23), "Killer Apps: Best Branded Mobile Applications," *Forbes*. Retrieved July 21, 2011, from http://www.forbes.com/2009/11/23/best-worst-apps-cmo-network-best-apps_slide_7.html

23. Brogan, Chris (2009, June 29), "Dunkin Run—Coffee Lovers Are Served." Retrieved July 21, 2011, from http://www.chrisbrogan.com/dunkin-run-coffee-lovers-are-served/

24. Fallon, Sean (2009, June 22), "Dunkin' Donuts 'Dunkin Run' iPhone App Will Change the Lives of Office Lackeys," Gizmodo. Retrieved July 21, 2011, from http://gizmodo.com/5299799/dunkin-donuts-dunkin-run-iPhone-app-will-change-the-lives-of-office-lackeys

25. Nicole, Kristen (2011, June 22), "Dunkin Donuts iPhone App, Great for Market Research?" bub.blicio.us. Retrieved July 21, 2011, from http://bub.blicio.us/dunkin-donuts-iPhone-ap/

26. Chen, Sande (2009, April 29), "The Social Network Game Boom," Gamasutra. Retrieved September 13, 2011 from http://www.gamasutra.com/view/feature/4009/the_social_network_game_boom.php

27. Verna, Paul (2011, January), "Social Gaming: Marketers Make Their Move," eMarketer. Retrieved September 13, 2011 from http://www.emarketer.com/Reports/All/Emarketer_2000759.aspx

28. Ibid.

29. Corwin, Peg (n.d.), "Virtual Currencies and Virtual Goods — Definitions and Revenue Streams in Social Networks," How To Start A Social Network. Retrieved September 13, 2011 from http://en.wikipedia.org/wiki/Virtual_currency

30. Verna, Paul (2011, January), "Social Gaming: Marketers Make Their Move," eMarketer. Retrieved September 13, 2011 from http://www.emarketer.com/Reports/All/Emarketer_2000759.aspx

31. Kaye, Kate (2010, October 18), "Farmers Insurance on FarmVille . . . What Took So Long?," ClickZ. Retrieved September 13, 2011 from http://www.clickz.com/clickz/news/1790530/farmers-insurance-farmvillewhat

32. Ibid.

33. Meraji, Shereen (2011, February 8), "Is That An Ad Growing In Your FarmVille Field?", NPR. Retrieved September 13, 2011 from http://www.npr.org/2011/02/08/133576017/is-that-an-ad-growing-in-your-farmville-field

34. Mack, Christopher (2011, April 15), "Social Gaming Roundup: Turner Broadcast, Foursquare Day, Branding, & More," Inside Social Games. Retrieved September 13, 2011 from http://www.insidesocialgames.com/category/playdom-2/page/3/

35. Hernandez, Brian Anthony (2011, May 3), "Why 5 Big Brand Marketing Campaigns are Betting Big on Social Gaming," Mashable. Retrieved September 13, 2011 from http://mashable.com/2011/05/03/social-gaming-marketing/

36. Foursquare (n.d.), *Wikipedia*. Retrieved September 27, 2011, from http://en.wikipedia.org/wiki/Foursquare#cite_note-2

37. Salt, Simon (2011), "Social Location Marketing: Outshining Your Competitors on Foursquare," Gowalla, Yelp & Other Location Sharing Sites. Que Publishing. Indianapolis, Indiana. pp. 66–70, 112–138.

38. Black, Leyl Master (2011, January 10), "5 Creative Facebook Places Marketing Campaigns," Mashable. Retrieved August 8, 2011, from http://mashable.com/2011/01/10/facebook-places-campaigns/

39. Grove, Jennifer Van (2011, January 12), "Google's Hotpot Recommendation Engine for Places Arrives on iPhone," Mashable. Retrieved August 8, 2011, from http://mashable.com/2011/01/12/googles-places-hotpot-iphone/

40. Salt, Simon (2011), "Social Location Marketing: Outshining Your Competitors on Foursquare, Gowalla, Yelp & Other Location Sharing Sites," Que Publishing. Indianapolis, Indiana. p. 132.

41. White, Charlie (2011, July 15), "Yelp Hits 20 Million Reviews [INFOGRAPHIC]," Mashable. Retrieved August 8, 2011, from http://mashable.com/2011/07/15/yelp-20-million-infographic/

42. Salt, Simon (2011), "Social Location Marketing: Outshining Your Competitors on Foursquare, Gowalla, Yelp & Other Location Sharing Sites," Que Publishing. Indianapolis, Indiana. p. 133.

43. Emarketer. (2010) Company reports. Retrieved July 21, 2011 from http://www.ignitesocialmedia.com/social-media-stats/foursquare-facebook-places-checkins/

44. SNL Kagan (2010, Oct. 21), "Economics of Location-Based Services," Ignite. Retrieved July 21, 2011, from http://www.ignitesocialmedia.com/social-media-stats/foursquare-facebook-places-checkins/

45. "Foursquare to Facebook Places: Insight into Check-ins" (2010, July 13), webroot survey, Ignite. Retrieved July 21, 2011, from http://www.ignitesocialmedia.com/social-media-stats/foursquare-facebook-places-checkins/

46. "Nearly 1 in 5 Smartphone Owners Access Check-in Services Via Their Mobile Phone" (2011, May 12), ComScore. Retrieved July 21, 2011, from http://www.comscore.com/Press_Events/Press_Releases/2011/5/Nearly_1_in_5_Smartphone_Owners_Access_Check-In_Services_Via_their_Mobile_Device

47. *JiWire Mobile Audience Insights Report* (2010, Q3), JiWire. Retrieved September 27, 2011, from http://www.jiwire.com/assets/htm/jiwire-download.php?type=pdf&file=JiWire_MobileAudienceInsightsReport_Q32010.pdf

48. "QR Codes" (n.d.), New Channel Direct. Retrieved July 22, 2011, from http://www.newchanneldirect.com/qr_codes/qr_codes.asp

49. Ibid.

50. Marie V-B (2011, January 26), "Location-Based Marketing for Newbies," PRBreakfastClub. Retrieved July 22, 2011, from http://prbreakfastclub.com/2011/01/26/location-marketing-for-dummies/#ixzz1SqclIaTK

51. Van Grove, Jennifer (2010, May 17), "Mayors of Starbucks Now Get Discounts Nationwide with Foursquare," Mashable. Retrieved September 27, 2011, from http://mashable.com/2010/05/17/starbucks-foursquare-mayor-specials/

52. Joraanstad Jake (2011, February 17), "Motorola Atrix – The Future of Mobile Computing," Techerator. Retrieved December 19, 2011, from http://www.techerator.com/2011/02/motorola-atrix-the-future-of-mobile-computing/

53. Wilcox, Cath (2011, November 17), "The Future of Mobile Computing is Context Aware," Overlay Media. Retrieved December 19, 2011, from http://www.overlaymedia.com/blog/?p=196

54. Brogan, Chris (2011, February 28), "The Future of Location-Based Applications," Chris Brogan Blog. Retrieved December 19, 2011, from http://www.chrisbrogan.com/futureoflocation/

55. Admin (2011, December 18), "Is Location Based Advertising the Future of Proximity Marketing?" SEO Optimisation Blog. Retrieved December 19, 2011, from http://www.cageymedia-dev.com/blogs/seo-optimisation-blog.co.uk/is-location-based-advertising-the-future-of-proximity-marketing

56. Ostrow, Adam (2010, January 12), "Conan Wins the Hearts and Minds of the Internet," Mashable, retrieved July 21, 2011, from http://mashable.com/2010/01/12/conan-obrien-statement/ and Carter, Bill (2010, January 12), "Conan O'Brien Says He Won't Host 'Tonight Show' after Leno," Media Decoder, retrieved July 21, 2011, from http://mediadecoder.blogs.nytimes.com/2010/01/12/conan-obrien-says-he-wont-do-tonight-show-following-leno/

57. Axon, Samuel (2010, January 11), "The Internet Is Laughing at NBC, Not with It," Mashable. Retrieved July 21, 2011, from http://mashable.com/2010/01/11/nbc-conan-leno-kimmel/

58. Parr, Ben (2010, February 24), "Conan O'Brien Officially Joins Twitter," Mashable, retrieved July 21, 2011, from http://mashable.com/2010/02/24/conan-obrien-twitter-2/ and "Conan O'Brien" (2011, July 21), Twitter, retrieved July 21, 2011, from http://twitter.com/#!/conanobrien

59. Parr, Ben (2010, April), "Conan O'Brien Drops in on Twitter HQ," Mashable. Retrieved July 21, 2011, from http://mashable.com/2010/04/23/conan-obrien-twitter-hq-pics/

60. Cashmore, Pete (2010, March 8), "Conan O'Brien Visits Google," Mashable. Retrieved July 21, 2011, from http://mashable.com/2010/05/08/conan-obrien-google/

61. Bergman, Cory (2010, November 8), "Will Conan's Social Marketing Blitz Turn into Ratings?" Lost Remote. Retrieved July 21, 2011, from http://www.lostremote.com/2010/11/08/will-conans-social-marketing-blitz-turn-into-ratings/

62. "Conan O'Brien" (2011, July 17), *Wikipedia*. Retrieved July 21, 2011, from http://en.wikipedia.org/wiki/Conan_obrien

63. "2010 Tonight Show Conflict" (2011, July 17), *Wikipedia*. Retrieved July 21, 2011, from http://en.wikipedia.org/wiki/Team_coco

64. Callari, Ron (n.d.), "Social Media's Geolocation Promotes Conan's Return to Late Night," InventorSpot. Retrieved July 21, 2011, from http://inventorspot.com/articles/social_medias_geolocation_promotes_conans_return_late_night

65. "Conan O'Brien Turns to Foursquare to Promote New Show, Launches His Own Badge" (2010, October 11), MobileMarketingWatch. Retrieved July 21, 2011, from http://www.mobilemarketingwatch.com/conan-obrien-turns-to-foursquare-to-promote-new-show-launches-his-own-badge-10171/

66. Carr, Austin (2010, October 12), "Conan O'Brien: King of Social Media," Fast Company. Retrieved July 21, 2011, from http://www.fastcompany.com/1694565/conan-obrien-king-of-social-media

67. Falconer, James (2010, October 11), "Conan O'Brien Debuts His Own Foursquare Badge," intomobile. Retrieved September 27, 2011, from http://www.intomobile.com/2010/10/11/conan-obrien-foursquare-badge/

68. Hall, Steve (2010, October 12), "Conan O'Brien Lets People Check In to His Blimp on Foursquare," AdRants. Retrieved July 21, 2011, from http://www.adrants.com/2010/10/conan-obrien-lets-people-check-in-to.php

69. "Spot the Conan Blimp and Unlock the Conan Blimpspotter Badge" (2010, October 8), About Foursquare. Retrieved July 21, 2011, from http://aboutfoursquare.com/conan-blimp/

70. "Conan O'Brien Presents: Team Coco" (2011, July 17), Appolicious. Retrieved September 27, 2011,from http://www.appolicious.com/omg/apps/415326-conan-obrien-presents-team-coco-tbs

71. "The Conan Blimp" (2011, July 17), Foursquare. Retrieved July 21, 2011, from https://foursquare.com/venue/10148291

72. "Location of the Year on Foursquare" (2011, July 18), Shorty Awards. Retrieved July 21, 2011, from http://shortyawards.com/special_awards/foursquare_location

73. "Conan" (2011, July 17), Foursquare, retrieved July 21, 2011, from https://foursquare.com/venue/10302784 and "TeamCoco" (2011, July 17), Foursquare, retrieved July 21, 2011, from https://foursquare.com/teamcoco

74. Van Grove, Jennifer (2010, October 8), "Conan O'Brien Gets His Own Foursquare Badge (and a Blimp)," Mashable. Retrieved July 21, 2011, from http://mashable.com/2010/10/08/conan-foursquare/

CHAPTER 14

Social Media Monitoring

Today, many organizations recognize that without social media monitoring, they are like ships at sea without navigation or radar, lacking the capacity to seek out opportunities and circumvent threats. This chapter draws upon the best practices in social media monitoring to help marketers find those elusive treasures and skirt the dangerous shoals of the social media seas.

LEARNING OBJECTIVES

After completing this chapter, students will be able to:

- Define social media monitoring
- Describe a brief history of social media monitoring
- Explain tracking social media
- Define social media measurement
- Identify how to measure social media
- Describe how to measure quantitative key performance indicators
- Explain how to measure qualitative key performance indicators

(Continued)

There seem to be as many definitions for the term "social media monitoring" as there are purposes for its use, ranging from simply listening to the social web to performing complex and sophisticated analyses of social media marketing activities. For current purposes **social media monitoring** is defined as the process of tracking, measuring, and evaluating an organization's social media marketing initiatives.

A Brief History of Social Media Monitoring

The earliest adopters of social media monitoring were public relations and advertising agencies, who used this monitoring as a means to detect negative comments posted to the social web about their clients.[1] These agencies were keen to head off potential PR nightmares resulting from disgruntled consumers. Unmonitored, damaging remarks on social media sites have the potential to snowball into a PR crisis, with deleterious effects on the client's brand reputation and the agency's future prospects of doing business with that client.

By detecting issues early on and taking swift action to mediate them, agencies sought to keep consumer outrage on social media from reaching mass media outlets, as happened with the "United Breaks Guitars" PR disaster discussed in Chapter 1. Social media monitoring was initially a time-consuming, expensive, and highly error-prone process because it was done manually and without the benefit of measurement guidelines. Nonetheless, the rewards outweighed the costs for the agencies.

As the social web rapidly grew, the importance of monitoring also increased. Software makers seized on the opportunities inherent in these trends and began developing social media monitoring tools and measurement standards. As power monitoring tools appeared, it became not only feasible but desirable for companies to move social media monitoring in-house.

As the implications and advantages of social media monitoring became known within organizations, its use spread to multiple departments. As an example, customer support departments started monitoring social media for complaints and questions about products and services. Public relations found social media monitoring useful as an early warning system of impending PR calamities. Companies discovered that they could gather valuable information about how they were perceived by consumers, how their competitors were viewed, and even how the industry as a whole was looked upon by the denizens of the social web.

Eventually, social media monitoring evolved beyond basic listening into active interaction. For example, customer support started responding to consumer concerns using the same social media sites where the issues were raised. PR departments took an active role in averting potential PR crises by using social media to instantly engage with the troubled parties to resolve the issues. In addition, public relations sought out and courted the influencers on the social web in an attempt to make them brand enthusiasts. Finally, marketing departments started using social media monitoring to track, measure, evaluate, and tune their social media marketing activities in order to maximize their chances of success.

- Describe how to use the Net Promoter Score
- Define return on investment (ROI)
- Explain how to evaluate social media monitoring tracking and measurements
- Describe how to select social media monitoring tools
- Identify key predictions about the future of social media monitoring

Tracking

Social media tracking is the process of finding and following content on the social web. Given the size and continued growth of the social web, finding specific content on it can be a daunting task. Moreover, marketers are frequently unsure what to search for. However, by following a sustainable and actionable tracking plan, marketers can significantly increase the odds of success.

One of the biggest challenges marketers face in setting up a tracking plan is to identify the keywords that will retrieve relevant data. Ill-defined search terms not only waste resources, but can produce misleading results that will do more harm than good.

To efficiently and effectively find relevant content on the social web, use the five-step approach below:

1. Choose Focus Areas: By defining what is being sought in detail, marketers can, for example, determine whether the organization's brand is the sole focus of the search, or if the search extends to competitor's brands. Marketers will likely want to track both to assess how well the company's brand is doing compared with the competition.

2. Select Target-rich Platforms By choosing the specific social media platforms where the target audience most heavily participates, marketers will not be buried in irrelevant returns or overwhelmed with spurious data when searching these platforms.

3. Identify the Appropriate Keywords and Phrases: By studying how people actually describe brands or other topics, it is possible to construct search queries using common language that will return the most pertinent results. The Google AdWords Keyword Tool provides a good way to find frequently used search terms. It shows the number of monthly searches on Google using variously related keyword phrases. Be carefully to avoid using insider industry jargon as search terms. Most consumers will not be familiar with the terms and hence will not use them on the social web. In addition, when people are talking about their work, they seldom use descriptors like *white-collar worker, blue-collar worker,* or *unemployed.* They are much more likely to use terms such as *attorney, doctor, carpenter, plumber,* or *laid off* and *outsourced.*

4. Restrict or Widen the Search: By using **Boolean operators**, such as AND, OR, and NOT, marketers can build search queries that either narrow or broaden a search. For example, the **Boolean AND operator**, often represented by a plus sign (+), constricts a search by specifying that the results must include all the keywords in the query, while the **Boolean NOT operator**, often represented by the minus sign (-), excludes results containing the specified keywords. For example, the search query *netbooks +laptops* will retrieve only content that contains both keywords. The search query *netbooks -laptops* produces results that have the keyword *netbooks* but not *laptops*. In addition to Boolean operators, **phrase searching** also narrows the results by only returning content that exactly matches the keywords within quotes (such as *"laptops that suck"*). Finally, the **Boolean OR operator** lets marketers widen a search to include content that has either of the keywords connected by the operator. For example, the search query: *netbooks OR laptops* generates a larger number of results because each retrieved item can have just one of the keywords.

5. Adjust Searches: By realizing that searches often do not produce the desired results, marketers can refine their search. For example, a start-up or relatively small company, with little presence on the social Web, may not return results for a general brand search. If this is the case, marketers can still find valuable information by searching for the brands of competitors or look for potential customers based on target market information, such as interests, tastes, behaviors, and demographics. It is also worth noting that mentions of companies that specialize in B2B sales will likely not be found on Facebook or Twitter where consumers hang out, but they might be found on LinkedIn where companies network[2]

Once key sources of information are found on the social web, marketers will want to follow these sources on a regular basis. Google Alerts, RSS, and more sophisticated tracking tools provide the means to receive automated updates from specified sources (these tools will be explored further in the "Social Media Monitoring Tools" section below).

Measuring

The reliability of social media measurement is a topic of debate, with some pundits questioning its precision and accuracy.[3] The notion that some marketing initiatives cannot be accurately accounted for is a longstanding one. For example, the department store mogul John Wanamaker, who passed away in 1922, noted that "[h]alf the money I spend on advertising is wasted; the trouble is I don't know which half."[4] Wanamaker's ancient quandary is equally applicable to modern attempts to measure social media marketing activities. The results may be accurate half the time, but which half?

This is a fact underscored by the Third European Summit on Measurement, held June 2011 in Lisbon, at which the 170 delegates made their first contributions on the need for standards in social media measurement.[5] However, after a lengthy discussion, these measurement professionals were unable to even agree on definitions, let alone how to measure the key elements of social media marketing.[6]

Furthermore, according to the *Social Media Marketing Industry Report*, the number-one question that over 3,300 social media marketers want answered is "How do I measure the effectiveness of social media?"[7] Clearly, there is a lack of consensus on how to answer this question, and that lack explains why less than one out of seven companies measured their return on investment for social media marketing during the first two years of implementation.[8]

Nonetheless, Jim Sterne, author of *Social Media Metrics*, writes that "measurement is no longer optional" for a company's social media marketing activities: "Whether money is tight or times are good, everybody is bent on improving their business performance based on metrics. You cannot continue to fly by the seat of your pants. Automated systems and navigational instrumentation are required on passenger planes, and your business deserves no less."[9]

Hence, the need to measure social media remains of paramount concern for businesses because it enables marketers to assess progress toward achieving marketing goals, determine how strategies are performing, and make necessary adjustments. Despite the absence of definitive standards for social media measurement, it is possible to provide useful guidelines for what to measure in social media and how to measure it.

WHAT IS SOCIAL MEDIA MEASUREMENT?

Social media measurement is the determination of the volume of content and the sentiment toward a brand or topic on the social web.[10] The volume of content is a **quantitative measurement**, while judging sentiment is a **qualitative measurement**. The number of posts, comments, tweets, retweets, likes, and follows are instances of quantitative metrics, while mentions, comments, conversations, and feedback about a brand are examples of qualitative metrics.[11]

HOW TO MEASURE SOCIAL MEDIA

Quantitative and qualitative metrics are called Key Performance Indicators. A Key Performance Indicator (KPI) is a social media metric that indicates the progress of strategies in achieving goals.[12] Quantitative KPIs measure return on investment from social media marketing efforts (i.e., X number of posts for X amount of dollars).[13] Qualitative KPIs assess the impact of social media marketing activities on "soft" goals, such as brand awareness, influence, and engagement.[14]

Choosing the right social media KPIs is reliant upon having a good understanding of which social media goals are important to an organization.[15] Understanding what an organization wants to accomplish defines what social metrics it should collect.[16] In other words, an organization's desired outcomes determine the most appropriate measurements.

Hence the first step to measurement is defining an organization's qualitative and quantitative social media goals.[17] Katie Delahaye Paine, author of *Measure What Matters*, writes that "[i]n order to be measureable, the goal or objective of your strategy or campaign must include not just the desired outcome but also a date, by which it should happen, and ideally, a budget and the audience it is designed to influence."[18]

Once measureable goals have been established, the second step is to choose a mixture of quantitative and qualitative KPIs that will accurately measure progress in achieving those goals. There are literally hundreds of KPIs to choose from, and therefore, the key is to find the ones that closely correlate (tie) with the company's social media goals. In addition, it can be useful to combine KPIs by turning them into ratios. For example, "comments per blog post, retweets per followers, help you measure audience activity and engagement."[19]

It is worth noting that according to a 2011 CMO Survey, companies are shifting away from measuring social media marketing efforts using financial KPIs, such as sales revenue, sales per customers, and profits per customer, toward behavioral measurements, such as the number of page visits and followers, buzz, text analysis, online ratings, and abandoned shopping carts, as depicted in Table 14.1.* However, it is still important to include at least a few KPIs that indicate if a company is turning a profit; otherwise, the KPIs can be reached, while the company actually loses money on the social media marketing initiative.[20]

The third step is to set a **baseline** or **benchmarks**, which will act as standards against which all social media KPIs are measured.[21] Benchmarks provide a starting point, enabling marketers to determine the progress of social media strategies toward achieving goals. To create this baseline, find and record the current values of the chosen KPIs. Once these values are established, it is important to measure the rate of change for these metrics: "[f]or example it's fantastic [to] get 1,000 followers in a day but not [to] get them over the year."[22] In addition, it is valuable to benchmark an organization's social media metrics against the competition to provide context. As an example, discovering that a company has 5,000 followers on Twitter is far more meaningful when compared with a competitor's 3,000 followers.[23]

The fourth and final step is to compare an organization's social media KPIs to its benchmarks over a period of time to assess the pace and degree of progress. It is important to record measurements on a regular basis (that is, weekly) so that marketers can instantly take advantage of massive shifts while remaining aware of general trends over time. By identifying seismic events and general trends in social media measurements, marketers can more precisely assess whether social media strategies have been successful.[24] It is worth noting that the relevancy of this data should also be taken into consideration in these evaluations. For example, identifying how many Facebook followers are potential customers is crucial information for accurately measuring the success of an organization's social media marketing efforts.

The question is sometimes raised about the possibility of global or general social media measurements standards across organizations. This possibility would indeed be the social media marketer's silver bullet. Unfortunately, such universal social media measurement standards currently do not exist. As highlighted by the Third European Summit on Measurement in Lisbon, in 2011, "one size does not fit all" in measuring social media.[25] Indeed, "[a]ll existing models are wrong at some level."[26] The bottom line from the summit participants is that social media marketers must each define custom meaningful metrics for their own organizations.[27]

Metrics	August 2010	August 2011
Hits/visits/page views	47.6%	52.2%
Repeat visits	34.7%	34.9%
Number of followers or friends	24%	34.1%
Conversion rates (from visitor to buyer)	25.4%	29.3%
Buzz indicators (web mentions)	15.7%	20.5%
Customer acquisition costs	11.8%	14.1%
Sales levels	17.9%	13.3%
Other text analysis ratings	6.6%	12.0%
Online product/service ratings	8.2%	10.4%
Revenue per customer	17.2%	9.6%
Net promoter score	7.5%	6.8%
Customer retention costs	7.7%	6.4%
Abandoned shopping carts	3.8%	4.8%
Profits per customer	9.4%	4.8%

Notable shifts

Metrics shift toward web-based customer behaviors:
- Page visits, followers, buzz, text analysis, online ratings, and abandoned shopping carts

Financial metrics decline:
- Sales levels, revenue per customer, profits per customer

No significant change:
- Repeat visits
- Net promoter score
- Customer retention costs

Source: The CMO Survey, comsurvey.org, August 2011 Highlights and Insights, Table 5.2.

Table 14.1 Social media metrics used by firms

---

*Key Performance Indicators, such as text (sentiment) analysis and Net promoter score, will be explained in detail below.

QUANTITATIVE SOCIAL MEDIA MEASURING

Quantitative social media measuring is a methodology that focuses on counting the volume of specific types of content on the social web. According to the study *Social Media Usage, Attitudes and Measurability*, the most popular social media quantitative measurements among marketers are those that directly measure the number of interactions. The vast majority of marketers (93%) count the number of visitors/page views, while 85% of marketers also measure the number of fans/followers, with 79% measuring the traffic arriving at company websites from the social web. In addition, 72% of marketers count the number of leads generated from social media, and 58% measure new customer conversions. Seventy-one percent assess the number of comments posted, and 55% count the number of shared links on bookmarking and social news sites.[28]

To make quantitative social media metrics useful, these metrics must be tied to specific marketing goals. The primary challenge of connecting quantitative KPIs to marketing goals is to make the goals specific, measurable, attainable, realistic, and timely (**SMART**).

In addition, goals and related KPIs must be established for each type of social media platform in order to maximize results. The following are examples of SMART goals and relevant quantitative KPIs for five popular social media platforms, a corporate blog, a microblog (Twitter), a social network (Facebook), a video sharing site (YouTube), and a social news site (Digg):

CORPORATE BLOG

- 30% increase in total number of unique visitors within six months
- 40% growth in total number of views within six months
- 20% increase in the ratio of visitors' comments to posts (comments/posts) within six months
- 10% growth of RSS subscribers within six months
- 5% growth of RSS feed requests within six months

TWITTER

- 20% growth in the number of followers within thirty days
- 30% growth in the number of retweets (message amplification) within thirty days
- 10% increase in click-through rate (CTR) of the links posted in tweets within thirty days (Note: observing which types of links garner the highest CTRs can help in tuning tweets to provide consumers with links they are interested in and hence further improve the CTRs.)
- 15% increase in visits to website from tweet links within thirty days
- 10% growth in time on website from tweet links within thirty days
- 5% increase in website conversions (i.e., sales) from tweet links within thirty days

FACEBOOK

- 20% growth in the number of fans within five months
- 30% growth in the number of comments within five months
- 20% increase in the number of comments and Likes on admin post within six months
- 5% growth in the number of wall response time within six months

- 40% increase in the number of Facebook Place check-ins within six months

- 30% increase in visits to company website from Facebook ads within three months

YOUTUBE

- 30% growth in the number of videos viewed within four months

- 20% growth in the number of unique visitors within four months

- 10% increase in the number of subscribers to company channel within four months

- 30% increase in the ratio of comments on videos to the number of videos uploaded within four months

- 15% growth in the number of embedded links to the videos (i.e., links from other sites to brand videos) within four months

- 30% increase in average rankings of images or videos by viewers within four months

DIGG

- 20% increase in number of Diggs within three months

- 30% growth in comments on the Digg site within four months

- 10% increase in traffic driven to the company website from Digg within five months

- 2% growth within five months in newsletter subscriptions from people visiting the company's landing page for Digg

- Getting an article about the company on the front page within one year[29]

Several important observations can be made about the quantitative goals and KPIs for the various social media platforms listed above. First, they provide only a brief glimpse at the countless ways to measure performance quantitatively on social media platforms. Second, quantitative KPIs must be closely tied to well-defined goals to be effective. Finally, they must be tailored for each platform.

Before turning to qualitative social media metrics, it is worth noting that marketers can easily get lost in measuring "hollow" metrics. According to marketing consultant Elaine Fogel, "[i]t's not important how many names we collect, but rather how many we engage, build relationships with, become our brand advocates, and exchange info with."[30]

However, if quantitative social media metrics are chosen carefully, using the techniques described above, the results can be impressive. For instance, the communication giant Avaya measures the number of social media mentions per week and the number of support issues resolved that week, according to their head of social media, Paul Duney.[31] That diligence has paid off not only in terms of lowering customer support costs and improving customer relations, but in one case— a conversation that began on Twitter— resulted in $250,000 sale for Avaya.[32]

Here are a few more examples of companies benefiting quantitatively:

- Southwest Airlines credits its activity on Twitter with bringing in more than $1 million in ticket sales.

- Marriott's corporate blog is attributed with delivering over $5 million in bookings by directing people to the reservation page.

- Dell Outlet's Twitter presence has generated over $6.5 million in sales.

- Lenovo credits the use of its community website for answering customer questions, a practice that has reduced call center activity by 20%.

- Naked Pizza attributes about 68% of total dollar sales to its Twitter presence.

- Blendtec's humorous YouTube "Will It Blend?" videos have garnered millions of views and increased sales by five times their previous rate.[33]

QUALITATIVE SOCIAL MEDIA MEASURING

Qualitative social media measuring is the process of accessing the opinions and beliefs about a brand.[34] According to the report *Social Media Usage, Attitudes and Measurability*, the most popular social media qualitative metrics among marketers are those that assess the impact of social media activities on customer relationships. For example, 84% of marketers measure dialogue with prospects and customers, while 68% measure the strength of existing customer relationships. Fifty-seven percent measure customer retention rates, while 43% of marketers calculate the ratio of negative to positive relationships with consumers. In addition, 68% of marketers track corporate/brand reputation.[35]

Another study, *The State of Social Media for Business*, supports these findings, with the notable exception that brand building was deemed more important than customer relationships by businesses.[36] This difference is unremarkable, given that it is typically easier and cheaper to measure changes in customer relationships than shifts in brand awareness and recognition. But this difference raises an interesting question.

With definitive quantitative measurements available, why perform these more "touchy-feely" qualitative measurements in social media? Simply put, quantitative data seldom reveals the whole story. This reality becomes increasingly the case as a brand grows in popularity when knowing how aware consumers are of the brand and their perceptions of it help shape social media marketing initiatives. In addition, qualitative metrics play a key role in identifying consumer satisfaction and dissatisfaction with a brand. For example, if a sizable number of people tweet, "iPhones suck" or alternatively "iPhones rock," quantitative metrics will simply count the number of tweets, not the (positive or negative) sentiment contained within them. And sentiments and beliefs can reveal much about brand perception.[37]

It is important to note that quantitative and qualitative measurements are not mutually exclusive. In fact, combining the two types of social media metrics provides a more realistic and accurate picture of an organization's progress in achieving its desired marketing goals.[38] Indeed, social media measurement "is unique in bringing both types of insights together to characterize performance and the value derived from social media efforts."[39]

Qualitative Key Performance Indicators (KPIs)

A number of Key Performance Indicators (KPIs) are available for measuring the qualitative performance of social media marketing activities. Perhaps the most influential qualitative KPI is sentiment analysis.[40] **Sentiment analysis**, or **opinion mining**, uses computer algorithms to automatically detect the basic mood, attitudes, or emotions of the creators of content on the social web.[41] Typically, sentiment analysis classifies social media opinions about a brand (or other topic) as positive, neutral, or negative.[42]

Although sentiment analysis enjoys widespread use, KPIs should be chosen based on the marketing goals of an organization, not popularity. Table 14.2 lists four common business objectives (social media goals) and the qualitative KPIs that have proven useful in tracking their progress, as well as the social media monitoring tools adept at measuring them (social media monitoring tools will be discussed later in this chapter).

Business Objective	Key Performance Indicator	Vendors to Watch
Foster Dialog	Share of Voice	Alterian SM2, Radian6, Scout Labs, Statsit, Trendrr, Visible Technologies
	Audience Engagement	Coremetrics, Webtrends, Radian6, Scout Labs, Converseon, Filtrbox (Jive), Visible Technologies
	Conversation Reach	Alterian SM2, Radian6, Scout Labs, Social Radar, Statsit, SWIX, Trendrr, Visible Technologies
Promote Advocacy	Active Advocates	Biz360, Filtrbox (Jive), Radian6
	Advocate Influence	Cymfony, Filtrbox (Jive), Lithium, Radian6, Razoriish (SIM Score), SAS, Telligent, Twitalyzer, Visible Technologies
	Advocacy Impact	Coremetrics, Lithium, Ornniture, Webtrends, SWIX, Telligent
Facilitate Support	Resolution Rate	Filtrbox (Jive), RightNow Technologies, Salesforce.com, Telligent
	Resolution Time	Filtrbox (Jive), RightNow Technologies, Salesforce.com, Telligent
	Satisfaction Score	ForeSEe Results, iPerceptions, Karnpyle, OpinionLab
Spur Innovation	Topic Trends	Alterian SM2, Cymfony, Filtrbox (Jive), Radian6, SAS, Scout Labs, Social Mention, Social Radar, Trendrr, Visible Technologies
	Sentiment Ratio	Alterian SM2, Converseon, Cymfony, Filtrbox (Jive), Radian6, SAS, Scout Labs, Social Radar, Trendrr, Visible Technologies
	Idea Impact	Biz360, Cymfony, Filtrbox (Jive), Luglron, RadianC, Scout Labs, Visible Technologies

Table 14.2 Social Marketing Analytics Business Objectives, Key Performance Indicators, and Vendors to Watch

The following section explores each of these qualitative KPIs in detail. It is excerpted and adapted from the report *Social Marketing Analytics*, courtesy of the Altimeter Group, a research-based advisory firm that helps companies and industries leverage disruption to their advantage, and Web Analytics DEMYSTIFIED, a leading consultancy firm that specializes in digital measurement and optimization solutions for business.*

KPIs for Measuring Dialog Creating dialog with consumers demands that businesses produce relevant and meaningful content to engage an audience and attract contributors. Organizations must embrace this element and accept that while dialog can be initiated by an organization, it often takes on a life of its own that spirals beyond the control of a corporate blog, site, or forum.

Three metrics for measuring progress in achieving the business objective of fostering dialog include: Share of Voice, Audience Engagement, and Conversation Reach.

Dialog Key Performance Indicator #1: Share of Voice Share of Voice indicates how a brand stacks up in comparison with its competitors. It is calculated by dividing the company's brand mentions by the total mentions of the industry in social channels (i.e., articles, blogs, comments, Tweets, videos, etc.), as shown in the equation below. Share of

---

*From Owyang, Jeremiah, and John Lovett (2010, April 22), *Social Marketing Analytics: A New Framework for Measuring Results in Social Media!*, Altimeter Group and Web Analytics DEMYSTIFIED. Retrieved September 22, 2011, from http://www.slideshare.net/jeremiah_owyang/altimeter-report-social-marketing-analytics Reprinted with permission.

Voice gains further meaning when measured over a period of time and accompanied by historical comparisons because these provide a baseline to assess progress.

This metric can also offer competitive insight when represented as a pie chart comparing the percentages of the company and its competitors.

Additionally, Share of Voice should be segmented by channel to identify which social channels (i.e., social media platforms) have the greatest impact.

Share of Voice

$$\frac{\text{Brand Mentions}}{\text{Total Mentions (Brand + Competitor A, B, C \ldots n)}} = \text{Share of Voice}$$

When Share of Voice deviates beyond a reasonable threshold, the first place to evaluate is the content produced by marketing. If the content freshness is waning, then it shouldn't be a surprise that Share of Voice is in decline as well. Alternatively, if competition is clobbering a company's Share of Voice, it's time to understand what the competition is doing right. A strong competitor's marketing campaign or hilarious YouTube video that's gone viral can send a company's Share of Voice plummeting. Understanding why Share of Voice is moving offers competitive intelligence that can help marketers tune and improve a social media marketing effort.

Dialog Key Performance Indicator #2: Audience Engagement **Audience Engagement** shows the level of a company's engagement in comparison to its viewership. It is calculated by dividing the proportion of visitors who participate in a specific marketing initiative by contributing comments, sharing or linking back by the total number of views (see equation below). A baseline or benchmark for this KPI should be established in order to track improvements (or declines). Organizations with a strong following can expect a consistent volume of audience engagement and can modify expectations based on advertising, search efforts, and promotional activity accordingly.

Audience Engagement is a leading indicator of dialog about a specific topic or product.

Audience Engagement

$$\frac{\text{Comments + Shares + Trackbacks}}{\text{Total Views}} = \text{Audience Engagement}$$

Variations in Audience Engagement should serve to identify hot issues and topics of lesser interest. Thus, rather than looking at the absolute metrics for Audience Engagement, it's important to understand the variations of engagement across unique marketing initiatives. An isolated number alone won't necessarily offer actionable information, yet when viewed in the context of alternative initiatives, it will serve to quantify the impact of a specific initiative and determine if more publicity or promotion is required. Audience Engagement should be tracked over time to understand the typical volume of dialog within a specific channel.

Dialog Key Performance Indicator #3: Conversation Reach **Conversation Reach** reveals the number of unique visitors who participate in a specific brand/issue/topic conversation across one or more social media channels. It is calculated by dividing the number of people participating in a social media conversation by total audience exposure (see equation below). When calculating Conversation Reach, the first challenge is identifying the scope of the conversation by associating it with a specific marketing initiative, a topic, and/or keywords. Once this breadth of the conversation is clear, companies can forecast the audience exposure within different social media channels and quantify the expected number of unique voices contributing to the dialog. Reach metrics will be highly variable depending on the topic and should be trended over time.

Organizations should formulate a Reach Benchmark of past initiatives to identify when the volume of participants in a conversation is expanding and traveling beyond the normal ripple of dialog venues. Recognizing such significant trends can help marketers properly allocate social media marketing resources.

Conversation Reach

$$\frac{\text{Total People Participating}}{\text{Total Audience Exposure}} = \text{Conversation Reach}$$

Conversation reach can be evaluated in both volume and location across social media channels. When Reach metrics exceed expectations, companies should explore the most active channels and influencers, while keeping an eye on sentiment to ensure that the reach is going in a positive direction. Low reach metrics can signify ineffective channels or marketing messages that are murky or poorly received. Conversation Reach can also indicate when it's time to spur on an organization's advocate community to add to the conversation.

KPIs FOR MEASURING ADVOCACY The Advocacy success metrics are largely focused on the dedicated audience in social media that a company can trust to support its brand, products, or services. Not all companies will need to manage advocacy programs, yet the majority of organizations out there will have both advocates and detractors at some time. By developing an advocacy program, organizations can build a stable of genuine enthusiast to support the brand and combat detractors of the company. Key Performance Indicators that reveal the health of an advocacy program include: Active Advocates, Advocate Influence, and Advocacy Impact.

Advocacy Key Performance Indicator #1: Active Advocates **Active Advocates** measures the number of individuals generating positive sentiment over a given time frame (i.e., past 30 days). It is calculated by dividing the number of active advocates by the total (passive and active) advocates for a brand (see equation below). Expectations for the Active Advocates metric should be established when setting up an organization's advocacy program. This metric will echo the corporate goals established for enlisting consumer support by leveraging social media channels. It will provide immediate context on the health of the advocacy program and determine if it's working as designed. Active Advocates should be benchmarked over time with annotations and reminders identifying when programs initiate or specific advocacy awards/incentives are offered.

Active Advocates

$$\frac{\text{\# of Active Advocates (w/in past 30 days)}}{\text{Total Advocates}} = \text{Active Advocates}$$

After establishing the appropriate number of Active Advocates required for an organization's advocacy program to remain healthy, taking action on this number becomes routine. Above average numbers require minimal feeding, while negative Active Advocate scores indicate that it's time to reach out to company fans and create some buzz. This metric can be adjusted based on specific programs or campaigns, but should be compared against a benchmark of overall corporate advocacy.

Advocacy Key Performance Indicator #2: Advocate Influence **Advocate Influence** indicates the unique advocate's influence across one or more social media channels. It is calculated by dividing a single advocate's influence by the total number of brand advocates (see equation below). Building an advocacy program involves enlisting people who are going to reverberate good will about a company's products on a consistent basis. Yet setting expectations for how far and wide each advocate's message will travel requires an advocacy influence calculation. Influence can be measured using the volume of relevant content, comments, shares, and reach. This measure can be used as an input to calculate Advocacy Influence by quantifying the relative influence of any given individual against a standard derived from all advocates (Total Advocate Influence) within the organization's advocacy program.

Active Influence

$$\frac{\text{Unique Advocate's Influence}}{\text{Total Advocates Influence}} = \text{Active Influence}$$

The Advocate Influence KPI is most valuable when evaluated in the context of a business objective (social media goal). Advocate Influence can be used to identify new individuals for brand advocacy program, incentivize participants, or penalize/ motivate others. This metric will also enable marketers to identify existing channels and social circles that influencers reach and allow marketers to identify new territory for soliciting advocates. To do this, establish a threshold for influence and evaluate individuals as compared to the threshold. This will also allow marketers to segment advocates by varying degrees of influence and associate individuals with specific topics.

Advocacy Key Performance Indicator #3: Advocacy Impact **Advocacy Impact** measures the direct or indirect contributions of advocacy on conversions. It is derived by dividing the number of advocacy driven conversions by the total volume of advocacy traffic (see equation below). Calculating Advocacy Impact is tricky because it quickly becomes complicated as conversions are often the consequence of many marketing events. So don't expect Advocacy Impact to be a definitive metric for all conversions resulting from advocacy activity. However, it is still possible to quantify direct conversion events resulting from advocacy programs or even individual advocates. The first step is identifying conversions; whether they are online sales, document downloads, or requests for information, the calculation will be the same. Track referral information to determine the source of conversion traffic and monitor all traffic generated from advocacy initiatives. Since marketers know where advocates commonly discuss company products and services, this is one method of tracking online activity back to individual advocate sources.

Advocacy Impact

$$\frac{\text{Number of Advocacy Driven Conversions}}{\text{Total Volume of Advocacy Traffic}} = \text{Advocacy Impact}$$

Understanding the impact of an advocacy program and, to a lesser extent, the impact of individual advocates is imperative in determining overall effectiveness of the business objective. Each advocacy program or individual can be armed with specific identifiers that will point back to the influence they have on a online conversions. As stated previously this won't be empirical due to multiple marketing events that result in conversions, but it can identify last touch conversion events and be used to recognize traffic generated by individual advocates and programs. Once this information is apparent, the actions are clear: Feed a company's most effective programs and fuel its active advocates.

KPIs FOR MEASURING CUSTOMER SUPPORT Support success metrics are largely focused on an organization's ability to listen and respond to the ongoing conversation about an organization's brand, products, services, and entire company. As mentioned previously, social media creates multiple opportunities for delivering customer support in rapid fashion. Although social support won't eliminate the need for traditional support channels, it can alleviate pressure from existing solutions and empower a company's staff to respond quickly and efficiently. Performance indicators for customer support include: Issue Resolution Rate, Resolution Time, and Satisfaction Score.

Support Key Performance Indicator #1: Issue Resolution Rate Social Media **Issue Resolution Rate** is the percentage of customer service inquiries resolved satisfactorily using social media channels. It is calculated by dividing the number of service issues resolved satisfactorily by total number of service issues (see equation below). The implicit factor within the Issue Resolution Rate is actively determining whether the issue was satisfactorily resolved or not. This can be accomplished by asking customers or interpreting satisfaction using some other means. Marketers can do this with a simple online survey question or other automated method, although results will not be all inclusive. Whenever possible, set expectations by comparing social media issue resolution with traditional call center metrics. This will provide a baseline of performance and offer strong indicators of channel quality.

Issue Resolution Rate	$$\frac{\text{Total \# Issues Resolved Satisfactorily}}{\text{Total \# Service Issues}} = \text{Issue Resolution Rate}$$

The Issue Resolution Rate should provide immediate recognition of the quality of an organization's social media support efforts. Low issue resolution rates signify that additional training is required for staff or that the issues in question may require more documentation. Use this metric to take cues on which channels or service agents are most effective and leverage their success throughout the organization.

Support Key Performance Indicator #2: Resolution Time **Resolution Time** indicates the amount of time required to produce a human-generated response to customer service issues posed in social media channels. It is calculated by dividing total inquiry response time by total number of service inquiries (see equation below). Customers expect near instantaneous response to their service inquiries and while organizations may not have sub 60-second response times, they should strive to respond in a timely manner. Again, expectations can be set based on traditional call center or email response times if available, keeping in mind that social interactions are much closer to real-time than other channels. Responses should most likely be measured in hours and benchmarked against baseline comparatives. Also recognize that automated responses are unlikely to satisfy a company's customers, thus genuine, quality answers from actual humans are the expected norm.

Resolution Time	$$\frac{\text{Total Inquiry Response Time}}{\text{Total \# Service Inquiries}} = \text{Resolution Time}$$

When Resolution Time performance declines, the first place to investigate is a company's front line social media service representatives. Was there a widespread issue that caused a delay in resolution time or was it an isolated event? In either case, understanding the response times and their contextual circumstances should illuminate potential issues. While calculating response time for service inquiries may require some simple tabulation of issue start and resolution times, many social media measurement solutions offer basic work flow tools to direct issues to appropriate staff. If service is a primary component of an online social media strategy, then a work flow tool baked into its monitoring solution is a must-have.

Support Key Performance Indicator #3: Satisfaction Score Customer Satisfaction Score indicates the relative satisfaction of customers. It is computed by dividing positive customer feedback by all customer feedback (see equation below). There are numerous calculations and established methods for determining customer satisfaction, which include inputs such as quality, delivery, perceived value, and overall performance. Any combination of these or other important metrics on a weighted scale should comprise a numeric satisfaction score. It's important to note that social channels should not act as a proxy for other proven methods of determining satisfaction like surveys.

The expectations for a customer Satisfaction Score should be established on benchmark figures derived from historical performance. If no historical track record exists, then a consistent set of scores can serve as the norm.

Satisfaction Score

$$\frac{\text{Customer Feedback (input A, B, C...n)}}{\text{All Customer Feedback}} = \text{Satisfaction Score}$$

When customer satisfaction scores plummet, companies should investigate the source of the decline and the channels involved. Satisfaction Scores are likely to change less quickly than other social media KPIs and will trend upward or downward over time. It's important to catch downward movement in trends early to prevent customer attrition and remedy issues before they become pervasive.

KPIs MEASURING FOR SPURRING INNOVATION The innovation success metrics are largely focused on a business's ability to recognize and take action on ideas generated by the general population. Organizations that develop methods for harnessing feedback and indirect cues will develop a competitive advantage. Further, organizations that do this in a transparent manner will develop loyal and dedicated customers. Performance indicators for Innovation include: Topic Trends, Sentiment Ratio, and Idea Impact.

Innovation Key Performance Indicator #1: Topic Trends Topic Trends measure key brand/product/service topics identified by monitoring social media conversations. It is calculated by dividing the number of specific topic mentions by all topic mentions (see equation below). Topic trends should be evaluated much like keywords because there will typically be a number of popular topics followed by a long tail of less common ones. The ability to pick up on topic threads that fall below the blockbuster categories can yield productive ideas for innovation. Organizations will require the help of commercial social media monitoring tools to effectively listen to the vast array of conversations happening across the web. Yet, the ability to understand the context of product and service conversations as well as where these conversations are taking place is critical for tapping into consumer knowledge. Expect topic trends to have some consistency in terms of leading topics, yet new topics can surface quickly.

Topic Trends

$$\frac{\text{\# of Specific Topic Mentions}}{\text{All Topic Mentions}} = \text{Topic Trends}$$

Organizations that are fast to react to both positive and negative Topic Trends will showcase their social media savvy. While popular topics should incite organizations to consider a new lexicon for company's product and service offerings, hidden gems can deliver the greatest value.

Companies should dedicate time to mining topic trend data on a regular basis to ensure that they are in touch with consumers and to seek out new ideas for innovation.

Innovation Key Performance Indicator #2: Sentiment Ratio **Sentiment Ratio** indicates the positive, neutral, and negative brand mentions about specific products or services over a given time period. It is calculated by dividing positive, neutral, and negative brand mentions by all brand mentions (see equation below). Sentiment Ratios should be trended over time and represented in context of positive: neutral: negative. Sentiment is only possible to attain using automated analysis available from commercial social media monitoring technologies.

Obviously all brands hope for positive sentiment, but marketers and PR professionals should be able to harness and learn from any type of sentiment especially when it comes to seeking feedback for new product or service ideas. Expectations should be adjusted according to a baseline of consistent results. However, sentiment can change quickly.

Sentiment Ratio

$$\frac{\text{Positive : Neutral : Negative Brand Mentions}}{\text{All Brand Mentions}} = \text{Sentiment Ratio}$$

Each type of sentiment (positive/neutral/negative) can be analyzed to determine the source and origin of the response. Positive sentiment can be used to identify advocates and communities where a brand is welcomed. Neutral sentiment can help to interpret where conversations about an organization's brand can be swayed through reinforcement, dialog, and advocacy. Negative sentiment should be addressed directly and countered with support, advocacy, dialog, or some combination therein. The ability to recognize these areas and take action on them will elevate a company's ability to innovate.

Innovation Key Performance Indicator #3: Idea Impact **Idea Impact** measures the rate of interaction, engagement, and positive sentiment generated from a new product or service idea. It is calculated by dividing the number of positive conversations, shares, and mentions by the total idea conversations (see equation below). It may be helpful to think about the Idea Impact metric as the next generation focus group. Rather than going through the exercise of running ideas through a finite number of target individuals, Idea Impact enables organizations to leverage the power of the Internet and social media to test the waters. While the challenge is to do this without revealing the entire secret sauce, organizations can test concepts, prototypes, and other innovation ideas through a wide net of consumers or controlled group of advocates. In either case, the ability to measure the impact of new ideas is paramount for innovation.

Idea Impact

$$\frac{\text{\# of Positive Conversations, Shares, Mentions}}{\text{Total Idea Conversations, Shares, Mentions}} = \text{Idea Impact}$$

Idea impact can be used as an indicator for success in numerous ways. For example, movie trailers released through controlled social media outlets can be measured according to the buzz generated through conversations, shares, and social mentions to accurately predict the box office success. Similarly, consumer product promotions can be measured according to the dialog generated among target audiences. By using Idea Impact organizations, an organization can gain insight into how consumers will receive a given product or service. This in turn is a metric for forecasting the success of an organization's innovation efforts.

There are several key points worth highlighting regarding the above qualitative KPIs. First, a few of them, such as resolution time as it pertains to customer support, are actually quantitative. This fact underscores how quantitative and qualitative can work hand-in-hand to reveal more than either can alone. Second, although this list is comprehensive, it is by no means exhaustive. There are many alternative and additional qualitatively KPIs for measuring progress in achieving social media marketing goals. Third, qualitative KPIs, like quantitative KPIs, must be meticulously tied to distinct goals to be measurable.

Fourth, it should always be kept in mind that measuring performance with qualitative KPIs is a subjective endeavor, based in large part on a marketer's best judgment.[43] Terms like "awareness," "perception," "advocacy," and "influence" can be interpreted in different ways.

Finally, "sentiment" is not the Holy Grail of qualitative metrics. Although almost every major monitoring tool provides some form of sentiment analysis, looking at these sentiment reports in isolation just reveals how happy people are with a brand.[44] Only when sentiment is tracked over time in combination with other measurements does it expose interesting data. For example, using sentiment scores to filter and segment data can uncover "prominent and emerging topics within negative- [or positive-] sentiment content."[45]

Examples of companies benefiting qualitatively abound. Here are just a few:

1. Starbucks spawns many new product ideas by asking customers what they want from the coffee giant.

2. TurboTax uses Twitter to provide answers to questions during key tax season, thus helping establish themselves as authorities in its field and creating a trusted brand.

3. Kogi Korean BBQ uses Twitter to notify customers when food trucks will be in their neighborhood, thereby increasing sales and customer satisfaction.

4. Comcast uses Twitter to provide customers with immediate support, which creates more satisfied consumers.

5. Home Depot uses Twitter and its associates (store employees) to offer technical support to customers. The store associates use hashtags in their tweets to make support information easier to find, plus the associates include their names, which makes customers more comfortable with the home improvement advice they receive because they know exactly who is supporting them, as well as boosting employee morale with public recognition and appreciation.[46]

The Net Promoter Score

One of the most popular and simplest qualitative measurements is the **Net Promoter Score** (NPS), which is a measurement used to gauge the loyalty of a company's customer relationships.[47] It was developed by Fred Reichheld, Bain & Company and Satmetrix and has been used as a replacement for customer satisfaction measurements.

The NPS assumes that every company's customer can be divided into three classes: Promoters, Passives, and Detractors. The score is obtained by asking customers to answer a single question using a 0-to-10 rating scale. The question is "How likely is it that you would recommend [company X] to a friend or colleague?" Customers are categorized as follows:

- Those with a 9-to-10 score are **Promoters**, loyal enthusiasts who will continue to buy and refer other consumer and fuel further growth.

- Those with a 7-to-8 score are **Passives**, satisfied but unenthusiastic customers, vulnerable to competitive offerings.

- Those with a 6-to-0 score are **Detractors**, unhappy customers likely to damage the brand and hinder growth through damaging word of mouth.[48]

The NPS is calculated by taking the percentage of customers who are Promoters and subtracting the percentage who are Detractors.[49] However, the NPS itself is not a percentage but rather uses a plus "+" or minus "-" to indicate the product. An NPS that is above zero (i.e., has a plus sign) indicates a good customer relation's rating, with a +50 being considered indication of excellent customer relations.[50]

Return on Investment

Return on Investment (ROI) is a ratio arrived at by subtracting expenses from sales and then dividing the result by the expenses.[51]

$$ROI = \frac{Sales - Expenses}{Expenses}$$

In some instances, calculation of ROI is straightforward. Thus, when an organization invests $100,000 in expanding its sale force and sales revenue increases by $500,000, the Return on Investment (ROI) is 400%.

$$400\% = \frac{\$500,000 - \$100,000}{\$100,000}$$

Although calculating ROI for situations like this one is fairly straightforward, other marketing initiatives, such as advertising and PR campaigns, lack a direct link between sales and expense. As an example, it is difficult, if not impossible, to directly link sales increases with money spent on a mass media ad campaign. In such cases it is necessary to develop new measurements of return to justify investments.

For instance, advertising professionals came up with *reach* and *frequency* as ways to measure progress. **Reach** is the percentage of people in a target market who are exposed to an advertising schedule at least once, while **frequency** is the number of times an individual views a commercial in a particular advertising schedule.[52] Together, these metrics provide mass media advertisers with a way to assess what they are getting for the ad dollars.[53]

Currently, the ability to measure social media marketing ROI is a hotly debated topic.[54] However, there is agreement that measuring quantitative ROI is usually a forthright process. For example, if a company spends $40,000 having its employees take time to answer product questions using Twitter and, as a consequence, saves $60,000 in customer support calls, then the ROI for this social media marketing endeavor is 50%.

$$50\% = \frac{\$60,000 - \$400,000}{\$40,000}$$

However, measuring qualitative ROI is a different story. For example, hiring a social media marketing specialist to increase Facebook fans for a company's page involves a specific cost (i.e., the salary of the specialist), but the return in terms of increased sales from the company's growing popularity on Facebook is difficult, if not impossible, to determine. Such obstacles may well explain why only about 40% of companies measure social media marketing ROI, and just 8% of marketers express satisfaction with the ROI of their social marketing campaigns.[55]

In terms of qualitative social media marketing efforts, the argument is made that **impact** (i.e., raising people's awareness of a brand and influencing their perception of the brand through engagement) should be the primary goal of social media marketing, not ROI, at least in the short term.[56] In other words, the organization's investment in social media marketing should be treated as an investment, creating additional value for the company until the time comes when it can be directly linked to business transactions, which result in measurable ROI: "[t]here is also the notion that many social media initiatives are in an investment phase, not [in the] return phase of maturity."[57]

The mere fact that measuring qualitative ROI is challenging at the moment should not be taken to mean that qualitative social media marketing initiatives do not contribute to an organization's bottom line. Building brand awareness, perception, and loyalty, as well as improving customer relationships through consumer engagement, certainly have a long-term effect in attracting customers and retaining them, which eventually translate into additional sales and hence increased ROI.[58]

Nonetheless, the pressing demand to demonstrate a fiscal return for social media expenditures, as well as the need to assess progress and tune social media endeavors, is spawning the development and use of a plethora of new qualitative social media metrics. It is important to remember that when choosing new qualitative metrics, begin by setting clear marketing goals and benchmarks, and then select the qualitative Key Performance Indicators (KPIs) that are most likely to reveal progress toward achieving those goals based on established benchmarks.

Finally, the following questions can be used to judge how far along an organization is in reaching its qualitative goals:

- Is the organization reaching new social media audiences?

- Is the company viewed in a more positive than negative light by social media users?

- Is the organization engaged in meaningful conversations on the social web?[59]

Evaluation

Evaluation is the process of interpreting data once it has been measured with the intention to derive insights and understanding from it.[60] Just measuring the impact of social media activity is insufficient—measurement only gains meaning through analysis. Such analysis enables management to determine whether social media strategies are achieving an organization's goals.

However, evaluation is where many organizations come up short, failing to connect the dots between social media metrics, strategies, and business goals.[61] The reasons for this failure are threefold. First, sound analysis of social media measurements relies on collection of the relevant data in the first place. If the data gathered does not accurately measure the performance of social media strategies in attaining goals, then any analysis generated from it will be not only unreliable but misleading. Second, it takes a significant commitment of time and resources by an organization to evaluate social media measurements, and that commitment demands a financial investment that some organizations are unwilling or unable to make. Third, social media measurement is still in the experimental stage, meaning that sometimes marketers lack the necessary methodologies and tools to identify "the connections between social media activity metrics and business outcomes."[62]

Only by establishing the relationship between social media metrics and business goals can marketers properly evaluate the impact and value (including but not limited to ROI) of social media marketing initiatives.[63] The aim of an appropriately focused evaluation, therefore, is to produce a thorough description of the progress of social media marketing activities over time in order to reveal where strategies have succeeded or nose-dived, along with how things went right or wrong and why. Accordingly, "[such analysis] allows the program team to see where it must focus its efforts and resources next. It identifies success and failure, opportunities and risks, potential improvements, and new courses of action."[64]

CASE STUDY

Pfizer Tracks and Measures Adverse Drug Effects with BuzzMetrics[*]

Introduction

[The Nielsen Company is a] global information and media company whose BuzzMetrics solution enables clients to make informed business decisions regarding their Internet, digital and marketing strategies. [Pfizer, Inc., is one] of the world's leading pharmaceutical companies—at the cutting-edge of the research and development of medicines for humans and animals. [Together, the two companies found a way to monitor consumer opinion and sentiment on the social web after negative press about possible side effects of Pfizer's Varenicline drug, a prescription pill designed to help smokers stop smoking.]

Champix

© iStockphoto/Thinkstock RF

History

[In 1849 cousins Charles Pfizer and Charles Erhart founded the Pfizer pharmaceutical company, which has been steadfastly dedicated to "discovering and developing new, and better, ways to prevent and treat disease and improve health and well-being for people around the world."[65]

---

*From Ammerman, Erika, and Little, Brad (2009), "case study: *Pfizer's Champix Brand*," Nielsen Company. Retrieved July 6, 2011, from http://blog.nielsen.com/nielsenwire/wp-content/uploads/2009/07/nielsen_case_study_buzzmetrics_and_pfizer.pdf

Chantix (Varenicline) is a trademark drug of Pfizer, which was approved by the FDA in May 2006.[66] In September 2006 Varenicline was approved for sale in the European Union under the trade name Champix.[67]

In March 2010 "[a]ccording to a report in the *Vancouver Sun*, three Canadian women . . . filed a class action law suit against Pfizer, Inc., the maker of the stop-smoking drug Champix (brand name Chantix in the U.S.), claiming that it causes depression and suicidality."[68]

Challenge ···

- Pfizer was concerned that media coverage of negative side effects allegedly associated with their smoking cessation product—Champix—were seriously undermining confidence in the brand

- Pfizer knew that online consumer generated media (CGM) was a potentially rich source of unprompted patient insight on the true health of the brand

- However, regulations unique to the prescription healthcare industry legally require pharmaceutical companies to "make every effort" to follow up all "Adverse Events" (AEs)—consumer experiences not intended by the drug or its usage—by notifying the Drug Safety Group (DSG) within 24 hours and following up with the patient to gain further details on the experience

- It was feared that spontaneous consumer feedback might contain high rates of AEs as consumers candidly, and sometimes anonymously, share their experiences online

- Consequently, adverse event reporting regulations have resource implications that effectively prohibit pharmaceutical companies from conducting and benefitting from CGM research. Additionally, the spontaneous and honest nature of CGM could be undermined if individuals receive unwanted contact from researchers.

Strategy ···

- Pfizer approached The Nielsen Company about how their BuzzMetrics solution could mine CGM as a rich source of patient insight without compromising European healthcare laws or research quality

- Nielsen worked with Pfizer's brand and market research teams, the Drug Safety Group and legal teams to establish a methodology that enabled Pfizer to monitor CGM and, consequently, improve their strategy, consumer insights and other critical parts of the business

- It was a simple piece of innovation in this area that allowed us to conduct a successful project, utilizing this new data source:

  1. Nielsen analysts were trained in the identification and reporting of AEs. Nielsen and the Pfizer teams determined a threshold number of AE reports that the DSG could deal with reasonably without being overloaded with additional work

  2. When the threshold number of AE reports were identified by Nielsen, all available patient information was forwarded to the DSG for follow-up, and the research halted

  3. Once all AEs had been processed by the DSG, the research resumed. This allowed Nielsen to be removed from patient outreach, and for the DSG to deal with the more manageable number of AE reports each time

Results

1. The research resulted in an immediate ROI by demonstrating that a potentially expensive marketing program wasn't necessary—consumer opinion and sentiment remained positive towards the Champix brand despite the negative press reports:

   "During the first 2–3 weeks, every time I took my tablets I felt sick, but this soon subsided....I would and have recommended them" Netdoctor.co.uk, 19 December 2007

   "decided that for the new yr i was going to give them up...i started champix and i am now on my 11 day but i am still smoking but i have cut down a lo, so far i feel good have a slight headache in the afternoon when i take my 2nd tab and i also get v tired too ,but to me it is still manageable just to get me through this..." Netdoctor.co.uk, 26 January 2008

2. The project broke down a company barrier to the use of such research—through the simple means of creating a flexible and sympathetic research process. The "template" can be used across other Pfizer brands and countries

3. One major website was identified that attracted a lot of smoking cessation chat that was ripe for further listening and unbranded patient support advertising

4. The project has brought new light to the ongoing understanding of ALL areas of drug products and uses—a new goldmine for Pfizer to help improve their strategy, marketing, consumer insights and many other critical parts of the business

The Client Perspective

"Apart from the obvious relevance for our brand, the general value to the pharmaceutical industry of understanding consumers' opinions of prescription medicines is evident for all to see. The research offered us the opportunity to understand what consumers were hearing about our brand, how this was being interpreted, and what impression of the brand was being created on-line for potential future users. Its most obvious business impact was that a potentially expensive marketing program was demonstrated not to be necessary." Michael Goff, Business Intelligence Manager, Pfizer U.K.

Furthermore, Pfizer was so happy with the work that they asked us to collaborate in submitting the partnership to the British Healthcare Business Intelligence Association's BOBI awards....

The Recognition

Nielsen received the award for "Most Innovative Approach" from the British Healthcare Business Intelligence Association for creating a bespoke research methodology commended for its business impact, cost effectiveness and novelty. The BOBI judging panel commented: "This was a unanimous and clear winner. Overall, we felt it was a smart, innovative, cost effective piece of research which demonstrated the business impact and could be used elsewhere in the business. It demonstrated innovation in two ways:

- Overcoming internal challenges to the research, which are faced on a regular basis and delivering a pragmatic, practical solution
- Learning from the consumer by using an emerging methodology to monitor online consumer discussions (Consumer-Generated Media)"

Selecting Social Media Monitoring Tools

In May 2011 there were 213 paid and free social media monitoring tools available.[69] As the number of tools for monitoring social media rapidly grows, so does the challenge in understanding which ones are most appropriate for an organization to use. In large part this dilemma can be resolved by determining which metrics to measure, which social media platforms to cover, and which price range an organization can afford.

As explained in the measurement section above, well-defined marketing goals should drive the decision regarding which social media metrics to measure and hence the selection of the most appropriate monitoring tool. This need is borne out by a 2011 study, which found that the number-one factor affecting a marketer's choice of a social media monitoring tool was what metrics it offers (ease of use and pricing were also considerations).[70]

Free monitoring tools, such as Google Alerts, SocialMention, and CoTweet, are suitable for listening to social media (i.e., observing what people are saying about a brand). However, these free tools tend to provide a flood of information that can quickly overwhelm the user. If marketers want to measure the impact of social media marketing efforts on a brand, they can use moderately priced monitoring services, such as Viral Heat, as shown in Table 14.3.[71] As the table indicates, if marketers want to listen, measure,

---

Nielsen Buzzmetrics—Pricing is $40,000/year.
Benefit: All reporting done by Nielsen Online
Pros: Total hands-off tool
Cons: Very costly service
Features/Notes: Quarterly or monthly reports. It specializes in engagement, measuring, and analyzing consumer-generated media (CGM). It offers a suite of products to measure CGM and online word-of-mouth to help companies understand and track consumer buzz, including opinions, preferences, reputation, image, issues, and up-and-coming trends.

Radian6—Price starts at $500/month.
Benefit: Industry leader
Pros: Innovative technologies and support team
Cons: Best suited for medium- to large-sized brands and businesses
Features/Notes: Offers the most complete platform to listen, measure, and engage. Customers can track and engage in ongoing conversations taking place on blogs, videos, forums, social networks, and mainstream news sites. Radian6 is currently helping over 10,000 brands track social media sites, including Comcast, MTV, Dell, UPS, GE, and Microsoft.

Sentiment Metrics—Pricing is based on the number of concurrent search terms and users.
Benefit: Offers various levels of monitoring services
Pros: Produces easy-to-understand graphs with a top-line analysis of message delivery and lead topics
Cons: Relatively new company located in Australia
Features/Notes: Comprehensive analysis providing sentiment, influencer, and demographic information that enables targeted marketing activities. Powerful engagement and work flow features allow clients to respond to questions and comments on the social web directly from the system.

Table 14.3 Review of Seven Top Social Media Monitoring Services, as of September 10, 2010

© The Phelps Group

Social Mention—Pricing is free.
Benefit: Allows for basic tracking and measurement of any term in social media in real time
Pros: Free
Cons: It is only a report so that engagement will have to be done manually, and nonrelevant items may be included in the results.
Features/Notes: Daily email activity report, basic analysis, and ability to generate Excel report from data. It is like Google Alerts but for social media, and it is a good top-line tool for tracking key terms in social media.

Viral Heat—Pricing is tiered three ways and ranges from basic, at $9.99 a month, to business, at $89.99 a month.
Benefit: Cost for features
Pros: Good combination of low cost and moderate monitoring/measurement/sentiment features
Cons: All hands-on so setup, tracking, measurement, and results will need to be done manually
Features/Notes: Moderate monitoring, measurement, sentiment features; can set up "profiles" to contain many advanced search terms; can identify key influencers by volume and impact. It is currently considered one of the best entry-level, paid social media monitoring tools for people who want moderate analysis and features and don't want to pay top dollar.

Scout Labs—Pricing is tiered and begins at $249 a month.
Benefit: Advanced features and team collaboration
Pros: Manipulation of great amounts of data; team collaboration allows for work flow assigning, and tracking
Cons: Difficult to use for those not familiar with social media monitoring tools; not the best solution for one person monitoring
Features/Notes: Advanced monitoring, measurement, sentiment, reporting, and team collaboration. It is a great social media monitoring tool for teams that need advanced features, work-flow capabilities, and easy reporting.

HootSuite—Pricing is tiered and ranges from free to $99.99 a month.
Benefit: Allows for engagement and monitoring directly within one platform
Pros: Amount of engagement and monitoring features
Cons: Interface is cumbersome due to engagement and monitoring features being fitted within one window; not a good solution for those just wishing to track social media
Features/Notes: Fully customizable; ability for work flow; ability to post to multiple sites. Although it has a lot of different features, they are limited in ability, crammed, and often difficult to navigate. It is geared more toward people looking to manage a social identity as opposed to a brand.

Table 14.3 *(continued)*

and engage the social web using a single monitoring platform, they will need to turn to higher-priced services, such as Nielsen Buzzmetrics and Radian6. Despite the advantages of the pricier platforms, the majority of marketing professionals (54.7%) spend less than $100 a month on social media monitoring tools, with 19.7% spending $100 to $500 per month, 19% shelling out $500 to $5,000 a month, 4.4% spending $5,000 to $10,000, and just 2.2% spending $10,000 or more per month.[72]

It is worth noting that marketers have expressed frustrations with both free and paid monitoring tools, noting an "excessive lag time and [failure] to provide reliable, accurate data," an excessive number of bugs and confusing user interfaces, a lack of tool innovation, and an unjustifiably high prices."[73] Fortunately, tool vendors continue to improve their offerings, and regardless of the frustration with the current batch of tools, marketers continue to rely on them to measure performance, as well as using them to justify expenditures on social media marketing activities.

Using Radian6, AAA Monitors and Interacts with the Social Web

Introduction

In 2009 AAA, formerly known as the American Automobile Association, became aware that its customers were complaining about the organization on social media sites instead of contacting its customer support services. The organization turned to Radian6, a maker of a popular social media listening platform, to help find and respond to customers complaints on the social web.

History

AAA (pronounced "triple A") is a not-for-profit organization, primarily known for its emergency roadside services, maps, and other travel amenities. It was launched in 1902 by nine motor clubs with fewer than 1,500 members. By July 2010, AAA was North America's largest motoring and leisure travel organization, with 51 million members in the United States and Canada.[74] AAA provides travel and automotive services as well as insurance and discounts. The organization's headquarters is located in Heathrow, Florida.

Founded in 2006, Radian6 provides a social media monitoring platform designed to help companies listen to and participate in the social web by identifying what is being said online about their brands, industries, and competitors: "The company's flexible dashboard enables monitoring all forms of social media with results appearing in real-time as discovered. Various analysis widgets give users the ability to uncover the top influencers as well as which conversations are having an impact online."[75]

Challenge

In 2009, AAA was confronted with the fact that new generations of customers were using the social web to discuss and criticize the organization. It wanted to provide the best customer service possible, so the challenge was to find a way to effectively locate these comments and conversations on the social web and then respond to them. AAA was also acutely aware that member concerns could rapidly go viral on the social web. Hence the organization needed the means to track the pace of negative comments so that it could catch and resolve potentially brand-damaging situations early on before they snowballed into public relations nightmares.

Strategy**

To satisfy its particular needs, AAA choose Radian6. This social media monitor software provided AAA with the ability to track what was being said about the AAA brand, industry, and competitors in real time, as well as the ability to identify the

---

**The quotations from this section taken from "AAA Rolls Out Radian6 to Monitor and Listen in Social Media" (2009, January 9), press release, Radian6. Retrieved July 10, 2011, from http://www.radian6.com/blog/2009/01/aaa-rolls-out-radian6-to-monitor-and-listen-in-social-media/ Reprinted with permission.

content that caused the greatest chatter about the organization. Moreover, Radian6 nicely integrated with the AAA's existing customer relation management (CRM) software and web analytical tools to give AAA an overall view of "website activity and performance through the lens of social media."[76]

"Social media provides AAA members and consumers with a powerful opportunity to make their opinions and experiences known. We are actively engaged in listening and responding to those on the Web who are talking about AAA," explains Janie Graziani, AAA's manager of new media and technology. "To do this better, AAA is using Radian6 to provide insight into who is talking and what kind of impact they are having in their online communities. In addition, AAA is able to track issues of interest to members, such as transportation infrastructure and senior mobility, and become involved in conversations which, logically, AAA should be providing information about."

"The fast moving nature of the web means that conversations about a company can get fractured and splintered across several channels. For example, a brand mention may start on a forum, and carry to a blog, then to Twitter," says Radian6's CEO Marcel LeBrun. "With Radian6, companies can better connect the dots online between these points of dialogue. Not only can they get a holistic view of how the conversation unfolds, but they can choose appropriate places to engage with their customers and provide a valuable connection with the brand."

The Radian6 software also allows users to focus their analysis and results on a specific set of sites or sources on the web or to exclude specific sources as needed. These capabilities allow companies to home in on targeted results for a particular issue or topic that's highly relevant to their community.

"Radian6 helps us discover which social media, such as comments, social bookmarks and on-topic inbound links, are working together to create influence," continues Graziani. "By learning who is leading the discussion in our industries, AAA can create more effective and efficient outreach efforts by focusing resources in those areas where they are most likely to have the greatest impact."

Results

With Radian6 in place, AAA soon began responding to a wide variety of comments on the social web, ranging from inquiries about roadside assistance to broken web site links. Consequently, "[o]f the 8,500 social media mentions the company generates per month, AAA responds to between 100 and 200 of those."[77] Complaints that cannot be handled in an expeditious manner are passed over to customer support for rapid response. However, the greatest value add for AAA has been the realization that listening to the social web is really an expansion of the role of public relations within the organization "because issues that have the potential to flare up on blogs and in chat rooms are addressed more quickly."[78]

© Radian6, a division of salesforce.com Canada

Radian6 Engagement Console provides an overview of the complete social web or filters by media type allowing a user to keep an eye on a company's most important social channels. It also has the ability to search and filter by keyword, thus enabling the user to locate relevant conversations happening in real time.

The Future of Social Media Monitoring

Without doubt the rapid pace of advances in social media monitoring techniques, metrics, and tools will continue into the foreseeable future. Increasingly useful and sophisticated metrics will reveal additional information about the performance of social media strategies in attaining marketing goals.

Beyond these obvious forthcoming developments, the evolution of the Internet into a social web has some interesting implications. As connections between people, posts, comments, discussions, articles, and reviews expand exponentially, these linkages capture untold information, which can be mined for valuable marketing insights.[79] **Data mining** is the process of automatically sifting through large amounts of data to reveal trends, patterns, and relationships in order to detect useful information.[80] Data mining the vast interconnections and content on the social web can uncover unique and valuable patterns about brands.[81] As Ashley Friedlei, CEO of eConsultancy, puts it, "[d]ata is the new oil—let's work on refining it."[82]

Lastly, improvements in natural language processing and the "Semantic Web" promise to deliver even more powerful ways to monitor the social web. The **Semantic Web** is a common framework that facilitates machine interpretation of the meaning of language.[83] Social media monitoring tools stand to gain much from incorporating advances in the Semantic Web to enhance analytics for brands.[84]

EXERCISE CASE STUDY

SAS Social Media Analytics: Monitoring a Brand with a Brand

Introduction ....

On November 7, 2010, KDPaine & Partners, a leading public relations and social media measurement firm, and SAS, the leader in business analytics software and services and the largest independent vendor in the business intelligence market, won the prestigious New Communications Award of Excellence for their breakthrough work in social media research.[85]

According to KDPaine, "SAS and [KDPaine & Partners] won the award in the Social Data Measurement/Measurement Innovation Division for their work transitioning traditional PR measurement into an integrated, consistent and comprehensive communications measurement program....The research program gathered information from thousands of traditional and social media outlets, including YouTube, Facebook, social bookmarking sites, as well as internal and external blogs. Each item was analyzed to determine the nature of the conversation, content of the posting, engagement level, and how the author positioned the company."[86]

History ....

SAS is the leader in business analytics software and services and the largest independent vendor in the business intelligence market. Through innovative solutions, SAS helps customers at more than 50,000 sites improve performance and deliver value by making better decisions faster. Since 1976 SAS has been giving customers around the world The Power to Know®.[87]

Challenge* ....

As a leading provider of business analytics solutions to organizations worldwide, SAS has long understood and valued the role that media, traditional as well as social, plays in the sales cycle. For more than a decade SAS has monitored and measured its competitive position in the media. With the rapid rise in influence of social media in the last two years, it became clear that the measurement and metrics program needed to be expanded to include social conversations. It was also clear that social media offered an entirely new opportunity to measure the success or failure of communications efforts through correlations with web activity. The challenge was how to accurately reflect and report on SAS' results in order to provide data on which to make better decisions. And specifically, would the metrics be able to be used to better understand what worked and didn't work around the launch of SAS' own SAS® Social Media Analytics product in April at their annual SAS Global Forum international user conference.

Issues To Be Addressed

The fundamental goal for SAS was to create a reliable, accurate and useful set of metrics that would help marketing, PR and communications professionals make better decisions. The metrics had to meet a rigid set of requirements including;

1. Accuracy of data—without management's trust in the data, the reports wouldn't be valuable. This was complicated by SAS' very name, given social media's predilection for abbreviation. One SAS employee has collected more than 400 unrelated "SAS" acronyms via Google alerts alone.

2. Timeliness of data—social media has increased the speed of mass communication, and thus demands reduced response times and quicker decision making. Not only did the data have to be available 24/7/365, but it also needed to be processed—read and coded—in record time if it was going to be effectively used to shape strategy.

3. Context and clarity—SAS didn't just need numbers; they needed to understand why the numbers came to be what they were. They needed to understand the competitive environment in which they were operating, and they needed to quickly understand what the data meant.

Define the Target Audience

The SAS PR team's traditional target audience has been IT decision makers—CEOs, CIOs, CFOs and senior executives in marketing and operations—in Fortune 1000 companies. But with its new SAS® Social Media Analytics—a SAS Solutions

*From "SAS with KDPaine & Partners" (2010), © Society for New Communications Research. Reprinted with permission.

OnDemand offering—the audience instantly became much broader. Any organization that needed to better understand its social media program—including employees at various levels within PR and advertising agencies, consumer package goods, services companies, retailers, and financial services firms across the board—essentially anyone working with customers was now part of their target audience.

Strategy ....

Goals and Objectives

With the above concerns in mind, SAS, in conjunction with KDPaine & Partners, designed a research program. The following major goals were decided upon:

1. Provide ongoing, accurate and timely data to help SAS make better decisions regarding the direction of external communication activities.

2. Correlate the data with online activity to determine levels of engagement and outcomes from specific programs

3. Advise the social media team on what it should or should not be doing in social media: What changes should it make to its present programs? What new programs should it add?

4. Set benchmarks against which future programs could be judged.

The Plan

Step 1: Data Collection
The first step in helping SAS achieve its goal of understanding social media was to standardize collection techniques for SAS and its competitors. The biggest challenge was simply getting relevant data. So much of the social media conversation happens in 140 characters; SAS can easily become an abbreviation for everything from Surfers against Sewage to Second Avenue Subway. While automation and exclusion tables helped, they posed a challenge as well: set your exclusionary tables too strictly and you miss relevant information. Set them too broadly and you drown in data. It was decided to observe and explore a predefined range of social media channels for SAS and its competitors, and then define a list of the top 100 channels or sites that would be read in depth. Typical patterns of traffic and usage could then be determined and used as a starting point for understanding where the institutions stood with respect to this new media.

Step 2: Standardizing Qualitative Data
As with any content analysis project, [KDPaine & SAS] also needed to establish standardized definitions of tone, positioning, and visibility. By establishing these metrics SAS would be able to see just how it and its peer institutions were being mentioned in social media, as well as measure how many people are potentially seeing these messages, whether good or bad.

Step 3: Establishing Benchmarks
The fourth and final step of developing SAS' plan included integrating web analytics data into the program to determine which programs were most successful at driving engagement and subsequent action.

The Deployment

Collection techniques were developed by testing and finalizing a master list of search terms that included all possible mentions of SAS and its peer competitive set. After experimenting with a number of different collection techniques, we selected Boardreader and eNR as the most comprehensive solution. We created a detailed set of coding and collection instructions that were approved internally at SAS. Next we collected data from traditional media and social media sources including: blogs, social bookmarking sites (e.g., Digg, Reddit, Farg, Newsvine), forums/message boards, micro-blogs (e.g., Twitter), photo sharing sites (e.g., Flickr), social networking sites (e.g., Facebook, Myspace, etc.) and video sharing sites (e.g., YouTube, Google Video, etc.). The third step of our plan involved standardizing and defining qualitative data for coding purposes. We wanted to define tone so we could know not just what people were saying about the organizations, but how they were saying it. We defined tone as follows:

- Positive—After reading the article, you are more likely to invest in, do business with, or work for the company.
- Neutral—The article either provides statements of fact (e.g., "xyz occurred"), doesn't give you enough information to feel either way, or it gives information that is both positive and negative, with neither side more convincing than the other.
- Negative—After reading the article, you are less likely to invest in, do business with, or work for the company.

In addition to tonality, we also characterized each item as either high visibility or low visibility depending upon where in the item the brand was mentioned. Tracking this metric would allow SAS to combine what people are saying, how they are saying it, and the likelihood of these mentions being read or seen by others. The idea behind this is that the more prominent a brand mention is in an item, the greater likelihood of a reader/viewer seeing and remembering it.

Additionally, we identified how each item positioned SAS and/or its competitors in relation to the industry or its place among competitors. Was it leading in the industry? Was it taking charge in a new initiative? Was it doing something that others have already done? We defined positioning as follows:

- Follower—The company was said to be following an industry trend, or taking actions already taken by its competitors.
- Laggard—The company was said to have failed to take an action that others have, and that has shown to be beneficial.
- Leader—The company was said to be a leader in its industry, or the first to take an action or make a business decision that may prove to be beneficial.
- No Positioning—The content does not discuss the company's position within the market, and does not compare it to its competitors.

We further identified what companies were mentioned, who authored the item and when, which spokespersons were quoted, what subjects were discussed, which business lines/industries were mentioned and how each item positioned SAS and/or its competitors on key issues. The selection of competitors to be tracked was made based on organizations SAS felt were their peers in specific marketplaces or competitors for particular offerings. Competitors were classified by one of two company types.

- List "A" included companies that only offer business analytics software and all mentions of the companies included in List "A" were analyzed.

- List "B" is comprised of companies that make business analytics software, but also sell data warehousing products, servers, operating systems or other types of software and/or hardware. Mentions of the companies included in List "B" were only analyzed when those mentions were specifically tied to their business analytics/business intelligence products as well as other products comparable to SAS to ensure an accurate competitive set.

Challenges and Obstacles

Establishing consistent collection methodologies was a challenge, particularly with Facebook and Social Bookmarking items. To deliver SAS with relevant findings, as well as methods that would be usable over time, we spent many hours developing coding categories for what we would track from media, such as Facebook and Social Bookmarking. Recording activity on these sites wasn't merely recording stories and related comments, such as in a typical blog. We had to understand and define entirely new terms such as walls, discussion threads, tags, and discussion boards, among others. Certain media types have different names for the same things (followers vs. friends vs. connections) while others offer options that are exclusive to that media type ("likes" on Facebook). Recognizing, grouping, and defining all of these metrics provided a large obstacle that was overcome through constant research and developing and testing definitions, categories, and coding results. Another obstacle was simply handling the large amounts of mentions found for each company. Social media has been gaining more and more popularity in recent years, which means working with thousands of mentions in various media. To overcome this issue we used a hybrid coding methodology inside our dashboard which allowed us to organize mass amounts of data and conduct data analysis across all variables.

Results ....

With an ongoing view of SAS volume of mentions, spikes generated by product launches and coverage specifically of product launches, events, etc. becomes a telling metric by which SAS can estimate where, when, why and how its specific messages or news of certain products can be found in traditional and social media. SAS introduced a new business offering, SAS® Social Media Analytics, in April, 2010. Figure 14.1 shows the volume of SAS Social Media Analytics mentions across all media in the months immediately before, during and after the official launch date.

Figure 14.2 shows where the mentions occurred, emphasizing what media channel was most often responsible for the April, 2010 volume spike associated with the product launch. Because SAS Social media Analytics is tailored specifically to the Social Media realm, visibility of the product IN social Media was essential. As Figure 14.2 demonstrates, news in Mainstream media outlets accounted for just 2% of all mentions of the launch. A whopping 90% of relevant mentions occurred on Twitter amongst a fairly savvy group of Social Media enthusiasts. The remaining 8% of all SAS Social Media Analytics mentions occurred on additional Social Media channels.

SAS considers its positioning among its competitors in the media to be an indicator of success. It strives to not just have more mentions, but values quality over quantity. For them, success sometimes means more positive mentions and

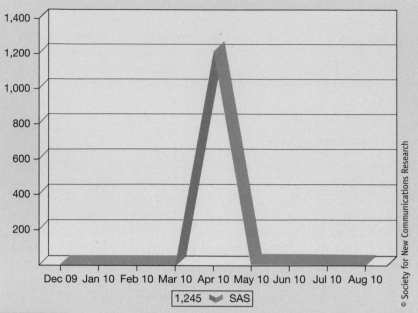

Figure 14.1

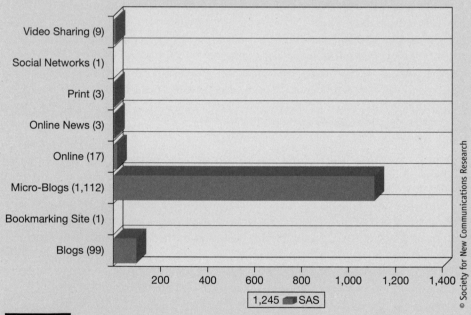

Figure 14.2

fewer negative mentions than its competitors; a larger share of positive coverage over time is often more important than earning the leading share of all coverage over time. Testing demonstrated that the sentiment of SAS mentions in comparison to its competitors was superior in terms of overall volume and positive mentions.

How do these test results specifically map to the objective(s) stated above?

Research Goal #1

Provide accurate and timely data to help SAS make better decisions. SAS now has a dashboard that it can access 24/7/365 to instantly get answers to its questions. Three members of the SAS team use it on a regular basis and as many as eight occasionally. They are able to monitor mentions of SAS as well as individual product lines specific to individual teams/departments within SAS communications. Team members can generate reports with the click of a button to share internally.

Research Goal #2

Correlate the data with online activity to determine levels of engagement and outcomes from specific programs SAS [and include] the ability to correlate online activity with media volume and the total opportunities to [display] SAS and/or a specific program or product line. By examining relationships between web analytics and media presence, SAS can demonstrate a link between the two in real time.

Research Goal #3

Advise SAS communicators on what they should or should not be doing in social media: What changes should they make to present programs, and/or what new programs should they add? The KDPaine team regularly dives into the SAS data, keeping a pulse on what is happening and continually looking for trends and changes occurring over time. The team is also acutely aware of many other trends within the technology industry, giving them an advantage when advising SAS on how to enhance their social media program. Regular consulting with the KDPaine team, as well as a data set that speaks for itself, gives SAS the information and drive to continually improve strategies and easily recognize success.

Research Goal #4

Set benchmarks against which future programs could be judged. KDPaine has been monitoring and measuring SAS mentions since 2004. With more than six years of data collected and analyzed in its dashboard, SAS has established an unlimited number of benchmarks for itself. Not only does SAS know at a glance where it stands in terms of media coverage amongst its competitors, it knows where it stands relative to yesterday, last year and five years ago. Every product launch, press release, special announcement, act of philanthropy over the last six years has been recorded. So, the media effects of every product launch, press release, special announcement and act of philanthropy can be measured against those recorded previously. Spikes in coverage over time are accounted for, whether they were the result of the inclusion of and gradual explosion in Twitter conversations or something that SAS did, like its SAS Social Media Analytics launch.

Notes

1. "Turning Conversations into Insights: A Comparison of Social Media Monitoring Tools" (2010, May 14), white paper, FreshMinds Research. Retrieved September 28, 2011, from http://shared.freshminds.co.uk/smm10/whitepaper.pdf
2. Naslund, Amber (2010, January 13), "5 Steps to a Better Social Media Monitoring Plan," Radian6 Blog, retrieved July 25, 2011, from http://www.radian6.com/blog/2010/01/5-steps-to-a-better-social-media-monitoring-plan/; Melin, Eric (2011, July 18), "Define and Refine: 5 Steps to Build Better Searches," *Spiral16 Blog*, MetricsMan, retrieved July 25, 2011, from http://www.spiral16.com/blog/2011/07/define-and-refine-5-steps-to-build-better-searches-2/; and Barker, Donald I., Melissa S. Barker, and Catherine T. Pinard (2013), Unit D, *Internet Research—Illustrated*, 6th ed. (Boston, MA: Cengage Learning), pp. 1–23.
3. Stelzner, Michael (2009, October 20), "Is Social Media Marketing Measurable? The Big Debate," Social Media Examiner. Retrieved July 28, 2011, from http://www.socialmediaexaminer.com/is-social-media-marketing-measurable-the-big-debate/
4. Wasserman, Todd (2011, March 31), "How the Pros Measure Social Media Marketing Success," Mashable. Retrieved July 25, 2011, from http://mashable.com/2011/03/31/measure-social-media-roi/
5. Third European Measurement Summit (2011, June 8–11), International Association for the Measurement and Evaluation of Communication. Retrieved July 26, 2011, from http://www.regonline.co.uk/builder/site/Default.aspx?EventID=921595
6. Watson, Tom (2011, June 8), "Social Media Metrics—Standards or Ritual Measurement?" DummySpit. Retrieved July 25, 2011, from http://dummyspit.wordpress.com/2011/06/08/social-media-metrics-%E2%80%93-standards-or-ritual-measurement/
7. Stelzner, Michael (2011, April), *2011 Social Media Marketing Industry Report: How Marketers Are Using Social Media to Grow Their Businesses*, Social Media Examiner. Retrieved July 28, 2011, from http://www.socialmediaexaminer.com/SocialMediaMarketingReport2011.pdf
8. *The State of Social Media for Business: Select Themes for 2010* (2010, June), SmartBrief and Summus. Retrieved August 3, 2011, from http://kevin.lexblog.com/uploads/file/SB-SocialMediaForBusiness-SelectThemes2010-3Nov10.pdf
9. Sterne, Jim (2010), *Social Media Metrics: How to Measure and Optimize Your Marketing Investment* (Hoboken, NJ: John Wiley), p. 2.
10. Li, Charlene, and Josh Bernoff (2008), *Groundswell: Winning in a World Transformed by Social Technologies*. (Boston, MA: Harvard Business Press), pp. 82, 126.
11. Blanchard, Olivier (2011, May 31), "The Basics of Social Media Measurement for Business," *BrandBuilder Blog*. Retrieved July 26, 2011, from http://thebrandbuilder.wordpress.com/2011/05/31/the-basics-of-social-media-measurement-for-business/

12. "Key Performance Indicators (KPI)" (n.d.), *BusinessDictionary*. Retrieved July 29, 2011, from http://www.businessdictionary.com/definition/key-performance-indicators-KPI.html

13. "Social Media Analytics. Simplified!" (2011, April 11), SocialF5. Retrieved July 29, 2011, from http://www.socialf5.com/blog/2011/04/social-media-analytics-simplified/

14. Ibid.

15. Reh, John (n.d.), "Key Performance Indicators (KPI): How an Organization Defines and Measures Progress toward Its Goals," About.com. Retrieved July 29, 2011, from http://management.about.com/cs/generalmanagement/a/keyperfindic.htm

16. Chaney, Paul (2011, July 12), "How to Measure Social Media Marketing; 3 Steps," Practical eCommerce. Retrieved July 25, 2011, from http://www.practicalecommerce.com/articles/2902-How-to-Measure-Social-Media-Marketing-3-Steps

17. Reid, Alexandra (2011, July 6), "Measuring Social Media: A Step-by-step Guide for Newbies," Francis Morgan. Retrieved July 30, 2011, from http://francis-moran.com/index.php/tag/qualitative-social-media/

18. Paine, Katie Delahaye (2011), *Measure What Matters* (Hoboken, NJ: John Wiley), pp. 34–35.

19. Kallas, Priit (n.d.), "48 Social Media KPIs (Key Performance Indicators)," DreamGrow Social Media. Retrieved July 29, 2011, from http://www.dreamgrow.com/48-social-media-kpis-key-performance-indicators/

20. Ibid.

21. Reid, Alexandra (2011, July 6), "Measuring Social Media: A Step-by-step Guide for Newbies," Francis Morgan. Retrieved July 30, 2011, from http://francis-moran.com/index.php/tag/qualitative-social-media/

22. Kallas, Priit (n.d.), "48 Social Media KPIs (Key Performance Indicators)," DreamGrow Social Media. Retrieved July 29, 2011, from http://www.dreamgrow.com/48-social-media-kpis-key-performance-indicators/

23. Ibid.

24. Reid, Alexandra (2011, July 6), "Measuring Social Media: A Step-by-step Guide for Newbies," Francis Morgan. Retrieved July 30, 2011, from http://francis-moran.com/index.php/tag/qualitative-social-media/

25. Jeffrey, Angela (2011, July 26), "Social Media Measurement: Are Global Standards Possible?" VMS Voice. Retrieved July 26, 2011, from http://vmsvoice.com/2011/07/social-media-measurement-are-global-standards-possible/

26. Ibid.

27. Jeffrey, Angela (2011, July 26), "Social Media Measurement: Are Global Standards Possible?" VMS Voice. Retrieved July 26, 2011, from http://vmsvoice.com/2011/07/social-media-measurement-are-global-standards-possible/

28. *Social Media Usage, Attitudes and Measurability: What Do Marketers Think?* (2010), King Fish Media, along with Hub Spot and Junta42. Retrieved July 30, 2011, from http://www.kingfishmedia.com/marketing-resources/research/social-media-usage-2010

29. Barker, Melissa (2010, July 27), "5 Steps to a Winning Social Media Marketing Plan," EzineArticles, retrieved July 30, 2011, from http://ezinearticles.com/?5-Steps-to-a-Winning-Social-Media-Marketing-Plan&id=4748691 and Joy, Kitin (2011, April 5), "Social Media Marketing—Validated, Time-Tested Ways to Grow Your Business," Social Media Marketing, retrieved July 25, 2011, from http://www.internetnewswire.com/socialmediamarketingcom-launches-page-free-social-media-marketing-ebook/22679

30. Stelzner, Michael (2009, October 20), "Is Social Media Marketing Measurable? The Big Debate," Social Media Examiner. Retrieved July 29, 2011, from http://www.socialmediaexaminer.com/is-social-media-marketing-measurable-the-big-debate/

31. Ibid.

32. Hibbard, Casey (2009, November 12), "It Pays to Listen: Avaya's $250K Twitter Sale," Social Media Examiner. Retrieved July 30, 2011, from http://www.socialmediaexaminer.com/it-pays-to-listen-avayas-250k-twitter-sale/

33. Giri, Radha (2011, April 13), "Social Media ROI—Measuring the Quantitative and Qualitative Results," *Radha Giri's Blog*. Retrieved July 25, 2011, from http://radhagiri.blogspot.com/2011/04/social-media-roi-measuring-quantitative.htm

34. Murdough, Chris (2009, Fall), "Social Media Measurement: It's Not Impossible," *Journal of Interactive Advertising*, vol. 10, no 1. Retrieved July 30, 2011, from http://jiad.org/article127

35. *Social Media Usage, Attitudes and Measurability: What do Marketers Think?* (2010), King Fish Media, along with Hub Spot and Junta42. Retrieved July 30, 2011, from http://www.kingfishmedia.com/marketing-resources/research/social-media-usage-2010

36. *The State of Social Media for Business: Select Themes for 2010* (2010, June), SmartBrief and Summus. Retrieved August 3, 2011, from http://kevin.lexblog.com/uploads/file/SB-SocialMediaForBusiness-SelectThemes2010-3Nov10.pdf

37. Bailey, Chris (2010, March 7), "Adding Qualitative to Your Social Media Measurement Mix," Bailey Work Play. Retrieved July 28, 2011, from http://www.baileyworkplay.com/2010/03/adding-qualitative-to-your-social-media-measurement-mix/

38. Ibid.

39. Murdough, Chris (2009, Fall), "Social Media Measurement: It's Not Impossible," *Journal of Interactive Advertising*, vol. 10, no 1. Retrieved July 30, 2011, from http://jiad.org/article127

40. Wright, Alex (2009, August 23), "Mining the Web for Feelings, Not Facts," *New York Times*. Retrieved August 30, 2011, from http://www.nytimes.com/2009/08/24/technology/internet/24emotion.html

41. "Sentiment Analysis" (n.d.), *Wikipedia*. Retrieved August 30, 2011, from http://en.wikipedia.org/wiki/Sentiment_analysis

42. Ibid.

43. Chaney, Paul (2011, July 12), "How to Measure Social Media Marketing; 3 Steps," Practical eCommerce. Retrieved July 28, 2011, from http://www.practicalecommerce.com/articles/2902-How-to-Measure-Social-Media-Marketing-3-Steps

44. Gilliatt, Nathan (2010, March 12), "Sentiment Analysis Is Not a Mood Ring," Net-Savvy Executive. Retrieved July 25, 2011, from http://net-savvy.com/executive/measurement/sentiment-analysis-is-not-a-mood-ring.html?utm_source=feedburner&utm_medium=feed&utm_campaign=Feed%3A+net-savvy+%28The+Net-Savvy+Executive%29

45. Ibid.

46. Giri, Radha (2011, April 13), "Social Media ROI—Measuring the Quantitative and Qualitative Results," *Radha Giri's Blog*. Retrieved July 25, 2011, from http://radhagiri.blogspot.com/2011/04/social-media-roi-measuring-quantitative.htm

47. "Net Promoter Score" (2010), REX: Process Excellent Network. Retrieved July 28, 2011, from http://www.processexcellencenetwork.com/glossary/net-promoter-score/

48. "How to Calculate Your Score" (n.d.), Net Promoter. Retrieved July 28, 2011, from http://www.netpromoter.com/np/calculate.jsp

49. Ibid.

50. "Net Promoter Score" (n.d.), *Wikipedia*. Retrieved July 31, 2011, from http://en.wikipedia.org/wiki/Net_promoter_score

51. Schumchenia, Greg (2011, July 29), "6 Best Practices for Calculating Return on Social Media," Business 2 Community. Retrieved August 1, 2011, from http://www.business2community.com/social-media/6-best-practices-for-calculating-return-on-social-media-046772

52. "Understanding Reach and Frequency" (n.d.), Riger Knowledge Base. Retrieved July 25, 2011, from http://www.riger.com/know_base/media/understanding.html

53. Cohan, Pablo (2011, May 26), "Make Reach and Frequency Work for You," CreativeZone. Retrieved August 1, 2011, from http://creativezone.mediamind.com/Blog/index.php/2011/05/26/make-reach-and-frequency-work-for-you/

54. Pick, Tom (2010, August 23), "The Social Media ROI Debate," Social Media Today. Retrieved August 1, 2011, from http://socialmediatoday.com/index.php?q=tompick/167269/social-media-roi-debate

55. Satya (2011, April 18), "Measuring ROI in Social Media," *Blueliner Blog*, retrieved July 26, 2011, from http://www.bluelinerny.com/blog/measuring-roi-in-social-media.php and "Roots of Social Media Marketing Rise and Social Monitoring Provider Evaluation" (2010, July), presentation transcript, Forrester Research, SlideShare, retrieved July 26, 2011, from http://www.slideshare.net/SOCIALtality/roots-of-social-media-marketing-rise-and-social-monitoring-provider-evaluation-2906943

56. "Social Media Measurement 2011: Five Things to Forget and Five Things to Learn" (2010, December 30), Metricsman. Retrieved July 26, 2011, from http://metricsman.wordpress.

com/2010/12/30/social-media-measurement-2011-five-things-to-forget-and-five-things-to-learn/

57. Ibid.

58. Stamoulis, Nick (2011, May 6), "Can Social Media Marketing ROI Be Measured?" *Search Engine Optimization Journal*. Retrieved July 25, 2011, from http://www.searchengineoptimizationjournal.com/2011/05/06/social-media-roi/

59. Allen, Elizabeth (2009, November 17), "Measuring Success: Qualitative and Quantitative," *Adaptivate Blog*. Retrieved August 1, 2011, from http://adaptivateblog.com/2009/11/17/measuring-success-qualitative-and-quantitative/

60. Blanchard, Olivier (2011), *Social Media ROI: Managing and Measuring Social Media Efforts in Your Organization* (Boston, MA: Pearson Education), p. 196.

61. Blanchard, Olivier (2011, May 31), "The Basics of Social Media Measurement for Business," *Brand Builder Blog*. Retrieved August 2, 2011, from http://thebrandbuilder.wordpress.com/2011/05/31/the-basics-of-social-media-measurement-for-business/

62. Ibid.

63. Ibid.

64. Blanchard, Olivier (2011), *Social Media ROI: Managing and Measuring Social Media Efforts in Your Organization* (Boston, MA: Pearson Education), p. 196.

65. "Pfizer Inc: Evolving to Meet the Needs of a Changing Society" (n.d.), History, Pfizer. Retrieved July 9, 2011, from http://www.pfizer.com/about/history/history.jsp

66. "FDA Approves Novel Medication for Smoking Cessation" (2006, May 11), FDA. Retrieved July 9, 2011, from http://www.fda.gov/NewsEvents/Newsroom/PressAnnouncements/2006/ucm108651.htm

67. "Champix—The 'Quit Smoking' Prescription Drug" (n.d.), champixinfo. Retrieved July 9, 2011, from http://www.champixinfo.co.uk/

68. Schimelpfening, Nancy (2010, March 23), "Three Women File Suit against Maker of Stop-Smoking Drug," About.com. Retrieved July 9, 2011, from http://depression.about.com/b/2010/03/24/three-women-file-suit-against-maker-of-stop-smoking-drug.htm

69. "Social Media Monitoring Tools and Services" (2011, May), *Ideya Market Report*, 2nd ed. Retrieved August 1, 2011, from http://ideya.eu.com/images/SMMTools%20Excerpt%20FINAL25052011.pdf

70. Ryan, Erin (2011, April 21), "Social Media Monitoring Dissected (Infographic)," *Socialeyezer Blog*. Retrieved July 25, 2011, from http://share.flowtown.com/b31e4482d249f163/?web=c1a800&dst=http%3A//socialeyezer.com/2011/04/21/social-media-monitoring-dissected-infographic/

71. "We Review Seven Top Social Media Monitoring Services" (2010, September 10), *Phelps Groups Blog*. Retrieved August 1, 2011, from http://blog.thephelpsgroup.com/blogs/thephelpsgroup/archive/2010/09/10/we-review-seven-top-social-media-monitoring-services.aspx

72. Ryan, Erin (2011, April 21), "Social Media Monitoring Dissected (Infographic)," *Socialeyezer Blog*. Retrieved July 25, 2011, from http://share.flowtown.com/b31e4482d249f163/?web=c1a800&dst=http%3A//socialeyezer.com/2011/04/21/social-media-monitoring-dissected-infographic/

73. Ibid.

74. "AAA Fact Sheet" (2010, July 14), press release, aaanewsroom. Retrieved July 10, 2011, from http://aaanewsroom.net/Assets/Files/2010841440280.General_Facts_2010.doc

75. "Brand Ownership Is No Longer Solely the Domain of the Institution" (n.d.), About Us, Radian6. Retrieved July 10, 2011, from http://www.radian6.com/company/about-us/

76. "Radian6 Social CRM Integration" (2010, March 5), Radian6. Retrieved July 10, 2011, from http://www.radian6.com/resources/library/radian6-social-crm-integration/

77. Peacock, Marisa (2010, June 7), "WEM Lessons: Case Studies on Social Media Monitoring," WMS Wire. Retrieved July 10, 2011, from http://www.cmswire.com/cms/web-engagement/wem-lessons-case-studies-on-social-media-monitoring--007702.php

78. Ibid.

79. Monica (2011, January 11) "5 Technologies Shaping the Future of Social Media Measurement," Market Sentinel. Retrieved August 2, 2011, from http://www.marketsentinel.com/blog/2011/01/5-technologies-shaping-the-future-of-social-media-measurement/

80. "Data Mining" (n.d.), *BusinessDictionary.com*. Retrieved August 2, 2011, from http://www.businessdictionary.com/definition/data-mining.html

81. Ibid.

82. Friedlein, Ashley (2011, January 14), "17 Digital Marketing Trends for 2011," eConsultancy. Retrieved August 2, 2011, from http://econsultancy.com/us/blog/7014-digital-marketing-trends-2011-by-econsultancy-ceo-ashley-friedlein

83. Herman, Ivan (2009, November 12), "W3C Semantic Web Frequently Asked Questions," W3C Semantic Web. Retrieved August 2, 2011, from http://www.w3.org/2001/sw/SW-FAQ

84. Russell, Matthew A. (2011), *Mining the Social Web* (Sebastopol, CA: O'Reilly Media), pp. 313–14.

85. Paine, Katie Delahaye (2010, November 7), "SAS and KDPaine & Partners Win 2010 Excellence in Communications Award," press release, KDPaine & Partners. Retrieved July 9, 2011, from http://www.kdpaine.com/tasks/sites/kdp/assets/File/SNCR_Award_release-2(1).pdf

86. Ibid.

87. Ibid.

CHAPTER

15

Social Media Marketing Plan

The single most important action a marketer can take to improve an organization's chances of success in executing social media marketing activities is to develop a solid plan. Indeed, one of the major reasons social media marketing efforts fail is poor planning.[1] This chapter draws on everything that has come before in the textbook in order to demonstrate how to craft the elements of an effective social media marketing plan.

Introduced in Chapter 2, the **Social Media Marketing Planning Cycle** provides an eight-step model for developing a social media marketing plan, as shown in Figure 15.1. In this chapter a fictitious **XYZ Coffee Company** (envision a nationwide chain of well-known coffee shops) will serve to illustrate how to effectively apply each of these steps in constructing the plan.

In addition to these steps, no social media marketing plan would be complete without a **budget** listing its costs and a **return on investment** analysis. These two additional elements will be covered in detail at the end of the chapter.

When combined, these ten steps provide the core components for building a winning social media marketing plan. A few finishing touches will make the plan presentable for dissemination and consumption. They include a title page, table of contents, and executive summary.

LEARNING OBJECTIVES

After completing this chapter, students will be able to:

- Define the key elements of a social media marketing plan
- Create a title page, table of contents, and executive summary
- Compose a brief plan overview
- Observe the social media presence of an organization
- Conduct a competitive analysis
- Identify the target market
- Set social media goals
- Determine social media strategies

(Continued)

- Describe how to implement the plan
- Explain how to monitor progress
- Create a budget
- Estimate return on investment
- Explain how to get C-Suite backing

Figure 15.1 Social Media Marketing Planning Cycle

Each of these elements will be explained in sequence, using sections from the imaginary XYZ Coffee Company's plan as points of reference. The appendix that follows contains the entire example plan and provides an overview of how these pieces fit together. It is worthwhile to frequently refer to this appendix while reading the chapter in order to avoid losing sight of the forest for the trees.

Creating an Informative and Eye-Catching Title Page

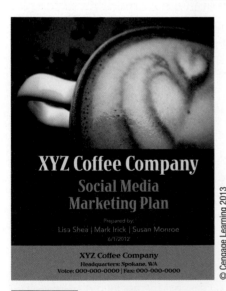

Figure 15.2 Sample Title (Cover) Page

A sharp **title page** makes a social media marketing plan not only stand out; it instantly provides the reader with the information necessary to identify the purpose and authors of the document as well as the release date. Using eye-catching graphics and tasteful fonts helps to accent important information on the title page.

A title page of the plan should begin with a descriptive name for the document, followed by the company name, address, contact information, and the authors who prepared it. Do not forget to include the publication date of the document. (A word of caution: avoid using lengthy or elaborate descriptions of the plan on the title page—they only serve to distract the reader from the key information on the page.)

Figure 15.2 shows the title page from the XYZ Coffee Company's social media marketing plan. Note the clean layout, snappy graphic, and the use of fonts to enhance the other relevant information on the page. In addition, observe the effective use of background colors to clearly differentiate the types of information on the page. The net effect is to attract attention and provide a tantalizing hint of what lies within the document.

Automatically Generating a Table of Contents

A table of contents is essential for a lengthy document such as a social media marketing plan. If manually prepared, a table of contents should not be assembled until the plan is finished. This approach requires going through the entire manuscript to find and record all the section headings, subheadings, and page numbers. This task is laborious, monotonous, and error-prone.

Fortunately, modern word processors, such as Microsoft Word®, provide the ability to automatically generate a table of contents from formatted section headings in the document.[2]

Formatting the sections of a social media marketing plan can be done either during or after the preparatory phrase. The most efficient and safest method is to designate the section heading levels during composition, thus minimizing the chances of missing important items and simultaneously creating the initial organization of the document. Further, this technique makes it easy and quick to modify the structure of the plan during its preparation by demoting sections (indenting them in the table of contents), promoting sections (reducing their level of indentation), and changing the sequence of sections (simply dragging and dropping heading names in the panel on the left side of the document moves the heading name and accompanying section to the new location).

Once the document is written, with the section headings properly formatted and arranged, the table of contents can be automatically generated, showing the heading levels and associated page numbers, as seen in Figure 15.3. This process provides a fast, flexible, and reliable way to structure and automatically generate a table of contents for a social media marketing plan.

Writing a Compelling Executive Summary

A persuasive executive summary highlights the main benefits and components of a social media marketing plan.[3] It provides the first impression of the plan. Research shows that it can take just "17 seconds to make a lasting impression."[4] Therefore, an executive summary is one of the most important parts of the plan because decision makers will use it to quickly determine whether the plan's ideas are worth pursuing.[5] This momentary glimpse will either inspire them to learn more or to lose interest.[6]

Given the importance of the executive summary, it is worthwhile to put in the time and effort to write a great one. The following tips offer direction in preparing an executive summary that makes the best possible first impression:

- **Lead with Why the Plan Should Be Adopted**: The executive summary should begin with a justification for management to make the investment necessary to take the actions proposed by the plan.[7] The reasons provided should resonate and be ones that decision makers consider important. In business this importance typically means a short-term monetary return, although long-term considerations, such as brand building and improved

Table of Contents

© Cengage Learning 2013

Figure 15.3 Sample Table of Contents

customer relationships, may also play a critical role in the decision to proceed.

- **Keep the Audience in Mind**: Use the language appropriate for the readership. How you word the executive summary will differ depending on what the intended audience cares most about. In other words, the wording must satisfy the audience's needs.[8] For example, top executives will expect business terminology that helps them determine the value of the proposal.

- **Organize the Summary to Reflect the Structure of the Plan**: Readers will expect to see a summary that mirrors the organization of the components in the social media marketing plan. Consequently, the executive summary should be written in the same sequence as that plan's components were introduced.[9]

- **Provide a General Overview of the Main Components**: The executive summary should provide a synopsis of the primary elements in the plan, such as a brief overview, the organization's current social media presence, a completive analysis, goals, strategies, target market, tools, implementation, monitoring, tuning, and budget.[10]

- **Limit the Length**: People reading executive summaries are habitually short on time. So keep the executive summary to a page, two at the most.[11] A careful balance must be struck between being too brief, which could indicate a lack of thoroughness, and too lengthy, which might be seen as unfocused and rambling.

- **Include the Names of the Plan's Authors**: This list should include the team leaders who prepared the plan, along with their respective titles.[12]

- **Compose the Executive Summary Last**: This maxim is well-known but often ignored in the haste to complete a plan. In reality, writing the executive summary before finishing the plan will actually lengthen the process. Once the plan is done, a comprehensive overview of the most significant components is available, making it not only simpler but faster to summarize the highlights in the executive summary. In addition, during the development of the plan, portions are typically in constant flux that will introduce inaccuracies in a prewritten executive summary and require that it be rewritten repeatedly.[13]

Figure 15.4 provides an example of an executive summary that makes use of all these tips.

Composing a Brief Overview

To maximize the chances that decision makers reading the social media marketing plan will fully appreciate its value, it is important to lay down a contextual foundation for readers to understand the information in the plan. This overview should not only lay the groundwork for reading the plan but should also stress the benefits of enacting it. The following tips provide suggestions for constructing an effective overview section:

- Describe the industry and company in order to set the stage for the decision makers by providing a quick look at the past, present, and likely future of the industry and the company's track record within that industry. [14]

- Explain the competitive advantage in order to show how the company can realize significant gains by using social media marketing. This explanation will help decision makers understand the importance of the plan.

- Describe how social media marketing can contribute by concisely listing the social media actions that will be required to secure the competitive advantage. It is dangerous to assume readers of the plan will readily grasp the value of social media marketing, let alone how it can deliver results.

Figure 15.5 demonstrates how to implement these recommendations in order to create an effective overview.

Executive Summary

XYZ Coffee Company has a wide range of market segments, ranging from luxury coffee drinkers to professionals. However, younger people are not typically coffee drinkers, and they represent a lucrative, massive, untapped market segment, especially the more affluent youths.

The primary focus of this social media marketing plan is to use the social web as a means to find, engage, attract, and retain this upscale youth market as XYZ Coffee Company patrons. It is based on comprehensive research of the company's current social media presence, competitive intelligence, and target market analysis. This thorough examination and appraisal has resulted in a set of specific actionable social media goals and in optimal strategies for reaching those goals as well as the best social media tools for successfully executing and monitoring the plan.

Social media goals for the XYZ Coffee Company include:
- Strengthening the brand, primarily among the more affluent youth market segment
- Driving word-of-mouth recommendations
- Improving customer satisfaction
- Generating and implementing new product ideas
- Promoting advocacy
- Increasing foot traffic in the stores
- Search Engine Optimization (SEO) to increase traffic and conversions

A set of comprehensive social media strategies will be employed to achieve the above goals. These strategies include listening, interacting, engaging, embracing, influencing, and contributing to the social web. In addition, this plan describes how the progress of social media efforts will be tracked, measured, and evaluated. These actions will enable the plan's execution to be tuned to obtain optimal results.

A detailed budget shows the cost of implementing the plan. The plan concludes with a return on investment analysis. The team leaders responsible for preparing, overseeing, and executing the plan include the VP of marketing, Lisa Shea; the director of communications, Mark Jones; and the social media marketing manager, Susan Monroe.

Figure 15.4 Sample Executive Summary

Brief Overview

Over the last two decades, coffeehouses have become part of the American landscape. Millions of people purchase an espresso-based coffee drink daily. The willingness to spend $3 to $5 for a cappuccino, mocha latte, or chocolate-ice-blended drink occurred within just the last decade, largely due to Starbucks. The specialty-coffeehouse industry continues to grow at a strong pace.

Affluent youth, not normally heavy consumers of coffee, represent a niche market that has yet to be tapped. As explained below in detail, social media can be used to observe, interact, engage, and influence this market segment. These actions will help attract and retain this youth market as XYZ Coffee Company patrons, in combination with XYZ Coffee Company's high-volume, upscale, inviting atmosphere, and high-quality products. Moreover, most of the XYZ Coffee Company's locations are near university or college campuses, locations that provide easy access for this target market.

Figure 15.5 Overview Section from the XYZ Coffee Company Social Media Marketing Plan

Observing Social Media Presence

Figure 15.6 Brand Health

© Cengage Learning 2013

The first step in the Social Media Marketing Planning Cycle is to listen to what people are saying about a company, thereby enabling the organization to determine its current social media presence. There are two primary ways to assess the social media presence of an organization: *holistically* and *granularly*. The holistic approach looks at **brand health**, a collective measure of a company's social media presence from many different sources.[15]

A useful analogy is to compare brand health with the general assessment a medical doctor might give a patient at the end of an examination. Rather than going through each test result separately, the physician might simply say that the patient has a clean bill of health. Likewise, brand health is "a high-level assessment that tells a company everything's alright or, conversely, there are problems that need to be addressed."[16]

If the sweeping pronouncement of social media brand health is good, then marketers have an overall indication that their social media marketing initiatives are working. On the other hand, if the news is bad, then, like the doctor, it is necessary to zero in on specific social media platforms and look at each site's Key Performance Indicators (KPIs) to identify the sources, nature, and extent of the problem.

Measuring social media brand health can be done in a number of ways. The most frequently used method is sentiment analysis of the entire social web (or at least as much of the social web as any given monitoring tool is capable of assessing). By listening to the conversations that are taking place about a particular company on the social web, marketers can determine if the general consensus about a brand are mostly positive, neutral, or negative.

In addition to measuring the sheer **volume** of positive, neutral and negative brand mentions, the **velocity** at which these brand mentions are changing, for better or worse, can provide clues about the future of brand health.[17] Brand health measurements should also include **visibility**—the number of people aware of the brand, who they are, and what they are saying about it.[18] Finally, the **volatility** of brand sentiment can expose rapid changes caused by ill-advised changes in product quality, licensing terms, customer support policies, and so on.[19] For example, when Starbucks changed its long-established logo, a spike in negative comments on social communities alerted the company to the problem, which they addressed in an expeditious and forthright manner, averting a PR disaster.

Finally, it is worth noting that analyzing a company's sentiment score in isolation only reveals how happy people are with the company, not how it compares with competitors or even with the entire industry. By comparing the company's sentiment score with the competition's scores, marketers can determine the company's brand health relative to its rivals.[20]

Even when the overall news about the social media health of a brand is good, it is still useful to look at the metrics for individual social media platforms as a means of determining where social media marketing efforts are performing well and where there is room for improvement. This practice also establishes benchmarks with which to measure progress in implementing platform-specific tactics and achieving social media goals (a topic that is discussed more fully in the implementing and monitoring sections below).

The following are five key metrics for auditing a company's social media presence on individual social media platforms:

- **Sentiment Analysis**: Shows the number of positive, neutral, or negative mentions on each social media platform where the company has a sizable presence[21]

- **Reach**: Indicates the number of Twitter followers, Facebook fans, LinkedIn group members, Flickr view count, and so on[22]

- **Company Posts**: Measure how often the company posts on each social media platform[23]

- **Feedback**: Shows the number of comments, likes, or replies to company-generated content[24]
- **Average Response Time**: Assesses response time to user comments on the company's social media properties

Table 15.1 depicts a granular view of XYZ Coffee Company's social media presence on six major social media platforms.

Metric	Sentiment	Reach	Company Posts	Feedback	Average Response Time to Feedback
Facebook Page	Positive 58% Neutral 31% Negative 11%	1,200,000 fans	2 daily	10 comments and 20 likes daily	2 hours
Twitter Account	Positive 60% Neutral 28% Negative 12%	350,000 followers	10 daily	50 @tweets 200 retweets daily	30 minutes
LinkedIn Page	Positive 50% Neutral 26% Negative 24%	25,000 followers	3 daily	6 replies daily	1 day
YouTube Channel	Positive 45% Neutral 27% Negative 28%	5,000 subscribers	2 per month	5 comments per video monthly	2 days
Flickr Photostream	Positive 45% Neutral 50% Negative 5%	3,000 monthly views	10 per month	2 comments per photo	1 week
EzineArticles	Positive 70% Neutral 21% Negative 9%	200 monthly views	3 articles per month	5 per article	1 week

Table 15.1 Platform-specific Measurements of the Social Media Presence of the XYZ Coffee Company

Conducting a Competitive Analysis

As mentioned before, the *first* step in the Media Marketing Planning Cycle is to listen to the social web. In addition to determining an organization's social media presence, these observations can provide valuable competitive intelligence. For example, a careful examination of what people are saying online about competitors can expose potential threats from competitors as well as possible lucrative opportunities.[25]

One useful way to conduct a competitive analysis of the social web is with a SWOT Analysis. SWOT is an acronym which stands for Strengths, Weaknesses, Opportunities, and Threats.[26] It was developed in the 1960s at Stanford Research Institute (SRI) by grants from Fortune 500 companies who wanted to improve the success of strategic planning.[27] A **Social Media SWOT Analysis** identifies a company's strengths and weaknesses on social media platforms as well as the opportunities and threats on the social web.[28] It is a useful decision-making technique to identify attractive social media opportunities for an organization.

In a Social Media SWOT Analysis, the internal factors within an organization that affect its performance on various platforms are classified as strengths and weaknesses,

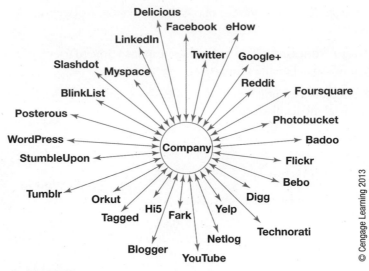

Figure 15.7 Visualizing a Competitive Analysis of the Social Web

© Cengage Learning 2013

while the external factors on the social web that impact the performance of the organization on social media platforms are categorized as opportunities and threats. This form of SWOT Analysis provides the means to match the organization's social media platform strengths and weaknesses with opportunities and threats in the social media environment in order to find areas of competitive advantage.

The first step in a Social Media SWOT Analysis is to find and list an organization's strengths and weaknesses on social media platforms, along with the relevant opportunities and threats in the social media realm.[29] This step can be accomplished by answering the questions in Table 15.2.

Strengths	Weaknesses
• Does the organization have a strong brand presence on multiple social media platforms?	• Does the organization have a weak brand presence on multiple social media platforms?
• Has the company a proven track record on social media platforms?	• Is the company's track record on social media platforms spotty?
• Are most of the company's actions successful on social media platforms?	• Do the majority of the company's actions on social media platforms fall short in expected outcomes?
• Does the organization have experienced staff adept at various social media platforms?	• Does the organization lack sufficient expertise to work effectively on social media platforms?
• Is the staff enthusiastic about working with social media platforms?	• Is the staff apathetic or apprehensive about working with platforms?
• Are all the company's social media marketing efforts monitored to assess progress in achieving marketing goals?	• Does the company lack the ability to fully monitor its social media marketing efforts in order to measure progress in achieving marketing goals?
• Are top executives supportive of social media efforts?	• Are top executives reluctant to fully commit to social media marketing?
• Are ample resources available for participating on social media platforms?	• Are resources insufficient for building and maintaining a presence on social media platforms?
• Does the company currently have a variety of vibrant social media properties?	• Does the company lack a variety of vibrant social media properties?
• Does the company have unique products or services that satisfy the needs of social media users?	• Does the company lack distinctive products or services or do the current offerings fail to satisfy the needs of social media users?

Opportunities	Threats
• Which social media platforms have the greatest concentration of the company's target audience? • What does the target market do on these sites? • Do they have any unfulfilled needs on the platforms that the company can satisfy? • Are there emerging target markets on these platforms with needs the company can satisfy? • What social media technologies provide opportunities for the company? • Are there ways the company and its competitors can benefit by working together on the platforms? • Are there opportunities for collaborating with customers to build brand presence on platforms? • Are suppliers present on these platforms? • What do customers value about the company? • Is market demand increasing?	• Who are the company's direct competitors on the major social media platforms? • Are there emerging competitors on these major platforms? • What are the social media strategies and tactics that competitors pursue on these platforms? • How successful are these strategies and tactics in building brand presence on the company's key social media platforms? • In what ways are competitors' products or services superior to the company's offerings? • How are competitors likely to respond to any changes in the way the company markets on the platforms? • Is the company behind in adopting new technologies? • Are international competitors taking away market share? • What do customers dislike about the company? • Is market demand decreasing?

Table 15.2 Profiling an Organization's Social Media Platform Strengths, Weaknesses, Opportunities, and Threats

© Cengage Learning 2013

Once all the factors for a company have been profiled using Table 15.2, it is possible to determine the appropriate strategy in the SWOT Matrix, shown in Table 15.3.[30] For example, if a company has many social media platform strengths and considerable opportunities on the social web, as depicted in Table 15.4, then the SWOT Matrix recommends the pursuit of an S-O (strength-opportunity) strategy, which encourages the company to follow opportunities on the social web that are a good fit for the organization's social media platform strengths. On the other hand, if the profile indicates substantial weaknesses in an organization's platform performance and many external threats exist on the social web, then a W-T (weakness-threat) strategy might prove helpful in preventing the company's weaknesses from making it highly susceptible to external threats.

The SWOT options are:

- **S-O Strategy**: Follow social media platform opportunities that match the organization's strengths on the social web.

- **W-O Strategy**: Overcome weaknesses in social media platform performance to follow opportunities on the social web.

- **S-T Strategy**: Identify ways the organization can use its platform strengths to reduce its vulnerability to external threats from competitors or new technologies on the social web.

- **W-T Strategy**: Create a protective strategy that reduces the chances the organization's social media weaknesses will make it vulnerable to external threats. This strategy would likely take the form of monitoring the social web to detect customer complaints and handling them before they become a PR disaster.

In conclusion, a SWOT Analysis of social media should always be part of a social media marketing plan because of its substantial contributions to crafting effective strategies for achieving marketing goals.[31]

SWOT Matrix	Strengths (S)	Weaknesses
Opportunities (O)	S-O strategy	W-O strategy
Threats (T)	S-T strategy	W-T strategy

Table 15.3 SWOT Matrix

© Cengage Learning 2013

Strengths	Weaknesses
• XYZ has a strong brand presence on the majority of the major social media platforms. • The company has a proven track on social media platforms, such as Facebook and Twitter. • Most of the company's actions result in the desired outcomes on social media platforms. • XYZ has an experienced staff adept at effectively using Facebook and Twitter to market the company. • The staff is enthusiastic about working with Facebook and Twitter. • XYZ's quantitative social media marketing efforts are monitored to assess progress in achieving marketing goals. • Most of XYZ's management is supportive of XYZ's social media efforts, especially on Facebook and Twitter because they have proven their usefulness in improving the company's bottom line. • Resources are adequate for participating on some social media platforms, such as Facebook and Twitter. • XYZ's Facebook and Twitter are lively social media properties. • The company's high-quality beans, distinctive coffee blends, and coffee shop atmosphere satisfy the needs of the current social media target market.	• XYZ has less than desirable brand presence on YouTube, LinkedIn, Flickr, and EzineArticles. It has no presence on Foursquare, an important platform for location marketing. • The company's track record on YouTube, LinkedIn, and Flickr is spotty. • The company's actions on YouTube, LinkedIn, Flickr, and EzineArticles have fallen short of expected outcomes. • XYZ currently lacks the expertise to effectively market on YouTube, LinkedIn, Flickr, and article directories like EzineArticles. • The staff is apprehensive about working with platforms such as YouTube, LinkedIn, Flickr, and article directories like EzineArticles. • The company presently lacks a comprehensive monitoring tool to track and measure qualitative progress across the social web and on specific platforms. • There has been an understandable reluctance by management to fully commit to an aggressive social media marketing campaign because of the inherent risks and costs in undertaking such an endeavor. • Resources are insufficient for building and maintaining a substantial presence on YouTube, LinkedIn, Flickr, Foursquare, and EzineArticles. • XYZ currently lacks a vibrant brand community where the company could directly engage with customers, eliciting valuable product feedback and new product ideas, as well as discussion forums for answering support questions. • The present social media presence does not satisfy the needs of the affluent youth market.

Table 15.4 XYZ Coffee Company SWOT Profile

Opportunities	Threats
• Facebook, Twitter, and YouTube have the largest concentration of the company's current target audience. • The target audiences on these sites tend to be spectators and joiners. • Significant portions of the affluent youth target audience are content creators and critics with needs that are not currently being met. • The affluent youth market is a strong emerging target market on all the major social media platforms, with need to observe, join, converse, create content, and criticize content. • The emergence of social location services like Foursquare, ubiquitous smartphone usage, and mobile apps for checking in from locations to earn awards, make these technologies a significant opportunity for XYZ. • Starbucks, McDonald's, and XYZ could cooperate in sponsoring social media events that support major charities. They could also work together to develop an open source wiki with information about coffee. • XYZ can collaborate with customers to build brand presence on social media platforms by engaging in activities such as inviting contributions from customers (e.g., YouTube videos). • Suppliers are present in large numbers on LinkedIn. • XYZ customers value the high-quality, unique coffee drink blends and the warm, friendly atmosphere of the company's coffee shops. • Market demand is currently slowly increasing.	• Starbucks is the closest direct competitor on the major social media platforms. • McDonald's low prices and widespread locations are making it an emerging competitor, especially on key social media platforms like Facebook and Twitter. • Starbucks pursues aggressive social media strategies across the social web, including its own brand community and location-marketing initiatives. • Starbucks has been extremely successful in building brand presence on the company's key current social media platforms, such as Facebook, Twitter, and YouTube. • Starbucks has more locations and a wider selection of coffee drinks and foods than XYZ. • Starbucks and McDonald's will likely duplicate XYZ's location-marketing efforts, so the company must continually innovate in this space. • XYZ has yet to use social location services like Foursquare to participate in location marketing. • International competitors have yet to make inroads In competing with XYZ, but their market penetration should be tracked carefully in case this situation changes. • The customers dislike the wait to get support and lack of opportunity for input about XYZ products. • Market demand for coffee drinks dropped off during the height of the recession.

Table 15.4 XYZ Coffee Company SWOT Profile *(Continued)*

Setting Goals

With the above reconnaissance and analysis complete, it is possible to determine the social media goals that stand the best chance of achieving a competitive advantage for the organization. Chapter 2 introduced a set of general social media goals, which provide a good starting point for crafting organization-specific goals. They include brand building, increasing customer satisfaction, driving word-of-mouth recommendations, producing new product ideas, generating leads, crisis reputation management, integrating social media with PR and advertising, and search engine optimization (SEO).

The process of adapting these overall goals to take advantage of a particular organization's unique opportunities will no doubt involve revising, integrating, or dropping a few of them. Figure 15.8 illustrates how this set of general social media goals has been modified to fit the situation and needs of the hypothetical XYZ Coffee Company.

Goals

In consideration of the above reconnaissance and analysis, it is apparent that a significant opportunity exists for the XYZ Coffee Company to attract and retain a new, younger generation of coffee drinkers with a comprehensive social media marketing campaign.

The following social media goals are designed to achieve this undertaking:
- Strengthening the brand, primarily among the upscale-income youth market segment
- Driving word-of-mouth recommendations
- Improving customer satisfaction
- Generating new product ideas
- Promoting advocacy
- Increasing foot traffic in the stores
- Search Engine Optimization (SEO) to increase traffic and conversions

Figure 15.8 Goal Section from the XYZ Coffee Company Social Media Marketing Plan

Determining Strategies

Once the social media goals have been set, the next step is to identify the strategies best suited for helping the organization reach them. Chapter 2 also introduced the **Eight C's of Strategy Development** (see the sidebar), which are guidelines for constructing social media marketing strategies for a particular organization.

Strategies

XYZ Coffee Company will pursue a highly aggressive set of strategies for its social media marketing campaign. Such a comprehensive approach is obviously not without risks because it represents a sizable investment in personnel, and is time consuming and expensive. In addition, since no one controls the social web and since blunders do harm to a brand, in-depth engagement standards will be established for company employees interacting on the social web.

XYZ Coffee Company's comprehensive social media strategies include:
- **Listening** to the social web to determine where the company brand is being mentioned, who is talking about it, and what attracts consumers to the brand, as well as what is being said about competitors' brands.
- **Interacting** with consumers on Facebook and Twitter, where high concentrations of the target audience reside. Always acting as a contributor, not an overt promoter, to strengthen the brand by improving brand awareness, recognition, and perception. In addition, connecting with suppliers on LinkedIn to improve provider relationships.
- **Engaging** customers to drive word-of-mouth recommendations with YouTube viral brand videos and Flickr pictures showing the warm, friendly atmosphere of the coffee shops, where people hang out looking trendy.
- **Embracing** customers by establishing **a vibrant brand community**, where customers can pose questions about products and receive answers. In addition, participants will be encouraged to use the discussion forums to suggest innovative product ideas and provide valuable feedback about existing products and services. These actions will fortify customer relationships, improve customer satisfaction, and hence improve customer retention.
- **Influencing** the target market with YouTube videos and podcasts that feature interviews with the thought leaders in the coffee industry (mass influencers), enlisting them to help shape opinions about the company's products and services to promote brand advocacy on the social web.
- **Connecting** with customers by starting a location marketing program that rewards consumers for regular mobile check-ins at store locations using Foursquare.
- **Contributing** content to EzineArticles for widespread syndication and consequence improvement in search engine ranking, which in turn will increase website traffic and sales.

Figure 15.9 Strategy Section from the XYZ Coffee Company Social Media Marketing Plan

However, like the general social media goals discussed above, these strategic guideposts only provide broad brushstrokes in the strategy design process. They must be fitted to fulfill a particular organization's social media goals. Figure 15.9 demonstrates how these overall strategies have been customized for the imaginary XYZ Coffee Company.

Identifying the Target Market

A company may already have an accurate understanding of the profile of its target audience; however, the behavior, interests, and tastes of that target market might be slightly or even radically different on the social web. As Chapter 3 describes in detail, **personas** provide an effective means for a company to categorize target audiences on the social web. A variety of characteristics can be used to group a target audience into personas, including *demographics* (such as age range, gender, income range, occupations, and education); *needs, interests, and tastes* (such as a desire for a friendly atmosphere, enjoying coffee drinking, an interest in sports, or the preference for exotic blends of coffee); and *behavior* (such as spending habits). Essentially, a persona is a detailed profile of a particular subset of people within the broad target audience.

One popular way to define personas is with Forrester Research's Social Technographics Profile, which enables marketers to use age, location, and gender to identify the type of activities that characterize people engaged on the social web: creators, critics, conversationalists, collectors, and spectators, among others.

For example, Figure 15.10 profiles the personas for the hypothetical XYZ Coffee Company. Depending on the behavior of the target market, it is possible to determine which social media platforms these personas are most likely to frequent. As an example, spectators are not likely to participate in such social networks as Facebook or LinkedIn, but they might watch YouTube videos and read blogs, but not comment on the posts.

Target Market

XYZ Coffee Company has a wide range of market segments, ranging from luxury coffee drinkers to professionals. However, the members of the current generation of young adults are not typically coffee drinkers, and hence they represent a lucrative, massive, untapped market segment, especially the slightly upscale higher-income youths.

Forrester's Social Technographics Profile Tool indicates that 93% of U.S. males in the age range eighteen to twenty-four are spectators on the social web. Eighty-four percent of this market segment exhibits the persona of joiners, with 53% acting as social media critics and only 44% creating content.[2] U.S. females in the same age range are slightly less inclined to engage in the social web as spectators (85%), and more likely to be joiners (86%) and creators (48%), but less inclined to be critics (47%).

Forrester Research surveys have determined that Generation Y online users constitute the largest group of creators, consisting of 37% of consumers ranging between ages eighteen and twenty-nine. In other words, young urban social media users are the most active of the personas in producing videos, blog posts, articles, discussion forum text, and so on. In addition, these studies have found young women to be far more active on the social web as conversationalists than young men.

© Cengage Learning 2013

Figure 15.10 Target Market Section from the XYZ Company Social Media Marketing Plan

Selecting Tools

Once the demographic and behavioral characteristics of the personas have been used to define a company's target market, the social media platforms with the highest concentration of the target audience should be chosen. For instance, if the personas for the target market primarily include conversationalists and content creators, then marketers will want to divide their attention between social networks and other online communities where people frequently converse and on social media platforms where people contribute content, such as video and photo sharing sites as well as article directories.

Implementing

Implementation is the process whereby the goals, strategies, target market, and tools are taken into consideration in creating actionable social media platform-specific tactics. In addition, implementation includes the generation and distribution of content as well as the assignment of staff to be responsible for preparing and carrying out platform-specific tactics and the development and dissemination of content on the various platforms.

SELECTING PLATFORM-SPECIFIC TACTICS

Each social media platform requires unique and customized tactics to successfully execute the company's overall strategies for reaching it marketing goals. Table 15.5 displays the chapters in which social media platform-specific marketing tactics and tools are covered.

The following sections summarize the marketing tactics for key social media platforms (these are drawn from the chapters in Table 15.5).

Platforms and Tools	Marketing Tactics
Blogs	Chapter 5: Publishing Blogs
Podcasts	Chapter 6: Publishing Podcasts and Webinars
Webinars	Chapter 6: Publishing Podcasts and Webinars
Article Directories	Chapter 7: Publishing Articles, White Papers, and E-Books
White Papers	Chapter 7: Publishing Articles, White Papers, and E-Books
E-Books	Chapter 7: Publishing Articles, White Papers, and E-Books
Video Sharing Sites	Chapter 8: Sharing Videos
Photo Sharing Sites	Chapter 9: Sharing Photos and Images
Social Networks	Chapter 10: Social Networks
Microblogs	Chapter 11: Microblogging
Discussion Boards	Chapter 12: Discussion Boards, Social News, and Q&A Sites
Social News Sites	Chapter 12: Discussion Boards, Social News, and Q&A Sites
Q&A Sites	Chapter 12: Discussion Boards, Social News, and Q&A Sites
Mobile Apps	Chapter 13: Mobile Computing and Location Marketing
Location Marketing Services	Chapter 13: Mobile Computing and Location Marketing

© Cengage Learning 2013

Table 15.5 List of the Chapters That Cover Social Media Platform-specific Tactics, Tools, and Services

FACEBOOK Facebook is the most popular social network, with more than 750 million users.[32] It is especially well suited for interacting with end consumers. Although not exhaustive, the following list of Facebook tactics can strengthen a brand by improving brand awareness, recognition, and perception.

Facebook tactics:

- If not already done, create an officially branded company Facebook page (not account) that represents the business and allows users to follow or become fans of a company.

- Customize the page to reflect the company's style and values, but provide some content distinct from the firm's primary website.

- Frequently update the company page with content that is relevant and engaging for Facebook users—no more than three updates per day. Be persistent, consistent, and genuine.

- Focus on content:
  o Create share-worthy content that encourages further discussions among the target market to advance a brand's position by making the brand more memorable or personable.
  o Content needs to be light, funny, and informative.
  o Offer a special deal or value.
  o Give away free products to encourage likes so that the company's brand will spread rapidly through Facebook friend networks.
  o Run contests or offer discounts to Facebook members to convince people to follow a Facebook profile. Contests should be tailored to the product being offered.
  o Give useful tips, or ask open-ended questions that will interest the audience.
  o Not every content item must be original; sharing links to interesting items can also be valuable.

- Facebook is about personal connections, so letting some personality through in updates and giving a human voice to a brand are some of the most powerful advantages of this social networking platform. Engage with users to create an emotional connection; this engagement will build brand loyalty. Used correctly, Facebook is an excellent tool for business-to-consumer marketing.

- Facebook users are often picky about which items they will like. To get an idea of what sort of content to post, look at other Facebook pages—particularly those of businesses offering a similar product or service to the one being marketed—and see which statuses or comments are being liked the most. This investigation will give some insight into what potential fans want to see. Often less serious posts will be liked more, so keep content funny, personable, and entertaining.

- To gain viewers for a page, put links on other websites, email signatures, business cards, and outgoing communications.

- To make the URL for the Facebook page easy to write and remember, use a shorter vanity URL. A customized URL makes the page more memorable, increasing the chance Facebook users will visit and become fans.

- Use Facebook Places to offer special deals when visitors check in.

- Create local market events, or host a charity drive to bring visitors to a Places page.

- Use Facebook ads to generate traffic to the company website.

- Use the Facebook ad tool to specify race, gender, interests, and location; the Estimated Reach section can give an idea of how many users fit the target market. Facebook ad costs can be set very low (well under $100 per month) depending on the budget.

Figure 15.11 shows how some of these Facebook tactics can be customized for a specific company.

Facebook
Facebook is the most popular social network, with more than 750 million users. It is especially well suited for interacting with existing and potential consumers. Hence XYZ Coffee Company will use its Facebook presence to strengthen the brand by improving brand awareness, recognition, and perception, especially with the affluent youth target market.
Following are the key tactics that will be implemented on Facebook to help build the company brand: • Post content that is of interest to the youth target market such as popular coffee drinks, music, teenage icons, and fashion, funny YouTube videos, community events, etc. • Post content three times each day • Light or funny ads to direct traffic to company website • Giveaways once every month to increase the number of likes • Facebook Places coupons for check-ins • Participate in industry pages • Include links to company Facebook page on all outbound communications such as promotional materials, brochures, and email signatures, as well as on the company website

Figure 15.11 Facebook Tactics for the XYZ Coffee Company

TWITTER Twitter is currently the fourth most popular social media platform, with over 200 million unique monthly visitors.[33] With Twitter it is possible to instantly reach a large (often mobile) audience with brief but focused messages, making it a great marketing platform for interacting with users on the go.

Twitter tactics:

- Customize the company's profile page, starting with a good avatar picture and customized background, text color, and company description.

- The profile's description should complement the avatar by providing context and important details. Writing space is limited, so the description will have to be concise.

- A custom-made background image can display personality, a longer explanation of the product or services, and past accomplishments. The background is also a place to put URLs for other social networking profiles, websites, or blogs.

- Use Twitter to start a discussion or to participate in an ongoing conversation.

- Twitter can operate as a "global human search engine" in almost any field of expertise. It is possible to find someone on Twitter with relevant information to share.

- Use *targeted follow* strategy—search for and follow target markets and always follow back. Use the phrase "You should follow me on Twitter."

- Putting out updates when people are online to see them is essential to make an impact; research shows that midday and midweek tend to produce the best results.

- Promptly respond to questions and comments.

- Providing useful information can build a brand's reputation and thought leadership.

- Ask for opinions or product reviews to seek feedback and engage the followers.

- Being kind, polite, and appreciative helps to grease the apparatus and keep it running smoothly.

- Tweet things that are of interest to your target market. Be sure to use appropriate hashtags.

- Twitter profile must answer the question "Why follow and listen to the messages being offered?"

- Offer special deals on Twitter including coupons, promotional discounts, special products, and free shipping.

- Use Twitter to increase brand awareness, connect with customers, provide support, and distribute information.

- Use Twitter to identify influential people and those who have common interests in order to create potentially valuable relationships.

- Provide content that is fun, interesting, and valuable, and people will come looking for more.

- Be creative in persuasively conveying much larger ideas.

- Use link-shortening services such as bit.ly to track real-time interest in posts.

Figure 15.12 depicts how several of these Twitter tactics can be tailored for a particular company.

Twitter

Twitter is currently the fourth most popular social media platform, with over 200 million unique monthly visitors. With Twitter it is possible to instantly reach a large (often mobile) audience with brief but focused messages, making the site a great marketing platform for interacting with users on the go, especially the upscale-income youth market that XYZ is targeting.

The following tactics will be pursued to take the utmost advantage of this platform for strengthening the brand among the target audience:
- Respond to questions and comments promptly
- Average of ten to fifteen tweets daily and use hashtags frequently
- Use shortened links to share interesting articles, videos, breaking news, etc.
- Use Twellow to search for targeted users to follow twenty new people daily to generate more followers
- Retweet to increase sharing of our content in return
- Giveaways once every month to increase followers
- Include links to company Twitter on all outbound communications such as promotional materials, brochures, and email signatures, as well as on the company website

Figure 15.12 Twitter Tactics for the XYZ Coffee Company

LINKEDIN LinkedIn is the one of the most popular social media platforms, with over 200 million unique monthly visitors in August 2011.[34] With 81% of business to business marketers using LinkedIn, it is the dominant B2B social network, making it ideal for a company to connect with suppliers in order to improve provider relationships.

LinkedIn tactics:

- Create a company page, and use it to showcase job openings, new positions, or similar information in order to develop a large company following and to raise awareness of a brand because more people will see that company as a suggestion based on their contacts' interests.

- All employees should strive to complete 100% of their profiles and optimize with appropriate key words. In addition, employees should include links to the company website, Facebook, Twitter, and blog, among others. Also include such applications as SlideShare to add relevant content and link to third-party articles in order to appear less self-promotional.

- Employees should ask contacts, past customers, industry analysts, and employees to join the group and/or follow the brand.

- Each employee should request recommendations from past employers, customers, supervisors, and so on to showcase expertise.

- Key employees should be assigned the responsibility of regularly participating in industry groups.

- Groups should be launched with descriptive names in order to address a common issue or problem.

- Content should be formatted so that it follows the group's theme, using a regular series of tips and showcasing the company's product's subtlety.

- Employees should post regularly in the group with contents of interest to the group members such as the latest industry information or thoughtful questions.

- Join associated group, first taking the time to learn what the group deems relevant before posting. Be courteous and show respect for other users' time by posting only relevant, well-considered, and valuable thoughts to group discussion boards.

- LinkedIn Answers should be used by employees to contribute valuable and well-considered answers in order to draw in business leads by highlighting personal expertise.

- Company representatives should focus on fostering relationships before asking for assistance and personalizing communications in order to demonstrate sincere interest in getting to know a person.

- Posted titles and summaries should use catchy, keyword-rich titles.

- Use InMail to ask to be connected. Send a personalized message, and explain why you would like to be connected.

Figure 15.13 shows how several of these LinkedIn tactics can be adapted for a particular company.

LinkedIn

LinkedIn is one of the most popular social media platforms, with over 200 million unique monthly visitors in August 2011. With 81% of business-to-business marketers using LinkedIn, it is the dominant B2B social network, making it ideal for XYZ to connect with suppliers to improve provider relationships.

The following LinkedIn tactical actions will be taken:
- Key employees should strive to complete 100% of their profiles and optimize with appropriate keywords
- Employee profiles should include links to the company website, Twitter, Facebook, YouTube, etc.
- Employees should ask recommendations to show credibility
- Participate in industry groups a minimum of once per week to establish credibility and build brand awareness.
- Connect with industry thought leaders.
- Build relationship with suppliers.

Figure 15.13 LinkedIn Tactics for the XYZ Coffee Company

YOUTUBE YouTube is the second most popular social media platform, with more than 450 million unique monthly visitors.[35] As more people choose to consume information visually, YouTube's vast (and growing) reach and compelling content make it the perfect platform for engaging consumers to drive word-of-mouth recommendations.

YouTube tactics:

- Create authentic videos with real people in actual locations to make the videos more persuasive in order to engage viewers. Offbeat and unusual videos tend to get more attention.

- Include links to videos on all other social media properties (Facebook, Twitter, etc.).

- Actively comment on videos that relate to your industry in order to make connections. The more influential you can appear in the community, the more credibility your business will have.

- **Choose keywords for videos carefully.** Tag videos with various keywords to rank higher in the YouTube search engine. Make them relevant to the subject matter or niche. Think about what customers will be searching for, and target those keywords.

- **Produce videos that are informative and entertaining.** Use videos to educate the audience about issues its members face in your industry. Be sure to provide helpful hints.

- Get to the point quickly, and make the video two minutes or less. Research shows that less than 45% stay past the one-minute mark, while only 24% of the viewers stay past the two-minute mark.

- Email the video links to customers.

- Cross-marketing: be sure to include links to your website or other social media properties in your videos, and promote the video on your company website and social media properties.

- Ask friends and associates to share the videos on their social media properties.

- Identify YouTube opinion leaders, and ask them to rate the videos.

- Create contests or feature user-submitted videos on the corporate website or blog. The result can be a series of testimonials, how-to tutorials, or other indirect promotions which cost nothing for a social media campaign that achieves substantial results.

- Start a video channel, and update contents regularly.

Figure 15.14 illustrates how several of these YouTube tactics can be adapted for implementing a particular company's overall strategies and marketing goals.

YouTube

YouTube is the second most popular social media platform, with more than 450 million unique monthly visitors in August 2011. As more people choose to consume information visually, YouTube's vast (and growing) reach and compelling content make it the perfect platform for engaging consumers to drive word-of-mouth recommendations.

The following YouTube tactical actions will be taken on behalf of the company:
- Creative, entertaining, light-hearted videos focused on the youth market
- Tag videos with relevant keywords to rank higher in the YouTube search engine
- Videos should be two minutes or less in length
- Embed company logo/image in all videos
- Post one video per month
- Reply to comments daily
- Cross-marketing by using Facebook and Twitter to promote videos

Figure 15.14 YouTube Tactics for the XYZ Coffee Company

FLICKR Flickr is the most popular photo sharing service, with over 90 million unique monthly visitors.[36] It is well suited for engaging customers with photos of the business, thereby personalizing the company in ways no other social media platform can match. For example, sharing photos of a coffee shop with a warm, friendly atmosphere humanizes the business. When a business creates a buzz on the social web by sharing photos, people start talking about it, causing others to become interested in knowing more about the company. This level of engagement with customers can help drive word-of-mouth recommendations.

Flickr tactics:

- Use the company's Flickr Photostream to share pictures with customers, thus keeping them up to date with current events at the business.

- Use Flickr to personalize the company by showing what is going on behind the scenes, featuring interesting and informative pictures of product preparation, customer service, festive holiday parties, or employees just enjoying doing their jobs.

- Use photo sharing on the company's Flickr Photostream as a teaser for more information elsewhere, such as the company's website and Facebook page.

- Share photos of employees at a philanthropic event, and provide a linking to the corporate blog for followers to learn more about the event.

- Ask customers to share photos of the business that capture distinctive aspects of it, such as a storefront's appearance during a beautiful sunset. Recognize the best submissions with some form of award.

- Create a positive buzz about the company by sponsoring a photo contest in which the person sharing the most innovative picture of the business wins a discount or other prize.

- Upload images of a product with detailed specifications and technical details. Place a link to the company website in the description that will bring traffic to the company website.

- Company pictures can be highly persuasive for potential buyers, even when they are not directly about the product. Posting photos online can give "a strong sense of culture and provide a human face to the company."[37]

- Use photo sharing to help draw traditional press attention. In addition, with appropriate keywords, a photo result often shows up on the first page of results, bringing many to view the content.

- Use multiple photo sharing sites to upload images in order to expand the company's reach to different audiences.

- Be diligent about using titles, descriptions, photo sets, and tags to secure top Google Search results.

- The most popular shared images tend to be humorous, unplanned, or spontaneous in appearance. Detailed, up-close photographs with a simple background draw more interest than landscapes.

- Post a link to images using Facebook, Twitter, and a company website to generate traffic.

Figure 15.15 illustrates how several of these Flickr tactics can be adapted for implementing a particular company's overall strategies and marketing goals.

BRAND COMMUNITY The central feature of a successful brand community is a vibrant discussion board, with a sizable number of avid participants who select topics and drive the conversations. Some of the benefits of engaging customers in a brand community include improved customer relations, reduced customer support costs, and the generation of innovative new product ideas.

Brand platform tactics:

- Create a friendly, comfortable, and responsive environment using well-designed discussion boards and forums with a specific target audience in mind.

- Appeal to the consumer personas that might be interested in the product, and let the conversation develop organically without directing the topics toward the product.

Flickr

Flickr is the most popular photo sharing service, with over 90 million unique monthly visitors. It is well suited for engaging customers with photos of the business, which can personalize the company in ways no other social media platform can match. For example, sharing photos of a coffee shop, with a warm, friendly atmosphere, humanizes the business. When a business creates a buzz on the social web by sharing photos, people start talking about it and cause others to become interested in knowing more about the company. This level of engagement with customers can help drive word-of-mouth recommendations.

The following Flickr tactical actions will be taken:
- Upload photos featuring funny pictures, interesting events, product preparation, customers enjoying coffee, festive holiday parties, or employees just enjoying doing their jobs
- Be diligent about using titles, descriptions, photo sets, and tags to secure top Google Search results
- Upload high-quality pictures weekly
- Reply to comments daily
- Cross-marketing by posting the most interesting pictures on Facebook and links on Twitter to photos, etc.

Figure 15.15 Flickr Tactics for the XYZ Coffee Company

- Offer memberships to close contacts, friends, customers, employees, and business partners, among others. Due to their prior engagement with the brand or product, some of these people may become core members (and potentially moderators) as the community develops.

- Encourage members to invite their friends to the community by offering a competition with prizes to reward members for bringing in new people.

- Participants should be encouraged to use the discussion forums to suggest innovative product ideas and to provide valuable feedback about existing products and services.

- Asking open-ended questions, having polls in which users vote, and recognizing quality posts are some classic methods. Allowing some democratic input makes forums more interesting for users.

- The most successful brand communities provide vibrant discussion boards where people actively participate because they find the topics useful, captivating, and rewarding.

- Stick to the topic. Discussions, or threads, always have a title and general topic that is obvious from reading just a few posts.

- Use common sense and read the rules of the discussion board and understand social norms before posting messages. Prior to asking the community for an answer, search the forum to see if the topic has already been discussed.

- Use good grammar and capitalization. Having solid grammar, good spacing, and proper punctuation makes a post easier and more enjoyable to read. For a similar reason, do not use ALL CAPITALS when posting; it is interpreted as shouting by forum users and will generate negative responses.

- No feeding the trolls. In discussion forum parlance, a troll is someone who attacks or personally insults another user, driving a thread off-topic with negative comments.

- Do not post repetitively (or double post). If a question or comment does not receive a response on one thread, it is unwise to post it elsewhere.

- Do not create fake online identities to praise, defend, or create the illusion of support for one's self, allies, or company.

- Members join and follow a discussion board because it provides useful information or entertainment. Therefore, all posts should serve one or both of those goals.

- As consumers increasingly look to each other for guidance on which products to buy or what companies to avoid, discussion boards can play a prominent role in a social media marketing campaign.

- Participate in highly relevant discussion boards with members who are potentially receptive to the marketing campaign.

- Observe discussion forums, and ask the right questions to garner product development ideas.

- Offer an incentive for users to provide information. Ask broad, open-ended questions to draw in thoughts from as many sources as possible.

Figure 15.16 shows how some of these brand community tactics can be customized for a specific company.

Brand Community

The central feature of a successful brand community is a lively discussion board with a sizable number of avid participants who select topics and drive the conversations. Some of the benefits of engaging customers in a brand community include improved customer relations, reduced customer support costs, and the generation of innovative new product ideas.

The following tactical actions will be taken to construct a vibrant brand community:
- Create a friendly, comfortable, and responsive environment using well-designed discussion boards and forums with a specific target audience in mind
- Appeal to the consumer personas that might be interested in the product and let the conversation develop organically without directing the topics toward the product
- Ask open-ended questions, have polls in which users vote, and recognize quality posts
- Allow some democratic input to make forums more interesting for users
- Answer questions and handle complaints promptly, within the hour whenever possible
- Ask broad, open-ended questions to draw in thoughts from as many sources as possible
- Encourage participants to use the discussion forums to suggest innovative product ideas and to provide valuable feedback about existing products and services
- Encourage members to invite their friends to the community by offering competitions with prizes to reward members for bringing in new people

Figure 15.16 Brand Community Tactics for the XYZ Coffee Company

---

FOURSQUARE Foursquare is the most popular location-based network (social location service), providing the ability for people to share their location with friends and to win prizes for visiting businesses and checking in.

Foursquare tactics:

- Create a Foursquare business page using a new automated system. As brands create a business page, Foursquare now automatically adds them to their Page Gallery.

- Upload photos to your Tips and check-ins.

- Add Tips and push them to associated Twitter and Facebook pages to increase a brand's reach and to help businesses integrate social media marketing efforts.[38]

- Offer coupons and special discounts.

- Offer free product after a certain number of check-ins.

- Offer badges or special status to loyal customers after a certain number of check-ins.

- Create special deals to encourage customers to bring their friends.

- Place a QR code on coupons and special offers in order to provide instant links to the company's social media properties such as Twitter, LinkedIn, Facebook, blog, and corporate website, etc.

Figure 15.17 demonstrates how several of these social location marketing tactics can be modified for a particular company.

> **Foursquare**
>
> Foursquare is the most popular location-based network (social location service), providing the ability for people to share their location with friends and win prizes for visiting businesses and checking in.
>
> The following Foursquare tactical actions will be taken:
>
> - Create a Foursquare business page using a new automated system
> - Upload photos to your Tips and check-ins
> - Offer coupons and special discounts
> - Offer free product after a certain number of check-ins
> - Offer badges or special status to loyal customers after a certain number of check-ins
> - Create special deals to encourage customers to bring their friends
> - Place a QR code on coupons and special offers in order to provide instant links to the company's social media properties such as Twitter, LinkedIn, Facebook, blog, corporate website, etc.

Figure 15.17 Foursquare Tactics for the XYZ Coffee Company

© Cengage Learning 2013

EZINEARTICLES EzineArticles is one of the top article directories on the social Web.[39] It is a favorite among Internet marketers because this highly trafficked site allows authors to link articles back to their websites, therefore substantially improving search engine rankings. EzineArticles has earned an authoritative reputation by employing human reviewers, who impose strict criteria for style and content, thus attracting real-world experts to publish tens of thousands of new articles each month. In turn, these articles have been syndicated on millions of sites around the world.

EzineArticles tactics:

- Produce article content that the target audience will be interested in reading.

- A good article can range in length from several hundred to several thousand words, depending on the topic and the target audience.

- Use proper grammar and punctuation; readers will typically expect more research, fact checking, and polish from articles than they do from blogs.

- Obtain Expert status by writing well-researched articles in order to develop a strong following.

- Choose a good title to draw in readers; the title should be concise, descriptive, and give a solid idea of what the article will be about.

- Follow the guidelines of article directories to avoid unnecessary complications on the path to publication, and produce articles that people will be willing and able to read.

- Article should start by describing a problem, offering some common solutions, and then discussing what special benefits the product being marketed has in solving that problem.

- Draw attention to the product, and develop a company's reputation for thought leadership; then use that expertise to generate sales.

- Use more subtle framing than a standard advertising pitch. Do not include the product name in the description or title.

- Put valuable, general information first and then specific details about the product's advantages toward the end.

Figure 15.18 shows how some of these article directory tactics can be tailored for a particular company.

EzineArticles is one of the top article directories on the social Web. It is a favorite among Internet marketers because this highly trafficked site allows authors to link articles back to their websites, a process that can substantially improve search engine rankings. EzineArticles has earned an authoritative reputation by employing human reviewers, who impose strict criteria for style and content, thus attracting real-world experts to publish tens of thousands of new articles each month. In turn, these articles have been syndicated on millions of sites around the world.

The following EzineArticles tactical actions will be taken:

- Produce article content that the target audience will be interested in reading
- Articles should be entertaining, easy-to-read, and no more than 500 words
- Obtain Expert Status by writing well-researched articles in order to develop a strong following
- Choose a good title to draw in readers that is concise, descriptive, and gives a solid idea of what the article will be about
- Follow the guidelines of article directories to avoid unnecessary complications on the path to publication and produce articles that people will be willing and able to read
- Use more subtle framing than a standard advertising pitch and do not include the product name in the description or title
- Post an article each week and respond to comments daily

Figure 15.18 Article Directory Tactics for the XYZ Coffee Company

© Cengage Learning 2013

CREATING CONTENT

Although each social media platform will require specific types of content, it is possible to provide some general guidelines for generating and using content across most platforms:

- **Developing or Acquiring Content**: A thorough analysis of the content needs for each social media platform should be conducted, identifying the specific needs of each community, finding the gaps in content, and either creating or acquiring the content. A careful inventory of existing content within an organization may uncover material that can be repurposed for use on social media platforms. In addition, third parties, such as freelance writers, can be contracted to prepare platform-specific content.

- **Managing Content**: Regardless of whether platform content is prepared in-house or outsourced, it will still require editing. Moreover, user content on private social networks, brand communities, and company-run discussion boards should be moderated, with careful grafting and pruning of discussion threads to keep them on-topic and generating productive conversations.

- **Cross-utilizing Content**: A great way to leverage content across platforms is to restructure it for cross-platform utilization. Be careful not to overutilize this procedure because it may trigger unwanted attention from search engines, which might deem too much similar content as spam and lower its search ranking. In some cases search engines may even exclude the content from their primary search index. Either situation would certainly reduce traffic to the company's sites via search engines.

- **Breaking Apart Content**: Making content into smaller chunks and reformatting it will stretch the utilization of the material, allowing it to appear in various forms on multiple platforms, such as article directories, blogs, microblogs, podcasts, webinars, and discussion boards.[40]

Figure 15.19 displays the content tactics for the imaginary XYZ Coffee Company.

Content Development

Although each social media platform will feature specific types of content, the following tactics will maximize the generation of quality content that can be repurposed multiple times, saving time and money and creating the greatest possible impact:

- **Developing Content**: A thorough analysis of the content needs for each social media platform will be conducted, identifying the specific needs for each community, finding the gaps in content, and filling them with content that satisfies consumer needs. A careful inventory of existing content within an organization will be undertaken to find material that can be repurposed for use on social media platforms.
- **Managing Content**: Social media content will be carefully edited before posting and consumer contributions will be moderated to ensure the brand community conversation stays on topic.
- **Cross-utilizing Content**: To leverage existing content, it will be adapted to each type of platform for proper cross-utilization. Care will be taken not to overutilize this procedure because it may trigger unwanted attention from search engines.
- **Breaking Apart Content**: Breaking content into smaller chunks and reformatting it will stretch the utilization of the material, allowing it to appear in various forms on multiple platforms, such as article directories, blogs, microblogs, podcasts, webinars, discussion boards, and so on.

Figure 15.19 Content Creation Tactics for XYZ Coffee Company

ASSIGNING ROLES

In order to execute platform-specific tactics and generate content, specific roles and responsibilities must be assigned based on expertise and availability of staff. Some traditional approaches to making these assignments include giving the job to the marketing, public relations, or advertising department or entirely outsourcing the undertaking to an agency. Unfortunately, these approaches have not met with a great deal of success because existing department personnel typically lack the skill and expertise to engage effectively in social media marketing and outside agencies lack the intimate knowledge of a company's products, customer support, and culture.[41]

The most successful social media marketing efforts result from having nontraditional roles lead the conversation. For example, Home Depot has its associates respond to questions on Twitter, Ford has its mechanics tweet about their automobiles, and Starbucks has its baristas lead the conversation.[42]

In short, roles for executing the social media marketing plan should be assigned to those with the knowledge, expertise, and training to effectively engage with consumers on the social web. These individuals can be employees with the proper social media training or social media marketing specialists and community managers hired by the company and then thoroughly trained in the use of its products and services, as well as indoctrinated with the organization's culture and values, as depicted in Figure 15.20.

Assignments

In order to execute platform-specific tactics and generate content, specific roles and responsibilities will be assigned based on expertise and availability of staff. Assignments for executing the social media marketing plan will be carried out by those with the knowledge, experience, and training to effectively engage with consumers on the social web. The following personnel will be involved in the implementation of the social media plan:

- VP of marketing, Lisa Shea
- Director of communications, Mark Irick
- Social media marketing manager, Susan Monroe
- Hire the following positions:
  1. A community manager
  2. Multimedia video specialist
  3. A professional writer
  4. Two social media marketing specialists

Figure 15.20 Role Assignments for XYZ Coffee Company

Monitoring

As defined in Chapter 14, social media monitoring is the process of tracking, measuring, and evaluating an organization's social media marketing activities. Each of these activities presents unique challenges and opportunities for marketers.

TRACKING

Tracking is the process of finding and following content on the social web. One of the biggest challenges marketers face in setting up a tracking plan is to identify the right keywords and phrases for finding and following relevant data. A tracking plan should choose optimal topics of focus, select platforms with the greatest concentration of the target audience, identify optimal keywords and phrases by studying how people actually describe brands or other topics, use Boolean operators to zero in the desired data, and adjust searches when they do not produce the desired results.

MEASURING

The process of measuring social media marketing endeavors is currently highly controversial and an incredibly fast moving field. The intense pressure to demonstrate the value of expenditures on social media marketing is driving the rapid development of new measurement techniques, metrics, methodologies, technologies, and tools. Although quantitative measurements remain a crucial part of assessing online marketing initiatives, the vast majority of research, debate, and innovations are centered on qualitative measurement because it has demonstrated the most promise in connecting the dots between social media marketing and financial performance.[43]

The impact of social media marketing on such qualitative goals as increasing brand awareness, perception, and loyalty, as well as increasing customer relationships and brand advocacy, is long-term in nature. Typically, it takes time on the social web to strengthen a brand, improve how customers view support, and convince influencers to become brand evangelists. However, no one doubts that these activities can eventually contribute significantly to a company's bottom line. The challenge lies in showing how.

Despite the obstacles, no social media marketing plan would be complete without well-defined quantitative and qualitative Key Performance Indicators (KPIs) to assess the headway being made in reaching the organization's marketing goals. Table 15.6 shows the quantitative KPIs for the XYZ Coffee Company. Note these metrics are granular, designed to measure progress on individual social media platforms where the company's target audience can be found in the highest concentration.

A number of Key Performance Indicators are available for measuring the qualitative performance of social media marketing activities. As previously explained, KPIs should be chosen based on the marketing goals of an organization.

Table 15.7 depicts the qualitative KPIs for the XYZ Coffee Company. These metrics are arranged by the qualitative social media goals, indicating the name of the KPI, its formula, and its performance target.

EVALUATING

As defined in Chapter 14, **evaluation** is the process of interpreting data once it has been measured with the intention to derive insights and understanding from it. Just measuring the impact of social media activity is insufficient—measurement only gains meaning through analysis. Such analysis enables management to determine whether social media strategies are achieving the organization's goals.

The aim of an appropriately focused evaluation is to produce a thorough description of the progress of social media marketing activities over time to reveal where strategies have succeeded or nose-dived, along with how things went right or wrong and why.

Social Media Platform	Quantitative Key Performance Indicators (KPIs) for the Next Year
Facebook	• 40% growth in the number of likes • 20% growth in the number of fans • 20% increase in the number of comments and likes on admin post • 5% growth in the number of wall response time • 40% increase in the number of Facebook Places check-ins • 30% increase in visits to company website from Facebook ads
Twitter	• 30% growth in the number of followers • 30% growth in the number of retweets (message amplification) • 30% growth in the number of mentions • 10% increase in click-through rate (CTR) of the links posted in tweets (Note: Observing which types of links garner the highest CTRs can help in tuning tweets to provide consumers with links they are interested in and hence further improve the CTRs.) • 20% increase in visits to website from tweet links • 5% increase in website conversions (i.e., sales) from tweet links
LinkedIn	• 20% growth in the number of connections • 10% increase in the number of recommendations • 20% growth in the number of posts and comments in discussion groups • 20% increase in the number of group members • 15% growth in the number of questions answered or asked
YouTube	• 30% growth in the number of videos viewed • 20% growth in the number of unique visitors • 10% increase in the number of subscribers to company channel • 10% increase in positive comments • 15% growth in visits to company website from YouTube • 10% increase in average rankings of videos by viewers
Flickr	• 20% growth in the number of views of video/photo • 30% growth in the number of replies • 20% growth in the number of page views • 30% growth in the number of comments • 30% growth in the number of subscribers • 15% growth in visits to company website from Flickr
Brand Community	• 30% growth in the number of visits • 20% growth in the number of relevant topics/threads • 30% growth in the number of individual replies • 20% growth in the number of sign-ups • 30% growth in the incoming links • 30% growth in the citations in other sites • 20% growth in the tagging in social bookmarking • 30% growth in the offline references to the forum or its members
Foursquare	• 30% growth in the number of impressions • 40% growth in the number of check-ins • 40% growth in the number of redemptions (comes from point-of-sale systems) • 30% growth in the number of visitors to business after viewing venue/special on foursquare (foot traffic)
EzineArticles	• 40% growth in the number of published articles • 20% growth in the number of article views • 30% growth in the article niches • 40% growth in the number of sites that pickups articles (syndication rate) • 20% growth in the number of inbound links from syndicated articles (required website analytics)

Table 15.6 Quantitative KPIs for XYZ Coffee Company

Social Media Goals	Key Performance Indicators	KPI Formula	KPI (One-year) Performance Targets
Brand Strengthening	Sentiment Ratio (SR)	$SR = \dfrac{\text{Postitive: Neutral: Negative Brand Mentions}}{\text{Expenses}}$	10% increase
Word of Mouth	Share of Voice (SV)	$SV = \dfrac{\text{Brand Mentions}}{\text{Total Mentions}}$	15% increase
	Audience Engagement (AE)	$AE = \dfrac{\text{Comments} + \text{Shares} + \text{Trackbacks}}{\text{Total Views}}$	20% increase
	Conversation Reach (CR)	$CR = \dfrac{\text{Total People Participating}}{\text{Total Audience Exposure}}$	10% increase
Customer Satisfaction	Issue Resolution Rate (IRR)	$IRR = \dfrac{\text{Total \# Issues Resolved Satisfactorily}}{\text{Total \# Service Issues}}$	10% increase
	Resolution Time (RT)	$RT = \dfrac{\text{Total Inquiry Response Time}}{\text{Total \# Service Inquiries}}$	20% increase
	Satisfaction Score (SC)	$SC = \dfrac{\text{Customer Feedback}}{\text{Total Customer Feedback}}$	25% increase
Generating New Product Ideas	Topic Trend (TT)	$TT = \dfrac{\text{\# of Specific Topic Mentions}}{\text{All Topic Mentions}}$	20% increase
	Idea Impact (II)	$II = \dfrac{\text{\# of Positive Conversations, Shares, Mentions}}{\text{Total Idea Conversations, Shares, Mentions}}$	15% increase
Promoting Advocacy	Active Advocates (AA)	$AA = \dfrac{\text{Total \# of Active Advocates within 30 days}}{\text{Total Advocates}}$	20% increase
	Advocate Influence (AIN)	$AIN = \dfrac{\text{Unique Advocate's Influence}}{\text{Advocate Influence}}$	15% increase
	Advocacy Impact (AIM)	$AIM = \dfrac{\text{Number of Advocacy Driven Conversations}}{\text{Total Volume of Advocacy Traffic}}$	20% increase

Table 15.7 Qualitative KPIs for XYZ Coffee Company

Accordingly, "[such analysis] allows the program team to see where it must focus its efforts and resources next. It identifies success and failure, opportunities and risks, potential improvements, and new courses of action."[44]

SELECTING MONITORING TOOLS

As explained in the measurement section above, well-defined marketing goals should drive the decision regarding which social media metrics to measure and, consequently, the selection of the most appropriate monitoring tools. Free monitoring tools work well for listening to social media (i.e., observing what people are saying about a brand). Google Alerts, Google Trends, Google Reader, and SocialMention are popular free tools for tracking quantitative metrics. Google Web Analytics is useful for assessing the effectiveness of social media efforts directed at driving traffic to the company website and the consequent conversions (e.g., sales). Paid monitoring tools, such as Radian6, provide all-in-one solutions for tracking, measuring, and aiding in the analysis of qualitative metrics. Pricing of these tools should also be a key consideration in the selection process. Chapter 14 lists some popular free and paid tools along with which tasks each is best suited to accomplish.

TUNING

As defined in Chapter 2, **tuning** is the constant and continuous process of adjusting and improving the elements of the plan to maximize the chances of success. This process involves assessing a company's progress in implementing its social media strategies and then adjusting the social media marketing plan based on this feedback to optimize goal achievement.

Reevaluating the goals, strategies, and execution of the plan is necessary because of the ever-changing nature of consumer tastes, countermoves by competitors, and the continual introduction of new social media technologies. For example, if the number of views of the company's YouTube channel begins to decline, marketers must react quickly to adjust the content to match the target market's evolving interests.

If comments on the YouTube Channel are falling off as well, marketers need to reexamine and modify platform-specific tactics, possibly creating more humorous or how-to videos, which better fit the target market's shifting tastes. If this does not work, then additional adjustments in content should be made until the number of audience comments pick up again. In short, planning and executing social media marketing activities is a never-ending cycle. Marketers must constantly monitor and tune the plan to attain the maximize results.[45]

BUDGETING

Although there are no hard and fast rules about how much a company should invest in social media marketing, a survey of 140 global corporations provides some valuable budgetary guidelines (the following material was adapted and excerpted from the report, *How Corporations Should Prioritize Social Business Budgets*, courtesy of the Altimeter Group)* This 2010 study found that these corporations had spent between $66,000 and $1,364,000 on social media marketing, largely dependent upon the maturity level of the company, as depicted in Table 15.8.

These 140 companies were categorized into *novice, intermediate*, and *advanced* groups using the the questionnaire shown in Figure 15.21. The questionaire assessed the

	Novice	Intermediate	Advanced
Average Budget	$66,000	$1,002,000	$1,364,000
Average Team Size	3.1	8.2	20.8
Most Common Organizational Models	Centralized (37%)	Hub and Spoke (49%)	Hub and Spoke (44%)
	Decentralized (23%)	Centralized (25%)	Centralized (28%)
	Hub and Spoke (23%)	Multiple Hub and Spoke (18%)	Multiple Hub and Spoke (19%)

© The Altimeter Group

Table 15.8 Maturity Drives Average Budget, Team Size, and How Corporations Organized for Social Business in 2010

*From Owyang, Jeremiah, and Charlene Li (2011, February 11), *Report: How Corporations Should Prioritize Social Business Budgets*, Altimeter. Retrieved August 12, 2011, from http://www.altimetergroup.com/2011/02/report-how-corporations-should-prioritize-social-business-budgets.html

Assess Your Social Business Maturity Level

For each section, choose the statement that best describes your social business program. Give yourself 1 point if you choose "1," 2 points if you choose "2," and 3 points if you choose "3." Add up your total score below to determine your social business maturity level.

A. Program
____ **1.** We are mostly experimenting with social media.
____ **2.** We've launched long-term initiatives that are part of an overall social strategy.
____ **3.** Social business permeates the enterprise — it's transcended the Marketing department, and impacts Product, Support, R&D, etc.

B. Leadership and Organizational Model
____ **1.** We do not have a formalized Social Strategist role or organizational model.
____ **2.** We've organized into a Hub and Spoke model with a formal Social Strategist role at the helm.
____ **3.** We've evolved to a Multiple Hub and Spoke or Holistic model, and business units can deploy on their own with little guidance from the Hub.

C. Processes and Policies
____ **1.** We have not conducted internal audits or established processes or policies for governance.
____ **2.** We've conducted internal audits and established processes and policies across the enterprise.
____ **3.** We've created clear processes and workflow across cross-functional teams.

D. Education
____ **1.** There is no formal education program to train internal associates.
____ **2.** We've launched an education program but it's not rolled out to the entire company.
____ **3.** We've formalized an ongoing education program that serves as a resource for all employees.

E. Measurement
____ **1.** We've tied our social media efforts back to engagement metrics, like number of clicks, fans, followers, RTs, check-ins, etc.
____ **2.** We've tied our social media efforts back to social media analytics, like share of voice, resonation, word of mouth, etc.
____ **3.** We've tied our social media efforts back to business metrics, like revenue, reputation, CSAT, etc.

F. Technology
____ **1.** We've invested in brand monitoring to listen to and develop understanding of our customers.
____ **2.** We've invested in scalable technologies such as community platforms or social media management systems (SMMS).
____ **3.** We've invested in social integration with other digital touchpoints like the corporate website, kiosks, mobile devices, etc., across the entire customer lifecycle.

Total score _____

If you scored between **0 and 6** points, your program is at the **Novice** level.
If you scored between **7 and 12** points, your program is at the **Intermediate** level.
If you scored between **13–18** points, your program is at the **Advanced** level.

Your Social Business Maturity Level _____

Figure 15.21 Social Media Marketing Budget Questionnaire

social business maturity level of the company based on six general areas: Program, Leadership and Organization Model, Processes and Policies, Education, Measurement, and Techonolgy. Companies with a score of below 6 are clasified as Novice, a score of 7-12 are Intermediate, and a score above 12 are Advanced.

According to Table 15.9, spending in social media will grow dramatically in 2011 in the following three categories:

1. **Internal Soft Costs in three areas**: staff to manage social media, training and education, and research and development.

2. **Customer-Facing Initiatives in four areas**: boutique agencies specializing in social media, spending on advertising and marketing, traditional agencies deploying social media campaign, and influencer/blogger program.

3. **Technology Investments in five areas**: custom technology development, community platforms, brand monitoring, social customer relation management (SCRM), and social media management systems (SMMS).

So how should a company prioritize its social media spending? It depends on a company's maturity level. When a company is just experimenting with social media, without much presence on any social media platform and, hence, is in the novice stage, a dedicated core team should start with monitoring the social web to create a social media plan and develop a training program for the core team before deploying a social media marketing campaign.

During the intermediate stage, with management buy-in and the core social media team garnering addition funding, the company is in a position to develop a brand community and utilize social media management systems (SMMS) to create "highly engaged communities across the social web."[46]

	Novice		Intermediate		Advanced	
	Adoption	Spending	Adoption	Spending	Adoption	Spending
Internal Soft Costs						
Staff to Manage	68%	$133,000	76%	$303,000	88%	$406,000
Training and Education	85%	$9,000	76%	$15,000	76%	$66,000
Research and Development	55%	$8,000	75%	$59,000	74%	$56,000
Customer-Facing Initiatives						
Boutique Agencies (specializing in SM)	32%	$31,000	55%	$96,000	59%	$233,000
Ad/Marketing Spend	63%	$36,000	78%	$204,000	76%	$195,000
Traditional Agencies (deploying SM)	52%	$51,000	49%	$162,000	35%	$87,000
Influencer/Blogger Programs	37%	$12,000	66%	$60,000	85%	$50,000
Technology Investments						
Custom Technology Development	28%	$11,000	58%	$55,000	66%	$272,000
Community Platforms	42%	$78,000	58%	$126,000	78%	$196,000
Brand Monitoring	60%	$42,000	87%	$108,000	89%	$150,000
Social CRM	6%	$1,000	42%	$27,000	44%	$116,000
Social Media Management Systems	39%	$4,000	60%	$28,000	72%	$23,000

Base: 140 Global Corporate Social Strategists; for spending, those who have adopted each social business category.

Table 15.9 Average Adoption and Spending on 12 Social Business Categories by Corporations in 2011 by Program Maturity Level

As the company graduates into the advanced stage, the focus will shift into integrating social media throughout the entire business. Instead of having a core team of social media strategists, the company is ready to develop a set of clearly defined social media guidelines to educate all employees, and unleash them onto the social web.

To allow employees to be brand ambassadors, it is crucial to develop "a social media policy that [goes] so far as to show employees the best way to be interesting, add value and build their own networks online."[47] Investment in a scalable social customer relations management (SCRM) is also required "to gather and analyze the increasing amount of data from social profiles and interactions, then connect this information to core customer data . . . to deepen relationships and anticipate customer needs."[48]

Figure 15.22 displays the budget for the XYZ Coffee Company.

Budget

The following are the estimated expenses to implement this plan and achieve the stated goals within the next year:

Community Platform Software	$50,000
Monitoring Tool	$10,000
A Community Manager	$80,000
A Video Specialist	$50,000
Content Creation and Copyediting	$50.000
Two Social Media Specialists	$100,000
Total expenses for the year	$375,000

Figure 15.22 Budget for the XYZ Coffee Company

ESTIMATING RETURN ON INVESTMENT

In finance, return on investment (ROI) is calculated by subtracting expenses from sales, and then dividing the result by the expenses. If the subsequent ratio is positive, then the investment shows a return (the larger the ratio, the higher the return.) Unfortunately, it is often difficult, if not impossible, to calculate a financial ROI for many social media marketing investments, especially those with qualitative goals, such as improving brand awareness, brand engagement, and word-of-mouth.[49]

In these situations, marketers have been forced to develop reasonable proxies for financial measures of success.[50] A **Proxy ROI** is an estimate of the long-term impact of social media marketing investments on customer response.[51] Common Proxy ROIs include brand awareness, customer satisfaction, sentiment analysis, share of voice, Net Promoter scores, and so on.

The majority of social media marketing initiatives are aimed at impacting these qualitative metrics, such as using Facebook and Twitter to strengthen a brand or using a brand community to improve customer relationships. Debates about the validity of Proxy ROIs are heated and ongoing, with some critics challenging whether they can actually measure ROI.[52] However, some studies have found direct linkages between Proxy ROIs and financial performance over the long run.[53]

Regardless of the ongoing debate about Proxy ROIs, they often provide the only viable alternative to justifying the investment in a social media marketing plan, thereby explaining why they are in widespread use today and continue to grow in popularity. Whenever it becomes unrealistic or infeasible to calculate financial ROIs for a social media marketing plan, estimates of proxy ROIs should be considered as a means to explain the expected rewards for investing in the plan, as illustrated in Figure 15.23.

Return on Investment

The location marketing and article marketing strategies aim at increasing website traffic and hence sales, so it will be possible to calculate their respective financial ROIs. However, the majority of the social media goals for the XYZ Coffee Company are not directly connected to sales, and consequently, standard ROI analysis will not be feasible. Fortunately, there are viable alternatives for estimating the return on investment for these social media goals.

Proxy ROIs measure the long-term impact of social media marketing investments on customer response. They include both quantitative and qualitative measurements, such as the number of views of the company's social media properties; the company's posting activity, and the customer responses rates, as well as sentiment analysis, share of voice, satisfaction scores, and advocacy impact. These proxy ROIs provide a meaningful way to judge the expected rewards for investing in this plan.

Figure 15.23 ROI for XYZ Coffee Company

Getting C-Suite Buy-In

With the social media marketing plan complete, the time has come to convince the "**C-Suite**" that the investment in social media will payoff for the company. The C-Suite is a term widely used for a corporation's top executives, who have titles that often start with the letter C, for chief, such as in chief executive officer, chief information officer, chief financial officer, and chief operating officer.[54] The following are few tips to help gain the buy-in of these top level decision makers:

- **Identify with the Mindset of These Executives**: These are busy big-picture people who want to hear the broad brushstrokes of the plan, not the minute details of how the company will gain followers on Facebook.

- **Show Them the Payoff**: In asking for a sizeable investment, the first question these top executives will want answered is "What is the return on investment?" With social media marketing efforts, the return on investment will likely have to be couched as proxy results, such as improved sentiment analysis scores showing brand strengthening or improved customer relationship metrics. Stress that it takes time to realize returns from social media efforts, but emphasize that payoff can be big—and have a few studies handy to back up this assertion.

- **Present a Detailed Budget Request**: These folks will also want to know how the company's money is being spent. Be as specific as possible as to what social media initiative will cost, and link the expenditures to desired outcomes.

- **Show Them the Timetable for Reaching Milestones**: Although social media marketing should be an ongoing activity for a company, progress in achieving marketing goals should have milestones. These milestones are often best given in conjunction with the Key Performance Indicators so that executives can quickly see the projected time it will take to reach each milestone (such as six months to increase the company's share of voice).

- **Close the Deal**: Summarize the key benefits of the implementing of the plan while being transparent about potential downsides and the preparations that will be taken to mitigate them if they occur. Underscore that having a plan and executing it efficiently enables the company to act proactively rather than retroactively on the social web.[55]

Review Questions for the XYZ Coffee Company Social Media Marketing Plan

1. Why should the XYZ Coffee Company observe its social media presence before moving forward with preparing a social media marketing plan? Explain.

2. How will the XYZ Coffee Company's social media strategies help it achieve the organization's marketing goals for the social web?

3. Where will the company's target audiences most likely reside on the social web and what are they likely to be doing on these social media platforms?

4. Beyond the social media platforms that the XYZ Coffee Company has chosen to focus on, what other platforms might be worthwhile in investing resources on to reach its target audiences? Explain your rationale.

5. Would you change how the company monitors its progress in achieving its social media marketing goals? If so, how? If not, why not?

Notes

1. Ballenthin, Andrew (2009, October 5), "5 Reasons Why 90% of Social Media Efforts Fail," *Community Marketing Blog*. Retrieved August 6, 2011, from http://communitymarketing. typepad.com/my_weblog/2009/10/5-reasons-why-90-of-social-media-efforts-fail.html
2. "Create a Table of Contents or Update a Table of Contents" (n.d.), Microsoft. Retrieved August 7, 2011, from http://office.microsoft.com/en-us/word-help/create-a-table-of-contents-or-update-a-table-of-contents-HP010368778.aspx
3. "Writing Guide: Executive Summaries" (n.d.), Colorado State University. Retrieved August 7, 2011, from http://writing.colostate.edu/guides/documents/execsum/index.cfm
4. Clay (2011, February 9), "Getting It Right: How to Write a Winning Executive Summary," Towson University. Retrieved August 5, 2011, from http://tuoutreach.com/2011/02/09/getting-it-right-how-to-write-a-winning-executive-summary/
5. Menzies, M. Dusty, M. Edward Rister, Saudah Sinaga, Victoria Salin, Eluned Jones, and Jenny Bialek (2009, August 31), *Agricultural Economics Undergraduate Writing Handbook—2009* (College Station: Texas A&M University). Retrieved August 8, 2011, from http://agecon2.tamu.edu/people/faculty/williams-gary/429/Complete%20Writing%20Guidelines.pdf
6. "How to Write an Executive Summary" (2011, January 10), Succeed as Your Own Boss. Retrieved August 5, 2011, from http://succeedasyourownboss.com/01/2011/how-to-write-an-executive-summary/
7. "Writing Executive Summaries: Justification" (n.d.), Colorado State University. Retrieved August 7, 2011, from http://writing.colostate.edu/guides/documents/execsum/pop2h.cfm
8. Foster, Lorne (2005, June), "Writing the Executive Summary," York University, Toronto. Retrieved August 7, 2011, from http://www.yorku.ca/lfoster/2005-06/soci4440b/lectures/PolicyPaperWriting_TheExecutiveSummary.html
9. Greenhall, Margaret (n.d.), "Writing an Executive Summary, with Examples," UoLearn. Retrieved August 7, 2011, from http://www.uolearn.com/reportwriting/writingexecutivesummaries.html
10. "How to Write Executive Summary" (2011, January 24), Invest Engine. Retrieved August 5, 2011, from http://investengine.com/blog/how-to-write-executive-summary
11. "Executive Summary" (n.d.), Howe Writing Initiative, Miami School of Business, Farmer School of Business. Retrieved August 7, 2011, from http://www.fsb.muohio.edu/fsb/content/

programs/howe-writing-initiative/student-resources/Writing%20an%20Executive%20 Summary.doc

12. "Suggestions for Improvement—Executive Summary Example" (2011, January 23), Executive Plan. Retrieved August 5, 2011, from http://www.businessplanexecutivesummary. com/2011/01/suggestions-for-improvement-executive-summary-example.html

13. "How to Write Executive Summary" (2011, January 24), Invest Engine. Retrieved August 5, 2011, from http://investengine.com/blog/how-to-write-executive-summary

14. "How to Write an Effective Business Plan" (2011, May 16), BigHospitality. Retrieved August 8, 2011, from http://www.bighospitality.co.uk/Business/How-to-write-an-effective-business-plan

15. Evans, Mark (2011, July 20), "Brand Health and Social Media," *Sysomos Blog*. Retrieved August 9, 2011, from http://blog.sysomos.com/2011/07/20/brand-health-and-social-media/

16. Ibid.

17. Engler, Glenn (2011, March 5), "Social Media—The Future of Your Brand Health," Random Patterns of Thoughts. Retrieved August 9, 2011, from http://www.glennengler.com/brands/ social-media-the-future-of-your-brand-health/

18. Rahman, Faria (2011, May 24), "Factors to Consider When Determining Brand Health," Retrieved August 9, 2011, from http://blog.openviewpartners.com/factors-to-consider-when-determining-brand-health-2/

19. Ibid.

20. Ogneva, Maria (2010, April 10), "How Companies Can Use Sentiment Analysis to Improve Their Business," Mashable. Retrieved August 9, 2011, from http://mashable.com/2010/04/19/ sentiment-analysis/

21. Qian, Albert (2011, May 22), "Is There a Standard Format for Preparing Social Media Audit?" Quora. Retrieved August 9, 2011, from http://www.quora.com/Is-there-a-standard-format-for-preparing-social-media-audit

22. Seiple, Pamela (2011, July 1), "Top 5 Metrics for Auditing Your Social Media Marketing ROI," *HubSpot Blog*, retrieved August 14, 2011, from http://blog.hubspot.com/blog/tabid/6307/ bid/18643/Top-5-Metrics-for-Auditing-Your-Social-Media-Marketing-ROI.aspx and "Social Media Metrics" (2009, August 11), *Emerging Technologies Librarian Blog*, retrieved August 14, 2011, from http://etechlib.wordpress.com/2009/08/11/social-media-plan-metrics/

23. Stephan, Nikki (2011, May 5), "How to Conduct a Comprehensive Social Media Audit," *Arik Hanson Communications Conversations Blog*. Retrieved August 14, 2011, from http://www. arikhanson.com/2011/05/05/how-to-conduct-a-comprehensive-social-media-audit/

24. Ibid.

25. Hoult, Kevin (n.d.), "Strategic Planning for Social Media Marketing: Strategic Planning Worksheet" [SWOT and Target Marketing template], Social Media Conference NW. Retrieved October 7, 2011, from http://www.socialmediaconferencenw.com/speakers/presentations/ Strategic%20Planning%20for%20Social%20Media%20Workbook.pdf

26. Kokemuller, Neil (n.d.), "Purpose of a SWOT Analysis," Chron, Small Business. Retrieved August 10, 2011, from http://smallbusiness.chron.com/purpose-swot-analysis-15364.html

27. Rothwell, Phil (2010, May 25), "What Is a SWOT Analysis?" FreshBusinessThinking. Retrieved August 10, 2011, from http://www.freshbusinessthinking.com/business_advice.php? AID=5743&Title=What+Is+A+SWOT+Analysis?

28. "Social Media SWOT Analysis" (n.d.), Entrepreneurship in Box. Retrieved August 8, 2011, from http://www.entrepreneurshipinabox.com/1484/social-media-swot-analysis/

29. "Social Media SWOT Analysis" (n.d.), Entrepreneurship in Box. Retrieved August 8, 2011, from http://www.entrepreneurshipinabox.com/1484/social-media-swot-analysis/

30. "SWOT Analysis" (n.d.), QuickMBA. Retrieved September 1, 2011, from http://www. quickmba.com/strategy/swot/

31. "Social Media SWOT Analysis" (n.d.), SEO Wizardry. Retrieved August 8, 2011, from http:// www.seowizardry.ca/social-media-swot-analysis

32. Kincaid, Jason (2011, June 23), "Facebook Now Has 750 Million Users," Tech Crunch. Retrieved August 11, 2011, from http://techcrunch.com/2011/06/23/facebook-750-million-users/

33. "Top 15 Most Popular Social Networking Sites" (2011, August 8), eBizMBA, retrieved August 11, 2011, from http://www.ebizmba.com/articles/social-networking-websites and "Top 15 Most Popular Web 2.0 Websites" (2011, August 8), eBizMBA, retrieved August 11, 2011, from http://www.ebizmba.com/articles/web-2.0-websites

34. "Top 15 Most Popular Web 2.0 Websites" (2011, August 8), eBizMBA. Retrieved August 11, 2011, from http://www.ebizmba.com/articles/web-2.0-websites

35. Ibid.

36. Ibid.

37. Borges, Bernie (2009), *Marketing 2.0* (Tucson, AZ: Wheatmark), p. 85.

38. Garcia, Nancy (2011, August 3), "New Features For Brands Using Foursquare Business Pages," *Piehead Blog*. Retrieve August 11, 2011, from http://www.piehead.com/blog/2011/08/new-features-for-brands-using-foursquare-business-pages

39. "Top 50 Article Directories by Traffic, Pagerank" (2011, August 11), Virtual Real Estate Toolbar. Retrieved August 11, 2011, from http://www.vretoolbar.com/articles/directories.php

40. Murthey, Steve (2010, October 13), "Eight Components for Social Media Success: #3 Content Plan/Programming Schedule," Social Media Considerations. Retrieved August 5, 2011, from http://stevemurthey.com/2010/10/13/eight-components-for-social-media-success-3-content-plan-programming-schedule/

41. Martin, Erroin A. (2010, June 7), "7 Components of a Winning Social Media Plan," Von Gehr Consulting. Retrieved August 5, 2011, from http://vongehrconsulting.com/Finding-Answers-Blog/2010/06/7-components-of-a-winning-social-media-plan/

42. Ibid.

43. "New Study: Deep Brand Engagement Correlates with Financial Performance," (2009, July 20), Altimeter. Retrieved August 12, 2011, from http://www.altimetergroup.com/2009/07/engagementdb.html

44. Blanchard, Olivier (2011), *Social Media ROI: Managing and Measuring Social Media Efforts in Your Organization* (Boston, MA: Pearson Education) p. 196.

45. Barker, Melissa S. (2011, April 14), "5 Steps to a Winning Social Media Marketing Plan," *New Social Media Marketing Blog*. Retrieved August 12, 2011, from http://www.new-social-media-marketing.com/blog/5-steps-to-a-winning-social-media-marketing-plan/

46. Swallow, Erica (2011, February 10), "HOW TO: Optimize Your Social Medial Budget," Mashable. Retrieved August 12, 2011, from http://mashable.com/2011/02/10/optimize-social-media-budget/

47. O'Dell, Jolie (2011, July 28), "HOW TO: Help Employees Talk about Your Brand Online," Mashable. Retrieved August 12, 2011, from http://mashable.com/2010/07/28/internal-brand-management-online/

48. Owyang, Jeremiah, and Charlene Li (2011, February 11), *Report: How Corporations Should Prioritize Social Business Budgets*, Altimeter. Retrieved August 12, 2011, from http://www.altimetergroup.com/2011/02/report-how-corporations-should-prioritize-social-business-budgets.html

49. Hoffman, Donna L., and Marek Fodor (2010, Fall), "Can You Measure the ROI of Your Social Media Marketing?" *MIT Sloan Management Review*, vol. 52, no. 1, SlideShare. Retrieved August 12, 2011, from http://www.slideshare.net/MichaelGaspar/mit-5769540

50. Briody, Kevin (2011, April 22), "Social Media ROI Revisited: 4 Ways to Measure," Ignite. Retrieved August 12, 2011, from http://www.ignitesocialmedia.com/social-media-measurement/social-media-roi-revisited-4-ways-to-measure/

51. Briody, Kevin (2011, April 22), "Social Media ROI Revisited: 4 Ways to Measure," Ignite, retrieved August 12, 2011, from http://www.ignitesocialmedia.com/social-media-measurement/social-media-roi-revisited-4-ways-to-measure/ and Hoffman, Donna L., and Marek Fodor (2010, Fall), "Can You Measure the ROI of Your Social Media Marketing?" *MIT Sloan Management Review*, vol. 52, no. 1, SlideShare, retrieved August 12, 2011, from http://www.slideshare.net/MichaelGaspar/mit-5769540

52. Briody, Kevin (2011, April 22), "Social Media ROI Revisited: 4 Ways to Measure," Ignite. Retrieved August 12, 2011, from http://www.ignitesocialmedia.com/social-media-measurement/social-media-roi-revisited-4-ways-to-measure/

53. "New Study: Deep Brand Engagement Correlates with Financial Performance" (2009, July 20), Altimeter. Retrieved August 12, 2011, from http://www.altimetergroup.com/2009/07/engagementdb.html

54. "C-Suite" (n.d.), *Investopedia*. Retrieved August 7, 2011, from http://www.investopedia.com/terms/c/c-suite.asp

55. Kelly, Nichole (2011, April 11), "7 Tips for Selling Executives on Social Media," Social Media Examiner. Retrieved August 8, 2011, from http://www.socialmediaexaminer.com/7-tips-for-selling-executives-on-social-media/

XYZ Coffee Company

Social Media Marketing Plan

Prepared by:

Lisa Shea | Mark Irick | Susan Monroe

6/1/2012

XYZ Coffee Company

Headquarters: Spokane, WA

Voice: 000-000-0000 | Fax: 000-000-0000

Appendix

XYZ Coffee Company Social Media Marketing Plan

Table of Contents

Executive Summary

XYZ Coffee Company has a wide range of market segments, ranging from luxury coffee drinkers to professionals. However, younger people are not typically coffee drinkers, and they represent a lucrative, massive, untapped market segment, especially the more affluent youths.

The primary focus of this social media marketing plan is to use the social web as a means to find, engage, attract, and retain this upscale youth market as XYZ Coffee Company patrons. It is based on comprehensive research of the company's current social media presence, competitive intelligence, and target market analysis. This thorough examination and appraisal has resulted in a set of specific actionable social media goals and in optimal strategies for reaching those goals as well as the best social media tools for successfully executing and monitoring the plan.

Social media goals for the XYZ Coffee Company include:

- Strengthening the brand, primarily among the more affluent youth market segment

- Driving word-of-mouth recommendations

- Improving customer satisfaction

- Generating and implementing new product ideas

- Promoting advocacy

- Increasing foot traffic in the stores

- Search Engine Optimization (SEO) to increase traffic and conversions

A set of comprehensive social media strategies will be employed to achieve the above goals. These strategies include listening, interacting, engaging, embracing, influencing, and contributing to the social web. In addition, this plan describes how the progress of social media efforts will be tracked, measured, and evaluated. These actions will enable the plan's execution to be tuned to obtain optimal results.

A detailed budget shows the cost of implementing the plan. The plan concludes with a return on investment analysis. The team leaders responsible for preparing, overseeing, and executing the plan include the VP of marketing, Lisa Shea; the director of communications, Mark Jones; and the social media marketing manager, Susan Monroe.

Brief Overview

Over the last two decades, coffeehouses have become part of the American landscape. Millions of people purchase an espresso-based coffee drink daily. The willingness to spend $3 to $5 for a cappuccino, mocha latte, or chocolate-ice-blended drink occurred within just the last decade, largely due to Starbucks. The specialty-coffeehouse industry continues to grow at a strong pace.

Affluent youth, not normally heavy consumers of coffee, represent a niche market that has yet to be tapped. As explained below in detail, social media can be used to observe, interact, engage, and influence this market segment. These actions will help attract and retain this youth market as XYZ Coffee Company patrons, in combination with XYZ Coffee Company's high-volume, upscale, inviting atmosphere, and high-quality products. Moreover, most of the XYZ Coffee Company's locations are near university or college campuses, locations that provide easy access for this target market.

Social Media Presence

XYZ Coffee Company began utilizing social media in 2009. Today, the social media health of the brand is good. Analysis of sentiment (opinion) across the social web shows that 55% of customer mentions of the company are positive. However, this sentiment analysis also reveals that 30% of company mentions are neutral, with a troubling 15% negative.

This last figure is less disturbing when compared with the negative sentiment analysis scores for the company's two closest competitors, ABC Coffee and Dolt Coffee Shops. Forty three percent of social mentions about ABC are negative, with a staggering 57% of social mentions of Dolt being negative. In this context XYZ's lower negatives indicate the company is doing a better job than the competition.

In addition to this holistic assessment of the social media presence of the company, it is useful to examine how the company is performing on individual social media platforms. The following are five key metrics for auditing a company's social media presence on individual social media platforms:

- **Sentiment Analysis**: Shows the number of positive, neutral, or negative mentions on each social media platform where the company has a sizable presence

- **Reach**: Indicates the number of Twitter followers, Facebook fans, LinkedIn group members, Flickr view count, and so on

- **Company Posts**: Measure how often the company posts on each social media platform

- **Feedback**: Shows the number of comments, likes, or replies to company-generated content

- **Average Response Time**: Measures response time to user comments on the company's social media properties[1]

Table A.1 uses several key metrics to provide a more granular look at the company's social media presence on six major social media properties.

Notice that the table indicates a strong and active social media presence on Facebook and Twitter, with respectable figures for LinkedIn and YouTube. The company's Flickr photostream metrics are low, but given the relatively lower traffic rate for this platform, the numbers are not unexpected. The table reveals that the company is making effective use of popular article directories, such as EzineArticles.

Competitive Analysis

By carefully listening to the social web and thoroughly assessing the company's social media resources, the following **Social Media SWOT Analysis** identifies the company's strengths and weaknesses on popular social media platforms, as well as the potential opportunities and threats posed by competitors and technological advancements on the social web, as shown in Table A.2.

Given the factors profiled in Table A.2, it is possible to determine a general strategy using the SWOT Matrix shown in Table A.3. Since XYZ Coffee Company's social media platform strengths and external opportunities are substantial, the SWOT Matrix recommends the pursuit of an S-O (Strength-Opportunity) strategy, which (according to the bulleted recommendations below) advises XYZ to pursue opportunities on the social

Metric	Sentiment	Reach	Company Posts	Feedback	Average Response Time to Feedback
Facebook Page	Positive 58% Neutral 31% Negative 11%	1,200,000 fans	2 daily	10 comments and 20 likes daily	2 hours
Twitter Account	Positive 60% Neutral 28% Negative 12%	350,000 followers	10 daily	50 @tweets 200 retweets daily	30 minutes
LinkedIn Page	Positive 50% Neutral 26% Negative 24%	25,000 followers	3 daily	6 replies daily	1 day
YouTube Channel	Positive 45% Neutral 27% Negative 28%	5,000 subscribers	2 per month	5 comments per video monthly	2 days
Flickr Photostream	Positive 45% Neutral 50% Negative 5%	3,000 monthly views	10 per month	2 comments per photo	1 week
EzineArticles	Positive 70% Neutral 21% Negative 9%	200 monthly views	3 articles per month	5 per article	1 week

© Cengage Learning 2013

Table A.1 Platform-specific Measurements of a Company's Social Media Presence

Strengths	Weaknesses
• XYZ has a strong brand presence on the majority of the major social media platforms. • The company has a proven track on social media platforms, such as Facebook and Twitter. • Most of the company's actions result in the desired outcomes on social media platforms. • XYZ has an experienced staff adept at effectively using Facebook and Twitter to market the company. • The staff is enthusiastic about working with Facebook and Twitter. • XYZ's quantitative social media marketing efforts are monitored to assess progress in achieving marketing goals. • Most of XYZ's management is supportive of XYZ's social media efforts, especially on Facebook and Twitter because they have proven their usefulness in improving the company's bottom line. • Resources are adequate for participating on some social media platforms, such as Facebook and Twitter. • XYZ's Facebook and Twitter are lively social media properties.	• XYZ has less than desirable brand presence on YouTube, LinkedIn, Flickr, and EzineArticles. It has no presence on Foursquare, an important platform for location marketing. • The company's track record on YouTube, LinkedIn, and Flickr is spotty. • The company's actions on YouTube, LinkedIn, Flickr, and EzineArticles have fallen short of expected outcomes. • XYZ currently lacks the expertise to effectively market on YouTube, LinkedIn, Flickr, and article directories like EzineArticles. • The staff is apprehensive about working with platforms such as YouTube, LinkedIn, Flickr, and article directories like EzineArticles. • The company presently lacks a comprehensive monitoring tool to track and measure qualitative progress across the social web and on specific platforms. • There has been an understandable reluctance by management to fully commit to an aggressive social media marketing campaign because of the inherent risks and costs in undertaking such an endeavor.

Table A.2 Social Media SWOT Analysis for the XYZ Coffee Company *(Continued)*

XYZ Coffee Company's comprehensive social media strategies include:

- **Listening** to the social web to determine where the company brand is being mentioned, who is talking about it, and what attracts consumers to the brand, as well as what is being said about competitors' brands.

- **Interacting** with consumers on Facebook and Twitter, where high concentrations of the target audience reside. Always acting as a contributor, not an overt promoter, to strengthen the brand by improving brand awareness, recognition, and perception. In addition, connecting with suppliers on LinkedIn to improve provider relationships.

- **Engaging** customers to drive word-of-mouth recommendations with YouTube viral brand videos and Flickr pictures showing the warm, friendly atmosphere of the coffee shops, where people hang out looking trendy.

- **Embracing** customers by establishing **a vibrant brand community**, where customers can pose questions about products and receive answers. In addition, participants will be encouraged to use the discussion forums to suggest innovative product ideas and provide valuable feedback about existing products and services. These actions will fortify customer relationships, improve customer satisfaction, and hence improve customer retention.

- **Influencing** the target market with YouTube videos and podcasts that feature interviews with the thought leaders in the coffee industry (mass influencers), enlisting them to help shape opinions about the company's products and services to promote brand advocacy on the social web.

- **Connecting** with customers by starting a location marketing program that rewards consumers for regular mobile check-ins at store locations using Foursquare.

- **Contributing** content to EzineArticles for widespread syndication and consequence improvement in search engine ranking, which in turn will increase website traffic and sales.

Target Market

XYZ Coffee Company has a wide range of market segments, ranging from luxury coffee drinkers to professionals. However, the members of the current generation of young adults are not typically coffee drinkers, and hence they represent a lucrative, massive, untapped market segment, especially the slightly upscale higher-income youths.

Forrester's Social Technographics Profile Tool indicates that 93% of U.S. males in the age range eighteen to twenty-four are spectators on the social web. Eighty-four percent of this market segment exhibits the persona of joiners, with 53% acting as social media critics and only 44% creating content.[2] U.S. females in the same age range are slightly less inclined to engage in the social web as spectators (85%), and more likely to be joiners (86%) and creators (48%), but less inclined to be critics (47%).[3]

Forrester Research surveys have determined that Generation Y online users constitute the largest group of creators, consisting of 37% of consumers ranging between ages eighteen and twenty-nine.[4] In other words, young urban social media users are the most active of the personas in producing videos, blog posts, articles, discussion forum text, and so on. In addition, these studies have found young women to be far more active on the social web as conversationalists than young men.

Tools

With the demographic and behavioral characteristics of the personas defined for the company's target market, the social media platforms with the highest concentration of the target audience have been chosen. The types of personas within the target market played a key role in the selection of each social media platform. For example, since the personas for both male and female demonstrate a high propensity to be joiners, the company's Facebook page was chosen to interact with them as a means of strengthening the brand.

Furthermore, females within the youth target audience are strong conversationalists, making the company's Twitter account an ideal social media platform for interacting with them, further strengthening the brand among this important target market. Moreover, given that many of the company's suppliers participate in LinkedIn, it was decided to also focus on this social network as a means to improve the quality of supplier relationships.

Since the males in the youth target market are more inclined to be critics of content while the females tend to be creators of content, it was deemed worthwhile to construct a brand community where the company could directly and more intimately embrace these groups by offering them a chance to provide feedback about the company's products, seek support assistance, and suggest new product ideas. The intent is to fortify customer relationships, improve customer satisfaction, and hence increase customer retention.

Given that Generation Y social media users constitute the largest group of creators, consisting of 37% of consumers ranging between ages eighteen and twenty-nine, YouTube was chosen in order to engage with this group by offering how-to videos about coffee drink selection and behind-the-scenes footage of how XYZ takes painstaking care preparing its own distinctive coffee blends. Additionally, there is an opportunity to use YouTube to show the company's above-and-beyond customer service with videos featuring employees helping customers in humorous nontraditional ways, such as running around and around a car in front of the store in order to help retrieve the customer's runaway pet.

Although Flickr is the home of professional and amateur photographers, it also attracts a large number of bloggers and marketers looking for photos to use. Businesses are also beginning to use Flickr as a way to convey the quality of their products, reveal a sense of their unique atmosphere and culture, and encourage brand enthusiasm.

In addition, mobile apps for smartphones will be used in conjunction with the social location service Foursquare to connect with customers using check-ins to reward regular patronage. Finally, EzineArticles, one of the top article directories that allows backlinks to the company's website from article submissions, was selected for its search-engine optimization potential (widely syndicated articles will likely increase search engine ranking, which has a direct correlation to increased website traffic, sales leads, and sales).

Implementation

The above goals, strategies, target market, and tools have been taken into consideration in creating the following actionable social media platform-specific tactics. In addition, this section of the plan indicates how content will be generated efficiently and effectively for each social media platform, as well as assigning staff to be responsible for carrying out these tactics and preparing content for dissemination on the various platforms.

PLATFORM-SPECIFIC TACTICS AND TOOLS

The social media platforms and tactics below where chosen as the optimal means for implementing the company's overall strategies and reaching its social media goals.

FACEBOOK Facebook is the most popular social network, with more than 750 million users.[5] It is especially well suited for interacting with existing and potential consumers. Hence XYZ Coffee Company will use its Facebook presence to strengthen the brand by improving brand awareness, recognition, and perception, especially with the affluent youth target market.

Following are the key tactics that will be implemented on Facebook to help build the company brand:

- Post content that is of interest to the youth target market such as popular coffee drinks, music, teenage icons, and fashion, funny YouTube videos, community events, etc.

- Post contents three times each day

- Light or funny ads to direct traffic to company website

- Giveaways once every month to increase the number of likes

- Facebook Places coupons for check-ins

- Participate in industry pages

- Include links to company Facebook page on all outbound communications such as promotional materials, brochures, and email signatures, as well as on the company website

TWITTER Twitter is currently the fourth most popular social media platform, with over 200 million unique monthly visitors.[6] With Twitter it is possible to instantly reach a large (often mobile) audience with brief but focused messages, making the site a great marketing platform for interacting with users on the go, especially the upscale-income youth market that XYZ is targeting.

The following tactics will be pursued to take the utmost advantage of this platform for strengthening the brand among the target audience:

- Respond to questions and comments promptly

- Average of ten to fifteen tweets daily and use hashtags frequently

- Use shortened links to share interesting articles, videos, breaking news, etc.

- Use Twellow to search for targeted users to follow twenty new people daily to generate more followers

- Retweet to increase sharing of our content in return

- Giveaways once every month to increase followers

- Include links to company Twitter on all outbound communications such as promotional materials, brochures, and email signatures, as well as on the company website

LINKEDIN LinkedIn is one of the most popular social media platforms, with over 200 million unique monthly visitors in August 2011.[7] With 81% of business-to-business marketers using LinkedIn, it is the dominant B2B social network, making it ideal for XYZ to connect with suppliers to improve provider relationships.

The following LinkedIn tactical actions will be taken:

- Key employees should strive to complete 100% of their profiles and optimize with appropriate keywords
- Employee profiles should include links to the company website, Twitter, Facebook, YouTube, etc.
- Employees should ask recommendations to show credibility
- Participate in industry groups a minimum of once per week to establish credibility and build brand awareness
- Connect with industry thought leaders
- Build relationship with suppliers

YOUTUBE YouTube is the second most popular social media platform, with more than 450 million unique monthly visitors in August 2011.[8] As more people choose to consume information visually, YouTube's vast (and growing) reach and compelling content make it the perfect platform for engaging consumers to drive word-of-mouth recommendations.

The following YouTube tactical actions will be taken on behalf of the company:

- Creative, entertaining, light-hearted videos focused on the youth market
- Tag videos with relevant keywords to rank higher in the YouTube search engine
- Videos should be two minutes or less in length
- Embed company logo/image in all videos
- Post one video per month
- Reply to comments daily
- Cross-marketing by using Facebook and Twitter to promote videos

FLICKR Flickr is the most popular photo sharing service, with over 90 million unique monthly visitors.[9] It is well suited for engaging customers with photos of the business, which can personalize the company in ways no other social media platform can match. For example, sharing photos of a coffee shop, with a warm, friendly atmosphere, humanizes the business. When a business creates a buzz on the social web by sharing photos, people start talking about it and cause others to become interested in knowing more about the company. This level of engagement with customers can help drive word-of-mouth recommendations.

The following Flickr tactical actions will be taken:

- Upload photos featuring funny pictures, interesting events, product preparation, customers enjoying coffee, festive holiday parties, or employees just enjoying doing their jobs
- Be diligent about using titles, descriptions, photo sets, and tags to secure top Google Search results
- Upload high-quality pictures weekly
- Reply to comments daily
- Cross-marketing by posting the most interesting pictures on Facebook and links on Twitter to photos, etc.

BRAND COMMUNITY The central feature of a successful brand community is a lively discussion board with a sizable number of avid participants who select topics and drive the conversations. Some of the benefits of engaging customers in a brand community include improved customer relations, reduced customer support costs, and the generation of innovative new product ideas.

The following tactical actions will be taken to construct a vibrant brand community:

- Create a friendly, comfortable, and responsive environment using well-designed discussion boards and forums with a specific target audience in mind

- Appeal to the consumer personas that might be interested in the product and let the conversation develop organically without directing the topics toward the product

- Ask open-ended questions, have polls in which users vote, and recognize quality posts

- Allow some democratic input to make forums more interesting for users

- Answer questions and handle complaints promptly, within the hour whenever possible

- Ask broad, open-ended questions to draw in thoughts from as many sources as possible

- Encourage participants to use the discussion forums to suggest innovative product ideas and to provide valuable feedback about existing products and services

- Encourage members to invite their friends to the community by offering competitions with prizes to reward members for bringing in new people

FOURSQUARE Foursquare is the most popular location-based network (social location service), providing the ability for people to share their location with friends and win prizes for visiting businesses and checking in.

The following Foursquare tactical actions will be taken:

- Create a Foursquare business page using a new automated system

- Upload photos to your Tips and check-ins

- Offer coupons and special discounts

- Offer free product after a certain number of check-ins

- Offer badges or special status to loyal customers after a certain numbers of check-ins

- Create special deals to encourage customers to bring their friends

- Place a QR code on coupons and special offers in order to provide instant links to the company's social media properties such as Twitter, LinkedIn, Facebook, blog, corporate website, etc.

EZINEARTICLES EzineArticles is one of the top article directories on the social Web.[10] It is a favorite among Internet marketers because this highly trafficked site allows authors to link articles back to their websites, a process that can substantially improve search engine rankings. EzineArticles has earned an authoritative reputation by employing human reviewers, who impose strict criteria for style and content, thus attracting real-world experts to publish tens of thousands of new articles each month. In turn, these articles have been syndicated on millions of sites around the world.

The following EzineArticles tactical actions will be taken:

- Produce article content that the target audience will be interested in reading

- Articles should be entertaining, easy-to-read, and no more than 500 words

- Obtain Expert Status by writing well-researched articles in order to develop a strong following

- Choose a good title to draw in readers that is concise, descriptive, and gives a solid idea of what the article will be about

- Follow the guidelines of article directories to avoid unnecessary complications on the path to publication and produce articles that people will be willing and able to read

- Use more subtle framing than a standard advertising pitch and do not include the product name in the description or title

- Post an article each week and respond to comments daily

CONTENT DEVELOPMENT

Although each social media platform will feature specific types of content, the following tactics will maximize the generation of quality content that can be repurposed multiple times, saving time and money and creating the greatest possible impact:

- **Developing Content:** A thorough analysis of the content needs for each social media platform will be conducted, identifying the specific needs for each community, finding the gaps in content, and filling them with content that satisfies consumer needs. A careful inventory of existing content within an organization will be undertaken to find material that can be repurposed for use on social media platforms.

- **Managing Content:** Social media content will be carefully edited before posting and consumer contributions will be moderated to ensure the brand community conversation stays on topic.

- **Cross-utilizing Content:** To leverage existing content, it will be adapted to each type of platform for proper cross-utilization. Care will be taken not to over-utilize this procedure because it may trigger unwanted attention from search engines.

- **Breaking Apart Content:** Breaking content into smaller chunks and reformatting it will stretch the utilization of the material, allowing it to appear in various forms on multiple platforms, such as article directories, blogs, microblogs, podcasts, webinars, discussion boards, and so on.

ASSIGNMENTS

In order to execute platform-specific tactics and generate content, specific roles and responsibilities will be assigned based on expertise and availability of staff. Assignments for executing the social media marketing plan will be carried out by those with the knowledge, experience, and training to effectively engage with consumers on the social web. The following personnel will be involved in the implementation of the social media plan:

- VP of marketing, Lisa Shea

- Director of communications, Mark Jones

- Social media marketing manager, Susan Monroe
- Hire the following positions:

1. A community manager

2. Multimedia video specialist

3. A professional writer

4. Two social media marketing specialists

Monitoring

Social media monitoring is the process of tracking, measuring, and evaluating an organization's social media marketing activities. The following sections explain how each of these activities will be executed to determine if the plan is achieving the desired social media goals laid out above.

TRACKING

The company will implement a sustainable and actionable tracking plan that identifies the right keywords to find and follow the relevant data on the social web. The tracking plan will choose optimal topics of focus, select platforms with the greatest concentration of the target audience, identify optimal keywords and phrases by studying how people actually describe brands or other topics, use Boolean operators to zero in the desired data, and adjust searches when they do not produce the desired results.

MEASURING

Social media measurement is the determination of the volume of content and the sentiment toward a brand or topic on the social web.[11] The volume of content is a quantitative measurement, while judging sentiment is a qualitative measurement. The number of posts, comments, tweets, retweets, likes, and follows are instances of quantitative metrics, while mentions, comments, conversations, and feedback about a brand are examples of qualitative metrics.[12]

Quantitative and qualitative metrics are called Key Performance Indicators. A Key Performance Indicator (KPI) is a social media metric that indicates the progress of strategies in achieving goals.[13] Choosing the right social media KPIs is reliant upon having a good understanding of which social media goals are important to an organization.[14] Understanding what an organization wants to accomplish defines which social metrics it should collect.[15] In other words, an organization's desired outcomes determine the most appropriate measurements.

To make quantitative social media metrics useful, they must be tied to specific marketing goals. The primary challenge of connecting quantitative KPIs to marketing goals is to make the goals specific, measurable, attainable, realistic, and timely (SMART).

QUANTITATIVE KPIS With the above considerations in mind, Table A.4 lists the quantitative KPIs that have been chosen to measure progress in achieving the company's marketing goals on the social media platforms where the highest concentration of the target audience resides.

QUALITATIVE KPIS Table A.5 shows the qualitative KPIs designed to measure the social media goals for the XYZ Coffee Company (naturally, benchmarks will be established for each of these metrics so that progress can be assessed).

Social Media Platform	Quantitative Key Performance Indicators (KPIs) for the Next Year
Facebook	• 40% growth in the number of likes • 20% growth in the number of fans • 20% increase in the number of comments and likes on admin post • 5% growth in the number of wall response time • 40% increase in the number of Facebook Places check-ins • 30% increase in visits to company website from Facebook ads
Twitter	• 30% growth in the number of followers • 30% growth in the number of retweets (message amplification) • 30% growth in the number of mentions • 10% increase in click-through rate (CTR) of the links posted in tweets (Note: Observing which types of links garner the highest CTRs can help in tuning tweets to provide consumers with links they are interested in and hence further improve the CTRs.) • 20% increase in visits to website from tweet links • 5% increase in website conversions (i.e., sales) from tweet links
LinkedIn	• 20% growth in the number of connections • 10% increase in the number of recommendations • 20% growth in the number of posts and comments in discussion groups • 20% increase in the number of group members • 15% growth in the number of questions answered or asked
YouTube	• 30% growth in the number of videos viewed • 20% growth in the number of unique visitors • 10% increase in the number of subscribers to company channel • 10% increase in positive comments • 15% growth in visits to company website from YouTube • 10% increase in average rankings of videos by viewers
Flickr	• 20% growth in the number of views of video/photo • 30% growth in the number of replies • 20% growth in the number of page views • 30% growth in the number of comments • 30% growth in the number of subscribers • 15% growth in visits to company website from Flickr
Brand Community	• 30% growth in the number of visits • 20% growth in the number of relevant topics/threads • 30% growth in the number of individual replies • 20% growth in the number of sign-ups • 30% growth in the incoming links • 30% growth in the citations in other sites • 20% growth in the tagging in social bookmarking • 30% growth in the offline references to the forum or its members
Foursquare	• 30% growth in the number of impressions • 40% growth in the number of check-ins • 40% growth in the number of redemptions (comes from point-of-sale systems) • 30% growth in the number of visitors to business after viewing venue/special on foursquare (foot traffic)
EzineArticles	• 40% growth in the number of published articles • 20% growth in the number of article views • 30% growth in the article niches • 40% growth in the number of sites that pickups articles (syndication rate) • 20% growth in the number of inbound links from syndicated articles (required website analytics)

Table A.4 Quantitative Key Performance Indicators for the XYZ Coffee Company

Social Media Goals	Key Performance Indicators	KPI Formula	KPI (One-year) Performance Targets
Brand Strengthening	Sentiment Ratio (SR)	$SR = \dfrac{\text{Postitive: Neutral: Negative Brand Mentions}}{\text{Expenses}}$	10% increase
Word of Mouth	Share of Voice (SV)	$SV = \dfrac{\text{Brand Mentions}}{\text{Total Mentions}}$	15% increase
	Audience Engagement (AE)	$AE = \dfrac{\text{Comments + Shares + Trackbacks}}{\text{Total Views}}$	20% increase
	Conversation Reach (CR)	$CR = \dfrac{\text{Total People Participating}}{\text{Total Audience Exposure}}$	10% increase
Customer Satisfaction	Issue Resolution Rate (IRR)	$IRR = \dfrac{\text{Total \# Issues Resolved Satisfactorily}}{\text{Total \# Service Issues}}$	10% increase
	Resolution Time (RT)	$RT = \dfrac{\text{Total Inquiry Response Time}}{\text{Total \# Service Inquiries}}$	20% increase
	Satisfaction Score (SC)	$SC = \dfrac{\text{Customer Feedback}}{\text{Total Customer Feedback}}$	25% increase
Generating New Product Ideas	Topic Trend (TT)	$TT = \dfrac{\text{\# of Specific Topic Mentions}}{\text{All Topic Mentions}}$	20% increase
	Idea Impact (II)	$II = \dfrac{\text{\# of Positive Conversations, Shares, Mentions}}{\text{Total Idea Conversations, Shares, Mentions}}$	15% increase
Promoting Advocacy	Active Advocates (AA)	$AA = \dfrac{\text{Total \# of Active Advocates within 30 days}}{\text{Total Advocates}}$	20% increase
	Advocate Influence (AIN)	$AIN = \dfrac{\text{Unique Advocate's Influence}}{\text{Advocate Influence}}$	15% increase
	Advocacy Impact (AIM)	$AIM = \dfrac{\text{Number of Advocacy Driven Conversations}}{\text{Total Volume of Advocacy Traffic}}$	20% increase

Table A.5 Qualitative Key Performance Indicators for the XYZ Coffee Company

EVALUATING

Once the social media data have been gathered and measured, they will be carefully evaluated. Only through establishing the relationship between social media metrics and business goals can the marketing team properly analyze the impact and value of social media marketing activities and then present the results to management.

The end game is to produce a thorough description of the progress of the company's social media marketing activities over time in order to reveal when strategies have succeeded or when they require adjustment. This evaluation process will uncover opportunities and threats, potential areas for improvement, and possible new courses of action. Such analysis will enable the marketing team to see where it must next focus its efforts and resources.

SOCIAL MEDIA MONITORING TOOLS

The selection of the social media monitoring tools was based upon four factors: the company's social media marketing goals, the metrics chosen to measure progress in achieving these goals, the training necessary to use the tools, and the costs.

Free monitoring tools, including Google Alerts, Google Trends, Google Reader, and SocialMention, will be used to track and measure most of the quantitative metrics. Google Web Analytics will provide measurements of the effectiveness of article marketing on driving traffic to the company website and the resulting sales.

The paid monitoring tool Radian6 is recommended to track and measure the qualitative metrics because it is priced reasonably and has the necessary features to accomplish the task with a high degree of accuracy. In addition, it has a relatively friendly user interface, requiring less training than other comparable monitoring tools. Radian6 also offers the ability to integrate with the company's CRM system in order to make engaging customers on the social web seamless and easy.

Tuning

The social media marketing team will constantly monitor and adjust the elements of the plan to maximize the chances of success. The company's progress in implementing its social media strategies will be continually assessed, and then, based on this assessment, strategies and tactics will be adjusted to optimize goal achievement.

Reevaluating the goals, strategies, and execution of the plan is necessary because of the ever-changing nature of consumer tastes, countermoves by competitors, and the continual introduction of new social media technologies. In short, planning and executing social media marketing activities is a never-ending process. Hence the marketing team will constantly monitor and fine-tune the plan to maximize results.

Budget

Table A.6 presents the estimated expenses for implementing this plan and for achieving the stated goals within the next year.

Community Platform Software	$50,000
Monitoring Tool	$10,000
A Community Manager	$80,000
A Video Specialist	$50,000
Content Creation and Copyediting	$50.000
Two Social Media Specialists	$100,000
Total expenses for the year	$375,000

© Cengage Learning 2013

Table A.6   Budget for the XYZ Coffee Company

Return on Investment

The location marketing and article marketing strategies aim at increasing website traffic and hence sales, so it will be possible to calculate their respective financial ROIs. However, the majority of the social media goals for the XYZ Coffee Company are not directly connected to sales, and consequently, standard ROI analysis will not be feasible. Fortunately, there are viable alternatives for estimating the return on investment for these social media goals.

Proxy ROIs measure the long-term impact of social media marketing investments on customer response. They include both quantitative and qualitative measurements, such as the number of views of the company's social media properties; the company's posting activity, and the customer responses rates, as well as sentiment analysis, share of voice, satisfaction scores, and advocacy impact. These proxy ROIs provide a meaningful way to judge the expected rewards for investing in this plan.

Notes

1. Qian, Albert (2011, May 22), "Is There a Standard Format for Preparing Social Media Audit?" Quora, retrieved August 9, 2011, from http://www.quora.com/Is-there-a-standard-format-for-preparing-social-media-audit; Seiple, Pamela (2011, July 1), "Top 5 Metrics for Auditing Your Social Media Marketing ROI," *HubSpot Blog*, retrieved August 14, 2011, from http://blog.hubspot.com/blog/tabid/6307/bid/18643/Top-5-Metrics-for-Auditing-Your-Social-Media-Marketing-ROI.aspx; "Social Media Metrics" (2009, August 11), *Emerging Technologies Librarian Blog*, retrieved August 14, 2011, from http://etechlib.wordpress.com/2009/08/11/social-media-plan-metrics/; and Stephan, Nikki (2011, May 5), "How to Conduct a Comprehensive Social Media Audit," *Arik Hanson Communications Conversations Blog*, retrieved August 14, 2011, from http://www.arikhanson.com/2011/05/05/how-to-conduct-a-comprehensive-social-media-audit/
2. "What's the Social Technographics Profile of Your Customers?" (2010, Q2), Forrester Research. Retrieved August 13, 2011, from http://www.forrester.com/empowered/tool_consumer.html
3. Ibid.
4. Bernoff, J. (2010, Jan. 19), "Social Technographics: Conversationalists Get onto the Ladder," *Forrester Research Blog*. Retrieved December 23, 2010, from <http://forrester.typepad.com/groundswell/2010/01/conversationalists-get-onto-the-ladder.html>
5. Kincaid, Jason (2011, June 23), "Facebook Now Has 750 Million Users," Tech Crunch. Retrieved August 11, 2011, from http://techcrunch.com/2011/06/23/facebook-750-million-users/
6. "Top 15 Most Popular Social Networking Sites" (2011, August 8), eBizMBA, retrieved August 11, 2011, from http://www.ebizmba.com/articles/social-networking-websites and "Top 15 Most Popular Web 2.0 Websites" (2011, August 8), eBizMBA, retrieved August 11, 2011, from http://www.ebizmba.com/articles/web-2.0-websites
7. "Top 15 Most Popular Web 2.0 Websites" (2011, August 8), eBizMBA. Retrieved August 11, 2011, from http://www.ebizmba.com/articles/web-2.0-websites
8. Ibid.
9. Ibid.
10. "Top 50 Article Directories by Traffic, Pagerank" (2011, August 11), Virtual Real Estate Toolbar. Retrieved August 11, 2011, from http://www.vretoolbar.com/articles/directories.php
11. Li, Charlene, and Josh Bernoff (2008), *Groundswell: Winning in a World Transformed by Social Technologies* (Boston, MA: Harvard Business Press), pp. 82, 126.
12. Blanchard, Olivier (2011, May 31), "The Basics of Social Media Measurement for Business," *BrandBuilder Blog*. Retrieved July 26, 2011, from http://thebrandbuilder.wordpress.com/2011/05/31/the-basics-of-social-media-measurement-for-business/
13. "Key Performance Indicators (KPI)" (n.d.), *BusinessDictionary.com*. Retrieved July 29, 2011, from http://www.businessdictionary.com/definition/key-performance-indicators-KPI.html
14. Reh, John (n.d.), "Key Performance Indicators (KPI): How an Organization Defines and Measures Progress toward Its Goals," About.com. Retrieved July 29, 2011, from http://management.about.com/cs/generalmanagement/a/keyperfindic.htm
15. Chaney, Paul (2011, July 12), "How to Measure Social Media Marketing; 3 Steps," Practical eCommerce. Retrieved July 25, 2011, from http://www.practicalecommerce.com/articles/2902-How-to-Measure-Social-Media-Marketing-3-Steps

Note: Page numbers in *italic* type indicate figures, illustrations or tables.

Y

Z